VENTURE CAPITAL CONTRACTING AND
THE VALUATION OF HIGH-TECHNOLOGY FIRMS

Venture Capital Contracting and the Valuation of High-technology Firms

Edited by

JOSEPH A. McCAHERY

LUC RENNEBOOG

OXFORD
UNIVERSITY PRESS

OXFORD

UNIVERSITY PRESS

Great Clarendon Street, Oxford OX2 6DP

Oxford University Press is a department of the University of Oxford.
It furthers the University's objective of excellence in research, scholarship,
and education by publishing worldwide in

Oxford New York

Auckland Bangkok Buenos Aires Cape Town Chennai
Dar es Salaam Delhi Hong Kong Istanbul Karachi Kolkata
Kuala Lumpur Madrid Melbourne Mexico City Mumbai Nairobi
São Paulo Shanghai Taipei Tokyo Toronto

Oxford is a registered trade mark of Oxford University Press
in the UK and in certain other countries

Published in the United States
by Oxford University Press Inc., New York

© the Editors and several Contributors 2003

The moral rights of the author have been asserted
Database right Oxford University Press (maker)

First published 2003

British Library Cataloguing in Publication Data

Data available

Library of Congress Cataloging in Publication Data

Data available

ISBN 0–19–927013–9

1 3 5 7 9 10 8 6 4 2

Typeset by Newgen Imaging Systems (P) Ltd., Chennai, India
Printed in Great Britain
on acid-free paper by
Biddles Ltd., Guildford and King's Lynn

Preface

This volume has grown out of a Conference on Venture Capital and the Valuation of High-technology Firms, organized jointly by the Faculty of Law and the Faculty of Economics, at Tilburg University in September 2000. The Conference was held at the Tias Business School. We are very grateful for their financial and organizational support. We were fortunate to have the generous financial assistance of Andersen Legal (Wouters), the Real Options Group, the Center for Company Law, CentER for Economic Research, the Department of Finance, and the Schoordijk Institute of the Faculty of Law. We would like to thank the Anton Philips Fund for generous research assistance.

The Conference brought together a large number of the leading economists and lawyers from England, Europe, and the USA to explore, from a range of standpoints, a series of questions about the contractual mechanisms employed in venture capital investments, the relevance of banks in the provision of finance to start up companies, the role of law in the venture capital process, the affect that organizational law has on both the supply and the demand side of venture capital finance, real option theory and its application to the valuation of IT firms, and the pricing and allocation of IPO shares. The collection benefited from the comments and insights from conference participants, many of which are reflected in the chapters in this volume.

We decided to divide the chapters into four parts, corresponding to the themes explored at the conference: (i) venture capital financing, (ii) innovation, law, and finance, (iii) valuation of high-tech firms, and (iv) venture capital exits and initial public offerings. The chapters in this collection should appeal to economists and lawyers working in the fields of finance, corporate law, and securities law.

We would like to thank the many individuals who have provided us with helpful comments and encouragement. We would particularly like to thank John Armour, Hugo Backx, Ronald Biemans, Bill Bratton, Michel van Bremen, Eric van Damme, Peter Essers, Marc Goergen, Leigh Hancher, Colin Mayer, Gerard Meussen, Piet Moerland, Phillipe Naert, Theo Nijman, Theo Raaijmakers, Ed Rock, Grzegorz Trojanowski, Adri Verboven, Erik Vermeulen, and Reinout Vriesendorp. We would also wish to acknowledge our gratitude to Connie Dollevoet for assisting us in organizing the conference. We would like to thank the authors of papers, commentators, and chairs of sessions for the contributions at the conference. We are particularly grateful for the outstanding group of contributors whom we have worked with to produce the present collection.

We would like to thank those who have helped us in preparing the volume. Barbara Gabor has assisted us with the preparation of the final submission to the press. We owe special thanks to our editor at Oxford University Press, Andrew Schuller, for improving the manuscript. We thank our respective faculties for the fine environment that they provide. Finally, we are grateful to the Tilburg Law and Economics Center for generating a stimulating environment for multidisciplinary research in law and economics.

Contents

Part III. Valuation of High-tech Firms

Part IV. Venture Capital Exits and IPOs

List of Figures

List of Tables

Abbrevations

AAR	Average abnormal return
ADRs	American Depositary Receipts
AIM	Alternative Investment Market
APR	Absolute priority rule
ASM	Annual Survey of Manufacturers
BES	Business Expansion Scheme
BHRs	Buy-and-hold returns
BVCA	British Venture Capital Association
CAAR	Cumulative average abnormal return
CARs	Cumulative average abnormal returns
CCIP	Chamber of Commerce and Industry
CTM	Control Transfer Model
CVCA	Canadian Venture Capital Association
DTA	Decision tree analysis
DVD	Digital video disc
EIS	Enterprise Investment Scheme
EMI	Enterprise Management Initiative
EPC	European Private Company
ERISA	Employee Retirement Income Security Act
Euro.NMs	European New Markets
FDA	Food and Drug Administration
FRS	Financial Reporting Standard
FSAP	Financial Services Action Plan
HPR	Holding period return
IPO	Initial public offering
IRS	Internal Revenue Service
LLC	Limited Liability Company
LLP	Limited liability partnership
LSE	London Stock Exchange
LSVCCs	Labour Sponsored Venture Capital Corporations
MFR	Minimum funding requirement
MMCD	Multimedia compact disk
NMAX	New Market of Amsterdam Exchanges
NPV	Net present value
NSF	National Science Foundation
RCAP	Risk Capital Action Plan
Re-RULPA	Revision of the Revised Uniform Limited Partnership Act
RPE	Relative pricing error

SAS	Société par actions simplifiée
SBIC	Small Business Investment Company
SDD	Super density disk
SGA	Selling, general, and administrative expenses
SIC	Standard Industrial Classification
SMEs	Small- and medium-sized enterprises
SRPE	Symmetrized relative pricing error
TASE	Tel Aviv Stock Exchange
TCC	Threshold criterion for continuance
TCI	Threshold criterion for investment
USPTO	US Patent and Trademark Office
VC	Venture capitalist
VCT	Venture Capital Trust

List of Contributors

John Armour, BA, BCL (Oxon), LLM (Yale) is a senior research fellow at the Centre for Business Research and university lecturer in Law at Cambridge University. He is interested in the economic analysis of corporate law and finance, with particular reference to insolvency. His work includes empirical and theoretical studies of the law and practice of corporate insolvency, the role of commercial norms in resolving financial distress, the effects of insolvency upon environmental liabilities, and the theory of secured credit. He is currently working on an empirical study of venture capital contracting practices in the Cambridge high-tech cluster.

Dirk Bergemann is an Associate Professor at the Department of Economics at Yale University. He is also a staff member of Cowles Foundation for Research in Economics. He received his BA from the J.W. Goethe University (Frankfurt) and his Ph.D. from the University of Pennsylvania (Philadelphia). His main research areas are information economics and financial contracting. He has published widely in journals such as *Econometrica, Journal of Economic Theory, RAND Journal of Economics,* and *Review of Economic Studies*, among others. He is an Associate Editor of the B.E. *Journals in Microeconomics* and the *RAND Journal of Economics*. His current research is supported by the National Science Foundation and the A. P. Sloan Foundation.

Bernard S. Black is Professor of Law at Stanford Law School. Previously, he was a Professor of Law at Columbia Law School. He received a JD degree from Stanford Law School, an MA degree from the University of California at Berkeley, and a BA degree from Princeton. He was also a law clerk for Judge Patricia M. Wald of the US Court of Appeals for the DC Circuit. He has been an adviser on company law reform in Russia and Indonesia. Currently, he teaches corporate law, corporate finance, corporate acquisitions, and foundations of the regulatory state. He has written numerous articles on topics in corporate law, corporate governance, and securities regulation. He is the co-editor of the leading American casebook of *Mergers and Acquisitions* and co-author of *A Guide to the Russian Law on Joint Stock Companies* (1998).

William W. Bratton is Professor of Law at Georgetown University. Prior to joining Georgetown University, he was Samuel Tyler Research Professor at George Washington University Law School, the Kaiser Professor of Law and Director of the Heyman Center on Corporate Governance at Cardozo Law School, and Professor of Law and Woodrow Wilson Scholar at Rutgers University School of Law, Newark. He has published articles on a variety of subjects in corporate law and law and economics. In addition, he is co-editor of the leading American textbook on corporate finance and an Oxford University Press collection on regulatory competition.

Michael J. Cooper is an Assistant Professor of Finance at Purdue's Krannert Graduate School of Management. He received his Ph.D. from the University of North Carolina.

His current research is focused on empirical asset pricing, including behavioural finance, and data-snooping issues. Some of his recent publications include 'A Rose.com by Any Other Name', with Orlin Dimitrov and P. Raghavendra Rau, in *The Journal of Finance*; 'On the Predictability of Stock Returns in Real Time', with R.Gutierrez and W. Marcum, in *The Journal of Business*, and 'Value versus Growth', with Jennifer Conrad and Gautam Kaul, in *The Journal of Finance*. Professor Cooper steadfastly denies that he exhibited any self-attribution bias during the dotcom bubble of the late 1990s, even though his brokerage account records tend to suggest otherwise.

Didier Cossin is Professor of Finance at HEC, University of Lausanne where he chairs the Institute of Banking and Finance, and is Adjunct Professor at IMD, Switzerland. He holds a Ph.D. in Business Economics from Harvard University and is a former Visiting Scholar (Fulbright Fellow) at the Massachusetts Institute of Technology. He is also a former student at ENS (rue d'Ulm) Paris and holds Masters degrees from Sorbonne University and EHESS. Didier's current research has three strands: credit risk issues (credit risk pricing, credit derivatives), the use of real options in finance, and corporate governance (international comparison of top management turnover and board interlockings). He is the author of two books, of several book chapters, and of more than fifteen refereed publications.

Douglas Cumming, BCom (Hons.) (McGill), MA (Queen's), JD/Ph.D. (Toronto), is Assistant Professor of Finance, Economics & Law at the University of Alberta School of Business, and Visiting Assistant Professor of Finance at the University of Amsterdam Graduate School of Business. His recent empirical papers on venture capital financial contracts and exits across Canada, Europe, and the USA were invited for presentation at the American Law and Economics Association at Harvard Law School (2002), the American Finance Association in Washington, D.C. (2003), and numerous other conferences.

Susanne Espenlaub completed a D.Phil. about initial public offerings at Oxford University in 1996. She did her undergraduate studies at Heidelberg University and Queen Mary and Westfield College in London. She has been a Lecturer in Finance at the Manchester School of Accounting & Finance since 1995. Her research areas are corporate finance and governance. She has published work on IPOs in *European Financial Management, The Journal of Business Finance & Accounting*, and *Venture Capital: An international journal of entrepreneurial finance*.

Ronald J. Gilson is the Meyers Professor of Law and Business at Stanford Law School and the Stern Professor of Law and Business at Columbia Law School. He was a reporter of the American Law Institute's Principles of Corporate Governance, and is the author of the *Law and Finance of Corporate Acquisitions* (with B. Black) and *Cases and Materials on Corporations* (with J. Choper and J. Coffee), as well as many articles on corporate governance, corporate acquisitions, and venture capital. Professor Gilson is one of the founders of the Legal Scholarship Network.

Marc Goergen, originally from Luxembourg, holds an MSc in Economics from the Free University of Brussels (ULB) and an MBA in European Business from Solvay Business School, Brussels. He completed his D.Phil. in Economics at Keble College, Oxford and subsequently joined the School of Accounting and Finance, University of Manchester and the Manchester School of Management, UMIST as a lecturer. In 1997, he lectured at the ISMA Centre, University of Reading and moved back to the Manchester School of Management, UMIST in 1999. Marc's areas of research include initial public offerings, corporate governance, ownership disclosure, dividend policy, and corporate investment. His books, *Corporate Governance and Financial Performance* and *Corporate Governance and Dividend Policy* were published by Edward Elgar and Oxford University Press, respectively.

John R. M. Hand is Professor and Chairman of the Accounting Faculty at the Kenan-Flagler Business School at UNC Chapel Hill. He has served on the faculties of the University of Chicago and Yale University, and is a two-time winner of the American Accounting Association's competitive manuscript competition. His current research, teaching, and consulting interests are at the intersection of accounting, finance, and entrepreneurship, particularly the business economics and valuation of high-tech companies. He is co-editor of *Intangible Assets* (Oxford University Press, 2003) with Baruch Lev of New York University.

Ulrich Hege is an Associate Professor in Finance at HEC School of Management (Hautes Etudes Commerciales) in Paris, France. He is also affiliated to the Centre for Economic Policy Research (CEPR) in London and to CentER in Tilburg (Netherlands). He earned his Ph.D. from Princeton University in 1994, and a Masters degree in economics from the University of Frankfurt (Germany). He has held teaching positions at Tilburg University and ESSEC (Paris). His research focuses on a variety of topics in corporate finance. Besides questions related to venture capital, he has worked on corporate governance, joint ventures, internal capital markets, the choice between bank debt and publicly traded debt, credit risk, debt restructuring and bankruptcy, as well as on topics in contract theory and in law and economics.

Thomas Hellmann is an Assistant Professor of Strategic Management at the Graduate School of Business, Stanford University, where he teaches a popular MBA elective on 'Strategy in Entrepreneurial Ventures'. His research on the process of entrepreneurship and the role of venture capital has been published in top economics and finance journals. He has also collaborated with Joseph Stiglitz, working on issues of financial systems development. He holds a Ph.D. in Economics from Stanford University and a BSc from the London School of Economics.

Steven N. Kaplan is the Neubauer Family Professor of Entrepreneurship and Finance at the University of Chicago Graduate School of Business (GSB). He is the faculty director of the GSB's entrepreneurship area. His research, teaching, and consulting focus on issues in private equity and entrepreneurial finance, corporate governance, corporate restructuring, mergers and acquisitions, and corporate finance. Professor Kaplan serves on the board of directors of Liberty Acorn Funds, Morningstar, and Vectiv. He also serves on a number of advisory boards.

Arif Khurshed is a lecturer at the Manchester School of Accounting and Finance, University of Manchester. He graduated from the University of Buckingham with an MSc in Business Economics and with a Ph.D. from the ISMA Centre, University of Reading, where he was a lecturer. His research interests include initial public offerings, venture capital, corporate governance, and investment trusts. He has published in *Journal of Business Finance and Accounting* and *Applied Financial Economics*.

Samuel Kortum is an Associate Professor of Economics at the University of Minnesota and a Research Associate at the National Bureau of Economic Research. He received a bachelor's degree from Wesleyan University and a Ph.D. in Economics from Yale. He has taught in the Economics Department at Boston University and served as an economist at the Federal Reserve Board. Kortum's research concerns technological change, spanning the topics of economic growth, innovation, technology diffusion, firm dynamics, and international trade. His research has appeared in top academic journals and has been supported by grants from the National Science Foundation.

Benoît Leleux is the Stephan Schmidheiny Professor of Entrepreneurship and Finance at IMD. He was previously Visiting Professor of Entrepreneurship and Director of the 3i VentureLab at INSEAD, and Associate Professor and Zubillaga Chair in Finance and Entrepreneurship at Babson College, Wellesley, MA (USA) from 1993 to 1999. He obtained his Ph.D. at INSEAD, specializing in corporate finance and venture capital. He holds an MSc in Agricultural Engineering and an MA in Education from the Université Catholique de Louvain (Belgium), and an MBA from Virginia Tech. He was a Fellow of the Sasakawa Young Leaders Program in Japan and the College for Advanced Studies in Management (CIM) in Brussels.

Josh Lerner is the Jacob H. Schiff Professor of Investment Banking at Harvard Business School, with a joint appointment in the Finance and Entrepreneurial Management Units, and is a Research Associate in the National Bureau of Economic Research. He graduated from Yale College in physics and history of technology and obtained a Ph.D. from Harvard's economics department. He worked for several years on issues concerning technological innovation and public policy, at the Brookings Institution, for a public–private task force in Chicago, and on Capitol Hill. Much of his research focuses on the structure and role of venture capital organizations. His work has been published in a variety of top academic journals.

Jeffrey MacIntosh (BSc, MIT, 1975; LLB, University of Toronto, 1981; LLM, Harvard Law School, 1982) has taught at the University of Toronto's Faculty of Law since 1983. He is currently Toronto Stock Exchange Professor of Capital Markets and spent one year (1987–88) as a John M. Olin Fellow in Law and Economics at the Yale Law School. He is a former Director of the Capital Markets Institute at the University of Toronto. His academic writings have been in the area of securities regulation, corporate law, and law and economics. More recently, his research has focused on venture capital.

Joseph A. McCahery is Professor of International Business Law at Tilburg University Faculty of Law and a research fellow at the Tilburg Center of Law and Economics. He holds a visiting appointment at Leiden University Faculty of Law. Previously he held an appointment at Warwick University, where he also received a Ph.D. degree. He was a law clerk for Judge Nathaniel R. Jones of the US Court of Appeals for the Sixth Circuit. He has published numerous articles on corporate law, corporate governance, regulation, and securities markets. In addition, he has co-written a book on corporate governance and is a co-editor on Oxford University Press collections on *Corporate Control and Accountability* (1993), *International Regulatory Competition and Coordination* (1997), *Corporate Governance Regimes* (2002), and forthcoming work on *Partnership and Close Corporation Law* (2003).

Enrico Perotti holds a Chair in International Finance at the University of Amsterdam. He obtained a Ph.D. in Finance from MIT in 1990; he taught courses at MIT, Boston University, and LSE. He has visited at the IMF, LBS, and CEU. His research is in corporate finance, banking, and international finance, with publications in top academic journals on leveraged recapitalizations, crosslistings, strategic real options, banking regulation, corporate governance, the Japanese keiretsu, transparency, emerging market development, privatization, and entrepreneurship. He is Director of the CIFRA research centre and a CEPR Fellow. He worked as consultant for the IMF, the World Bank, the EC, the NYSE, private financial institutions, and Eastern European governments.

Raghuram Rajan joined the Graduate School of Business, University of Chicago in 1991 after completing a Ph.D. at MIT. In 1995, Rajan was promoted to Professor of Finance. He visited the Kellogg School in 1996–97 and in 1997 he was appointed the first Joseph L. Gidwitz Professor of Finance at the GSB. In 2000–1, he held the Fischer Black visiting chair at MIT. His research focuses primarily on economic institutions ranging from banks to property rights. His papers have been published in all the top economics and finance journals including the *Journal of Political Economy, American Economic Review, Quarterly Journal of Economics, Journal of Monetary Economics, Journal of Finance, Review of Financial Studies*, and others. Rajan is a director of the American Finance Association and the Program Director for the Corporate Finance Program at the NBER. He has also served as a consultant to the World Bank, the Federal Reserve Board, the Swedish Parliament, finance companies, and banks.

Raghavendra Rau is an Assistant Professor of Finance at the Krannert School of Management at Purdue University. He received his Ph.D. from INSEAD. His current research is focused on empirical corporate finance, concerning issues relating to the speed of information acquisition and incorporation into stock prices. Some of his recent publications include 'Investment bank market share, contingent fee payments and the post-acquisition performance of acquiring firms' in the *Journal of Financial Economics* and 'Investor reaction to corporate event announcements: Under-reaction or over-reaction?', with Padma Kadiyala, in the *Journal of Business*. Professor Rau admits to being influenced by Professor Cooper's self-attribution bias during the dotcom bubble, and his brokerage account reflects this.

Luc Renneboog is Associate Professor at the Department of Finance of Tilburg University and a research fellow at the CentER for Economic Research (Tilburg), the Tilburg Center of Law and Economics, and the European Corporate Governance Institute (Brussels). He held appointments at the Catholic University of Leuven (Belgium) and Oxford University, and visiting appointments at London Business School, European University Institute (Florence), Venice University, and CUNEF (Madrid). He graduated from the University of Leuven with degrees in management engineering (MSc) and in philosophy (BA), from the University of Chicago with an MBA, and from the London Business School with a Ph.D. in financial economics. His research interests are corporate finance, corporate governance, dividend policy, insider trading, financial distress, and the economics of art.

Edward Rock received his JD from the University of Pennsylvania in 1983. He joined the Penn faculty in 1989 from the Philadelphia law firm of Fine, Kaplan, and Black, where he specialized in antitrust, corporate, and securities litigation. He has written widely on corporate law: on the role of institutional investors in corporate governance; closed corporations; the overlap between corporate law and antitrust; the overlap between corporate law and labour law; comparative corporate law; and the regulation of mutual funds. In 1994, he was a Visiting Professor of International Banking and Capital Markets at the Goethe Universität (Frankfurt) and in 1995–96 he was a Fulbright Senior Scholar at the Hebrew University (Jerusalem). In 2001, he was appointed the first Saul A. Fox Distinguished Professor of Business Law. His current research focuses on mergers and acquisitions and corporate constitutionalism.

Silvia Rossetto is a post-doctoral fellow in finance at the IDEI at the University of Toulouse. She obtained her Ph.D. in Finance at the University of Amsterdam in 2002 with a thesis 'Optimal Timing of Financial Decisions'. Her research interests are in corporate finance, strategic real options, venture capital, law, and finance. She has presented her work at several international conferences, including at the University of Chicago and at the American Finance Association. Before turning to academia, she worked in the aerospace industry creating procedures for the optimization of R&D processes.

Entela Saliasi is a Ph.D. student at the University of Lausanne (Switzerland). He is doing his research in FAME (Financial Asset Management and Engineering) which is a joint institute of the University of Geneva, the University of Lausanne, and the Graduate Institute of International Studies (Geneva). His research focuses on venture equity investment contracts, on financial engineering techniques, on the impact of the default risk on the optimal trading strategies of a levered investor, and on the role of collateral for allocation strategies of a constrained investor and in credit spreads. He holds an MPhil in International Relations with a specialization in International Economics from the Graduate Institute of International Studies (Geneva), as well as a Certificate of Studies in Finance from Oxford University.

Henri Servaes is Professor of Finance at London Business School. He holds a BBA from the European University and a MSIA and Ph.D. in finance from Purdue University. His areas of interest include corporate control, corporate diversification, initial public offerings, capital structure, and mutual funds. He has published articles on these topics in the leading finance journals, including the *Journal of Finance, Journal of Financial Economics*, and *Review of Financial Studies*. He serves as an associate editor of the *Journal of Finance, Financial Management*, and a number of other finance journals. He has held previous appointments at the University of Chicago, the Katholieke Universiteit Leuven (Belgium), Duke University, and the University of North Carolina at Chapel Hill.

Han Smit is the HAL Professor of Private Equity at Erasmus University Rotterdam. He has been visiting fellow at NIAS (Netherlands Institute of Arts and Sciences), Harvard

University, Boston University, and Columbia University. His research interests are in the field of private equity, valuation, and strategy. He published early articles that combine real options valuation with game theory to value competitive strategies in *Financial Management*, the *Journal of Applied Corporate Finance*, and elsewhere, and has a forthcoming book (with Lenos Trigeorgis) titled *Strategy: Options and Games* (Princeton University Press).

Per Strömberg is Associate Professor of Finance at the Graduate School of Business of the University of Chicago, research fellow of the NBER, and research affiliate of the CEPR. He received his Ph.D. in Finance from Carnegie Mellon University in 1997. Professor Strömberg's research has been in the areas of financial distress and venture capital finance, and is published in *Journal of Finance, American Economic Review*, and *Review of Economic Studies*. In 2001 he received the Brattle Prize for best corporate finance paper in the *Journal of Finance*. He has also consulted on valuation and performance of VC backed companies.

Lenos Trigeorgis is President of the Real Options Group and is a Professor of Finance at the University of Cyprus. He previously taught at Boston University, Columbia University, and the University of Chicago. He holds a Ph.D. (DBA) from Harvard University. He has published widely in numerous journals on corporate finance, competition, and strategy, and has written a number of books on real options published by the MIT Press, Oxford University Press, Princeton University Press, and others. He is internationally known as the author of *Real Options* (recently translated into Japanese), which is considered path-breaking for the field.

Erik Vermeulen is a research fellow at the Center for Company Law, Tilburg University. His research interests are the economics of law, partnership and corporation law, and venture capital financing. He has published articles on legal business forms in the venture capital industry and regulatory competition.

1

Venture Capital Financing of Innovative Firms: An Introduction

JOSEPH A. MCCAHERY AND LUC RENNEBOOG

1.1. INTRODUCTION

Venture capitalists are specialized intermediaries that direct capital to firms and professional services to companies that might otherwise be excluded from the corporate debt market and other sources of private finance. Venture capital financing is used to invest mainly in small- and medium-size firms with good growth and exit potential. Typically, venture capital firms concentrate in industries with a great deal of uncertainty, where information gaps among entrepreneurs and venture capitalist are commonplace. These ventures are identified as financially constrained. Start-up firms rely on venture capital as one of their main sources of funding. Recent empirical research has found that the effect of venture capital on the success of these ventures is considerable. The value of venture capital investment is borne out by the figures which show that venture capital-backed firms grow on average twice as fast as those not backed by venture capital firms (EVCA 1996).

Venture capital has been a critical component in the innovation process in the USA over the last two decades. Venture capital disbursements are more productive in generating patents, compared to corporate R&D. The strong link between venture capital and innovation is reflected in recent research that discovered that venture-backed firms in the USA accounted for 8 per cent of US industrial innovation during the decade ending in 1992 (Kortum and Lerner, Chapter 9, this volume). Not surprisingly, the rapid increase in venture capital funding in continental Europe has also led to a significant rise in patent applications, particularly in Germany (Tykvová 2000). The importance of venture capital for economic growth is now widely accepted. Audretsch and Thurik (2001) disclose that a positive relationship exists between the degree of entrepreneurial activity in a country and its economic growth performance. Empirical evidence from OECD countries over different time periods suggests moreover that an increase in entrepreneurial activity tends to result in subsequent higher growth rates and a reduction in unemployment.

In the USA, the depth of venture capital finance and equity financing for innovative firms is large. Pension funds and corporations still contribute the bulk of the funds raised;

namely 70 per cent. Gompers and Lerner (1998) identify a number of factors influencing the US pattern of venture capital fundraising. First, the lower capital gains tax rates (Poterba 1989). A decrease in capital gains taxes increases the number of entrepreneurs looking for capital, therefore leading to an increase in demand for new venture capital funds. Second, regulatory changes such as the US Department of Labor's shift in ERISA[1] policies in 1979 that allowed pension funds to invest in venture capital funds. Third, venture capital funds' returns positively influence the amount of funds raised. Finally, a strong initial public offering (IPO) market can increase the flow of capital from pension funds to venture capital funds. Bottazzi and Da Rin (2002) calculate that the amount of venture capital funds raised in the USA, during the 1990s, increased by a factor of 80. In contrast, European venture capital funds increased during the same period by a factor of 12 (Bottazzi and Da Rin 2002). For example, a recent EVCA (2001) study reveals that total private equity investment increased from approximately €5 billion per year during the 1989–96 period to €24 billion in 1999 and €34.7 billion in 2000. During the same period, venture capital fundraising has increased dramatically from about €5 billion in 1995 to approximately €48 billion in 2000. Still, it is hardly surprising that private equity investment and fund-raising has dropped off dramatically since 2000, when the stock market collapsed, the IPO market dried up, and a negative investor sentiment towards risk arose.

In the USA, institutional investors have been the main contributors to venture capital funds, which is consistent with a market-oriented financial system with a large and well-established corporate bond and equity market. In contrast, European institutional investors invest a relatively small amount in venture capital finance. The limited involvement of institutional investors and pension funds supports the view that banks remain the largest source of European venture capital funding. Recent data shows that banks, insurance companies, and other investors contributed almost 50 per cent of venture capital funding in 2000 (EVCA 2001). European pension funds contributed less than a quarter of total funding in 2000. It is worth pointing out, however, that European venture capitalists are now raising an increased portion of funds from institutional investors. As in the case of Germany, which is the largest venture capital market in Europe, 25 per cent of new capital raised is from pension funds (Becker and Hellmann 2001; Jeng and Wells 2000). Moreover, European pension funds increased the level of funding to 27 per cent in 2001 (EVCA 2001). Notwithstanding the increasing amounts of institutional investment, the European market is still lagging considerably behind the US venture capital industry, as reflected in the striking difference between the USA and Europe in terms of the percentage of GDP invested into venture capital (EVCA 2000; NVCA 2000). The growth in venture capital investment has been accompanied by a shift in the nature and composition of the US market. Before the 1980s, the venture capital market was dominated by small investment companies, limited partnerships, and some closed-end funds (Gompers and

---

[1] Employee Retirement Income Security Act. This is the 1974 legislation that codified the regulation of corporate pension plans. Prior to 1979, the prudent man rule provision prohibited pension funds from investing substantial amounts of money in venture capital or other high-risk asset classes. In 1979, the US Department of Labor promulgated which provided that pension fund investment decisions should be evaluated using standard analytical methods of portfolio choice. See CFR section 2550.404a-1.

Lerner 2000). Today, with the growth of funds flowing into the industry, the composition of the sector has changed with the investment adviser playing an important role in advising large pension funds and other institutions about their existing and potential investments.

As a consequence of the dominant role of banks, the majority of European venture capital has been dedicated to the later-stage financing of new equity (Boot and Verheyen 1997). However, a shift in the pattern in venture capital spending is also taking place. In recent years, venture capital financing has moved in the direction of backing early-stage technology companies. A number of factors are influencing the changing pattern of investment. To the extent that local venture capital firms are increasingly exposed to foreign competition coming from the USA and the UK, European venture capital firms are becoming more specialized. This is reflected in the recent European data that suggests that venture capital firms are restricting their investments to specific stages of development, investment sizes, or sectors. For example, Dutch venture capital firms are currently investing more capital in early stage ventures (seed, start-up, and expansion stages) compared to a few years ago. Indeed, early stage investment accounted for approximately 20 per cent of European equity investment in 2000. The preference of European venture capitalists for later-stage investments (buy-outs and turnarounds) continues unabated however. Investment in late-stage ventures (buy-outs and turnarounds) has increased from 40 per cent in 2000 to 45 per cent in 2001.

Europe has sought to emulate the success of the USA by taking steps to design institutions that support the development of an EU-wide venture capital market (Gilson and Black, Chapter 2, this volume). However, the European venture capital market is constrained by regulatory and market barriers that limit early-stage investment, and capital market structures that hinder the ability of portfolio companies to liquidate their positions in start-ups. While there is widespread agreement about the growth in the size of the European venture capital industry over the last decade, there is much less agreement on what should be done to catch up with the USA in its ability to fund venture-backed technological development. To be sure, there is a common thread to the strategies designed to bridge the gap between the USA and European venture capital markets. Most policymakers recommend that it is desirable to emulate US techniques and institutions. For instance, there is a consensus view of the importance of a liquid and deep stock market for the growth of a venture capital market. In response to the absence of a trading market for young companies with bright prospects, many advocated the creation of new stock markets that offered issuers suitable admissions and listing rules similar to NASDAQ. The creation of the (former) European New Markets (Euro.NM), an alliance of stock exchanges in Amsterdam, Brussels, Paris, Frankfurt, and Milan, facilitated the raising of capital for a large population of Europe's new companies (Goergen *et al.*, Chapter 18, this volume). There is also widespread agreement among policymakers on the need to stimulate the supply of risk capital for new businesses (European Commission 1998). The argument is that there are shortcomings in the provision of funding to small- and medium-size firms in Europe. In 2000, the Netherlands Ministry of Economic Affairs, for example, introduced a range of policy initiatives designed to eliminate the barriers in the financing of entrepreneurial firms. In the UK, the Myners Report (2001) considered revisions to pension fund regulation that might be needed to increase the flow of funds into the venture capital sector (Armour, Chapter 7, this volume). There is disagreement, however, about whether government-sponsored venture capital programs are cost-effective or merely crowd out private investment flows to venture capital funds (Cumming and MacIntosh 2002). Others emphasize that aspects of contract and organization law, bankruptcy law, tax legislation, labour regulation, and the regulation of pension funds have substantially contributed to the competitiveness of the US venture capital industry (Baums and Gilson 2000).

Even if government policymakers agree on the optimal menu of legal reforms needed to support the interests of investors and entrepreneurs, there will still exist a problem: innovative start-ups, particularly small and newly established firms, face difficulties in gaining access to sources of finance (Keuschnigg 2003). While the reported research has emphasized the maturity and development of the European venture capital market over the last decade, the difficulties encountered by small- and medium-size firms in securing external sources of funding are well documented. Saunders and Schmeits (2002) show that, even prior to the recent downturn in the IPO market, smaller businesses faced considerable barriers in obtaining equity finance and longer-term bank loans. The difficulties faced by innovative firms in gaining access to funding have been exacerbated by the substantial growth deceleration of the US economy. Start-up firms, which have limited access to capital due to their characteristics, are highly sensitive to the state of the economy since their future expectations are usually based on high growth rates. The post-bubble economic downturn has made it difficult for venture-backed firms to sustain high levels of growth. Over the two years between 2000 and 2002, total venture capital investment declined by almost half, worldwide (Megginson 2002). Activity in the IPO market has also decreased dramatically. The collapse in the IPO market in Europe—from 249 IPOs in 2000 to 47 IPOs in 2001—serves to reinforce this point. Thus, venture capital funds and entrepreneurs must, in the absence of a liquid IPO market, rely exclusively on trade sales to exit their investments. Perhaps not surprisingly, the organizational structure and legal practices of venture capital firms are changing in response to current market conditions.

The aim of this volume is to provide an analysis of the main legal and contracting structures that play a crucial function in the genesis and development of a venture capital market and the economic performance of portfolio firms. This volume will inevitably explore the differences between the US and European venture capital markets to determine which legal and financial elements are best suited to overcoming the problems of uncertainty and agency problems that arise at each stage of development. Specifically, this book will focus on the various organization and contractual techniques, such as staged financing, convertible securities, board and other forms of control, and the role of exit. At the same time, the theoretical chapters focus on the valuation of entrepreneurial firms and the liquidation preference in venture convertible securities. Along with the analyses of the different monitoring devices, the collection seeks to develop our understanding of the diverse exit routes available to venture capitalists.

This introduction reviews the organization and contractual structure of venture capital investments. Section 1.2 surveys the governance of venture capital partnerships and the determinants of venture capital compensation. Section 1.3 looks at how venture capital investments are made in the context of information problems, uncertainty, and agency costs. After analysing the techniques that venture capitalists have developed to screen and monitor their investments, this section then considers the main securities used by venture capitalists in making their investments in their portfolio companies. This section also considers the IPO as an important exit route for venture capitalists. Section 1.4 supplies an overview of the chapters in this collection. Section 1.5 concludes.

1.2. THE VENTURE CAPITAL INVESTMENT PROCESS

1.2.1. *The Organizational and Legal Structure of Venture Capital Partnerships*

Examining the source of funding helps to address the basic concerns of venture capital investors and provides a basis to survey the venture capital market. In the main, there are two types of venture capitalists: institutional venture capital funds and angel capitalists, who are wealthy individuals who make private equity investments in entrepreneurial firms (Gompers and Lerner 1999). Until recently, angel investors provided a significant amount of the financing to entrepreneurial companies each year in the USA. However, institutional venture capital funds have become the main funding source for entrepreneurial firms. There are four main types of venture capital funds: small business investment companies (SBICs), financial venture capital funds, corporate venture capital funds, and venture capital limited partnerships. In the USA, the limited partnership organizational form is the most popular type of venture capital fund (Gompers and Lerner 1999; McCahery and Vermeulen, Chapter 8, this volume). Even in the UK, where the limited partnership form under the Limited Partnership Act was seldom used, this form enjoys unusual prominence (Law Commission 2001). There are a variety of reasons for this, such as tax benefits, the flexibility surrounding its structure and terms, and its fixed life. Individuals and institutions who invest in a limited partnership can delegate investment and monitoring decisions to the venture capitalist, who acts as the general partner. The limited partnerships share aspects of publicly and closely held firms: passive owner–investors entrust their money to powerful and entrenched owner–managers who have substantial discretion over the funds (Armour, Chapter 7, this volume).

The flexibility of the limited partnership form allows the internal and external participants to enter into covenants and schemes that align the incentives of venture capitalists with those of outside investors and reduce agency costs. For instance, limited partners are usually permitted, despite restrictions on their managerial rights, to vote on important issues such as amendments of the partnership agreement, dissolution of the partnership agreement, extension of the fund's life, removal of a general partner, and the valuation of the portfolio (Sahlman 1990). Gompers and Lerner (1996) find that limited partners use several restrictions when structuring the partnership agreement. In their empirical analysis, they formulate two hypotheses: (1) the costly contracting hypothesis and (2) the supply and demand hypothesis. The first one predicts that a positive relationship exists between the use of restrictions and the propensity of the venture capitalist to behave opportunistically. Hence, in situations such as when the venture capitalist raises funds to invest in early stage ventures, the limited partner will use more restrictions to structure the partnership.[2] Gompers and Lerner (1999) find in their sample of 140 partnership agreements, 14 distinct covenants that address problems relating to the management of the fund, conflicts of interests, and restrictions on the type of investment the fund can make. The number and type of covenants correspond to the uncertainty, information asymmetry, and agency costs in the portfolio company. Other factors affecting the use of restrictions are the fund's size, the compensation system of the venture capitalist, and the reputation of the venture capitalist. The second hypothesis contends that relative supply and demand conditions in the venture capital market affects the covenants and restrictions in long-term contracts. This hypothesis predicts that when demand for the services of well-established venture capitalists changes rapidly, while the supply of those venture capitalists is fixed in the short term, less restrictions should be observed in the partnership agreements. Accordingly, it can be inferred that financial contracts can assist to limit the use of contractual restrictions in the partnership agreement. Thus, limited partners use restrictive covenants to limit the value erosion caused by uncertainty and agency problems, because they are not able to take an active role in selecting and monitoring ventures (Sahlman 1990). However, contractual restrictions can lead to the erosion of value, as they limit the flexibility of the venture capitalist to diversify risk and deal with the agency problems in each venture. This puts extra pressure on the average return of the venture capital funds (Gompers and Lerner 2000).

Despite several drawbacks, such as limited partnerships shares not being publicly traded and the archaic law governing this form,[3] UK limited partnerships have become the standard structure used by European venture capitalists in general (McCahery and Vermeulen, Chapter 8, this volume). That said, the UK's prominent position is under threat from other jurisdictions that have introduced or plan to design modern legislation on limited partnerships. It not surprising, therefore, that policymakers are planning to revise the Limited Partnerships Act 1907 by proposing to abolish the rule on maximum number of partners (presently limited to twenty) and introduce 'safe harbour' provisions similar to those found in the Delaware Revised Uniform Limited Partnership Act and Jersey's limited partnership form. These provisions clearly establish that limited partners may participate in the control of the firm so as to improve certainty and accessibility to foreign investors. The threat of competition, combined with the lobbying efforts of venture capitalists and sophisticated investors, will arguably make the UK limited partnership law more sophisticated and suitable for venture capital investment (Armour, Chapter 7 this volume).

The relationship between the limited partners and the general partners can be characterized as a principal–agent relationship, in which the principal is required to take

[2] Given that the contractual framework addresses the monitoring and information asymmetry problems effectively, it might be argued that in venture capital fund limited partnerships the role of fiduciary duties should be limited (Ribstein 2002).

[3] See Myners (2001) who argues that English limited partnership law is particularly cumbersome because of strict constraints on the number of partners and on limited partners' involvement in investment advisory work. At the time partnership law was under construction in the UK, there was another deficiency in English partnership law: English partnerships were not legal entities. This explains why Scottish limited partnerships with separate legal personality were used as vehicles for investment in Lloyds, which only permitted separate legal persons to be Lloyds names.

precautionary measures to ensure that the agent will be less inclined to act opportunistically. The compensation of the venture capitalist is comprised of two main sources for managing investments in each limited partnership. First, venture capitalists are typically entitled to receive 20 per cent of the profits generated by each of the funds (Klausner and Litvak 2001). A second source of compensation is the management fees the venture capitalists charge to each venture (Gompers and Lerner 1999). The compensation system plays a critical role in aligning the interests of venture capitalists and limited partners (Sahlman 1990). Yet, in contrast to the corporate governance structure of the public corporation, where dispersed shareholders have disproportionately less control than equity, the governance structure of venture capital backed firms tends to allocate greater control to investors (Baums and Gilson 2000).

1.2.2. *Venture Capitalist Compensation*

The portfolio company's compensation structure also provides a means to reduce the agency costs that arise from allocating the venture capitalists with the discretion to control rate and type of the investments. There are two sources of compensation for the venture capitalist. First, venture capitalists are typically entitled to receive 20 per cent of the profits and 2.5 per cent of the assets (Baums and Gilson 2000). Second, the general partner will receive a management fee for each venture. The compensation rate is fairly uniform across the industry (Klausner and Litvak 2001). However, Gompers and Lerner (1999) point out that older and more established funds receive a lower fixed fee. Apparently, the reason for the lower compensation is a matter of incentives, that is, newer venture capitalists firms have powerful market-based incentives needed to develop a reputation for quality, which gradually over time leads to increased market share. While we may think that the compensation structure works in the main to reduce agency costs, its effectiveness can be questioned. For instance, Baums and Gilson (2000) argue that agency costs result from the details of the general partner's option-like carried interest. Indeed, it is here, in particular, that questions about whether the compensation system is effective in reducing the opportunism which grows out of giving the general partner the discretion to choose when, and under what conditions, to realize investments. In this context, Baums and Gilson argue that a clawback provision is perhaps the best mechanism to limit the distorted incentives of general partners. Moreover, similar problems may also emerge from the allocation of control to venture capitalists in respect of mandatory distributions. By accepting that contractual devices are unlikely to limit this type of agency cost problem, investors must rely ultimately on the reputation market to sort this problem out.

1.3. INVESTMENT SCREENING

The analysis in the previous section suggests that portfolio company compensation, which comes from a small management fee and carried interest, can resolve some of the agency problems between venture capitalists and investors. In this section, we turn to discuss how the screening techniques used by venture capitalists to evaluate business prospects serve to reduce the uncertainty and information problems associated with early stage financing.

Some of the success of the portfolio company's returns will be influenced by the effort and skill expended in screening 'good' from 'bad' entrepreneurs (Fried and Hisrich 1994).

The basic approach to the screening of venture capital investments involves a direct and indirect component. First, direct screening serves to overcome the information problem in two important respects. Direct screening involves selecting the 'good' projects based on the examination of the prospective pool of entrepreneurs' business plans (Tyebjee and Bruno 1984). Because venture capitalists specialize in specific technologies and markets, and evaluate many potentially good investment opportunities, the information asymmetries between portfolio firms and entrepreneurs are reduced. Empirical evidence on how venture capitalists evaluate potential investment opportunities is provided by Kaplan and Strömberg (2000) for the USA. In this study of forty-two ventures by ten venture capital firms, they point out that portfolio companies use four groups of criteria when evaluating an investment opportunity: (1) attractiveness of the project analysed in terms of market size and growth, product attractiveness, the strategy, the likelihood of customer adoption, and the competitive position of the venture; (2) the quality of the management team and its performance to date; (3) deal terms; and (4) the financial or exit condition. Based on these analyses, the venture capitalist can make reasonable projections about the project's risks and the likelihood of success. Venture capitalist firms also specialize by investing in companies at a specific development stages of the venture or in a particular industry (Sahlman 1990). For example, particular skills or expertise, besides financial analysis, will often lead venture capitalists to focus their activities on an industry or sector, such as biotechnology, where the critical factor for success is the optimal allocation of resources to R&D (Lerner 1994). Venture capitalists will also build up expertise in a distinct development stage, such as early stage investments, which reinforces their ability to evaluate potentially good investment opportunities. Even though specialized venture capitalists are able to build on their expertise and experience to reduce some of the risk associated with their investment, this does not imply that they are not subject to additional risks. As specialized venture capitalists will often build concentrated portfolios, they may actually expose themselves to higher levels of risk, particularly if their portfolios are not well diversified (Norton and Tennebaum 1993). It is noteworthy that as venture capitalist funds become larger, the degree of specialization tends to decline (Gupta and Sapienza 1992).

Second, the contractual terms of venture capitalists' securities, especially in the USA, contribute to the screening process. As in the case of convertible preferred securities, the stock provides for a preference for dividends and liquidation, conversion rights and anti-dilution provisions, pre-emptive rights, go-along rights, and information rights. As a consequence of making this investment, venture capitalists will be induced to make analyses about product market competition, technology, customer and adoption, management team proficiency, financial projections, and exit strategies. The results of these findings will contribute to venture capitalists becoming ever more informed about the valuation of the company and whether to extend further financing.

Staged financing represents one of the most important contractual terms that increase the expected value of the portfolio project and make it possible for venture capitalists to extend financing to early stage projects. In the next section, we show that staged financing provides the necessary incentives to align the interests of the entrepreneur and venture capital fund.

1.3.1. *Staged Financing of Venture Capital Investment*

Thus far we have argued that the venture capitalist fund's screening techniques tend to limit the problems of adverse selection and ensure that they are in a position to judge accurately the portfolio company's prospects. We address the special development technique— staged financing—which is designed to reduce the uncertainty associated with early stage, high-tech financing and supply high-powered incentives for entrepreneurs by creating performance incentives. An important advantage of staged financing is that it allows venture capitalists the real option to stop financing the venture. In most deals, the venture capitalist provides the entrepreneur with just enough capital to reach specific milestones. Specific milestones are linked to important events such as the completion of a business plan, the production of a prototype, the receipt of a patent, and the marketing of a product (Klausner and Litvak 2001). The fact that when a milestone has not been reached venture capitalists can abandon the project limits the downside risk (Bergemann and Hege, Chapter 5, this volume). If the initial funding runs out before the management team of the portfolio company fails satisfactorily to meet a milestone, the venture capitalist has the option either to abandon financing or reduce the level of financing by making a lower valuation of the portfolio company (Black and Gilson, Chapter 2, this volume). As such, the staging of investment commitment performs the same function as debt in a leveraged buyout (Gompers 1995). Even though the entrepreneur can take steps to locate new financing, the first-round backers' unwillingness to fund future rounds of the project is information revealing, and may serve to deter other venture capital funds from taking on the risk. Nor will potential new investors want to extend new finance to projects where the incumbent venture capitalist fund has a contractual right of first refusal to future financing.[4] Second, staged investment tends to limit the asymmetric information and agency problems associated with early stage investment. Accepting a contract that includes staged financing allows the entrepreneur to send a costly signal about the true quality of his project. Thus, only entrepreneurs confident about their skills and the quality of the venture will accept the incentive contract.

Staged investment also helps to attenuate the commitment problem of the entrepreneur. Given that the venture consists mainly of intangible assets at the beginning of the relationship and that the entrepreneur has the unique human capital that is critical to the success of the venture, the entrepreneur has considerable bargaining power over the claims to the venture's returns in the subsequent rounds. As a consequence, the technique of staged investing offers a potential solution to the hold-up problem. Moreover, it creates high-powered incentives for the entrepreneur to exert optimal effort to increase, for example, the speed of product development. In each stage of funding, the investors provide capital in exchange for shares of the venture. Because the entrepreneur is financially constrained, his ownership of the venture will be reduced after each round of financing. The entrepreneur can limit this effect by achieving a high valuation of the firm at each new stage of financing. The valuation determines the number of shares that will be sold. The venture

---

[4] Gilson (2002) claims that potential investors face a serious risk of the winner's curse. Having been permitted to make the investment, the new, uninformed, venture capitalists will likely overvalue the project.

capitalists and the entrepreneur fix the amounts of funds necessary to reach the next mile-stone. A positive correlation between high valuation and share price reduces the number of shares that must be sold. Thus, the threat of dilution supplies the entrepreneur with a high-powered incentive to exert more effort.

So far we have focused on the positive benefits of staged financing. There are, how-ever, a number of recent articles in the literature showing how staged financing can give rise to opportunistic behaviour by both parties. First, staging creates incentives for the entrepreneur to focus on increasing the likelihood of the short-term positive performance of the venture ('window-dressing') (Barry 1994; Cornelli and Yosha 2002). In order to increase the probability of gaining another round of financing, the entrepreneur will have an incentive to manipulate short-term performance either by emphasizing the conditions that affect the valuation more favourably or by focusing on short-term goals. Staging shifts the entrepreneur's focus from long-term goals to short-term signal manipulation, which consists of making a positive news more likely to appear.[5] Signal manipulation reduces the probability that the venture will be terminated. However, as this reduces the value of the option to abandon the project, it may become less likely that the venture capitalist will provide finance in the first place. Second, staging also puts the venture capitalist in a position to behave opportunistically. Both the initial venture capitalist and the entrepreneur know that by not investing in a future round, the initial venture capitalist sends a negative signal to other potential investors about the quality of the venture. As the signal is particularly important for early stage companies, the initial venture capitalist can misuse his bargaining power by extracting additional returns at the expense of the entrepreneur. Moreover, if the expected return is not sufficient to cover the opportunity costs of time, knowledge, and capital, the venture capitalist can choose to prematurely liquidate a venture that has economic value (Barry 1994). Convertible preferred stock, discussed in the next section, can attenuate the window-dressing problem caused by staging. Additionally, syndicating investments can serve to alleviate the hold-up problem of the venture capitalist.

1.3.2. *The Monitoring Process*

In exchange for their investments, monitoring, and advice, venture capitalists usually demand control rights that are disproportionate to their shareholdings. From the perspect-ive of the venture capitalist, monitoring of the entrepreneur and the interim performance of the venture is crucial to making the optimal continuation decision. During the post-contracting stage, the venture capitalist combines monitoring with advising activities, which are typically arranged by contract. The venture capitalist's control extends to advising management on strategic decisions, assisting in recruiting key personnel, repla-cing management, and providing assistance on other issues such as investment banking and legal advice (Sahlman 1990; Hellman and Puri 2000).

---

[5] An implicit assumption is that at intermediate stages the venture capitalist cannot observe the true quality of the venture due to the information asymmetry between venture capital funds and the entrepreneur.

Lerner (1995) finds that venture capitalists are more likely to join or be added to the board of ventures in periods when there is a change in chief executive officer (CEO). Therefore, one would expect venture capitalists to intensify their monitoring activities at times when it is more necessary. The board mechanism also allows the venture capitalist to have access to key information about the potential profitability of the venture. In addition, most venture capitalists demand timely access to information, including detailed monthly financial statements and other operating statements. They can demand to inspect the venture's financial accounts at will. Gorman and Sahlman (1989) find that venture capitalists spend approximately half of their time monitoring an average of nine ventures. Furthermore, one of their most frequent activities is to assist management in raising additional funds. Gupta and Sapienza (1992) find that the frequency of interaction between the entrepreneur and the venture capitalist depends on a number of factors: (*a*) the extent of the CEO's new venture experience; (*b*) the venture's stage of development; (*c*) the degree of technological innovation pursued by the venture; and (*d*) the extent of the congruence between the CEO and the venture capitalist. The result shows that the degree of management ownership has no impact on the frequency of interaction. These findings are important since they show that, even with a high degree of goal congruence, extreme levels of uncertainty may weaken signals about the appropriate course of action, therefore requiring actions to generate extra information (Wright and Robbie 1998).

1.3.3. *Replacement of Management*

This section considers the circumstances under which the entrepreneur will voluntarily relinquish control over the company. In their study of 173 Silicon Valley start-ups, Hellmann and Puri (2000) provide evidence that venture capital backed ventures are more likely than firms without venture capital support to adopt professionally designed stock option plans and hire a vice-president of sales. These firms, moreover, are twice as likely to hire CEOs from outside the firm.[6]

Hellmann (1998) offers a theoretical explanation for the entrepreneur's decision whether to step aside and make room for a professional CEO. There are a number of trade-offs that must be considered. On the one hand, venture capitalists point out that that top management teams add value to ventures whereas entrepreneurs are prone to undertake actions that are in their best interest as opposed to the company's interest. On the other hand, entrepreneurs typically do not want to be replaced since they would forego considerable private benefits of control. In addition, replacement may have a negative effect on their reputational capital. To be sure, venture capitalists will only fund a project if they are protected against the entrepreneur hold-up problem. As a consequence, the entrepreneur faces a trade-off to give the venture capitalist either a larger equity stake in the firm or more control. This trade-off, in turn, results in a number of further conflicts. One source of conflict occurs when the entrepreneur is left with an equity stake that is not large enough to induce him to exert optimal effort. A related problem is when the

---

[6] It is worth noting, however, that Baker and Gompers (2000) find that the likelihood of venture capital financing is not a good proxy for the probability that a CEO will be replaced.

venture capitalist does not hold control and therefore lacks the power to appoint a new management team. Hellmann's model presents a solution in which giving control to the venture capitalist will provide him with sufficient incentives to contract for professional management of the firm.

1.3.4. *Convertible Preferred Stock*

Some commentators suggest that the most suitable type of security to use in early stage ventures is convertible preferred stock (Gompers 1995; Schmidt 2000; Cornelli and Yosha 2002; Bergmann and Hege, Chapter 5, this volume). Convertible preferred equity is considered optimal because it secures downside protection for venture capitalists by providing seniority over straight equity, while it supplies entrepreneurs with sufficient incentives to take risks in order to create higher final firm value (Bratton, Chapter 6, this volume). Convertible preferred stock gives the venture capitalist a fixed claim on the returns of the venture in the form of a dividend. The unpaid dividends accrue and must be paid to the convertible preferred equity holders before the dividend is paid out to common stock holders (Sahlman 1990; Gompers 1998; Kaplan and Strömberg, Chapter 4, this volume). Common shares provide incentives to the entrepreneur as compensation is thus based on the performance of the venture (Jensen and Meckling 1976). Using convertible preferred stock also gives venture capitalists a senior claim on cash flow and distributions in the case where the venture is liquidated (Armour, Chapter 7, this volume).

There are a number of explanations for the popularity of convertible preferred equity. One possible explanation for this pattern is that convertible preferred stock—which confers a voting right—ensured venture capitalists protection against burdensome amendments that favour other classes. Furthermore, this class voting mechanism allows holders of preferred stock to elect half or more of the board of directors, which gives the venture capitalist substantial control over the board. Recall that if the venture capitalist gains control through the board of directors, he can thus opt to replace the management team. Next, we note that with convertible preferred stock investors have the option to convert their preferred shares into common shares, which allows them to capture part of the firm's upside gains. The conversion price is usually set equal to the purchase price of the security, ensuring a one-to-one conversion. In addition, the contract contains anti-dilution protections that limit opportunistic behaviour of entrepreneurs. Another often cited reason is that convertible preferred stock is made redeemable at the option of the venture capitalist, which ensures that they will secure some compensation for their investment (Sahlman 1990).

From a theoretical perspective, some economists argue that convertible preferred stock provides an efficient means for dealing with the double-sided moral hazard problem. Such a double-sided moral hazard problem exists when two principal–agent relationships arise between two parties. This is very common in venture capital contracting since both the entrepreneur and the venture capitalist are agents as well as principals (Berglöf 1994). Schmidt (2000) explains that convertible securities can be used to allocate cash flow rights contingent on the state of nature and the entrepreneur's efforts. As such, this contract reduces the double-sided moral hazard problem by inducing both the venture capitalist and the entrepreneur to invest optimally in the project. A critical assumption is that a positive relationship exists between the ultimate success of the project, project quality, the efforts of the entrepreneur, and the commitment of the venture capitalist.[7] He argues that convertible preferred stock outperforms all other mixtures of debt and equity. The model assumes that convertible preferred stock is used only by active investors, as the venture's success is highly dependent upon their final efforts. The critical component of the convertible debt contract is the conversion ratio. It must be set at such a level that it induces the venture capitalist to invest and convert only if the entrepreneur chooses at least the efficient effort level. This in turn induces the venture capitalist to choose the right level of effort even though he loses some portion of ownership. In the event of a bad state, the venture capitalist chooses not to convert, the entrepreneur defaults on the debt, and the venture capitalist, as the holder of the debt claims, would accordingly liquidate the venture.

It is widely acknowledged that convertible preferred stock is the dominant form of security used by venture capitalists in the USA (Triantis 2001). This may be due to the standardization of purchase agreements (Gilson and Schizer 2001). Recently a number of empirical studies have confirmed the importance of convertible preferred stock in the USA. For instance, Kaplan and Strömberg (2003) find in their study of 200 venture capital investments in 118 companies by fourteen venture capital firms in the USA that convertible preferred securities have been used in 79.8 per cent of financing rounds, while in about half of these convertible preferred were participating. Commentators argue that there are a number of reasons for the significantly higher usage of convertibles in the USA compared with Europe[8] and Canada.[9] First, it is assumed that US venture capitalists are more sophisticated and established than venture capitalists elsewhere, which accounts for the significantly less frequent use of these instruments by non-US venture capitalists. Second, the size of the European venture debt market and the preference on the part of venture capitalists in Europe for straight debt may account for the lower rate of use of convertibles (Cumming 2001). Third, Gilson and Schizer (2002) argue that US venture capitalists are attracted to the tax advantage associated with preference stock, which allows them to make a lower valuation for the entrepreneur's common shares. Implicit in this argument is the view that the tax incentives connected with the reduced initial valuation of common stock for venture capitalists is the reason for the significantly higher use of convertible

---

[7] Typically venture capitalists provide both funding and advice to each venture they invest in. Consequently, the quality of the venture capitalist is considered an important factor for the success of the venture (Hellmann and Puri 1999).

[8] Bascha and Walz (2001) show that German venture capitalists typically use equity and silent partnerships and other financial instruments to fund their investments (see Schwienbacher 2002).

[9] Cumming (2001) examines the use of different types of securities in financing transactions in Canada for the 1991–98 period. For this period, he finds that common stock is used in 41.0% of the transactions, straight debt in 14.6%, convertible debt in 12.7%, mixes of debt and equity in 4.7%, and other combinations in 13.6%. Canadian venture capitalists invest in several different types of entrepreneurial firms. These firms are distinguished by stage of development, first venture capital round, technology, number of employees, syndication, and deal size. Cumming found that start-ups more frequently use convertible preferred equity. In addition, the use of straight preferred equity and straight debt securities are equally likely for start-ups. In contrast, expansion stage firms are equally likely to use straight preferred debt, common stock, and warrants. The empirical analysis shows that the stage of development determines the type of security used to fund Canadian start-up firms, and that the differences in the use of convertibles cannot be attributed to institutional differences (taxation and securities regulation).

preferred stock, rather than the agency cost-reducing qualities of the instrument identified by models created by finance scholars.

1.3.5. *The Exiting Strategy of Venture Capital Firms*

The exiting of the portfolio company investment is the final stage in the venture capital process. Venture capital firms have several options when considering exiting a venture (Cumming and MacIntosh, Chapter 15, this volume). Indeed, Gladstone (1989) suggests that there are six ways in which a venture capital firm can exit a venture, namely: (1) the sale of a company's shares through an initial public offering; (2) the sale of shares to another company or a trade sale; (3) the repurchase of the shares by the company by leveraging the company or by buy-backs;[10] (4) the sale of shares to another investor; (5) the reorganization of the company; and (6) corporate liquidation. According to Barry *et al.* (1990), the first two techniques are the most popular exit routes for US venture capitalists. Unsurprisingly, the pattern in Europe presents a different picture, as data from most countries show that the most common exit strategy is the sale of shares to another company and liquidation (Jeng and Wells 2000; Schwienbacher 2002). Yet, there has been a marked increase in IPO activity in recent years (but prior to 2001) (Bottazzi and Da Rin 2002). The growth in listings can be largely explained by the rapid development of the new market segments created in continental Europe and the UK (Goergen *et al.*, Chapter 19, this volume).

It is claimed that the possibility of an exit through an IPO allows the venture capitalist to enter into an implicit contract with the entrepreneur concerning future control of the company (Black and Gilson, Chapter 2, this volume). Clearly, this creates a strong incentive for the entrepreneur to refrain from behaving opportunistically. However, Gompers (1996) shows that 'younger', as compared with 'older', venture capital firms have strong incentives to behave opportunistically by taking companies quicker to exit through an IPO. The reason is that a successful IPO allows the young venture capitalists to send a quality signal about their ability to potential investors. Moreover, experienced venture capital firms, with solid reputations, appear to be very good at taking companies public close to market peaks (Lerner 1994). It is worth pointing out that venture capital backed companies have less of a positive return on their first day of trading compared with non-venture backed IPOs (Barry *et al.* 1990). This finding supports the view that capital markets recognize the monitoring quality of venture capital firms. In other words, venture capital firms' reputational capital enables them to credibly certify the quality of the companies they take to the stock market (Megginson and Weiss 1991).

1.4. ISSUE COVERAGE

This book is divided into three parts. Part I considers which legal and institutional structures are necessary to stimulate a vibrant venture capital industry. The experience of the USA suggests that a vibrant venture capital market requires a contracting structure, labour

---

[10] This option is generally not feasible for the fast-growing, capital-consuming companies that are the typical focus for venture capital firms (Black and Gilson 1998).

mobility, risk tolerance, a well-developed stock market, and large, independent sources of venture capital funding (Gilson 2002). The authors in this part explore the relationship between the stock market and venture capital market and the contractual arrangements that facilitate investment in entrepreneurial enterprises. Part II examines the sources of venture capital's advantage in funding innovation and investigates direct effects of legislation on the venture capital market. The authors in this part also consider whether the introduction of new legal business forms can stimulate the start-up rate of new companies and whether regulatory competition can give momentum to the creation of US-type closely held business forms in Europe. Part III addresses the problem of valuation. The authors in this part explore the alternatives to traditional valuation techniques using discounted cash flows. These chapters are devoted to real options analysis, and the study of the return premiums of internet stocks. Part IV focuses on the importance of exit vehicles for venture capital funds. In light of their importance, the chapters in this part assess the relative merits of the full range of exit vehicles, the value of a US listing for foreign high-tech firms, the important function of IPOs in providing finance for start-up firms, and explanations for the performance of IPOs. These chapters also provide a critical assessment of current research on the new issues puzzle.

1.4.1. *Venture Capital Financing*

In Chapter 2, Bernard Black and Ronald Gilson consider the reasons for the relative strength of the stock market-centred venture capital markets. They argue that the ability of venture capitalists to exit is crucial to their decision to invest in start-up companies. In stock market-oriented markets, exit occurs through the IPO process in which the venture capitalist disposes of part of his investment in the firm. The provisions for mandatory conversion of venture capital in the event of a qualifying IPO also aligns the incentives by constraining the form of the venture capital's upside pay-offs. In contrast, investors in bank-oriented markets have a restricted exit route, namely by sales (or mergers) to third parties. In this chapter, Black and Gilson submit that the incentive properties of exit, via the automatic conversion of the IPO, provide parties with an implicit contract that offers the entrepreneur a call option on control exercisable on the firm's success. The absence of a similar market and regulatory structures in some European jurisdictions places their start-up firms at a competitive disadvantage.

Thomas Hellmann shows in Chapter 3 the potential disagreements between an entrepreneur and a venture capitalist about the desirability of taking a company public. To the extent that there is a potential conflict of interest between the parties, Hellmann asks the question whether the parties can bargain to obtain an optimal governance structure that resolves the conflict. In this case, the optimal structure would entail the transfer of control from the venture capitalist to the entrepreneur. It is suggested that convertible preferred stock provides the optimal contracting solution. That is, the transfer is effected by the automatic conversion of preferred stock, which at the time of the IPO takes away the option value of the convertible security. This provides an optimal incentive for the venture capitalist not to push the company too hard (or too early) into going public. In this chapter, Hellmann also derives the optimality of demand registration rights.

In Chapter 4, Steven Kaplan and Per Strömberg focus on the principal–agent problem in financial contracting. They argue that while the theoretical finance literature has developed a number of mechanisms to address incentive problems, there is little empirical work that has assessed the ability of different financial contracts to resolve the conflicts of interest between principal and agent. In order to fill in the gap, Kaplan and Strömberg, provide an overview of their recent empirical studies on real world venture capital contracts. In their study of 213 actual contracts between venture capitalists and entrepreneurs, they find that venture capitalists separately allocate control and cash flow rights, voting rights, board rights, liquidation rights, and other rights. It follows that these rights are linked to the performance of the firm. As discussed earlier in the introduction, they also find that convertible securities are used by most venture capitalists in the USA and report on recent work on the screening and monitoring of venture capital investments. Kaplan and Strömberg show, based on a sample of sixty-seven portfolio companies, that venture capitalists, when making an investment analysis, screen potential ventures using a range of factors, including market size, the strategy, technology, management team, customer adoption, competition, and deal terms. They also report about how venture capitalists' analyses relate to the design of financial contracts used in practice. Venture capital ownership is less important when there is less external and internal uncertainty and vice versa. Finally, they demonstrate that monitoring and post-investment information collection is a key element to the success of venture capital sponsored projects.

In Chapter 5, Dirk Bergemann and Ulrich Hege consider the provision of venture capital in a dynamic model with multiple research stages, where time and investment needed to meet each benchmark are unknown. The allocation of funds is subject to moral hazard. They note that the optimal contract provides for incentive payments linked to attaining the next benchmark. These incentive payments must be increasing in the funding horizon of each stage. Benchmarking reduces agency costs, directly by shortening the agent's guaranteed funding horizon, and indirectly via an implicit incentive effect of information rents in future financing rounds. Bergemann and Hege argue that the *ex ante* need to provide incentives and the venture capitalist's desire to cut information rents create a hold-up problem. The venture capitalists can overcome the hold-up problem by providing all funds in every stage in a single up-front payment. The entrepreneur controls the application of the funds that are supplied by the venture capitalist. Finally, Bergemann and Hege show that the optimal compensation of the entrepreneur should consist of a nested sequence of options contracts.

William Bratton examines the law and economics of the downside arrangements in venture capital contracts in Chapter 6. For Bratton, downside protection in venture capital contracts means two things: first, power to replace the firm's managers (or alternatively to force sale or liquidation of the firm), and, second, power to protect the venture contract from opportunistic amendments. Recent empirical work has shed considerable light on the fact that venture capital investments possess this protection in varying degrees, depending on the mode of their participation and the governing contracts' terms. The venture capitalist, however, remains vulnerable in a significant number of cases, lacking voting and boardroom control and relying entirely on terms articulated *ex ante* in the preferred stock contract. In these cases, Bratton argues that there is a risk of exposure to issuer opportunism in downside situations. He evaluates the risk, reviewing the contract terms employed in venture capital transactions and the case law on preferred stock. A mixed picture emerges. The terms of venture capitalist's contracts show marked improvement in most respects compared with the traditional preferred stock contracts. Yet, the convertible preferred stock contracts are far from optimal in terms of reducing the incentives of issuer opportunism. Moreover, venture capitalists holding preferred stock cannot simply rely on courts for protection. In particular, Delaware has taken the lead, sustaining a classic case of preferred stock victimization in a venture capital context. Contract law's good faith duty can be used to protect venture capital preferred without a risk of unproductive judicial interference in corporate affairs. Drawing on the control transfer model of Aghion and Bolton (1992), Bratton shows that the interests of senior security holders are aligned in a larger set of cases than previously supposed. He concludes by arguing that when disputes between venture capitalists and entrepreneurs come to court, a presumption favouring the common stockholder is not defensible on efficiency grounds.

1.4.2. *Innovation, Law, and Finance*

In Chapter 7, John Armour explores the role of the law and lawyers in the venture capital process, particularly in the UK and continental Europe. Armour documents a number of institutional and organizational forms that provide investors in ventures and entrepreneurs with high-powered incentives and mechanisms to protect their rights. A number of economic studies further support the claim of the importance of legal rules and contractual structures for solving the central agency problems of venture capital contracting. In order to assess the importance of law, Armour surveys the differences in legal and institutional structures across countries. In particular, he points out that venture capitalists in Europe use convertibles significantly less frequently. There are a number of explanations for the international differences in legal and financial regulation of convertible preferred stock: (1) a Darwinian explanation of the evolution and dissemination of the 'better-adapted' terms; and (2) the ubiquity of convertible preferred stock in the USA is the product of regulatory and tax regulations. Overall, Armour suggests that there is sufficient support for the tax argument (the reason why US venture capitalists compared with those in continental Europe prefer convertible preferred stock). The extent that venture capitalists in the UK—which also has a favourable treatment of convertible preferred stock—use convertibles at a rate similar to the USA provides further support for the 'law matters' thesis. Armour also highlights the importance of law for the venture capital market by showing how changes in the regulation of pension fund investment contribute to the upsurge of venture capital fundraising in the USA during the 1980s. If the UK government were to implement the Myners Review recommendation to eliminate the minimum funding requirement for defined-benefit pension schemes, he speculates that the financing of start-up firms would most certainly increase.

In Chapter 8, Joseph McCahery and Erik Vermeulen explore the circumstances under which European lawmakers will contemplate taking steps to design new legal business forms that could support the further development of a European-wide venture capital market. In this chapter, the authors argue that flexible business forms must play a central role in the development of a robust venture capital industry. If there is a trade-off between the cost of entry and the success rate of business start-ups backed by venture capital, it seems more important to reduce government sponsorship programmes and stimulate business law reform which benefits entrepreneurs, venture capitalists, and outside investors alike. McCahery and Vermeulen survey the recent history of legal business form innovation in Europe, noting that the absence of new business vehicles may be due to a status quo bias. Most European close corporations tend to rely on standard legal rules: as most parties are familiar with these, the costs of using them are reduced. This is not to say that many of the standard rules are cumbersome and inefficient. They note that even if a firm had additional incentives to employ a different legal form, it is unlikely to select the vehicle due to the lack of certainty about legal rules and the signal it would send to suppliers of capital. The authors consider the possibility of making new business forms based on the US Limited Liability Company available in Europe. Prospects for the emergence of a corporate-type partnership entity depend in the main on the removal of legal and non-legal barriers. In terms of assessing the likelihood of the enactment of new business forms, the authors compare and weigh the competing interests on the supply and demand side of legislation. They conclude that the outcome will depend largely on the alliance of market sector interests groups. As far as a national government acts as an entrepreneur, it may be plausible to assert that a small state could seek to further its comparative advantage by making particular adjustments to its company law such that its partnership laws meets the needs of all types of firms.

In Chapter 9, Samuel Kortum and Josh Lerner focus on the public programmes designed to support the creation of venture capital funds. These programmes are justified on the grounds that venture capital has become an important source of funding for entrepreneurs. Indeed, an important source of funding for some of the early high-tech firms was the Small Business Investment Company. Moreover, the role of government funds in Israel is also viewed as an important factor in the formation of venture capital funds in the early 1990s. Similarly, a number of European and Asian countries have supported the development of venture capital funds. Kortum and Lerner's concern is to evaluate systematically the policies that promote venture capital and determine the effect of programmes in terms of stimulating innovation. The aim of this chapter is to model the relationship between venture capital, R&D, and innovation. Kortum and Lerner study the annual data for twenty US manufacturing industries for the period 1965–92. They report that the patenting patterns across the industries for the time period tends to support the view that venture capital is crucial for innovation. The evidence reveals that venture capital was responsible for 8 per cent of the innovations in the decade ending in 1992. Kortum and Lerner show, furthermore, that venture funding accounted for approximately 14 per cent of US innovations for the period ending in 1998. They conclude that the increased level of venture funding during the 1990s was primarily responsible for the increase in innovative activities.

1.4.3. *Valuation of High-tech Firms*

Hans Smit and Lenos Trigeorgis introduce the reader in Chapter 10 to the real options valuation techniques developed to cope with the high uncertainty of cash flows of projects or corporations. They demonstrate that in volatile markets the strategic position of a firm can be vulnerable not just to the actions of known competitors, but also to the unanticipated entry of new competitors, substitute products, or entirely new technologies that can modify the very competitive landscape it operates under. Embracing a new conceptual approach, Smith and Trigeorgis consider a firm's growth opportunities as a package of corporate real options. These options are actively managed by the firm, and may be affected by competitive actions, such that various strategic considerations of importance to practising managers can be finally brought into the analysis in a rigorous fashion consistent with the tenets of both industrial organization and modern finance. They assert that a combination of real options analysis and game theory can help answer many strategic questions that are important for corporate success in dynamic and volatile industries. Questions addressed by Smith and Trigeorgis include: What is the value of the growth opportunities in the business? When is it appropriate to speed up investment in order to capture a larger market share or pre-empt competitive entry altogether, and when is it better to maintain the flexibility of a 'wait-and-see' approach? Should the firm compete in R&D or is it more beneficial to take an accommodating stance vis-à-vis competition (e.g. via a joint research venture or another form of strategic alliance)?

In Chapter 11, John Hand examines how and why the stock market values high technology by examining the pricing of 606 publicly traded biotechnology firms in the USA. Contrary to the common view that the primary value drivers of biotechnology are 'soft' variables such as intellectual human capital, patents, strategic alliances, and joint ventures, the author shows that simple but 'hard' balance sheet, income statement, and statement of cash flows data explains some 70 per cent of the variance in biotech firms' equity market values within a log-linear regression framework. Given the size and economic importance of R&D to biotech firms, the mapping between the biotech firms' R&D expenditures and equity market values is also investigated. John Hand hypothesizes that the elasticity of equity market value with respect to R&D is a function of five factors: where the R&D lies in the biotech value chain of discovery, development, and commercialization; the growth rate in R&D spending; the scale of R&D expenditures; the human capital of the firm's employees; and the age of the firm. Using financial statement proxies for these factors, he finds that the elasticity of biotech firms' equity market values with respect to R&D is significantly larger the earlier the R&D expenditure is in the value chain, and the greater is the growth rate in R&D spending. The value elasticity of R&D is also reliably decreasing in the scale of R&D expenditures, and the maturity of the firm. Once can infer from the results of this chapter that despite the typically huge uncertainty inherent in the production and investment functions of biotechnology companies, particularly with regard to R&D, investors appear to price the equity of such firms in a more sophisticated manner than would be supposed from a popular viewpoint. Investors map the components of shareholder equity and net income into equity market values for biotech firms in similar directions to non-biotech firms. Investors also seem to value the key R&D intangible in a manner that recognizes the stage that the firm's R&D is at in the value chain, the likelihood that the firm will obtain property rights on its R&D, and the firm's maturity. Such sophistication would seem to bode well for the growth and accuracy of capital allocation in this growing area of high technology.

Enrico Perotti and Silvia Rossetto advance in Chapter 12 a theoretical approach using real options methodology to value entry options. They investigate the valuation of new Internet projects like platform investments (e.g. software operating systems or an Internet portal). Platform investment is the creation of an innovative distribution and production infrastructure that increases access to customers; as a result it reduces entry costs in related products. Relative to conventional producers, firms built around platforms enjoy strategic pre-emptive advantages, creating a set of entry options in uncertain market segments, to be exercised once demand ensures profitability. In a context of increased uncertainty, the relative value of platform to traditional strategies increases; moreover, the value of waiting to invest rises, but the value of platforms increases even more.

In Chapter 13, Michael Cooper and Raghavendra Rau argue that there is a strong positive stock price reaction to the announcement of corporate name changes into Internet-related dotcom names. This 'dotcom' effect produces cumulative abnormal returns on the order of 77 per cent for the ten days surrounding the announcement day. The effect does not appear to be transitory; there is no evidence of a post-announcement negative drift. These results may be driven by a degree of investor mania—investors seem to be eager to be associated with the Internet at all costs. This is supported by the fact that announcement returns are similar across all firms, regardless of the company's actual involvement with the Internet. Evidence of investor mania seems especially true when we consider the finding that firms with little or no sales generated from the Internet experience the greatest long horizon returns. The returns to firms announcing dotcom name changes are much greater during the months in which more name changes occur. This suggests that there has been a 'hot' name change period. The question which remains however is why an Internet firm should command such a premium from investors. Some suggest that Internet stock prices are influenced by non-financial data such as web usage data or the supply and demand for Net stocks. This result is surprising since the ultimate determinant of the stock price of any company should be the cash flows the company earns. In this chapter, Cooper and Rau examine if the pricing of Internet stocks is rational by examining the cross-section of return premiums earned by a very unique set of Internet firms, namely those firms which change their names to dotcom names. They are unique because these firms provide us with a 'pure' Internet premium; the firms have not undergone any change in fundamentals, yet they appear to be 'repriced' as Internet stocks after the name change. In a multivariate setting, the relative importance of variables that ought to capture fundamental value is investigated along with a number of proxies for 'irrational' pricing, such as changes in firm volume measure price pressure effects, dummy variables measuring the degree to which a dotcom name change firm is involved with the Internet, and others.

In Chapter 14, Didier Cossin, Benoît Leleux, and Entela Saliasi argue that valuing early stage high-tech companies is a challenge to current valuation methodologies. They suggest that the inability to come up with robust point estimates of value should not and does not lead to the breakdown of market liquidity. Instead, efforts are redirected towards the design of investment contracts that materially skew the distribution of pay-offs in favour of the venture investors. In effect, they submit that limitations in valuation abilities are addressed by designing the investment contracts as baskets of real options instead of linear pay-off functions. In this chapter, the authors investigate one common feature of venture capital contracts, namely the liquidation preference. By employing a real options perspective, using closed-form analytics and numerical analysis to draw inferences for future contract design, they conclude that it is possible to design optimal contracts that balance incentives, risk protection, and the sharing of the upside potential.

1.4.4. *Venture Capital Exits and IPOs*

In Chapter 15, Douglas Cumming and Jeffrey MacIntosh consider the issue of when venture capitalists make a partial, as opposed to a full exit, for the full range of exit vehicles. A full exit for an IPO involves a sale of all of the venture capitalist's holdings within one year of the IPO; a partial exit involves a sale of only part of the venture capitalist's holdings within that period. Usually, a full acquisition exit involves the sale of the entire firm for cash whereas, in a partial acquisition, the venture capitalist receives (often illiquid) shares in the acquirer firm. In the case of a buyback exit (in which the entrepreneur buys out the venture capitalist) or a secondary sale, a partial exit entails a sale of only part of the venture capitalist's holdings. A partial write-off involves a write down of the investment. In the chapter, Cumming and MacIntosh consider the determinants of full and partial venture capital exits for all five exit vehicles. They also perform a number of comparative empirical tests on samples of full and partial exits derived from a survey of Canadian and US venture capital firms. The evidence offers support to the central hypothesis, namely that the greater the degree of information asymmetry between the selling venture capitalist and the buyer, the greater the likelihood of a partial exit to signal quality. The evidence also indicates the differences between US and Canadian venture capital industries, and highlights the impact of legal and institutional factors on strategies across countries.

In Chapter 16, Edward Rock critically evaluates Black and Gilson's view that venture capital can flourish especially if venture capitalists can exit from successful portfolio companies through an initial public offering. He demonstrates that there is nothing in the Black and Gilson analysis that suggests the IPO exit must take place through a domestic stock market. Evidence from Israeli high-tech companies going public on the NASDAQ is used to explore the connection between a venture capital industry and domestic markets in a world of global capital and product markets. Rock argues that an important aspect of the success of the Israeli venture capital market has been the ability of start-ups to list their shares on NASDAQ and the NYSE and 'piggyback' on the securities law of the USA. In this empirical investigation of more than forty Israeli high-tech firms, Rock assesses the value of a US listing for a high-tech firm. For an Israeli firm, the process of going public requires fundamental changes in the internal organization of the company and the governance structure of the firm. In practice, Israeli firms relocate to the USA because it provides them with access to investors and product markets. As a consequence of the flow of IPOs on the NASDAQ in the 1990s, the Tel Aviv Stock Exchange has played a limited role in the development of the Israeli venture capital market. To the extent that Israel has become successful in the high-tech field, Rock concludes that this reflects the driving influence of US corporations and US venture capitalists in funding Israeli projects.

In Chapter 17, Susanne Espenlaub, Marc Goergen, Arif Khurshed, and Luc Renneboog provide a comprehensive overview of lock-in agreements contained in IPO prospectuses in the UK. A lock-in agreement restricts the original shareholders from tendering their shares for a given period of time after the listing of a firm. The chapter shows the effect of UK lock-in agreements on the abnormal returns of stocks with and without venture capital backed finance. The authors argue that an analysis of the lock-in agreements is particularly relevant due to the UK's distinct institutional and regulatory framework. Unlike the USA, where there is a trend towards a standardized 180-day lock-agreement, there is much greater diversity in lock-in agreements in the UK. They note, moreover, that regulatory requirements also contribute to the differences between the US and UK pattern. For instance, the London Stock Exchange required, until 2000, that only certain types of companies (i.e. mineral, scientific, and scientific research-based companies) seeking a listing—and did not satisfy the minimum age requirement of three years—were subject to a mandatory lock-in period. There is evidence that the length of the lock-in period is important to venture capitalists that seek to use the IPO as an exit route. Studies focusing on the efforts of venture capitalists to limit agency costs show that the length of the lock-in period is shorter for venture capital backed firms than non-venture capital backed firms. The authors examine the lock-in agreements of 186 UK IPOs issued during the 1992–98 period. First, they confirm the view that the lock-in period is substantially longer in the UK than the USA. The average period in the UK is 561 days. Second, they find significantly lower abnormal returns for venture capital-backed IPOs compared with other firms, which is consistent with results reported in the USA.

Raghuram Rajan and Henri Servaes take up in Chapter 18 the question of why initial public offerings underperform over time. They hypothesize that cycles in underpricing, long-run underperformance, and fluctuations in IPO volume are related to behaviour that can be explained as irrational on the part of investors. While Rajan and Servaes are aware of the limitations of explicit models relying on irrational behaviour, they attempt to take account of the effect of irrational behaviour on share price effects by modelling two forms of irrationality: (1) investor sentiment or price-insensitive demand; and (2) feedback tracer risk or the propensity of investors to chase trends. The empirical evidence confirms that these factors partially explain the three anomalies associated with the IPO market: (i) underpricing, (ii) windows of opportunity for new issues, and (iii) long-term underperformance. The study also provides evidence that investor interest in IPOs is related to the extend of underpricing, that strong growth predictions by analysts about IPOs forecast long-run underperformance, and that fluctuations in investor overoptimism about IPOs create windows of opportunity for firms to seek a stock exchange listing.

In Chapter 19, Marc Goergen, Arif Khurshed, Joseph McCahery, and Luc Renneboog argue that firms with high growth rates and volatile cash flows should go public early in their life cycle and allow their founders to diversify their investments. The lack of a possible future diversification of entrepreneurs' portfolios has been seen to be one of the major obstacles to the creation of high-tech businesses in Europe. Meantime, several European countries have launched new secondary markets in order to facilitate the financing of innovative companies with high growth potential. These were the type of companies that continental European listing rules would have earlier excluded. The aim of this chapter is to analyze whether the Euro.NMs fulfill their role of promoting new set-up firms by providing an adequate level of liquidity and a device for separating ownership and control quickly after the foundation of high-risk/high-growth businesses. The authors observe that the early success of the Euro.NMs was remarkable: at the end of May 2000, 438 companies from thirteen countries were listed across all the Euro.NMs, the total amount of new capital raised exceeded €23.5 billion, and the total market capitalization was around €234 billion. However, since the dissolution of the Euro.NMs in 2000, the markets have suffered from the decline in technology stocks with losses on some markets exceeding 80 per cent. Moreover, the Deutsche Börse AG announced in September 2002 that the Neuer Markt, which has seen its market capitalization decline by more than 95 per cent of its value in the last two years, would be closed for trading in 2003. The authors argue that further consolidation (and perhaps liquidation) is inevitable given the failure of the New Markets to attract foreign companies. The announcement that NASDAQ is quitting Europe appears to confirm that claim. While it is clear that the Euro.NMs developed a very active IPO market, the authors also focus on the important questions as to the specific causes of high-tech IPO underpricing and the subsequent severe underperformance. In this study, the entire population of IPOs from all five markets from the first day of trading until the end of 2000 is examined. In terms of initial returns, the authors show that underpricing ranges from only 4 per cent on the Nouveau Marche (Paris) to 86 per cent in the Netherlands (Amsterdam). It is argued that the performance discrepancies can largely be explained by differences in firm and industry characteristics and by agency conflicts between issuers and investment banks rather than by differences in (stock exchange) regulation. Inspection of the data also shows substantial long-run underperformance of Euro.NMs.

1.5. CONCLUSION

The debate on the development of an efficient venture capital market has forced policy-makers to consider which financial instruments, legal rules, labour laws, contracts, and other institutional structures are necessary to create a venture capital market. The contributions to this book have offered insights on the structure of venture capital fund financial contracts, the screening, monitoring, and staging of potential investments, the importance of partnership and other legal business forms for investors and start-up firms, the funding of innovation, the valuation of investments, and the exit routes for venture capitalists. The chapters in this volume, which draw upon international evidence and ideas from financial economics and law, will hopefully contribute to further research on the relationship between venture capitalists and entrepreneurs.

References

Aghion, P. and Bolton, P. (1992), 'An incomplete contracts approach to financial contracting', *Review of Economic Studies* 59, 473–94.

Audretsch, D. B. and Thurik, R. (2001), 'Linking entrepreneurship to growth, organization for economic cooperation and development', Working paper, STI.

Baker, M. and Gompers, P. A. (2000), 'The determinants of board structure and function in entrepreneurial firms', Working paper, Harvard University.

Barry, C. B. (1994), 'New directions in research on venture capital finance', *Financial Management* 23, 3–15.

——, Muscarella, C. J., Peavy, J. W. III., and Vetsuypens, M. R. (1990), 'The role of venture capital in the creation of public companies', *Journal of Financial Economics* 27, 447–71.

Bascha, A. and Walz, U. (2001), 'Financing practices in the German venture capital industry: an empirical assessment', Working paper, University of Tübingen.

Baums, T. and Gilson, R. J. (2000), 'Comparative venture capital contracting', Working paper, Stanford University.

Becker, R. and Hellman, T. (2001), 'The Genesis of Venture Capital: Lessons from the German Experience', Working paper, Stanford University.

Berglöf, E. (1994), 'A control theory of venture capital finance', *Journal of Law, Economics, and Organization* 10, 247–67.

Black, B. S. and Gilson, R. J. (1998), 'Venture capital and the structure of capital markets: banks versus stock markets', *Journal of Financial Economics* 47, 243–77.

Boot, A. W. A. and Verheyen, P. A. (1997), 'Financiering en macht: van financiële structuur naar beheersstructuur', Deventer: Kluwer BedrijfInformatie.

Bottazzi, L. and Da Rin, M. (2002), 'Venture capital in Europe and the financing of innovative companies', Economic Policy: A European Forum, 231–63.

Cornelli, F. and Yosha, O. (2002), 'Stage financing and the role of convertible debt', Working paper, London Business School.

Cumming, D. J. (2001), 'The convertible preferred equity puzzle in Canadian venture capital finance', Working paper, University of Alberta.

—— and MacIntosh, J. G. (2002), 'Crowding out private equity: Canadian evidence', Working paper, University of Alberta.

European Commission (1998), 'Risk capital: a key to job creation in the European Union', Brussels 31 March 1998, SEC (1998) 552 final.

EVCA (1996), (European Private Equity and Venture Capital Association), *1996 Yearbook*, Bruges: EVCA.

—— (2000), (European Private Equity and Venture Capital Association), *2000 Yearbook*, Bruges: EVCA.

—— (2001), (European Private Equity and Venture Capital Association), *2001 Yearbook*, Bruges: EVCA.

Fried, V. H. and Hisrich, R. D. (1994), 'Toward a model of venture capital investment decision making', *Financial Management* 23, 28–37.

Gilson, R. J. (2002), 'Engineering a venture capital market: Lessons from the American Experience', Working paper, Stanford Law School.

—— and Schizer, D. M. (2001), 'Understanding venture capital structure: a tax explanation for convertible preferred stock', Working paper, Stanford University.

Gladstone, D. (1989), *Venture Capital Investing*, Englewood Cliffs: Prentice Hall.

Gompers, P. A. (1995), 'Optimal investment, monitoring, and the staging of venture capital', *Journal of Finance* 50, 1461–89.

—— (1996), 'Grandstanding in the venture capital industry', *Journal of Financial Economics* 42, 133–56.

—— (1998), 'Ownership and control in entrepreneurial firms: an examination of convertible securities in venture capital investments', Working paper, Harvard University.

—— and Lerner, J. (1996), 'The use of covenants: an analysis of venture partnership agreements', *Journal of Law and Economics* 39, 463–98.

—— and Lerner, J. (1999), *The Venture Capital Cycle*, Cambridge, MA: MIT Press.

—— and Lerner, J. (2000), 'Money chasing deals? The impact of fund inflows on private equity valuations', *Journal of Financial Economics* 55, 281–325.

Gorman, M. and Sahlman, W. A. (1989), 'What do venture capitalists do?', *Journal of Business Venturing* 4, 231–48.

Gupta, A. K. and Sapienza, H. J. (1992), 'Determinants of venture capital firms' preferences regarding the industry diversity and geographical scope of their investments', *Journal of Business Venturing* 7, 347–62.

Hellman, T. (1998), 'The allocation of control right in venture capital contracts', *Rand Journal of Economics* 29, 57–76.

—— and Puri, M. (1999), 'Venture capital and the professionalization of start-up firms: empirical evidence', Working paper, Stanford University Business School.

—— and Puri, M. (2000), 'The interaction between product market and financial strategy: The role of venture capital', *Review of Financial Studies* 13, 959–84.

Jensen M. C. and Meckling, W. H. (1976), 'Theory of the firm: managerial behaviour, agency costs, and ownership structure', *Journal of Financial Economics* 3, 305–60.

Jeng, L. A. and Wells, P. C. (2000), 'The determinants of venture capital funding: evidence across countries', *Journal of Corporate Finance* 6, 241–89.

Kaplan, S. N. and Strömberg, P. (2003), 'Financial contracting theory meets the real world: an empirical analysis of venture capital contracts', *Review of Economic Studies*, 70, 281–315.

—— and —— (2000), 'How do venture capitalists choose investments', Working paper, University of Chicago.

Keuschnigg, C. (2003), 'Optimal public policy for venture capital backed innovation', Working paper, University of St Gallen.

Klausner, M. and Litvak, K. (2001), 'What economists have taught us about venture capital contracting', in M. J. Whincop (ed.), *Bridging the Entrepreneurial Gap: Linking Governance With Regulatory Policy*, Aldershot: Ashgate, 54–74.

Law Commission of England and Wales and Scotland Law Commission (2001), *The Limited Partnership Act 1907: A Joint Consultation Paper* (London: TSO) LCCP 161, SLCDP 118.

Lerner, J. (1994), 'The syndication of venture capital investments', *Financial Management* 23, 16–27.

—— (1995), 'Venture capitalists and the oversight of private firms', *Journal of Finance* 50, 301–18.

Megginson, W. L. (2002), 'Toward a global model of venture capital', *Journal of Applied Corporate Finance* (forthcoming).

—— and Weiss, K. A. (1991), 'Venture capital certification in initial public offerings', *Journal of Finance* 46, 879–903.

Myners, P. (2001), *Institutional Investors in the United Kingdom: A Review*, HM Treasury.

Norton, E. and Tennebaum, B. H. (1993), 'The effects of venture capitalists' characteristics on the structure of the venture capital deal', *Journal of Small Business Management* 1, 32–41.

NVCA (1998), 'Eight annual economic impact of venture capital study: a study conducted by Coopers & Lybrand and Venture One', Arlington, VA.

Poterba, J. M. (1989), 'Capital gains tax policy toward entrepreneurship', *National Tax Journal* 42, 375–89.

Ribstein, L. A. (2002), 'Confining fiduciary duties', Working paper, University of Illinois.

Sahlman, W. A. (1988), 'Aspects of financial contracting in venture capital', *Journal of Applied Corporate Finance* 1, 23–36.

Sahlman, W. A. (1990), 'The structure and governance of venture-capital organizations', *Journal of Financial Economics* 27, 473–521.

Saunders, A. and Schmeits, A. (2002), 'The role of bank funding for the corporate sector: the Netherlands in an international perspective', Working paper, Amsterdam Center for Corporate Finance.

Schmidt, K. M. (2000), 'Convertible securities and venture capital finance', Working paper, University of Munich.

Schwienbacher, A. (2002), 'An empirical analysis of venture capital exits in Europe and US', Working paper, University of Namur.

Triantis, G. G. (2001), 'Financial contract design in the world of venture capital', Working paper, University of Chicago.

Tyebjee, T. T. and Bruno, A. V. (1984), 'A model of venture capital investment activity', *Management Science* 30, 1051–66.

Tykvová, T. (2000), 'Venture capital in Germany and its impact on innovation', Working paper, Centre for European Economic Research, University of Mannheim.

Wright, M. and Robbie, K. (1998), 'Venture capital and private equity: a review and synthesis', *Journal of Business Finance and Accounting* 25, 521–70.

PART I

VENTURE CAPITAL FINANCING

2

Venture Capital and the Structure of Capital Markets: Banks versus Stock Markets

BERNARD S. BLACK AND RONALD J. GILSON

2.1. INTRODUCTION

Contrasting capital markets in the USA with those of Japan and Germany has become a commonplace activity. The USA has a large number of comparatively small banks that play a limited role in the governance of large corporations, and a well-developed stock market with an associated market for corporate control that figures prominently in corporate governance. In contrast, Japanese main banks and German universal banks are few in number but larger in size, relative to Japanese and German firms, and are said to play a central corporate governance role in monitoring management (e.g. Aoki 1994; Roe 1994). Neither country has an active market for corporate control.

Advocates of bank-centred capital markets claim that this structure fosters patient capital markets and long-term planning, while a stock market-centred capital market is said to encourage short-term expectations by investors and responsive short-term strategies by managers (e.g. Porter 1992; Edwards and Fischer 1994). Advocates of stock market-centred systems (e.g. Gilson 1996) stress the adaptive features of a market for corporate control, which are lacking in bank-centred systems, and the lack of empirical evidence of short-termism.

Paralleling the assessment of the comparative merits of stock market and bank-centred capital markets, scholars have also sought to explain how the USA, Germany, and Japan developed such different capital markets. Recent work has stressed that the characteristics of the three capital markets do not reflect simply the efficient outcome of competition between institutions, in which the most efficient institutions survive. The nature of the

The authors are grateful for helpful suggestions from the editors and an anonymous referee, and from Anant Admanti, Erik Berglof, Stephen Choi, Kevin Davis, Uri Geiger, Victor Goldberg, Paul Gompers, Joseph Grundfest, Ehud Kamar, Michael Klausner, Joshua Lerner, Ronald Mann, Paul Pfleiderer, Mark Ramsayer, Charles Sabel, Allen Schwartz, and Omri Yadlin, and from participants in workshops at Columbia Law School, Harvard Law School, Stanford Law School, the Max Planck Institute (Hamburg), and the American Law and Economics Association. Research support was provided by Columbia Law School and the Roberts Program in Law and Business, Stanford Law School. We thank Laura Menninger, Nishani Naidoo, Annette Schuller, and Ram Vasudevan for research assistance. This article was published in *Journal of Financial Economics* 47, 243–77 (1998) and is printed here with permission.

American capital market—a strong stock market, weak financial intermediaries, and the absence of the close links between banks and non-financial firms said to characterize the Japanese and German capital markets—reflects, at least in part, politics, history, and path-dependent evolution, rather than economic inevitability (e.g. Black 1990; Roe 1994; Gilson 1996). Much the same seems to be true of Germany and Japan (Hoshi 1993; Roe 1994). To be sure, competitively driven evolution hones efficiency, but institutions that emerge are shaped at critical stages by the random hand of events and the instrumental hand of politics.

In this chapter, we seek to contribute to two literatures. First, we extend the debate about the relative efficiency of bank- and stock market-centred capital markets by documenting and explaining a second systematic difference between the two systems: the existence of a much stronger venture capital industry in stock market-centred systems.

We define 'venture capital', consistent with American understanding, as investment by specialized venture capital organizations (which we call 'venture capital funds') in high-growth, high-risk, often high-tech firms that need capital to finance product development or growth and must, by the nature of their business, obtain this capital largely in the form of equity rather than debt. We exclude 'buyout' financing that enables a mature firm's managers to acquire the firm from its current owners, even though in Europe so-called 'venture capital' firms often provide such financing—more often, in many cases, than the financing that Americans call venture capital.

Other countries have openly envied the US venture capital market and have actively, but unsuccessfully, sought to replicate it. We offer an explanation for this failure: we argue that a well-developed stock market that permits venture capitalists to exit through an initial public offering (IPO) is critical to the existence of a vibrant venture capital market.

Understanding this critical link between the stock market and the venture capital market requires that we understand the implicit and explicit contractual arrangements between venture capital funds and their investors, and between venture capital funds and entre-preneurs. This brings us to our second contribution: we extend the literature on venture capital contracting by offering an explanation for two characteristics of the US venture capital market. First, we explain the importance of exit—why venture capital providers seek to liquidate their portfolio company investments in the near to moderate term, rather than investing for the long term like Japanese or German banks. Second, we explain the importance of the form of exit: why the potential for the venture capital provider to exit from a successful start-up through an IPO, available only through a stock market, allows venture capital providers to enter into implicit contracts with entrepreneurs concerning future control of start-up firms in a way not available in a bank-centred capital market. Thus, we make explicit a functional link between private and public equity markets: the implicit contract over future control that is permitted by the availability of exit through an IPO helps to explain the greater success of venture capital as an organizational form in stock market-centred systems.

Section 2.2 motivates the theoretical analysis by contrasting the venture capital markets in the USA and Germany. Section 2.3 develops the importance of exit from venture capital investments to the viability and structure of the venture capital industry. Exit serves two key functions. First, venture capital investors specialize in providing portfolio companies with a combination of financial capital, monitoring and advisory services, and reputational capital. The combination of financial and non-financial services loses its efficiency advantages as the portfolio company matures. Thus, recycling venture capital investors' capital through exit and reinvestment is jointly efficient for the provider and the portfolio company. Second, exit facilitates contracting between venture capital managers (persons with expertise in identifying and developing promising new businesses) and providers of capital to venture capital managers. The exit price gives capital providers a reliable measure of the venture capital manager's skill. The exit and reinvestment cycle also lets capital providers withdraw capital from less skilled venture capital managers or managers whose industry-specific expertise no longer matches the nature of promising start-up firms. It supports an implicit contract under which capital providers reinvest in the future limited partnerships of successful venture capital managers.

Section 2.4 focuses on the implicit contract over control between the entrepreneur and the venture capital fund. The potential to exit through an IPO allows the entrepreneur and the venture capital fund to enter into a self-enforcing implicit contract over control, in which the venture capital fund agrees to return control to a successful entrepreneur by exiting through an IPO. This implicit contract cannot readily be duplicated in a bank-centred capital market. Section 2.5 compares the predictions from our informal model with evidence about the success of venture capital in other countries, including Canada, Great Britain, Israel, and Japan. Section 2.6 considers alternative explanations for the observed international patterns of venture capital development, especially differences in legal rules. Some of these reasons may have predictive power, but none has enough power to displace our theory as an explanation for a substantial portion of the observed intercountry variation. Section 2.7 considers the implications of the symbiosis between stock markets and venture capital markets for efforts by other countries to expand their venture capital markets. Section 2.8 concludes.

2.2. THE VENTURE CAPITAL INDUSTRY IN THE USA AND GERMANY

In this section, we compare the venture capital industries in the USA and Germany in order to motivate the theory developed in Sections 3 and 4, in which a stock market-centred capital market (present in the USA but absent in Germany) is a precondition of a substantial venture capital industry.

The USA has a much more fully developed venture capital market than Germany. The differences are of both size and substance. The USA has a larger number of funds and the funds themselves are larger relative to each country's economy. Substantively, US funds are more heavily invested in early stage ventures and high-tech industries, while German venture capital provides primarily later-stage financing in lower-technology industries.

The US venture capital market is quite large. As of the end of 1994, 591 US venture capital funds had total investments (from which the fund had not yet exited or been written off) of around $34 billion (Venture Capital Yearbook, 1995). New investment in venture capital funds in 1996 was $6.5 billion (Fig. 2.1). In recent years, venture capital-backed firms have raised several billion dollars annually through IPOs, including a 1996 total

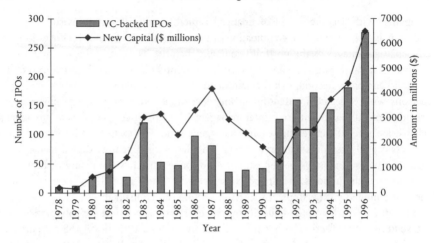

Figure 2.1. *Venture Capital-backed IPOs: New Venture and Capital Commitments. Number of initial public offerings of venture-capital-backed companies (left-hand scale), and amount of new capital commitments to venture capital funds (right-hand scale), between 1978 and 1996.*

Source: Venture Capital Journal and Venture Capital Yearbook (various dates); *The Economist*, March 29, 1997 (survey of Silicon Valley).

of $12 billion; they form a significant portion of the total IPO market (Venture Capital Yearbook, various years through 1997; Brav and Gompers 1997).[1] Between 1991 and 1996, there were 1,059 venture capital-backed IPOs, an average of over 175 per year (see Table 2.1), as well as 466 exits through acquisition of the venture-capital-backed firm.

Figure 2.1 shows the annual variation in the number of venture-capital-backed IPOs, as well as the amount of new capital committed to venture capital funds. Inspection of Fig. 2.1 suggests a correlation between the availability of exit through IPO (proxied by the number of venture capital-backed IPOs) and investor willingness to invest in venture capital funds (measured by new capital commitments), with perhaps a one-year lag between a change in the number of IPOs and a resulting change in the amount of capital committed (see Table 2.2). This correlation is consistent with the theory developed below on the link between the stock market and the venture capital market.

The visual impression of a correlation between venture-capital-backed IPOs and new capital commitments to venture capital funds is confirmed by a simple regression of capital contributions in year $X + 1$ (as a dependent variable) against number of venture-capital-backed IPOs in year X. Regression 1 below shows that the number of IPOs in year X correlates strongly with new capital contributions in year $X + 1$. Regression 2 adds year as an additional possible explanatory variable. The correlation between number of IPOs in year X and new capital commitments in the following year remains statistically significant

---

[1] An alternative way to measure the importance of venture-capital-backed IPOs is to measure the firms' market capitalization rather than the amount of funds raised in the IPO. The 276 venture-capital-backed firms taken public in 1996 had a mean market capitalization of $209 million and total market capitalization of $58 billion (Venture Capital Journal, April, 1997).

Table 2.1. *VC-backed IPOs, public acquisitions, and private acquisitions.*
Number of IPOs of venture-capital-backed companies and number of sales of
venture-capital-backed companies, between 1984 and 1996

Year	VC-backed IPOs	Exits via acquisitions		
		Of private companies	Of already public companies	
1984	53	59	27	86
1985	47	83	18	101
1986	98	90	30	120
1987	81	113	27	140
1988	36	106	29	135
1989	39	101	45	146
1990	42	76	33	109
1991	127	65	19	84
1992	160	90	4	94
1993	172	78	14	92
1994	143	99	No data	No data
1995	183	98	No data	No data
1996	276	94	No data	No data

Source: *Venture Capital Journal and Venture Capital Yearbook* (various dates);
The Economist, March 29, 1997 (survey of Silicon Valley).

Table 2.2. *Correlation between venture capital-backed IPOs and new capital commitments to venture capital funds*

	Dependent variable	Independent variable(s)			R^2	Number of observations
		Intercept	VC-backed IPOs in year X	Year		
1	Capital contribution in year $X + 1$	1015 ($t = 2.35$)*	20.2 ($t = 4.54$)***			
					0.56	18
2	Capital contribution in year $X + 1$	137846 ($t = 0.93$)	15.1 ($t = 2.17$)*	70.1 ($t = 0.94$)		
					0.59	18

Least-squares regression of capital contributed to venture capital funds ($ millions) in year $X + 1$ against number of IPOs of venture-capital-backed companies in year X. Based on data from 1978 to 1996 as shown in Fig. 2.1. t-statistics in parentheses. ***(**)(*) = significant at 0.001 (0.01) (0.05) level, respectively.
US venture capital funds obtain capital from a range of sources, but pension funds are the largest contributor. Pension funds have provided roughly 40% of the capital raised by venture capital funds over the last ten years or so (Table 2.3). In Germany, on the other hand, banks supply the majority of venture capital commitments.

Table 2.3. *USA and Germany: capital raised by venture capital funds by type of investor*

	1992	1993	1994	1995
United States				
Corporations	3%	8%	9%	2%
Private individuals & families	11	8	9	17
Government agencies	—	—	—	—
Pension funds	42	59	46	38
Banks and insurance companies	15	11	9	18
Endowments and foundations	18	11	21	22
Other	11	4	2	3
Total	100%	100%	100%	100%
Germany				
Corporations	7%	9%	8%	10%
Private individuals & families	6	7	8	5
Government agencies	4	6	7	8
Pension funds	—	—	—	9
Banks	53	52	55	59
Insurance companies	10	12	12	6
Endowments and foundations	—	—	—	—
Other	17	14	10	2
Total	100%	100%	100%	100%

Percentage of capital raised by venture capital funds in the USA and Germany, by type of investor, for 1992–1995.

Sources: *European Venture Capital Association Yearbook* (1995); *Bundesverband Deutsche Kapitalbeteiligungsgesellschaften Jahrbuch* [German Venture Capital Association Yearbook] (various years through 1996); *Venture Capital Yearbook* (various years through 1997).

as a predictor of new capital commitments in the following year. These regressions are not intended to fully capture the factors that affect capital commitments to venture capital funds, but do confirm the visual correlation evident from Fig. 2.1.

Seed, start-up, and other early stage investments that take a company through development of a prototype and initial product shipments to customers accounted for about 37 per cent of new capital invested by venture capital funds in 1994 (Tables 2.3 and 2.4). Later-stage expansion financing represented another 45 per cent of 1994 investments. Because venture capitalists usually stage their investments (Sahlman 1990; Gompers 1995), most expansion financing goes to companies that received early stage financing. Thus, the bulk of venture capital investments go to firms that receive venture capital financing very early in their life. Moreover, most investments go to technology-based companies; in 1994, 68 per cent of new investments went to these companies (Venture Economics 1995).

Lest venture capital be dismissed as trivial in amount, and therefore not an important factor in comparing corporate governance systems, we note that mature firms that began with venture capital backing assume macroeconomic significance in the US economy.

Table 2.4. *USA and Germany: venture capital
disbursements by stage of financing*

	1992	1993	1994	1995
United States				
Seed	3%	7%	4%	
Startup	8	7	15	
Other early stage	13	10	18	
Expansion	55	54	45	
LBO/Acquisition	7	6	6	
Other	14	16	12	
Total	100%	100%	100%	
Germany				
Seed	1%	1%	2%	2%
Startup	6	7	8	6
Expansion	45	66	54	65
LBO/Acquisition	24	25	36	18
Other	25	—	—	8
Total	100%	100%	100%	100%

Percentage of capital disbursed by venture capital funds in the
USA and Germany, by nature of investment, for 1992–1995.

Sources: European Venture Capital Association Yearbook (1995);
Bundesverband Deutsche Kapitalbeteiligungsgesellschaften Jahrbuch
[German Venture Capital Association Yearbook] (various years
through 1996); *Venture Capital Yearbook* (various years through
1997).

They play a major, often dominant role in several important and rapidly growing sectors where the USA is recognized as a world leader, including biotechnology (e.g. Genentech and Biogen); personal computers and workstations (e.g. Apple, Compaq, and Sun Microsystems); many personal computer components and related devices such as hard drives and routers (e.g. Seagate Technologies, Connor Peripherals, and Cisco Systems); personal computer software (e.g. Lotus Development and Harvard Graphics); and semiconductors (e.g. Intel and Advanced Micro Devices).

The German venture capital industry is a fraction of the size of the US industry. Only 85 venture capital organizations existed at the end of 1994, with DM 8.3 billion ($5.5 billion) in cumulative capital commitments (European Venture Capital Yearbook, 1995) and annual investments of under $400 million. Venture capital investments were 0.01 per cent of German GDP in 1994; only one-sixth of the US level. This comparison understates the difference in venture capital activity between the two countries because the European definition of venture capital is broader than the American definition. These organizations received the majority of their capital from banks (55 per cent) and insurance companies (12 per cent). Pension funds are not a factor in the German market because German corporate and government pension obligations are largely unfunded.

Table 2.5. *Exits by German venture capital funds, 1995*

Exit type	Number of Firms
Buyback by portfolio company	166
Sale of portfolio company	74
Block sale of venture capital fund's stake	8
IPO	12
(IPOs on foreign stock markets)	(11)
Other	4
Total	264

Type of exit from portfolio companies by German venture capital funds for 1995.

Source: *Bundesverband Deutsche Kapitalbeteiligungsgesellschaften Jahrbuch* [German Venture Capital Association Yearbook] (1996).

The German venture capital industry also differs from the USA in its aversion both to early stage investment (Table 2.4) and to investment in high-tech industries (Harrison 1990). In 1994, only 8 per cent of the venture capital invested went to start-up companies, and only 2 per cent to seed financing. Technology-related investments comprised only 11 per cent of all new investments.

In Germany, as in the USA, exit by the venture capital fund is the norm, but the form of exit differs. Exit through the stock market is largely unavailable, although a handful of German venture capital-backed firms have gone public on Britain's Alternative Investment Market (AIM). The venture capital fund's exit therefore comes principally through the company's repurchase of the venture fund's stake (a strategy not available to the rapidly growing firms that are the predominant recipients of venture capital financing in the USA), or through selling the company. Table 2.5 shows the exit strategies employed by German venture capital funds for 1995. Of the twelve exits through IPO, only one was in Germany; the rest were on foreign markets.

This section has only sketched the US and German venture capital markets. But it demonstrates the pattern we seek to explain: the existence in the USA of a dynamic venture capital industry centred on early stage investments in high-tech companies and the absence of a comparable industry in Germany.

2.3. THE IMPORTANCE OF EXIT BY THE VENTURE CAPITAL FUND

The first step in understanding the link between the stock market and the venture capital market involves the importance of exit by the venture capital fund from its investments. We develop below an informal theory for why exit by venture capital providers from their successful investments is critical to the operation of the venture capital market, both for the relationship between a venture capital fund and its portfolio companies, and for the relationship between the fund and its capital providers. Florida and Martin (1990) argue that US venture investors' refusal to act as long-term investors in portfolio companies weakens US competitiveness. Our analysis provides an efficiency justification for exit.

The need for an exit strategy does not itself explain the distinctive properties of exit through an IPO and, therefore, the special role of an active IPO market. We develop that relationship in Section 2.4.

2.3.1. *Exit from the Venture Capital Fund—Portfolio Company Relationship*

Venture capitalists provide more than just money to their portfolio companies. Three additional contributions loom large (Gorman and Sahlman 1989; Bygrave and Timmons 1992; Barry 1994; Lerner 1995): management assistance to the portfolio company, analogous to that provided by a management consulting firm; intensive monitoring of performance, reflecting the incentives to monitor arising from equity ownership and the power to act using the venture capitalist's levers of control; and reputational capital, that is, the venture capitalist's ability to give the portfolio company credibility with third parties, similar to the role played by other reputational intermediaries such as investment bankers.

2.3.1.1. *Management Assistance*
The typical venture capital fund is a limited partnership run by general partners who are experienced at moving companies up the development path from the start-up stage and have market knowledge based on other investments in the portfolio company's industry and related industries (Sahlman 1990; Gompers and Lerner 1996). With this experience, the venture capitalist can assist a management-thin early stage company in locating and recruiting the management and technical personnel it needs as its business grows, and can help the company through the predictable problems that high-tech firms face in moving from prototype development to production, marketing, and distribution. The venture capital fund's industry knowledge and experience with prior start-up firms helps it locate managers for new start-ups (Carvalho 1996).

2.3.1.2. *Intensive Monitoring and Control*
Venture capital funds have strong incentives to monitor entrepreneurs' performance, deriving from equity ownership. They also receive strong control levers, disproportionate to the size of their equity investment. One control lever results from the staged timing of venture capital investment. The initial investment is typically insufficient to allow the portfolio company to carry out its business plan (Sahlman 1990; Gompers 1995). The venture capitalist will decide later whether to provide the additional funding that the portfolio company needs. The company's need for additional funds gives its management a performance incentive in the form of a hard constraint, analogous to the use of debt in leveraged buyouts.[2]

---

[2] Gompers (1995) explains the extra control rights given to the venture capital fund as a response to adverse selection problems in early stage financing, where information asymmetries between the entrepreneur and the venture capital fund are greatest.

The typical contractual arrangements between a venture capital fund and a portfolio company provide other control levers. The venture capitalist typically receives convertible debt or convertible preferred stock that carries the same voting rights as if it had already been converted into common stock (Benton and Gunderson 1993; Gompers 2000).[3] The venture capital fund commonly receives greater board representation—often an absolute majority of the board—than it could elect if board representation were proportional to overall voting power. Board control lets the venture capital provider replace the entrepreneur as chief executive officer if performance lags.[4] Even where the venture capitalist lacks board control, the investor rights agreement gives the venture capital provider veto power over significant operating decisions by the portfolio company.

2.3.1.3. *Reputational Capital*

Much like an investment bank underwriting an IPO (Gilson and Kraakman 1984; Booth and Smith 1986), the venture capital fund acts as a reputational intermediary. Venture capital financing enhances the portfolio company's credibility with third parties whose contributions will be crucial to the company's success. Talented managers are more likely to invest their human capital in a company financed by a respected venture capital fund, because the venture capitalist's participation provides a credible signal about the company's likelihood of success. Suppliers will be more willing to risk committing capacity and extending trade credit to a company with respected venture capital backers. Customers will take more seriously the company's promise of future product delivery if a venture capitalist both vouches for and monitors its management and technical progress. Moukheiber (1996) provides an account of the reputational power of Kleiner, Perkins, Caufield, and Byers, a leading venture capital fund. Later on, the venture capitalist's reputation helps to attract a high-quality underwriter for an IPO of the portfolio company's stock (Meginson and Weiss 1991; Lerner 1994*a*).

The venture capital fund's proffer of its reputation to third parties who have dealings with a portfolio company is credible because the fund is a repeat player, and has put its money where its mouth is by investing in the portfolio company. The fund's reputation is crucial for its own dealings with investors in its existing and future limited partnerships, with other venture capitalists in syndicating investments in portfolio companies and in negotiating with entrepreneurs concerning new portfolio investments (Sahlman 1990; Lerner 1994*b*). Consistent with a reputational analysis, Brav and Gompers (1997) report that venture-capital-backed IPOs do not suffer the long-run underperformance reported for IPOs in general.

---

[3] The standard contractual package for an early stage venture capital investment consists of a convertible preferred stock purchase agreement; the portfolio company's certificate of incorporation; and an investor rights agreement. The purchase agreement, through detailed representations and warranties, documents the portfolio company's condition at the time of the venture capital investment. The certificate of incorporation sets out the voting and other rights of the venture capital fund's convertible debt or preferred stock. The investor rights agreement contains the portfolio company's ongoing obligations to the venture capital fund, including detailed negative covenants and such things as registration rights.

[4] Hellmann (1995) explains why an entrepreneur would give the venture capitalist this right: to reduce the cost of capital, thereby increasing the share of the equity the entrepreneur retains. We discuss the reputation market necessary to prevent the venture capitalist from misusing this power in Section 2.4.

Like a venture capitalist's provision of financial capital, its non-financial contributions are also staged, albeit informally. A venture capitalist can choose not to make or return telephone calls to or from a portfolio company or its suppliers, customers, or prospective employees. The fund's power to withhold its management assistance and reputational capital reinforces its incentive and power to monitor.

The management assistance, monitoring, and service as a reputational intermediary that a venture capitalist provides share a significant economy of scope with its provision of capital. This scope economy arises from a number of sources. The portfolio company must evaluate the quality of the venture capital fund's proffered management assistance and monitoring. Similarly, potential employees, suppliers, and customers must evaluate the credibility of the fund's explicit and implicit representations concerning the portfolio company's future. Combining financial and non-financial contributions both enhances the credibility of the information that the venture capitalist provides to third parties and bonds the venture capitalist's promise to the portfolio company to provide non-financial assistance. The venture capitalist will suffer financial loss if it reneges on its promise of non-financial support. Combining financial and non-financial contributions also lets investors in venture capital funds evaluate a fund's non-financial contributions by measuring its return on investment. Lin and Smith (1995) also link the venture capitalist's financial and non-financial investments. Finally, there is the customary role of monitoring in ensuring that the portfolio company's managers do not divert to themselves some of the company's income stream.

The non-capital inputs supplied by venture capital providers have special value to early stage companies. As the portfolio company's management gains its own experience, proves its skill, and establishes its own reputation, the relative value of the venture capital provider's management experience, monitoring, and service as a reputational intermediary declines.[5] Thus, by the time the portfolio company succeeds, the venture capital provider's non-financial contributions can be more profitably invested in a new round of early stage companies. But because the economies of scope discussed above link financial and non-financial contributions, recycling the venture capitalist's non-financial contributions also requires the venture capitalist to exit—to recycle its financial contribution from successful companies to early stage companies.

2.3.2. *The Exit and Reinvestment Cycle for Venture Capital Funds and Capital Providers*

The efficiency of exit for the venture capitalist–portfolio company relationship complements a similar efficiency arising from the relationship between the venture capitalist and the investors in its limited partnerships. The cycle of financial commitment to early stage firms, followed by exit from these investments, responds to three contracting problems in

---

[5] Compare Rajan's (1992) analysis of the trade-off between a bank-like lender who has the ability to monitor the borrower's ongoing performance and public investors who cannot monitor. As the borrower's quality improves, the returns to monitoring decrease, and the most efficient capital provider shifts from a monitoring bank-like lender to a non-monitoring investor. Diamond (1991) discusses a similar generational theory in which optimal investor type depends on a firm's stage in its life-cycle.

the venture capitalist—capital provider relationship. First, capital providers need a way to evaluate venture capitalists' skill, in order to decide to which managers to commit new funds. Second, capital providers need to evaluate the risks and returns on venture capital investments relative to other investments, in order to decide whether to invest in venture capital, and how much to invest. Third, capital providers need to be able to withdraw funds from less successful managers, or from managers whose industry-specific expertise no longer matches current investment opportunities. Yet the very specialization that explains why capital providers hire venture capitalists rather than invest directly ensures that capital providers cannot easily assess whether a venture capital fund's ongoing investments are or are likely to become successful, or how successful they are likely to be.

Exit by the venture capital manager from specific portfolio investments provides a benchmark that lets capital providers evaluate both the relative skill of venture capital managers and the profitability of venture capital relative to other investments (Gompers 1996). At the same time, payment of the exit proceeds to capital providers lets the capital providers recycle funds from less successful to more successful venture capital managers.

Conventional limited partnership agreements between venture capital funds and capital providers reflect the efficiency of exit for this relationship. The limited partnership agreement typically sets a maximum term for the partnership of 7–10 years, after which the partnership must be liquidated and the proceeds distributed to the limited partners (Sahlman 1990). During the term of the limited partnership agreement, the proceeds from investments in particular firms are distributed to limited partners as realized. Moreover, venture capital funds have strong incentives to exit from their investments, when feasible, well before the end of the partnership period. A fund's performance record, based on completed investments, is the fund's principal tool for soliciting capital providers to invest additional funds in new limited partnerships.

The explicit contract between capital providers and the venture capitalist, requiring liquidation of each limited partnership, is complemented by an implicit contract in which capital providers are expected to reinvest in future limited partnerships sponsored by successful venture capital funds. The expectation of reinvestment makes it feasible for venture capital funds to invest in developing infrastructure and expertise that will outlive the term of any one limited partnership, and could not be justified by the returns on the modest amount of capital that a venture capitalist without a track record can expect to raise. Figure 2.2 illustrates the explicit and implicit contracts between venture capitalists and their investors.

In sum, exit is central to the venture capital manager's accountability to capital providers. The efficiency of exit for the venture capital fund—capital provider relationship complements its efficiency properties for the portfolio firm—venture capital fund relationship. Taken together, they provide a strong rationale for exit from individual portfolio investments as a critical component of a viable venture capital industry.

2.4. THE AVAILABILITY OF EXIT BY IPO: IMPLICIT CONTRACTING OVER FUTURE CONTROL

The analysis in Section 2.3 establishes the importance of an exit strategy to the venture capital market. But it does not differentiate between stock market- and bank-centred

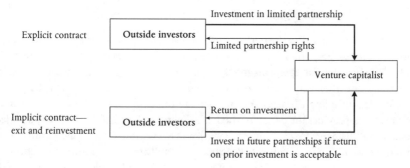

Figure 2.2. *Implicit and explicit contracts between venture capitalists and outside investors.*

capital markets. A stock market makes available one special type of exit—an IPO. But another exit strategy is available to venture capital funds in both bank-centred and stock market-centred capital markets: the fund can cause the portfolio company to be sold to a larger company. Indeed, even in the USA, venture capitalists frequently exit through sale of the portfolio company rather than through an IPO (Table 2.1). A third exit option—leveraging the portfolio company so it can repurchase the venture capitalist's stake—is generally not feasible for the fast-growing, capital-consuming companies that are the typical focus of venture capital investing in the USA.

Exit through sale of the portfolio company is likely to be the most efficient form of exit in some cases. For example, innovation may be better accomplished in small firms while production and marketing may be better accomplished in large firms. In this circumstance, selling a start-up company to another firm with manufacturing or marketing expertise can produce synergy gains. These gains can be partly captured by the start-up firm through a higher exit price (Bygrave and Timmons 1992).

In other cases, an IPO may be the most efficient form of exit. The potential for an IPO to provide a higher-valued exit than sale of the company must be considered plausible, given the frequency with which this exit option is used in the USA. Viewed *ex ante*, venture capital financing of firms for which exit through IPO will (or might turn out to) maximize exit price could be a positive net present investment in a stock market-centred capital market, but not in a bank-centred capital market. But this difference should affect investment decisions only at the margin. Thus, it cannot easily explain the dramatic differences between the venture capital industries in the USA and Germany, both in size and in type of investment.

Thus, we are only part of the way towards a theory that explains the observed link between venture capital markets and stock markets. We have shown why venture capital providers need an exit strategy. What remains to be shown is that the potential for exit through an IPO, even if exit often occurs through the portfolio company's sale, is critical to the development of an active venture capital market. This section shows that the potential for exit through an IPO allows the venture capital provider and the entrepreneur to enter into an implicit contract over future control of the portfolio company in a manner that is not readily duplicable in a bank-centred system.

2.4.1. *The Contracting Framework*

In a contracting framework, the relevant time to assess the influence of an IPO's availability (and therefore the importance of a stock market) on the operation of the venture capital market is when the entrepreneur and venture capital provider contract over the initial investment, not when exit actually occurs. A number of authors have modelled aspects of this contract, including the staging of the venture capitalist's funding, which vests in the venture capital provider the decision whether to continue the portfolio company's projects (Admati and Pfleiderer 1994; Gompers 1995), and the venture capital fund's purchase of a convertible security both to mitigate distributional conflicts between the entrepreneur and the venture capitalist associated with a future sale of the firm (Berglof 1994), and to solve an adverse selection problem among prospective entrepreneurs (Marx 1994; Gompers 2000). Our informal model seeks to explain three additional characteristics of venture capital contracting: (1) the parties' *ex ante* joint preference that the venture capital fund exit through an IPO; (2) how the entrepreneur's preference that the fund use this exit strategy if it becomes available *ex post* is expressed through a self-enforcing implicit contract over future control; and (3) how this implicit contract provides the entrepreneur with incentives that are not easily duplicated if sale of the portfolio company is the only exit option. Because the incentive properties of this contract go to the heart of the entrepreneurial process, its availability in a stock market-centred capital market links the venture capital market and the stock market and can explain the absence of vigorous venture capital in countries with bank-centred capital markets.

Our IPO exit model requires three non-controversial assumptions: (i) the entrepreneur places substantial private value on control over the company she starts; (ii) it is not feasible for an untested entrepreneur to retain control at the time of the initial venture capital financing; and (iii) it is feasible for a successful entrepreneur to reacquire control from the venture capitalist when the venture capitalist exits. We discuss each assumption below.

A private value for control is a standard feature in venture capital models and, more generally, in models that seek to explain the incentive properties of capital structure (Grossman and Hart 1988; Harris and Raviv 1988; Holmstrom and Tirole 1989). Moreover, for entrepreneurs, the assumption appears to be descriptively accurate. The failure rate for start-up companies is high enough[6] that, without a large private value for control, many potential entrepreneurs would decide not to leave a secure job to start a new company. It is also apparent that ceding to the venture capital provider the power, frequently exercised, to remove the entrepreneur from management is a significant cost to the entrepreneur (Hellmann 1995).

Even if entrepreneurs value control highly, they cannot demand its retention at the time that they are seeking venture financing. The typical entrepreneur has not previously run a start-up company. Venture capitalists rationally insist on retaining control to protect

---

[6] See Gompers (1995) (16% of portfolio companies are liquidated or go bankrupt), Barry (1994) (one-third of venture capital investments result in losses), Sahlman (1990) (one-third of venture capital investments result in losses). Additionally, a significant percentage of would be entrepreneurs never secure venture funding at all.

themselves against the risk that the entrepreneur won't run the firm successfully or will extract private benefits from the firm instead of maximizing its value to all investors.

The situation changes once a start-up firm has succeeded. The entrepreneur has proved her management skill and provided some evidence that she can be trusted with other peoples' money. Returning control to the entrepreneur could now maximize firm value. Even if not, the value lost may be less than the entrepreneur's private value of control. The opportunity to regain control also provides an incentive, beyond mere wealth, for the entrepreneur to devote the effort needed for success. This possibility squarely raises the contracting problem that we address below: how can the venture capitalist commit, *ex ante*, to transfer control back to the entrepreneur, contingent on a concept as nebulous as 'success'?

2.4.2. *The Entrepreneur's Incentive Contract*

When the entrepreneur sells an interest in her company to a venture capital fund, the venture capitalist receives both a residual interest in the firm's value, typically in the form of convertible preferred stock or debt, and significant control rights, both explicit (e.g. the right to remove the chief executive officer) and implicit (e.g. the right to decide whether the firm can continue in business through staged funding). In return, the company and the entrepreneur get three things. The portfolio company receives capital plus non-financial contributions including information, monitoring, and enhanced credibility with third parties. This explicit contract is illustrated in Fig. 2.3. In addition, the entrepreneur receives an implicit incentive contract denominated in control. The structure of this incentive contract depends on the availability of an IPO exit strategy.

To begin with, an IPO is available to the portfolio company only when the company is successful. Indeed, the frequency with which a venture capital fund's portfolio companies go public is a central measure of the venture capitalist's success in the eyes of investors in venture capital funds (Gompers 1996). When an IPO occurs, the entrepreneur receives two things. Like the venture capital provider, the entrepreneur gets cash to the extent that she sells some of her shares in the offering, plus increased value and liquidity for unsold shares. In addition, the entrepreneur reassumes much of the control originally ceded to the venture capitalist. The venture capitalist's percentage stake is reduced by its direct sale of

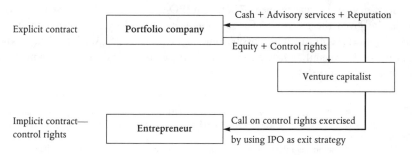

Figure 2.3. *Implicit and explicit contracts between venture capitalist and entrepreneur.*

shares,[7] by the venture capitalist's in-kind distribution of shares to its investors (Gompers and Lerner 1997), and by the company's sale of new shares in the IPO to dispersed shareholders. The now-public firm also no longer depends on the venture capitalist for continuation decisions through staged funding; the public equity market is available. The greater liquidity of the venture capitalist's remaining investment after the IPO also reduces the venture capitalists' incentive to monitor (Coffee 1991 discusses the trade-off between monitoring and liquidity).[8] The venture capitalist's need to monitor the portfolio company intensively is further reduced because some of the monitoring task will now be undertaken by stock market analysts. On average, venture capital funds reduce their holdings of a portfolio company's shares by 28 per cent within one year after an IPO (Barry *et al.* 1990). Three years after the IPO, only 12 per cent of lead venture capitalists retain 5 per cent or more of the portfolio company's shares (Lin and Smith 1995).

Finally, and most significantly, the explicit contract between the venture capital fund and the portfolio company ensures that important control rights that were initially given to the fund, including guaranteed board membership and veto power over business decisions, disappear on an initial IPO whether or not the fund sells any shares at all in the IPO. Typically, the terms of the convertible securities held by the venture capital fund require conversion into common stock at the time of the IPO (Gompers 2000); the negative covenants contained in the investor rights agreement also terminate on an IPO (Benton and Gunderson 1993). In short, the venture capital fund's special control rights end at the time of an IPO, leaving the fund with only the weaker control rights attendant on substantial stock ownership. Even this control will diminish over time as the venture capital fund reduces its remaining stock position. Control becomes vested in the entrepreneur, who often retains a controlling stock interest and, even if not, retains the usual broad discretion enjoyed by chief executives of companies without a controlling shareholder.

The opportunity to acquire control through an IPO exit if the company is successful gives the entrepreneur a powerful incentive beyond the purely financial gains from the increased value of her shares in the firm. In effect, the prospect of an IPO exit gives the entrepreneur something of a call option on control, contingent on the firm's success.

Contrast this outcome with what the entrepreneur receives when the venture capital provider exits through sale of the portfolio company to an established company. As in an IPO, the entrepreneur receives cash or the more liquid securities of a publicly traded acquirer. Control, however, passes to the acquirer, even if the entrepreneur remains in charge of day-to-day management. Thus, if an IPO exit is not available, the entrepreneur cannot be given the incentive of a call option on control exercisable in the event of success. Exit through an IPO is possible only in the presence of a stock market; its role in the contract between the venture capitalist and the entrepreneur links the venture capital market and the stock market.

---

[7] Over the years 1979–1990, lead venture capitalists sold shares in some 27% of IPOs of venture capital backed companies. The incidence of venture capitalist sales increased to 37% in the last three years of that period (Lin and Smith 1995).

[8] The increased liquidity and the venture capitalist's ability to sell off its investment gradually after the IPO is critical because the underwriter will typically limit the amount that the venture capitalist can sell in the IPO and over the following six months lest the market draw an unfavourable inference about the portfolio company's future value from the venture capitalist's sales (Benton and Gunderson 1993).

2.4.3. *Feasibility of the Implicit Contract Over Control*

It remains to demonstrate the feasibility of the implicit incentive contract over control and its superiority to an explicit contract. We undertake these tasks in this section and Section 2.4.4. The difficulty of defining success and the potential advantages of an implicit contract are suggested by the parties' use of an implicit contract involving staged funding to handle the pre-IPO decision as to whether and on what terms the venture capitalist will provide additional financing.

The feasibility problem is to specify a self-enforcing implicit contract: (i) whose terms are clear; (ii) whose satisfaction by the entrepreneur is observable; and (iii) whose breach by the venture capital provider would be observable and punished by the market. Consider the following stylized implicit contract: the entrepreneur will be deemed sufficiently successful to exercise her call option on control and the venture capital provider will exit through an IPO, so long as a reputable investment banker will underwrite a firm commitment offering. The need to clearly specify the conditions under which the entrepreneur can exercise the call option on control is met, not by defining numerical performance standards that the portfolio company must meet, but by delegating the performance assessment to a third party. Investment bankers have an incentive to seek out (or respond to inquiries from) portfolio companies whose performance has been strong enough to allow a successful public offering. A central feature of the investment banker's role in a public offering is as an information intermediary that proffers its reputation on behalf of the portfolio company much as the venture capitalist provides credibility to the portfolio company at an earlier stage in its development. The investment banker's internal standards for companies it is willing to take public, made credible by its willingness to commit its own capital and reputation to the offering, provide a self-enforcing statement of the conditions for exercise of the entrepreneur's call option.

The second requirement, that the entrepreneur's satisfaction of the exercise conditions be observable, is met in the same way. The investment banker's offer to take the portfolio company public is directly observable by the venture capital provider and the entrepreneur and is credible because the investment banker has the right incentives to honestly evaluate a portfolio company's performance.

The final requirement, that the venture capitalist's breach of the implicit contract be observable and punishable by the market, is also met. Observability results from the character of the venture capital market. The universe of portfolio companies sufficiently successful to merit a public offering is limited, as is the number of venture capital providers. Both sides of the market are relatively concentrated, with a significant number of portfolio companies geographically concentrated and the offices of a significant percentage of US venture capital providers found along a short strip of Sand Hill Road in Silicon Valley (Saxanian 1994). Moreover, venture capital funds typically specialize in portfolio companies geographically proximate to the fund's office.[9] While proximity

---

[9] Lerner (1994*a*) reports that venture capital providers located within five miles of a portfolio company are twice as likely to have a board representative than providers located more than 500 miles distant. The fact that in 1996, 40% of total venture capital disbursements were to portfolio companies in California (Venture Capital Yearbook 1997) provides further evidence of venture capital provider concentration sufficient to support a reputation market.

facilitates monitoring, it also facilitates the emergence and maintenance of a reputation market. A claim by an entrepreneur that a venture capital provider declined to allow a portfolio company to go public when a reputable investment banker was available would quickly circulate through the community. Finally, venture capital providers are repeat players, who typically seek at regular intervals to raise funds for new limited partnerships, which must then invest in new portfolio companies, before prior limited partnerships are completed (Sahlman 1990). In the competition to be lead venture investor in the most attractive companies, a reputation for breaching the implicit contract for control is hardly an advantage.

The viability of reputation market constraints on venture capitalist behaviour is confirmed by another aspect of the overall venture capitalist–entrepreneur relationship. The venture capitalist's staged capital commitment gives the venture capitalist the option to abandon short of providing the portfolio company sufficient funds to complete its business plan. This gives the entrepreneur an incentive to perform, gives the venture capitalist incentives to monitor, and reduces agency costs by shifting the continuation decision from the entrepreneur to the venture capitalist. However, this pattern, coupled with the right of first refusal with respect to future financing typically given to the venture capitalist (Sahlman 1990), also permits the venture capitalist to act opportunistically. What can the entrepreneur do if the venture capitalist opportunistically offers to provide the second-stage financing necessary for the entrepreneur to continue at an unfair price? The entrepreneur could seek financing from other sources, but the original venture capitalist's right of first refusal presents a serious barrier: who would incur the costs of making a bid when potential bidders know that a bid will succeed only when a better informed party—the original investor—believes the price is too high? A reputation market can police this potential for opportunism.[10]

2.4.4. *Superiority of the Implicit Contract Over Control*

An explicit contract that specifies the operating performance necessary to entitle the entrepreneur to reacquire control is a difficult undertaking. Creating a state-contingent contract that specifies the control consequences of the full range of possible states of the world over the four- to ten-year average term of a venture investment, without creating perverse incentives, is a severe challenge both to the parties' predictive powers and their drafting capabilities. It is in precisely these circumstances that an implicit contract is likely to have a comparative advantage over an explicit contract.

Moreover, the venture capitalist will be willing to cede control only at the time of exit, not before. Yet a mechanical formula cannot ensure that a reputable underwriter will be willing to take the portfolio company public. In addition, the venture capitalist must actively cooperate for an IPO to succeed. At the same time, the venture capitalist cannot unduly 'puff' the portfolio company's prospects, because the capital markets will punish this behaviour through reduced marketability of IPOs of other portfolio companies.

---

[10] Admati and Pfleiderer (1994), who model the shift of the continuation decision to the venture capitalist, do not address this problem.

Thus, a supposedly explicit contract, defining when the entrepreneur and the venture capital fund have the right to take the portfolio company public, cannot easily be enforced. Such a contract would be substantially implicit in fact, even if explicit in form. Thus, it is not surprising that entrepreneurs and venture capitalists, for the most part, do not seek to contract explicitly over control.

Finally, the implicit/explicit dichotomy presented above oversimplifies the real world. In fact, some elements of the contract over control are explicit, while others are left implicit. For example, cessation of the venture capital fund's special control rights at the time of an IPO is explicitly required, while the timing of the triggering event—the IPO—is left implicit. Conversion of the venture capitalist's convertible securities into common stock special rights is sometimes explicitly required if the portfolio company achieves defined financial milestones, even without an IPO (Benton and Gunderson 1993; Gompers 2000). Also, consistent with the greater importance of control earlier in a firm's life, the venture capitalist's explicit control rights are generally stronger, the earlier the stage of the investment (Gompers 2000).

2.4.5. *Consistency with Empirical Evidence*

In our model, successful entrepreneurs often prefer exit by IPO, and have the implicit contractual right to demand this form of exit not only when it maximizes firm value compared with the alternative of sale of the firm, but also when the entrepreneur's private value of control outweighs the entrepreneur's loss in share value. Our model predicts that the venture capitalist's successful exits will take place disproportionately through IPOs. If so, IPO exits will be more profitable than exits through sale of the portfolio company, by more than can plausibly be explained by the different values available through these different forms of exit.

This prediction is confirmed. Gompers (1995) reports that venture capital funds earn an average 60 per cent annual return on investment in IPO exits, compared with 15 per cent in acquisition exits; see also Sagari and Guidotti (1993); Petty *et al.* (1994). MacIntosh (1996) reports that IPO exits are more profitable in Canada as well. It is not plausible that these large differences could arise if the venture capitalist chose in each case the exit that maximized return on investment.

2.5. EVIDENCE FROM OTHER COUNTRIES

We have developed an informal theory in which the success of early-stage venture capital financing of high-growth, often high-tech, firms is linked to the availability of exit through an IPO. The weak form of the theory is that IPO exit is preferred by entrepreneurs. This preference leads to an implicit contract over control between the entrepreneur and the venture capitalist, in which the entrepreneur's success is rewarded by giving the entrepreneur the option to reacquire control through an IPO exit. This theory is consistent with the evidence discussed in Section 2.2 of a correlation between frequency of IPO exit and amount of new capital contributed to venture capital funds, and the evidence in Section 2.4.5 that successful exits occur disproportionately through IPOs.

The strong form of our theory is that the entrepreneur's preference for control is strong enough to significantly impair the development of a venture capital market in countries where exit by acquisition is the only viable option. This section offers an informal test of the strong form of our theory: does the theory predict the observed success of venture capital in different countries with different types of capital market? We provide data on Germany and the USA in Section 2.2; we survey several other countries below.

2.5.1. *Japan*

We have only limited quantitative data on the size of the venture capital industry in Japan. However, the quantitative and qualitative data that we have (primarily from Milhaupt 1997) is consistent with our theory: Japan, with its bank-centred capital market, has relatively little venture capital. In 1995, there were only 121 venture capital funds, of which more than half were affiliated with banks and run by the parent bank's employees. The employees of bank-affiliated funds commonly rotate through jobs in the bank's venture capital affiliate and then return to the parent bank. Thus, they are unlikely to develop the special skills needed to evaluate high-tech investments. Another 25 Japanese venture capital funds were run by securities firms or insurance companies.

Unlike American venture capital funds, which primarily provide equity financing, Japanese funds, perhaps reflecting their parentage, provide funds mostly through loans. Where American venture capital funds concentrate on high-tech businesses, and are the principal capital source for many start-up high-tech firms, Japanese venture capital firms rarely invest in high-tech firms. Instead, they concentrate on manufacturing and services, including such mundane investments as small shops and restaurants. As of 1995, Japanese venture capital funds owned more than 10 per cent of the stock of only one biotechnology company, two new materials firms, and twelve electronics firms.

2.5.2. *Great Britain and Other European Countries*

The similarity between Germany and Japan in the weakness of their venture capital industries strengthens the empirical support for the claim that bank-centred capital markets do not develop a strong venture capital industry. The converse claim is that stock market-centred capital markets can develop a strong venture capital industry. In particular, our theory predicts that Great Britain, with its active stock market, should have comparatively strong venture capital industries. This prediction is also supported by the evidence. British GDP is only about two-thirds of Germany's, yet its venture capital industry is almost five times larger, measured by cumulative capital committed (*Economist* 1996); new capital commitments are comparable to the USA as a percentage of GDP. Ireland, with its easy access to the London stock market, also has relatively high-venture capital as a percentage of GDP. Britain and Ireland are the clear European leaders in venture capital, with everyone else far behind.

Table 2.6 shows new funds raised by venture capital funds in 1993 and 1994 as a percentage of GDP. Great Britain's lead over everyone else would be greater still if the data

Table 2.6. *New capital committed to venture capital funds, 1993–94 (per cent of GDP)*

Country	Year		Average: 1993–94
	1993	1994	
United States	0.03%	0.06%	0.05%
Great Britain	0.09	0.27	0.18
France	0.06	0.07	0.06
Italy	0.02	0.02	0.02
Germany	0.01	0.01	0.01
Netherlands	0.04	0.07	0.05
Spain	0.03	0.01	0.02
Sweden	0.06	0.06	0.06
Ireland	0.04	0.25	0.15
Portugal	0.06	0.07	0.06
Belgium	0.04	0.03	0.04
Denmark	0.01	0.08	0.04
Switzerland	0.03	0.02	0.03
Norway	0.05	0.03	0.04
Finland	0.01	0.04	0.02
Iceland	0.06	0	0.03
Austria	0	0	0

New capital commitments to venture capital funds, as percent of national GNP, for various countries between 1993 and 1994.

Source: European Venture Capital Association, 1995.

were classified by the venture capital fund's home country, because British-based venture capital funds invest substantial amounts through affiliates in other European countries.

These data understate the relative size of the US venture capital industry. European venture capital firms are less specialized than their American counterparts and are often affiliated with commercial banks. The European Venture Capital Association defines 'venture capital' to include leveraged buyouts and buy-ins, and replacement of a firm's existing financing. In contrast, leveraged buyout firms in the USA are a distinct industry from venture capital firms; venture capital is also distinct from non-venture private equity financing. Non-venture uses of funds by European 'venture capital' firms are substantial. For example, in Great Britain, 47 per cent of capital commitments in 1994 went to buy-ins and buyouts, and only 8 per cent to early stage financing. In France, 40 per cent of venture capital comes from banks, and in 1994, 51 per cent of funds committed went to buyouts, buy-ins, and replacement financing, while only 9 per cent went to early stage financing.

2.5.3. *Canada*

Our evidence on Canada is drawn primarily from the recent survey by MacIntosh (1996). Canada has a relatively open IPO market—both domestic IPOs and access to the US IPO market. Thus, our theory predicts that Canada should have a relatively active venture capital industry. The Canadian data are difficult to interpret because of heavy government intervention in the venture capital industry. Labor Sponsored Venture Capital Corporations (LSVCCs), which must be formed by a labour union, receive substantial tax benefits. As a result, they dominate the Canadian venture capital industry. These funds tend to invest more conservatively than other venture capital funds. The largest single LSVCC fund, the Solidarité fund, is owned by the government of Quebec.

Still, there is substantial evidence that Canadian venture capital funds, especially private funds, play a large role in early stage financing of high-tech Canadian firms. In 1994, private independent funds had C$1.8 billion under management, and all Canadian venture capital firms had C$4.5 billion under management. The latter figure is comparable to the USA after adjusting for the size of the economy. Moreover, 25 per cent of new capital went to early stage financing—a figure similar to that for the USA, and much higher than for European and Japanese venture capital firms. The percentage of early stage investments is likely higher than this for non-LSVCC funds. In Canada, as in the USA, IPO exit is common and the highest-return exits are through IPOs.

2.5.4. *Israel*

Israel offers an interesting case study of how an existing venture capital industry can adapt when the option of a domestic IPO is taken away through regulation. The Israeli economy has grown rapidly during the 1990s, partly in response to deregulation of a formerly heavily government-controlled economy. High-tech start-ups, often financed by venture capital funds, have been an important element in this growth (Gourlay 1996). Multiple elements have contributed to the Israeli high-tech and venture capital industries, including government guarantees against large losses by publicly traded venture capital funds in the form of a put option on the fund's shares, government creation of incubator facilities for start-up firms, and a substantial influx in the early 1990s of immigrant scientists from Russia.

In the early 1990s, Israeli high-tech firms often went public on the Tel Aviv Stock Exchange at a very early stage. After a stock price crash in early 1994, the Tel Aviv Stock Exchange adopted listing rules that limited IPOs by early stage companies. Israeli venture capital funds have nonetheless continued to flourish by shifting their IPOs from the Tel Aviv Stock Exchange to the NASDAQ market. Giza Group (1996) reports the results of 16 IPOs of venture capital-backed Israeli companies from 1993 through early 1996, of which 14 were on NASDAQ, one on the British AIM small-firm market, and one on the Tel Aviv Stock Exchange. As of March 31, 1997, 62 Israeli companies had listed securities on NASDAQ, including 22 in 1996 alone; most were high-tech companies. The cumulative total exceeds any other country's except Canada's, and far exceeds any other country's relative to GDP.

2.6. ALTERNATIVE EXPLANATIONS FOR INTERCOUNTRY VARIATIONS IN VENTURE CAPITAL

We have developed in this chapter an informal theory, based on the stock market's role in providing contracting options not available in a bank-centred capital market, that may partially explain cross-country variations in venture capital. In this section, we evaluate briefly several alternative explanations for the different levels of venture capital financing in stock market- and bank-centred capital markets. We first consider a claim of functional irrelevance: institutional differences between stock market- and bank-centred systems do not affect economic outcomes because bank-centred systems have developed functionally equivalent means for financing early stage entrepreneurial activities. We then turn to explanations that acknowledge differences between countries in their ability to provide financing for high-tech ventures, but assign causation differently than we do.

While our analysis here is only suggestive, differential performance between the USA and Germany in industries where venture capital plays a significant role in the USA suggests that Germany has not yet developed a functional substitute for venture capital. Alternative explanations may account for some of this functional difference, but none appears able to fully displace the account of cross-national differences offered here.

2.6.1. *Institutional but not Functional Differences*

Different methods of organizing capital markets do not necessarily dictate corresponding functional or performance differences. For example, empirical research by Kaplan (1994*a,b*) and Kaplan and Minton (1994) suggests that Japanese and German companies change top management in response to poor earnings and stock price performance about as often and as quickly as US companies, despite the three countries' quite different corporate governance institutions. The similar outcomes could reflect the impact of selection on path-dependent corporate governance systems. That three leading industrial economies change senior management under roughly the same circumstances may reflect a selection bias. By limiting the sample to these successful systems, we observe only systems that, within the constraints established by their particular institutions, have solved reasonably well the central corporate governance problem of replacing poorly performing managers (Gilson 1996; Kaplan and Ramseyer 1996).

The same functional equivalence argument can be made with respect to differences in how successful economies finance entrepreneurial activities. If other financing methods, such as bank financing of start-up companies or internalization of the entrepreneurial process by large companies, yields the same performance as the US venture capital market, then the institutional differences are historically interesting but not functionally significant.

The empirical evidence needed to assess the functional equivalence argument for venture capital financed industries is not available, but anecdotal evidence makes us sceptical about functional equivalence. The USA has become a world leader in precisely those industries, notably biotechnology and computer-related high technology, in which the venture capital market figures centrally (Powell 1996). Moreover, in both Europe and the USA, large pharmaceutical companies are responding to biotechnology entrepreneurship not by funding the entrepreneurs directly, but instead by providing later-stage financing and partnering arrangements to entrepreneurial companies, mostly US-based and originally financed through US venture capital. (Powell 1996; Hellmann 1996; Lerner and Merges 1997). The result is not functional equivalence but specialization: different activities are allocated to different countries on the basis of differences in their venture capital markets.

2.6.2. *The Role of Pension Fund Financing of Venture Capital*

In both Japan and Germany, pension funds do not invest in venture capital. In Germany, corporate pension obligations are typically unfunded, so large private pension plans do not exist. Japan has moderate-sized corporate pension plans, but these plans are barred by law from investing in venture capital (Milhaupt 1997). In the USA, in contrast, the Department of Labor in 1979 explicitly sanctioned pension fund investment in venture capital. As shown in Table 2.3, pension plans now provide over 40 per cent of total investment in US venture capital funds.

Differences in pension fund size and regulation can explain part, but in our judgment only part, of the cross-national differences in the size of the venture capital industry. Funded pension obligations, as in the USA, as opposed to unfunded pension obligations in Germany, dictate only who makes employee pension investments, not the investments themselves. A company with an unfunded pension plan, in effect, incurs an unsecured debt—its promise to pay pensions when workers retire. The company can invest the funds thus made available in any way it chooses, including in venture capital. German firms could also voluntarily fund their pension obligations, as many American firms did even before ERISA established minimum funding requirements in 1973. The pension plan could then invest in venture capital, if it so chose.

In the USA, the unclear legality of pension fund investments in venture capital between 1973 and 1979 sterilized this pool of investable funds. Not surprisingly, the 1979 regulatory change resulted in a flow of funds into the previously restricted area. German firms have never been subject to an investment restriction similar to 1973–79 US regulation.

More generally, money is the ultimate fungible commodity, and venture capital commitments are a tiny fraction of total business investment—in the USA, around $5 billion annually compared with gross investment of over $1 trillion. If there were attractive profits to be made from venture capital investing, it seems likely that funds would be available from other sources, even if not from pension plans. After all, the Germans and the Japanese save more than Americans as a percentage of GDP, merely in different forms.

2.6.3. *Differences in Labour Market Regulation*

Germany and a number of other Western European countries impose substantial restrictions on layoffs, especially severance payment obligations. These rules impose costs on start-up businesses and thus could discourage their formation. Variations in labour market restrictions correlate with observed national variations in venture capital. Germany has strong layoff protections and little venture capital. Japan has few formal restrictions on layoffs, but the common practice by large companies of hiring only recent college graduates and promising them lifetime employment reduces labour market mobility (Gibson and Roe 1997). In contrast, the USA and Britain have more flexible labour markets and more active venture capital markets.

Labour market regulation and practices could well affect the vitality of venture capital. For example, Gilson (1999) argues that weak enforcement of covenants not to compete is a factor in the strength of venture capital in California; Hyde (1997) argues that the concentration of venture-capital-backed firms in Silicon Valley both supports and depends on what he calls 'high-velocity' labour markets. But labour market regulation, as a partial explanation for the vitality of venture capital markets, seems unlikely to fully displace our explanation, based on differences in capital markets.

Consider Germany as an example. Severance obligations build over time; they are much less burdensome for a start-up firm that fails after a few years of operation than for a mature firm that closes a plant that has operated for decades. Moreover, unpaid severance obligations are of little significance if a firm goes bankrupt—they merely expand the pool of unsecured claims on the firm's assets.

Moreover, labour market restrictions do not map perfectly onto national patterns in venture capital activity. Canada has moderately strong labour market restrictions; Ireland and Israel have strong restrictions comparable to West Germany's. Yet these countries also have strong venture capital. This pattern is consistent with their access to stock markets: the London market for Ireland; the US market for Israel; and US and domestic stock markets for Canada.

2.6.4. *Cultural Differences in Entrepreneurship*

A final explanation is cultural. Germans and Japanese could be less entrepreneurial and less willing to risk failure than Americans, leading to lesser demand for venture capital services (Milhaupt 1997 discusses Japanese culture). Cultural explanations for different patterns of economic activity are hard to evaluate. They can be partly tautological. In economically successful countries like Germany and Japan, the forces of economic selection will cause cultural and economic institutions to become mutually supportive. Because both are endogenously determined, observing that cultural institutions support existing economic patterns tells us nothing about causation. For present purposes, the more interesting issue is not a static inquiry into the current equilibrium of culture and economic institutions, but a dynamic one: how can culture and institutions change in response to exogenous changes in the economic environment (North 1990, 1994). We briefly consider this issue from an instrumental perspective in Section 2.7.

However, there is some reason for scepticism about claims of large cultural differences in willingness to take risks. People in all countries found large numbers of businesses, most of which fail. The empirical regularity to be explained is not why the Germans and Japanese do not start risky new businesses, but why they do not start many high-tech businesses, with few tangible assets on which a bank can rely for partial return of its investment. The success of immigrant entrepreneurs in countries with strong venture capital (e.g. Russian immigrants in Israel and Asian immigrants in the USA) suggests that entrepreneurs will emerge if the institutional infrastructure needed to support them is available. After all, Russia and India are also not known for their cultural support of entrepreneurship. Moreover, efforts to find large cross-cultural differences in entrepreneurship between the USA and Russia at the close of the Communist period have failed, even though these two countries ought to exhibit much larger differences than the USA, Germany, and Japan (Shiller *et al.* 1991, 1992).

2.7. IMPLICATIONS FOR VENTURE CAPITAL IN BANK-CENTRED CAPITAL MARKETS

Exploring the implications of the link between venture capital markets and stock markets is more complicated than the simple admonition that bank-centred capital markets should create a stock market. That straightforward approach has been tried before and failed. For example, France and Germany created special stock exchange segments for newer, smaller companies during the 1980s that, by the mid-1990s, had been shuttered or marginalized (Rasch 1994). Nonetheless, the financial press still stresses the absence of a venture capital market as being at the root of the European high-tech sector's poor performance, particularly with respect to Germany (e.g. Fisher 1996*a,b*), and three efforts are underway to try again to create stock markets that cater to small high-tech companies. The Alternative Investment Market of the London Stock Exchange began trading in June 1995 and now lists over 200 firms (Price 1996). Euro NM, a consortium of the French Le Nouveau Marché, which began trading in February, 1996, the German Neuer Markt, and the Belgian New Market, is scheduled to begin full operation in 1997. Finally, EASDAQ, an exchange explicitly patterned after the US NASDAQ and of which the NASD is a part owner, opened on September 30, 1996 (Pickles 1996). This flurry of stock market creation, taken with the explicit goal of enhancing the European venture capital market, suggests that there may be value in exploring the normative implications of the stock market–venture capital market link.

We begin our analysis of this link by stressing the path dependency of national capital markets. It is not merely a stock market that is missing in bank-centred systems. The secondary institutions that have developed in bank-centred systems, including the banks' conservative approach to lending and investing, and social and financial incentives that less richly reward entrepreneurial zeal and more severely penalize failure (see Harrison 1990 (Germany); Milhaupt 1997 (Japan)), are less conducive to entrepreneurial activity than the secondary institutions of stock market-centred capital markets. More critically, experienced venture capitalists, able to assess the prospects of new ventures and to provide the non-financial contributions that venture capitalists supply in the USA are absent, as are investment bankers experienced in taking early-stage companies public. Neither institution will develop quickly. A strong venture capital market thus reflects an equilibrium of a number of interdependent factors, only one of which is the presence of a stock market.

For example, Germany today faces a chicken and egg problem: a venture capital market requires a stock market, but a stock market requires a supply of entrepreneurs and deals which, in turn, require a venture capital market. In addition, German entrepreneurs who care about future control of their company must trust venture capitalists to return control to them some years hence and must further trust that the stock market window will be open when they are ready to go public. The institutional design issue is how to simultaneously create both a set of mutually dependent institutions and the trust that these institutions will work as expected when called upon.

In such a path-dependent equilibrium, the cost of change is the guard rail that keeps us on the path. We remain in an equilibrium less efficient than would be possible without the transaction costs of creating the institutions needed to support alternatives (Kohn 1995). While we do not aspire to offer a solution here, our analysis suggests an approach to creating the conditions conducive to a vigorous venture capital market: avoid the problem of creating multiple new institutions by piggybacking on another country's institutions. If this is successful, a profit opportunity and corresponding potential for the development of local institutions will be created.

Most obviously, in the increasingly global capital market, the German venture capital market could follow Israel's lead in relying on the US stock market and its supporting infrastructure. A German company that maintains accounting records in a fashion consistent with US standards—arguably much less of a burden when done from the beginning than if implemented by a conversion, as when Daimler-Benz listed its shares on the New York Stock Exchange—confronts no regulatory barrier to listing on NASDAQ, the exchange most suitable to venture-capital-backed IPOs. At present, over 100 European companies, including one German company, list their shares on NASDAQ. Many of these listings represent the IPO of the company's stock. With NASDAQ comes its institutional infrastructure. For example, both Hambrecht and Quist and Robertson, Stephens and Co., leading investment bankers for venture-capital-backed IPOs in the USA, are opening European offices and holding conferences to introduce American venture capital funds to European entrepreneurs (Lavin 1996). Silicon Valley law firms are also actively recruiting European IPO candidates.

The availability of this institutional infrastructure, without the costs of establishing it from scratch, can shorten the shadow of the past and, in the medium term, induce the development of competing local institutions. For example, in the near term, foreign venture capitalists will likely find it profitable to hire and train locals to help them find profitable investment opportunities. In the medium term, some of these people, once trained, will form their own firms and compete with their former employers.

2.8. CONCLUSION

In this chapter we have examined one of the path-dependent consequences of the difference between stock market- and bank-centred capital markets: the link between an active stock market and a strong venture capital market. We have shown that economies of scope among financial and non-financial contributions by venture capital providers, plus venture capital investors' need for a quantitative measure of venture capital funds' skill, can explain the importance of an exit strategy. Moreover, the potential for exit through an IPO, possible in a stock-market-centred capital market, allows the venture capitalist and the entrepreneur to contract implicitly over control, in a manner that is not easily duplicable in a bank-centred capital market. Finally, we have suggested that the best strategy for overcoming path dependent barriers to a venture capital market in bank-centred systems is to piggyback on the institutional infrastructure of stock-market-centred systems.

Our model seeks to explain the importance of a possible IPO exit for a high-growth firm financed by a venture capital fund, for which exit by the fund is desirable at a stage in the firm's life when it is still consuming rather than generating capital. For a mature, cash-generating firm, another exit strategy that preserves the entrepreneur's control is possible: the firm itself can buy back the venture capital fund's stake, perhaps by borrowing the needed funds. This strategy permits a somewhat different implicit contract over control between the fund and an entrepreneur: if the firm is successful enough to buy out the fund, the fund will acquiesce in this strategy even if this form of exit does not maximize the fund's return on an individual investment. In the USA, this form of exit is associated not with venture capital funds but with 'leveraged buyout' funds. In Europe, which has a less clear distinction between venture capital and leveraged buyouts, this form of exit is common when venture capital funds invest in management buyouts of mature firms. We plan to explore in future work the possible extension of our model to the leveraged buyout industry.

References

Admati, A. and Pfleiderer, P. (1994), 'Robust financial contracting and the role of venture capitalists', *Journal of Finance* 49, 371–402.

Aoki, M. (1994), 'Monitoring characteristics of the main bank system: An analytical and developmental view', in M. Aoki and H. Patrick (eds), *The Japanese Main Bank System: Its Relevance for Developing and Transforming Economies*, Oxford: Oxford University Press.

Barry, C. (1994), 'New directions in venture capital research', *Journal of Financial Management* 23, 3–15.

——, Muscarella, C., Peavy J., III, and Vetsuypens, M. (1990), 'The role of venture capitalists in the creation of a public company', *Journal of Financial Economics* 27, 447–71.

Benton, L. and Gunderson, R. Jr. (1993), 'Portfolio company investments: Hi-tech corporation, venture capital and public offering negotiation', in M. Halloran, L. Benton, R. Gunderson, Jr., K. Kearney, and J. del Calvo (eds), *Law & Business*, New York: Harcourt Brace Jovanovich.

Bergloff, E. (1994), 'A control theory of venture capital finance', *Journal of Law, Economics, and Organization* 10, 247–67.

Black, B. (1990), 'Shareholder passivity re-examined', *Michigan Law Review* 89, 520–608.

Booth, J. and Smith, R. (1986), 'Capital raising, underwriting and the certification hypothesis', *Journal of Financial Economics* 15, 261–81.

Brav, A. and Gompers, P. (1997), 'Myth or reality? The long-run underperformance of initial public offerings: Evidence from venture and non-venture capital-backed companies', *Journal of Finance* 52, 1791–812.

Bygrave, W. and Timmons, J. (1992), *Venture Capital at the Crossroads*, Cambridge, MA: Harvard Business School Press.

Carvalho, A. (1996), 'Venture capital as a network for human resources allocation', Working paper, University of Illinois.

Coffee, J. (1991), 'Liquidity versus control: The institutional investor as corporate monitor', *Columbia Law Review* 91, 1277–368.

Diamond, D. (1991), 'Monitoring and reputation: The choice between bank loans and directly placed debt', *Journal of Political Economy* 99, 689–721.

Economist (1996), 'Going for the golden egg', Sept. 28, 89.

Edwards, J. and Fisher, A. (1994), *Banks, Finance and Investment in Germany*, Cambridge: Cambridge University Press.

European Venture Capital Association (1995), *EVCA Yearbook 1995*, London: Ernst & Young.

Fisher, A. (1996a), 'A venture across the pond', *Financial Times*, July 24, 1996, 12.

—— (1996b), 'Germans urged to take a risk for jobs', *Financial Times*, July 16, 1996, 2.

Florida, R. and Martin, K. (1990), *The Breakthrough Illusion: Corporate America's Failure to Move From Innovation to Mass Production*, New York: Basic Books.

Gilson, R. (1996), 'Corporate governance and economic efficiency', *Washington University Law Quarterly* 74, 327–45.

—— (1999), 'The legal infrastructure of high-technology industrial districts: Silicon Valley and covenants not to compete', *New York University Law Review* 74, 575–629.

—— and Kraakman, R. (1984), 'The mechanisms of market efficiency', *Virginia Law Review* 70, 549–644.

—— and Roe, M. (1997), 'Lifetime employment: Labor peace and the evolution of Japanese corporate governance', *Columbia Law Review* 99, 508–40.

Giza Group (1996), *Survey of Venture Capital and Investment Funds in Israel, August 1996*, Tel Aviv: Giza Group.

Gompers, P. (1995), 'Optimal investment, monitoring, and the staging of venture capital', *Journal of Financial Economics* 50, 1461–489.

—— (1996), 'Grandstanding in the venture capital industry', *Journal of Financial Economics* 42, 133–56.

—— (2000), 'An examination of convertible securities in venture capital', Working paper, Harvard Business School.

—— and Lerner, J. (1996), 'The use of covenants: An empirical analysis of venture partnership agreements', *Journal of Law and Economics* 39, 463–98.

—— and Lerner, J. (1997), 'Venture capital distributions: Short-run and long-run reactions', Working paper, Harvard Business School.

Gorman, M. and Sahlman, W. (1989), 'What do venture capitalists do?', *Journal of Business Venturing* 4, 231–48.

Gourlay, R. (1996), 'The development of a venture capital industry lies behind the economic success of a new breed of high-tech Israeli company', *Financial Times*, April 30, 1996, 14.

Grossman, S. and Hart, O. (1988), 'One share-one vote and the market for corporate control', *Journal of Financial Economics* 20, 175–202.

Harris, M. and Raviv, A. (1988), 'Corporate governance: voting rights and majority rules', *Journal of Financial Economics* 20, 203–35.

Harrison, E. (1990), *The West-German Venture Capital Market*, Frankfurt am Main: Peter Lang.

Hellmann, T. (1995), 'The allocation of control rights in venture capital contracts', *RAND Journal of Economics* 29, 57–76.

—— (1996), 'Competition and cooperation between entrepreneurial an established companies: The viability of corporate venture investments', Paper for the second annual Conference of Strategic Management, Stanford University.

Holmstrom, B. and Tirole, J. (1989), 'The theory of the firm', in R. Schmalensee and R. Willig (eds), *Handbook of Industrial Organization*, Vol. 1, Handbooks in Economics No. 10, Amsterdam: North-Holland, 62–133.

Hyde, A. (1997), 'High-velocity labor markets', Working paper, Rutgers Law School.

Hoshi, T. (1993), 'Evolution of the main bank system in Japan', Working paper, University of California at San Diego.

Kaplan, S. (1994*a*), 'Top executive rewards and firm performance: A comparison of Japan and the United States', *Journal of Political Economy* 102, 510–46.

——(1994*b*), 'Top executives, turnover, and firm performance in Germany', *Journal of Law, Economics, and Organization* 10, 142–59.

—— and Minton, B. (1994), 'Appointments of outsiders to Japanese boards: determinants and implications for managers', *Journal of Financial Economics* 36, 225–58.

—— and Ramseyer, J. (1996), 'Those Japanese firms with their disdain for shareholders: another fable for the academy', *Washington University Law Quarterly* 74, 403–18.

Kohn, M. (1995), 'Economics as a theory of exchange', Working paper, Dartmouth College Department of Economics.

Lavin, D. (1996), 'The sky's the limit', *Convergence* 2, 8.

Lerner, J. (1994*a*), 'The syndication of venture capital investments', *Financial Management* 23, 16–17.

—— (1994*b*), 'Venture capitalists and the decision to go public', *Journal of Financial Economics* 35, 293–316.

—— (1995), 'Venture capitalists and the oversight of private firms', *Journal of Finance* 50, 301–18.

—— and Merges, R. (1997), 'The control of strategic alliance: an empirical analysis of biotechnology collaborations', Working paper No. 6014, National Bureau of Economic Research.

Lin, T. and Smith, R. (1995), 'Insider reputation and selling decisions: the unwinding of venture capital investments during equity IPOs', Working paper, Claremont Graduate School.

MacIntosh, J. (1996), 'Venture capital exits in Canada and the U.S.', Working paper, University of Toronto Faculty of Law.

Marx, L. (1994), 'Negotiation of venture capital contracts', Working paper, University of Rochester.

Megginson, W. and Weiss, K. (1991), 'Venture capital certification in initial public offerings', *Journal of Finance* 46, 879–903.

Milhaupt, C. (1997), 'The market for innovation in the United States and Japan: Venture capital and the comparative corporate governance debate', *Northwestern University Law Review* 91, 865–98.

Moukheiber, Z. (1996), 'Kleiner's web', *Forbes*, March 25, 1996, 40–2.

North, D. (1990), *Institutions, Institutional Change, and Economic Performance*, Cambridge: Cambridge University Press.

—— (1994), 'Economic performance through time', *American Economic Review* 84, 359–68.

Petty, W., Bygrave, W., and Shulman, J. (1994), 'Harvesting the entrepreneurial venture: A time for creating value', *Journal of Applied Corporate Finance* 7, 48–58.

Pickles, C. (1996), 'One answer to Europe's capital needs', *Wall Street Journal Europe*, October 23.

Porter, M. (1992), 'Capital disadvantages: America's failing investment system', *Harvard Business Review* 70, 65–82.

Powell, W. (1996), 'Inter-organizational collaboration in the biotechnology industry', *Journal of Institutional and Theoretical Economics* 152, 197–215.

Price, C. (1996), 'EASDAQ pins hopes on NASDAQ', *Financial Times*, Sept. 30, 23.

Rajan, R. (1992), 'Insiders and outsiders: the choice between informed and arm's length debt', *Journal of Finance* 47, 1367–400.

Rasch, S. (1994), 'Special stock market segments for small company shares in Europe—what went wrong?', Discussion Paper No. 93–13, Center for European Economic Research.

Roe, M. (1994), *Strong Managers, Weak Owners: The Political Roots of American Corporate Finance*, Princeton: Princeton University Press.

Sahlman, W. (1990), 'The structure and governance of venture capital organizations', *Journal of Financial Economics* 27, 473–522.

Sagari, S. and Guidotti, G. (1993), 'Venture capital: The lessons from the developing world for the developing world', *Financial Markets. Instruments and Investments* 1, 31–42.

Saxanian, A. (1994), *Regional Advantage: Culture and Competition in Silicon Valley and Route 128*, Cambridge MA: Harvard University Press.

Shiller, R., Boycko, M., and Korobov, V. (1991), 'Popular attitudes toward free markets: The Soviet Union and the United States compared', *American Economic Review* 81, 385–400.

——, ——, and —— (1992), 'Hunting for Homo Sovieticus: Situational versus attitudinal factors in economic behavior', Brookings Papers on Economic Activity, 127–81.

Venture Capital Yearbook (various years through 1997), New York: Venture Economics Publishing.

3

Going Public and the Option Value of Convertible Securities in Venture Capital

THOMAS HELLMANN

3.1. INTRODUCTION

Venture capitalists specialize in the financing of new growth-oriented companies. As such they are sometimes hailed as one of the few investors that provides long-term finance. A closer look at venture capital, however, reveals that while venture capitalists do indeed provide financing with a long horizon they also insist on defining the limits of the horizon as clearly as possible. Venture capitalists are not interested in becoming long-term owners of start-up companies, but they rather specialize in raising new companies up to a certain level of maturity, at which time they want to hand off the investment to other investors. Venture capitalist are thus concerned about the 'exit options' of their investments.

The main exit options in venture capital are liquidation, acquisition, and going public. Liquidation applies essentially to failed companies where only some asset value can be recuperated; acquisitions can range from a disguised liquidation all the way to a sale of a highly successful company; in an initial public offering (IPO) the venture capitalists can either sell some of their shares directly by including them in the offering, or they can sell them subsequently on the market (subject to some legal restrictions, such as a lock-up period).

There are several benefits for a venture capitalist in taking a company public. Venture capitalists have particular expertise in selecting, monitoring, and supporting early stage high-risk ventures (see Hellmann and Puri 2000*a, b*). As companies mature the opportunity cost of holding onto these investments becomes very high for the venture capitalists. Venture capitalists thus value the opportunity to obtain liquidity on their investments. An IPO provides a natural venue for liquidity (see also Lerner 1994). The completion of an IPO also creates some 'bragging rights' for a venture capitalist. Apart from the obvious profitability measures, venture capitalists typically measure their success in terms of the number of companies they have taken public. Outsiders trying to evaluate the performance of a venture capitalist find it very difficult to value the investment of the venture capitalist's portfolio, since it consists of privately held companies that publish only limited information about themselves. Once a company has gone public, however, its value becomes much more apparent to outsiders. By taking a company public, venture capitalists can thus demonstrate their success. This may be particularly useful to a venture capitalist who is currently raising a new fund. Gompers (1996) finds some evidence of what he calls 'grandstanding': he shows that venture capitalists are more likely to take a company public early if they are engaged in raising a fund at the same time or in the near future.

While an IPO thus brings venture capitalists a number of benefits, it also involves a number of costs, which are typically borne by the company and/or the entrepreneur. There are obviously the direct costs of going public, and IPOs are traditionally under-priced. The public company is held to a much higher standard of accountability that constrains the activities of senior management. In some cases going public requires some fundamental changes in the internal organization of the company, ranging from merely hiring an experienced CFO all the way to formalizing and possibly changing the com-pany's internal processes and culture. In addition, some entrepreneurs dislike the very idea that their company is partly owned and controlled by an anonymous set of investors who may have a different set of objectives.

If the exit decision is a potentially contentious issue it would seem that the entrepreneur and the venture capitalist would want to anticipate this conflict and create a governance structure to address this problem. The question we ask in this chapter is how a venture capitalist and an entrepreneur can structure an optimal contract in the light of a potential conflict of interest about exit. We focus on the conflict of interest as to whether the company should go public. In the simplest case, the alternative to not going public is keeping the company private. Sometimes the alternative may also be more subtle. For example, it may be that the entrepreneur and the venture capitalist disagree on the timing of an IPO, so that the entrepreneur wants to keep the company private for a certain period of time, to allow it to first mature and prove its viability, before dealing with the exposure of public markets.

At this point it is useful to mention a few stylized facts about venture capital contracts (see also Sahlman 1990; Bartlett 1995; Kaplan and Strömberg 2000). First, the most common financial arrangement is for the entrepreneurs to hold ordinary stock while the venture cap-italists hold convertible preferred stock. The main difference between these two securities is that the preferred stock gives the venture capitalists some 'downside' protection, while it still allows them to participate on the 'upside' by converting their stock. Second, a standard clause in venture capital contracts is that the preferred stock automatically con-verts into ordinary stock in the event of an IPO. Third, the venture capitalists are usually accorded 'demand registration rights'. This is the right to force the company into going public by asking that the venture capitalists' shares be sold on a stock exchange.

The main hypothesis of this chapter is that the common use of these three contractual features can be explained as an efficient response to the conflict of interest described above. To make this argument we develop a simple model where an entrepreneur and a venture capitalist design a contract that attempts to align the incentives of each party and provides an efficient governance structure. The model contains a double moral hazard, where the entrepreneur provides non-contractible effort to increase the operational performance of the company and the venture capitalist provides non-contractible effort to increase the financial options available to the firm. In particular the venture capitalist can invest in preparing the company to go public. We assume that the IPO benefits the venture capitalist more than the entrepreneur.

The optimal contract prescribes a transfer from the venture capitalist to the entrepreneur that compensates the latter for his disutility of an IPO. Such a transfer can be implemented by using convertible preferred stock that automatically converts in the event of an IPO. The cost of the automatic conversion of preferred stock is the loss of the option value of convertibility. This option value depends on the maturity of the company. If the company is still in a relatively early stage where there still exists a significant risk of failure, preferred stock is valuable since it affords some downside protection to the venture capitalist. Automatic conversion thus imposes a real cost to the venture capitalist in case of an early IPO. An interesting implication of the analysis is that if the company is taken public at a later, more mature stage the automatic conversion is much more harmless, since the venture capitalist no longer needs the downside protection.

The use of demand registration rights is also related to the issue of compensating the entrepreneur for the disutility of an IPO. If the entrepreneur were to control the exit decision, then he could hold up the benefits of going public by demanding a large transfer from the venture capitalist. If the venture capitalists anticipate such a hold up, they no longer have an incentive to adequately prepare the company to go public. In order to prevent such a hold-up it is efficient to give the venture capitalist control over the decision to take the company public.

This chapter contributes to the emerging literature on convertible securities in venture capital. Berglöf (1994) considers the advantage of the convertible security in terms of allocating bargaining power. Cornelli and Yosha (1999) show that convertibility might reduce or eliminate incentives for inefficient window dressing. Schmidt (1999) explains the use of convertible securities in a sequential investment framework. Repullo and Suarez (1998) also focus on a two-sided moral hazard problem and find that the optimal security resembles convertible preferred equity. Other recent papers include Marx (1998), Bergemann and Hege (1998), and Dessi (1999). With the exception of a brief discussion in Schmidt (1999), none of these papers address the issue of automatic conversion. In a companion paper, Hellmann (2000) focuses on the trade-off between acquisitions and IPOs. It provides a detailed analysis of the optimality of convertible securities, including their automatic conversion in case of an IPO. The new aspect of this paper is to focus on the option value of the convertible security. Fundamentally, the convertible security gives the investor a choice between two distinct sets of cash flow rights. At the time of the IPO, this choice disappears because of the automatic conversion. This means that the investor losses the option value of convertibility. This option value has not received any attention in the literature so far. In this chapter I show how it can play a role in mediating the concerns of the investor and the entrepreneur with respect to going public.

The remainder of the chapter is structured as follows. In Section 3.2, I present the basic model. In Section 3.3, I develop the optimal contract when all states of the world are verifiable. In Section 3.4, I show how a contract with convertible preferred stock that automatically converts in the event of an IPO implements the optimal solution, even if the states of the world are not verifiable. In Section 3.5, I explain the rationale for giving demand registration rights, where the venture capitalist obtains control over the decision to go public. Section 3.6 examines an extension of the model where the decision to go public affects not only private benefits, but also cash flows. It is followed by a brief conclusion.

3.2. THE BASE MODEL

In the model there is an entrepreneur denoted by E. He has no wealth but the idea or human capital to create a company that may create value in the future. There is a venture capitalist denoted by V. She has the funds and expertise to finance the company. There are other private equity investors, denoted by P, who can make later-stage investments in companies (and V may also join them in the late stage investments). Finally, there are stock market investors, denoted by S, who can also make investments in later stage companies. All parties are risk-neutral and there is no discounting. All parties have symmetric information.

There are three dates in the model. At date 0 the company requires an investment I_0. At date 1 the company can be in three different states denoted σ_A, σ_B, and σ_C. In state σ_A it is efficient to liquidate the company at a value L. In states σ_B and σ_C it is efficient to refinance the company with an investment I_1. If refinanced the company can be in two possible states at date 2 denoted by σ_D and σ_E. For σ_D the company has a value r, and for σ_E it has a value R. I assume that all rounds of financing are perfectly competitive so that, in order to finance the investment, investors at dates 0, 1, and 2 need to receive an expected utility of I_0 and I_1, respectively. We make three straightforward assumptions about the payoff structure, namely (i) $I_0 > L$; (ii) $I_1 > r - L$; and (iii) $R > r > L$; (i) and (ii) say that the returns may fall below the cost of investment, so that investors at date 0 and date 1 cannot make a riskless investment; (iii) merely provides a simple ordering of the states. We also assume that R is sufficiently large to make the project feasible.

At date 0, V finances the company. At date 1, there are two states under which the project may get refinanced. If σ_B occurs the company is not ready to go public, so that it can only be refinanced by P. If σ_C occurs the company is ready to go public. In this case a decision has to be made whether it will be refinanced by P or S.

Throughout the chapter I use the notation $\bar{\mu}_1 = 1 - \mu_1$, and similarly for all other probabilities. State σ_A occurs with a probability $\bar{\mu}_1$; state σ_B occurs with a probability $\mu_1\bar{\lambda}$; state σ_C occurs with a probability $\mu_1\lambda$; state σ_D occurs with a probability $\mu_1\bar{\mu}_2$; state σ_E occurs with a probability $\mu_1\mu_2$.

μ_2 is the probability of success after date 1. It reflects the notion that at date 1 there is some fundamental uncertainty about the viability of the company that has not been resolved yet. μ_1 is the probability that the project can be refinanced at date 1. It reflects the progress of the company in its early phase. This performance depends on the amount of private non-verifiable effort that E puts into the company. We denote the effort costs by $c_E(\mu_1)$ with $c_E(0) = 0$, $c_{E'} > 0$ and $c_E'' > 0$ and $c_{E'}(1) = \infty$.

λ is the probability that the company is ready to go public at date 1. At date 1 there is still considerable uncertainty about the value of the firm, as reflected in the difference between R and r. This uncertainty gets resolved after date 1. We can think of date 2 as a reduced form of a game where the company pays out dividends to its owners without ever going public. This would essentially be a profitable private company. Alternatively we can think of date 2 as a late IPO, where the company goes public at a mature stage, where the conflicts of interest between the entrepreneur and the venture capitalists are considerably lower. The event r at date 2 is best interpreted as a late liquidation event.

The model focuses on the decision to go public at date 1. Depending on what exit event we have in mind for date 2, we can think of the date 1 decision either as a timing decision about the IPO, or else about the fundamental decision whether or not to go public at all. In either case, the possibility of go public depends on the 'level of understanding' in the public market. To take a company public a certain amount of public relations effort needs to be done, to explain to investors the underlying value proposition of the company. Going public may also require the company to make the company 'presentable', such as by improving the quality of its bookkeeping or formalizing some of its management practices.

Consider the venture capitalist's costs associated with an early IPO. Venture capitalists maintain relationships with investment bankers and analysts. They can spend a significant amount of time explaining the concept of the business and preparing the investment banking community for an upcoming IPO. To model this we assume that λ depends on the private non-verifiable effort of V which is given by $c_V(\lambda)$ with $c_V(0) = 0$, $c_{V'} > 0$ and $c_{V''} > 0$ and $c_{V'}(1) = \infty$.

Both P and S can finance the company at date 1, with different implications to V and E. We begin our analysis with a simple specification, where the venture has the same cash flows under P- and S-financing, but where V and E associate different private benefits with the two modes of financing. In Section 3.6, we extend the model to also allow for different cash flows under P- and S-financing and show that the model remains valid. In the base model, we assume that V prefers S while E prefers P. With an IPO, V receives a private benefit γ, and E perceives a private cost ϕ. We first assume that γ and ϕ are both constants, but relax this assumption in Section 3.5. Moreover, we assume that $\gamma > \phi > 0$, so that if possible an IPO is always efficient.

The choice of the initial financial instruments used by V and E is the focus of the analysis. Initially assume that all the states of the world $\{\sigma_A, \sigma_B, \sigma_C, \sigma_D, \sigma_E\}$ are verifiable. Afterwards we relax this assumption and ask which financial contract can implement the optimal (second-best) contract even if the states of the world are observable but not verifiable. The optimal contract between E and V specifies V's percentage share α_i, which depends on the following states: $i = A, D|B, E|B, D|C, E|C$. In addition E and V will have to cede some returns to the investor at date 1. We denote the share of P or S by ζ_i, where $i = D|B, E|B, D|C, D|E$. They must satisfy

$$\mu_2 \zeta_{E|B} R + (\bar{\mu}_2)\zeta_{D|B} r = I_1 \quad \text{and} \quad \mu_2 \zeta_{E|C} R + (\bar{\mu}_2)\zeta_{D|C} r = I_1.$$

The expected utilities at date 0 of E and V are respectively given by

$$U_E = \mu_1 u_E + \bar{\mu}_1(1 - \alpha_A)L - c_E(\mu_1) \quad \text{and} \quad U_V = \mu_1 u_V + \bar{\mu}_1 \alpha_A L - c_V(\mu_1),$$

where

$$u_E = \mu_2\lambda((1 - \alpha_{E|C} - \zeta_{E|C})R - \phi) + \mu_2\bar{\lambda}(1 - \alpha_{E|B} - \zeta_{E|B})R)$$
$$+ \bar{\mu}_2\lambda((1 - \alpha_{D|C} - \zeta_{D|C})r - \phi) + \bar{\mu}_2\bar{\lambda}(1 - \alpha_{D|B} - \zeta_{D|B})r),$$
$$u_V = [\mu_2\lambda(\alpha_{E|C}R + \gamma) + \mu_2\bar{\lambda}\alpha_{E|B}R + \bar{\mu}_2\lambda(\alpha_{D|C}r + \gamma) + \bar{\mu}_2\bar{\lambda}\alpha_{D|B}r.$$

The optimal contract maximizes U_E subject to $U_V = I_0$ and subject to incentive constraints developed below. E's reservation utility is assumed to be satisfied at all times. For very large I_0 the project cannot be financed, so we limit the analysis to the relevant range of I_0 where the project can be financed. The contract between E and V can be renegotiated at no cost and at any time.

3.3. OPTIMAL CONTRACTS WITH VERIFIABILITY

In this section, we derive the optimal (second-best) contract when the states of the world are verifiable. To begin the analysis we first derive the socially optimal (first-best) solution, which cannot be implemented in general.

Define $\rho = \mu_2 R + \bar{\mu}_2 r - I_1$. In order to maximize their joint utility

$$\bar{\mu}_1 L + \mu_1[\rho + \lambda(\gamma - \phi)] - c_E(\mu_1) - c_V(\lambda) - I_0,$$

E and V would both have to provide an efficient amount of private effort. The efficient levels of μ_1 and λ, denoted by μ_1^{FB} and λ^{FB}, which are given by

$$\rho + \lambda(\gamma - \phi) - L = c_{E'}(\mu_1^{FB}) \text{ and } \mu_1(\gamma - \phi) = c_{V'}(\lambda^{FB}).$$

Since μ_1 and λ are not contractible, these first-best levels may not occur in general. Consider first V's privately optimal choice of λ^*, given by

$$\mu_1\mu_2(\gamma + \alpha_{E|C}R - \alpha_{E|B}R) + \mu_1\bar{\mu}_2(\gamma + \alpha_{D|C}r - \alpha_{D|B}r) = c_{V'}(\lambda^*).$$

We can actually achieve the efficient level $\lambda^* = \lambda^{FB}$ by setting

$$(\mu_2\alpha_{E|B}R + \bar{\mu}_2\alpha_{D|B}r) - (\mu_2\alpha_{E|C}R + \bar{\mu}_2\alpha_{D|C}r) = \phi.$$

This implies the following proposition.

Proposition 3.1. *In the optimal contract V's expected pay-off is higher and E's expected pay-off lower by an amount ϕ at date 1 whenever the company is financed by S rather than P.*

Proposition 3.1 says that V must make a transfer to E if she wants to take the company public. This transfer exactly compensates E for his disutility of going public. The reason for this transfer is to control the incentives of V to take the company public. In the absence of this transfer V would over-invest in taking the company public. This would create an inefficiency since V does not take into account the loss of utility of E. By imposing a transfer, however, she is forced to take account of E's disutility and this somewhat curtails her otherwise excessive enthusiasm to take the company public.

Consider next E's privately optimal choice of μ_1^*, which is given by

$$u_E - (1 - \alpha_A)L = c_{E'}(\mu_1^*).$$

Proposition 3.2. *The optimal contract gives all the liquidation value at date 1 to V, that is, $\alpha_A = 1$. E always provides less effort than in the first-best contract, that is, $\mu_1^* < \mu^{FB}$.*

Proof. Take λ as given. We rewrite E's first-order condition as

$$[\rho + \lambda(\gamma - \phi)] - u_V + \lambda(\gamma - \phi) - L + \alpha_A L = c_{E'}(\mu_1).$$

For any given λ the joint utility is increasing in μ_1 as long as the left-hand side of this expression is not larger than $\rho + \lambda(\gamma - \phi) - L$. The joint utility is thus increasing in μ_1 as long as $u_V - \alpha_A L > 0$. Using $\mu_1 u_V + \bar{\mu}_1 \alpha_A L - c_V(\mu_1) = I_0$, this condition is equivalent to $\mu_1(u_V - \alpha_A L) = I_0 + c_V(\mu_1) - \alpha_A L > 0$ since $I_0 > L \geq \alpha_A L$. This proves that E provides too little effort. Moreover, since μ_1 is decreasing in $(1 - \alpha_A)L$, the optimal contract has $(1 - \alpha_A)L = 0$. $\qquad\square$

The intuition for this result is straightforward. Because of the wealth constraint E cannot obtain a sufficiently large stake in the company to have the efficient incentive to maximize the value of the company, as opposed to pursuing other objectives or providing less effort. In order to provide the highest possible incentives the optimal contract therefore rewards E only in case of success. It is thus optimal to give V first rights to the liquidation proceeds in case of failure.

3.4. CONVERTIBLE PREFERRED EQUITY

In this section, we show how the optimal contract from the previous section can be implemented even if the states of nature are not verifiable. Specifically we assume that the states of nature $\{\sigma_A, \sigma_B, \sigma_C, \sigma_D, \sigma_E\}$ are observable but not verifiable. If a contract cannot be made contingent on the states of the world, it can still be made contingent on verifiable actions, and in particular on events such as liquidation, refinancing, or going public. It is useful to introduce the following definition:

Definition 3.1. We call a contract 'convertible preferred stock with automatic conversion in case of an IPO' if it satisfies the following conditions:

- E receives n_E ordinary stock where n_E is an arbitrarily fixed number.
- V receives redeemable convertible preferred stock. The redeemable value of the preferred stock has a total face value δ and the stock can be converted into n_V ordinary shares.
- V's preferred stock automatically converts to ordinary stock in the event of an IPO.

We will now solve for the optimal contract. For simplicity we assume that at date 1 all investors use ordinary stock, although all the results continue to hold if they use other securities. In state σ_B, P requires n_B number of stocks and in state σ_C, S requires n_C number of stocks, where

$$\mu_2 \frac{n_B}{n_V + n_E + n_B} R + \bar{\mu}_2 \frac{n_B}{n_E + n_B} \text{Max}[0, r - \delta] = I_1,$$

$$\frac{n_C}{n_V + n_E + n_C} (\mu_2 R + \bar{\mu}_2 r) = I_1. \tag{3.1}$$

Moreover,

$$U_V(n_V, n_B, n_C, \delta) = \bar{\mu}_1 \text{Min}[\delta, L] + \mu_1 \lambda \gamma - c_V(\lambda)$$

$$+ \mu_1 \lambda \frac{n_V}{n_V + n_E + n_C} (\mu_2 R + \bar{\mu}_2 r)$$

$$+ \mu_1 \bar{\lambda} \mu_2 \frac{n_V}{n_V + n_E + n_B} R + \mu_1 \bar{\lambda} \bar{\mu}_2 \text{Min}[\delta, r] = I_0.$$

Solving (1) for n_C we can replace $\mu_1 \lambda (n_V/(n_V + n_E + n_C))(\mu_2 R + \bar{\mu}_2 r)$ in U_V with $\mu_1 \lambda (n_V/(n_V + n_E))\rho$. Moreover, using $r \geq \delta$, and from proposition 2 using $\delta \geq L$, we get

$$U_V = \bar{\mu}_1 L + \mu_1 \lambda \left(\gamma + \frac{n_V}{n_V + n_E} \rho \right) - c_V(\lambda)$$

$$+ \mu_1 \bar{\lambda} \mu_2 \frac{n_V}{n_V + n_E + n_B} R + \mu_1 \bar{\lambda} \bar{\mu}_2 \delta. \tag{3.2}$$

The first-order condition for λ is

$$\mu_1 \left[\gamma + \frac{n_V}{n_V + n_E} \rho - \mu_2 \frac{n_V}{n_V + n_E + n_B} R - \bar{\mu}_2 \delta \right] = c_V'(\lambda).$$

To satisfy the optimality condition from proposition 1, choose δ to satisfy

$$-\phi = \frac{n_V}{n_V + n_E} \rho - \mu_2 \frac{n_V}{n_V + n_E + n_B} R - \bar{\mu}_2 \delta$$

or

$$\delta = \frac{1}{\bar{\mu}_2} \left[\phi + \frac{n_V}{n_V + n_E + n_B} \mu_2 R - \frac{n_V}{n_V + n_E} \rho \right]. \tag{3.3}$$

With this we immediately state the main proposition of this section.

Proposition 3.3. *A contract with convertible preferred stock with automatic conversion in case of an IPO implements the optimal contract, even though the states of the world are not verifiable. There exist $\bar{\phi} > \underline{\phi} \geq 0$, so that for $\phi < \underline{\phi}(\phi > \bar{\phi})$ the contract also allocates additional stock options to $V(E)$.*

Proof. Consider the solution to eqns (1–3). As we will see below, for $\phi \in [\underline{\phi}, \bar{\phi}]$ we have $r \geq \delta \geq L$. To verify that this contract implements the optimal contract, note first that since $\delta \geq L$, V retains all the claims on L in state σ_A. Now if the company goes public at date 1 (i.e. in state σ_C) then V's stock automatically converts. The expected cost of conversion to V is value that she forgoes by not retaining her preferred stock position. This position is only valuable if the company is liquidated at date 2, that is, its expected value is given by $\bar{\mu}_2(\delta - (n_V/(n_V + n_E + n_C))r)$ which just equals ϕ. This represents a transfer from V to E that satisfies the condition of Proposition 1. To find $\underline{\phi}$ and $\bar{\phi}$ we simply use $\delta = L$ and $\delta = r$ in eqn 3. For $\phi < \underline{\phi}$ we can reduce the transfer in state σ_C by setting $\delta = L$ and giving V some additional stock options in case of IPO. For $\phi > \bar{\phi}$ we can increase the transfer in state σ_C by setting $\delta = r$ and giving E some additional stock options in case of IPO. Assume for simplicity that these stock options are granted at zero cost. Let o_V and o_E denote the number of shares allocated to V or E. The optimal choice o_V and o_E are given by

$$\mu_2 \frac{n_B}{n_V + n_E + n_B} R + \bar{\mu}_2 \frac{n_B}{n_E + n_B} \text{Max}[0, r - \delta] = I_1,$$

$$\frac{n_C}{o_V + o_E + n_V + n_E + n_C}(\mu_2 R + \bar{\mu}_2 r) = I_1 \qquad (3.1')$$

$$U_V = \bar{\mu}_1 L + \mu_1 \lambda \left(\gamma + \frac{o_V + n_V}{o_V + o_E + n_V + n_E} \rho \right) - c_V(\lambda)$$

$$+ \mu_1 \bar{\lambda} \mu_2 \frac{n_V}{n_V + n_E + n_B} R + \mu_1 \bar{\lambda} \bar{\mu}_2 \delta, \qquad (3.2')$$

$$\delta = \frac{1}{\bar{\mu}_2} \left[\phi + \frac{n_V}{n_V + n_E + n_B} \mu_2 R - \frac{o_N + n_V}{o_V + o_E + n_V + n_E} \rho \right]. \qquad (3.3')$$

$\square$

Proposition 3.3 says that for a central range of parameters a contract with convertible preferred stock with automatic conversion in case of an IPO is optimal. From Proposition 3.2 we know that V should get all the proceeds of a liquidation L. By setting $\delta \geq L$ the preferred feature allows V to secure these proceeds in case of liquidation. In order to break even V also needs to participate in the proceeds in case of success. This is naturally done by converting her preferred stock into ordinary stock that participates in the success of the company. The most intriguing part of Proposition 3.3 is thus the automatic conversion of the preferred stock in case of an IPO. With an IPO, there is real cost to converting the preferred stock. The convertible preferred stock contains an option value of convertibility. If in fact the company does well, then the convertible stock can simply be converted.

But if the company does not do well and needs to be liquidated at date 2, then it is better not to convert the preferred stock and demand the face value of the preferred option. The automatic conversion in case of an IPO thus takes away the option value of convertibility.

Formally, the option value of convertibility is given by $\bar{\mu}_2(\delta - (n_V/(n_V + n_E + n_C))r)$. The optimal contract chooses δ so that the option value of convertibility just equals ϕ in case of an IPO. This implies that V is paying a price for taking the company public at date 1. This implements the requirement of the optimal contract derived in Proposition 3.1 that there needs to be some transfer from V to E in case of an IPO. This guarantees an optimal level of preparation for the IPO. The elegant part of the optimal contract is that this transfer depends on the option value of convertibility. A simple combination of debt and equity could not replicate this state-contingent transfer.

Proposition 3.3 holds for a central range of the parameter ϕ. The idea is that for central values of ϕ we can design a contract where the cost of automatic conversion (i.e. the option value of convertibility) just equals E's disutility of going public ϕ. But because the key variable δ can only be chosen in a bounded range $L \leq \delta \leq r$, the cost of automatic conversion is bounded itself in the range $[\underline{\phi}, \bar{\phi}]$. If $\phi < \underline{\phi}$ the conversion of all the preferred stock implies a transfer from V to E that is too large relative to the disutility of going public. In this case giving V some additional stock options reduces the cost for choosing an IPO. And if $\phi > \bar{\phi}$ the cost of conversion is not high enough to optimally deter V from striving to take the company public. In this case it is possible to allocate additional stock options to E, which increases the cost for choosing an IPO.

3.5. REGISTRATION RIGHTS

So far we implicitly assumed that in state σ_C it is not only efficient to go public, but that both E and V agree to go public without any renegotiation. This assumption is valid for the model so far, since E is indifferent between going public, while V has a strict preference for going public. Consider now a minor extension of the model where there is some uncertainty about how much E dislikes going public: this uncertainty may reflect idiosyncrasies in the entrepreneur's preferences, and of the particular situation in which the company may go public. This uncertainty is resolved at date 1. We use the simplest possible specification, where ϕ can take two values, ϕ_1 with probability ψ and ϕ_2 with probability $\bar{\psi}$, where $\phi_2 < \phi_1 < \gamma$ and $\psi\phi_1 + \bar{\psi}\phi_2 = \phi$.

If the states of nature are not verifiable we must examine the incentives of the decision-maker to take a decision. In particular, either E or V can have the right to decide whether the company goes public. Control rights by themselves may not determine the outcome of the decision itself, since the two parties can always renegotiate. They matter, however, since they affect the bargaining positions of the two parties at the time of renegotiation (see also Hellmann 1998).

Suppose first that V controls the decision to go public and suppose that the implicit cost of converting her preferred stock is given by T^*. From Proposition 3.1 we know that the optimal transfer is given by $T^* = \phi$. In state σ_C the net gain of going public to V is $\gamma - T^* = \gamma - \phi > 0$, so that whenever possible V takes the company public. This says that giving V control rights yields an efficient outcome.

The interesting insight is that this is no longer the case if E has the decision rights. To see this, suppose that E controls the decision to go public and suppose first that $T^* = \phi$. If ϕ_2 occurs, E's net gain of going public is given by $T^* - \phi_2 = \psi(\phi_1 - \phi_2) > 0$. But if ϕ_1 occurs, E's net gain of going public is given by $T^* - \phi_1 = \bar{\psi}(\phi_2 - \phi_1) < 0$. E refuses to go public if ϕ_1 occurs. Naturally, the two parties can renegotiate. We use the generalized Nash bargaining solution to describe the outcome of the renegotiation. Let $\theta \in (0, 1)$ denote V's relative bargaining power and note that the total bargaining surplus is $\gamma - \phi_1$. In a renegotiation E accepts to go public in return for a transfer payment $\tilde{T}$ such that $\tilde{T} - \phi = (1 - \theta)(\gamma - \phi_1) \Leftrightarrow \tilde{T} = \theta\phi_1 + (1 - \theta)\gamma$. The problem with the above solution is that E now receives a higher expected transfer than in the optimal solution (i.e. $\psi\tilde{T} + \bar{\psi}T^* > \phi$). This would lead to an inefficient investment of V to take the company public. One may be tempted to reduce T^* to bring the expected transfer back to its optimal level. Suppose that the initial transfer is set at a level $T = \phi_2$. The expected transfer is then $\psi(\theta\phi_1 + (1 - \theta)\gamma) + \bar{\psi}\phi_2 = \phi + (1 - \theta)(\gamma - \phi_1) > \phi$, that is, it is still too high relative to the first-best solution. But if the transfer is set at any level $T < \phi_2$, then E renegotiates even if ϕ_2 occurs: the renegotiated transfer is given by $\tilde{T}_2 = \theta\phi_2 + (1 - \theta)\gamma$ and the expected transfer is $\psi\tilde{T} + \bar{\psi}\tilde{T}_2 = \theta\phi + (1 - \theta)\gamma > \phi$. This proves that it is impossible to implement the efficient level of the transfer T^* if E has control over the decision to go public. We have thus shown:

Proposition 3.4. *The efficient contract gives V the right to take the company public through demand registration rights.*

V thus needs to have control over the decision to go public since E is likely to 'abuse' any control he has over this decision. While the company would still go public in state σ_C with E control, this would only happen after a renegotiation in which E can extract some rents from V. Because of the this hold-up potential V would under-invest in taking the company public.

3.6. CASH FLOW EFFECTS OF IPOs

The analysis so far made the simplifying assumption that an IPO affects private benefits but not the cash flows of the venture. There may be many reasons why cash flows too are affected by an IPO. On the positive side, the cost of capital may be lower in the stock market than with private equity investors. The company may also benefit from greater visibility and accountability etc. All of these should increase the net profit and valuation in case of an IPO. On the other hand, however, an IPO may also involve underpricing and significant registration costs, as well as ongoing costs of being a public company, such as investor relations and litigation costs. We do not model these in detail, but consider only the following simple reduced form. Consider R_i and r_i, $r = P, S$ and define

$$\Delta = \mu_2(R_S - R_P) + \bar{\mu}_2(r_S - r_P) = \rho_S - \rho_P,$$

Δ is the incremental net profits of going public.

Proposition 3.5. *All the results of the model continue to hold in the model where cash flow differs between P and S by an arbitrary amount Δ.*

Proof. The joint utility is now given by

$$\bar{\mu}_1 L + \mu_1 [\mu_2 R_P + \bar{\mu}_2 r_P + \lambda(\Delta + \gamma - \phi) - I_1] - c_E(\mu_1) - c_V(\lambda) - I_0.$$

The efficient level λ^{FB} is determined by

$$\mu_1(\Delta + \gamma - \phi) = c_{V'}(\lambda^{FB}).$$

The higher Δ, the higher the optimal level of λ. To implement the efficient level of λ, the analysis is analogous to before. We have

$$\mu_2 \frac{n_B}{n_V + n_E + n_B} R_P + \bar{\mu}_2 \frac{n_B}{n_E + n_B} \text{Max}[0, r_P - \delta] = I_1,$$

$$\frac{n_C}{n_V + n_E + n_C}(\mu_2 R_S + \bar{\mu}_2 r_S) = I_1, \qquad (3.1'')$$

$$U_V = \bar{\mu}_1 L + \mu_1 \lambda \left(\gamma + \frac{n_V}{n_V + n_E} \rho_S \right) - c_V(\lambda)$$

$$+ \mu_1 \bar{\lambda} \mu_2 \frac{n_V}{n_V + n_E + n_B} R_P + \mu_1 \bar{\lambda} \bar{\mu}_2 \delta. \qquad (3.2'')$$

The first-order condition for λ is

$$\mu_1 \left[\gamma + \frac{n_V}{n_V + n_E} \rho_S - \frac{n_V}{n_V + n_E + n_B} \mu_2 R_P - \bar{\mu}_2 \delta \right] = c_V'(\lambda)$$

so that the optimal δ must satisfy

$$\delta = \frac{1}{\bar{\mu}_2} \left[\phi + \frac{n_V}{n_V + n_E + n_B} \mu_2 R_P - \frac{n_V}{n_V + n_E} \rho_S - \Delta \right]. \qquad (3.3'')$$

We have thus shown that the model continues to hold even if we allow for the IPO to have a positive or even a negative effect on the net cash flows of the venture. □

The main insight from Proposition 3.5 is that the result from the main model continues to hold in a model where going public affects not only the private benefits, but also the cash flows of the company. Normally we would think that $\Delta > 0$, that is, that an IPO will increase the net profits of the company. However, there may also be some cases where $\Delta < 0$, such as if an IPO at date 1 commands a large underpricing premium. An interesting observation is that for $\Delta < 0$ all the results of the model go through, even if $\phi = 0$. This says that even if E has no private costs of going public, there may still be a problem, namely if V has an excessive incentive to push the company to go public prematurely.

3.7. CONCLUSION

Venture capitalists have an interest in exiting their investment once a company has reached a certain level of maturity. Entrepreneurs and venture capitalists may disagree about the best way to exit the investment. We examine a conflict of interest around the decision to go public, and derive an optimal contract. The model explains a number of stylized facts about venture capital contracts, namely that venture capitalists hold convertible preferred stock that automatically converts in the event of an IPO, and that has demand registration rights attached to it. An interesting aspect of the model is that we can also interpret the conflict of interest as a disagreement on the timing of going public. An interesting line of future research is to further analyse the dynamics of when such a conflict is most likely to arise.

References

Bartlett, J. (1995), *Equity Finance: Venture Capital Buyouts, Restructurings and Reorganizations*, 2nd edn., New York: John Wiley and Sons.

Bergemann, D. and Hege, U. (1998), 'Venture capital financing, moral hazard, and learning', *Journal of Banking and Finance* 22, 703–35.

Berglöf, E. (1994), 'A control theory of venture capital', *Journal of Law, Economics, and Organization* 10, 247–67.

Cornelli, F. and Yosha, O. (1999), 'Stage financing and the role of convertible debt', CEPR Discussion Paper 1735.

Dessi, R. (1999), 'Financing entrepreneurs: optimal contracts and the role of intermediaries', Mimeo, IDEI, Toulouse.

Gompers, P. (1996), 'Grandstanding in the venture capital industry', *Journal of Financial Economics* 42, 133–56.

Hellmann, T. (1998), 'The allocation of control rights in venture capital contracts', *RAND Journal of Economics* 29, 57–76.

—— (2000), 'IPOs, Acquisitions and the use of convertible securities in venture capital', Mimeo, Stanford University.

—— and Puri, M. (2000*a*), 'The interaction between product market and financing strategy: the role of venture capital', *Review of Financial Studies* 13, 959–84.

—— and Puri, M. (2000*b*), 'Venture capital and the professionalization of start-ups: empirical evidence', Mimeo, Stanford University.

Kaplan, S. and Strömberg, P. (2000), 'Financial contracting meets the real world: an empirical study of venture capital contracts', Working paper, University of Chicago.

Lerner, J. (1994), 'Venture capitalist and the decision to go public', *Journal of Financial Economics* 35, 293–316.

Marx, L. (1998), 'Efficient venture capital financing combining debt end Equity', *Review of Economic Design* 3, 371–87.

Repullo, R. and Suarez, J. (1998), 'Venture capital finance: a security design approach', Mimeo, CEMFI, Madrid.

Sahlman, W. (1990), 'The structure and governance of venture capital organizations', *Journal of Financial Economics* 27, 473–521.

Schmidt, K. (1999), 'Convertible securities and venture capital finance', Mimeo, University of Munich.

4

Evidence on the Venture Capitalist Investment Process: Contracting, Screening, and Monitoring

STEVEN N. KAPLAN AND PER STRÖMBERG

4.1. INTRODUCTION

There is a large academic literature on the principal–agent problem in financial contracting.[1] This literature focuses on the conflicts of interest between an agent—an entrepreneur with a venture that needs financing—and a principal—an investor with the funds to finance the venture. Theory has identified a number of ways that the investor/principal can mitigate these conflicts. First, the investor can engage in information collection before deciding whether to invest, in order to screen out *ex ante* unprofitable projects and bad entrepreneurs. Second, the investor can structure financial contracts, that is, the allocation of cash flow and control rights, between the entrepreneur and investor to provide incentives for the entrepreneur to behave appropriately. And third, the investor can engage in information collection and monitoring once the project is under way.

Despite the large volume of theory, empirical work has lagged behind in comparing the contracts and actions of real world principals to their counterparts in financial contracting theory. In this chapter, we describe recent empirical work and its relation to theory for one prominent class of such principals—venture capitalists (VCs). In our view, VCs are real world entities that closely approximate the investors of theory. VCs invest in entrepreneurs who need financing to fund a promising project or company. VCs have strong incentives to maximize value, but, at the same time, receive few or no private benefits of control. Although they are intermediaries, VCs typically receive at least 20 per cent of the profits on their portfolios.[2]

In addition to being interesting from a theoretical perspective, VC actions and contracts of are interesting from a practical perspective. VCs have been extremely prominent (despite the 'tech crash') in the last several years: (1) they have been associated with a number of the prominent corporate successes like Cisco, eBay, and Yahoo; (2) they have generated substantial returns and wealth for their investors; (3) the amount of venture capital raised

---

[1] For a recent summary, see Hart (2001).   [2] See Hart (2001) and Gompers and Lerner (1999).

and invested has increased markedly in the last ten years, particularly in the USA and Europe;[3] and (4) policymakers have tried to encourage more investment in start-ups and innovation.

In this chapter, we describe recent empirical work—both ours and that of others—on the three things that VCs do—contracting, screening, and monitoring. Unlike previous empirical work that has relied largely on surveys, our work (and much of the work we describe) relies on detailed information collected from actual VC financings. We describe our data in Section 4.2. We then present a description of our work on contracting in Section 4.3. In Sections 4.4 and 4.5, we discuss recent work on screening and monitoring. We proceed in this order because the screening and monitoring discussions assume an understanding of contracting.

4.2. DATA

The data we use in our papers are taken from 213 VC investments in 119 portfolio companies by fourteen VC firms. Each VC firm provided the contractual agreements governing each financing round. The VC firm also provided (if available) the company's business plan, internal analyses evaluating the investment, and information on subsequent performance.

4.3. CONTRACTING

In Kaplan and Strömberg (2003), we compare the characteristics of real world financial contracts to their counterparts in financial contracting theory.[4] We do so by conducting a detailed study of the 213 actual contracts between VCs and entrepreneurs.

We obtain the following findings: First, a key feature of VC financings is that they allow VCs to separately allocate cash flow rights, voting rights, board rights, liquidation rights, and other control rights. We explicitly measure and report the allocation of these rights. Table 4.1 summarizes several of our results for cash flow rights and control rights. The separation is apparent, for example, in that VCs control roughly 50 per cent of the cash flow rights on average, but have a majority of board seats in only 25 per cent of the investments.

Second, while convertible securities are used most frequently, VCs also implement the same set of rights using combinations of multiple classes of common stock and straight preferred stock. We also point out that VCs use a variant of convertible preferred called participating preferred in roughly 40 per cent of the financings. Participating preferred, under most circumstances, behaves like a position of straight preferred stock and common stock rather than like a position of convertible preferred. Hence, the VC claim corresponds in most cases to a holding of (zero-coupon) debt and voting equity.

For example, assume a VC pays $10m for a convertible preferred that converts into one million shares. Assume, also, there are one million other shares outstanding. Now, assume

---

[3] For example, see Botazzi and Da Rin (2001) and Christofidis and Debande (2001).

[4] For earlier, related work, see Sahlman (1990), Gompers (1998), and Black and Gilson (1998).

Table 4.1. *Venture capitalist cash flow and control rights (Kaplan and Strömberg, 2003)*

Mean (Median)	Total sample (N = 213)				First VC rounds only (N = 98)				Pre-revenue rounds only (N = 79)			
	Best case	Worst case	Difference	Control switch % of cases	Best case	Worst case	Difference	Control switch % of cases	Best case	Worst case	Difference	Control switch % of cases
A. Cash flow rights												
% VC equity	46.7 (47.3)	55.5 (57.5)	−8.8 (−4.2)	—	40.4*** (41.0)	53.0* (50.5)	−12.6*** (−8.0)	—	51.3*** (50.0)	65.0*** (66.6)	−13.7*** (−8.9)	—
B. Control rights												
VC has majority of votes, % of cases	52.8	68.9	—	17.8	40.8***	61.2***	—	24.5%	60.8*	83.5***	—	22.7
VC has majority of board seats, % of cases	25.4	35.8	—	10.4	11.6***	27.4**	—	15.8%	28.2	37.2	—	9.0
Automatic conversion price/round price	3.6 (3.0)	—	—	—	4.4*** (3.0)	—	—	—	4.3*** (3.2)	—	—	—

Post-round allocations of rights for 213 investments in 119 portfolio companies by 14 venture capital partnerships. Investments were made between 1987 and 1999. VC allocations are aggregated over all claims from VCs present in a particular round. Best case occurs if management meets all performance and vesting milestones or contingencies. Worst case occurs if management does not meet performance milestones and stock and options do not vest. Asterisks indicate significant differences compared to the total sample using a Mann–Whitney test at: 1% ***; 5% **; and 10% * levels.

the company is sold for $30m. If the preferred does not have participation rights, the VC will convert its preferred into one million shares; each share will be worth $15–30m divided by 2m total shares; and the VC will end up with $15m. If the preferred has participation rights, the VC gets the first $10m; each common share will be worth $10m as the remaining $20m is shared among the two million shares; and the VC ends up with $20m—$10m from the preferred and $10m from the common. This is the same pay-off the VC would receive if it owned straight preferred and common.

Third, cash flow rights, voting rights, control rights, and future financings are frequently contingent on observable measures of financial and non-financial performance. As is evident in Table 4.1, these state contingencies are more common in the early stages of the VC–entrepreneur relationships (first VC rounds) and in earlier stage investments.

Fourth, voting rights, board rights, and liquidation rights are allocated such that if the company performs poorly, the VCs obtain full control. As company performance improves, the entrepreneur retains/obtains more control rights. If the company performs very well, the VCs retain their cash flow rights, but relinquish most of their control and liquidation rights through the automatic conversion provision that is present in virtually all our financings. As Table 4.1 shows, this conversion does not occur unless the venture earns the VC a sizable multiple of its investment. *Ex ante*, the investors are likely to be in control in more states of the world for early stage ventures that have not yet started to generate revenues, while previously successful entrepreneurs get to retain more control in their new ventures.

Fifth, we find that it is typical for VCs to include non-compete and vesting provisions that make it more expensive for the entrepreneur to leave the firm, thus mitigating the potential hold-up problem between the entrepreneur and the investor. Vesting provisions are more common in early stage financings where it is more likely that the hold-up problem is more severe.

Finally, we find that cash flow incentives, control rights, and contingencies implemented in these contracts are used more as complements than as substitutes. Ventures in which the VCs have voting and board majority are also more likely to have the entrepreneur's equity claim as well as the release of committed funds being contingent on performance milestones.

Our results have the following implications: First, cash flow rights matter in a way that is consistent with the principal–agent theories of Holmström (1979), Harris and Raviv (1979), Lazear (1986), and others. VCs change the entrepreneur's equity compensation function, making it more sensitive to performance when incentive and asymmetric information problems are more severe.

Second, the allocation of control rights between the VC and the entrepreneur is a central feature of the financial contracts. This strongly suggests that despite the prevalence of contingent contracting, contracts are inherently incomplete. This finding gives support to the incomplete contracting approach pioneered by Grossman and Hart (1986) and Hart and Moore (1990, 1998).

Third, cash flow rights and control rights can be separated and made contingent on observable and verifiable measures of performance. This is most supportive of theories that predict shifts of control to investors in different states, such as Aghion and Bolton (1992) and Dewatripont and Tirole (1994).

Fourth, the widespread use of non-compete and vesting provisions indicates that VCs care about the hold-up problem explored in Hart and Moore (1994).

4.4. SCREENING

Before making an investment and designing the financial contracts, VCs spend a significant amount of time and effort evaluating and screening the investment opportunity. Kaplan and Strömberg (2002) focus empirically on this information collection and evaluation.

To help the VC partnership evaluate an investment in a company, it is common for the individual VC who is sponsoring the investment to prepare a detailed investment analysis or memorandum for the other partners. We analyse the investment memoranda from eleven VC partnerships for investments in sixty-seven portfolio companies. We complement our analysis with information from the company business plans, as well as data on the financial contracts from Kaplan and Strömberg (2003).

First, we describe the VC analyses. These analyses include a set of investment theses or rationales for making the investment and a discussion of the concomitant risks. Consistent with academic and practitioner accounts, VCs explicitly consider the attractiveness of the opportunity—the market size, the strategy, the technology, customer adoption, and competition—the management team, and the deal terms. VCs also explicitly delineate the risks involved in the investments. The risks typically relate to the same characteristics that the VCs evaluate for attractiveness.

Table 4.2. *Ranking of rationales and risks in VC analyses (from Kaplan and Strömberg 2002)*

Top 10 investment rationales	% of cases mentioned	Top 10 investment risks	% of cases mentioned
1. Large market size and growth	68.7	1. Weak/incomplete management	61.2
2. Strong management team	59.7	2. Risky business strategy/model	50.7
3. Attractive business strategy/model	53.7	3. Risky competitive position	40.3
4. Attractive product/technology	40.3	4. Product/technology risk	31.3
5. Favourable competitive position	32.8	5. Uncertain market size/growth	31.3
6. Customer adoption likely	29.9	6. Uncertain customer adoption	22.4
7. Favourable performance to date	26.9	7. High valuation	19.4
8. Low valuation	20.9	8. Costly to monitor investment	14.9
9. Limited downside/funds at risk	19.4	9. Large downside/funds at risk	13.4
10. Good fit in VC portfolio	17.9	10. Unfavourable performance to date	7.3

Explicitly mentioned rationales for investing and investment risks according to VC analyses for investments in 67 portfolio companies by 11 venture capital partnerships. Investments were made between 1987 and 1999.

Table 4.2 summarizes the investment theses or rationales and the investment risks. Two observations are worth making about the table. First, many of the same considerations appear as both rationales/positive and as risks/negatives indicating that there is a great deal of variation in the VC analyses. Second, management risk is one of the most common sources of uncertainty that the VC identifies. It is present in more that 60 per cent of the sample investments. This sometimes reflects a concern with the founder's incentives, for example, that the founder seems to show a lack of focus or have a difficult personality. More often, however, the concern is less about undesirable characteristics of the founders and more about the management team being incomplete in some sense. It is very common that a VC identifies a need to complete the management team with experienced executives.

We then consider how the assessments in the VCs' analyses interact with the design of the financial contracts. We focus on the risks or uncertainties identified by the VCs in each transaction, dividing them into risks that are: (1) associated with external uncertainty—the relevant information is external to the firm and, we argue, it is more likely that the VC and the entrepreneur are equally informed; (2) associated with internal uncertainty—the relevant information is internal to the firm and, we argue, it is more likely that the VC is less informed than the entrepreneur; and (3) associated with complexity. Greater external and internal risks are associated with more VC ownership, more VC control, and more contingent compensation. Greater internal risk is also associated with more contingent financing. Greater complexity is associated with less contingent compensation.

Finally, we examine the relation between the ultimate investment outcome/performance and the VC's initial analysis of the company. On the margin, one might expect there to be no relation because the contracts (and valuations) would adjust to differences in quality and risk. However, if VCs have some monopoly power, if some investments are infra-marginal, or if VCs, too, are learning, a relation could exist. Subsequent performance, as measured by an IPO, is unrelated to the risks the VCs identify. Subsequent performance is, however, modestly related to the VC's initial positive appraisal of the management team.

These results confirm that VCs expend a great deal of time and effort in evaluating and screening transactions. This is consistent with anecdotal accounts that the scarcest commodity a VC has is time not capital.[5] This suggests that theoretical models can benefit by including investor effort in evaluating potential investments[6] and by assuming that investors are particularly well informed.[7]

4.5. MONITORING

Finally, several recent papers focus on post-investment information collection, monitoring, and other actions by the VC. Anecdotal accounts stress an important role for VCs in monitoring management, finding management, and providing advice.[8]

---

[5] For example, see Gladstone (1988) or Quindlen (2000).   [6] See Dessein (2001).
[7] See Dessein (2001).   [8]For example, see Gorman and Sahlman (1989) or Quindlen (2000).

Hellman and Puri (2000) study a hand-collected sample of 173 start-up firms from California's Silicon Valley. They find that venture capital is associated with a significant reduction in the time to bring a product to market. They provide some evidence that this association holds after controlling for VC ability to select a more successful company.

Hellman and Puri (2002) study another aspect of the same data set. They find that VC-financed firms are more likely and faster to professionalize by adopting stock option plans and hire a vice president of sales. They also find VC-financed firms are more likely and faster to bring in CEOs from outside the firm.

Hsu (2002) studies start-ups that receive multiple financing offers from VCs. He finds that the acceptance of an offer is not related to the valuation placed on the company by the VCs. He also finds some evidence that the valuations are negatively related to measures of VC prominence. This is consistent with entrepreneurs believing that the value-added by VCs is important.

The four studies described in the previous paragraphs find indirect evidence of post-financing VC actions. Kaplan and Strömberg (2002) complement these studies by presenting direct evidence on VC actions or monitoring. We rely on the investment analyses at the time of the initial investment that describe actions that the VC took before investing and that the VC expects to undertake conditional on investing. In addition, for a subset of the portfolio companies, we describe subsequent status reports on the investments. These reports summarize undertaken and anticipated monitoring actions.

Our primary finding is to confirm that VCs play a large role in shaping and recruiting the senior management team. In 16 per cent of the investments, the VC plays a role in shaping the management team before investing; in 43 per cent, the VC explicitly expects to play a role after investing. In more than half, therefore, the VC has played or expects to play such a role. Sometimes this involves replacing a founding manager, but more often it is an issue of strengthening and broadening the existing management team by hiring experienced executives. Moreover, in more than a third of the investments, the VC expects to be active in other areas, such as developing a business plan, assisting with acquisitions, facilitating strategic relationships with other companies, or designing employee compensation. Table 4.3 summarizes these findings.

Because the investment memoranda vary in the amount of detail they provide and because they only mention the monitoring actions that are expected *ex ante*, these numbers almost certainly understate the VCs' monitoring and support activities. Still, there seem to be limits to the extent to which VCs are willing to monitor and support their portfolio companies. In our analysis of risks identified by the VCs, the VC was worried that the investment might require too much time in roughly 20 per cent of the investments. In two cases, this involved the VC becoming chairman of the company. This indicates that while VCs regularly play a monitoring and advisory role, they do not intend to become too involved in the company.

Overall, these studies corroborate the anecdotal evidence that VCs exert effort in monitoring and aiding the companies in which they invest. In addition to actions traditionally associated with investor monitoring, such as replacing management after poor performance, there is substantial evidence of VCs assisting the founders in running and professionalizing the business, what Hellman and Puri (2002) term the supporting role of

Table 4.3. *Venture capitalist monitoring and support (Kaplan and Strömberg 2002)*

	Number (%) of companies	
Management		
VC active in recruiting or changing management team before investing	11	(16%)
VC expects to be active in recruiting or changing management team after investing	29	(43%)
Any of the above	34	(51%)
Strategy/business model		
VC explicitly active in shaping strategy/business model before investing	6	(9%)
VC explicitly expects to be active in shaping strategy/business model after investing	20	(30%)
Any of the above	23	(34%)
Examples		
Design employee compensation		
Arrange vendor financing agreements		
Install information and internal accounting systems		
Have company exit non-core businesses		
Implement currency hedging program		
Hire market research firm to help with new store locations		
Assist with development of marketing plan		
Assist with mergers and acquisitions		
Develop business plan, budget, financial forecasts		
Monitor R&D and product management efforts		
Refine pricing model and work on major account strategy		
Assist technical service team		
Leverage VC strategic relationships		

VC actions before investment and anticipated at the time of investment for investments in 67 portfolio companies by 11 venture capital partnerships. Investments were made between 1987 and 1999.

venture capital. From a theoretical perspective, these studies suggest that certain types of investors (such as VCs) should be modelled as exerting costly effort to improve outcomes.[9]

4.6. IMPLICATIONS AND CONCLUSION

The empirical studies of VCs indicate that VCs attempt to mitigate principal–agent conflicts in the three ways suggested by theory—through sophisticated contracting, pre-investment screening, and post-investment monitoring and advising. The evidence also suggests that

---

[9] See Repullo and Suarez (1999), Casamatta (2000), and Inderst and Muller (2002) for theoretical treatments along these lines.

contracting, screening, and monitoring are closely interrelated. In the screening process, the VCs identify areas where they can add value through monitoring and support. In the contracting stage, the VCs allocate rights in order to facilitate monitoring and minimize the impact of the identified risk factors, for example, by allocating more control to investors when management is weak, or make founder cash flow rights and release of funds contingent on management actions. Also, the allocations of equity to VCs provide incentives to engage in costly support activities that increase the upside value of the venture, rather than just minimizing potential losses. There is room for future empirical research to study these activities in greater detail both for VCs and for other intermediaries such as banks.

The empirical studies also suggest two avenues for additional theoretical research. First, such research can better illuminate the rationales behind the actual contracts that are written. Understanding the interaction and complementarity between different types of cash flow, control, and liquidation rights seems particularly relevant. Dewatripont and Tirole (1994) and Hart (2001) are important first steps. Second, such research should take into account the fact that VCs exert costly effort both in pre-investment screening and post-investment monitoring and advising, and that these activities affect the design of the financial contracts.

References

Aghion, P. and Bolton, P. (1992), 'An incomplete contracts approach to financial contracting', *Review of Economic Studies* 77, 338–401.

Black, B. and Gilson, R. (1998), 'Venture capital and the structure of capital markets: Banks versus stock Markets', *Journal of Financial Economics* 47, 243–77.

Botazzi, L. and Da Rin, M. (2001), 'Venture capital in Europe: Euro.nm and the financing of European innovative firms', Working paper, Università Bocconi.

Cassamata, C. (2000), 'Financing and advising: optimal financial contracts with venture capitalists', Working paper, University of Toulouse.

Christofidis, C. and Debande, O. (2001), 'Financing innovative firms through venture capital', Working paper, European Investment Bank Sector Papers.

Dessein, W. (2001), 'Information and control in alliances and ventures', Working paper, University of Chicago.

Dewatripont, M. and Tirole, J. (1994), 'A theory of debt and equity: Diversity of securities and manager-shareholder congruence', *Quarterly Journal of Economics* 109, 1027–54.

Gladstone, D. (1988), *Venture Capital Handbook*, Englewood Cliffs: Prentice Hall.

Gompers, P. (1998), 'An examination of convertible securities in venture capital investments', Working paper, Harvard Business School.

—— and Lerner, J. (1999), *The Venture Capital Cycle*, Cambridge, MA: MIT Press.

Gorman, M. and Sahlman, W. (1989), 'What do venture capitalists do?', *Journal of Business Venturing* 4, 231–48.

Grossman, S. and Hart, O. (1986), 'The costs and benefits of ownership: A theory of vertical and lateral Integration', *Journal of Political Economy* 94, 691–719.

Harris, M. and Raviv, A. (1979), 'Optimal incentive contracts with imperfect information', *Journal of Economic Theory* 20, 231–59.

Hart, O. (2001), 'Financial Contracting', *Journal of Economic Literature* 39, 1079–100.

—— and Moore, J. (1990), 'Property rights and the nature of the firm', *Journal of Political Economy* 98, 1119–58.

—— and —— (1994), 'A theory of debt based on the inalienability of human capital', *Quarterly Journal of Economics* 109, 841–79.

—— and —— (1998), 'Default and renegotiation: A dynamic model of debt', *Quarterly Journal of Economics* 113, 1–41.

Hellman, T. and Puri, M. (2000), 'The interaction between product market and financial strategy: The role of venture capital', *Review of Financial Studies* 13, 959–84.

—— and —— (2002), 'Venture capital and the professionalization of start-up firms: Empirical Evidence', *Journal of Finance* 57, 169–97.

Holmström, B. (1979), 'Moral hazard and observability', *Bell Journal of Economics* 10, 74–91.

Hsu, D. (2002), 'Do entrepreneurs pay for affiliation?', Working paper, MIT.

Inderst, R. and Mueller, H. (2002), 'Competitive search markets for durable goods', *Economic Theory* 19, 599–622.

Kaplan, S. and Strömberg, P. (2003), 'Financial contracting theory meets the real world: An empirical analysis of venture capital contracts', *Review of Economic Studies* 70, 281–315.

—— and —— (2002), 'Characteristics, contracts, and actions: evidence from venture capitalist analyses', Working paper, University of Chicago,

Lazear, E. (1986), 'Salaries and piece-rates', *Journal of Business* 59, 405–31.

Lerner, J. (1995), 'Venture capitalists and the oversight of private firms', *Journal of Finance* 50, 301–18.

Quindlen, R. (2000), *Confessions of a Venture Capitalist*, New York: Warner Books.

Repullo, R. and Suarez, J. (1999), 'Venture capital finance: A security design approach', Working paper, CEMFI.

Sahlman, W. (1990), 'The structure and governance of venture capital organizations', *Journal of Financial Economics* 27, 473–521.

5

The Value of Benchmarking

DIRK BERGEMANN AND ULRICH HEGE

5.1. INTRODUCTION

5.1.1. *Motivation*

The venture capital industry, which has become the main source of financing of innovative projects, offers unique insights into how financiers and managers of innovative start-ups align their interest and resolve agency conflicts. The most frequently cited agency problems in venture capital contracting are that entrepreneurs may invest into efforts that have high-personal return (scientific recognition, investment in human capital, etc.) but add little or no value to the venture, and the tendency of the entrepreneurs to continue their projects beyond the efficient stopping time. The importance of the latter problem has arguably been reaffirmed by the slow and expensive wind-down of many cash-burning internet start-ups after March 2000.

Stage financing stands out as 'the most potent control mechanism a venture capitalist can employ' (Gompers and Lerner 1999: 139). Venture capitalists do not commit to future financing rounds, but will only agree to future financing rounds if their intermediate evaluation of the project is positive. By staging their financing, venture capitalists retain the real option to abandon the project periodically. Often, explicit benchmarks—technological or financial in nature—are written into the contracts, giving the venture capitalists additional contingent control rights that can be exercised if the benchmarks are missed, including the rights to change the management of the venture or to initiate liquidation procedures. Typically, the estimated cash need for the entire stage is injected at the beginning of the round, putting a large cash reserve at the disposal of the firm that is gradually drawn down.

Empirical research has revealed that the precise use of staging instruments depends on the risk and the characteristics of the project. The riskier is the project, the less information venture capitalists have about the venture, or the larger is the discretion of the entrepreneurs,[1] the shorter are the staging intervals, and hence the more frequently

The authors would like to thank Dima Leshchinskii and participants at the Tilburg University conference 'Legal and Valuation Issues of E-Business' for valuable comments. Bergemann gratefully acknowledges financial support from the National Science Foundation (SBR 9709887) and the Sloan Foundation. Hege acknowledges financial support from the European Commission (HPSE–CT–2002–00140).

[1] Kaplan and Stromberg (2001), Kaplan *et al.* (2002), Gompers and Lerner (1999).

are venture capitalists reevaluating the project and pondering the abandonment option. The larger is the total funding received of a venture, the more financing rounds are used. There is further empirical evidence on typical patterns of stage financing over the lifetime of a project. Typically, the duration of stages are increasing from one stage to the next. Also, the amount of cash injected per round is increasing over time. The rate of return seems to be highest in the early stages of a project, both measured by the internal valuations estimated at the start of every financing round, and by market-based exit valuations.[2] Practitioners apply considerably higher discount rates in early stages, reflecting a perceived higher failure risk there than in later stage investments.

While it has long been recognized in the literature that stage financing is a tool to mitigate agency conflicts, explicit dynamic studies on how projects are benchmarked, and how the optimal staging policy interacts with the typical conflicts in the financier–entrepreneur relationship, are surprisingly rare. Agency considerations are, however, an important determinant of the optimal funding policy of an innovative project. They influence the research intensity, research layout and, the research budget. This chapter aims to provide a more detailed understanding of this link by looking at the role of benchmarking.

We propose a simple model of a venture project over multiple stages to analyse this interaction. The venture capitalist controls the investment opportunity but she needs a wealth constrained entrepreneur to run it. The project consists of several stages, each characterized by a benchmark, and successful completion of the project requires that every benchmark is met. Time and money needed to meet each benchmark are subject to uncertainty, since in each period the research effort can either make progress or fail. As the project continues to receive financing without achieving the next benchmark, the investor gets closer to the point where she wishes to abandon the entire project. When one of the benchmarks is attained, the probability of the entire project jumps upwards.

The investment effort is unobservable to the investor and the entrepreneur can divert the funds to his private ends. The entrepreneur's control of the fund allocation introduces a conflict meant to capture in a stylized way the two main agency conflicts in the venture financing cited earlier, namely self-serving investments and the bias towards inefficient continuation. In each period, the solution of the agency conflict has to take into account the intertemporal incentives for the entrepreneur. If the entrepreneur diverts the capital flow for private purposes, she knows that she continues to receive funding for sure. In contrast, if she invests the funds, she knows that with a certain probability she is successful and the funding in the current stage will end. The longer the funding horizon of the current stage, the larger is this option value of the diversion.

5.1.2. *Results and Empirical Implications*

We first analyse the optimal funding when the venture capitalist cannot observe whether the intermediate benchmarks have been attained. In this case, the venture capitalist can only define a total funding horizon for the entire project, and make sure that the reward to the entrepreneur in case of completion of the last benchmark provides sufficient incentives

---

[2] See for these observations Cochrane (2001), Das *et al.* (2002), Gompers and Lerner (1999: 139).

to invest. This solution is inefficient compared with benchmarking for three reasons: First, there is no abandonment if the early benchmarks are not completed in time, adding to the entrepreneur's discretion and information rent. Second, if the early stages take longer than expected, the remaining budget for the last stages is inefficiently small. Finally, since the venture capitalist is in a position of asymmetric information with respect to the number of benchmarks that have already been met, the incentive payments must be tailored to fit all several possible 'types' of entrepreneur, which again increases the information rent.

We then consider the case where the benchmarks are observable. The optimal contract uses stage financing, the conclusion of a new contract upon reaching each benchmark. This offers the advantage of exploiting the value of the real option to abandon the project over time. The necessary incentive payments are an increasing function of the entrepreneur's discretion over the funds, and thus of the funding horizon of each stage. It reduces agency costs, because the agent's guaranteed funding horizon is reduced by the introduction of intermediate benchmarks. Agency costs are also reduced by the fact that the informal promise of information rents in future financing rounds acts as an implicit incentive device. A hold-up problem emerges between the *ex ante* incentive potential of implicit contracts and the venture capitalist's desire to cut information rents *ex post*. The supply of excess cash to the venture, as implied by providing all funds in a given stage in a lump-sum payment at the beginning of each stage, is a commitment device to overcome this problem.

We find that the optimal funding horizon is increasing from one stage to the next. This effect is exacerbated by the impact of the agency costs, and by the implicit incentive effect of future information rents. Thus, our model shows that the principal stylized facts of the evolution of funding over time can be explained as optimal choices: the research intensity is lower for early stages, explaining that a smaller budget is allocated to them, that their duration is shorter, and their success probability smaller. This is turn explains why the research risk is larger in early stages, and thus the observed return, conditional on success in early stages, is larger.

5.1.3. *Related Literature and Overview*

While the importance of stage financing has been widely documented in the empirical literature on venture capital contracting,[3] only a small number of theoretical papers have explicitly tried to provide a rationale for the use of benchmarks in venture finance. Cornelli and Yosha (2003) analyse the problem of an entrepreneur manipulating short-term results for purposes of 'window-dressing'. Neher (1999) shows that stage financing can serve as an instrument to reduce the bargaining power of an opportunistic entrepreneur who can repudiate her financial obligations. Berk *et al.* (2000) distinguish between purely technical risk in early stages and diverse sources of risk in later stages. They show that the systematic risk component is strongest in early stages, justifying a larger risk premium. Elitzur and Gavious (2002) have a model with several stages, where the probability of attaining each benchmark is determined by the entrepreneur's one shot effort choice. In their setting,

---

[3] Kaplan and Stromberg (2001, 2002), Kaplan *et al.* (2002), Gompers and Lerner (1999), Cochrane (2001), and Das *et al.* (2002).

optimal incentives contracts give rewards only upon completion of the last stage, in contrast to our results.

The basic set-up of our model closely follows our earlier papers on venture funding and the financing of innovation (Bergemann and Hege 1998, 2003), where we studied the dynamics of the optimal contract, the role of hard claims, the impact of time consistency on the stopping decision, and distinguished between arm's length and relationship financing. The innovation in this chapter is the inclusion of intermediate benchmarks.

The agency problem in this chapter is also related to papers emphasizing the role of hard budget constraints in the funding of innovation, like Ambec and Poitevin (2001) and Qian and Xu (1998). Finally, a large literature has investigated capital structure design, and in particular the use of convertible securities, as a tool for the venture capitalist to force abandonment of unprofitable projects, and thus as an alternative or complementary instrument to staged financing. Recent papers have frequently looked at two-sided moral hazard situations between entrepreneur and venture capitalist, for example, Casamatta (2003), Repullo and Suarez (2000), and Schmidt (2003).

The chapter is organized as follows. The model is presented in Section 5.2. The single stage project is reviewed in Section 5.3. The structure and efficiency of multi-stage projects without benchmarking is examined in Section 5.4. We then consider stage financing with benchmarking in Section 5.5. Section 5.6 discusses possible extensions and concludes.

5.2. THE MODEL

We consider a project with uncertain return that needs continuous financing over several stages and that can be undertaken by an entrepreneur or agent with zero wealth. The project is financed by a venture capitalist providing the necessary funds. The entrepreneur and venture capitalist are both risk-neutral and have a common discount rate $r > 0$. We introduce first the technological characteristics of stage financing before turning to the contracting environment.

5.2.1. *Project and Stages*

The innovative project needs to go through N sequential stages, which we denote by $n = 1, 2, \ldots, N$, to be successful. At the end of each stage, there is a discernible output, or benchmark. This may be a first research result, a key module, a prototype, or a beta version, a product ready for mass production, and finally the production, distribution, and marketing facilities necessary for the launch of operations. The stages are sequential in the sense that the successful completion of the stage $n - 1$ is a technological prerequisite for entering into the stage n.

If the last stage is completed, the output is verifiable and a gain of R is realized. The value of an incomplete project is zero (discussed in Section 5.6). We assume that it is worthwhile to undertake the project for at least one period, $R > c$.

The uncertainty of the project is resolved over time by a discovery process. In every stage, experimentation is needed to preserve the chances that the benchmark is eventually met, and experimentation requires time and money. If experimentation is undertaken in a given period t, then the stage of the project is successfully completed with probability λ, and costs $c\lambda$ arise. Therefore, the probability of completion of each stage per period is either λ (if there is investment), or 0 (if there is none). These conditions are the same for every stage. The nature of uncertainty in our model essentially is about the time and investment needed within each stage.

The investment only influences the conditional probability of success in every period and independent of time. In particular, the investment flow does not influence the value of the successful realization, R.

As the experimentation process unfolds over time, agent and venture capitalist learn more about the prospects of the project. Suppose then that for each stage, experimentation is undertaken for a total of T^n periods, where $T^n = T^1, T^2, \ldots, T^N$ denotes the maximum duration or horizon for the completion of each of the stages $n = 1, 2, \ldots, N$. The *ex ante* probability of successful completion of the first stage is thus $1 - (1 - \lambda)^{T^1}$. Since the completion of each earlier stage is required to move on, if there is no success in the nth stage within the horizon of T^n periods, it means that the entire project is abandoned. The *ex ante* probability that the entire project will be successful is then

$$p_0^1 = \prod_{n=1}^{N}(1 - (1 - \lambda)^{T^n}).$$

We next determine the evolution of the posterior beliefs. Denote by p_t^n the jointly held belief that the project will eventually be a success, held in the tth period of the nth stage based on continuous experimentation prior to t:

$$p_t^n = (1 - (1 - \lambda)^{T^n - t}) \prod_{i=n+1}^{N}(1 - (1 - \lambda)^{T^i}).$$

Thus, as long as the entrepreneur continues to invest in any given stage, the belief about the project's success is gradually diminishing as a result of the shorter number of chances of a yet successful experiment, $T^n - t$. However, once stage n is successfully completed, the belief discontinuously jumps to a higher level. We get a stochastic see-saw pattern of the evolution of the belief as follows: the belief slopes down within each stage but has an upwards trend overall, representing the improvement in beliefs as the projects nears completion of the final stage. The timing of the jumps are stochastic due to the uncertain nature of each stage (see Fig. 5.1).

5.2.2. *Moral Hazard and Financing*

Entrepreneur and venture capitalists have initially the same assessment about the likelihood of success, which is given by the prior belief p_0^1. The funds are supplied by the venture capitalist, but they can only be allocated by the agent to generate the desired success R. The venture capitalist, however, cannot observe whether the funds are correctly applied to the experiment, and thus a moral hazard problem arises between financier and entrepreneur. The entrepreneur can in fact 'shirk' and decide to divert the capital flow to her private

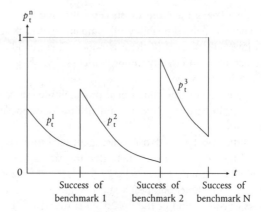

Figure 5.1. *Evolution of final success probability. The success times of intermediate benchmarks are random.*

ends, gaining a utility of $c\lambda$ in the process.[4] In contrast, the successful completion of any stage $n = 1, \ldots, N - 1$ is observable and verifiable.

The venture capitalist proposes a contract to the entrepreneur which can be contingent on time, the capital provided by the investor, as well as on new agreements between the two parties. Then the entrepreneur accepts or rejects the proposal, implying that the venture capitalist captures the entire surplus of the project.[5] Because of the moral hazard problem of the financing, however, the contract cannot be made contingent on the use of the funds. The design of the contract has to ensure that incentive compatibility and individual participation constraints are satisfied.

We will argue below that stage contracts of the following form are the optimal arrangements in this environment. The venture capitalist proposes such a stage contract at the entry into each new stage n. The contract specifies the maximal stage duration T^n to complete the stage n, and a dynamic schedule of monetary reward payments s_t^n that the agent receives in the event of meeting the benchmark of the nth stage after t periods.

The contract contains provisions effectively inhibiting the continuation of the project once T^n periods have lapsed; the project will have to be irrevocably abandoned. In other words, we assume that the venture capitalist can choose T^n and commit to the following horizon.[6]

5.3. A SINGLE STAGE

We prepare the ground by looking at the simple case where there is just a single possible stage, $N = 1$. This case is a version of the model analysed in our earlier papers

---

[4] An equivalent interpretation of the moral hazard problem is that running the experiments requires effort, which is costly for the agent. By reducing the effort, the agent also reduces the probability of success and hence the efficiency of the employed capital.

[5] The opposite assumption about the distribution of bargaining power is made in Bergemann and Hege (1998, 2003).

[6] See Bergemann and Hege (2003) for an extensive discussion of renegotiation in this game.

(Bergemann and Hege 1998, 2003, where details for the expressions of this section can be obtained) with a simplified belief process, but with two important differences: first, the venture capitalist has the bargaining power; and second, the number of periods is determined by the venture capitalist's profit maximization objective rather than efficiency.

Value of the venture. We denote by $V_t(T)$ the value of the project in stage t if the total horizon comprises T periods. Suppose the optimal number of financing periods is fixed at T which we assume for now (and show later) to be finite. Note that in the first best, $T = \infty$ since we have assumed that $\lambda R - c\lambda \geq 0$. If the project should be funded once, it should receive funds indefinitely since the problem is stationary. Hence we obtain the value of the venture in the terminal period T as $V_T(T) = \lambda R - c\lambda$, and in earlier periods recursively via the following dynamic programming equation:

$$V_t(T) = \max_{i_t \in \{0,\lambda\}} \left\{ i_t R - ci_t + \frac{1 - i_t}{1 + r} V_{t+1}(T) \right\}, \tag{5.1}$$

where $i_t \in \{0, \lambda\}$ is the venture capitalist's allocation of funds. Clearly, the linear form of the value function (5.1) indicates that it is optimal to invest at the level of $c\lambda$ for as long as $t \leq T$.

We consider the transition to the continuous time limit of our model, as in Bergemann and Hege (2002), from where details can be gleaned. Let Δ denote the time elapsed between two periods t and $t + 1$. With this notation, eqn (5.1) can be rewritten as:

$$V_t(T) = R\Delta\lambda - c\Delta\lambda + \frac{1 - \Delta\lambda}{1 + \Delta r} V_{t+\Delta}(T).$$

Letting $\Delta \to 0$ and solving yields, the continuous-time expression of the project value function at $t = 0$:

$$V_0(T) = \frac{1 - e^{-(r+\lambda)T}}{r + \lambda}(R - c)\lambda. \tag{5.2}$$

The value function $V_0(T)$ offers an intuitive explanation. $c\lambda$ is invested in each period, and the prize R is obtained with probability λ, conditional on no earlier discovery. The value of the project is then discounted with an effective factor of $r + \lambda$, compounding pure time, discounting r and the probability of success λ in each period. Total project uncertainty is then captured by the first term in eqn (5.2), which can be understood as a stochastic discount factor over T period, discounting the uncertain arrival time of the risky success.

Incentive contracts. Since successful completion of the project is the only verifiable evidence on the agent's effort, the incentives provided to the entrepreneur should maximally discriminate with respect to the signal R. With the wealth constraint of the entrepreneur, the optimal contract is a share contract, where the agent receives a positive reward $s_t \geq 0$ if the project was a success and nothing otherwise. The minimal reward s_t of the entrepreneur is chosen so that she truthfully carries out the proposed investment policy.

We consider only optimal share contracts from the venture capitalist's point of view, with full scope for intertemporal transfers, that is, long-term contracts.

We start from the incentive compatibility constraint for the entrepreneur in the last period, which immediately leads to the last period requirement on the entrepreneur's reward, $\lambda s_T \geq c\lambda$, and hence an expected value to the entrepreneur of $E_T(T) = c\lambda$. Moving backwards in time, we obtain a sequence of value functions, denoted by $E_t(T)$, and characterized recursively by the incentive problem:

$$E_t(T) = \min_{s_t} \left\{ \Delta \lambda s_t + \frac{1 - \Delta \lambda}{1 + \Delta r} E_{t+1}(T) \right\}, \tag{5.3}$$

where s_t is the minimum cash reward satisfying the entrepreneur's incentive constraint.[7] We notice the intertemporal structure of the problem. The incentives to divert for the agent arise (i) via a contemporaneous effect, namely the utility from the diverted funds $c\lambda$, and (ii) via the dynamic effect that the contract continuation into the next period becomes more likely.

The solution s_t of the minimization problem (5.3) delivers the expected value $E_t(T)$ the entrepreneur receives for a given funding policy, taking into account the sequence of incentive constraints. Taking again limits as $\Delta \to 0$, the value function $E_t(T)$ of the entrepreneur and his reward in case of success is given by:

$$E_t(T) = s_t = c\lambda \frac{1 - e^{-r(T-t)}}{r}. \tag{5.4}$$

The compensation s_t ensures that the entrepreneur employs the capital in every period towards the discovery process. The behaviour of the shares s_t over time is thus determined by an underlying option problem. The value of this particular option is determined as any regular option by the volatility of the underlying state variable (represented by the conditional probability, λ) and the maturity (the remaining length of the funding, $T - t$). Therefore, two forces help to realign the interest of the entrepreneur with the ones of the investor: (i) sufficiently strong discounting and (ii) shares are decreasing over time and hence penalize late discovery.

Optimal stopping. As the market for venture capital is competitive, in equilibrium the net value of the project will belong entirely to the venture capitalist. Prior to stopping the project, the venture capitalist will decide to fully fund the project; therefore, the decision on the optimal stopping time T sufficiently summarizes the venture capitalist's investment policy. The venture capitalist's initial problem is then given by:

$$\max_{\{T,(s_t)\}} \left\{ V_t(T) - E_t(T) \right\} \tag{5.5}$$

---

[7] The incentive constraint takes the form:

$$\Delta \lambda s_t + \frac{1 - \Delta \lambda}{1 + \Delta r} E_{t+1}(T) \geq c\Delta\lambda + \frac{1}{1 + \Delta r} E_{t+1}(T).$$

We have already characterized the optimal function of rewards s_t in eqn (5.4). To determine the optimum stopping time T, we investigate the maximum of eqn (5.5) and obtain the following solution (from the first-order condition):

$$T = -\frac{\ln(c/R - c)}{\lambda}. \tag{5.6}$$

Thus, unlike the first best solution, which always would be to choose $T = \infty$, the presence of agency costs implies a reduction in the horizon that maximizes the venture capitalist's profits.

5.4. FUNDING WITHOUT BENCHMARKS

We first consider the case where the venture capitalist has no benchmarking technology, that is, no capacity to observe or verify the completion of earlier stages. Only the realization of the last stage remains verifiable. Completion of all stages is indispensable for the project to create value, namely the prize R. Therefore, in this case, the venture capitalist can budget only for a single investment stage of total length T. For simplicity, we restrict this discussion to the case where there are just two stages, with $N = 2$, which is sufficient to analyse the structure of the solution. For this analysis, we make the additional assumption that

$$R > c\left(2 + \frac{1}{\lambda}\right). \tag{5.7}$$

This assumption guarantees that the venture capitalist is willing to offer a share s_T that is sufficient to ensure the entrepreneur's incentives in period $T - 1$, even if the entrepreneur has not yet completed the first benchmark.

5.4.1. *Value of the Venture*

Let us then consider the value of the firm in this problem. Assume that the entrepreneur has successfully completed the first stage. We use the superscript $i \in \{1, 2\}$ for the value functions to indicate that the entrepreneur knows to be in stage $i = 1, 2$. Thus, if the entrepreneur knows to be in the second stage, the value of the venture is obtained recursively by the dynamic programming equation:

$$V_t^2(T) = \max_{i_t} \left\{ \Delta i_t R - c\Delta i_t + \frac{1 - \Delta i_t}{1 + \Delta r} V_{t+\Delta}^2 \right\}, \tag{5.8}$$

where $i_t \in \{0, \lambda\}$ indicates the funding policy of the venture capitalist. We know that the entrepreneur may try to complete the first stage for T periods, and the second stage for $S = T - U$ periods, where U is the (random) completion time of the first stage. If the last stage is a failure in all of its S periods, the final prize will be $R_1 = 0$. Again, maximum investment $i_t = \lambda$ will be optimal in all S periods. Thus,

$$V_t^2(T) = \frac{1 - e^{-(r+\lambda)(T-t)}}{r + \lambda}(R - c)\lambda.$$

Similarly, the agent's value function in the first stage is,[8]

$$V_t^1(T) = \max_{i_t \in \{0, \lambda\}} \left\{ \frac{\Delta i_t}{1 + \Delta r} V_{t+\Delta}^2(T) - c\Delta i_t + \frac{1 - \Delta i_t}{1 + \Delta r} V_{t+\Delta}^1(T) \right\}. \qquad (5.9)$$

Solving recursively, and considering the limit as $\Delta \to 0$ (see the appendix for a derivation),

$$V_0^1(T) = \frac{\lambda}{r + \lambda} \left[\frac{1 - e^{-(r+\lambda)T}}{r + \lambda} - Te^{-(r+\lambda)T} \right] (R - c)\lambda \qquad (5.10)$$

In this expression, the second term in the square bracket indicates the increasing loss from the temporal limit being unconditional in the following sense: the later is the entry t into the second stage, the shorter will be the remaining time $T - t$ to complete successfully this final round. The first two terms in expression (5.10) represent the stochastic discounting of the final value, which occurs over the two stages. Finally, the last term $Te^{-(r+\lambda)T}$ expresses loss from suboptimal exploitation of the second stage.

5.4.2. *Information Rent and Optimal Stopping*

We turn then to the entrepreneur's rent in this case. The optimal continuation contract at the entry into the last stage is exactly as the contract would be for a single stage problem with a maximum of T periods. That is, the entrepreneur can secure herself at least a rent of

$$E_t^1(T) = c\lambda \frac{1 - e^{-r(T-t)}}{r}. \qquad (5.11)$$

Since only the entrepreneur observes whether the first benchmark has been attained or not, asymmetric information between venture capitalist and entrepreneur emerges as the project is undertaken—the entrepreneur knows whether he is of 'type 1'—still trying to meet the first benchmark—or already of 'type 2'—that is, advanced to the second stage—while the venture capitalist must design a contract that is incentive-compatible for one or for both types. Clearly, the project cannot succeed if it is not incentive compatible at least initially for type 1, and later for type 2. It is intuitive that, as the funding horizon T draws to a close, it is easier to ensure the incentives of type 2 than of type 1, who is in a more remote position, i.e. still two benchmarks away from final success. The critical question is, therefore, whether the optimal contract will provide incentives for both types throughout, or whether it will abandon the type 1 entrepreneur at some point and only provide incentives to the more advanced type 2.

We will show in the appendix that under assumption (5.7), the lower bound of the entrepreneur's value in eqn (5.11) represents at the same time the value function of the agent in the optimal incentive-compatible contract, that provides incentive compatibility

---

[8] Whether $V_t^2(T)$ or $V_t^1(T)$ is the true value is private knowledge of the entrepreneur, since he alone observes the first benchmark.

for both types for the longest time possible, namely for the first $T - 1$ periods. Since maximal incentive compatibility can be ensured with a contract that costs no more than the lower bound (5.11) of the entrepreneur's value, this contract must be optimal.

Taking the difference of expressions (5.10) and (5.11) yields the venture capitalist's objective function as:

$$V_0^1(T) - E_0^1(T) = \frac{\lambda}{r + \lambda} \left[\frac{1 - e^{-(r+\lambda)T}}{r + \lambda} - Te^{-(r+\lambda)T} \right] (R - c)\lambda - c\lambda \frac{1 - e^{-rT}}{r}.$$

The first-order condition yields the solution, which is given as the solution T of

$$Te^{-\lambda T} = \frac{c}{\lambda(R - c)}. \tag{5.12}$$

There two cases are then to be considered: either the project has a positive value for the venture capitalist and the optimal project horizon corresponds to the larger solution of eqn (4.6) which is the only candidate for a maximum; or, if the project is 'poor', that is, R is small relative to c, it may be optimal to choose $T = 0$.

5.5. STAGE FINANCING

In this section, we assume that the venture capitalist is able to observe and verify the completion of the first stage. The optimal contract is then a succession of stage financing contracts: only after successful completion of the first stage will the contract for the second stage be drafted. Contingent stopping, after failure in the first stage, is a valuable, real option in this case (as we will show), ensuring that continuing finance is only taking place if there is success in the preceding stage.

5.5.1. *Value of the Venture and Agency*

Proceeding again in a backwards fashion from the last stage, the value of the venture in the last stage, $V_t^N(T^N)$, corresponds exactly to the value in the single stage problem, where the optimal funding horizon in the stage N will now be denoted as T^N.

Consider then the value function in the penultimate stage. This value is a function of both the current duration T^{N-1} and the last stage duration T^N. To keep the notation short, let $\mathbf{T}^n = (T^n, T^{n+1}, \ldots, T^N)$ denote the vector of the durations of the remaining stages in stage n. The value function is recursively determined as

$$V_t^{N-1}(\mathbf{T}^{N-1}) = \max_{i_t \in \{0,\lambda\}} \left\{ \Delta i_t V_0^N(T^N) - c\Delta i_t + \frac{1 - \Delta i_t}{1 + \Delta r} V_{t+\Delta}^{N-1}(\mathbf{T}^{N-1}) \right\}. \tag{5.13}$$

Taking again limits as $\Delta \to 0$ and solving recursively, this value can be expressed as:

$$V_0^{N-1}(\mathbf{T}^{N-1}) = \frac{1 - e^{-(r+\lambda)T^{N-1}}}{r + \lambda}(V_0^N(T^N) - c)\lambda \tag{5.14}$$

$$= \frac{1 - e^{-(r+\lambda)T^{N-1}}}{r + \lambda}\left(\frac{1 - e^{-(r+\lambda)T^N}}{r + \lambda}(R - c)\lambda - c\right)\lambda,$$

where the last equation is obtained after using the expression for the last stage derived in Section 5.3. More generally, the value function for n stages can be stated as:

$$V_0^1(\mathbf{T}^1) = \left(\prod_{n=1}^N \lambda \frac{1 - e^{-(r+\lambda)T^n}}{r + \lambda}\right)(R - c) - \sum_{i=1}^N \left(\prod_{n=i}^N \lambda \frac{1 - e^{-(r+\lambda)T^n}}{r + \lambda}\right)c. \tag{5.15}$$

Clearly, as we construct recursively the value function of the multi-stage problem $V_0^{(n)}(T^n, \ldots, T^N)$, we find that the value function exhibits the following time pattern: with the completion of one stage, synonymous to entry into the next stage, the value experiences a discontinuous jump upwards; but within each stage, as the time runs towards the horizon set for its completion, the value is decreasing. Thus, the value function follows a stochastic see-saw pattern with an upwards drift just as the belief function does.

We turn then to the entrepreneur's rent at entry into the last stage. The optimal continuation contract at the (stochastic) entry point into the last stage is exactly as the contract would be for a single stage problem. That is, the entrepreneur can secure herself at least a rent of $E_0^N(T^N) = c\lambda((1 - e^{-rT^N})/r)$, where T^N is the funding horizon of the last stage. In fact, this rent is independent of the exact time when the last stage is reached. Thus, since the problem at the beginning of the last period is isomorphic to the single stage problem investigated above, the venture capitalist's preferred solution will be the same. The venture capitalist designs this contract to maximize $V_0^N(T^N) - E_0^N(T^N)$, and the solution will be as in (5.6), $T^N = -1/\lambda \ln(c/(R - c))$.

The situation becomes more complicated though as we move backwards in time. Consider the penultimate stage. Since the successful completion of this stage is verifiable, the agent can be paid a reward upon meeting the benchmark of this stage, and this reward can be conditional on the timing of the success. We will denote this time-contingent reward by s_t^{N-1}, where t is the period within the second to last stage where the agent meets the benchmark. Moreover, the agent knows that success carries with it the implicit compensation of moving on to the last stage, with its information rent $E_0^N(T^N)$. This information rent has an incentive effect in the second to last period. As it turns out, the size of this incentive effect, relative to the required incentive payment schedule within the stage, leads to an important distinction in the construction of the agent's value function.

5.5.2. *Always Immediate Incentives*

If T^{N-1} periods have passed without discovery, the project is liquidated, and the agent gets nothing, that is, $E_{T^{N-1}+\Delta}^{N-1}(\mathbf{T}^{N-1}) = 0$. Therefore, and considering again the continuous-time case in the last period of stage 1, the entrepreneur expects a rent of

$$E_{T^{N-1}}^{N-1}(\mathbf{T}^{N-1}) = \lambda[s_{T^{N-1}}^{N-1} + E_0^N(T^N)]. \tag{5.16}$$

In fact, incentive compatibility requires that this expected value be larger than $c\lambda$, which is the entrepreneur's option value from shirking. Hence if $\lambda E_0^N(T^N) < c\lambda$, then $s_{T^{N-1}}^{N-1} > 0$ is required. This condition can be rewritten as:

$$\lambda < \hat{\lambda} \equiv \frac{r}{1 - e^{rT^N}}. \tag{5.17}$$

Note that $\lambda > \hat{\lambda}$ will generally hold if (i) $\lambda > r$ and if (ii) T^N is large enough. In essence, the promise of the minimum of future information rents suffices by itself to guarantee incentive compatibility, and further contemporaneous incentives are not needed.

We consider then first the case where $\lambda < \hat{\lambda}$, that is, (5.17) is satisfied, since this case is easier to analyse, leaving the complementary case to the next subsection. With this condition, a positive reward payment is needed whenever the agent successfully completes one of the stages. We denote by $s_t^n > 0$ the minimum reward required upon completion of the nth stage in period t of stage n. The following simple observation is important to understand the structure of feasible contracts if $\lambda < \hat{\lambda}$:

Lemma 5.1. *Feasible stage financing contracts require that the agent be paid with an immediate cash reward of at least s_t^n.*

Proof. See the appendix.

In particular, it is not sufficient to pay the agent with equity or other claims contingent on R, that can only be cashed in if all stages are successfully completed. Immediacy of incentive rewards is the key observation here, and the reason for this immediacy is that a hold-up problem would arise otherwise: if the payments to the agent were contingent on achieving further benchmarks, they would have incentive effects in the next stage. As a result, the investor would cut back the rewards offered *ex post*, at entry into the subsequent stage. Anticipating this reduction *ex ante*, the agent would find it more attractive to shirk rather than to work. The investor needs to commit to the level of incentive payments required *ex ante*, and pledging immediate rewards that are not contingent on further achievements are the obvious way to do it.

This observation is interesting because, in principle, one would expect that the highest power of incentives could be attained by making all rewards contingent on completion of the final benchmark: in our nested model, the last stage has the highest information value on effort, since its completion means that the agent has truthfully invested in all prior stages. By contrast, success in any earlier stage gives information regarding the agent's effort only up to that benchmark. Although, incentives contingent on meeting the final benchmark appear to be the cheapest device for the investor, since actual reward payments will have to be paid only if the entire project is successful. Indeed, Elitzur and Gravious (2002) obtain a result that incentives should be based on the accomplishing of the last benchmark in a different model of stage financing, which shares with our model the feature that stages are nested.[9]

The fact that we obtain a different result here clearly points to a trade-off in our model, a trade-off between the advantage of high-powered incentives (which pleads in favour of postponing compensation) and the need to be time-consistent. An important practical implication of our immediacy result is:

Corollary 5.1. *Contracts can guarantee immediate incentives by providing all the funding needs for any stage up-front.*

Up-front financing of the funding needs in current stage, and hence the build-up of potentially important cash reserves, is not the only way to achieve the required immediate rewards; other forms are possible as well. But it is the way that is frequently observed in practice. Stage financing typically implies that cash is raised discontinuously, at the beginning of each stage, while the cash outflow from the venture is often much smoother. Our analysis interprets this discontinuous evolution in the venture's cash position as a deliberate choice to guarantee the agent's required information rents. In our view, the cash paid up-front is cash at the discretion of the agent, and this discretion protects the agent against any possible hold-up by the investor. Notice that a lower bound of the entrepreneurs' information rent at any given moment is the remaining stream of cash in-flows up to the maximum horizon of the current stage; and any excess cash that the entrepreneur holds in the current stage, after reaching the benchmark early, will be used in the subsequent stage since the new can easily provide the right incentives for mutual advantage.

We will continue with the analysis of the optimal contract in the case of $\lambda < \hat{\lambda}$, and in particular determine the optimal horizon T^n in a typical stage n. Starting from condition (5.16) in period T^n and moving backwards in time, suppose the agent accomplishes the benchmark of this stage in period $t < T^n$. When discovery is made, the entrepreneur will get a future rent that is at least equal to $E_0^{n+1}(T^{n+1}, T^{n+2}, \ldots)$, and this regardless of the period in which discovery occurs. We assume that immediate incentives are always needed, that is, $s_t^n > 0$ is necessary throughout to satisfy this incentive constraint. Taking this into account, the continuous time incentive constraint at any time must satisfy

$$E_t^n(\mathbf{T}^n) = \lambda \left[s_t^{(n)} + E_0^{n+1}(\mathbf{T}^{n+1}) \right] + (1 - \lambda) E_t^n(\mathbf{T}^n) \geq c\lambda + E_t^n(\mathbf{T}^n). \tag{5.18}$$

Since $s_t^n > 0$, clearly the inequality in eqn (5.18) will be binding. Hence, after solving recursively,

$$E_t^n(\mathbf{T}^n) = \lambda c\lambda \frac{1 - e^{-rT^n}}{r}. \tag{5.19}$$

---

[9] The logic of making compensation contingent on the most informative output is also reminiscent of Innes' (1990) moral hazard model.

As we would expect, the entrepreneur's rent is monotonically decreasing within the first stage, that is, $E_t^n(\mathbf{T}^n) > E_\tau^n(\mathbf{T}^n)$ for $\tau > t$.

We can then determine the optimal budgeting decision in this case. The investor recursively solves the contract design problem and chooses the optimal funding horizon T^n by maximizing her net value $V_0^n(\mathbf{T}^n) - E_0^n(\mathbf{T}^n)$. Substituting and solving the maximization problem (5.33) yields the following results:

Proposition 5.1. *Suppose immediate rewards are needed in every period, that is, $s_t^n > 0$ for all n and t. Then the optimal horizon in stage n is given by:*

$$T^n = -\frac{1}{\lambda} \ln\left(\frac{c}{V_0^{n+1}(T^{n+1}) - c} \right). \tag{5.20}$$

The optimal horizon T^n is strictly increasing in n.

Proof. See the appendix.

5.5.3. *Implicit Incentives*

We turn now to the case where $\lambda > \hat{\lambda}$. Consider the entrepreneur's incentives in the last period of the penultimate stage. If the benchmark is accomplished, the entrepreneur will get a future rent that is at least equal to

$$E_0^N(T^N) = c\lambda \frac{1 - e^{-rT^N}}{r}.$$

Thus, the entrepreneur's current value can be evaluated as

$$E_{T^{N-1}}^{N-1}(\mathbf{T}^{N-1}) = \max\left\{ c\lambda, \lambda c\lambda \frac{1 - e^{-rT^N}}{r} \right\}.$$

But in the case $\lambda > \hat{\lambda}$, we know the entrepreneur's implicit incentives given by the prospect of moving on the last stage exceed the minimal incentives required, and hence

$$E_{T^{N-1}}^{N-1}(\mathbf{T}^{N-1}) = \lambda c\lambda \frac{1 - e^{-rT^N}}{r},$$

meaning that $s_{T^{N-1}}^{N-1} = 0$ is sufficient.

Taking this into account, clearly incentive compatibility will be satisfied in the last period of stage $N - 1$. Moving backwards in time, in each prior period of this stage incentive compatibility requires that:

$$E_t^{N-1}(\mathbf{T}^{N-1}) = \lambda\left[s_t^{N-1} + c\lambda \frac{1 - e^{-rT^N}}{r} \right]$$

$$+ (1 - \lambda)E_t^{N-1}(\mathbf{T}^{N-1}) \geq c\lambda + E_t^{N-1}(\mathbf{T}^{N-1}). \tag{5.21}$$

Inequality (5.9) reveals that $s_t^{N-1} = 0$ is sufficient as long as

$$\lambda \left(c\lambda \frac{1 - e^{-rT^N}}{r} - E_t^{N-1}(\mathbf{T}^{N-1}) \right) \geq c\lambda. \tag{5.22}$$

Let us consider any general funding stage n. Now, as we would expect, the entrepreneur's rent is monotonically decreasing within each stage, that is, $E_\tau^n(\mathbf{T}^n) > E_t^n(\mathbf{T}^n)$ for $\tau > t$. To see this, note that $E_t^n(\mathbf{T}^n) \leq (c\lambda/r)$ for all $t \in [0, T^n]$, that is, the agent's rent will never exceed the value of a perpetual stream of funding of $c\lambda$ (since this is the maximum rent she can divert). Thus, there will be at most a single transition period where inequality (5.22) switches from being violated (and hence $s_t^n > 0$ for all periods prior to the transition period) to being satisfied (hence $s_t^n = 0$). We denote this transition period by $\hat{t}^n$. That is, $\hat{t}^n$ is the first period where implicit incentives are wholly sufficient to guarantee incentive compatibility. We can then express the value of the information rent as

$$E_t^n(\mathbf{T}^n) = \begin{cases} \lambda \left(\frac{1 - e^{-(r+\lambda)(t - \hat{t}^n)}}{r+\lambda} \right) E_0^{n+1}(\mathbf{T}^{n+1}) & \text{if } t \geq \hat{t}^n, \\ c\lambda \frac{1 - e^{-r(\hat{t}^n - t)}}{r} + e^{-r(\hat{t}^n - t)} \lambda \left(\frac{1 - e^{-(r+\lambda)(T^n - \hat{t}^n)}}{r+\lambda} \right) E_0^{n+1}(\mathbf{T}^{n+1}) & \text{if } t < \hat{t}^n. \end{cases}$$

$$\tag{5.23}$$

An investigation of the investor's problem allows us to establish the following key insight:

Proposition 5.2. *The optimal stopping time T^n will be such that the reward function $s_t^{(n)}$ is initially strictly positive, for an initial interval of $t \geq 0$.*

Proof. See the appendix.

The observation that the rewards s_t^n are initially strictly positive is equivalent to saying that the transition point $\hat{t}^n$ in eqn (5.24) is strictly positive. This observation allows us to write the agent's value, at entry into stage n, as:

$$E_0^n(\mathbf{T}^n) = c\lambda \frac{1 - e^{-r\hat{t}^n}}{r} + e^{-r\hat{t}^n} \lambda \left(\frac{1 - e^{-(r+\lambda)(T^n - \hat{t}^n)}}{r + \lambda} \right) E_0^{n+1}(\mathbf{T}^{n+1}). \tag{5.24}$$

In other words, the experimentation will be long enough for the agent initially to require additional contingent compensation via contemporaneous information rents $s_t^n > 0$. As time is running out in the current stage, however, the option value that the agent obtains by deviating diminishes, and with it the need to compensate for the loss in this value. Once $\hat{t}_1$ is passed, the experimentation in the current stage comes essentially free for the investor, since the implicit promise of future rents is sufficient; but that second phase cannot be prolonged without increasing the first, costly phase.

Note that the distance $T^n - \hat{t}^n$ is determined in a recursive fashion, via condition of eqn (5.22), and is therefore independent of T^n. We adopt the notation $I^n \equiv T^n - \hat{t}^n$ for the duration of this second phase. The agent's value function E^n follows again the by now

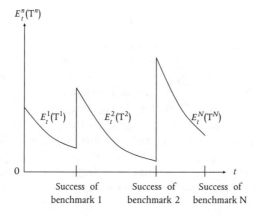

Figure 5.2. *Evolution of the entrepreneur's value function. The success times of intermediate benchmarks are random.*

familiar stochastic see-saw pattern, decreasing within each stage and upwards jumping at the entry into a new stage (Fig. 5.2). After substituting (5.14) and (5.24) and transiting to continuous time, the investor's problem of maximizing $V_0^n(\mathbf{T}^n) - E_0^n(\mathbf{T}^n)$ can be analysed. We find:

Proposition 5.3. *(i) Suppose $\lambda > \hat{\lambda}$. Then there is at least one stage, namely the penultimate stage, where implicit incentives are eventually sufficient.*

(ii) In a stage where implicit incentives are eventually sufficient, the optimal total horizon T^n is given by:

$$T^n = I^n + \frac{1}{\lambda} \ln \frac{V_0^{n+1}(T^{n+1})e^{-(r+\lambda)I^n}}{c - rE_0^{n+1}(T^{n+1})\left(\frac{1-e^{-(r+\lambda)I^n}}{(r+\lambda)}\right)}, \qquad (5.25)$$

where I^n, the duration of the phase where implicit incentives are sufficient, is:

$$I^n = -\frac{1}{r+\lambda} \ln \left(\frac{c(r+\lambda) - rE_0^{n+1}(T^{n+1})}{\lambda E_0^{n+1}(T^{n+1})} \right). \qquad (5.26)$$

(iii) I^n is increasing in n, and $I^n > 0$ in the final stages of the project (except for the last stage), but not necessarily in the early stages. If $I^n > 0$ in stage n, then the funding horizon T^n is strictly larger compared with the same stage with only immediate incentives ($\lambda < \hat{\lambda}$).

Proof. See the appendix.

The important insight of this analysis is that the potential power of implicit incentives is indeed increasing in the funding horizon. Since the funding horizon is always too short compared to the first-best (where it is infinite), and since the funding horizon is in principle increasing as more stages are completed and the overall value of the project increases, this is a welcome mechanism to overcome agency-driven capital budgeting constraints. Recall that the funding horizon in the last stage, T^N, will be the same with immediate or implicit incentives. Thus, a longer horizon in earlier stages is unambiguously good news. Intuitively, this increase in the funding horizon is due to the fact that part of the compensation in the current stage need not be provided contemporaneously. It is implied by the continuation values, making an extension of the current round less costly in terms of information rents. This effect may be so strong that the total funding horizon is not monotonically increasing from one stage to the next.

It is also intuitive why I^n is increasing over time. Since the agent's value must be strictly increasing from stage to stage (otherwise the incentive constraint would be violated), the potential power of implicit incentives is also increasing over time. Thus, typically implicit incentives will be prevalent in the last stages of a project (while still requiring immediate cash incentives in the early periods of each stage, according to Lemma 5.2). But in the early stages, it is more likely that the compensation must rely on immediate cash incentives in every period.

5.5.4. *Synopsis*

We can summarize our observations as follows: If the investor cannot use benchmarks, then the capital budget allocated to the project will be severely curtailed. The information rent has to be compounded over the entire horizon. Moreover, the experimentation horizon is defined for the project as a whole, and not fine-tuned to every stage. This will often lead to unwanted distortions in time allocations between various stages. For example, if most of the horizon has elapsed but the agent did not yet succeed in meeting the first benchmark, he will nevertheless continue to run the experiments for the first stage. The problem of continuing for too long in the first stage is made worse by the fact that the horizon for the subsequent stages will automatically be shortened, since the continuation budget becomes history-dependent.

Benchmarking introduces a sequential real option to abandon. In the context of our dynamic agency model, option value of these imbedded real options is comprised of the following four effects:

First, since the project is abandoned once a benchmark is not met within its pre-defined horizon, the information rent of the agent is dramatically reduced. In the simplest and perhaps most instructive case (immediate incentives), the compounding period of the information rent is shortened to the maximal duration of a single stage, rather than the maximal duration of the entire project.

Second, benchmarking makes it possible to define optimal and intertemporally consistent research budgets (research horizons) for every single stage. An important advantage is that these budgets will be independent of the history of delays and cost overruns in past financing rounds.

Third, the optimal research horizon increases from one stage to the next. Early stages should stop relatively rapidly because the chance for an overall success is remote. As more benchmarks are realized, the value of the project increases, and it becomes rational to persevere for longer. This finding explains that the first steps in a research project are the riskiest (and deserve the application of a higher risk-adjusted discount rate). Importantly, this decreasing trend in research risk is explained as an endogenous decision in a dynamic model, and not by technological characteristics. We would obtain a similar result if, say, λ was larger in early stages, making them a priori more likely to succeed.

A fourth, and more subtle, option value of benchmarking is that it permits the use of implicit incentives comprised by the relational promise of future contingent financing rounds if earlier rounds are successfully completed. The promise of future information rents serves as a powerful incentive device in earlier stages, making the extension of the funding horizon in earlier stages cheaper. The power of implicit incentives will notably be strong if the project's success probability is high relative to the time discount effect ($\lambda > r$). This is a welcome effect from a social point of view since the presence of agency costs means that all research horizons are too short when compared with the first best. The interdependence between the optimal sequencing of research horizons and the implicit incentive effect is perhaps the most intriguing finding of our analysis.

The benefits of benchmarking are reflected in the following comparative findings on the project duration:

Proposition 5.4. *(i) The total research horizon over all stages will always be strictly larger if stage financing is used compared with funding without benchmarking.*

(ii) If the project is relatively poor, $(R/c) < 1 + 3.71828$, then the last stage of stage financing alone will have a longer funding horizon than the entire horizon if there is no benchmarking.

Proof. See the appendix.

Thus, for a given research budget amounting to the total expected outlays at the beginning (real investments and compensations for the agent), the research horizon and the success probability will be the larger, and the better defined, the better monitored the intermediate benchmarks are. Its initial value and return to investors, as well as the value appreciation of the portfolio company from one financing round to the next, should be increasing functions of the benchmarking intensity.

5.6. ROBUSTNESS AND CONCLUSION

This chapter investigated the provision of venture capital in a research venture with sequential development stages. The binary outcome of each stage of the project is uncertain, and a steady investment flow is needed to safeguard the chances for success in each stage. The entrepreneur controls the application of the funds which are provided by the venture capitalist.

The optimal compensation of the entrepreneur is akin to a nested sequence of option contracts. The options express the value of the intertemporal incentive constraint, and the relational promise of future options works to alleviate the pressure to provide contemporaneous performance-related cash incentives.

A natural extension is to consider what happens if there are intermediate values of the project, that is, if upon realization of the intermediate benchmark n, a positive value R_n is realized if the project is unsuccessful in the next stage and hence abandoned after n stages.

In this case, the combined result of the current and all previous intermediate stages, worth R_n, will be sold to outsiders for a cash payment of R_n at the time of the sale. The project will then be irreversibly terminated, since neither the incumbent entrepreneur nor the acquiring outsiders will have a possibility to complete the missing stages. We assume of course that the successive intermediate values of the project satisfy, $R_1 < R_2 < \cdots < R_{N-1} < R_N$, and that in a perfect world every stage until the final stage N is worthwhile undertaking.

It is easy to see that this generalization has no impact on our finding whatsoever: as argued in Section 5.5, in principle the optimal incentive instrument would exploit the highest incentive power possible and grant a rent to the agent only upon completion of the last stage. But this leads frequently to a time consistency conflict between the *ex ante* level of required investments, and immediate cash compensations are needed to overcome the hold-up problem. Nothing changes in the structure of the optimal incanting contracts, when intermediate results are introduced. The only effect is in the investor's objective function, and indeed the appreciation of the values V^n from one stage to the next may be substantially reduced, and with it the increase in the optimal funding horizons form one stage to the next.

The chapter focuses on the financing of venture projects, but the problem analysed here is present in the financing of R&D in general. We show that the optimal funding horizon or research intensity in each of the sequential stages is derived endogenously, and identify the key determinants, namely future project risks and information rents and their interaction in the current stage. The present work contributes to the understanding of how agency costs and optimal research policy interact.

Appendix

Derivation of eqn (4.4): In discrete time, the value function can be written as follows (where we use the notation $\delta = (1/(1+r))$ for the discount factor):

$$V_0^1(T) = \delta\lambda V_1^2(T) + \delta(1-\lambda)V_1^1(T) = \delta\lambda \frac{1-\delta^{T-1}(1-\lambda)^{T-1}}{1-\delta(1-\lambda)}(R-c)\lambda$$

$$+ \delta(1-\lambda)\left[\frac{1-\delta^{T-2}(1-\lambda)^{T-2}}{1-\delta(1-\lambda)} + \delta(1-\lambda)\frac{1-\delta^{T-3}(1-\lambda)^{T-3}}{1-\delta(1-\lambda)}\right]$$

$$+ \cdots \left.\right]\delta\lambda(R-c)\lambda$$

$$= \frac{\delta\lambda}{1-\delta(1-\lambda)}\left[\frac{1-\delta^{T-1}(1-\lambda)^{T-1}}{1-\delta(1-\lambda)} - T\delta^{T-1}(1-\lambda)^{T-1}\right](R-c)\lambda.$$

For the transition to continuous time, we introduce again the notation Δ, hence replace $\delta = 1/(1+r)$ by $1/(1+\Delta r)$ and λ by $\Delta\lambda$. Taking the limit as $\Delta \to 0$, (4.4) obtains.

Derivation of eqn (5.11): We develop the argument in discrete time. We denote by E_t^i the entrepreneur's value function in t if he is of type $i = 1, 2$, and drop the argument T for simplicity. Suppose the entrepreneur is of type 1 in period $T - 1$, that is, he still has not completed the first stage. To ensure incentive compatibility for the last two periods, the last period reward s_T must at least satisfy

$$E_{T-1}^1 = \delta\lambda^2 s_T + \delta(1 - \lambda)c\lambda \geq c\lambda(1 + \delta). \tag{5.27}$$

Note that the venture capitalist is willing to offer this compensation since, from assumption (4.1), the minimum reward s_T satisfying (5.27) is such that $R - c > s_T$, so the net expected profit of the venture capitalist is positive. The value function of the type 1 entrepreneur in period $t \leq T - 1$ can also recursively be expressed as:

$$E_t^1 = \delta\lambda E_{t+1}^2 + \delta(1 - \lambda)E_{t+1}^1 \geq c\lambda + \delta E_{t+1}^1, \tag{5.28}$$

where $E_T^1 = c\lambda$ is the value that a type 1 entrepreneur receives in the last period (only diverting the capital can be rational). Hence, to satisfy incentive compatibility of type 1,

$$E_t^2 \geq E_t^1 + \frac{c\lambda}{\delta\lambda} \tag{5.29}$$

is required, and the sequence s_t, s_{t+1} must be chosen so as to satisfy (5.29). Note also that

$$s_T = c\lambda + \frac{c\lambda}{\delta\lambda} \tag{5.30}$$

satisfies this condition (5.29) in period $T - 1$ and, hence, also (5.27) with equality. Consider then incentive compatibility for type 2 which requires that

$$E_t^2 = \lambda s_t + \delta(1 - \lambda)E_{t+1}^2 \geq c\lambda + \delta E_{t+1}^2 \Leftrightarrow s_t \geq c + \delta E_{t+1}^2. \tag{5.31}$$

Using (5.30) and (5.29), it is possible to construct recursively a sequence of rewards $s_{T-1}, s_{T-2}, \ldots$ such that the incentive compatibility constraints (5.28) and (5.31) for types 1 and 2 hold with equality, everywhere for $t \leq T - 1$ and for type 2 at $t = T$. Then, by substituting (5.27) (holding with equality) into (5.28) (also holding with equality), we can recursively solve for the type 1 value function as

$$E_t^1 = c\lambda \frac{1 - \delta^{T-t}}{1 - \delta}, \tag{5.32}$$

and since (5.32) corresponds to the lower bound (5.12) and guarantees incentive compatibility for both types in the maximum number of periods, this contract must be optimal.

Proof of Lemma 5.1. Suppose that the reward with expected value of s_t^n is paid only conditional on termination of the next benchmark $n + 1$, for example, by paying a cash payment of $\hat{s}^{n+1} = (r + \lambda/(1 - e^{-(r+\lambda)T^{n+1}}))s_t^n$ if the benchmark of stage $n + 1$ is completed. Recall that $E_0^{n+1}(T^{n+1})$ is the minimum incentive compatible value of the agent upon entry in the subsequent stage. Suppose that, in the contract signed at entry in stage $n + 1$, the investor pledges new incentive compatible rewards worth $E_0^{n+1}(T^{n+1})$.

But since s_t^n is paid only conditional on success at least in the new stage $n + 1$, this reward has incentive power in stage $n+1$ as well: the effective value that the entrepreneur expects when never deviating in the new stage is worth $s_t^n + E_0^{n+1}(\mathbf{T}^{n+1})$. It follows that the investor can propose another contract for stage $n + 1$, where every success reward is reduced by $\hat{s}^{n+1}$, and yet this contract is incentive-compatible *ex post*. Thus, incentive payments worth $s_t^n + E_0^{n+1}(\mathbf{T}^{n+1})$ are required *ex ante*, but only $E_0^{n+1}(T^{n+1})$ will be offered *ex post*, showing a contradiction.

Finally note that $\lambda > \hat{\lambda}$ is the critical condition: this condition ensures that immediate compensation is required in every period of the last stage, and since $E^{n-1} < E^n$ and $T^{n-1} < T^n$, it follows immediately that the same holds in all prior stages. $\qquad\square$

Proof of Proposition 5.1. The optimal stopping horizon T^n is obtained by substituting (5.3) and (5.19) into the optimization problem:

$$\max_{T^n} V_0^n(\mathbf{T}^n) - E_0^n(\mathbf{T}^n) \tag{5.33}$$

and solving for the first-order condition. The fact that T^n is strictly increasing in n is an immediate consequence of the fact that $V_0^{n+1} > V_0^n$. $\qquad\square$

Proof of Proposition 5.2. Assume to the contrary that $s_t^n = 0$, implying $\hat{\imath}^n = 0$. Then, according to (5.23), the investors problem becomes:

$$\max_{T^n} \left(\frac{1 - e^{-(r+\lambda)T^n}}{r+\lambda} \right) \lambda (V_0^{n+1}(\mathbf{T}^{n+1}) - E_0^{n+1}(\mathbf{T}^{n+1})) \tag{5.34}$$

and since $V_0^{n+1}(\mathbf{T}^{n+1}) - E_0^{n+1}(\mathbf{T}^{n+1}) > 0$ as a consequence of recursive optimization, there is no finite solution T^n of (5.34). But then observe that, as $T^n \to \infty$, the agent can secure a perpetual rent of $c\lambda$ simply by always deviating. Thus, incentive compatibility of the contract in stage 1 requires that

$$\lim_{T^n \to \infty} E_0^n(\mathbf{T}^n) \geq \frac{c\lambda}{r}. \tag{5.35}$$

Finally, note that $E_0^n(\mathbf{T}^n) \geq (c\lambda/r)$ in (5.24) requires that $\hat{\imath}^n \to \infty$ as well, contradicting our assumption that $\hat{\imath}^n = 0$. $\qquad\square$

Proof of Proposition 5.3. In a stage where $I^n > 0$, the investor's initial problem can be written as (dropping bracket arguments for simplicity):

$$\max_{\hat{\imath}^n} \left(\frac{1 - e^{-(r+\lambda)I^n}e^{-(r+\lambda)\hat{\imath}^n}}{r+\lambda} \right) \lambda V_0^{n+1} - \left(\frac{1 - e^{-r\hat{\imath}^n}}{r} \right) c\lambda$$

$$- e^{-r\hat{\imath}^n} \left(\frac{1 - e^{-(r+\lambda)I^n}}{r+\lambda} \right) \lambda E_0^{n+1}. \tag{5.36}$$

Maximizing the objective function (5.36) and solving for T^n gives (5.26). The solution of I^n is obtained by solving the equivalent condition for (5.22) for an arbitrary stage n, and evaluated with equality at $t = \hat{t}^n$,

$$\lambda \left(E_0^{n+1} - \lambda \left(\frac{1 - e^{-(r+\lambda)I^n}}{r + \lambda} \right) E_0^{n+1} \right) = c\lambda. \tag{5.37}$$

Next, $E_0^n(T^n)$ must be strictly increasing in n, since otherwise the incentive constraint could not hold at the beginning of each stage. Inspection of (5.26) shows then that I^n is strictly increasing as well. Then consider the first-order condition of problem:

$$e^{-(r+\lambda)T^n} \lambda V_0^{n+1} = e^{-r(T^n - I^n)} \left(c\lambda - r \frac{(1 - e^{-(r+\lambda)I^n})}{r + \lambda} \lambda E_0^{n+1} \right), \tag{5.38}$$

Since we are looking at a stage where $I^n > 0$, it must be the case that

$$e^{-rI^n} \left(\frac{1 - e^{-(r+\lambda)I^n}}{r + \lambda} \right) \lambda E_0^{n+1} > e^{-rI^n} \frac{1 - e^{rI^n}}{r} c\lambda, \tag{5.39}$$

which implies that, for a given T^n,

$$e^{-r(T^n - I^n)} \left(c\lambda - r \frac{(1 - e^{-(r+\lambda)I^n})}{r + \lambda} \lambda E_0^{(n+1)} \right) < e^{-rT^n}. \tag{5.40}$$

But then compare the first-order condition (5.39) to condition (5.33) in the case of immediate incentives. Taking into account (5.40) then implies that for the same stage n, with identical V_0^{n+1} on the left hand side, the optimal T^n must be larger in the case of implicit incentives compared with the case of immediate incentives. □

Proof of Proposition 5.4. (i) Assume that a project with $N = 2$ will be stage financed, but contains the following contract provision: the duration of the second stage is a 1:1 decreasing function of the effective length of the first stage. That is, if the duration of stage 2 is T^2 when discovery of the first benchmark is immediate at $t = 0$, then the duration of stage 2 will be shortened to $T^2 - \tau$ if the first-stage discovery is alone made at $\tau > 0$.

Assume that $\lambda < \hat{\lambda}$. The value function of the project is identical to (5.10), and because of $\lambda < \hat{\lambda}$, the agent's value function is identical to (5.19). Let $T = T^1 + T^2$. The objective function is then:

$$\frac{\lambda}{r + \lambda} \left(\frac{1 - e^{-(r+\lambda)T}}{r + \lambda} - Te^{-(r+\lambda)T} \right) (R - c)\lambda - c\lambda \frac{1 - e^{-r(T - T^1)}}{r} \tag{5.41}$$

and differentiation with respect to T leads to the following first-order condition:

$$\lambda Te^{-\lambda T} = \frac{c}{R - c} e^{rT^1}. \tag{5.42}$$

Comparison of (5.42) and (5.12) clearly shows that the total funding horizon T is larger than without benchmarking. It is easy to extend this argument to $N > 2$. Moreover, note that the total funding horizon is weakly larger if $\lambda > \hat{\lambda}$, so the result holds a fortiori in this case.

(ii) As for the comparison of the length of the last stage under benchmarking, note that comparing (5.6) and (4.12) shows that

$$e^{-\lambda T^1} = \lambda T^2 e^{-\lambda T^2} = \frac{c}{R - c}, \qquad (5.43)$$

where T^1 is the solution of (5.6). Hence $T^2 > T^1$ iff $\lambda T^2 > 1$ in (5.12). Thus, for $\lambda T^1 = 1$, $T^2 = T^1$, and from (5.6), $\lambda T^1 = 1$ implies that $c/(R-c) = 1/e$. Then assume $\lambda T^1 > 1$, implying $e^{-\lambda T^1} = c/(R - c) < 1/e$. Hence also $\lambda T^2 e^{-\lambda T^2} = (c/R - c)) < 1/e$. Consider then the inequality $\lambda T^2 e^{-\lambda T^2} < 1/e$. Rearranging and taking logs,

$$\lambda T^2 > \ln \lambda T^2 + 1,$$

which can only hold if $\lambda T^2 > 1$, hence $T^2 > T^1$. $\qquad\qquad\square$

References

Ambec, S. and Poitevin, M. (1999), 'Organizational design of R&D activities', Mimeo, University of Montreal.

Bergemann, D. and Hege, U. (1998), 'Venture capital financing, moral hazard and learning', *Journal of Banking and Finance* 22, 703–35.

——— and ——— (2003), 'The financing of innovation: learning and stopping', Mimeo, Yale University and HEC School of Management.

Berk, J. B., Green, R. C., and Naik, V. (2000), 'Valuation and return dynamics of new ventures', Mimeo, UC Berkeley Haas School of Business, Carnegie Mellon University, and University of British Columbia.

Casamatta, C. (2003), 'Financing and advising: optimal financial contracts with venture capitalists', *Journal of Finance* (forthcoming).

Cochrane, J. H. (2001), 'The risk and return of venture capital', Mimeo, University of Chicago.

Cornelli, F. and Yosha, O. (2003), 'Stage financing and the role of convertible debt', *Review of Economic Studies* 70, 1–32.

Das, S., Jagannathan, M., and Sarin, A. (2002), 'The private equity discount: an empirical examination of the exit of venture backed companies', Mimeo, Santa Clara University.

Elitzur, R. and Gavious, A. (2002), 'A multi-period theoretic model of venture capitalists and entrepreneurs', *European Journal of Operations Research* (forthcoming).

Gompers, P. and Lerner, J. (1999), *The Venture Capital Cycle*, Cambridge, MA: MIT Press.

Innes, R. (1990), 'Limited liability and incentive contracting with ex-ante action choices', *Journal of Economic Theory* 52, 45–67.

Kaplan, S. and Stromberg, P. (2001), 'Financial contracting theory meets the real world: an empirical analysis of venture capital contracts', *Review of Economic Studies*, forthcoming.

——— and ——— (2002), 'Financial contracting, legal institutions and learning: a study of international venture capital contracts', Mimeo, University of Chicago.

———, ———, and Martel, F. (2002), 'Venture capital contracts around the world', Mimeo, University of Chicago.

Neher, D. (1999), 'Stage financing: an agency perspective', *Review of Economic Studies* 66, 255–74.

Qian, Y. and Xu, C. (1998), 'Innovation and bureaucracy under soft and hard budget constraints', *Review of Economic Studies* 65, 151–64.

Repullo, R. and Suarez, J. (1999), 'Venture capital finance: A security design approach', Working paper, CEMFI.

Schmidt, K. (2003), 'Convertible securities and venture capital finance', *Journal of Finance* 58, 1135–66.

6

Venture Capital on the Downside: Preferred Stock and Corporate Control

WILLIAM W. BRATTON

6.1. INTRODUCTION

When stock indices drop precipitously, when the start-up companies fizzle out, and when it stops raining money on places like Wall Street and Silicon Valley, attention turns to downside contracting. Law and business lawyers, sitting in the back seat as mere facilitators on the upside, move up to the front and sometimes even take the wheel. The job is the same on both the upside and downside, to maximize the value of going concern assets. But what comes easily on the upside can be dirty work on the down, where assets need to be separated from dysfunctional teams of business people so as to stem the flow of red ink to disappointed investors. The team members rarely go quietly, no matter how unsuccessful. The outcome can turn on provisions in contracts entered into on the upside—cookie cutter paragraphs in boilerplate forms, barely noticed when the cash flows easily.

This chapter takes the occasion of the simultaneous collapse of the high-technology stock market and the failure of the dotcom start-ups, along with the subsequent retrenchment of the venture capital business, to examine the law and economics of downside arrangements in venture capital contracts. The subject matter implicates core concerns of legal and economic theory of the firm. Debates about the separation of ownership and control, relational investing, takeover policy, the law and economics of debt capitalization, and bankruptcy reform all grapple with the downside problem of controlling and terminating unsuccessful managers for the benefit of outside debt and equity investors (and the related upside problem of incentivizing effective but fallible managers). The factors motivating these debates bear on venture capital contracting. But venture capital also presents a special puzzle for solution. Convertible preferred stock is the dominant financial contract in the venture capital market (Trester 1988; Sahlman 1990), at least in the USA.[1] This contrasts with other contexts in US corporate finance, where preferred stock is thought to be a financing vehicle long in decline. The only mature firms that finance with preferred, which

---

The ideas of this chapter arise out of 'Venture Capital on the Downside: Preferred Stock and Corporate Control', 100 Michigan Law Review (2002).

[1] Cumming (2000) reports that preferred is not extensively utilized in Canadian venture capital financing.

once was ubiquitous in American capital structures, tend to be firms in regulated industries having a little choice in the matter. Tax rules favouring debt finance provide the primary explanation for preferred's decline. But many corporate law observers would suggest dysfunctional downside contracting as a concomitant cause. Simply, preferred performs badly on the downside, where senior security contracts should be at their most effective. Preferred stockholders routinely have been victimized in distress situations by opportunistic issuers who strip them of their contract rights, transferring value to the junior equity holders who control the firm's management. The accumulation of bad experiences adds impetus to a wider trend to favour debt as the mode of senior participation. Venture capital finance is the exception to the trend. With preferred stock as the investing vehicle of choice, the number of venture capital funds increased from 34 with capital of $1.69 billion in 1991 to 228 funds with committed capital of $67.7 billion in the peak year of 2000 (Gompers and Lerner 2001: 151). Given preferred stock's history of contract failure, the question arises as to why American venture capitalists employ preferred instead of debt or common stock. This chapter draws on the economics of incomplete contracts to offer an answer.

Downside protection for a venture capitalist means two things—first, power to replace the firm's managers (or alternatively to force sale or liquidation of the firm), and, second, power to protect the venture contract itself from opportunistic amendment. Venture capital investments possess this protection in varying degrees, depending on the mode of their participation and the governing contracts' terms. At the best-protected end of the range of possibilities lie transactions where the venture capitalist holds a majority of the voting shares, whether of common or preferred. This imports control of the board and all necessary power to effect results in the firm. Thus situated, a holder of venture capital preferred can block any opportunistic stripping of its priorities and need not overly concern itself with the completeness of the protections specified in its contracts. At the opposite, least-protected end of the range of possibilities lie transactions where the venture capitalist holds preferred in the absence of either a voting stock majority or control of the board of directors. With no control whatsoever, the venture capitalist has the burden to extract protection in the form of express terms of the type conventional in contracts governing senior securities— promises to pay, negative covenants, liquidation provisions, conditions on commitments to make additional investments, and so forth. In many cases these provide a cumbersome, unreliable means to achieve the fundamental downside objective of removing mangers or forcing a sale. To see why, consider the archetypical case of a payment default on a bond contract. This is a governance event because it as a practical matter means a bankruptcy reorganization. But US reorganization practice under Chapter 11 is designed in the first instance to prevent the removal of managers and to avert a sale of the business. The proceeding will be controlled by the incumbent management, biased towards the status quo, and at the bottom line will lack a strong commitment toward protection of the contract rights of senior securityholders.[2]

---

[2] Under Section 1121(c) of the Bankruptcy Code the debtor in possession has the exclusive right to propose a plan during the first 120 days of a proceeding. Section 1129(a),(b) contemplates that seniors can be asked to give up value to juniors subject to the limit that seniors must at least receive liquidation value. 11 U.S.C. Sections 1121(c), 1129(a),(b).

Until recently, many academic observers assumed that venture capitalists always insist on full protection, taking voting control of their portfolio companies' shares and dominating their boardrooms. New empirical work shows that venture capitalists emerge with such full control at both the shareholder and board level in only a significant minority of cases (Kaplan and Stromberg 2001). In another significant minority of cases, the venture capitalist emerges at the vulnerable end of the range of protection, lacking voting and boardroom control and relying entirely on terms articulated *ex ante* in the preferred stock contract. In these cases, there arises a risk of exposure to issuer opportunism.

The most likely venture capital transaction structure entails neither full protection nor classic preferred stock vulnerability. In this majority of transactions, the venture capitalist emerges at a mid-point on the protection range, sharing control with the entrepreneur. Here the defining characteristic is an open-ended balance of power in the boardroom. The venture capitalist accordingly gets no unilateral power to control the assets and terminate the entrepreneur on the downside. Instead these matters are left open to contest. In a majority of this subset of transactions, the venture capitalist takes a majority of the voting stock even as it does not take a majority of board seats. The stock majority imports determinative protection against the stripping of contract rights. In a significant minority of these shared control transactions, however, the entrepreneur holds a majority of the shares with control in the boardroom being shared. This arrangement opens up a possibility of exposure to opportunism respecting the preferred stock contract.

In a majority of US venture capital transactions, then, the venture capitalist takes a cognizable risk of not getting the results it wants on the downside. Why should this be? This chapter addresses this question with a model of optimal capital structure in start-up investment contexts drawn from the economic literature of incomplete contracts. The model, which abstracts from the leading description of control transfer between entrepreneurs and outside capitalists from Aghion and Bolton (1992),[3] lets us explain the pattern of venture capital contracting in terms of rational provision of production incentives. More particularly, shared control arrangements are governance processes that avert problems of non-contractibility. When parties enter into venture capital contracts they are in a position to legislate respecting some but not all future outcomes. Fabulous success, for example, presents allocational problems but no questions respecting the entrepreneur's future control of the assets. Total failure is similarly cut and dried—the contracts trigger liquidation for the benefit of the venture capitalist subject to the constraints of the bankruptcy system. Middling outcomes are less amenable to advance specification. Here control transfers implicate complex business judgments outside the scope of existing contract technologies. Such scenarios are better suited to treatment through the operation of a contractually instituted governance process than through advance specification of a clear-cut outcome. Venture capital's shared control arrangements achieve this, making the entrepreneur's day-to-day control of assets and management contestable and facilitating

---

[3] In so doing, this chapter follows the suggestion of Kaplan and Stromberg (2001) that the Aghion–Bolton model is the most cogent of the theoretical explications of venture capital relationships. Hellman (1998) makes the same commendation.

control transfer at low cost even while giving the entrepreneur some assurance that control transfer power will not be arbitrarily exercised.

Section 6.2 sets out recently reported data on business practices respecting venture capital contracts. The data displace a longstanding assumption that venture capitalists always take complete voting control of their portfolio companies. Section 6.3 describes incomplete contracts and explains its appropriateness as a framework of inquiry respecting capital structure. Section 6.4 sets out an incomplete contracts model of a control transfer capital structure (the control transfer model or CTM), abstracting from the model of Aghion and Bolton. Section 6.5 brings the real world contracting pattern to the model and the model to the real world pattern. These results are an expansion of the model's framework, yielding a menu of contract specifications and governance processes from which parties to venture capital contracts can select. We emerge with a thick but workable description of control relationships between venture capitalists and entrepreneurs. Section 6.6 suggests a normative implication: control disputes arise respecting venture capital arrangements call for neutral umpires unconstrained by US law's rule of common equity primacy.

6.2. CONTRACTS AND CONTROL ARRANGEMENTS IN VENTURE CAPITAL FINANCE

In the once-prevailing story about venture capital transactions, entrepreneurs so need venture capital that they cede both a majority of stock and control of the boardroom. The control transfer to the venture capitalist (VC) is only temporary, however. If the portfolio company succeeds, control returns to the entrepreneur (*E*) when VC sells its stock in an initial public offering (IPO). Thus in the description of Ronald Gilson and Bernard Black (Chapter 2, this volume), the problem for solution with venture capital contracts is *E*'s lack of assurance against opportunistic retention of control by VC through undue delay of the IPO. They suggest that an 'implicit contract' backed by reputational constraints and financial incentives assures *E* that VC will voluntarily surrender the reins. Note that so long as VC has control its senior status is completely protected. Indeed, according to Gilson and Black (Chapter 2, this volume), the practice in venture capital transactions gives VC double protection, investing it with veto power over business decisions through provision of a full set of business covenants.

The VC control story, however, has turned out to be incomplete.[4] The reversal is understandable. Venture capital transactions are private placements. There is accordingly no public database respecting their financial terms and contracting structures. Actors in the industry, moreover, can be expected to take a proprietary view respecting their transactions' documentation. Kaplan and Stromberg break new ground just by gathering data respecting the contract governing venture capital investments in 118 start-ups (200 separate instances

---

[4] It also should be noted that the IPO is not the only means of VC exit on the upside. Four additional routes are available: (1) the VC can retain all or part of its shares and sell them into the trading market subsequent to the IPO; (2) the firm can be sold to a third party acquirer, with the VC taking a share of merger consideration upon exit; (3) the VC can sell its shares to a third party acquirer; and (4) the VC can sell its shares back to the issuer or to *E*. Any of these exits can be partial or full. For discussion of possibilities and practices, including empirical results in the USA and Canada, see Cumming and MacIntosh (2001).

Table 6.1. *Venture capital contracts—the control range: Kaplan and Stromberg's results*

	Traditional contracts—*E* voting control (%)	Shared control (%)	Voting control in *VC* (%)
Power to control assets/control of board of directors	13	62	25
Exposure to contract opportunism			
Majority of voting shares			
No vesting	11.6	17.6	70.8
Full vesting	23.1	21.1	55.8

of investment) made by 14 venture capital firms located across the USA. The data displace the standard story, showing that VCs do not always take control of their portfolio firms.[5] The theory of the firm has a lot of explaining to do as a result.

Kaplan and Stromberg find that one or the other party, VC or *E*, has control of the board in only 38 per cent of their cases (see Table 6.1). In this subset, the VC takes control in two thirds of the cases and the *E* takes control in one third of the cases; also, cases of VC control are more likely to occur in respect of late-stage financings. In the remaining 62 per cent of the cases, neither side takes control (Kaplan and Stromberg 2001: 17). Instead, each of the VC and the *E* designates a director for a seat or seats. They then are to agree on a candidate to fill the remaining seat or seats. Under standard corporate law on allocation of authority, control of the boardroom means control of the assets and personnel. The upshot on the downside, assuming conflicting views in *E* and VC as to the best course of action, or, indeed, assuming that VC wishes to remove *E* from the position of CEO, is that the views and votes of the third director are outcome determinative.

Kaplan and Stromberg (2001) also collect data on voting control at the shareholder level. At this point recall that while a majority of the voting shares means boardroom control with plain vanilla corporate documentation, standard corporate practice permits shareholders to make special contractual arrangements respecting boardroom control. Such is the case with venture capital transactions, which tend to provide separate voting schemes for board election, on the one hand, and for other matters on which shareholders vote, on the other hand. The latter proceed on a one vote per share basis.[6] Accordingly, voting control over matters like charter amendments and mergers goes to the actor, *E* or VC, holding the largest number of shares. The number and proportion of shares held by *E* and VC in turn will vary depending on how well *E* performs. It is customary in venture capital contracting to use stock ownership as a performance incentive for *E*, setting out

[5] Significantly, the touchstone discussion of venture capital contracting, Sahlman (1990: 506), makes no assertion respecting the frequency of VC control. It does note the incidence of shared control in the boardroom.

[6] Or, in the case of the VC, votes equal to the number of shares of common stock into which its shares are convertible.

performance targets and providing that more stock vests in E as the targets are met. Here are Kaplan and Stromberg's figures respecting the allocation of these votes for all rounds of financing: In 70.8 per cent of the cases, the VC controls a majority of the votes, assuming no performance-based stock allocations to the E ever come to vest. Given full vesting, the number of cases in which VC controls a majority decreases to 55.8 per cent. E controls in 11.6 per cent of the cases, rising to 23.1 per cent given full vesting. Neither party controls in 17.6 per cent, rising to 21.1 given full vesting. Some variance comes into the figures in subsets broken down by round of investment. VC control is higher (86.8 per cent, no vesting; 65.8, full vesting) in rounds conducted where the start-up has not yet produced revenues and lower (59.0 no vesting; 48.7 full vesting) in post-revenue rounds. The net on the downside, where full vesting of E performance-based stock is unlikely to have occurred, strongly favours VC voting control.

Kaplan and Stromberg (2001) show strong correlations between share voting control and board control. Where VC has voting control, VC also has board control in 22.5 per cent of the cases; but board control is shared in 70 per cent of the cases where VC has voting control. Where VC never has voting control, board control is shared in 58.1 per cent of the cases; E controls in 38.7 of the cases. Where VC has voting control subject to divestment given E equity vesting, board control is shared in 94.1 per cent of the cases. A correlation between voting rights and cash flow rights also can be noted. The VC mean economic ownership claim in all transactions assuming no vesting is 55.7 per cent and 47.6 per cent with full vesting.

Finally, Kaplan and Stromberg (2001: tables 6 and 7) report that in 15 per cent of the cases, the documentation defines a state of unacceptable suboptimal performance in advance by reference to financial information and provides for a state-contingent transfer of control to the venture capitalist.

Summing up, shared control in the boardroom is the dominant governance mode in the portfolio companies in Kaplan and Stromberg's sample. It even prevails in a majority of the cases where one or the other of VC or E has a majority of voting shares. But, at the same time, each of VC and E have boardroom control in significant numbers of portfolio companies. This data complicates the explanatory task for theory of the firm. The question is neither why VC control, nor why E control. It is, first, why shared control in most cases with outlier cases of VC control and E control? Second, how, if at all, do the shared control arrangements described in Kaplan and Stromberg's sample function so as to assure full realization of a given start-up's profit potential?

6.3. INCOMPLETE CONTRACTS THEORIES OF THE FIRM

This chapter's principal assertion is that the value of shared control lies in the fact that it makes E's day-to-day control of assets and management contestable, facilitating control transfer at low cost even as it gives E a degree of assurance against arbitrary and capricious exercise of that control transfer power. To see why these factors are important, look at the situation *ex ante*, before VC commits its money. VC knows that E could have a valuable business idea even while simultaneously turning out to be a poor manager. E knows that VCs bring this sceptical point of view to their review of portfolio companies, but also knows that VCs are not immune to adverse selection and may not be infallible in their business judgments. Both parties also know that as events unfold E and VC may interpret them differently, with E as the inside party having an advantage respecting hard information. There results a nascent conflict of interest, which may or may not ripen depending on future events. A shared control arrangement holds out advantages as a solution. It gives VC a governance structure which contemplates *ex ante* that E may have to replaced by a professional manager. At the same time, shared control lets E take charge of the business without being VC's at will employee, as would be case if VC had control of the board. The shared control arrangement leaves the matter of E's performance evaluation open and waits for events to unfold.

VC will want to take control of the assets and replace E on a moderate downside scenario[7]—the portfolio company still has prospects but E does not appear to be equipped to realize them. Such mediocre or poor performance can stem from adverse selection or moral hazard problems. In either case, it would not give rise to conflict of interest and contracting problems between E and VC in a world where E derives no private benefits from the control of assets. Oliver Hart (1995) shows that in such an ideal (and taxless) world, first-best results can easily be achieved with an all common stock capital structure and a simple incentive compensation system. Hart describes a simple two-period situation where the firm is founded at $t = 0$ and liquidated at $t = 2$, with an intermediate decision respecting liquidation or continuance to be made at $t = 1$, along with a dividend payment. Hart would make the compensation of the managing participant E depend entirely on the dividend d. That is, incentive compensation I should equal $\pi(d1 + d2)$, where π is a proportion of the firm's total returns. If the payment also covers liquidation proceeds— $I = \pi[d1 + (d2, L)]$—the E can be expected to make an optimal decision respecting liquidation at $t = 1$. If at $t = 1$, the expected value of L is greater than the total returns expected at $t = 2$, the firm is liquidated at $t = 1$ and no costly contracting designed to align the manager's incentives with those of outside investors is necessary (Hart 1996: 146–8). Under this incentive structure there is no *ex ante* prospect of firm continuance in the event of poor results.

The real world problem is that managers like E do derive private benefits from asset management. In Hart's conception, the bribe π required align their incentives with those of the outside security holders is unfeasibly large.[8] Accordingly, a complex capital structure must be devised in order to align incentives in the direction of optimal investment and management and insure that the actor with the appropriate incentives controls the assets.

Incomplete contracts models of capital structure seek to describe such incentive compatible capital structures. They start with a common sense definition of contracts—contracts are comprised of advance specifications of future results. To the extent that a given outcome cannot successfully be specified in advance, the subject matter is non-contractible.

---

[7] A catastrophic downside scenario arises when the portfolio company's business has no prospects under anyone's management. Here VC contracts in the end provide for termination with the VC taking the crumbs off the table.

[8] The treatment of Hellmann (1998) should be contrasted at this point. In that set up, E's private benefits from control may be outweighed by the upside prospects of a pay-off on E's common stock in the firm, which pay-off will be realized only if E gives up control.

The models make three assertions about corporate contracts and capital structures. First, corporate contracts can be expected to omit important future variables due the difficulty or impossibility of *ex ante* description. That is, the particular posture of events on which critical governance outcomes will depend later on may not be sufficiently specifiable in advance so as to permit the parties to draft in advance a contract term setting out appropriate instructions. Second, corporate contracts can be expected to omit important future variables due the difficulty or impossibility of *ex post* observation and verification (Grossman and Hart 1986; Hart and Moore 1988; Holmstrom and Milgrom 1992). That is, even if the parties can anticipate and describe future contingencies, once events have unfolded in the future there may be no concrete factual basis for the operation of an advance legislative directive. To enforce a contractual specification, you have to be able make a proof in court. Complex facts of business life do not always lend themselves to such presentations, especially by those outside the firm, whether government regulators or VCs. Meanwhile, hard accounting numbers produced by a firm do not by themselves direct business judgments and are in any event subject to manipulation by insiders. Finally, non-contractibility may obtain because the requisite transactional technologies do not yet exist.[9] Third, given the forgoing problems of non-contractibility, important outcomes in corporate contracts will be determined not by advance specification but by the firm's structure of ownership. The specification of the owner and any associated contingent control allocations built into the firm's contracts—in particular the contracts making up the capital structure—substitute for contract terms absent due to the condition of contractual incompleteness (Aghion and Bolton 1992: 479).

As the zone of non-contractible contingencies expands, the ownership specifications become more important. Ownership and control of the assets will not be vested in perpetuity in a single actor because so doing would both imply a low-powered performance incentive and leave the firm without defence against adverse selection and opportunism. In this conceptualization, the firm's present owners are the actors who direct its ongoing management and investment policies, or, in the alternative, who determine whether to sell or liquidate the firm.[10] In the event of suboptimal performance, control transfer to an actor possessing more compatible incentives may be advisable. The firm's performance thus depends on the incentives of not only its present owners but of its contingent future owners. Optimal capital structure depends on the control transfer arrangements that shape these incentives.[11]

---

[9] Unlike most law and economics, which tends to include any voluntary economic relation within its notion of the *ex ante* contract, incomplete contracts theory restricts the reach of the *ex ante* contract to cases where actors make explicit specifications about the future. That is, to have 'contract' terms that govern future states, those contingent states must be specified and the future outcomes must be computable. Since many future states of nature clearly are not computable, transacting parties as a result lack the technology necessary to enable the negotiation and composition of a contract term *ex ante* (Anderlini and Felli 1994).

[10] Notably, 'owner' is here specially defined as the party who has the right to control all aspects of the asset that have not been given over to contractual specification *ex ante* (Grossman and Hart 1986). Under this definition, ownership and control cannot be separated, although they can be shared. Since asset control is ownership, residual claimants who do not manage are not owners, whatever the law's contemplation.

[11] It should be noted that the basic assertions of the incomplete contracts school are a subject of debate in economic theory. Maskin and Tirole (1999) argue that parties can indeed design contracts that overcome

Significantly, incomplete contracts economics makes no resort to 'implicit contracts' as it describes governance structures. The term implicit contracts, as used in law and economics, describes counterparty conduct which a given contract party expects (often in a situation of trust or reliance), but as to which there is no explicit requirement in the contract. Such expectations often arise respecting future events as to which a contractual specification satisfying all parties is difficult or impossible. Implicit contracts fill these gaps. But they do not do so as implied, legally enforceable duties, as do the implied contracts of contract law. In the law and economics usage, no legal constraints follow from the identification of an implicit contract. More often than not the dependent party is left exposed to counterparty opportunism and remitted to self-protection through explicit contracting the next time around. In giving this instruction, the implicit contracts approach makes a significant assumption—that the zone of contractibility is universal and incomplete contracts always can be completed. Given that assumption, it appears to make good policy sense to deploy the law so as to force the parties to conclude their own contracts rather than insert contract terms devised by judges acting *ex post* (Easterbrook and Fischel 1993: 445).

Incomplete contracts economics holds out a distinctly different approach to contracts because it does not assume universal contractibility. Indeed, it holds that transacting actors can create producing institutions that assuredly evolve toward the first-best only to the extent that they deal with contractible subject matter. Absent contractibility, we are of necessity in a second-best world, where the function of economics is to identify and explain barriers that prevent the evolution of first-best transaction structures. In this second-best world there arises no all-pervasive presumption against regulation. Where subject matter is non-contractible, problems have to be sorted out *ex post* and it makes no sense to remit parties to *ex ante* contract. It does not necessarily follow that a given judicial or other regulatory intervention will move actors in a productive direction. In theory, given ideal circumstances, incompleteness only means that the parties themselves renegotiate *ex post* once the requisite facts are on the table. In the real world, however, such renegotiations do not necessarily occur under ideal conditions. Determinations about the desirability of judicial intervention to protect against opportunism accordingly have to be made case by case.

6.4. THE CONTINGENT CONTROL MODEL

There follows a contingent CTM abstracted from precedent work by Aghion and Bolton (1992) so as to appear in an accessible form keyed to the description of real world venture capital arrangements.[12] The CTM is well-suited to the exposition of the control transfer problem in venture capital contexts. This section recounts its main properties. The section that follows discusses is implications for real world venture capital contracting.

---

the problems the school describes as 'non-contractible', and that irrelevance obtains as between a incomplete contract left open to *ex post* renegotiation and a contract with described trades. The response appears in Hart and Moore (1999). The dispute in part turns on whether the parties can credibly commit not to renegotiate. If they can, then the case for investing resources in advance specification strengthens.

[12] See Bratton (1997: 429–34) for an application in the context of a discussion of dividend policy.

6.4.1. *The Set Up*

Once again we get a two-period model built on a stylized picture of the relationship between E and VC (see Table 6.2). The two period framework follows the life of a firm from birth to liquidation, facilitating a dynamic inquiry into the incentive effects of different capital structures. An amount K is invested in the firm at $t = 0$; all of K comes from VC. The firm is liquidated at $t = 2$, when monetary returns r are realized. The amount of the payout will depend on an action a to be taken from amongst the set of feasible actions A by the actor in control of the firm after the realization of a state of nature θ at $t = 1$. There only two possible future states of nature, a good business state θ_g and a bad business state θ_b. Different actions a will be optimal depending on which state occurs. More particularly, action set A contains only two possible actions, a_g and a_b in each of the two states of nature θ_g and θ_b. In state θ_g the maximizing choice of action a^* is a_g; and in state θ_b the first-best choice of action a^* is a_b. Just which θ is going to occur is not clear at $t = 0$, when E and VC enter into a contract which must address the contingency respecting the future choice of a. At $t = 1$, immediately prior to the time for the choice of a, the operation of the business will produce a signal s as to the state of nature θ_g or θ_b (Aghion and Bolton 1992: 475–6).

The model works the classic conflict of interest problem between E and VC through this framework. The interests come into conflict because returns to E and VC are received in different forms such that choices of different actions a can impact on them differentially. Monetary returns of the project r are payable to VC at $t = 2$, minus amounts of compensation payable to E pursuant to a compensation schedule in the contract concluded at $t = 0$ by E and VC. The compensation arrangement provides a transfer $t > 0$, the precise amount of which is a function of s and r. Thus VC's payout $y = r - t$. Critically, E also receives significant non-monetary private benefits b, such as reputation, which are not also received by VC. The quantum of b is a legitimate part of the overall yield of value from the project, but is neither observable nor verifiable by third parties. Yields of both r and b will depend on the state of nature θ and the choice of a. E's yield is a function of $r(a, \theta) + b(a, \theta)$, and VC's yield is solely a function of $r(a, \theta)$. The conflict of interest devolves on the choice of a because the choice of a can differentially impact r and b, and open up a significant differential of returns between VC and E.

E and VC confront significant problems of non-contractibility at $t = 0$. It would be easy if the state of nature θ could be specified *ex ante*. Then it might be possible for the contract between E and VC to direct the party in control, presumably E, to take a jointly maximizing action a^*. Unfortunately θ is impossible or very costly to describe

Table 6.2. *Contingent control model—time sequence*

Investment	Signal s	Returns r	Realization of K as to θ
$t = 0$	$t = 1$		$t = 2$
	action a taken		

ex ante, although the parties will be able to identify θ *ex post*, at $t = 2$. The model does, however, assume that even though the E–VC contract cannot be made directly contingent on θ, it can be made contingent on the signal s, which is verifiable although imperfectly correlated with θ. Even so, the occurrence of s at $t = 1$ does not enable the drafting of a complete contract. For even if s were perfectly correlated with θ, the project still would be too complex to permit an *ex ante* specification of the optimizing response a_g or a_b upon the realization of s. Although the set of choice will be limited to a_g and a_b, the model makes the realistic assumption that both will lie wholly within the realm of traditional management business judgment to be exercised by the actor in control of the firm. Neither is susceptible either to direct specification or to indirect specification through a constellation of affirmative and negative covenants.[13]

The upshot is that the capital structure's allocation of control rights between E and VC will determine the choice of a and the level of value, optimal or suboptimal, yielded by the firm (Aghion and Bolton 1992: 476–7). The capital structure, as set out in the E–VC contract, inevitably specifies an allocation of control which in turn determines which actor has the privilege to chose action a. Control can lie in E or in VC or in both. The CTM works through the scenarios of E control, VC control, and joint control to ascertain the distance between the set of results built in by the incentive structure and first-best set of results. Where E controls, a first-best choice of action follows automatically only when the choice of a^* also happens to maximize y, b, and the transfer payment t. Here E's incentives are perfectly aligned with the general maximizing result (Aghion and Bolton 1992: 480–1). But, given the way the CTM is set up, on some outcomes the incentives are misaligned—when E controls, its private benefits cause it to make the wrong choice on a bad outcome. VC's choice of action is suboptimal on a good outcome.

The CTM runs two modes of working around the misaligned incentives. The first is Coasian bargaining, modelled on the assumption that the entrepreneur has all the bargaining power. The second is control transfer specified in advance in the E–VC contract and triggered by the signal s.

6.4.2. *Coasian Bargaining*

It is a truism of law and economics that even given misaligned incentives, an optimal result, here a^*, can result from a round of Coasian bargaining *ex post*. Given a subject matter presenting contractibility problems, Coasian bargaining is a particularly attractive alternative, because it lets the parties leave the matter open *ex ante*, saving on transaction costs and avoiding use of dysfunctional provisions. In the CTM, a round of negotiation would occur after the realization of s at $t = 1$ in which a non-controlling party benefited by the choice of a^* purchases its choice by the controlling party with a side payment (Hart 1996: 98). Assuming θ_b, we speak of a case where $a^* = a_b$, but the private benefit

---

[13] Direct specification might be possible in a different case, where a_g and a_b entail a selection between a limited set of choices identifiable in advance, for example, either merger, liquidation, or sale of assets. But, even given the feasibility of that sort of specification, *ex post* judicial enforcement of the contractual directive could still fall short of feasibility if information asymmetries led to problems of third party verification.

return b to E yielded by a choice of a suboptimal choice of a_g is greater than value of b yielded by the choice of a^*. In addition, the yield of y to VC is greater if a^* is chosen over a_g. For simplicity, the model assumes that E has all the bargaining power. Given the above alignment of values, E will offer to choose a^* (here $\theta_b a_b$) if VC pays E the sum equal to the difference between the value of y yielded on the choice of a^* and the value of y yielded on a suboptimal choice of a. VC can be expected to accept the offer provided that amount offered is greater than its original investment K. Assuming θ_g, then $a^* = a_g$, and a round of bargaining results if the private benefit return b to E yielded by a suboptimal choice of a_b is greater than the yield of b on a choice of a^* and the yield of y to VC is greater where a^* is chosen over a_b. Since E has all the bargaining power, E will offer to choose a^* (here $\theta_g a_g$) if VC pays E the difference between the value of y yielded on the choice of a^* and the value of y yielded on a suboptimal choice of a. Once again, VC can be expected to accept the offer provided that amount offered is greater than its original investment K. Restating, on a bad state with E in control, if the increase in returns to VC that results from substituting an optimal choice of action is greater than the differential in returns to E that results from abandoning the suboptimal action, then, VC, given the signal of a bad outcome, will bribe E with a payment that at least makes up E's differential so long as the returns to VC net of the payments pay back at least its original investment and make it better off than it would be with the suboptimal choice.

The problem is that, given the CTM's set up, Coasian bargaining does not always lead to an efficient result. This stems from the fact that renegotiation leading to a^* does not result in every case. The model assumes, realistically enough, that the return of at least K constitutes a rationality constraint for VC. Thus the renegotiation fails and the first-best result will not be chosen if the value of K is so high that it exceeds the yield on offer by E. The very possibility that this situation could arise has destabilizing implications for the whole deal: VC can be expected to refuse to invest at $t = 0$ unless some form of protection against E's opportunism is included in the contract package (Aghion and Bolton 1992: 480–3).[14]

Generalizing, Coasian bargaining fails to assure optimal results in midstream corporate contexts where the interests of the party controlling the assets (usually E or management) in the conduct of the business differ from those of contributors of capital (usually VC or outside equity). The generalization is intuitively attractive, and obtains even in the absence of bargaining costs, endowment effects, or collective action problems, the latter being the factor usually cited against midstream renegotiation of corporate contracts (Coffee 1989: 1664–5). The key to the result is the CTM's ascription of bargaining power

---

[14] The CTM runs the VC control scenario with similarly equivocal results. Here first-best choices of action will follow only where the choice of a that maximizes y happens to be a^*, meaning that VC's incentives are perfectly aligned with the general maximizing result. Where the choice of a that maximizes y is not first-best there can be room for Pareto improving renegotiation in the form of a bribe paid to the actor in control by the actor disadvantaged by the suboptimal choice of a. But, once again, it turns out that the optimal choice a^* does not result in every case. The model's reasonable assumption of a wealth constraint on E's part (VC provides all of K) substantially limits the possibility of renegotiation where VC controls. Simply, since b and t constitute E's entire wealth, E lacks the resources to make the bribe. For VC control to assure first-best results, then, the amount of t has to be set high enough to give E sufficient cash for the bribe. But this adjustment, in turn, returns us to the same place as the search for the first-best under E control. As t increases, projected investment returns to VC fall short of K at some point and VC refuses to invest (Aghion and Bolton 1992: 483–4).

to E. With that power, E can negotiate VC down to an *ex post* return y that is less than VC's original investment K. That result kills the deal *ex ante*. In the real world, in the absence of fiduciary constraints, protective contract terms, or an immediately exercisable contingent control power to terminate E, E will have significant bargaining power along the lines assumed in the CTM. The power arises in the first instance from the information asymmetries favouring E. Costs and other frictions in the way of E's removal enhance that bargaining power. As the power grows, VC's investment returns shrink.

It follows, logically enough, that VC (or any other outside equity investor) needs one of three things—fiduciary protection, protective contract terms, or an immediately exercisable contingent control power. The CTM proceeds to the third of these alternatives.

6.4.3. *Control Transfer by Advance Specification*

The CTM employs the device of contingent control to solve the problem presented by the misalignment of the incentives of E and VC so as to yield results superior to that of Coasian renegotiation. Two additional assumptions have to be made to support the contingent control device's operation—that VC's returns are higher when a suboptimal choice of a is made in θ_g states and a E's returns are higher when a suboptimal choice of a is made in θ_b states. With this alignment, VC will make a first-best choice in θ_b and E will make a first-best choice in θ_g, and a contract that accords control to VC in θ_b and E in θ_g will be optimal. These assumptions reflect an appealing intuition about the governance of start-ups. E knows the business and should not be disturbed on θ_g scenarios. But, since E also derives private benefits from control of the business, E is ill-suited to make an optimal choice of business plan, or an optimal decision between termination and continuance, in θ_b states.

Since θ is unverifiable, the feasibility of a contingent control arrangement depends on the degree of correlation between s and θ (Aghion and Bolton 1992: 484–6). Given the requisite correlation, an optimal arrangement can be made operational with relative ease in a world with a frictionless bankruptcy process. Thus does the CTM use a contract provision to avert difficulties stemming from the noncontractible nature of θ. More particularly, VC's participation in the firm takes the form of debt. The realization of s at $t = 1$ is made a default/no-default event, with default occurring in a θ_b state. In the event of default, E becomes bankrupt and VC takes control, choosing the first-best a; in θ_g states there is no default and E stays in charge (Aghion and Bolton 1992: 487). The same result can be effected with preferred stock (in a frictionless world). The realization of s signalling a $_b$ state triggers a redemption of VC's stock. If E does not have a source of substitute capital, the duty to redeem causes bankruptcy and the same result as debt finance.[15]

6.4.4. *Implications*

The CTM has a number of intuitively attractive implications. The assertion that hard-wired contingent control transfers dominate over backroom renegotiations resonates well. The

---

[15] Provided there is not a significant amount of debt, which by definition is senior to VC's preferred stock, in the capital structure.

model also raises a pertinent question respecting the relative effectiveness of employment contracts and control transfer structures as means to channel E's incentives in productive directions. The model implies that where crucial management choices—selections of a from sets A—are noncontractible due to problems of observability and verifiability and where E enjoys private benefits b, monetary incentive schemes based on firm profitability or stock market performance cannot be expected to import adequate discipline. Control structures allowing outsider investors to take actions that managers dislike in the event of poor firm performance, although a second-best solution, can be expected to do a more effective job of manipulating management incentives in productive directions (Dewatripont and Tirole 1994: 1028).

But the CTM's exclusive reliance on bankruptcy control transfer makes its transition to real world practice problematic. Bankruptcy, after all, is a drastic and costly step to have to take. The next section works past this sticking point.

6.5. THE CTM AND THE PEOPLE OF SENIOR SECURITIES IN VENTURE CAPITAL CONTRACTING

This section moves the CTM a step in the direction of the real world practice described in Section 6.2 above by relaxing some assumptions and expanding the menu of contractual devices implicating control and control transfer.

At first inspection, the data set out in Section 6.2 appear to suggest that the CTM's analytical structure lacks predictive power in the venture capital context. Recall that the most likely real world arrangement is shared control, and the next most likely is vesting of control in one party or the other. Contingent control transfer devices based on advance specification of an s show up in a minority of the cases. But the data nonetheless instantiate the CTM's dynamic in significant ways. For one thing, the real world venture capital contracts' boardroom control arrangements have to be read together with their financial provisions. These invariably provide for redemption of the preferred held by VC in the intermediate term. This means that in an extreme θ_b state the contracts provide for a bankruptcy transfer of control, exactly as predicted by the CTM. On the other hand, the CTM has less immediate relevance with respect to control transfer in θ_b states where turnaround remains a possibility and θ_g states where retention of E will be profitable but suboptimal. But the framework can be adopted to assist our understanding of these situations. The CTM's limitations stem from two components. First, it effects its contingent control transfer through a bankruptcy proceeding on the assumption that bankruptcy is frictionless. In the real world bankruptcy costs are onerous (Altman 1984). Venture capital practice shows us that these costs do not have to be incurred to effect a contingent control transfer. Second, the model limits itself to a contract term as it attempts to deal with the problem of noncontractibility. In so doing it hypothesizes an imperfect but plausible element of contractible subject matter: Although θ is unverifiable, the trigger s is verifiable even though it is not a perfect proxy for θ. But what of cases where there is no reliable s or the parties cannot agree on one? In these cases some other control transfer device must be employed. The discussion that follows expands the menu of possibilities to include processes implicating control transfer and operating on an open-ended basis, dispensing with contractual triggers.

6.5.1. *Bankruptcy versus Boardroom Control Transfer*

The CTM's assumption that control transfer occurs on a bankruptcy scenario can be relaxed easily by reference to standard tools of corporate law practice. In a close corporation context, changes of control in the boardroom can be contracted for in advance, even if the VC takes preferred stock. E and VC simply enter into a 'pooling agreement', contracting in their capacity as shareholders with respect to their future votes. In the context of the CTM, they would execute a voting agreement pursuant to which the occurrence of s signalling an θ_b state would trigger the extension of a contingent irrevocable proxy from E to VC. The proxy would give VC the votes to elect a majority of the board and to remove incumbent directors. With boardroom control, VC can choose the CEO who will choose a_b^*.[16]

The two different methods of control transfer, in the boardroom and through liquidation, are suited to different business outcomes. One accordingly would expect to see both employed in real world arrangements. Significantly, the CTM interpolates only two business situations—the selection of a from the range A in θ_g and θ_b states. In practice, there will be an open-ended range of such future choices, a from A, b from B, c from C, and so on, and θ_g and θ_b will cover a range of outcomes. When such a choice concerns a change in the business plan or the replacement of key personnel, whether in an θ_g or θ_b state, the boardroom control transfer mode is indicated. The liquidation trigger, in contrast, is better suited to severe θ_b states calling for disinvestment.[17]

Another distinction between control transfer by redemption and bankruptcy and control transfer by boardroom election should be noted. The former mode of transfer implies VC financing by a senior security, whether debt or preferred. That is because when redemption causes insolvency, control devolves to VC because it holds a liquidation preference over E in the bankruptcy distribution. Boardroom control transfer can be (and often is) effected in a firm funded entirely with common stock and does not implicate an insolvency proceeding. This implies a real world preference for transfer by boardroom control transfer provision over control transfer through redemption and liquidation, if only because bankruptcy is costly in the real world. But the prediction must be qualified because redemption does not necessarily lead to a bankruptcy proceeding. If the going concern retains value, the triggering of the redemption right can become the occasion for renegotiation between VC and E. Since VC now has the option of forcing insolvency, it comes to the table with cognizable bargaining power.[18]

[16] Dewatripont and Tirole (1994: 1031–4), although still a model denominated as a debt–equity model, captures the dynamic of a boardroom control transfer.

[17] For a model amplifying the efficiency properties of creditors' liquidation rights, see Hart and Moore (1998).

[18] If the going concern retains more value still, E can refinance and pay off VC. If VC is the party positioned to choose a^* the result is suboptimal.

6.5.2. *Debt, Preferred, or Common?*

The foregoing discussion gives rise to two further questions about venture capital contracts: why preferred stock and not debt? And, why preferred and not common stock? To put the former question is to note that the periodic payment properties of noncumulative convertible preferred can be mimicked in part with a convertible income bond.[19] Such a security would import the same high-powered incentives to the E as does convertible preferred. Where the preferred holder gets an intermediate term right to put the stock back to the issuer, the convertible bondholder gets the substance of that right with intermediate term maturity. Either way, VC gets a liquidation preference which has the effect of raising the cost to E of poor performance. Packaging this convertible senior security as debt would carry two additional benefits for VC: a higher and harder bankruptcy priority and a chance for a tax deduction on interest payments.

But American corporate law holds out a significant disincentive to the packaging of venture capital participations as debt. VCs commonly do more than monitor their investments and facilitate the hiring of professional managers by their portfolio companies. They often control or influence the decision to replace the CEO and other key business decisions. To the extent that the transaction structure holds out the prospect of significant VC input in management, including the power to specify business results, VC should act in the capacity of an equity securityholder at the time it exercises such control power. A debtholder who exercises control power in that capacity loses its limited liability status, and could be personally liable to other creditors of the firm or even to E in the event its management decisions work out badly.[20] Debtholders can influence control while retaining limited liability only indirectly, by specifying default events *ex ante* in negative covenants. In order to structure meaningful control by a debtholder, then, a basis of contractible subject matter is needed. In the alternative, a contingent control transfer to a debtholder can be effected without risk of unlimited liability on the scenario posed by the CTM—default, bankruptcy, emergence with VC in charge, presumably as the holder of all of the equity of a reorganized firm. But as noted above, bankruptcy costs make this a second-best alternative in real world planning.

The preferred/common stock choice turns in part on priorities. In the CTM, E takes periodic return in salary t. If VC takes its position in common stock and E also holds some common as an incentive device, VC and E would share what is left of r at $t = 2$ pro rata, which would mean a double dip for E. If VC holds stock with an income preference, VC takes $r - t$, to the extent of the preference and any common stock held by E would pay in addition to t only to the extent that VC's preference is satisfied fully. More generally, in

---

[19] Kaplan and Stromberg (2001: 18) report that preferred dividends are cumulative in only 46 per cent of the cases. This suggests that periodic income is not a primary concern here.

[20] The classic case, Martin v. Peyton, 246 N.Y. 213, 158 N.E. 77 (1927), concerns a loan to a partnership. The liability of bank lenders to small businesses is the subject of leading cases in recent years. See, for example, K.M.C. Co. v. Irving Trust Co., 757 F.2d 752 (6th Cir. 1985); State Nat'l Bank of El Paso v. Farah Mfg. Co., 678 S.w. 2D 661 (Tex. Ct. App. 1984). There is of course a way to deflect this risk for a debt holding VC with control power. If the VC is a human being one forms a wholly owned shell corporation or limited liability company to hold the debt; if the VC is a corporation it forms a shell wholly owned subsidiary. Both steps are costly, and there remains a residual risk of veil piercing.

small business planning, preferred and debt are standard tools for compensating financial participants where the entrepreneurs take much of their share of free cash flows in the form of salary payments. In addition, on downside scenarios preferred means a priority to whatever is left in liquidation.[21] Tax concerns play an important role as well. The overhang of preferred rights lowers the value of the common for tax purposes, permitting E to buy the common stock at low prices without reporting taxable income on the differential between the amount paid and the greater amount paid by VC (Sahlman 1990: 510). Finally, there is an exogenous regulatory concern. Regulated institutional investors participating in the venture capital partnership, such as insurance companies, will prefer to take their equity in the form of convertible senior securities so as to satisfy legal constraints on the amount of common stock in their investment portfolios.

6.5.3. *Shared Control*

We turn now to the CTM's assumption that even though a^* cannot be specified in advance, the parties can, to the extent they deem s reliable, contract *ex ante* to change control for the purpose of making the selection of a^* more likely. This set up is descriptive of innumerable instances in practice. Financial contracts routinely utilize such imperfect but verifiable signals. Such real world manifestations of s are the accounting and performance data utilized in the drafting of representations, closing conditions, covenants, and default triggers. Indeed, 15 per cent of the cases in Kaplan and Stromberg's sample specify boardroom control transfers to VC based on financial or accounting performances.

More difficult contracting problems arise where governance intervention needs to be specified but s is unreliable, unverifiable, or there is no s. If we stay within the confines of the CTM, the lack of s means that there is nothing to trigger a transfer of control and VC has to let the investment ride until $t = 2$. At that point, given an a_b state, VC's dividend and liquidation priorities assume paramount importance, but the pay-off may be suboptimal.

Let us abandon the CTM's hard assumptions respecting payouts to E and VC and the choice of action a, and instead assume that the choice among a_g and a_b on θ_g and θ_b states depends on complex and probabilistic factors so that there is no clear-cut connection between E or VC control and the optimal choice of a. Where in the model, it is always optimal to leave E in charge on θ_g states, now it is plausible to suggest that VC could effect $a^*\theta_g$ simply by removing E and undertaking a search for a substitute a chief executive better suited to grappling with the problems at hand and bringing about a^*. But because the decision that a substitute is better fitted to effect $a^*\theta_g$ follows from a complex business judgment, there may be no basis with which to provide for this control allocation *ex ante*. The same sort of problem could arise in an θ_b state where correction remains possible, with the new CEO being charged with the job of turning the operation around. Such

---

[21] It is noted that one could presumably replicate the preferred stock outcome by placing in VC combination of common stock and debt. This would, however, mean a process burden on VC in the event of exercise of control to make it clear that it acted in the capacity of a common stockholder. A residual litigation risk would endure even so.

scenarios are better suited to treatment through the operation of a contractually instituted governance process than through advance contractual specification of a clear-cut outcome.

Joint control suggests itself as a solution in these cases.[22] In Aghion and Bolton's CTM, joint control is defined very narrowly to mean that either E and VC both agree, or that in the event of disagreement, E will make a one-time take it or leave it offer to VC as to choice of a; in the event that VC refuses the offer, deadlock results and the returns to both parties are 0. Such a joint control set-up means that hold-ups are a possibility in every case. As a result, in Aghion and Bolton's model, joint control always is dominated by unilateral or contingent control (Aghion and Bolton 1992: 486).

But joint control is not dominated if we change the CTM's assumptions. Contingent control dominates only because the model assumes a reliable s. Without a reliable s, the negotiating parties would have a high-powered incentive to find a way to contract around the deadlock the model assumes. It comes as no surprise that any number of such devices show up in real world business planning practice. For example, VC could contract for a seat on the board of directors.[23] This ameliorates information asymmetries and imports voice without the power to direct results—VC can attempt to influence E without having a power to specify the choice of a. Alternatively, the parties could contract for 50–50 boardroom representation and interpolate a deadlock breaker, such as arbitration. Since this would be contingent on their failure to agree, it would not depend on the identification of an s. Such sharing arrangements are common in the world of contracts among equity participants in small businesses. Although not perfect, such solutions do amount to a plausible second best given the absence of a contractible contingency clearly indicating that control should be vested in E or VC.

With this we return to Kaplan and Stromberg's results and the practice of shared control in venture capital start-ups. The contracting pattern suggests an interesting modification of the CTM's set-up. As noted, contracts providing for contingent control transfer to the VC upon an s specified in advance are a small minority. But this point also confirms the theoretical prediction that contracts in this context will manifest strategies for dealing with noncontractible subject matter.[24] The small number of such provisions bespeaks a judgment that the available signals are unreliable. It appears that both the VC and E prefer to grapple with unverifiable facts attending θ_b states in the black box of the boardroom.

During the noncontractible period between $t = 0$ and $t = 2$, VC, instead of waiting for a verifiable signal, takes a noncontrolling position inside the firm's boardroom. In the boardroom there are three directors, E, VC, and a neutral third actor selected by both. So long as the three agree, control is shared. In the event of disagreement between VC and E,

---

[22] Kirilenko (2001) offers a formal model of joint control in venture capital contexts in which control is a continuous variable to be adjusted through different contract provisions. This model, by opening up control to a range, moves the formal theory of the firm closer to Kaplan and Stromberg's real world picture. It does not, however, specify any direct connections between its formal terms and real world institutions.

[23] Venture capital transactions tend to include a separate 'Investor Rights Agreement' entered into between the issuer and individual purchasers of preferred. These contracts customarily include a right attend board meetings in a non-voting capacity (Dauchy 2000: 300).

[24] The practitioner literature shows that this is effected by a shareholder voting agreement pursuant to which, in the event that performance targets are not met, E promises to vote for additional directors nominated by VC (Dauchy 2000: 243).

the mutually selected third director holds the balance of power. By hypothesis, VC and *E* will compete to influence the third director. Suppose performance has been mediocre and VC would like to remove and replace *E* as CEO. If the third director is motivated to enhance firm value and VC persuades the third director that the move is necessary for achievement of an θ_g state, *E* is out. At the same time, *E* also has access the third director and can state a defence.[25]

Compare the more limited menu of control transfer devices in the CTM. There, if there is no transfer by advance specification but performance incentives turn out to be dysfunctional, you contract into the optimal performance state only by means of a Coasian bribe. Interestingly, this item is always on the real world menu. Nothing stops a VC in the tripartite shared control arrangement from making a similar bribe to either the third director or *E*. Nor does anything stop the third director from initiating this discussion and holding out for a side payment. But a persuasive substantive pitch to the third director costs VC less than a bribe. By hypothesis, then, the ideal third director has a strong reputational interest in being seen as an impartial, expert maker of good-faith business judgments who pursues firm value from a neutral stance and is impervious to Coasian bribes. This lets the firm reach a^* without barriers stemming from *ex ante* wealth endowments or insufficient expected value of the project in θ_b. For the reputational constraint to work, the third director would have to be an actor known in a business community common to both *E* and VC. Here, as in Gilson and Black's description, the real world pattern of close geographic proximity between *E* and VC would be facilitative: The third director should also live in the neighbourhood. Similar reputational concerns may constrain the VC before forming an alliance with the third director against *E*. The VC who engineers too many *E* replacements or, worse, abuses its power can be shut out of future deals with the best *E*s.

6.5.4. *Implications*

The shared control structure's real world dominance over the alternative of VC control or hardwired control transfers suggests that *E*s have significant but not decisive bargaining power, presumably because VCs compete to finance the most promising entrepreneurs. It also suggests that an arrangement positioning cooperation in the shadow of a threatened control transfer has productivity advantages. Certainly, there is evidence of significant CEO turnover in the venture capital field.[26] Thus, to the extent the venture capital interest can be protected satisfactorily without outright boardroom control, one would expect shared control to dominate over venture capitalist control.

A recent story in the business press reinforces this description of shared control in venture capital portfolio companies. Robert E. Davoli, a VC with a notable number of wildly successful high-technology investments in the years preceding 2000, is also known

---

[25] Halloran *et al.* (2000: 8–23) offers a comparison venture capital form, which provides for VC control on a three out of five basis.

[26] Gompers and Lerner (2000: 176–7) report turnover in 40 out of 220 venture capital rounds in their data set. Hannan *et al.* (1996) finds that in the first twenty months following a firm's initial round of venture capital finance, 20 per cent firms replace *E* with a non-founder CEO; the percentage goes up to 40 after forty months and 80 after eighty months.

for an aggressive posture respecting the tenure of his *E*s. He has fired six of twenty-four in a five-year period. The result is a reputation as an impatient VC, in contrast to the more passive postures of the 'instant' VCs who, chasing the trend, entered the business in the late 1990s. This is said to make Davoli a throw-back to the heroic days of venture capital in the 1960s, when pioneers like Arthur Rock and Thomas J. Perkins took a hands-on role. Meanwhile, Davoli is said to be subject to a constraint when attacking an *E* for missing a performance target. He must first mobilize the board.

Even as this story describes a world of shared control, it suggests caution with the foregoing account. First, venture capital arrangements may have evolved in history, with VC control being the practice in an early phase and shared control becoming more prominent as more capital came to pursue fewer deals with a more sophisticated generation of *E*s. Second, shared control may mean different things in different portfolio companies. Many factors can come to bear when the third director is selected. VC is likely to have the more extensive network of potential candidates. Information asymmetries and differentials in bargaining power and skill could mean that the 'independent' third director is highly susceptible to the influence of the VC (or, as seems less likely, to the influence of *E*). If negotiations work systematically to favour VC influence, the real world of shared control may not be materially dissimilar from that of the standard picture of VC control.

Consider in this regard a technical point respecting the control sharing mechanism. As a matter of contract planning, it is never enough for *E* and VC to agree to agree on the third director. One must also provide for the possibility that *E* and VC might fail to agree on a candidate.[27] Without a deadlock-breaking arrangement at the selection stage, a board of two can emerge and make costly deadlock a possibility. The standard close corporation drafting solution is to provide for the intervention of a neutral arbitrator at this point.[28] The legal literature suggests that a low-cost but somewhat arbitrary alternative approach is utilized in some venture capital deals. Under this, the charter provides that *E*'s class of stock elects one director, VC's class of stock elects one director, and the third director is elected by all the stock, voting as a single class (Duchy 2000: 316). Assuming that each of *E* and VC each have one vote per share and do not hold exactly the same number of shares, the result in a case of disagreement is that the winning third-seat candidate will be nominated by the actor with the larger absolute number of shares. Absent some other arrangement constraining the exercise of voting power, this means that in the event of disagreement, the party with the share voting majority controls all significant firm decisions. According to Kaplan and Strömberg's numbers, this contracting solution favours the VC in the majority of cases.

We have assayed the dynamics of shared control without asking a fundamental question: Why shared control in most cases, full VC control in a significant minority of cases, and full *E* control in a smaller minority of cases? What factors distinguish the three classes of transaction? A line of theoretical economics addresses these questions. Thomas Hellmann (1998: 58) focuses on bargaining power and productivity variables. He asks why *E* would surrender control in the first place, since surrender of control creates the possibility that

[27] One also needs to control the size of the board.
[28] See Ringling Bros.-Barnum & Bailey Combined Shows v. Ringling, 53 A.2d 441 (Del. 1947).

at some point after start-up VC will terminate E as chief executive officer and substitute a professional manager. If VC always has all the bargaining power, the question is easily answered—E has no other way to access capital. But, notes Hellmann, a puzzle arises in a world where Es can access alternative (and more passive) sources of capital. Alternatively, an E with an attractive-looking project acquires bargaining power when multiple VC's compete for the opportunity to participate. In Hellmann's model, VC control is more likely and replacement of E more frequent where professional management substitutes add value, Es tend to be unproductive, Es derive low private benefits from control, and VCs have greater bargaining power (Hellmann 1998: 60). By extension, we should expect to see greater control rights in VC in transactions holding out greater potential information asymmetries. Finally, Kirilenko offers an incomplete contracts model which shows that more control comes to VC with higher degrees of adverse selection. In this model, as control is surrendered to VC, E can be expected to take a give-back in the form of more advantageous financial terms.

6.6. CONCLUSION

This chapter's choice of incomplete contracts economics to describe venture capital contracts has normative implications. The economics suggest that *ex post* Coasian bargaining is not a vehicle well-suited to optimal incentive alignment in corporations. Accordingly, when governance disputes break out, a set of instructions needs to come from somewhere. The economics also suggest a zone of preference for shared control and process over advance specification. Accordingly, instructions will not always come in the form of advance contract specifications and the legal system will be on call to provide third party umpires.

On the matter of judicial umpiring, standard law and economics (Macey 1991) joins the Delaware courts[29] to counsel against intervention to protect relational victims on the theory that transacting parties should be encouraged to specify everything in advance in contracts. Alternatively, when the interests of common and senior holders conflict, law and economics again joins with Delaware in presuming in favour of the common. Here the theory is that short of an extreme distress situation, value is maximized when management decisions are aligned with the interests of the residual risk-holder.

The incomplete contracts economics presented in this chapter suggests a more circumspect approach. Where subject matter is non-contractible, a blanket presumption against *ex post* intervention on the grounds of forced contract is incoherent. Furthermore, the CTM shows that efficient results and the interests of senior securityholders are aligned in a larger set of cases than previously supposed. When disputes between venture capitalists and entrepreneurs come to court, a rote presumption favouring the common stockholder is not defensible on efficiency grounds.

---

[29] See Equity-Linked Investors, L.P. v. Adams, 705 A.2d 1040 (Del.Ch. 1997); Dalton v. American Investment Co., 490 A.2d 574 (Del. Ch. 1985); Jedwab v. MGM Grand Hotels, Inc., 509 A.2d 584 (Del. 1986).

References

Aghion, P. and Bolton, P. (1992), 'An incomplete contracts approach to financial contracting', *Review of Economic Studies* 59, 473–94.

Altman, E. (1984), 'A further empirical investigation of the bankruptcy cost question', *Journal of Finance* 39, 1067–89.

Anderlini, L. and Felli, L. (1994), 'Incomplete written contracts: indescribable states of nature', *Quarterly Journal of Economics* 109, 1085–124.

Bratton, W. W. (1997), 'Dividends, non-contractibility, and corporate law', *Cardozo Law Review* 19, 409–74.

Coffee, J. C. (1989), 'The mandatory enabling balance in corporate law: an essay on the judicial role', *Columbia Law Review* 89, 1618–91.

Cumming, D. J. (2000), 'The convertible preferred equity puzzle in venture capital finance', Working paper, University of Alberta.

—— and MacIntosh, J. G. (2001), 'The extent of venture capital exits: evidence from Canada and the United States', Working paper, University of Toronto.

Dauchy, C. E. (2000), 'Venture capital financings', in *Practicing Law Institute, Doing Deals*, New York: Practicing Law Institute.

Dewatripont, M. and Tirole, J. (1994), 'A theory of debt and equity: diversity of shareholders and manager-shareholder congruence', *Quarterly Journal of Economics* 109, 1027–54.

Easterbrook, F. H. and Fischel, D. R. (1993), 'Contract and fiduciary duty', *Journal of Law and Economics* 36, 425–46.

Gompers, P. and Lerner, J. (2000), *The Venture Capital Cycle*, Cambridge, MA: MIT Press.

—— and —— (2001), 'The venture capital revolution', *Journal of Economic Perspectives* 15, 145–64.

Grossman, S. and Hart, O. (1986), 'Costs and benefits of ownership: a theory of vertical and lateral integration', *Journal of Political Economy* 94, 691–719.

Halloran, M. J., Benton, L. F., Gunderson, R. V., Kearney, K. L., and de Calva, J. (2000), *Venture Capital and Public Offering Negotiation*, 3rd edn., Englewood Cliffs, NJ: Aspen Law and Business.

Hannan, M. T., Burton, M. D., and Barron, J. N. (1996), 'Inertia and change in early years: employment relations in young high-technology firms', *Industrial and Corporate Change* 5, 503–36.

Hart, O. (1996), 'Firms, contracts, and financial structure', *Journal of Finance* 51, 1555–8.

—— and Moore, J. (1988), 'Incomplete contracts and renegotiation', *Econometrica* 56, 755–85.

—— and —— (1998), 'Default and renegotiation: a dynamic model of debt,' *Quarterly Journal of Economics* 113, 1–41.

—— and —— (1999), 'Foundations of incomplete contracts', *Review of Economic Studies* 66, 115–38.

Hellman, T. (1998), 'The allocation of control rights in venture capital contracts', *RAND Journal of Economics* 29, 57–76.

Holmstrom, B. and Milgrom, P. R. (1992), 'Multitask principal–agent analyses: incentive contracts, asset ownership, and job design', *Journal of Law, Economics, and Organization* 7, 24–52.

John, A. B. (2000), 'How a VC does it', *Business Week*, July 24, 97–104.

Kaplan, S. and Stromberg, P. (2001), 'Financial contracting theory meets the real world: an empirical analysis of venture capital contracts', Working paper, Graduate School of Business, University of Chicago.

Kirilenko, A. A. (2001), 'Valuation and control in venture finance', *Journal of Finance* 56, 565–87.

Klausner, M. and Litvak, K. (2001), 'What economists have taught us about venture capital contracting', Working paper, Stanford Law School.

Macey, J. R. (1991), 'An economic analysis of the various rationales for making shareholders the exclusive beneficiaries of corporate fiduciary duties', *Stetson Law Review* 21, 23–44.

Maskin, E. and Tirole, J. (1999), 'Unforeseen contingencies and incomplete contracts', *Review of Economic Studies* 66, 83–114.

Sahlman, W. A. (1990), 'The structure and governance of venture capital organizations', *Journal of Financial Economics* 27, 473–521.

Trester, J. J. (1998), 'Venture capital contracting under asymmetric information', *Journal of Banking and Finance* 22, 675–99.

PART II

INNOVATION, LAW, AND FINANCE

7

Law, Innovation, and Finance

JOHN ARMOUR

7.1. INTRODUCTION

Venture capital is used to finance a small minority of companies with the potential and ambition to grow rapidly. It is thought to be of disproportionate importance in stimulating innovation. Start-up companies with new business ideas and high-growth potential, but lacking liquid assets, may be unable to obtain bank finance because of the high risk they present. Venture capital involves the supply of equity finance—so the investor shares in the benefits of high growth—alongside 'hands-on' governance so as to assist in bringing about the success of such companies.

Venture capital investment differs widely from country to country, both in terms of the aggregate sums invested and the way in which the venture capitalists (VCs) structure their relations with investee companies. In keeping with the comparative program of much recent corporate finance scholarship, how to account for these differences is an important question for positive social science. It is also a question that has considerable interest for policymakers. A number of recent national and EU initiatives have sought explicitly to encourage innovative firms and venture capital finance. For example, the European Commission's Risk Capital Action Plan (RCAP) is designed to stimulate this type of activity throughout Member States (European Commission 1998, 2000a). The UK Government has set itself the goal of making Britain the 'best place in the world to start and grow a business' (SBS 2001: 3). The stimulation of the market for venture capital will clearly play an important part in this process, and an understanding of the determinants of venture capital investment is of obvious importance in achieving this objective.

This chapter reviews evidence about the extent to which law and lawyers 'matter' for venture capital investment. As such, it relates both to the policy debate about financing innovative firms and more generally to the comparative finance literature that has investigated the extent to which law may be one of the determinants of differing patterns of corporate finance across various countries. The review is organized around the idea that law may 'matter' in a variety of ways for corporate finance. The starting point is a model of what venture capital investment involves, derived from empirical studies in the USA.

The VC is a financial intermediary, who raises funds from end-investors which are then used to finance small entrepreneurial firms. The contracts between the VC and the investee firms have complex terms which can be understood as responses to agency problems inherent in the financing relationship. The first way in which laws may 'matter' is by affecting the way in which the practice of venture capital investment is structured—most obviously, in the terms of the contracts used. Empirical studies of the contracting practices of VCs show clear differences between national practices, and it is plausible that some at least of these may be driven by differences in the legal regimes. Most obviously, these might arise due to mandatory legal rules—for example, local tax laws—which distort choices of inframarginal investors in favour of a particular type of financial contract.

A related possibility is that the variety in contracting practices is partly caused by learning externalities in the market for contract terms. These could arise wherever the costs of contract drafting make it economic to rely on 'standard forms' which are customized in individual cases. Once a particular form has been used, it may be cheaper for lawyers negotiating a similar transaction simply to apply the terms used the first time rather than start again from scratch. As a given set of terms is used over and over, familiarity with its contents will spread, in time becoming acquired by judges called upon to decide its meaning. These factors can give rise to situations where contract terms are chosen not for their intrinsic merit, but simply because the learning and network costs of using an 'unusual' term would outweigh the benefits. Term choice is then said to be 'path dependent', because what determines the outcome is not current relative usefulness, but the historical reasons for the original selection. Empirical studies show that venture capital contracts are written by lawyers who customize and apply standard terms. Path dependencies created by the use of such standards might give rise to differences in contracting practices between legal systems. The meaning of contract terms is likely only to arise for consideration by lawyers qualified in the jurisdiction of their governing law, and hence learning and network benefits are likely to be limited to a particular jurisdiction—implying differences in terms used from one legal system to another, but less so within a given legal system.

Laws may also 'matter' for the aggregate levels of venture capital investment. At the margins, distortions introduced by mandatory rules can be expected to lead to more or less investment in aggregate. Such rules may affect either investors' willingness to supply venture capital finance, or entrepreneurs' demand for such finance. From a policy perspective, demand-side factors such as the taxation of entrepreneurs' returns or the potential consequences of personal bankruptcy are probably much more important for stimulating innovative businesses than factors which affect the supply-side. This is because investors' funds can travel across borders much more readily than can entrepreneurs. Thus if domestic laws—for example, pension fund regulations—inhibit domestic investors, entrepreneurs may still be able to raise finance from overseas investors whose jurisdictions do not impose such restrictions. However, overseas investors from such 'supply friendly' jurisdictions will not invest in domestic firms unless there is demand from local entrepreneurs. Thus for policymakers seeking to foster innovative firms, measures which stimulate demand are likely to produce a greater return on reform energies than changes designed to foster supply.

The rest of the chapter is structured as follows. Section 7.2 considers the way in which law and legal institutions may affect the content of the VC portfolio company relation.

It is striking that the financial contracts used in US venture capital investment agreements seem to be uniquely homogeneous, almost all making use of convertible preferred stock, whereas in other countries for which data are available terms tend to be much more diverse. This does not appear to be driven by any evolution towards the 'best' terms in the USA, but rather is likely to be the result of aspects of US law, and possibly learning externalities generated amongst the close-knit community of venture capital lawyers.

Section 7.3 then describes how the incidence of venture capital finance differs across countries. Consideration is paid in Section 7.4 to a range of mandatory rules of law which may affect the incidence of venture capital finance. In each case, the enquiry proceeds first by hypothesizing how the relevant rules may affect the practice of venture capital investment as described in the model. These are categorized according to whether the posited effect will be on the supply of venture capital— that is willingness to invest—or the demand—i.e. the creation of entrepreneurial projects or the attractiveness of venture capital finance. After the hypotheses are identified, relevant evidence is reviewed and UK developments are considered. Section 7.5 considers the impact of cross-border movements of funds, and in so doing seeks to sort the potentially relevant variables into some sort of hierarchy to assist a policymaker in deciding which may be the most urgent issues to address. Section 7.6 is a brief conclusion.

7.2. HOW MIGHT LAW AFFECT THE PRACTICE OF VENTURE CAPITAL INVESTMENT?

7.2.1. *Terms in Venture Capital Investment Agreements*

'Start-up' firms developing new technologies commonly do not generate steady cash flows which can be used to make interest payments on debt. By contrast, their cash flows are often negative, with large sums being 'burnt' in order first to develop a product and second to grow the market. This leads to a long lag-time before any repayment to investors can be made. Furthermore, the extreme uncertainty associated with developing new technologies makes it difficult to predict how much return (if any) will be generated. These factors make debt investment unsuitable, as the 'upside' returns are fixed by the rate of interest charged (Bank of England 2001), and at very high interest rates an 'adverse selection' problem would emerge (Stiglitz and Weiss 1981). A second problem for start-ups seeking debt finance is that many lack liquid assets. The key feature of debt that allows the financial contract to work is the ability of the financier to take control of the assets should default occur which makes credible their threat to enforce in bad states (Hart 1995). However, the value (if any) of a start-up firm will inhere in the ideas—the 'human capital' of the entrepreneur, and their opportunities for growth, which are not amenable to enforcement by an investor.

Through their specialist knowledge, VCs are able to add value through 'active monitoring' of the firm's business operation, as well as financial backing (Black and Gilson 1998). The terms on which VCs are willing to invest are thought by financial economists to play a crucial role in maximizing the benefits of the investment.[1] They respond to the same information asymmetry concerns as debt contracts, but are adapted to the context of the start-up firm with few liquid assets. The terms used in US investment agreements have been investigated empirically (Sahlman 1990; Kaplan and Stromberg 2000), and their structure is now fairly well understood.

Finance is not advanced all at once, but rather is 'staged'. Subsequent 'rounds' of finance may not be available, or only on considerably more expensive terms, if performance targets are not met in the interim. This process gives the VC control rights over the decision whether or not to continue the project. Instead of pulling assets out of a firm (default on debt) the VC simply refuses to put more assets in. In either case, the denial of assets leads to closure of the firm's business.

Venture capitalists typically take preferred shares, usually convertible on demand into ordinary shares, whereas the entrepreneur takes 'plain' ordinary shares. Conversion by the VC will of course remove the liquidation preference, and so will only be done where the portfolio company is doing well. Investment agreements usually provide for automatic conversion on a successful IPO.

Investment agreements usually also provide for a range of control rights to be given to the VC. The VC can arrange for their preferred shares to carry enhanced voting rights in the general meeting, usually by providing that they can be voted on an 'as-converted' basis. If a controlling stake is accorded, this will entitle them to remove the members of the board of directors. The VC can demand entitlements to appoint directors to the board.

It is impossible for the entrepreneur to alienate her human capital. However, by making greater cash flow rights vest over time, the entrepreneur can be 'locked in' to the business. This is typically achieved through option vesting schemes, whereby the executives are given options to purchase stock provided that they remain with the firm for a fixed period. Furthermore, entrepreneurs usually also sign covenants not to compete, which apply should they cease to work for the firm.

Whilst a good deal is known about the standard terms used in US venture capital investment agreements, many more questions have yet to be answered. One particularly troublesome issue is that the theoretical explanations do not fully explain why convertible preferred stock appears to be the financial contract of choice. The indeterminacy has two aspects. On the one hand, the liquidation priority it affords is unlikely to be of much value to VCs, for the same reason as debt finance is inappropriate. A typical start-up firm will have few liquid assets and therefore the returns from liquidation, if the 'downside' outcome eventuates, will be small. Thus it is unclear why the venture capitalist does not simply take ordinary stock (Bratton, Chapter 6, this volume; Gilson and Schizer 2002). On the other hand, in cases where the assets do have some downside value and liquidation priority may be worth taking, theoretical accounts of the value of convertibility do not distinguish between convertible debt and preferred equity (e.g. Cornelli and Yosha 1997; Repullo and Suarez 1998; Hellmann, Chapter 3, this volume; Schmidt 2001). Thus we

---

[1] For reviews of the extensive literature on venture capital investment contracts, see Gompers and Lerner (2001), Hart (2001), and Klausner and Litvak (2001).

might expect in some cases to see convertible debt, and in others ordinary equity. Yet convertible preferred is the instrument of choice in the USA.

A number of studies have also been done of the financial contracts employed in venture capital investments outside the USA. None of these found convertible preferred stock to be ubiquitous in the same way. Bascha and Walz (2001) found that convertible preferred was only used in a small subset of German venture capital investment agreements, as did Cumming (2000) in respect of Canadian venture capital contracts, and Cumming (2002) in respect of contracts taken from a range of European countries. Furthermore, Cumming (2001) found that US VCs who invested in Canadian start-up companies did not use convertible preferred stock with anything like the frequency observed in their US investments. Rather, each of these studies found a heterogeneous mix of financial instruments were used in their samples—including ordinary shares, preference shares, and convertible debt. The next two subsections consider whether these differences are in whole or in part explicable by reference to varying domestic legal rules, or the practices of lawyers in particular jurisdictions. It seems likely that 'law matters' here in the sense of being able to determine the contents of financial contracts.

7.2.2. *The Role of Law*

There are several possible explanations for the international differences in financial contracts revealed by the empirical literature. Nor are these accounts necessarily mutually exclusive. The first story is that a Darwinian process of 'survival of the fittest' is occurring, whereby terms gradually evolve towards the optimal financial instrument—in this case, the convertible preferred share favoured by US VCs for their domestic investments. The reason that contracting practices in other jurisdictions differ is that their venture capital markets are less mature, and consequently the process of evolution has not yet progressed so far. This theory receives some support from the findings of Bascha and Walz (2001). In their sample, investments made by private venture capital funds employed more convertible instruments and more covenants than those made by public funds, suggesting that the latter were perhaps less incentivized to control the actions of their portfolio companies. However, this theory cannot recover from the problem that there is no satisfactory explanation for the posited superiority of convertible preferred stock over ordinary equity or (as the case may be) convertible debt. Furthermore, the idea that funds in the USA are somehow further along a process of evolutionary development than those in other jurisdictions is flatly contradicted by the findings of Cumming (2001) that US funds do not use convertible preferred stock when investing in Canadian companies. If the Darwinian explanation were right, then it would be precisely these investors we should expect to see leading the dissemination of 'better-adapted' terms.

A second theory suggests that the ubiquity of convertible preferred as the financial contract of choice in the USA is driven by regulatory or institutional constraints, as opposed to its innate efficiency. On this 'law matters' view, the evolution of US terms has been artificially curtailed. The normative implication is that convertible preferred may represent a laggard, as opposed to a leader, in an evolutionary race. Gilson and Schizer (2002) develop a tax-based explanation (first suggested in Sahlman 1990) of the fact that

US VCs rarely take ordinary shares in investee companies. They argue that the entrepreneur will usually take compensation in the form of shares. As start-ups rarely pay dividends, the entrepreneur will be unlikely to see any cash return until he eventually sells these shares, which typically he will not be permitted to do for a number of years. Under the US federal tax regime, the value (at the date he receives them) of the entrepreneur's shares will be taxed as income. The difference between this value and that which he obtains when he sells them will then be taxed—when it is eventually realized—as a capital gain. The entrepreneur will wish to 'finesse' matters so that as much as possible of his return is taxable as a capital gain. This is because marginal rates of CGT are much lower than for income tax, and because CGT is not payable until the realization occurs whereas income tax is payable annually and may create liquidity problems for the entrepreneur. Thus to minimize income tax liability (and thereby increase the portion of his ultimate return which is assessable for CGT), the entrepreneur will wish to attribute as low a valuation as possible to the shares. Yet the entrepreneur will want to attribute as high a value as possible to shares taken by the VC so as to minimize dilution. This difficulty is finessed, for the benefit of the tax authorities, by issuing preferred stock to the VC and ordinary shares to the entrepreneur, each of which can be valued differently.

A complementary explanation is given by Bratton (Chapter 6, this volume) for the non-observance of convertible debt in US investment agreements. This is, he argues, because of fears of lender liability which might accompany a holding of debt. Under US corporate law, lenders who, as VCs do, become involved in making management decisions, may face direct liability to other creditors or even to shareholders should their decisions work out badly. This provides a significant disincentive to combining debt investment with active governance. These explanations could be tested by comparisons with the tax codes of other jurisdictions. In particular, in countries where capital gains tax liability is lower, or more substantial tests as to the valuation of shares are used, then it predicts that convertible preferred shares would be used less frequently, in favour of ordinary stock; and in countries with less stringent lender liability laws, we would expect to see more convertible debt.

The evidence from other jurisdictions is not inconsistent with the predictions of the 'law matters' view. As has been noted, a much wider range of financial contracts are employed in virtually every other jurisdiction that has been studied apart from the USA. To test these theories, it would be necessary to compare the relevant US laws with those in other jurisdictions where convertible preferred stock is not the financial contract of choice. Gilson and Schizer (2002) briefly consider the position in Canada, suggesting that it is unnecessary to create a separate class of stock to enable the manager to have entirety of his compensation assessable for CGT, rather than income tax. This is because the tax code does not treat stock or options received by entrepreneurs as income, and allows their capital gains assessment to be at particularly favourable rates. A similar regime obtains in the UK, where since 1984 employees who are compensated with stock options will thereby incur no liability to income tax and no CGT until exercise, provided that the options were held for a specified period. This favourable treatment has since 1999 been extended in the guise of the 'Enterprise Management Initiative' (EMI), which allows 'small, high-risk' firms to offer options to employees which not only incur no income tax liability, but also no CGT liability until the sale of the shares. Under the UK system, there would appear to be no need for the sort of 'finessing' described by Gilson and Schizer, and hence if their explanation is valid, convertible preferred should not be the financial contract of choice for UK VCs. As yet, good evidence on this question is not available, although anecdotal accounts suggest a plurality of contracts are used.

7.2.3. *The Role of Lawyers*

A third possible explanation for the differences in financial contracts has to do with the role played by lawyers in designing contract terms. As we have seen, the legal structure of venture capital investments is something that is primarily contractual. This implies, therefore, that the lawyers who are involved in the design of the contracts may have a crucial role to play in facilitating venture capital finance. Gilson (1984) posits that, contrary to the popular myth that lawyers simply destroy value through adding an extra layer of costs, business lawyers play the role of 'transaction cost engineers', adding value by structuring transactions in such a way as to facilitate parties' reaching their desired outcomes.

Qualitative studies of the services provided by Silicon Valley law firms suggest that these lawyers at least perceive themselves as offering benefits to their clients—principally high-tech local businesses—which are unavailable elsewhere. An initial study conducted by Friedman *et al.* (1989) revealed that lawyers who advised 'start-ups' provided not only general legal advice, but often also more general business advice, and through their networks were able to broker meetings between their clients and VCs, thus facilitating access to finance. The interviewees also described their approach as being geared towards finding the 'work-around' for any legal problem. They considered their transaction documentation to contain less verbiage than that of their Manhattan contemporaries, with the gaps in these incomplete contracts filled by norms of trust and reciprocity engendered by the fact that they, and both parties to the deal, were members of a relatively close-knit community in which reciprocity and reputation were important.

A more wide-ranging subsequent study elaborated upon these findings. Suchman and Cahill (1996) present interview evidence suggesting that Silicon Valley lawyers help to reduce the uncertainty experienced by participants to high-tech financing deals in a variety of ways. For example, Silicon Valley law firms are allegedly much more willing than their counterparts elsewhere to agree to defer billing until a start-up client has made revenues (effectively bearing the risk that it will never do so) or indeed to bill by taking equity in the client.[2] Furthermore, these firms are willing to give opinion letters to allay venture capital investors' due diligence concerns without undergoing the same level of scrutiny (because of the intense pressure of time) as counterpart firms elsewhere might do. In effect, the result is that the law firm provides insurance to the high-tech client.

Moreover, Silicon Valley law firms are the first 'port of call' for entrepreneurs seeking to obtain venture capital finance. The lawyers can investigate the entrepreneur's quality, and reject those whose business plans are obviously unlikely to get funded. More importantly,

---

[2] This practice, and the ethical concerns to which it gives rise, is considered in more detail by Puri (2001), who explains how it has now spread to other parts of the USA, Canada, and even some English firms.

they can act as a valuable intermediary by channeling clients towards VCs with preferences for particular types of project. In each case, the recommendation of the entrepreneur by a law firm with an interest in maintaining its reputation serves as a 'bond' of the quality of the client.[3]

A third way in which Suchman and Cahill identify lawyers as adding value is through 'coaching' clients about the norms of the venture capital community—what to expect and what not to expect. This can reduce transaction costs by ensuring homogeneity of expectations, thereby minimizing the likelihood that a dispute will break out. However, to the extent that VCs rely on the degree to which a potential investee is aware of community norms as a signal of quality, then coaching by law firms may be detrimental. Rock (Chapter 16, this volume) argues that VCs look favourably on potential investees who 'know the rules of the game' as this signals their seriousness of commitment. However, if law firms coach clients, then this reduces the cost to entrepreneurs of becoming informed, and hence the signal becomes noisier.

Finally, Suchman and Cahill argue that the use of standardized terms helps reduce the transaction costs of negotiation in any individual deal. This seems intuitively plausible: whilst the hypothetical 'best' contract may require significant customization to fit the needs of the parties *ex post*, this may not be the best where *ex ante* negotiation and drafting costs are included in the equation. It may be cheaper simply to use a 'standard form' which is understood by, and therefore acceptable to, both sides. Furthermore, a standard form may be better understood by courts and therefore offer greater benefits of certainty of interpretation.

Of all the apparently beneficial practices identified by Suchman and Cahill, the issue of standardization of terms is perhaps most interesting in the context of venture capital finance. Whilst standardization may generate savings, it is not necessarily optimal. Difficulties could arise where (i) there is a subset of firms for whom a different type of investment agreement would be preferable; or (ii) circumstances change such that the original standard terms are no longer the best 'average' fit to the requirements. In each case, the 'network externalities' which are created by the dominant term—that is, the ease for lawyers of understanding, the ease of judicial interpretation, etc.—and the fact that the full costs of moving from that network must be borne by the first party to do so—will create a powerful impediment to change unless lawyers can coordinate on the design of a new set of terms (Kahan and Klausner 1996, 1997). Furthermore, Bernstein (1995) questions whether the terms are likely not also to be systematically redistributive in favour of VCs, who are repeat players, and away from entrepreneurs, who usually are not.

To conclude this section, it is in principle possible that the ubiquity of convertible preferred stock in US investment agreements could be explicable by reference to the close-knit communities of lawyers advising high-tech firms, and their influence in standardizing contracts. However, not enough is known about contracting practices in other jurisdictions

[3] Bernstein (1995) offers an explanation why lawyers might have comparative advantage over VCs in doing this: for a VC, if screening returns a negative result, there is no pay-off. However, for lawyers, there is a pay-off in a wider range of cases because they can match entrepreneurs to a range of VCs. This explanation, however, ignores the point that a VC's upside pay-off is much larger than of lawyers[1].

to be able to say with any degree of confidence whether or not this is a significant influence. On the evidence presently available, the most promising theoretical explanation for the differences between financial contracts remains that legal rules matter for the terms of parties' contracts.

7.3. HOW DOES THE INCIDENCE OF VENTURE CAPITAL INVESTMENT VARY ACROSS COUNTRIES?

The main sources of data on venture capital investment activity in different countries are the annual reports published by the trade associations, such as the NVCA in the USA and EVCA in Europe. There are some difficulties in comparing the data, because of differences in measurement between associations, and even between years within a particular series of reports (Baygan and Freudenberg 2000). These drawbacks notwithstanding, it is possible to illustrate several important trends by reference only to aggregated data.

First, venture capital investment is cyclical, and Fig. 7.1 shows how early stage funds invested rose during the late 1990s in both Europe and the USA. However, 2001 has seen a sharp decline in US investment, and although comparable data are not available for Europe, it is to be expected that the trend will be similar.

Second, the overall level of venture capital investment varies significantly from country to country. Figure 7.2 shows levels of early-stage investment in 1998 and 2000 for a range of European countries and the USA, divided by GDP so as to allow comparison in relation to the size of the economies. More than twice as much early stage venture capital per million dollars of GDP is invested in the USA than in any European country. Within Europe, the UK in 1998 ranked behind Germany, Finland, Ireland, and, perhaps surprisingly, Belgium and the Netherlands. The UK's position had advanced within Europe by 2000, but in the light of subsequent events this looks to be a 'bubble year', and so it is difficult to know how much reliance to place upon these data. The relative levels of early-stage investment have themselves changed over time. During the mid-1980s, more early-stage venture capital was invested per million dollars of GDP in the UK than in the US, as Graph 3 shows. By the mid-1990s, this trend had been reversed.

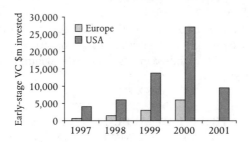

Figure 7.1. *Recent trends.*

Sources: PwC MoneyTree, EVCA.

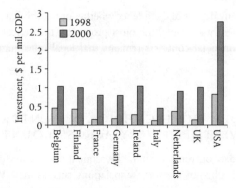

Figure 7.2. *Early-stage VC investment, by country.*
Sources: PwC MoneyTree, EVCA, OECD.

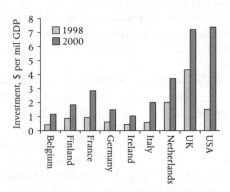

Figure 7.3. *Expansion and buyout private equity investment, by country.*
Sources: PwC MoneyTree, EVCA, OECD.

A third observation is that relative national levels of investment of later-stage private equity finance—that is, expansion and buyouts—are quite different to those of early-stage venture capital. Figure 7.3 shows levels of expansion and buyout finance, adjusted for GDP, between the same range of countries. These data are sufficient to raise some intriguing puzzles. Why is early stage investment made at such a lower rate in countries like the UK than in the USA, or indeed in other European countries? And why have these differences changed over time?

7.4. HOW MIGHT LAW AFFECT THE INCIDENCE OF VENTURE CAPITAL FINANCE?

We now turn to consideration of a range of different legal rules which may affect either the supply of (investors' willingness to provide funds) or the demand for (entrepreneurs' willingness to develop new projects) early-stage venture capital finance. We begin with the most obvious—taxes and subsidies—and then look at the regulation of banks and pension funds, listing rules, organizational law, labour law, and finally insolvency law. In each case, hypotheses are established, relevant empirical literature is reviewed, and the position in the UK is considered.

7.4.1. *Taxes and Subsidies*

The use of tax incentives or subsidies to stimulate venture capital investment is very topical, as it features centrally in many countries' policies towards fostering entrepreneurship. Clearly, these incentives could operate either on the supply or the demand side.

7.4.1.1. *Capital Gains Tax*
Lower rates of capital gains tax could be expected to stimulate either or both the supply of venture capital and its demand, by increasing the returns to both investors and entrepreneurs. Mason and Harrison (2000) conducted a questionnaire study of UK angel investors, and concluded that CGT was a high-order factor influencing their decisionmaking about investments. The usefulness of these findings is diminished by the fact that they necessarily do not include extramarginal investors. Conversely, Gompers and Lerner (2000), in their study of fundraising by US VCs from 1972 to 1994, found that reductions in the rate of CGT increased the level of venture capital funds raised at state, industry, and firm level.[4] However, the changes in CGT did not, as one might expect if the effect were supply-side driven, result in relatively greater commitments of funds from taxable as opposed to tax-exempt investors. Rather, all investors put up proportionately more. This led Gompers and Lerner to conclude that the primary impact of capital gains tax was felt not by investors, but by potential entrepreneurs.

In the UK, CGT was modified in 1998 through the introduction of 'taper relief' for assets held for more than a certain number of years, the scope of which was broadened in 2000. For 'business assets' held for four years or more, the applicable rate of CGT for higher-rate taxpayers falls from 40 to 10 per cent.[5] All shares in unquoted trading companies are classed as business assets. For quoted trading companies, shares held by employees are classed as business assets, as are shares held by outside investors comprising more than 5 per cent of the company's share capital (Inland Revenue 2001*a*: 34–55). This relief can be expected to stimulate both supply and demand for venture capital finance, as it reduces the CGT payable both by outside investors and entrepreneurs. The extension of relief to quoted companies is important, as it ensures that exits after an IPO are not penalized.

---

[4] Specifically, the introduction in 1993 of a relief for 'small business stock' permitted gains on shares held in qualifying corporations for more than five years to be taxed at 14 per cent instead of the standard 28 per cent (IRC Section 1202).
[5] This now compares favourably with the maximum capital gains tax rate applied in the USA for long-term gains (i.e. where the asset has been held for more than twelve months) of 20 per cent. However, non-corporate taxpayers may reduce the tax payable on gains from 'small business stock' to 14 per cent, up to a statutory ceiling (IRC Section 1202).

7.4.1.2. *Subsidies*

Many countries have sought to stimulate investment in venture capital through granting subsidies. These can take various forms, ranging across a spectrum from targeted tax reliefs to investors in venture capital funds, through 'partnership' funds which are partially state-funded and raise private investment as well, and which invest in specific types of firm, to tax relief on stock options and finally direct state investment in high-tech enterprise. We would expect investment tax relief primarily to stimulate supply of finance, direct subsidies and tax relief on stock options to stimulate demand, and 'partnership' funds to do both.

It is undoubtedly the case that appropriately designed subsidy schemes can stimulate the provision of venture capital finance. For example, the US Small Business Investment Company (SBIC) scheme, a federally-guaranteed risk capital form in operation from 1958 to 1969, led to the provision of more than $3bn to small firms, more than three times the money that was privately provided during this period. Furthermore, the more recent Small Business Innovation Research programme (SBIR), in operation from 1983 to 1995, provided as much funding for small, high-tech companies in 1995 as the entire private supply of early stage venture capital in that year (Lerner 1996: 2).

However, careful setting of the eligibility criteria is necessary. The problems of failure to do so are illustrated by the Business Expansion Scheme (BES) set up by the UK government during the 1980s. This gave tax relief on investments in unquoted companies, but had criteria which were too widely drawn to prevent substantial abuse, and little funds were actually raised for the benefit of small high-risk companies at which the scheme was originally aimed (DTI 1999: 30).

A less obvious problem is that inappropriately targeted subsidized schemes may 'crowd out' the private provision of funds. In Canada, Cumming and MacIntosh (2001) provide evidence that the introduction of legislation setting up subsidized Labour-Sponsored Venture Capital Corporations (LSVCCs) actually led to an overall reduction of the supply of venture capital funds. One possible cause is that the LSVCCs' cheaper cost of capital and readily available funds meant that the valuations attributed to private equity investments were driven up, making returns unattractive to private funds.

Another important criterion for assessment is whether the schemes produce good returns. Subsidies are not well spent on funding poor projects. Over the years, various German subsidy schemes have produced very poor investments. Becker and Hellmann (2000) present a fascinating case study of the first German venture capital fund, the WFG. Inexperienced managers and fears by bank co-investors that the fund might become a competitor for their small firm business led to the adoption of very poor contractual protection mechanisms, and the WFG's average internal rate of return was −25 per cent. Even today, Bascha and Walz (2001) document that German public–private partnership funds do not make use of such sophisticated contractual protection as their purely private counterparts.

In contrast, Lerner (1996) provides evidence that investee firms of the publicly funded SBIR programme experienced greater long-run growth (measured in terms of sales and employee numbers) than matching firms which did not receive such investment. Interestingly, however, this outperformance was limited to investee firms which were located in areas where there were substantial levels of private venture capital investment as well.

Public funds invested in companies in areas where venture capital investment was not already prominent did not produce returns better than matched firms in those areas.

A range of tax incentives specifically targeted at venture capital are on offer in the UK. The Venture Capital Trust (VCT) form, introduced in 1993, offers investors relief from both income and capital gains tax on funds invested for more than five years.[6] In 1994, the Enterprise Investment Scheme (EIS) was introduced, providing extensive tax reliefs to encourage individuals to invest in ordinary shares in small, high-risk unquoted companies.[7] The recently launched Enterprise Fund employs the 'partnership fund' model (Bank of England 2001: 67–8). Its first element is the UK High Technology Fund, which invests in venture capital funds that specialize in providing early stage finance to high-tech firms. The second element consists of Regional Venture Capital Funds set up throughout England to specialize in the provision of small-scale equity finance to local firms. In each case, the funds invested are only partially public money, with the majority being privately sourced.

Similarly, the granting of tax relief towards stock options, which as we have seen are widely used as a means of incentivizing employees, has been used in an attempt to stimulate demand for venture capital finance. The Finance Act 1984 provided that stock options would not be subject to income tax provided they were held for a specified period, and if held as part of a formal scheme would create no CGT liability until exercise. A further scheme known as the 'EMI' was introduced in 1999. This allowed 'small, high-risk' firms to offer options to employees which not only incur no income tax liability, but also incur no CGT liability on their exercise, deferring this until the sale of the shares. Furthermore, the four-year holding period for taper relief under CGT is deemed to start at the time of grant, rather than exercise, of the options. The scheme was extended in 2000 to allow an individual company to grant options within the scheme to employees to purchase shares up to a total value of £3m (at the time of grant) (Inland Revenue 2001*b*).

7.4.2. *Regulation of Institutional Investment: The Case of Pension Funds*

Much of the finance raised by VCs in the USA and the UK comes from pension funds, insurance companies, and other collective investment mechanisms. The simple theory here is that regulations which inhibit fund managers from investing in 'high-risk' asset classes such as private equity and venture capital may hinder supply in economies where a large amount of private wealth is tied up in such schemes.

The effect of pension regulation on venture capital investment in the USA has been documented by Gompers and Lerner (1999, 2001). They point to a dramatic rise in fundraising and disbursements by venture capital firms which followed the liberalization

---

[6] More specifically, an individual subscribing for up to £100,000 of shares in a VCT will get income tax relief at 20 per cent on his investment, provided the shares are held for at least five years, and will pay not CGT on the disposal of his VCT shares; furthermore, the VCT itself will not be subject to CGT on the sale of shares it holds in investee companies (SJ Berwin 1997: 5).

[7] The scheme allows an individual to invest up to £100, 000 per annum in unquoted companies, and provided that they are held for more than five years, will confer income tax relief at 20 per cent on those investments and exempt disposals from CGT (SJ Berwin 1997: 6).

of the law. Under the Employee Retirement Income Security Act (ERISA), pension fund trustees are required to select investments according to the standard which a 'prudent man' would apply. It was once thought that certain asset classes—such as private equity—were inherently too risky to be within the rule. However, in 1979 the US Department of Labor explicitly clarified that private equity could fall within the prudent man rule.[8] Over the next three years, there was a huge upsurge in venture capital fundraising, and a much greater proportion came from pension funds. Gompers and Lerner (2000) demonstrate a significant link between the liberalization of the ERISA rules and the supply of venture capital finance, which is robust to controls for a range of other possible influencing factors.[9]

During the late 1990s, there was an absolute decline in private equity investment by UK pension funds. (Myners 2001: 174–5). Thus by 1999, only 0.5 per cent of the assets under management by UK pension funds were held in private equity, compared with 6.6 per cent of US funds. Could the regulation of institutional investment in the UK be a hindrance to the supply of venture capital finance? This issue was considered in a recent Treasury-commissioned review of institutional investment conducted by Paul Myners (The Myners Review 2001), which concluded that inappropriately designed pension regulation could well be impeding inflows of capital to UK private equity.

There have been significant reforms in UK pension regulation in recent years. The Maxwell affair and related scandals in the early 1990s led to the enactment of the Pensions Act 1995, which was designed to tighten safeguards for pension fund beneficiaries. One such mechanism was the introduction of a 'minimum funding requirement' (MFR) for defined-benefit pension schemes. This was designed to ensure that pension funds remained adequately capitalized, protecting employees against the risk of their employer's insolvency and the risk of gross mismanagement by their fund trustees. It operates by requiring that current assets of the fund (marked-to-market value) exceed liabilities by a defined margin. Clearly, with long-term obligations such as pensions the way in which future liabilities are discounted to present value is crucial.

The MFR links liability valuations to the rates of returns on a specific portfolio of assets.[10] Unfortunately this creates an additional risk for pension fund managers who invest in assets outside these classes—that of 'mismatch' between prevailing rates of return on their assets and the 'MFR portfolio' rates which will be used to discount their liabilities. The Myners Review concluded that this had tended to bias decisions about 'asset classes' in favour of those which were included within the MFR portfolio, leading to underinvestment in venture capital.

The Myners Review recommended the abolition of the MFR, a proposal which had already found favour with government. A consultation paper published by the Department

---

[8] Provided that a fund's portfolio is appropriately diversified, and consideration is paid to the risk-reward profile of a particular investment class, then 'riskiness' per se is not a reason to make investment imprudent.

[9] Jeng and Wells (2000) did not find any correlation between the size of the pension funds under management in a particular country and the levels of venture capital finance. This is not, however, surprising, as the study did not control for differing regulation of pension funds in different jurisdictions.

[10] Under the MFR, liabilities to current pensioners are discounted by the current rate of gilts, and liabilities to current employees are discounted at the current rate for equities for their projected remaining time in employment, and at the rate for gilts for the expected period for which they will be pension recipients.

of Work and Pensions in September 2001, The Minimum Funding Requirement: The Next Stage of Reform, explains plans to scrap the MFR. Also recommended by Myners was the introduction of a Cadbury-style 'voluntary' regime of transparency and disclosure, with pension trustees being required annually to explain asset allocation decisions, or give reasons for not so doing. It was argued that this would generate more communication between managers and trustees on this issue, and also encourage trustees to think more in absolute terms about the assessment of managers' performance.

However, the problem may be reincarnated as the new Financial Reporting Standard (FRS 17) which is to be introduced for the compilation of pension fund balance sheets. Again, this creates a possibility of 'mismatch risk' because assets are marked-to-market, whereas liabilities are discounted using a reference portfolio—in this case the yield on AA-grade bonds. It is thought that this will stimulate demand for bonds and further depress the supply of pension fund money into venture capital.

Pension reform is also on the EU's legislative agenda, under the twin guises of the Financial Services Action Plan (FSAP) and the RCAP. Under the RCAP, the European Commission is seeking to promote investment in, and employment and growth by, high-tech SMEs throughout Europe. A key facet of the strategy is linked to the FSAP: the liberalization of pension fund rules will, it is hoped, facilitate the supply of funds into venture capital finance. The FSAP, in a bid to enhance the performance of European pension funds, proposes to introduce a pan-European standard of prudential pension regulation based on a 'prudent person' standard. Under this approach, the trustee is given discretion to select the appropriate mix of investments, according to the stand-ard of prudence, based upon requirements of risk and return, liquidity, etc. specific to the fund in question (European Commission 2000b). At present, many European coun-tries mandate that pension trustees invest according to quantitative lists defining the mix of investments which trustees must make. However, historical returns on pension assets in countries adopting the prudent person standard have been much higher than those in other European jurisdictions which have adopted a quantitative list approach (Bolkestein 2000).

The introduction of a pan-European prudent person standard would undoubtedly increase the supply of funds available for investment in VC. In many jurisdictions, pension trustees are simply prohibited by the scope of the 'legal list' according to which they must invest from putting funds into risk capital. Under the proposed reforms, this would be legitimate—even desirable—provided that the overall portfolio balance of risk and returns was appropriate. However, the reforms may yet be modified in a way which will be much less likely to stimulate the supply of venture capital finance. Following dissent from various Member States whose prudential pension regulation schemes currently adopt a quantitative approach, the Spanish Presidency has suggested that a compromise standard, dubbed 'prudent person plus' might be adopted instead. Whilst the details of the proposal have not been made clear, the fear is that it may involve quantitative restrictions of some type, especially on the level of high-risk investments such as venture capital and private equity. Because of the pan-European effect of any Directive, this would be binding on the UK and therefore might amount to a net retrograde step from the current position (*Financial Times* 2002).

7.4.3. *Organizational Law*

Organizational law may affect the incidence of venture capital finance on both the supply and the demand side. On the supply side, the impact will be felt through the design of business organizations used by VCs to structure their funds. On the demand side, it will be through the organizational structures available to entrepreneurs seeking to incorporate their businesses.

7.4.3.1. *Supply Side: Limited Partnerships*
The standard organizational form used by VCs in the USA is the limited partnership (Gompers and Lerner 1999: 9–10). The VC himself is a general partner, and is exposed to unlimited personal liability, whereas the end-investors are limited partners. This structure is typically adopted because of its tax transparency: profits are for tax purposes allowed to 'pass through' the partnership and are taxed as income in the hands of the end-investors. This allows tax-exempt investors such as pension funds to invest alongside others, without losing their privileged status. In order to minimize the costs of conflicts of interest between VCs and end-investors, their action space is usually circumscribed by a range of covenants, for example restricting the size of any investment in a given firm, restricting co-investment in portfolio companies by general partners and restricting the fund from investing in particular types of firm (Gompers and Lerner 1999: 29–55). If it is difficult to employ an organizational form which allows for 'pass-through' taxation, then we might expect this to have a negative impact on the supply of venture capital finance, at least by tax-exempt investors.

In the UK, the limited partnership vehicle has also become an important form of organization for VCs (Myners 2001). They are structured under the Limited Partnerships Act 1907. There are two key problems under the current law. First, the maximum number of partners is limited to twenty.[11] This prevents risk-sharing amongst more than 20 investors, forcing parties to set up parallel partnerships which add to organizational complexity (DTI 2001*b*: 4). The rule was introduced by the Joint Stock Companies Act of 1844 in order to 'channel' parties towards incorporation by registration, because of the procedural difficulties encountered in suing a large partnership at the time. Procedural developments in the interim mean that partnerships can now sue and be sued in their own name, and so this rationale no longer exists. The DTI consulted on the removal of the limit in 2001 (DTI 2001*a*), and the government have announced their intention to abolish it (DTI 2001*c*).[12]

Second, the 1907 Act provides that limited partners shall lose the benefit of limited liability if they take part in the management of the partnership business.[13] The Act thus envisages limited partners as purely passive contributors of capital. According to the Myners review (Myners 2001: 168), this can create problems in practice as end-investors usually want some degree of oversight of the business. The 1907 Act does allow for limited partners to inspect the books and 'examine into the state and prospects of the partnership

---

[11] Companies Act 1985 s 716; Limited Partnerships Act 1907 s 4(2).

[12] A special relaxation of rule will apply from 22 March 2002 for limited partnership collective investment schemes authorized under the Financial Services and Markets Act 2000.

[13] Limited Partnerships Act 1907s 6(1).

business and . . . advise with the partners thereon'. However, its precise scope is unclear, particularly as to whether a distinction should be drawn between 'advice' and veto power exercised in respect of covenants.

The structure of limited partnership law is currently under review by the Law Commission. Their recent consultation paper (Law Commission 2001) has proposed the introduction of 'safe harbour' provisions along the lines of those found in Delaware and Jersey limited partnership statutes, which would make it clear that specified actions do not constitute participation in management. Under the proposed rule, participation in 'extraordinary' business decisions would not result in a loss of limited status.[14] Activities falling into this category would be further clarified by a 'safe harbour' list, as including: consulting and advising a general partner on the limited partnership business; investigating or approving accounts; being an employee of the firm or of its general partner; or voting on 'fundamental' business decisions such as an amendment to partnership deed, a change in nature of business activities, conflict of interest transactions between general and limited partners, and resolutions to wind up the partnership.

7.4.3.2. *Supply Side: Private Companies*

Organizational law may also affect venture capital investment at the level of the investee company. Where legal entity structures are excessively rigid and do not adequately facilitate contracting with a concentrated investor—such as a VC—over rights to returns and control in the manner discussed in the preceding sections, this will make the investment less attractive. Although little empirical work has been done on the extent to which these issues do in fact impede venture capital investment, it is possible to identify some key concerns in the theoretical literature.

First, it must be possible for parties to customize corporate constitutions. McCahery and Vermeulen (Chapter 8, this volume) document the problems which Dutch law's mandatory terms concerning the corporate constitution would create for a US-style venture capital contract. Second, the legal treatment of shareholder remedies is crucial. On the one hand, expressly bargained for rights—for example, those held by the VC—should be afforded adequate protection from opportunistic acts which seek subsequently to dilute them (Bratton, Chapter 6, this volume). On the other hand, the too-ready availability of a 'minority oppression' remedy in circumstances other than where parties have expressly bargained for protection can serve to undermine the investment process, by weakening non-legal governance mechanisms to which the parties might otherwise turn (Rock and Wachter 1999). Third, if an IPO is desired as an exit mechanism, organizational law should not place impediments in the way of the firm's subsequent listing. In the USA, it is common for start-up firms to make use of the public corporation form, notwithstanding that these are less flexible than forms designed specifically for small businesses, such as partnerships and LLCs (Bankman 1994). It is thought that this is due first to investors'

---

[14] The scope of the proposed safe harbour would draw on the distinction between 'ordinary' and 'extraordinary' business matters which is already found in the default management provisions of the 1907 Act (Law Commission 2001: s 6(5)). Ordinary business decisions may be decided upon by a majority of general partners, it being implicit that 'extraordinary' decisions require the consent of all partners.

greater familiarity with the public company statutes, and second to certain tax advantages which are available to corporations but which are not to other entities—for example, the relief on CGT granted to holders of 'small business stock' (Steel, undated).[15]

In the UK, a range of mandatory rules of company law may create difficulties for VCs. For example, directors' mandatory fiduciary duties to act in the best interests of the company may hinder a VC's nominees from exercising their governance function in situations of partisan conflict between the interests of the VC and of the founders.[16] This duty, which will be breached if consideration is only given to the interests of their VC appointee, cannot be modified through the terms of the articles of association.[17] Comben and Wilkinson (2000: 172), authors of a practitioner manual on the drafting of shareholder agreements, state that the common understandings of parties are usually that a nominee director will act in the interests of his appointor, such that there is a 'considerable divergence between the law and the practical reality'.

Similarly, the 'maintenance of capital' principle, in its statutory incarnation, prohibits a shareholder from claiming damages from the company for breach of a promise to redeem shares, and makes such promises unenforceable by specific performance unless the company is able to pay for the repurchase out of distributable profits.[18] This makes it impossible to replicate the term frequently found in US investment agreements whereby the VC has the right to 'put' his shares to the firm—in effect, the ability to bring about its liquidation on demand. That said, it is possible for the VC to contract for liquidation rights by other means—as, for example, through 'exploding votes' in a winding-up resolution,[19] or through a voting agreement under which the entrepreneur agrees to vote in conformity with the VC on resolutions for liquidation.[20]

7.4.3.3. *Demand Side: The Accessibility of Corporate Forms to Entrepreneurs*

To the extent that the organizational law of a jurisdiction hinders incorporation by small firms, it may restrict the demand for venture capital finance. We would expect that the availability of a limited liability business entity at minimal cost will be a primary concern for entrepreneurs, a point that is borne out by empirical studies which show that limited liability is a primary motivation for incorporation by very small businesses.[21] Furthermore, entrepreneurs will wish to be able to operate such an entity with minimum regulatory costs, such as requirements that they perform a costly annual audit. As documented by Djankov *et al.* (2000), the costs of forming an incorporated business entity vary widely across jurisdictions. Although these authors do not test for this, it might be anticipated that in states where incorporation is easy, demand for venture capital finance would be strongest. However, Djankov *et al.* (2000) indicate that, whilst involving more red tape than some

---

[15] I.R.C. 1202. Cf. Callison (2000), who argues that the relative unattractiveness of the LLC form to venture capital investors is because of its governance attributes, which assume that every investor will be an active participant in all business decisions.

[16] Scottish Co-operative Wholesale Society v. Meyer [1959] AC 324; Kuwait Asia Bank EC v. National Mutual Life Nominees Ltd [1991] AC 187.   [17] Companies Act 1985 s 310.

[18] Companies Act 1985 s 178.   [19] Bushell v. Faith [1970] AC 1099.

[20] See Russell v. Northern Bank Development Corporation Ltd [1992] 1 WLR 588.

[21] Freedman and Godwin (1994) and Hicks *et al.* (1995).

jurisdictions (most notably Canada), the UK is still one of the easiest places in the world to incorporate a business, taking into account all of the regulatory measures which must be complied with.

English company law appears relatively attractive to the entrepreneurial business. A potential problem in many European jurisdictions is the incidence of rules mandating a minimum share capital prior to incorporation, often coupled with a ban on payment for shares other than in cash or with a requirement for costly valuation of non-cash consideration. This may make it more difficult for a wealth-constrained entrepreneur to establish a limited company at the pre-funding stage. Fortunately, UK company law contains no minimum capital requirement for private companies, and provides no impediment to the issue of shares in exchange for non-cash consideration to be supplied by an entrepreneur. Similarly, the approach of English courts to all questions involving the 'corporate veil' has been to ensure it remains as impermeable as possible.

7.4.4. *Labour Law*

It is arguable that labour law may have an impact on the demand side of the venture capital market. This could operate in a number of ways. On the one hand, extensive redundancy entitlements designed either to insure employees against the risk of redundancy, or to protect their investments in firm-specific human capital against employer opportunism, may hamper a start-up firm's ability to recruit staff (Black and Gilson, Chapter 2, this volume). If the business is extremely risky, then the potential cost of employee redundancy entitlements will have to be taken into account in hiring decisions—it will not be enough simply to offer employees stock in the firm and thereby allow them to bear the risk themselves. Credence is given to this account by Jeng and Wells (2000) finding in their cross-country study of the determinants of venture capital finance that labour market rigidities were negatively correlated with venture capital investment. The study used employee mobility as a proxy for labour market rigidities, and so is not a perfect test of the hypothesis considered above. Further qualitative work is necessary to establish what link, if any, exists in practice.

Another way in which labour law might hamper demand for start-ups is suggested by Gilson (1999). He argues that a key factor in the relative success of the Silicon Valley 'cluster' over the earlier-established 'Route 128' corridor is the difference in the willingness of courts in each jurisdiction to enforce covenants not to compete. In California, such covenants are routinely not enforced. This might at first glance seem detrimental to the success of a region—surely it would enhance concerns about the appropriation of new technologies by competitors, and reduce willingness to invest in their development? This is conceded by Gilson, who counter-argues that such losses must be offset against gains in second-stage agglomeration economies—the facilitation of the transfer of new information throughout players in the region. Provided that departing employees remain in the region, going to another local firm, and that traffic is multilateral, then firms can expect on average to recoup such losses. Furthermore, the benefits in information transfer may allow new discoveries to be exploited much more rapidly, and in different ways, than in a jurisdiction where covenants to compete are rigidly enforced.

7.4.5. *Insolvency Law*

The possible impact of insolvency law on the incidence of venture capital finance is not something which has been explored in the literature in any sustained way. The insolvency literature has, until very recently, tended to focus on the case of publicly traded firms, and has only just begun to focus on the incentives the law offers to those running small businesses. This section will argue, perhaps counter-intuitively, that personal insolvency law is likely to have a more important impact on the incidence of venture capital finance than corporate insolvency law.

7.4.5.1. *Supply Side: Corporate Insolvency Law*

Much has been written elsewhere about the differences between 'creditor friendly' and 'debtor friendly' corporate insolvency laws. An intriguing argument which may repay closer consideration is that a 'debtor friendly' corporate insolvency law may be able to increase the supply of venture capital finance.

An important difference is whether or not the corporate insolvency law promotes adherence to the so-called 'absolute priority rule' (APR): namely, that the priorities of payments agreed between investors should be respected in the making of distributions in insolvency proceedings. Almost all corporate insolvency regimes involve some amount of divergence from this. The most obvious is the elevation of certain types of claimant to 'preferred' status, such as employees and tax claims. Additionally, insolvency laws may distribute wealth away from secured creditors, by restricting their rights to enforce against their collateral. More fundamentally, however, under some systems it is possible for shareholders to receive payments even if the creditors are not paid in full.

An example of a system where this type of breach of the APR occurs routinely is Chapter 11 reorganization in the USA. Under this procedure, creditors and the debtor engage in a form of structured bargaining over a plan of reorganization. When the plan is confirmed by the court, the debtor emerges from Chapter 11 proceedings and the parties' pre-confirmation claims are extinguished and replaced with the claims against the firm detailed in the plan. Typically, creditors will agree to accept payment of less, and later, than they had originally contracted for. If the APR were respected, then we would expect shareholders not to receive any payment under these plans where the firm's assets are worth less than its liabilities. Yet empirical studies have confirmed that it is normal for the old shareholders to receive claims in the reorganized firm—worth somewhere in the region of five per cent of its market value—notwithstanding that the creditors are receiving claims that are worth less than their outstanding debts.[22] Insolvency scholars believe this outcome occurs in the USA because of the way the law is structured so as to give considerable bargaining leverage to the debtor.

By contrast, in a 'creditor-friendly' jurisdiction such as the UK, there is no question of the law facilitating such outcomes. Creditors are firmly in control of insolvency proceedings, and the only way in which the shareholders will retain any claim on a reorganized firm is if the creditors consider they are contributing value to it, for example, through their

---

[22] For a review, see Armour (2001).

human capital. We would think that, *ceteris paribus*, breaches of the APR would make debt investment *ex ante* less desirable, and equity more desirable. Might this therefore have the effect of stimulating venture capital finance for high-risk, high-growth firms?

This argument encounters a significant objection. Reorganization law is likely to be less relevant for 'start-up' firms than for others. Not that, if the VC decides not to continue funding the firm, then it is unlikely to be able to obtain finance from elsewhere. The fact that the VC, an insider with knowledge about the project, has decided it is not going to succeed will send a clear signal to potential alternative funders which will deter them from investing. For the same reasons, a sale of the business as a going concern in insolvency will not be feasible. So what will be left? Given that there will be few liquid assets, there is unlikely to be much to fight over at all (Gilson and Schizer 2002; see also Gerhard 2000; Corcoran 2002). On this view, therefore, the priorities of distribution directed by insolvency law are largely irrelevant: there is nothing to distribute.[23]

A second dimension on which corporate insolvency laws vary is the legal consequences of firm failure for executives. In the UK, managers of insolvent firms may face personal liability for 'wrongful trading' if a court considers that, from the point in time when they should have realized that the company had no reasonable prospect of avoiding insolvent liquidation, they did not take every reasonable step that they might to protect the interests of creditors. This liability may be incurred not only by those who are in fact directors of the company, but also by 'shadow directors': those in accordance with whose instructions the board of directors habitually act. Similarly, directors (and shadow directors) whose companies go into insolvency proceedings will find that their conduct is investigated, and they may be disqualified by the court from participating in the management of companies for a period of 3–15 years if their conduct is found to have been such as to make them 'unfit' to act as directors. Similar penalties for those in control of companies which become insolvent do not exist under US corporate insolvency law. It might be thought that these extra penalties could serve as a deterrent to venture capital investment.

A problem with the application of the UK regime is that it depends on the ability of the court to decide appropriately as to the managers' conduct. When business decisions are judged with hindsight, it may be all too easy for a court to conclude that a director should have realized that insolvency was inevitable, and should have done more to protect the interests of creditors. Thus the VC's nominees, who sit as board members in portfolio firms, or the VCs themselves—who in certain circumstances may constitute themselves 'shadow directors'—may fear that an inappropriate court decision will lead to the imposition of liability or disqualification. Might this be a factor which would inhibit the supply of venture capital finance at the margin?

This second apparent comparative disadvantage to investment in UK start-up companies also vanishes on closer inspection. First, a legal comparison that looks solely at 'insolvency

---

[23] The effect of corporate insolvency law on venture capital supply might not, however, be direct. If creditors fare worse in traditional manufacturing businesses, and shareholders fare better, then the range of industries in which venture capital becomes the cheapest form of outside finance may increase. This might have a knock-on effect of stimulating the growth of venture capital funds, which in turn then develop expertise sufficient to invest in other, more risky firms.

law' may be misleading. Directors in other jurisdictions may owe duties to creditors which arise from corporate law, once their firm becomes insolvent.[24] As a result, they too may face personal liability to contribute to the insolvent company's assets if they do not act sufficiently in the interests of creditors.

Second, and more importantly, the structure of the VC's incentives under the investment agreement are likely to mean that there is little chance of any tardiness in bringing about liquidation. Recall that the VC typically has preferred shares. These will allow him to rank ahead of the entrepreneur for the purposes of repayment of capital in a liquidation, if there is any money left over after creditors have been paid. Thus, as soon as the VC decides that the company is not going to be a success, he will have an incentive to liquidate it as soon as possible so as to maximize his chances of getting something back. A court would be most unlikely to seek to second-guess the decision of a VC as to whether the firm is likely to prosper: not only does the VC have greater expertise than the court, but the sincerity of his belief is credibly demonstrated by his willingness to invest funds.

7.4.5.2. *Demand Side: Personal Insolvency Law*

So far, we have argued that it unlikely that the structure of a country's corporate insolvency law will have a significant impact on the supply of venture capital finance in that jurisdiction. By contrast, personal insolvency law may be a much more important factor than would seem apparent at first blush. Superficially, we may point to the limited liability which incorporation of the business will generate for entrepreneurs. Of course, it is possible to 'contract out' of limited liability through the grant by shareholders of personal guarantees of business indebtedness. Such guarantees are indeed demanded as a matter of course by banks lending to small firms (Freedman and Godwin 1994). Yet for start-up companies without major debt investors, such guarantees may not be so prevalent. To see the possible relationship between venture capital finance and personal insolvency, it is necessary to consider the process of business initiation.

Imagine a putative entrepreneur who is considering starting a firm. He will not be able to obtain venture capital finance until a reasonably advanced stage of development. To begin with, he will likely seek investment from family and friends, and run up credit card debt. When these sources are exhausted, he may seek 'angel' finance, and only by the time he has a defined business plan and a reasonably well-developed technology will the firm become an attractive proposition to VCs. From here on, let us focus on three broad sectors of outcome. First, he might not succeed in raising venture capital finance. In this case, it is quite possible that he will have over-extended his personal finances to reach this point, and will face personal insolvency. Second, he may raise venture capital finance and the firm subsequently prospers. In this case, his personal debt load will be paid off. Third, he may raise venture capital finance and the firm subsequently fails. Whilst in the interim he may have received salary from the firm, it is still quite possible that he is so over-extended that the collapse of the firm will precipitate personal insolvency as well. Thus in the first and third cases, the content of personal insolvency law will matter a great

---

[24] See, for example, *Credit Lyonnais Bank Nederland NV v. Pathe Communications Corp* (1991 Del Ch).

deal to the entrepreneur. *Ex ante*, at the point in time immediately before our story starts, the putative entrepreneur will have made a decision to go into business on his own. One factor in this decision will be the potential 'downside' consequences if scenarios one or three eventuate.[25]

If personal insolvency law imposes harsh consequences upon the individual, then *ex ante* the attractiveness of entering into a risky entrepreneurial endeavour will be reduced, particularly if the individual is risk-averse. This theory would predict that a harsher personal insolvency law should be related to a reduced demand for venture capital finance, as less entrepreneurs are willing to initiative high-risk businesses.

An initial test of this theory might be to compare the personal insolvency laws of the UK and the USA, two jurisdictions with readily accessible legal materials. In the UK, the estate of the bankrupt, minus certain exemptions, is taken over by a trustee and sold for the benefit of his creditors (Fletcher 1996). The exemptions include items for the bankrupt's personal use in employment and clothing and household items required for his basic domestic needs and those of his family. The bankrupt is then subject to certain legal disabilities for a three-year period,[26] including an inability to incur credit of more than £250 without disclosing his status as a bankrupt, a ban on trading under a different name without disclosing the name under which he was declared bankrupt, and being disqualified from participating in the management of a limited liability company.[27] During this time, the whole of the bankrupt's income apart from a very modest living allowance must be transferred to the trustee for the benefit of his creditors. At the end of three years, the 'first time' bankrupt receives a 'discharge' and all legal disabilities cease.[28]

This position may be contrasted with that which obtains in the USA (Tabb 1997). An individual debtor may opt to enter bankruptcy proceedings under either Chapter 7, Chapter 11, or Chapter 13 of the Bankruptcy Code. Chapter 7, the most frequently used, normally provides a debtor with an immediate automatic discharge from most of his debts, in return for handing over all of his non-exempt assets for the benefit of creditors.[29] From this point onwards, no creditor may seek to collect pre-bankruptcy debts from the debtor, and the debtor may keep the proceeds of any subsequent earnings.[30] There is no specified period during which the debtor is subject to legal disabilities, and proceedings typically take around 3–4 months to finalize. Indeed, the Bankruptcy Code specifically protects debtors from any discriminatory treatment on account of the fact that they have filed for bankruptcy.[31] The range of property which is exempt from the bankrupt estate is largely defined by reference to the state in which the debtor has been domiciled for the

---

[25] It may be argued that entrepreneurs are by nature optimistic, and will have sufficient belief in their project to discount the risk of failure. In this case, the consequences of personal bankruptcy will be less important to them *ex ante*. This may well be accurate as a description of those who choose to become entrepreneurs, but it proves nothing about those who choose not to do so because of the fear of bankruptcy.

[26] The period may be reduced to two years for cases involving total debts of less than £20,000.

[27] There are a range of other disabilities, including being barred from sitting as a Member of Parliament or of the House of Lords.

[28] If the individual was previously discharged from bankruptcy less than nine years beforehand, then discharge is not automatic.　　　　　　　　　　　　　　　　　　　[29] 11 USC Sections 524, 727(a).

[30] 11 USC Sections 524(a); 541(a)(6).　　　　　　　　　　　　　　　[31] 11 USC Section 525.

180 days preceding the filing.[32] The level of exemptions varies widely, the most notoriously generous being the 'homestead' exemptions under Florida and Texas law, which allow the debtor to retain an interest in his home of unlimited value. However, in some other states, such as Pennsylvania, the debtor is allowed to exempt no more than a total of $300-worth of property.[33]

Given that UK personal insolvency law is considerably stricter than its US counterpart, we might expect that this would lead to a reduced demand for venture capital finance, particularly amongst start-up firms. The data on comparative incidence of venture capital appear to bear this out. Further, albeit indirect, support for this hypothesis comes from a recent study by Fan and White (2000). This found a significant correlation between incidence of owner-managed businesses and the total value of property which might be exempted from bankruptcy under state law in the USA.

The UK's Enterprise Bill 2002 contains a number of features designed to reduce the harshness of personal insolvency for individuals who have become bankrupt simply because of bad luck, as opposed to irresponsible risk-taking on their part. Under the new legislation, the time to automatic discharge will be reduced to twelve months, although if fraud is shown then the bankrupt may be made subject to a Bankruptcy Restraining Order which will, *inter alia*, prohibit him from being involved in the management of a company for a period of 5–15 years. Furthermore, the legal disabilities associated with the status of undischarged bankrupt will be scrapped, as a bid to send a signal to society that bankruptcy should carry less stigma. At the European level, the EC's RCAP has identified the need to facilitate the 'softening of bankruptcy laws to allow failed entrepreneurs a second chance...' (European Commission 2000*b*), although specific proposals for reform have yet to be tabled.

Ironically, proposed reforms in the USA will move personal bankruptcy law in the opposite direction. The proposals will see the introduction of means-testing for debtors who wish to make use of Chapter 7 proceedings, requiring those whose incomes are above a certain threshold instead to make use of the Chapter 13 procedure, which involves a composition with creditors as opposed to an outright discharge (American Bankruptcy Institute 2001). The reforms will also restrict the ability of fraudulent debtors to rely on the homestead exemption, meaning that a debtor convicted of securities fraud or certain types of felony would be unable to shield more than $125,000 of real estate (*Washington Post* 2002). These reforms may have the effect of making entrepreneurship less attractive at the margins.

[32] 11 USC Section 522(b). The same subsection also provides a federal list of exemptions which the debtor may elect to apply instead of state exemptions (Section 522(d)), provided that his state of domicile has not legislated to deny its debtors this choice. Tabb (1997: 643–4) notes that 'as of 1997, 35 states had opted out of the federal scheme, rendering Section 522(d) a dead letter in much of the nation'.

[33] The US bankruptcy system is not quite as reckless in its generosity to debtors as it at first may seem. There are a number of grounds for denying discharge, perhaps the most important of which is that a discharge may not be granted more than once every six years. Furthermore, if the court considers that the debtor is committing a 'substantial abuse' of the system by not filing for Chapter 13, under which a debtor enters into a repayment compromise with his creditors lasting three years, then he may also dismiss the case. Finally, a range of debts such as those incurred on the basis of fraud, student loans, alimony payments, and certain tax claims may not be discharged.

7.5. THE IMPACT OF REGULATORY COMPETITION

The hypotheses considered in Section 7.4 all proceeded on the strong assumption that entrepreneurship and venture capital investing is primarily a domestic affair. We now relax this assumption to look at the possible impact of regulatory competition on venture capital investment. As a first observation, it is worth noting that funds for investment in venture capital flow readily across borders. Baygan and Freudenberg (2000) present an analysis of trade association data which shows the extent to which this took place in Europe during the 1990s. Some of their findings are replicated in Table 7.1. This has important implications for policy, suggesting that law reform efforts designed to stimulate venture capital finance should be directed at the demand rather than the supply side. Transnational capital flows may simply bypass several of the supply side legal 'barriers' to venture capital considered in Section 7.4. Of course, entrepreneurs are also able to repatriate themselves in favour of jurisdictions where demand-side variables are more favourable to their endeavours. Yet it seems plausible that the necessary differential between national legal systems so as to provoke substantial movements would have to be much greater than for movements of funds.

Consider first the case of pension fund regulation. The Myners Report itself notes that there was a spectacular growth in funds committed to UK venture capital during the second half of the 1990s—but that most of the influx was from abroad, particularly from US pension funds (Myners 2001: 175). The problem with pension fund governance is therefore probably not one of undersupply of venture capital finance to UK firms. Rather, it is a problem for pension fund beneficiaries, who cannot reap the benefits of such investment. This view is echoed by Mayer (2001: 7), who questions whether the relatively low levels of venture capital investment in early-stage companies in the UK is not due to demand-side problems, such as the availability of entrepreneurs with good projects.

Second, if a domestic law, such as that of England, creates significant barriers to using the Limited Partnership form for venture capital funds, then a fund may simply engage

Table 7.1. *Cross-border private equity investment flows, 1999 (% of domestic investments)*

	Outflows (to other countries)	Inflows (from other European countries)	Net inflows
Ireland	10	372	362
Finland	16	76	60
Italy	5	13	8
Germany	17	22	5
France	25	22	−3
Netherlands	50	38	−12
Belgium	54	41	−13
UK	33	5	−28

Source: Baygan and Freudenberg (2000).

in 'forum shopping' by using a Delaware or Jersey business form instead. The logic of the same argument may be extended to choice of state of incorporation for start-up firms seeking to raise venture finance. To the extent that domestic organizational forms hinder their ability to contract effectively with VCs, they may simply opt to incorporate elsewhere, even if the business does not physically move (see Rock 2001).

Factors which affect the demand for venture capital—that is, those legal variables which may have an impact on the level of entrepreneurial activity—would therefore appear to be more important areas to address if policymakers are keen to promote early-stage venture capital finance. In a world of global capital flows, demand-side factors such as capital gains tax, personal insolvency law, and labour law (to the extent that these may be shown to affect entrepreneurial activity) will be more important than the more supply-side oriented factors considered above.

7.6. CONCLUSION

This chapter has reviewed theories and evidence as to the extent to which law 'matters' for the provision of venture capital finance, and a central theme has been that it may do so in a variety of ways. Clearly, regulatory provisions may affect the incentives of marginal investors and entrepreneurs, thereby affecting the aggregate levels of venture capital investment in a country. Theoretically, a range of different regulatory provisions may have an impact on the incentives for investors to supply, or for entrepreneurs to demand, venture capital finance. The available empirical evidence tends to support the claims that taxes and pension fund regulation may be determinants of investment. The evidence as respects the effects, if any, of organizational law, labour law, and insolvency law is still equivocal or non-existent, and these issues constitute important questions for future research. The advent of globalization is likely to mean that law reform which seeks to stimulate the supply of domestic venture capital will make less of a difference to overall levels of investment than efforts to stimulate demand.

Law may also matter for inframarginal investors, by determining the content of their venture capital investment agreements. Theoretical studies of the agency problems in financing innovation suggest that there are several different financial contracts which might be adequate to overcome the worst difficulties, but are somewhat ambivalent as to which is optimal. As we have seen in Section 7.2, it appears that US tax law may be a reason for US VCs' propensity to take convertible preferred stock in their American investee companies—but not when they invest in Canadian companies, where a different tax regime applies. Although the law determines the form of the contracts, the theoretical studies suggest there will be little effect, if any, on their optimality.

References

American Bankruptcy Institute (2001), 'Major effects of the comsumer bankruptcy provisions of the 2001 bankruptcy legislation (H.R. 333 and S. 420)', available online at http://www.abiworld.org/mainpoints.pdf.

Armour, J. (2001), 'The law and economics of corporate insolvency: a review', in R. D. Vriesendorp, J. A. McCahery, and F. M. J. Verstijlen (eds), *Comparative and International Perspectives on Bankruptcy Law Reform in the Netherlands*, The Hague: Boom Juridische uitgevers, 99–138.

Bank of England (2001), *Financing of Technology-based Small Firms*, London: Bank of England.

Bankman, J. (1994), 'The structure of Silicon Valley start-ups', *UCLA Law Review* 41, 1737–68.

Bascha, A. and Walz, U. (2001), 'Financing practices in the German Venture capital industry: an empirical assessment', Working paper, University of Tübingen.

Baygan, G. and Freudenberg, M. (2000), 'The internationalisation of venture capital activity in OECD countries: implications for measurement and policy', OECD STI Working Paper 2000/7.

Becker, R. and Hellmann, T. (2000), 'The genesis of venture capital—lessons from the German experience', Working paper, Stanford University.

Bernstein, L. (1995), 'The Silicon Valley lawyer as transaction cost engineer?', *Oregon Law Review* 74, 239–55.

Black, B. S. and Gilson, R. J. (1998), 'Venture Capital and the structure of capital markets: Banks versus stock markets', *Journal of Financial Economics* 47, 243–77.

Bolkestein, F. (2000), 'Addressing the challenges for European pensions', Speech given at Chatham House, London, 29 February (http://europa.eu.int/comm/internal_market/en/speeches/spch060.htm).

Callison, J. W. (2000), 'Venture capital and corporate governance: evolving the limited liability company to finance entrepreneurial business', *Journal of Corporation Law* 26, 97–124.

Comben, A. and Wilkinson, C. (2000), *Joint Ventures and Shareholders' Agreements*, London: Butterworths.

Corcoran, E. (2002), 'Digital diaspora; from the internet wreckage, the spirit of Silicon Valley emerges', *Forbes* 169, 4.

Cornelli, F. and Yosha, A. (1997), 'Stage financing and the role of convertible debt', London Business School Working Paper No 253–1997.

Cumming, D. J. (2000), 'The convertible preferred equity puzzle in Canadian venture capital finance', Working paper, University of Alberta School of Business.

—— (2001), 'United States venture capital financial contracting: evidence from investments in foreign securities', Working paper, University of Alberta School of Business.

—— (2002), 'Contracts and exits in venture capital finance', Working paper, University of Alberta School of Business.

—— and MacIntosh, J. G. (2001), 'Law, finance and the Canadian venture capital cycle', Paper presented at CLEA meeting, University of Toronto, Sept 2001.

Department of Trade and Industry (DTI) (1999), *Addressing the SME Equity Gap: Support for Regional Venture Capital Funds*, London: DTI URN 99/876.

—— (2001a), *Removing the 20 Partner Limit*, London: DTI URN 01/752.

—— (2001b), *Removing the 20 Partner Limit: Summary of Responses*, London: DTI.

—— (2001c), 'Government to remove the 20 partner limit on company partnerships', Press Release P/2001/619, 9 November.

Djankov, S. La Porta, R., Lopez de Silanes, F., and Shleifer, A. (2000), 'The regulation of entry', NBER Working Paper 7892.

European Commission (1998), 'Risk capital: a key to job creation in the European Union', Brussels, 31 March, SEC (1998) 552 final.

—— (2000a), 'Progress report on the risk capital action plan', Brussels, 18 October, COM (2000) 658 final.

European Commission (2000*b*), 'Proposal for a directive of the European parliament and for the Council on the Activities of Institutions for Occupational Retirement Provision', Brussels, 11 October, COM (2000) 507 final.

Fan, W. and White, M. J. (2000), 'Personal bankruptcy and the level of entrepreneurial activity', Working paper, University of Michigan.

Financial Times (2002), 'Fears for European private equity projects', 31 March.

Fletcher, I. F. (1996), *The Law of Insolvency*, 2nd edn, London: Sweet & Maxwell.

Freedman, J. and Godwin, M. (1994), 'Incorporating the micro business: perceptions and misperceptions', in A. Hughes and D. J. Storey (eds), *Finance and the Small Firm*, London: Routledge, 232–50.

Friedman, L. M. Gordon, R. W., Pirie, S., and Whatley, E. (1989), 'Law, lawyers, and legal practice in Silicon Valley: a preliminary report', *Indiana Law Journal* 64, 555–67.

Gebhard, R. S. (2000), 'Dot-com bankruptcies: a preview from Silicon Valley?', *American Bankruptcy Institute Journal* (19 Sep.), 6–8.

Gilson, R. J. (1984), 'Value creation by business lawyers: legal skills and asset pricing', *Yale Law Journal* 94, 239–313.

—— (1999), 'The legal infrastructure of high technology industrial districts: Silicon Valley, route 128, and covenants not to compete', *New York University Law Review* 74, 575–629.

—— and Schizer, D. M. (2002), 'Understanding venture capital structure: a tax explanation for convertible preferred stock', Working paper, Columbia Law School and Stanford Law School.

Gompers, P. A. and Lerner, J. (1999), *The Venture Capital Cycle*, Cambridge, MA: MIT Press.

—— —— (2000), 'What drives venture capital fundraising?' NBER Working Paper 6906.

—— —— (2001), 'The venture capital revolution', *Journal of Economic Perspectives* 15, 145–68.

Hart, O. (1995), *Firms, Contracts, and Financial Structure*, Oxford: Clarendon Press.

—— (2001), 'Financial contracting', HIER Discussion Paper 1924/HLS, John M. Olin Center for Law, Economics and Business Discussion Paper 327, Harvard University.

Hicks, A., Drury, R., and Smallcombe, J. (1995), 'Alternative company structures for the small business', ACCA Research Report No 42, London: Certified Accountants Educational Trust.

Inland Revenue (2001*a*), 'Capital gains tax: an introduction', leaflet CGT1 available from www.inlandrevenue.gov.uk.

—— (2001*b*), 'Tax boost to employee share ownership', Inland Revenue Press Release REV3, available from www.inlandrevenue.gov.uk.

Jeng, L. A. and Wells, P. C. (2000), 'The determinants of venture capital fundraising: evidence across countries', *Journal of Corporate Finance* 6, 241–89.

Kahan, M. and Klausner, M. (1996), 'Path dependence in corporate contracting: increasing returns, herd behavior and cognitive biases', *Washington University Law Quarterly* 74, 347–66.

—— —— (1997), 'Standardization and innovation in corporate contracting (or 'the economics of boilerplate')', *Virginia Law Review* 83, 713–69.

Kaplan, S. and Strömberg, P. (2000), 'Financial contracting theory meets the real world: an empirical analysis of venture capital contracts', Working paper, University of Chicago Graduate School of Business.

Klausner, M. and Litvak, K. (2001), 'What economists have taught us about venture capital contracting,' in M. J. Whincop (ed.), *Bridging the Entrepreneurial Finance Gap: Linking Governance with Regulatory Policy*, Aldershot: Ashgate, 54–74.

Law Commission of England and Wales and Scottish Law Commission (2001), 'The Limited Partnerships Act 1907: a joint consultation paper', London: TSO, LCCP 161, SLCDP 118.

Lerner, J. (1996), 'The government as venture capitalist: the long-run effects of the SBIR Program', NBER Working Paper No 5753.

Mason, C. M. and Harrison, R. T. (2000), 'Influences on the supply of informal venture capital in the UK: an exploratory study of investor attitudes', *International Small Business Journal* 18, 11–28.

Mayer, C. (2001), 'Institutional investment and private equity in the UK', Paper for the conference on 'Corporate governance: reassessing ownership and control' at Cambridge University, May.

Myners, P. (2001), *Institutional Investment in the United Kingdom: A Review*, London: TSO.

Puri, P. (2001), 'Taking stock of taking stock', *Cornell Law Review* 87, 99–156.

Repullo, R. and Suarez, J. (1998), 'Venture capital finance: a security design approach', CEMFI Working Paper No 9804.

Rock, E. B. and Wachter, M. I. (1999), 'Waiting for the omelet to set: match-specific assets and minority oppression in close corporations', *Journal of Corporation Law* 24, 913–48.

Sahlman, W. A. (1990), 'The structure and governance of venture-capital organizations', *Journal of Financial Economics* 27, 473–521.

Schmidt, K. M. (2001), 'Convertible securities and venture capital finance', Working paper, University of Munich.

SJ Berwin & Co (ed.) (1997), *Venture capital incentives in Europe*, London: EVCA.

Small Business Service (SBS) (2001), *Think Small First*, London: SBS.

Steel, J. (undated), 'Choice of entity: corporations vs. LLCs', available on Gray Cary website: http://www.gcwf.com/articles/vcp/vcp_sum00_1.html.

Stiglitz, J. E. and Weiss, A. (1981), 'Credit rationing in markets with incomplete information', *American Economic Review* 71, 393–409.

Suchman, M. and Cahill, M. (1996), 'The hired gun as facilitator: lawyers and the suppression of business disputes in Silicon Valley', *Law and Social Inquiry*, 679–712.

Tabb, C. J. (1997), *The Law of Bankruptcy*, Westbury, NY: Foundation Press.

Washington Post (2002), 'Millionaire's loophole', Editorial, 23 April, Page A16.

8

Business Organization Law
and Venture Capital

JOSEPH A. MCCAHERY AND ERIK P. M. VERMEULEN

8.1. INTRODUCTION

The subject of this chapter is the reform of business organization law in Europe. An inquiry into the relationship between the development and diffusion of new business forms invites a discussion of the inherent advantages and disadvantages of alternative business structures. Our discussion of the European landscape of partnerships and close corporations focuses on the tendencies of businesses to favour existing arrangements, which makes it hard to consider (let alone develop) alternative business vehicles.

Establishing business forms that are flexible and limit transaction costs is arguably most important at this time when entrepreneurs are facing increased risks to starting a business. The significance of unincorporated businesses for productivity growth, innovation, and job creation explains the high priority given to the attempt to create new legal structures that are more favourable to the needs of these enterprises. It has become widely noted that a number of countries are moving towards fostering an institutional framework designed to make available the advantages of limited liability to an increasing number of unincorporated businesses. The significance of new business forms for firm performance derives from the observation that the level of regulatory burden and creditor protection varies appreciably across Europe depending on the nature of the company law regime. To an important degree, a high number of European closely held firms are organized under a legal structure that is designed simply to meet the needs of the public corporation. It is therefore natural to give attention to the significant differences between firms when attempting to supply legal forms designed to meet their needs. Concerns about the diversity of business activities and firm structures mean that policy must work at different levels, and may involve considerable complexity. As a consequence, the debate on the appropriate design and expansion of business forms is gathering momentum.

This chapter will examine the theoretical arguments for and against the importance of new business forms for the growth of start-ups. We begin with a brief review of the recent history of business form innovation within Europe. Our review reveals that the absence of new business entities (or structural reforms) may be due to a status quo bias and other network externalities. Turning to the importance of new business forms to a robust economy, Section 8.2 assesses which organizational and legal structures are favourable for the growth of high-tech start-ups. We argue in Section 8.3 that introduction of an efficient organizational form is crucial to further stimulate the development of a successful venture capital market in Europe. Here we give consideration to the possibility of developing new business forms, based on the US Limited Liability Company (LLC), which could lead to an increase in the level of start-ups. Prospects for the emergence of a corporate-type partnership entity depends, in the main, on the removal of legal and non-legal barriers. In Section 8.4, we assess the implications of the introduction of a new form and the stimulation of competitive lawmaking across Europe. We argue that, despite the potential for firms to choose business forms from among many European states, regulatory competition may be limited due to the absence of significant supply- and demand-side benefits. But, of course, we do not rule out stepped up regulatory competition (and the fast diffusion of innovative codes) if some states were to induce capital movement by, for instance, lowering tax rates for certain limited liability businesses. Finally, we explore in Section 8.5 the consequences of regulatory arbitrage in guiding legal reform. We compare and weigh the competing interests on the demand side of legislation, finding there is no clear-cut story about the possibility of enactment of an LLC-type statute. The outcome will depend largely on the power of the venture capital associations, lawyers and professional intermediaries, and business groups to bring pressure to bear so as to roll back the otherwise mandatory EC company laws. As far as a national government acts as an entrepreneur, it may be plausible to conjecture that a small state, such as Ireland or the Netherlands, could seek to further its comparative advantage—via other Member States—by making particular adjustments to its company law, through introducing a menu of defaults (e.g. the reform of partnership law) so as to place its rules on a more equal footing, thereby offering a degree of diversity to firms making decisions about incorporations.

8.2. THE EVOLUTION OF CLOSELY HELD BUSINESS FORMS IN EUROPE

For many years, European policymakers have been concerned with the design of legal and institutional structures intended to enhance small- and medium-sized businesses (SMEs) in their entrepreneurial and risk-taking activities.[1] SMEs are responsible for productivity growth, contribute to innovative processes in manufacturing, and are the primary source

---

[1] See Commission of the European Communities (1999), The Competitiveness of European Enterprises in the Face of Globalisation—How it can be encouraged, COM(98) 718 final, Brussels, 20.01.1999; Commission of the European Communities, Challenges for enterprise policy in the knowledge-driven economy, Proposal for a Council Decision on a Multiannual Programme for Enterprise and Entrepreneurship (2001–2005), COM(2000) 256 final/2, Brussels, 11.5.2000; European Commission, Green Paper on Innovation (1995); European Commission, Risk Capital: A Key to Job Creation in the European Union (1998).

of job creation and development across Europe's regions.[2] But a core problem for Europe remains how to stimulate the development of an efficient institutional and legal structure that satisfies entrepreneurs' concerns for limiting the regulatory burden and providing low cost legal rules that contracting parties would prefer. The European Commission, in their attempts at convincing the European Council and the Member States to take action, has stated frequently that, if the constraints are not tackled in the near term, Europe will fall even further behind in the competitive race with the USA. Since European lawmakers are reluctant to interfere with closely held business statutes, the Member States will have the responsibility for revising their own laws. Whilst many observers admit that if jurisdictions were to respond effectively to these concerns by introducing new business forms that would promote savings for several classes of firms, the legislation would likely serve to attract new investment. To the extent this is correct, it follows that many states would take the necessary steps to attract business investment. Still, despite the benefits that well-positioned reforms would have for governments, previous attempts to bring about company law reforms in many countries have not been very successful.

8.2.1. *Recent Developments in European Corporate Law*

There have been a number of developments in the context of company law recently. We have witnessed a series of UK initiatives that involve the establishment of new partnership arrangements that may entail economic benefits for individual firms. Prompted by competition from the Channel Islands, English lawmakers recently promulgated a Limited Liability Partnership Act (Young 2000; McCahery 2003). The legislation introduces a vehicle that has legal personality, a partnership governance structure, limited liability, and partnership tax treatment. In drafting this legislation, the Department of Trade and Industry responded to the pent-up demand from existing partnerships—international accounting firms—which wished to transfer to limited liability partnership (LLP) status. Although the LLP Act was initially drafted to address the liability concerns of large accounting and other service providers in England, the statutory provisions, as enacted, cover all types of businesses. However, the new vehicle, even if it represents a new policy direction in company law legislation, cannot be viewed as creating a successful, low cost solution for SMEs notwithstanding the flexibility and access to lower cost rules afforded by the introduction of the Act.

French legislators have been more active in the supply of new legislation directed to creating new types of limited liability forms for small businesses that wish to operate with management structures that resemble corporations. The 1994 introduction of the *société par actions simplifiée* (SAS), and its subsequent modification in 1999, creates the opportunity for partners in a joint venture—and for other purposes—to adopt a legal structure that is truly flexible in the organization and control of the firm. Some argue that the new form holds out the potential to provide cost saving benefits that may attract new incorporations, allowing France to compete effectively with Germany and England. By

[2] See OECD, Small and Medium Enterprises Outlook (OECD 2000).

making the corporate structure more adaptable to business needs of SMEs and allowing its shareholders to be both individuals and legal entities, the French government would probably have increased the number of new domestic businesses, and perhaps a small subsection of SMEs. Regardless whether the activity increases as a result of the adoption of the SAS, critics argue that the complexity of the SAS may lead to incomplete contracting, since the statute fails to supply a comprehensive statutory template that the parties can fall back upon when establishing the distribution and allocation of powers and responsibilities. There are a substantial number of issues that parties cannot content themselves *ex ante* due to the absence of sufficient legal precedent necessary to write joint venture agreements.

At a European level, a group of business leaders and legal experts of different nationalities,[3] brought together on the initiative of CREDA, the research centre of the Paris Chamber of Commerce and Industry (CCIP), has proposed the introduction of a European Private Company (EPC) (Helms 1998). In contrast to the European Company, that is grounded on the German *Aktiengesellschaft* and therefore mainly aimed at publicly held firms, the EPC has been designed in order to offer closely held firms, which are particular SMEs, wishing to develop on the European market a Europe-wide, simple, effective form, meeting their specific requirements. The draft Regulation is very concise. It comprises only thirty-eight articles. If an EPC is to be established, the articles of incorporation must necessarily contain the rights of the shareholders, the organization and operation of the company, and the powers of its governing bodies. At first blush, this makes the EPC less complicated and a more flexible form of business entity. For instance, like the US LLC, it is possible to establish a 'shareholder managed' EPC and a 'manager managed' EPC. Consequently, since the close corporation is often viewed as an owner-controlled firm, the EPC meets a practical wish. However, few believe that the new draft EPC regulation could resolve the practical difficulties that prevent its immediate adoption by jurisdictions. Indeed, although the draft Regulation has few mandatory rules, the drafters have created a barrier by failing to supply adequate default rules on important issues. Besides the resistance from national groups, there is concern that the draft regulation will not totally satisfy the needs of new incorporators.

Allowing the choice of business forms for new firms was recently addressed by the European Court of Justice's decision in *Centros*, which recognized the right of a Danish firm to incorporate in the UK without the intent to conduct business operations in the jurisdiction.[4] The Centros case could be a forerunner of a completely different approach to corporate regulation and may eventually yield some tangible results in this field. This case shows that incorporating firms will migrate to countries that offer internal processes and legal regimes that lower their costs. Some doubts however persist whether this is a perfect choice for Europe. In any event, the harmonization route proposed implicitly by *Centros* could eventually require a European Delaware. The UK seems to be the natural choice because of its flexible structure and the efficiency of its measures. It is true that the UK, like its US counterpart, Delaware, invests considerable resources in developing its company code, case law, and administrative proceedings for the benefit of its wide range

[3] Among others, Jeanne Boucourechliev, Robert Drury (Exeter), Yves Guyon (Paris), Peter Hommelhoff (Heidelberg), Levinus Timmerman (Groningen).
[4] Case C-212/97 Centros Ltd. v. Erhvervs-og Selskabsstryelsen [1999] ECR I-1459. See Deakin (2001).

of incorporating businesses. Legal feasibility considerations aside, some doubts persist about whether the UK is a viable alternative for incorporating SMEs. Whilst responsive to the productive concerns of private businesses seeking transferable shares and limited liability, a large number of SMEs tend to be precluded by the large firm bias of the present Company Act legislation. From this perspective, there are a number of legislative amendments required to create real cost savings for a number of firms in the class of SMEs.

8.2.2. *Network and Learning Benefits*

Despite the potential benefits for governments, like tax revenue and economic growth, national lawmakers had, until recently, few incentives to introduce legal innovations. In most jurisdictions, the provisions of the closely held business forms are somehow linked to the publicly held corporation form, which may account for the 'lock-in' to the existing mandatory provisions (Lutter 1998). Many law and economics scholars take it for granted that when network or learning effects are present, the value of a contractual term or legal rule increases (Kahan and Klausner 1996). The standardization of provisions in corporate codes has the effect of creating network benefits. For example, the fact that a majority of firms select Delaware law to govern their rights leads to a network benefit for the firms that incorporate in Delaware. At the same time, Delaware maintains its position by providing a corporate dispute resolution centre of extraordinary sophistication (Romano 1993, 2001). The learning benefits (which come from the use of Delaware law) explain why most parties that originally opted into the framework have an incentive to continue to use the regime.[5]

If we take these benefits into account, we expect to see that newly formed companies will likely migrate to the business forms that confer large network benefits to the user. This will mean that the demand will be higher than it otherwise might be, which in turn will lead to the supply of standard rather than customized terms. Because standardized terms offer certainty, business lawyers, when advising clients about incorporation decisions, will tend to recommend a standardized term—even if suboptimal—rather than draft a customized term that could lead to higher expected value for a client.[6] The result, in turn, is that continuous use of the dominant business form, even if not ideally suited for some firms, will serve to reduce the incentives for lawmakers (and lawyers) to innovate.

Like other areas of law reform in continental Europe, the reluctance to diverge from the existing company law framework means that even if new business forms were adopted, parties might be unwilling to substitute the standard form for non-standard terms. From the perspective of legal change, firms are often able to overcome the learning and network costs when selecting a new legal arrangement that gives rise to economic benefits that

---

[5] Delaware's case law and judges also play an important role in developing its market share for charters. To be sure, its code's advantages are less distinct than its case law, given the convergence of statutes among states. Interestingly, Delaware does not control the production of its case law since other jurisdictions may litigate Delaware law issues. See Bratton and McCahery (1995).

[6] See Bernstein (1995: 248) (arguing that most Silicon Valley lawyers urge their clients to adopt a standardized contract in complex venture capital transactions).

maximize firm value. To be sure, there are a number of other reasons that reduce legal innovation in company law. The involvement of the European Community in developing a harmonization program, designed to create a degree of uniformity in the law regarding creditor and shareholder protection throughout the European Union, has tended to restrict innovations in the field of company law (Cheffins 1997). The harmonization process, which introduces an essential minimum floor and tolerates a degree of diversity at the national level, applies mainly to the public corporation, which arguably explains why SMEs, in contrast to the USA, employ a separate business organization form. Even though the EC directives were initially focused on public corporations, we observe that both national and EC lawmakers tend to extend their reach to the close corporation when introducing policy reforms (Bisacre 1999). Quite apart from the normative concerns of employing a harmonization process to develop a system of uniform rules, the imposition of such a mandatory rule—without the opportunity of opting out—will have the effect of increasing the incidence of standardization and may well lead to a number of legal and institutional barriers to innovation in corporate law (Whincop 2000; Wouters 2000; Hertig and McCahery 2004). Consequently the prospects for changing the main elements of European corporate law, given the petrification and network effect, are rather slim (Romano 1996).

8.2.3. *Default Rules and Business Forms*

In this section, we ask how an inquiry into the relationship between transaction costs and the introduction of new business statutes is crucial for understanding the problems that closely held firms face at the early phase of their development. Specifically, how do new business forms help solve the internal affairs of European closely held firms? Ideally, the introduction of a new business statute, designed to supply firms with limited liability, flexible legal rules, and preferential tax treatment, enables business ventures to better structure their legal identity in respect of their organizational requirements. In making this projection, US scholars have argued that new business forms tend to be efficient because they offer small firms with comprehensive sets of terms which limit the drafting and information cost burdens while providing them with limited liability and the free transferability of shares. The creation of an off-the-rack standard form contract designed to meet the needs of SMEs is the legal equivalent of a simple, low-cost incorporation. To the extent that the new business statutes offer firms and legal decisionmakers a set of simple and coherent terms, the language of the legislation should provide an acceptably low cost vehicle for planning and operation of their business and the resolution of conflicts. We suspect that the supply of clear and simple default rules will, in the absence of transaction costs, be regarding as value enhancing (Easterbrook and Fischel 1991). Adoption of default terms would serve to provide firms with value-enhancing opportunities that otherwise might not be available.

Given the learning and network costs discussed earlier, it could be anticipated that a particular default rule might as well entail a lock-in effect (Klausner 1995). Consequently some class of firms, if they are relatively numerous and have sufficient incentives, may adopt a separate default term if the transaction costs are low and the network effects are positive. For example, one menu of defaults could focus on high-tech, start-ups, while another menu could furnish expansion investments with the optimal terms. Adoption of an alternative menu will tend eventually, even in the presence of status quo bias, to establish its own network and learning benefits. Participants in business ventures may sometimes decide to draft their own stylized terms by attempting to contract around the traditional business forms (e.g. partnership and corporate forms). If the gains from introducing new structures are large, parties will create customized structures that reflect their own preferences and legal priorities. However, even though lawyers and other professionals will draft contractual terms that promote the interests of their clients, several studies show that lawyers have mixed objectives in recommending an innovative term, especially when the reputational pay-off does not exceed the professional risk and uncertainty of drafting a standard term (Bernstein 1995).

In comparison with the USA, even if the traditional business statutes in Europe were sufficiently flexible to allow opting out by firms, there are substantial transaction costs in developing highly customized terms that would satisfy the needs of this class of entrepreneur. For instance, use of convertible equity is possible under Dutch law if the articles of incorporation allow for it. Yet in practice it turns out to be a rather cumbersome mechanism because of the existing legal standards that require mandatory capital maintenance and certification of transfers of shares. Moreover, the parties most likely to be concerned with the adoption of new legislation would be seriously disinclined to move in this direction due to uncertainty arising from the legal gaps in the case law relating to the enforcement of contracts and disputes amongst business partners. Participants in closely held firms are therefore more likely, in the absence of responsive competitive pressures from other states for new law developments, to demand amendments to their local closely held business statutes. Meantime, the organizational benefits that could flow from the adoption of new amendments to the existing legal regime (e.g. protection of minority investors) are only slightly inferior to the introduction of new business forms aimed at promoting the efficiency considerations of this particular sub-class of businesses.

Since national policymakers are inclined to refrain from making wholesale changes in their legal regimes, due to the mandatory quality of the EC's directives on company law, critics suggest that lawmakers should resolve the high costs of internal and external rules by adopting a deregulatory policy in respect of the laws relating to the governance of closely held firms (Bachmann 2001). To take an example, one is inclined to point to the troublesome nature of 'over-regulation' with respect to quasi-partnership relationships (Raaijmakers 1994, 2000; De Kluiver 1995). Central to this view is the claim that relaxing the provisions of investor and creditor protection will provide a clear set of benefits to the participants of closely held firms. The goal of regulatory reform must be to balance the interests of third parties and the benefits to firms offered from modifying the salutatory structure to meet the interests of entrepreneurs. However an efficient regulatory response, involving a determination of the appropriate level of regulation, ultimately requires the application of cost/benefit decisions to ascertain the policy changes that must be undertaken. In pursuing this goal, policymakers could better focus on designing legislation that supplies greater flexibility for participants of small firms while offering them low-cost access to limited liability.

Proponents insist that closely held corporations in Europe are in fact a quasi-partnership. In an archetypical quasi-partnership form, the participants in the enterprise are understood as partners, mandating that the governance problems of the firm be resolved by reference to partnership law principles. In contrast to the USA, there really is something to this analogy. Participants in small firms across Europe select the quasi-partnership organizational form to take advantage of limited liability and the advantageous tax rules, even though corporate law governance norms are not optimal for this class of firms. However, courts increasingly attempt to resolve conflicts between parties in such closely held firms by reference to partnership law. Hence, equal rights in management, automatic buyout rights, and broad fiduciary duties govern 'partnership corporations'.

Still there may be problems with this approach to the legal control of closely held firms, since lawmakers run the risk of ignoring the needs of fast growing start-up firms that are in need of high levels of capital investment. There are roughly two types of firms that operate as closely held corporations. Historically, the family-run enterprise has formed the most significant component of business ventures that operate in this category (Rock and Wachter 1999). It is well known that legal rules differ for firms with capital symmetry than those without. However, recently the introduction of high-tech start-ups, which are a by-product of the changes in the business environment in some European countries, have contributed to a new demand for the use of this legal structure. The latter group of firms require a flexible enough set of legal rules to accommodate a wide range of financial incentive contracts, the effectiveness of which will depend on the characteristics of the external investors, the entrepreneurs, and other suppliers of capital to the firm. One might suspect that the mandatory nature of the legal rules governing closely held firms will not serve the needs of start-ups, consequently participants in such firms will be drawn to new forms that allow, to the greatest possible extent, modification of the statutory structure to suit their own needs. The questions raised by allowing firms to contract out of the terms set by the private company law statutes, and simultaneously allowing parties to create another menu tailored to their own purposes, is the main issue facing corporate law reformers within Europe.

8.3. THE IDEAL GOVERNANCE STRUCTURE FOR HIGH-TECH START-UPS

Some have widely ascribed the competitive strength of the US economy to the robust venture capital industry and the promotion of innovative start-ups. After we have briefly surveyed the central features of the venture capital cycle, we explore the importance of the corporate form in the USA, which seems to guide the venture capital process towards efficient outcomes. We expand on the legal discussions of the economic importance of its features for the growth of high-tech start-ups. We seek to show that the introduction of a similar cost-saving business form in Europe, which features a management governance structure and limited liability, promises to benefit the venture capital industry.

8.3.1. *The Venture Capital Process and the Legal Control of the Start-up Firm*

The venture capital process is often characterized as a 'pure agency relationship',[7] in which the entrepreneur is the agent and the venture capitalists are the principals (Gompers and Lerner 1999; Triantis 2001). Against the background of high risk and informational uncertainty, the venture capitalist may encounter complex and costly problems that are best addressed contractually. Given high asset input and uncertain valuations, the agency costs can be substantial in high-growth start-ups (Cossin *et al.*, Chapter 14, this volume). Typically, venture capitalists invest large stakes in 'entrepreneurs', whose abilities are often difficult to evaluate (Hellmann, Chapter 3, this volume). Accordingly, given the high probability of conflict between the venture capitalist and entrepreneur, investors will find it necessary to both monitor and bond the entrepreneur to reduce the agency costs that occur throughout the venture capital cycle.[8] It would seem that the absence of complete risk diversification and active market for shares holds out the potential for greater risk and reinforces the demand for high-level monitoring of entrepreneurs. A growing literature shows that agency costs will increase as assets become less tangible, which adds to the importance that monitoring can play in managing the relation between investor and entrepreneur.

Note that venture capitalists will monitor their investments through a combination of traditional corporate governance techniques (Barry *et al.* 1990; Gompers 1995; Hellmann 1998). For some firms, the active involvement by venture capitalists in key corporate functions and decisionmaking may limit a range of agency problems.[9] Yet information asymmetries are likely to persist because entrepreneurs control the flow of information, and consequently have the potential to create significant value dilution for investors. While there are many reasons for information infirmities within the start-up firm, the two dominant explanations are: (a) the entrepreneur has information unavailable to the venture capitalist, and (b) the entrepreneur's information is often distorted by reason of overestimation of his chances (Norton 1993). On the one hand, the former information regards the actual product, technology, and market as well as the quality, ethics, and fortitude of the entrepreneurial team whereas, on other hand, the latter could diverge dramatically from reality on account of the entrepreneur's personal attachment to the concern. In any event, the venture capitalists must be prepared, despite the entrepreneur's commitment in time and resources, to develop a course of action—which is contrary to

---

[7] Which is comparable to the relationship between the shareholders and managers in a publicly held corporation.

[8] See Gorman and Sahlman (1989); Hellmann (1998) (observing that, according to venture capitalists, entrepreneurs are prone to pursue actions that are in their personal interest as opposed to the company's interest).

[9] We acknowledge, however, that active involvement in the management of the firm may have the opposite and perverse effect; see Holmstrom and Tirole (1993).

the entrepreneur's interests—so as to protect the interests of other investors and ensure that the firm has a chance of going public (Hellmann and Puri 2000).

This conflict is naturally more contested when there is a control change decision as in the case of taking the company public (Sahlman 1990). Venture capitalists prefer to exit the start-up either through an initial public offering (IPO) or by way of a merger agreement (Holmén and Högfeldt 2000). In the context of the automatic conversion in the case of an IPO, the venture capitalist seeks to obtain the returns from his investment, while the entrepreneur aims to retain control and achieve an optimal payout (Black and Gilson, Chapter 2, this volume). It is worth pointing out that the nature and costs of exit are shaped also by the firm's underlying corporate governance structures, *ex ante* contracts, and the reputation of the underwriters (Holmén and Högfeldt 2000).

Proponents' claims about the importance of organizational forms and legal structures for the growth of start-ups suggest that certain corporate forms prove more successful in the long run. There is a burgeoning US literature on the relationship between organizational structure and firm performance. To be sure, commentators explain that, if Europe were to replicate the US market, it should give priority to establishing high labour mobility and risk tolerance (Milhaupt 1997); a well-developed stock market;[10] and large, independent sources of venture capital funding. However, despite these arguments, it is submitted that the availability of efficient business organizational forms must also play a central role in the development of a robust venture capital industry across Europe.

8.3.2. *The Employment of the Public Corporation Form in the USA*

When the economic environment is uncertain, US entrepreneurs seeking venture capital financing will select a business form that attenuates information problems (board structure and control) and incentive concerns (stock options) while retaining a flexible reward structure and providing tax advantages for investors. In this context, entrepreneurs have a variety of well-developed and standardized legal forms to choose from. However, many commentators have dismissed the importance of business forms as an ingredient in the success formula of the US venture capital market. The success of the US venture capital market is attributed mainly to the admixture of a vibrant and liquid capital market, which facilitates IPOs, and the critical use of financial instruments, which mitigate agency costs and support the efficient structuring of staged financing and the sustained level of new entrepreneurs with high capacity to realize their commercial aims. Nevertheless, the success of the venture capital market is arguably due to the availability of a corporate form that combines strong management and control characteristics with contractual flexibility. In this subsection, we assess the comparative advantages of the respective legal forms available to venture capital investors and their advisers.

In the USA, start-ups are structured predominantly as public corporations (Bankman 1994). Contracting into this regular corporate form even seems to attract venture capitalists in their own decisionmaking about one-time legal decisions. This is surprising in that the

---

[10] See Black and Gilson (Chapter 2, this volume) (arguing that a well-developed stock market permitting venture capitalists to exit through an IPO is critical to the existence of a vibrant venture capital market).

choice to incorporate entails that the predictable tax savings, which arise from the pass through tax treatment, are not accessible. These alleged tax savings may supply them with a respectable amount of money. The usual losses from the start-up venture do not flow through to the 'partner–shareholders' in a corporation while these tax-deductible losses could offset other sources of income at the parties' level. The use of other business forms, like a general partnership, limited partnership, or LLC, which couples internal flexibility with limited liability for all players and pass-through tax treatment, can yield more favourable benefits.

Naturally a question arises as to why venture capital players forgo tax savings by selecting the public corporation (Bankman 1994; Klausner 1995). The determination of the factors prompting venture capitalists to prefer the corporate legal form, as compared to other vehicles, is the subject of considerable controversy in the USA. For instance, William Callison and Deborah DeMott have argued that the governance structure rather than lower tax rate is the main consideration for venture capitalists selecting the corporate form (DeMott 1997; Callison 2000). With respect to determining the optimal business arrangement, it is submitted that the general partnership is not a viable alternative due to the excessive risks and agency costs in combination with personal liability for the partnership's debts. Although venture capitalists endeavour to avoid taking control of a start-up firm, the limited partnership is not a viable option as a consequence of the higher liability costs associated with downside risks. Furthermore, it is not to be expected, at least in Europe and increasingly in the USA, that entrepreneurs will leave their well-paid employment without *ex ante* liability protection.

The reluctance by high-tech start-ups to choose the LLC is explained in terms of a preference to save on transaction costs and time during the course of the venture capital cycle. For instance, by forming a public corporation they avoid the high costs of converting the LLC into the corporate form prior to an IPO. Indeed, underwriters in the USA rarely employ unincorporated business forms that can be utilized to issue equity interests (Bankman 1994). Yet from an efficiency standpoint, the legal, accounting, and organizational costs of a conversion do not explain why venture capitalists and their legally literate advisers are reluctant to experiment with other business forms, if tax savings exceed these costs. Paradoxically, venture capitalists and entrepreneurs, who are usually fond of innovations in the context of firm ventures, are apparently not especially eager, absent high-powered incentives, to experiment with other legal forms (Kahan and Klausner 1996).

In the context of staged financing, entrepreneurs tilt away from other business forms relative to the corporate form because their investors and independent advisers prefer a vehicle that provides parties with, in addition to a strong management and control structure, a set of well-developed, standardized, and widely used contractual structures. Thus, the learning and network effects, which respectively arise from prior and future usage of terms and/or statutes, confer benefits such as existing and prospective judicial precedents, common business practices, cheaper legal services, and positive effects on the valuation of businesses. The use of stock options as a compensation system for entrepreneurs reflects the prevalence of standardized venture capital contracts. Stock options, as distinct from fixed cash salaries, function as a contingent compensation that is linked to the business performance (McCahery and Renneboog 2001). Ideally, stock options provide an incentive to entrepreneurs to benchmark their performance in accordance with the venture capital-ists' expectations and prevent overly risky actions and opportunism. Although the great flexibility of the LLC statutes warrants a similar compensation system, parties prefer the use of stock options, thereby forgoing tax savings (Bankman 1994; Klausner 1995).

Furthermore, the competition for corporate charters among the states has broken down anachronistic mandatory state laws in the USA. As a result, general corporation laws have become more flexible allowing a closely held business to modify its charters in accordance with their special needs. Another benefit of the general corporate form is the uniformity among the state laws, whereas the LLC statutes vary according to state (Callison and Vestal 2001). It is, however, to be expected that the federal 'check-the-box' tax rule[11] will be responsible for the rapid development of corporate-type LLC statutes.[12] Within these considerations, the corporation as the preferred business form is likely to dominate until reputation or incentive reasons alter the preference profile of upstart incorporators.

8.4. THE INTRODUCTION OF A CORPORATE-TYPE LLC IN EUROPE

The European legal and commercial venture capital environment contrasts significantly with the US template. The European model relies on traditional legal techniques and financial instruments attuned to the needs of the large public corporation. Despite the importance of SMEs in the high-tech sector, there have been few legal reforms to enhance the wider dispersion of start-ups generally. Moreover, the legal rules that entrepreneurs must contract into have the tendency to create high barriers and, as a consequence, limit opportunity. In this section, we give consideration to the possibility of European lawmakers—who have not been very forthcoming—creating a corporate-type LLC which would meet the needs of start-ups.

The role of legal innovation is crucial to address the uncertainties which characterize the venture capital industry, and to accommodate the needs of both the entrepreneurs and venture capitalists, respectively. It may be that deregulation of corporate law is preferable to the multiplication of business forms, which can undoubtedly lead to uncertainty and a problem of choice (Freedman 1999). However attractive deregulation may be, it does not offer a swift and complete solution to the lock-in effect. Moreover, there are few jurisdictions in the EU which are responsive to the productive concerns of businesses seeking transferable shares and limited liability. In practice a large number of start-ups and close corporations are excluded from the large firm bias towards incorporating in a foreign jurisdiction. Under the circumstances, we would expect foreign corporations to migrate

---

[11] Under the Internal Revenue Service's (IRS) 'check-the-box' regulations, which became effective 1 January 1997 (Treas. Reg. Sections 301.7701–1 to –3, 61 Fed. Reg. 66,584 (1996)), unincorporated associations are taxed as partnerships unless they affirmatively elect to be taxed as corporations.

[12] See Ribstein (1995: 432) (arguing that, freed from the tax constraints, statutory business forms could proliferate further. According to Ribstein, the check-the-box tax treatment could signal the beginning of new corporate-type partnership and accelerate the demise of the close corporation). See also Callison (2000); Hamilton (1998: 161–2); Keatinge (1997).

to business friendly jurisdictions only if the negative externalities were sufficiently high. Since incorporation in a foreign state involves substantial transaction costs, it would not be immediately obvious that the benefits would outweigh the costs of foreign incorporation. We conclude that despite the potential for large public firms to select business forms from among the many European states, regulatory competition may be limited due to the absence of significant benefits for the incorporating firm. But we do not, of course, rule out the possibility of stepped-up regulatory competition if some states were to innovate by creating new vehicles that could encourage high-tech start-ups to migrate. We submit that the emergence of a new limited liability vehicle in Europe, that ideally suits the venture capital process, is better positioned to offset the inefficiencies resulting form the lock-in effects and could prompt the evolution of new forms across the EU.

Given the apparent demand for new business forms, we might expect the proliferation of new statutes from a range of EU domestic producers. One can plausibly project the legislatures of many Member States offering a variety of statutes, several of which provide different sets of default rules for distinct types of firms. The very novelty of this thesis is that introducing multiple business forms could benefit firms by supplying a flexible bundle of rules designed to meet the needs of different types of businesses, which provide an attractive means to limit information and transaction costs.[13] If there is sufficient demand from firms, we can expect a number of jurisdictions to provide the new forms so long as the costs of innovation are not too onerous. As a consequence, the introduction of new legal rules and structures (namely the reform of partnership forms) could overcome the barriers and opposition by interest groups to innovative legal rules. At a more general level, we might expect the introduction of a partnership-like business form to serve as a framework to assess the level of flexibility in the organizational rules of the new business forms (Ribstein 2001). However, this legal innovation story is unlikely to prove compelling since it is submitted that the negative externalities and other costs could deter the proliferation of new forms.

As we see it, the debate over innovation in European business organization law turns on the credibility of national lawmakers finding a compelling reason to abandon the defence of well-entrenched legal forms and the mandatory rules that reinforce their position (and consequently block the diffusion of new innovative legal rules). Provided that the proposed statutes afford a workable menu of beneficial provisions and are attractive enough to be widely used, the new legal forms could supply a focal point around which new networks arise. If the new forms were to offer the appropriate protections and incentives that draw (potential) venture capital firms into its framework, we should expect support from a number of organized businesses and professional groups. The new form's inherent benefits exceeding the lost benefits of leaving the current private corporate law form is a prerequisite

---

[13] See Ribstein (1995, 2001). For instance, commentators have suggested that the UK LLP could satisfy the needs of venture capitalists and their investors (see Jones 2001: 1–2 and 12–13). However, we submit that an LP-type form conceived along the lines of the US limited liability limited partnership (LLLP) (see the Revision of the Revised Uniform Limited Partnership Act: Re-RULPA) might better meet the contracting requirements of the European venture capital funds. The business form we suggest in this paper would complement the 'LLLP' since it could be an efficient means to organize the venture capitalists' portfolio investments in high-tech start-ups.

for its success. It might be argued that these arguments alone do not support a convincing counter-story to the foregoing analysis. But if we look to the governance benefits that emerge from the introduction of new business statutes, we expect that innovative forms will attract those new style, high-tech firms that cannot benefit from the older, existing legal forms.[14] Furthermore, evidence from the USA shows that the introduction of a new form could provide the necessary impetus to help erode the mandatory nature of EC corporate law rules (Ribstein 2001).

8.4.1. *Towards a Venture Capital Organizational Form*

If we accept the view that the introduction of new legal vehicles could stimulate the evolution of business organization forms in Europe, then this account of legal change has very sharp implications for the way we might alter the structure and form of the different legal rules relating to venture capital-backed firms. Looking just at the venture capital industry, investors and entrepreneurs take advantage of a combination of contractual and organizational structures to manage the allocation of resources and the monitoring and control of agents within the venture. This subsection will consider the potential benefits that an LLC business form—with management-based structures—could have for the monitoring and control of high-tech start-ups.

The attractiveness of the US LLC statutes can be seen in contrast with other similar-styled business forms in Table 8.1.

The US form provides virtually a complete shield against personal liability—this is important given the risk inherent to a highly innovative start-up—without cumbersome formation and capital maintenance rules. As for the consideration for the payment of 'shares', most LLC statutes provide that contributions may be made to the firm in many different forms, such as 'tangible or intangible property or other benefit to the company, including money, promissory notes, services performed, or other agreements to contribute cash or property, or contracts for services to be performed'.[15] Most LLC statutes provide extreme flexibility with respect to the internal organization. Although a legal entity, an LLC is best viewed as a contract among the members of the firm. The operating agreement even overrides the articles of organization in the case of a conflict. However, a great majority of LLC statutes provide for decentralized management directly by the members unless otherwise provided.

Even though several features of this form may be suitable to entrepreneurs and venture capitalists, this default rule for the governance structure of the LLC is, as we argued in Section 8.3, not optimal for the typical venture capitalist who attempts to limit his exposure to risk and opportunism through a combination of contractual measures (e.g. covenants) and the active monitoring of management. The principal–agent literature shows that the

---

[14] See Oesterle (1995) (stating that the adoption of LLC statutes expresses displeasure with evolving case law affecting small business); Ribstein (2001) (stating that a menu of business forms allows firms to adopt a set of rules that is coherent, invites efficient gap-filling by courts, and helps ensure efficient application of regulatory provisions). See also Rock and Wachter (1999).

[15] See Uniform Limited Liability Company Act, Section 401.

Table 8.1. *Comparison of US LLC and other business forms*

	LLP (UK)	Partnership (US) (RUPA)	LLC (US)	GmbH (Germany)	EPC (Proposal)
Legal personality	Entity by registration	Entity	Entity	Entity	Entity
Partnership property	LLP holds property	Partnership holds property	LLC holds property	GmbH holds property	EPC holds property
Management	Decentralized	Decentralized	Decentralized (default)/Centralized	Centralized	Opt-in
Agents	Partners	Partners	Member–manager(s)	Manager–director(s)	Opt-in
Liability	Limited	Joint and several Limited by filing a statement	Limited	Limited (capital requirements)	Limited (capital requirements)
Fiduciary duties	No general duty of good faith. Specific duties in the regulations to account for competing activities and use of partnership property.	Duties of loyalty and care Obligation of good faith and fair dealing	Information right/ Good faith and fair dealing	Information right (Sections 51a and 51b GmbHG) If 'incorporated partnership' strong 'fiduciary' duties	Information rights Opt-in
Management rights	Agreement. In absence of agreement every member may take part in management	Every partner may take part in management	Every member may take part in management Agreement may provide for classes of voting	Member–shareholders may participate in the control of the business	Opt-in
Financial rights	Agreement. In absence of agreement equal sharing rights	Equal sharing	If no agreement, sharing in proportion to the partner's contribution to capital	Sharing in proportion to the partner's contribution to capital	Opt-in

Table 8.1. *Continued*

	LLP (UK)	Partnership (US) (RUPA)	LLC (US)	GmbH (Germany)	EPC (Proposal)
Transferability of interest	Yes	Generally, no	Yes, restrictions are imposed by state laws, securities laws, and LLC operating agreement	Yes, but shares cannot be publicly traded	Opt-in
Continuity of life	Continuation of existence in spite of any change in membership	Continuation on buy-out of dissociated partner's interest	Withdrawal does not dissolve the LLC	Perpetual life unless the articles of incorporation provide to the contrary	Opt-in
Dissolution and winding-up	Corporate insolvency and winding-up procedures	Specified events	Specified events	Specified events	National regime
Formation	Incorporation document (two or more members)	Informal (two or more partners)	Public filing with the Secretary of State (one or more members)	Public filing of notary deed of incorporation and fulfilment of capital requirements (one or more members)	Public filing in one of the Member States and fulfilment of capital requirements (one or more members)
Taxation	Partnership	Pass-through 'check-the-box'	Pass-through 'check-the-box'	Corporate	National regime

failure to separate ownership from control will limit the benefits of specialization in the firm's decisionmaking. For example, if members are prepared to undertake the financial risk, and supply services for the firm's ventures, it does not follow necessarily that these members will be equally suited and talented to make the appropriate management decisions about the allocation of firm resources. Second, the integration of ownership and control means undifferentiated management decisionmaking, which entails a more cumbersome, costly, and restricted process. Finally, a member-dominated firm will suffer higher costs due to absence of monitoring and intervention devices to intervene on behalf of investors.

To be sure, the difficulty of the failure to separate ownership from control could be overcome by careful drafting of the firm's LLC agreement. In fact, some LLC statutes provide that a firm may be centrally managed if the statute provides for decentralized management but allows the parties to contract around the statute (Ribstein and Keatinge 1999). However, devising the optimal LLC structure is difficult to achieve. On the one hand, the flexibility afforded by the LLC statutes takes into account the diverse organizational needs of a variety of firms. In this regard, the LLC statute can play a significant role in transaction planning and design. On the other hand, there is an important trade-off between a high degree of flexibility and the cost of specificity. Extensive tailoring of default rules of an LLC statute, to satisfy the needs of venture capitalists, may be problematic due to the effort and transaction costs involved in contracting around the statutory defaults. Indeed, as US evidence shows, venture capitalists are reluctant to choose and modify an LLC statute despite it beneficial tax treatment and flexible structure. In such an environment, we expect that a successful and attractive LLC statute, which captures the needs of venture capitalists, will supply a set of 'off-the-rack' rules that include corporate governance-style provisions.

An optimal business form should also allow investors to exit their investments via an IPO. Even though the US LLC allows for publicly traded 'units', which are nothing more than depository receipts for the owners' property interests, the efficiency of selling units is called into question because underwriters are probably unwilling to employ 'units' on a large scale. If European lawmakers wish to create a favourable business environment for new firms, they should design an LLC vehicle that allows owners to have a share capital that is similar to corporate forms.[16] We suspect also that the incentive and protection mechanisms, which are necessary to prevent opportunistic behaviour, may be best achieved by the employment of corporate-type stock.

8.5. REGULATORY COMPETITION

The potential introduction of new business forms holds out the prospects of overcoming the negative effects of lock-in. We now turn to regulatory competition theory and ask whether there are sufficient incentives to create adequate demand for the introduction and diffusion of new LLC and partnership-like forms.

---

[16] In this case, the new form is in a sense analogous to a limited partnership with a share capital.

In terms of assessing the likelihood of the enactment of new business forms, there are several classes of start-ups that might be attracted by its cost-saving benefits. The first class is made of future start-ups that come into existence in the new limited liability form, but will never come into existence if this form is not available. It is expected that low formation costs will appeal to potential entrepreneurs who cannot afford a private company on their savings. A new business form could encourage them to undertake the risk of working out an innovative idea. Furthermore, if the new form provides an extensive set of protective default provisions for both the venture capitalists and the entrepreneurs, the number of start-ups may increase. The second class consists of future start-ups, which, but for the new form, would incorporate in the more expensive private company. The third class contains prospective portfolio companies that, at the insistence of the venture capitalists, will convert into the VC form. A fourth class contains the existing portfolio firms for which cost savings will accrue in the event of reorganization to the VC form, with the savings exceeding the cost of reorganization. Presumably, the number of firms in this last class will be very small, as dramatic contractual changes are not likely during the process of venture capital funding.

The appearance of more successful start-ups could foster prosperity and economic welfare. However, the powerful forces of efficiency and public welfare alone are not always sufficient to prompt lawmakers to undertake reforms along these lines. Granted that special interest groups can sometimes help to persuade the legislature that this is a propitious moment for reform, the question remains which powerful groups will support the proposal and what are the chances of its eventual enactment? In this case, the alliance of market sector interest groups, especially those groups tied to or affiliated to the venture capitalists themselves, may emerge as a strong lobby group. In most jurisdictions, the domestic equity exchanges conceivably could join in the lobbying process. In a period of fierce competition among European stock markets, good listing opportunities for an attractive venture capital vehicle could result in the desired spurt of listings. Finally, SME organizations will have a high-powered incentive to lobby for this innovative business form, which disposes of the cumbersome, time-consuming formation requirements and bolsters entrepreneurship.

On the positive side, we expect that some business lawyers may have sufficient incentives to support reform proposals. They can expect increased fees as a consequence of many classes of firms being attracted to a new, low-cost business vehicle. Conversely, the notaries—lawyers who specialize in incorporations and have qualified to issue a notarial deed—could organize themselves as a significant interest group, blocking innovative measures and frustrating attempts at effective implementation. In continental Europe, a notary deed is usually required for all incorporations. Given their well-entrenched position and proximity to the lawmaking process, it is advised that establishment of new forms preferably does not require issuance of such a deed. If the venture capital vehicle (and allied forms) were to gain adherence amongst investors and popularity with business lawyers, notaries' fee revenues might therefore drop substantially. Since their losses are probably more acute than the possible gains of the business lawyers generated by the pent-up demand, the notaries will have a particularly high-powered incentive to block this new form. Since both types of lawyers often practice together in law firms, these professionals will strongly disfavour reform. We expect further that Treasury and Revenue officials employed by national government will be opposed to legislative action to the extent that the new business form's flow-through tax treatment implies revenue losses, and could well organize interest group opposition to the introduction of new forms.

If we compare and weigh the competing interests on the 'demand-side' of legislation, we do not have a clear-cut story about the likelihood of enactment. The outcome will depend largely on the power of the alliance of market sector interest groups. However, we cannot make an adequate prediction without taking into account the 'supply side' (Laffont and Tirole 1993) of the legislation process. Legislative procedures reduce the stakes interest groups have in regulation, and, as a consequence, the supply side, that is, the political and regulatory institutions, plays a decisive role with respect to a new legal form. As far as the governmental institutions are maximizers of public welfare, an innovative business form might be enacted if policymakers are convinced that it is beneficial to job-creation and technology developments.

8.5.1. *Responsive Lawmaking and the Demand for Venture Capital Finance*

Governments, given the supply and demand for venture capital finance, have incentives to act entrepreneurally by undertaking legal reform efforts designed to stimulate venture capital investment (Bratton and McCahery 1997*a*). They may act to lift the curse that rests on Europe's regulatory competition's black box by actively attempting to 'attract investment or business activity or to promote the competitiveness of indigenous industries by providing a more favourable' business form (Woolcock 1996). Regulatory competition appears most unequivocally when rent incentives induce jurisdictions to compete for nominally sited legal relationships (Bratton and McCahery 1997*b*). These are unbundled legal products that can be sold separately to foreign consumers. Their provision leads to a two-party transaction resembling a conventional sale of goods. But strong competitive incentives do not show up, even among these horizontally situated suppliers of law—in these cases small jurisdictions tend to take leading competitive roles. Delaware, one of the smallest states, is the jurisdiction of incorporation of about half the firms listed on the NYSE. Small states tend to offer themselves as tax havens (Bratton and McCahery 2001). The explanation prevailing for Delaware probably applies across the board. The incentive effects of legal business of this sort loom large in a small jurisdiction. Even if, as with corporate law, incentives to compete clearly are present, legal competition may be subject to structural barriers that inhibit the evolution of efficient legal rules. In fact, states will have few incentives to invest the necessary resources for innovation if there are insufficient rents. The incentive picture on the supply and demand side become more complex when we shift our analysis to the production of a single legal product. Here, unlike the cost–benefit calculations in conventional product markets, political cost–benefit calculations tie bundles of issues together and, when legislation is involved, involve rent incentives and the welfare of multiple actors.

An innovative business organization form that makes it possible to emulate the most efficient US venture capital contracts may well attract sceptical foreign venture capitalists and entrepreneurs. The future may likely bring a significant increase in the number of start-up firms migrating to the most favourable jurisdiction to venture capital contracting, as envisaged by the ECJ's opinion in Centros.[17] An entrepreneurial state could reap the benefits (particularly if it changed its tax levels for certain business vehicles) by coming to the fore with a set of rules that are ideally suited to the venture capital process.[18] Indeed, the recent history of the reform of the private equity limited partnership, the standard organization form used by venture capitalists in the USA, UK, and continental Europe to supply finance to start-up companies (Gompers and Lerner 1999; Lerner and Schoar 2002), suggests that governments have strong incentives to create efficient legal rules designed to meet the needs of firms.[19]

In the UK, the limited partnership organizational form has enjoyed an upsurge of popularity in the venture capital industry since venture capital funds were allowed to employ LPs in 1987 (Law Commission 2001). Especially, the tax benefits, the flexibility surrounding its structure and terms, and its fixed life make the limited partnership the dominant venture capital fund vehicle. Despite several drawbacks, like limited partnership shares not being publicly tradable and the archaic law governing this form,[20] UK limited partnerships have become the standard structure used by European venture capitalists in

---

[17] See Case 21/297 Centros Ltd. v. Erhvervs-og Selskabsstryelsen [1999] ECR I-1459, §27: 'It is contrary to Articles 52 and 58 of the EC Treaty for a Member State to refuse to register a branch of a company formed in accordance with the law of another Member State in which it has its registered office but in which it conducts no business where the branch is intended to enable the company in question to carry on its entire business in the State in which the branch is to be created, while avoiding the need to form a company there, thus evading application of the rules governing the formalities of companies which, in that State, are more restrictive as regards the paying up of a minimum share capital'.

[18] See Goforth (1995); Ribstein (1995); Ribstein and Kobayashi (1997, 2001). US data on LLC and LLP forms demonstrates that sufficient demand for new unincorporated business forms could give legislators and interest groups an incentive to supply these forms.

[19] It should be noted, however, that few European jurisdictions have responded rapidly to the competitive pressures by enacting new limited partnership legislation more suitable for venture capital investment. German academics, for example, recommend that domestic lawmakers become more involved in responsive (i.e. competitive) lawmaking. Yet, corresponding interest group pressures have not sufficiently emerged so as to warrant German legislative attention to the competitive pressures highlighted by the academic debate (Bachman 2001). Nevertheless, Germany's popular commercial partnership-type business form, the GmbH & Co KG, which already has created considerable learning and network effects in Germany, has the potential to increase Germany's share of the European venture capital industry. Moreover, the limited partnerships with shares (Komanditgesellschaft auf Aktien, KgaA), in which the general partners have exclusive management control and limited partners may transfer their shares freely, appears to respond to the pent-up demand for more easily tradable private equity investments. Indeed, as interests in venture capital funds already change hands increasingly in the secondary market, the conversion to a combination of a limited partnership and a public corporation, which offers ready access to liquidity and market price, could be a viable alternative. However, in order to be competitive, legal and fiscal complications regarding the hybrid business forms should be minimized. Although Germany has recently created laws and regulations to clarify the position of these vehicles, more needs to be done to make them the standard structure for European venture capital funds. For instance, consideration should be given to codifying 'safe harbour' provisions. Moreover, the law should be more generous in liability protection for a limited partner, if the formation of the limited partnership or the admission of the limited partner have not been filed in the commercial register.

[20] See Myners (2001) (arguing that English partnership law is particularly cumbersome because of imposing strict constraints on the number of partners and on limited partners' involvement in investment advisory work). At the time partnership law was under construction in the UK, there was another deficiency in English partnership law: English partnerships were not legal entities. This explains why Scottish limited partnerships with separate personality have been used for as investment vehicles in Lloyds, which only permitted separate legal persons to be Lloyds names. Presumably Guernsey has recently given its limited partnerships the possibility to opt for legal personality so as to attract underwriting members of Lloyds. See Law Commission (2001: 2).

general. However, the UK's position is under threat of losing its prominent position to other jurisdictions that have introduced or planned to design modern legislation on limited partnerships.[21] It is not surprising, therefore, that policymakers are planning to revise the Limited Partnership Act 1907 by proposing to abolish the rule on the maximum number of partners (presently limited to 20) and introduce 'safe harbour' provisions similar to those found in the Delaware Revised Uniform Limited Partnership Act and Jersey's limited partnership form, which would make it clear that limited partners may participate in the control of the firm so as to improve certainty and accessibility to foreign investors.[22] The threat of competition in combination with the lobbying efforts of venture capitalists and sophisticated investors will arguably make UK limited partnership law more sophisticated and suitable for venture capital investment (see Table 8.2).[23] As a consequence, the limited partnership law reform fits the UK government's objectives of creating modern business organization forms supporting the needs of a competitive economy.

8.6. CONCLUSION

We conclude that if an entrepreneurial state (i.e. England, Ireland, Luxembourg, etc.) were the first to create a corporate-type LLC form, it could very well create a focal point leading a significant number of domestic and foreign firms to select from a new generation of business forms.[24] This could give such a state a lead in start-up formations and, due to favourable IPO opportunities, a more vibrant and competitive financial market. While the best available evidence indicates that the barriers to innovation are substantial, we submit that a number of states may have a financial incentive to compete for venture by offering new organization forms to business. There is, however, one impediment to this generally positive regulatory competition scenario: the possibility that other states free-ride on the efforts and resources of the national legislatures of small states by copying their statutes might entail that the lead will be exhausted in a very short space of time. Free-riding by other jurisdictions could act as a disincentive to invest any resources in legal innovation (Bratton and McCahery 1995). The only solution to this supply-side problem is for the first-mover states to develop less easily replicated expertise or other long-run advantages, like good securities regulations and a deep capital market, or a highly specialized commercial court (Romano 1993, 2001).

---

[21] The Joint Consultation Paper on the Limited Partnership Act 1907 alludes to Bermuda, the Cayman Islands, Delaware, Guernsey, Ireland, and Jersey.

[22] See Delaware Revised Uniform Limited Partnership Act (Title 6, chapter 17 of the Delaware Code) available at www.legis.stat.de.us/; Law Commission (2001).

[23] In this respect, the Chairmen of the Law Commission agree that: 'The limited partnership is a very important vehicle in certain specialized fields, such as venture capital and property development. It has flourished despite the obvious imperfections of the 1907 Act. There is now strong pressure from those operating in this specialized field for improvements to enable the law in the UK to continue to compete effectively with foreign jurisdictions, such as Delaware and the Channel Islands, which have recently overhauled their limited partnership statutes'. See Law Reform, News from the Law Commissions, Limited Partnership Act 1907 Consultation.

[24] US data also show that competitive pressures could play a significant role in the drafting and enactment of unincorporated business forms. In the UK, the creation of the LLP form in Jersey and subsequently in England supports the regulatory competition hypothesis. We should note, however, that there are greater barriers to the creation of a cross-border market for incorporations for close corporations.

Table 8.2. *Comparison of US LP and traditional LP*

Characteristic	LP (traditional)	LP (Re-RULPA)
Relationship to general partnership act	Linked	De-linked (but many RUPA provisions incorporated)
Duration	Specified	Perpetual; subject to change in partnership agreement
Use of limited partner name in entity name	Prohibited	Permitted
Limited partner liability for entity debts	None unless limited partner participates in the control of the business and persons transacting with the limited partnership could believe that the limited partner is a general partner	None, regardless of whether the limited partnership is an LLLP, 'even if the limited partner participates in the management and control of the limited partnership'
Limited partner duties	None specified	No fiduciary duties 'solely by reason of being a limited partner'; each limited partner is obliged to 'discharge duties . . . and exercise rights consistently with the obligation of good faith and fair dealing'
Partner access to information—required records/information	All partners have right of access; linked to general partnership	List of required information; Act expressly states that partner does not have to show good cause; however, the partnership agreement may set reasonable restrictions on access to and use of required information, and limited partnership may impose reasonable restrictions on the use of information
General partner liability for entity debts	Complete, automatic, and formally inescapable (n.b.—in practice, most modern limited partnerships have used a general partner that has its own liability shield, e.g. a corporation)	LLLP status available via a simple statement in the certificate of limited partnership; LLLP status provides a full liability shield to all general partners; if the limited partnership is not an LLLP, general partners are liable just as under RULPA
General partner duties	Linked to general partnership	RUPA general partner duties imported; general partner's non-compete duty continues during winding up
Allocation of profits, losses, and distributions	Linked to general partnership	Allocates distributions according to contributions made

Limited partner voluntary dissociation	Linked to general partnership	No 'right to dissociate as a limited partner before the termination of the limited partnership'; power to dissociate expressly recognized, but can be eliminated by the partnership agreement
General partner voluntary dissociation	Linked to general partnership	Right exists; dissociation before termination of the limited partnership is defined as wrongful
Dissolution following dissociation of a general partner	Occurs automatically unless agreements states otherwise; linked to general partnership	If at least one general partner remains, no dissolution unless 'within 90 days after the dissociation . . . partners owning a majority of the rights to receive distributions as partners' consent to dissolve the limited partnership; if no general partner remains, dissolution occurs upon the passage of 90 days after the dissociation, unless before that deadline limited partners owning a majority of the rights to receive distributions owned by limited partners consent to continue the business and admit at least one new general partner and a new general partner is admitted
Conversions and mergers	Generally no provision; however, German Merger Act permits conversions, etc.	Re-RULPA permits conversions to and from and mergers with any 'organization', defined as 'a general partnership, including a LLP, limited partnership, including a LLLP; LLC; business trust; corporation; or any other entity having a governing statute . . . [including] domestic and foreign entities regardless of whether organized for profit'

Source: Uniform Limited Partnership Act (2001) drafted by the National Conference of Commissioners on Uniform State Laws.

References

Bachmann, G. (2001), 'Grundtendenzen der Reform geschlossener Gesellschaften in Europa', *Zeitschrift für Unternehmens- und Gesellschaftsrecht* 351–84.

Bankman, J. (1994), 'The structure of Silicon Valley start-ups', *UCLA Law Review* 41, 1737–68.

Barry, C. B., Muscarella, C. J., Peavy III, J. W., and Vetsuypens, M. R. (1990), 'The role of venture capital in the creation of public companies', *Journal of Financial Economics* 27, 447–71.

Bernstein, L. (1995), 'The Silicon Valley lawyer as transaction cost engineer', *Oregon Law Review* 74, 239–55.

Bisacre, J. (1999), 'A European perspective on small business and the law', in B. A. K. Rider and M. Andenas (eds), *Developments in European Company Law Volume 2/1997: The Quest for an Ideal Legal Form for Small Businesses*, The Hague: Kluwer Law International, 87–96.

Bratton, W. W. and McCahery, J. A. (1995), 'Regulatory competition, regulatory capture, and corporate self-regulation', *North Carolina Law Review* 73, 1861–948.

—— (1997a), 'An inquiry into the efficiency of the limited liability company: of theory of the firm and regulatory competition', *Washington & Lee Law Review* 54, 629–86.

—— (1997b), 'The new economics of jurisdictional competition: devolutionary federalism in a second-best world', *Georgetown Law Journal* 86, 201–78.

—— (2001), 'Tax coordination and tax competition in the European Union: evaluating the code of conduct on business taxation', *Common Market Law Review* 38, 677–718.

Callison, J. W. (2000), 'Venture capital and corporate governance: evolving the limited liability company to finance the entrepreneurial business', *Journal of Corporation Law* 26, 97–124.

—— and Vestal, A. W. (2001), ' "They've created a lamb with mandibles of death": secrecy disclosure, and fiduciary duties in limited liability firms', *Indiana Law Journal* 76, 271–313.

Cheffins, B. (1997), *Company law, theory structure and operation*, Oxford: Oxford University Press.

De Kluiver, H. J. (1995), 'The European private company? A Dutch perspective', in H. J. De Kluiver and W. Van Gerven (eds), *The European private company?*, Antwerpen: MAKLU, 109–28.

Deakin, S. (2001), 'Regulatory competition versus harmonization in European company law', in Esty, D. C. and Geradin, D. (eds), *Regulatory Competition and Economic Integration*, Oxford: Oxford University Press, 190–217.

DeMott, D. A. (1997), 'Agency and the unincorporated firm: reflections on design on the same plane of interest', *Washington & Lee Law Review* 54, 595–612.

Easterbrook, F. H. and Fischel, D. R. (1991), *The Economic Structure of Corporate Law*, Cambridge, MA: Harvard University Press.

Freedman, J. (1999), 'The quest for an ideal form for small businesses—A misconceived enterprise?', in B. A. K. Rider and M. Andenas (eds), *Developments in European Company Law Volume 2/1997: The Quest for an Ideal Legal Form for Small Businesses*, The Hague: Kluwer Law International, 5–34.

Goforth, C. R. (1995), 'The rise of the limited liability company: evidence of a race between the states, but heading where?', *Syracuse Law Review* 45, 1193–289.

Gompers, P. A. (1995), 'Optimal investment, monitoring, and the staging of venture capital', *Journal of Finance* 50, 1461–89.

—— and Lerner, J. (1999), *The Venture Capital Cycle*, Cambridge, MA: MIT Press.

Gorman, M. and Sahlman, W. H. (1989), 'What do venture capitalists do?', *Journal of Business Venturing* 4, 231–48.

Hamilton, R. W. (1998), *Corporations Including Partnerships and Limited Liability Companies, Cases and Materials*, St. Paul: West Group.

Hellmann, Th. (1998), 'The allocation of control rights in venture capital contracts', *RAND Journal of Economics* 29, 57–76.

Hellmann, Th. and Puri, M. (2000), 'Venture capital and the professionalization of start-ups: empirical evidence', Working Paper, Stanford University.

Helms, D. (1998), *Die Europäische Privatgesellschaft*, Köln: Verlag Dr. Otto Schmidt.

Hertig, G. and McCahery, J. A. (2004), 'Company law and takeover law reforms in Europe: Misguided harmonization efforts or regulatory competition? in G. Ferrarini, K. Hopt, J. Winter and E. Wymeersch (eds.), A Modern Regulatory Framework for Company and Takeover Law in Europe, Oxford: Oxford University Press.

Holmén, M. and Högfeldt, P. (2000), 'A law and finance analysis of initial public offerings', Working Paper, Stockholm School of Economics.

Holmström, B. R. and Tirole, J. (1993), 'Market liquidity and performance monitoring', *Journal of Political Economy* 101, 678–709.

Jones, L. (2001), 'The UK's new LLP corporate entity could help stimulate entrepreneurship and innovation', *EuroWatch 2001*, 1–2 and 12–13.

Kahan, M. and Klausner, M. (1996), 'Path dependence in corporate contracting: increasing returns, behavior and cognitive biases', *Washington University Law Quarterly* 74, 347–366.

Keatinge, R. R. (1997), 'Corporations, unincorporated organizations, and unincorporations: check the box and the balkanization of business organizations', *Journal of Small and Emerging Business Law* 1, 201–48.

Klausner, M. (1995), 'Corporations, corporate law, and networks of contracts', *Virginia Law Review* 81, 757–852.

Laffont, J-J. and Tirole, J. (1993), *A Theory of Incentives in Procurement and Regulation*, Cambridge, MA: MIT Press.

Law Commission of England and Wales and Scottish Law Commission (2001), 'The Limited Partnerships Act 1907: A joint consultation paper', London: TSO, LCCP 161, SLCDP 118.

Lerner, J. and Schoar, A. (2002), 'The illiquidity puzzle: theory and evidence from private equity', Working paper, Harvard Business School.

Lutter, M. (1998), 'Limited liability companies and private companies,' in D. Vagts (ed.), *International Encyclopaedia of Comparative Law*, Vol. XIII, chapter 2, Tübingen: Mohr Siebeck.

McCahery, J. A. and Renneboog, L. (2001), 'Management remuneration: the indirect pay for performance relation', *Journal of Corporate Law Studies* 1, 317–32.

—— (2003), 'The Evolution of the unincorporated firm: an introduction', in J. A. McCahery, T. Raaijmakers, and E. Vermeulen (eds), Governance of close corporations and partnerships, Oxford: Oxford University Press.

Milhaupt, C.J. (1997), 'The market for innovation in the United States and Japan: venture capital and the comparative corporate governance debate', *Northwestern University Law Review* 91, 865–98.

Myners, P. (2001), *Institutional Investors in the United Kingdom: A Review*, London: AB.

Norton, E. (1993), 'Venture capital finance: review and syntheses', in C. F. Lee (ed.), *Advances in Quantitive Analysis of Finance and Accounting*, Greenwich: JAI Press, 141–65.

OECD (2000), 'Small and Medium Enterprises Outlook', Paris: OECD.

Oesterle, D. A. (1995), 'Subcurrents in LLC statutes: limiting the discretion of state courts to restructure the internal affairs of small business', *University of Colorado Law Review* 66, 881–920.

Raaijmakers, M. J. G. C. (2000), *Vennootschaps—en Rechtspersonenrecht*, Deventer: Gouda Quint.

—— (1994), 'Besloten vennootschappen': quasi-nv of quasi-vof?, *Ars Aequi* 43, 76–84.

Ribstein, L. E. (1995), 'Statutory forms for closely held firms: theories and evidence from LLCs', *Washington University Law Quarterly* 73, 369–432.

—— and Keatinge, R. P. (1999), Limited Liability Companies, St. Paul: West Group.

—— (2001), 'The evolving partnership', *Journal of Corporation Law* 26, 819–54.

—— and Kobayashi, B. H. (1997), 'Federalism, efficiency and competition', Working Paper, George Mason University.

—— (2001), 'Choice of form and network externalities', *William and Mary Law Review* 43, 79–140.

Rock, E. B. and Wachter, M. L. (1999), 'Waiting for the omelet to set: match-specific assets and minority oppression in the close corporation', *Journal of Corporation Law* 24, 913–48.

Romano, R. (1993), *The Genius of American Corporate Law*, Washington: American Enterprise Institute Press.

—— (1996), 'Explaining American exceptionalism in corporate law', in W. W. Bratton, J. A. McCahery, S. Picciotto, and C. Scott (eds), *International Regulatory Competition and Coordination, Perspectives on Economic Regulation in Europe and the United States*, Oxford: Clarendon Press, 127–52.

—— (2001), 'The need for competition in international securities regulation', *Theoretical Inquiries in Law* 2, 387–562.

Sahlman, W. A. (1990), 'The structure and governance of venture-capital organizations', *Journal of Financial Economics* 27, 473–521.

Triantis, G. G. (2001), 'Financial contract design in the world of venture capital', Working Paper, University of Chicago.

Whincop, M. (2000), 'An empirical investigation of the terms of corporate charters and influences on term standardization in a laissez-faire environment', Working Paper, University of Cambridge.

Woolcock, S. (1996), 'Competition among rules in the single European market', in Bratton, W. W., McCahery, J. A., S. Picciotto, and C. Scott (eds), *International Regulatory Competition and Coordination, Perspectives on Economic Regulation in Europe and the United States*, Oxford: Clarendon Press, 189–321.

Wouters, J. (2000), 'European company law: quo vadis?', *Common Market Law Review* 37, 257–307.

Young, S. (2000), 'Limited liability partnerships—a chance for peace of mind', *Business Law Review* 2000, 258–60.

9

Venture Capital and Innovation: Clues to a Puzzle

SAMUEL KORTUM AND JOSH LERNER

9.1. INTRODUCTION

Over the past decade, there has been a dramatic expansion of public programs around the globe to encourage the formation of venture capital funds. These programs share a common rationale: that venture capital has spurred innovation in the USA, and can do so elsewhere (see, for instance, the European Commission's Green Paper on Innovation 1995).

The rationales for these programs, however, have not been scrutinized, even though there appear to be several successes: many founders of pioneering independent venture firms in the 1960s received their initial experience in funds that were established as part of the Small Business Investment Company programme in the USA. Observers also attributed much of the initial formation of high-tech firms and business intermediaries in the 'Silicon Valley' and 'Route 128' regions to this program.

The Israeli government initiated two programs to encourage the formation of venture capital funds in 1991. Many analysts claim that the Yozma and Inbal initiatives led to not only an increase in venture capital under management (from $29 million in 1991 to over $550 million in 1997), but to a burst of investment by foreign high-tech companies in Israeli R&D and manufacturing facilities.

Singapore began aggressively promoting venture capital funds in 1985. The impact on venture capital activity has been dramatic—in 1996, over 100 funds managed over $7.7 billion, up from two funds and $42 million in 1985—and a number of observers have argued that these programs have led to a more general increase in high-tech R&D activity.

This chapter takes a first step towards systematically assessing policies to promote venture capital. It examines not the success of the initiatives themselves, but rather the

We thank Chris Allen, Ben Conway, Kay Hashimoto, Justin Jow, Bac Nguyen, and Patty Pitzele for research assistance. Jim Hirabayashi, Adam Jaffe, Jesse Reyes, and F. M. Scherer generously provided assistance with patent and venture capital data. Helpful comments were provided by Eli Berman, Jonathan Eaton, Simon Gilchrist, Zvi Griliches, Kevin Lang, Kaivan Munshi, Robert Porter, Joel Waldfogel, three anonymous referees, and various seminar participants. The US National Science Foundation and the Harvard Business School's Division of Research provided financial support. This chapter is an expanded version of Kortum and Lerner (2000). All errors are our own.

reasonableness of an essential premise behind the efforts: that venture capital funds spur technological innovation.

We proceed by exploring the experience of twenty industries covering the US manufacturing sector over a three-decade period. We first examine in reduced-form regressions whether, controlling for R&D spending, venture capital funding has an impact on the number of patented innovations. We find that venture capital is associated with a substantial increase in patenting. The results are robust to a variety of specifications of how venture capital and R&D affect patenting and to different definitions of venture capital.

We then consider the limitations of this approach. We present a stylized model of the relationship between venture capital, R&D, and innovation. This model suggests that simple reduced-form regressions may overstate the effect of venture funding. Both venture funding and patenting could be positively related to a third unobserved factor: the arrival of technological opportunities.

We address this concern in two ways. First, we exploit the major recent event in the venture capital industry. In 1979, the US Department of Labor clarified the Employee Retirement Income Security Act (ERISA), a policy shift that freed pensions to invest in venture capital. This shift led to a sharp increase in the funds committed to venture capital. This type of exogenous change should identify the role of venture capital, because it is unlikely to be related to the arrival of entrepreneurial opportunities. We exploit this shift in instrumental variable regressions. Second, we use R&D expenditures to control the arrival of technological opportunities that are anticipated by economic actors at the time, but that are unobserved to us as econometricians. In the framework of our model, we show that the causality problem disappears if we estimate the impact of venture capital on the patent–R&D ratio, rather than on patenting itself.

Even after addressing these causality concerns, the results suggest that venture funding does have a strong positive impact on innovation. The estimated parameter varies according to the techniques we employ, but focusing on a conservative middle ground, a dollar of venture capital appears to be about three times more potent in stimulating patenting than a dollar of traditional corporate R&D. Our estimates therefore suggest that venture capital, even though it averaged less than 3 per cent of corporate R&D from 1983 to 1992, is responsible for a much greater share—about 8 per cent—of US industrial innovations in this decade.

One natural concern is that changes in the legal environment may be confounding our results. In earlier work (1998), we have highlighted how the creation of a centralized appellate court for patent cases in 1982 nearly coincided with an increase in the rate of US patent applications. To address this concern, we employ in all regressions dummy variables for each year, which should control for changes in either the propensity to file for patents or for these applications to be granted. Year effects control for changes in the overall legal environment unless the 1982 policy shift boosted patenting disproportionately in particular industries, which does not appear to have been the case (Kortum and Lerner 1998).

Finally, we address concerns about the relationship between the dependent variable in our analyses (patents) and what we really wish to measure (innovations). Venture capital may spur patenting while having no impact on innovation if venture-backed firms simply patent more of their innovations to impress potential investors or to avoid expropriation of their ideas by these investors. To investigate this possibility, we compare indicators of the quality of patents between 122 venture-backed and 408 non-venture-backed companies based in Middlesex County, MA. Venture-backed firms' patents are more frequently cited by other patents and are more aggressively litigated: venture backing does not appear to lead to lower-quality patents. Furthermore, the venture-backed firms are more frequent litigators of trade secrets, which suggests that they are not simply patenting more in lieu of relying on trade secret protection.

It is important to acknowledge the limits of our analysis. We have followed a somewhat crude 'production function' approach to assess the contribution of venture capital. In so doing, we face many of the fundamental issues raised by Griliches (1979) in his critique of attempts to assess the contributions of R&D to productivity. Due to the lack of previous research in this arena, our paper should be seen as a first cut at quantifying venture capital's impact on innovation. We hope that it will stimulate additional investigations of the relationship between the institutions through which innovative activities are financed and the rate and direction of technological change.[1]

The plan of the chapter is as follows. Section 9.2 provides an overview of the US venture capital industry. Section 9.3 presents the data while Section 9.4 provides a set of reduced-form regressions. In Section 9.5 we build a simple model of venture capital, R&D, and innovation, in light of which we refine our estimates of the potency of venture capital. We address concerns about patenting as a measure of innovation in Section 9.6. The final section concludes.

9.2. VENTURE CAPITAL AND THE FINANCING OF YOUNG FIRMS[2]

The formal venture capital industry in the USA dates back to the formation of American Research and Development in 1946. (Venture capital can be defined as equity or equity-linked investments in young, privately held companies, where the investor is a financial intermediary who is typically active as a director, an adviser, or even a manager of the firm.) A handful of other venture funds were established in the decade after the pioneering fund's formation. The annual flow of money into new venture funds between 1946 and 1977 never exceeded a few hundred million dollars and was usually much less.

As Figure 9.1 demonstrates, funds flowing into the venture capital industry and the number of active venture organizations increased dramatically during the late 1970s and early 1980s, and the ratio of venture disbursements to R&D shortly thereafter. An important factor accounting for the increase in money flowing into the venture capital sector

---

[1] In addition to the literature on the contribution of R&D to productivity (Griliches 1979) and on the relationship between R&D and patenting (reviewed in Griliches 1990), this chapter also relates to the empirical literature on the relationship between cash flow and R&D expenditures at the firm level (e.g. Bernstein and Naidri 1986; Himmelberg and Petersen 1994). But as far as we are aware there is only one other study examining the relationship between innovation and the presence of particular financial institutions: Hellmann and Puri (1998) compare the survey responses of 170 venture-backed and non-venture-backed firms.

[2] This section is based in part on Gompers and Lerner (1998, 1999).

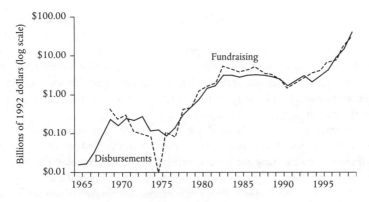

Figure 9.1. *Venture capital fundraising and disbursements, 1965–99.*

Notes: Data on venture capital fundraising are not available prior to 1969. No capital was raised by venture funds in 1975.

was the 1979 amendment to the 'prudent man' rule governing pension fund investments. Prior to 1979, the ERISA limited pension funds from investing substantial amounts of money into venture capital or other high-risk asset classes. The Department of Labor's clarification of the rule explicitly allowed pension managers to invest in high-risk assets, including venture capital. In 1978, when $424 million was invested in new venture capital funds, individuals accounted for the largest share (32 per cent). Pension funds supplied just 15 per cent. Eight years later, when more than $4 billion was invested, pension funds accounted for more than half of all contributions. In the years 1996 and 1997, there was another leap in venture capital activity. These patterns were mirrored in the investments by venture capitalists into young firms, also depicted in Figure 9.1.

Before considering the mechanisms employed by venture capitalists, it is worth highlighting that a lengthy literature has discussed the financing of young firms. Young firms, particularly those in high-tech industries, are often characterized by considerable uncertainty and informational asymmetries that make the selection of appropriate investments difficult and permit opportunistic behaviour by entrepreneurs after financing is received. This literature has also highlighted the role of financial intermediaries in alleviating moral hazard and information asymmetries.

To briefly review the types of conflicts that can emerge in these settings, Jensen and Meckling (1996) demonstrate that agency conflicts between managers and investors can affect the willingness of both debt and equity holders to provide capital. If the firm raises equity from outside investors, the manager has an incentive to engage in wasteful expenditures (e.g. lavish offices) because he may benefit disproportionately from these but does not bear their entire cost. Similarly, if the firm raises debt, the manager may increase risk to undesirable levels. Because providers of capital recognize these problems, outside investors demand a higher rate of return than would be the case if the funds were internally generated.

Even if the manager is motivated to maximize shareholder value, informational asymmetries may make raising external capital more expensive or even preclude it entirely.

Myers and Majluf (1984) and Greenwald *et al.* (1984) demonstrate that equity offerings of firms may be associated with a 'lemons' problem (first identified by Akerlof 1970). If the manager is better informed about the investment opportunities of the firm and acts in the interest of current shareholders, then managers only issue new shares when the company's stock is overvalued. Indeed, numerous studies have documented that stock prices decline upon the announcement of equity issues, largely because of the negative signal that it sends to the market.

These information problems have also been shown to exist in debt markets. Stiglitz and Weiss (1981) show that if banks find it difficult to discriminate among companies, raising interest rates can have perverse selection effects. In particular, the high-interest rates discourage all but the highest-risk borrowers, so the quality of the loan pool declines markedly. To address this problem, banks may restrict the amount of lending rather than increasing interest rates.

These problems in the debt and equity markets are a consequence of the information gaps between the entrepreneurs and investors. If the information asymmetries could be eliminated, financing constraints would disappear. Financial economists argue that specialized financial intermediaries, such as venture capital organizations, can address these problems. By intensively scrutinizing firms before providing capital and then monitoring them afterwards, they can alleviate some of the information gaps and reduce capital constraints.

To address these information problems, venture investors employ a variety of mechanisms. First, business plans are intensively scrutinized: of those firms that submit business plans to venture organizations, historically only 1 per cent have been funded. The decision to invest is frequently made conditional on the identification of a syndication partner who agrees that this is an attractive investment. Once the decision to invest is made, venture capitalists frequently disburse funds in stages. Managers of these venture-backed firms are forced to return repeatedly to their financiers for additional capital, in order to ensure that the money is not squandered on unprofitable projects. In addition, venture capitalists intensively monitor managers. These investors demand preferred stock with numerous restrictive covenants and representation on the board of directors. (Various aspects of the oversight role played by venture investors is documented in Gompers and Lerner (1999).) Thus, it is not surprising that venture capital has emerged as the dominant form of equity financing in the USA for privately held high-tech businesses.[3]

9.3. THE DATA

We analyse annual data for twenty manufacturing industries between 1965 and 1992. The dependent variable is US patents issued to US inventors by industry and date of application. Our main explanatory variables are measures of venture funding collected by

---

[3] While evidence regarding the financing of these firms is imprecise, Freear and Wetzel's (1990) survey suggests that venture capital accounts for about two-thirds of the external equity financing raised by privately held technology-intensive businesses from private-sector sources.

Venture Economics and industrial R&D expenditures collected by the US National Science Foundation (NSF).

Before discussing the use of these data, two challenges that these measures pose should be acknowledged. First, our dependent variable is problematic. Since the US Patent and Trademark Office (USPTO) does not compile patent statistics by industry and many firms have multiple lines-of-business, patenting in each industry can be only be indirectly inferred. We rely on a concordance that relates a patent's industry to the primary technological classification to which it is assigned by the patent examiner.[4]

Second, while we distinguish conceptually between R&D financed by corporations and R&D financed by venture capital organizations, the data do not allow a clean division. The industrial R&D data that we use, while based on a survey that overlooks the activities of many smaller firms, undoubtedly includes some research financed by venture capital organizations. Similarly, while the bulk of venture financing supports innovative activities at technology-intensive firms, some is used for other purposes. For instance, some of the venture financing goes to low-technology concerns or is devoted to marketing activities. It should be noted that by leaving some venture funding in our measure of corporate R&D, it is less likely that we will find an impact of venture capital on patenting conditional on the R&D measure.

Venture funding and patents are then aggregated into essentially the industry scheme used by the NSF in tabulating its survey of industrial R&D. We consolidate a few NSF industries that account for little R&D.[5] The resulting twenty industries are listed in Table 9.2. Additional details about the sources of the data are described in the appendix.

Table 9.1 summarizes the time-series dimension of the main data series. The table highlights the rapid growth of the venture capital industry. The ratio of venture capital to R&D jumped sharply in the late 1970s and early 1980s, and fell a bit thereafter. Patenting declined from the early 1970s to the mid-1980s, but then rose sharply.[6]

---

[4] This concordance relies on industry assignments of patents issued by Canada (the majority of which are issued to US inventors) to determine the likelihood of a particular industry assignment given a patent's technological classification (Kortum *et al.* 1997). Industry counts for the USA are based on the International Patent Classification assigned to each patent issued by the USPTO. The patent assignments differ depending on whether the assigned industry corresponds to the user or the manufacturer of the patented invention. We focus on the industry of use series, but our results about the impact of venture capital are robust to replacing industry of use with industry of manufacture. In either case, the industry assignment of patents may not correspond precisely to the industry doing the R&D or receiving the venture capital funding that led to the underlying invention.

[5] We focus on the manufacturing industries, since survey evidence (summarized in Cohen 1995) suggests that the reliance on patenting as a means of appropriating new technological discoveries is much higher in these industries (as opposed to, for instance, trade secrecy or first-mover advantages). Patenting is thus likely to be a better indicator of the rate of technological innovation in the manufacturing sector. The time period is determined on the one end by the availability of data on venture capital investment and on the other end by our inability to observe the detailed technological classifications of US patent applications before they are issued (applications are held confidential until issue).

[6] A natural concern is the extent of correlation between the venture capital and private R&D measures. While the two variables are positively correlated, the extent of correlation is less than the aggregate numbers in Table 9.1 might lead one to believe. In particular, the correlation coefficient between the logarithms of the dollar volume of venture financings and private R&D in each industry is 0.43. The partial correlation, once the year and industry are controlled for, is 0.31. The correlation between the number of companies receiving venture financing and private R&D is even lower.

Table 9.1. *Patenting activity of, R&D expenditures by, and venture capital disbursements for US manufacturing industries, by year*

Year	No. of patent applications	R&D expenditures ($m)	Venture capital disbursements		Ratio of venture capital to R&D	
			No. of firms	Amount ($m)	All VC (%)	Early stage only (%)
1965	50,278	25,313	8	13	0.05	0.02
1966	48,740	27,573	3	2	0.01	0.00
1967	48,900	29,515	9	24	0.08	0.07
1968	49,980	31,387	25	37	0.12	0.08
1969	51,614	33,244	66	149	0.45	0.38
1970	53,950	32,883	63	126	0.38	0.24
1971	54,776	32,360	57	224	0.69	0.41
1972	49,777	33,593	52	209	0.62	0.44
1973	45,807	36,169	74	235	0.65	0.30
1974	44,465	37,323	42	81	0.22	0.13
1975	44,082	35,935	41	118	0.33	0.24
1976	44,026	38,056	47	83	0.22	0.10
1977	41,550	39,605	57	138	0.35	0.21
1978	42,648	42,373	116	255	0.60	0.37
1979	44,941	45,318	152	301	0.66	0.28
1980	41,726	48,700	231	635	1.30	0.80
1981	39,137	52,012	408	1,146	2.20	1.39
1982	38,039	55,033	466	1,388	2.52	1.29
1983	34,712	58,066	656	2,391	4.12	1.97
1984	33,905	63,441	709	2,347	3.70	1.95
1985	36,732	66,860	646	1,951	2.92	1.42
1986	41,644	68,476	639	2,211	3.23	1.62
1987	46,434	67,700	713	2,191	3.24	1.57
1988	51,355	69,008	660	2,076	3.01	1.54
1989	55,103	70,456	669	1,995	2.83	1.56
1990	58,358	69,714	557	1,675	2.40	1.11
1991	58,924	69,516	422	1,026	1.48	0.71
1992	60,771	70,825	469	1,571	2.22	1.05

Patent applications refer to the number of ultimately successful patent applications filed in each year. All dollar figures are in millions of 1992 dollars. The ratios of venture capital disbursements to R&D expenditures are computed using all venture capital disbursements and early stage venture disbursements only.

Tables 9.2–9.4 summarize the industry dimension of the data on patents, venture capital, and R&D, respectively. It should be noted that disbursements are concentrated in certain industries. The top three industries—drugs, office and computing, and communication equipment—represent 54 per cent of the venture disbursements. The comparable figure for R&D expenditures is 39 per cent.

Table 9.2. *Patenting activity of US manufacturing industries, by industry and five-year period*

No.	Industry	SIC Codes	1965–69	1970–74	1975–79	1980–84	1985–89	1990–92
1	Food and kindred	20	1,790	1,957	1,365	1,201	1,555	1,138
2	Textile and apparel	22,23	3,246	3,004	2,639	2,339	3,787	2,923
3	Lumber and furniture	24,25	3,028	3,052	2,877	2,160	3,149	2,539
4	Paper	26	2,738	2,312	1,924	1,626	2,493	1,859
5	Industrial chemicals*	281,282,286	22,124	22,353	18,507	15,612	15,882	11,673
6	Drugs*	283	2,099	2,873	3,561	4,399	8,262	6,281
7	Other chemicals	284,285,287–289	14,559	14,403	11,760	10,461	11,283	8,405
8	Petroleum refining and extraction*	13,29	892	794	850	827	744	450
9	Rubber products	30	8,504	8,169	6,726	5,823	9,028	6,641
10	Stone, clay, and glass products	32	2,677	2,671	2,366	2,062	2,790	2,147
11	Primary metals	33	2,245	2,183	1,689	1,340	1,710	1,156
12	Fabricated metal products	34	19,805	19,484	18,479	14,894	18,359	13,211
13	Office and computing machines*	357	5,487	5,752	4,931	4,922	6,638	5,905
14	Other non-electrical machinery*	351–356,358–359	60,790	61,139	52,426	42,634	48,135	35,534
15	Communication and electronic*	366,367	30,838	28,380	24,679	24,302	30,417	25,793
16	Other electrical equipment*	361–365,369	23,768	22,403	19,213	16,995	19,736	14,197
17	Transportation equipment*	371,373–375,379	10,829	12,119	9,715	7,096	8,579	6,610
18	Aircraft and missiles*	372,376	1,634	1,434	1,200	905	1,113	835
19	Professional and scientific instruments*	38	18,690	19,244	17,287	15,683	21,026	17,235
20	Other manufacturing	21,27,31,39	13,769	15,050	15,054	12,237	16,582	13,521
	Total		249,512	248,775	217,247	187,518	231,268	178,053

Patent applications refer to the number of ultimately successful patent applications filed in each year. Industries marked with a * had an R&D-to-sales ratio above the median in 1964. These industries define a 'High R&D' sub-sample used for some of the later regressions.

Table 9.3. *Number and dollar amount of venture capital disbursements for US manufacturing industries, by industry and five-year period*

No.	Industry	1965–69	1970–74	1975–79	1980–84	1985–89	1990–92
Panel A: Venture Capital Investments (#s)							
1	Food and kindred	1	9	6	23	80	41
2	Textile and apparel	4	12	9	19	27	33
3	Lumber and furniture	2	8	6	24	62	16
4	Paper	2	2	2	2	12	4
5	Industrial chemicals	1	1	1	6	18	10
6	Drugs	1	12	34	245	554	337
7	Other chemicals	1	7	8	10	52	25
8	Petroleum refining and extraction	3	3	26	92	27	8
9	Rubber products	1	5	6	19	11	3
10	Stone, clay, and glass products	0	1	3	14	48	23
11	Primary metals	0	3	5	20	44	15
12	Fabricated metal products	0	0	0	2	1	1
13	Office and computing machines	39	84	108	744	641	205
14	Other non-electrical machinery	12	12	32	254	280	98
15	Communication and electronic	23	65	60	497	736	298
16	Other electrical equipment	0	6	16	36	52	28
17	Transportation equipment	1	7	5	6	24	10
18	Aircraft and missiles	0	0	0	12	20	2
19	Professional and scientific instruments	13	37	70	383	549	252
20	Other manufacturing	7	14	16	62	89	39
	Total	111	288	413	2,470	3,327	1,448
Panel B: Venture Capital Disbursements (millions of 1992 $s)							
1	Food and kindred	4	19	7	25	212	128
2	Textile and apparel	6	15	14	27	45	83
3	Lumber and furniture	4	17	9	26	200	30
4	Paper	1	8	3	3	22	1
5	Industrial chemicals	0	1	1	41	34	16
6	Drugs	0	15	136	623	1,869	1,317
7	Other chemicals	1	40	4	9	155	27
8	Petroleum refining and extraction	12	6	92	359	110	12
9	Rubber products	1	3	15	28	8	8
10	Stone, clay, and glass products	0	1	5	34	99	40
11	Primary metals	0	8	11	25	67	19
12	Fabricated metal products	0	0	0	1	0	1
13	Office and computing machines	67	404	288	3,253	2,491	613
14	Other non-electrical machinery	64	17	37	677	669	140
15	Communication and electronic	44	189	82	1,746	2,646	1,042
16	Other electrical equipment	0	8	53	78	107	41
17	Transportation equipment	0	10	4	9	47	42
18	Aircraft and missiles	0	0	0	19	19	7
19	Professional and scientific instruments	13	86	114	811	1,449	606
20	Other manufacturing	7	28	22	113	176	102
	Total	$225	$874	$895	$7,907	$10,423	$4,273

The count of venture capital investments in each five-year period is the sum of the number of firms receiving investments. All dollar figures are in millions of 1992 dollars.

Table 9.4. *R&D expenditures by US manufacturing industries, by industry and five-year period*

No.	Industry	1965–69	1970–74	1975–79	1980–84	1985–89	1990–92
1	Food and kindred	3,271	3,741	4,333	5,643	7,231	4,032
2	Textile and apparel	962	909	869	1,002	1,376	781
3	Lumber and furniture	269	945	1,204	1,111	936	670
4	Paper	2,419	2,871	3,554	4,019	3,980	3,520
5	Industrial chemicals	14,780	13,582	14,376	18,587	22,023	15,518
6	Drugs	6,384	9,033	12,365	17,870	25,730	21,395
7	Other chemicals	3,191	4,105	4,504	6,776	10,826	7,086
8	Petroleum refining and extraction	7,135	7,423	8,784	13,657	12,207	7,270
9	Rubber products	3,089	3,738	3,559	4,330	4,054	3,572
10	Stone, clay, and glass products	2,430	2,535	2,734	3,625	4,898	1,521
11	Primary metals	4,293	4,231	5,070	4,916	4,222	2,006
12	Fabricated metal products	2,812	3,664	3,578	4,343	4,390	2,278
13	Office and computing machines	10,802	17,045	23,398	35,485	53,779	33,061
14	Other non-electrical machinery	8,455	10,226	12,543	15,849	14,596	9,445
15	Communication and electronic	16,902	20,262	22,106	37,661	50,187	20,711
16	Other electrical equipment	12,483	13,903	13,764	13,597	8,560	7,722
17	Transportation equipment	19,713	25,133	30,340	34,324	46,152	28,489
18	Aircraft and missiles	19,104	16,631	17,043	27,177	34,692	18,113
19	Professional and scientific instruments	6,958	10,259	14,748	24,186	30,321	21,101
20	Other manufacturing	1,580	2,094	2,417	3,094	2,342	1,763
	Total	$147,032	$172,328	$201,288	$277,251	$342,501	$210,055

All figures are in millions of 1992 dollars.

Table 9.5 presents venture capital disbursements as a percentage of R&D spending. When normalized by total R&D, a number of low-tech industries such as textiles and apparel appear to be relatively reliant on venture funding. Note also the high degree of persistence over time in the set of industries in which venture funding is a substantial fraction of R&D. This pattern is maintained when looking only at early stage financing, as in Panel B.

9.4. REDUCED-FORM REGRESSIONS

We begin our empirical analysis by investigating whether, conditional on R&D spending, venture capital funding influences innovation. We estimate and report on patent production functions in the next two subsections. In undertaking this analysis, we will employ many of the conventions of the literature on 'innovation production functions' reviewed in Griliches (1990).[7] In the last subsection, we estimate a simpler linear specification that we will return to later in the chapter. Throughout Section 9.4, we treat venture financing as exogenous, deferring the discussion of its determinants until the next section.

9.4.1. *The Patent Production Function*

We estimate a patent production function of the form: $P_{it} = (R_{it}^{\rho} + bV_{it}^{\rho})^{\alpha/\rho} u_{it}$. Patenting ($P$) is a function of privately funded industrial R&D (R) and venture disbursements (V), while an error term (u) captures shifts in the propensity to patent or technological opportunities, all indexed by industry (i) and year (t). We focus on the parameter b, which captures the role of venture capital in the patent production function. For any $b > 0$, venture funding matters for innovation, while if b equals zero, the patent production function reduces to the standard form, $P_{it} = R_{it}^{\alpha} u_{it}$. The parameter α captures returns to scale, that is, the percentage change in patenting brought about by a 1 per cent increase in both R and V. The parameter ρ measures the degree of substitutability between R and V as means of financing innovative effort. When ρ equals one, the function reduces to $P_{it} = (R_{it} + bV_{it})^{\alpha} u_{it}$. As ρ goes to zero, the patent production function approaches the Cobb–Douglas functional form, $P_{it} = R_{it}^{\alpha/(1+b)} V_{it}^{\alpha b/(1+b)} u_{it}$.

9.4.2. *Estimates*

Non-linear least squares estimates of the patent production function are shown in Table 9.6. The dependent variable is the logarithm of the number of (ultimately successful) patent applications filed by US inventors in each industry and year. The two independent variables of interest are privately financed R&D in that industry and year and either the dollar volume of venture disbursements or the number of firms in the industry receiving venture backing.[8] We use as controls the logarithm of the federally funded R&D in the industry,

---

[7] As in this literature, we initially ignore the impact of such factors as the uncertainty about technological success on the propensity to patent innovations. In Section 9.6, we show that the results are robust to the use of alternative measures that at least partially address these problems.

[8] The parameter b is generally not invariant to the units in which venture activity is measured. To facilitate comparisons across regressions, we scale the measure based on the number of companies funded by venture

Table 9.5. *Ratio of venture capital disbursements to R&D expenditures for US manufacturing industries, by industry and five-year period*

No.	Industry	1965–69 (%)	1970–74 (%)	1975-79 (%)	1980–84 (%)	1985–89 (%)	1990–92 (%)
Panel A: All venture capital disbursements/R&D spending							
1	Food and kindred	0.14	0.50	0.16	0.44	2.93	3.18
2	Textile and apparel	0.57	1.68	1.59	2.72	3.24	10.59
3	Lumber and furniture	1.44	1.77	0.72	2.32	21.39	4.40
4	Paper	0.06	0.28	0.10	0.08	0.56	0.03
5	Industrial chemicals	0.00	0.00	0.01	0.22	0.15	0.10
6	Drugs	0.01	0.17	1.10	3.49	7.26	6.16
7	Other chemicals	0.03	0.98	0.09	0.13	1.43	0.38
8	Petroleum refining and extraction	0.16	0.08	1.04	2.63	0.90	0.17
9	Rubber products	0.04	0.07	0.42	0.64	0.20	0.21
10	Stone, clay, and glass products	0.00	0.02	0.19	0.93	2.01	2.62
11	Primary metals	0.00	0.19	0.21	0.51	1.59	0.94
12	Fabricated metal products	0.00	0.00	0.00	0.03	0.01	0.03
13	Office and computing machines	0.62	2.37	1.23	9.17	4.63	1.85
14	Other non-electrical machinery	0.75	0.16	0.30	4.27	4.58	1.48
15	Communication and electronic	0.26	0.93	0.37	4.64	5.27	5.03
16	Other electrical equipment	0.00	0.06	0.38	0.57	1.25	0.53
17	Transportation equipment	0.00	0.04	0.01	0.03	0.10	0.15
18	Aircraft and missiles	0.00	0.00	0.00	0.07	0.05	0.04
19	Professional and scientific instruments	0.19	0.84	0.77	3.35	4.78	2.87
20	Other manufacturing	0.46	1.34	0.90	3.65	7.51	5.81
Panel B: Early stage venture capital disbursements/R&D spending							
1	Food and kindred	0.14	0.22	0.05	0.14	1.69	2.17
2	Textile and apparel	0.36	0.90	0.79	0.67	1.46	3.05
3	Lumber and furniture	0.00	0.74	0.51	1.19	11.23	2.07
4	Paper	0.00	0.28	0.00	0.08	0.21	0.01
5	Industrial chemicals	0.00	0.00	0.00	0.21	0.04	0.07
6	Drugs	0.01	0.14	0.92	2.53	4.40	3.39
7	Other chemicals	0.00	0.62	0.03	0.10	0.55	0.21
8	Petroleum refining and extraction	0.13	0.08	0.56	1.40	0.59	0.11
9	Rubber products	0.00	0.05	0.32	0.41	0.17	0.00
10	Stone, clay, and glass products	0.00	0.02	0.00	0.50	1.37	1.46
11	Primary metals	0.00	0.15	0.12	0.46	1.35	0.17
12	Fabricated metal products	0.00	0.00	0.00	0.00	0.01	0.00
13	Office and computing machines	0.55	1.32	0.73	4.21	1.74	0.87
14	Other non-electrical machinery	0.68	0.08	0.12	2.08	2.11	0.49
15	Communication and electronic	0.19	0.46	0.16	2.68	2.69	1.97
16	Other electrical equipment	0.00	0.04	0.20	0.33	0.69	0.27
17	Transportation equipment	0.00	0.03	0.00	0.00	0.04	0.01
18	Aircraft and missiles	0.00	0.00	0.00	0.02	0.01	0.04
19	Professional and scientific instruments	0.10	0.65	0.26	1.95	2.86	1.39
20	Other manufacturing	0.31	1.12	0.36	2.34	3.54	1.84

All dollar figures are in millions of 1992 dollars. The ratios of venture capital disbursements to R&D expenditures are computed using all venture capital disbursements and early-stage venture disbursements only.

Table 9.6. *Non-linear least squares regression analysis of the patent production function*

	Using firms receiving venture backing		Using venture disbursements	
	Unconstrained	Constrained ($\rho = 1$)	Unconstrained	Constrained ($\rho = 1$)
Returns to scale parameter (α)	0.22	0.23	0.20	0.20
	[0.02]	[0.02]	[0.02]	[0.02]
Venture capital parameter (b)				
Firms receiving funding	58.51	39.57		
	[67.31]	[10.97]		
Venture disbursements			58.71	46.94
			[77.52]	[13.66]
Substitution parameter (ρ)	1.08	1.00	1.04	1.00
	[0.24]	—	[0.26]	—
Federally funded industrial R&D	0.01	0.01	0.01	0.01
	[0.01]	[0.01]	[0.01]	[0.01]
R^2	0.99	0.99	0.99	0.99
R^2 relative to dummy variable only case	0.26	0.26	0.27	0.27
Number of observations	560	560	560	560
Likelihood ratio statistic		0.2		0.0
p-Value, likelihood ratio test		0.65		0.99

Standard errors are in brackets. The dependent variable is the logarithm of the number of patents. Year and industry dummy variables are included in each regression.

as well as dummy variables for each industry (to control for differences in the propensity to patent) and year.

The results suggest that venture funding matters. The magnitude of b estimated in the unconstrained equation is substantial, in fact implausibly large, an issue we will return to below. Although the estimates are imprecise, a likelihood ratio test overwhelmingly rejects the special case of b equal to zero (with a p-value of less than 0.005).

We also find that R&D and venture capital are highly substitutable, with the point estimate of ρ close to one. A likelihood ratio test does not come close to rejecting the restriction that $\rho = 1$. On the other hand, $\rho = 0$ (the Cobb–Douglas special case) is strongly rejected (with a p-value of less than 0.005). As a consequence, in the remainder of the chapter we focus on the restricted equation, $\ln P_{it} = \alpha \ln(R_{it} + bV_{it}) + \ln u_{it}$, in which R&D and venture funding are perfect substitutes. In the restricted equation, b has

capitalists to have the same overall mean as the dollar disbursements measure (in 1992 dollars). For both measures of venture finance, we add a minuscule amount (the equivalent of $1000) to each observation so that we can consider the Cobb–Douglas limiting case in which the log of venture funding is what matters.

the interpretation of the potency of a dollar of venture funding relative to a dollar of R&D (this interpretation of b holds for either measure of venture funding, as discussed in footnote 8).

The results for the restricted equation are shown in the second and fourth columns of Table 9.6. Together, variation in R&D and venture funding explain over one quarter of the variation in the logarithm of patenting not captured by industry or time effects.[9] The returns-to-scale parameter α is about one quarter, small but not implausible. What does strain credibility, however, are the point estimates of b in the two regressions, implying as they do that venture funds are about forty times as potent as R&D. Below we explore a number of reasons why these estimates might be biased upward.

9.4.3. *A Linear Specification*

Before turning to the more difficult issues arising from the endogeneity of venture funding (which we address in Section 9.5), we first consider estimating b through a linear approximation of the patent production function (again with $\rho = 1$). Such an approximation is valid when venture funding is small relative to R&D. The linear specification has the advantage of simplicity. It is also inherently conservative in its empirical implications for the potency of venture capital. It interprets the observed average impact of V/R on patenting as the maximum marginal impact (i.e. the marginal impact as V/R approaches zero). Since our task is to evaluate the null hypothesis that venture capital is impotent, we find this inherent conservatism reassuring.

After linearizing the equation, we get $\ln P_{it} = \alpha \ln R_{it} + \alpha b(V_{it}/R_{it}) + \ln u_{it}$. This approximation is analogous to that employed by Griliches (1986) in his analysis of the impact of basic research, which like venture capital represented a small fraction of total R&D expenditures, on productivity growth. Note that in this equation, the potency of venture funding is calculated by dividing the coefficient on V/R by the coefficient on $\ln(R)$. Table 9.7 presents regressions employing the linear specification. The basic equations are in the first two columns. Consider the second regression, which estimates the coefficient on venture capital as 1.73. Because this is an estimate for the product of α and b, we must divide by our estimate of α, 0.24, to obtain the implied potency of venture funding, $b = 7.26$. The implied estimates of potency and the associated standard errors (calculated using the delta method) are shown in the last two rows. In both regressions, the estimate of potency is significantly positive.[10] The estimates suggest that a dollar of venture capital is over seven times more powerful in stimulating patenting than a dollar of corporate R&D. Although these estimates are large, note that they are substantially more modest than the estimates of b from the non-linear regressions.

---

[9] In all of the regression tables we present two measures of the goodness of fit: the overall R^2 and the R^2 when compared against a regression with just year and industry dummies. The latter is computed as ($SSR_{dummy\ only}$ − $SSR_{new\ regression}$)/$SSR_{dummy\ only}$, where SSR refers to the sum of squared residuals of the various regressions.

[10] Our error term consists of shocks to the propensity to patent and technological opportunities, which are likely to be persistent over time. To avoid inflating the statistical significance of the results, we calculate the standard errors using the autocorrelation-consistent covariance estimator of Newey and West (1987), with a maximum lag of three years.

Table 9.7. *Ordinary least squares regression analysis of the linear patent production function*

	Levels with year and industry effects		Long differences with period effects	
Privately funded industrial R&D (α)	0.25	0.24	0.24	0.22
	[0.06]	[0.06]	[0.07]	[0.07]
Venture capital/privately funded R&D (αb):				
Firms receiving funding	2.13		2.42	
	[0.63]		[1.21]	
Venture disbursements		1.73		2.29
		[0.69]		[1.04]
Federally funded industrial R&D	0.01	0.01	0.03	0.02
	[0.01]	[0.01]	[0.02]	[0.02]
R^2	0.99	0.99	0.81	0.82
R^2 relative to dummy variable only case	0.21	0.20	0.24	0.25
Number of observations	560	560	60	60
Implied potency of venture funding (b)	8.49	7.26	9.98	10.39
	[2.62]	[3.16]	[5.82]	[6.21]

Standard errors are in brackets. For the levels specifications they are based on the Newey–West autocorrelation-consistent covariance estimator (with a maximum of three lags). The standard errors for the parameter b are calculated using the delta method.

These linear results appear to be quite robust. We have explored changing the specification,[11] the measures of venture capital,[12] and the sample,[13] adding additional controls,[14] and using lags of the explanatory variables.[15]

[11] If the errors in the patent production function follow a random walk, then the equation should be estimated in differences rather than in levels. The difference regressions are shown in the last two columns of Table 9.7. In order to reduce the errors-in-variables problem, which tends to be magnified in a first-difference approach (Griliches and Hausman 1986), we compute averages of the logarithm of each variable over a four-year period. We then compute the change in the industry measures at eight-year intervals. Since we difference out the industry effects, we drop industry dummies from these regressions, but maintain a set of period dummies (not shown). The results of the long difference regressions are very similar to those of the levels regressions except that the precision of the estimates declines.

[12] It might be thought that the financing of start-ups and very young companies would pose the greatest information problems, and that the contributions of the venture capitalists would be most valuable here. In regressions reported in the first two columns of Table 9.8, we replace the venture funding measures with the count and dollar volume of only seed and early-stage financings. The estimated potency of a dollar of venture funding increases by 45–80 per cent.

[13] Our analysis may be distorted by the inclusion of numerous industries with very little innovative activity. In regressions reported in the last two columns of Table 9.8, we drop industries whose R&D-to-sales ratio was below the median in 1964, the year before the beginning of the analysis. (These industries appear with a^* in Table 9.2.) Once again, there is an increase in the estimated potency of venture funding relative to our baseline regressions.

[14] In unreported regressions, we also control for the logarithms of gross industry product or of industry employment. The effect of adding these controls is to reduce the coefficient on the logarithm of R&D, α (although it remains significantly positive). Both the magnitude and significance of the coefficient on V/R are essentially unchanged by the addition of either control.

[15] Another robustness check concerns possible lags between R&D spending, venture financing, and patenting. The empirical literature suggests that R&D spending and patent filings are roughly contemporaneous

9.5. ADDRESSING THE CAUSALITY PROBLEM

The empirical results in Section 9.4 suggest that there is a strong association between venture capital and patenting and that corporate R&D and venture funding are highly substitutable in generating innovations. The mechanisms behind this relationship and the extent to which our estimates of the impact of venture funding may be inflated by unobserved factors, however, are not addressed by our reduced-form regressions.

To explore these issues, we build a theoretical model of venture capital, corporate research, and innovation. We then use the model to illustrate under what conditions the approach of Section 9.4 is appropriate and when it may be problematic. The final two subsections present refinements of our empirical approach, motivated by the model. We do not seek to determine which single model is the best representation of the impact of venture capital on innovation. Rather, we seek to demonstrate the robustness of the results in Section 9.4 by showing that they hold up across a variety of models.

9.5.1. *Modeling the Relationship*

We consider an industry in which inventions can be pursued through either corporate R&D funding or venture capital. We make four major assumptions. First, we assume that the production function for innovations I in each industry i and time period t is essentially the one we settled upon empirically:

$$I_{it} = (R_{it} + bV_{it})^{\alpha} N_{it} = H_{it}^{\alpha} N_{it}, \qquad (9.1)$$

where $0 < \alpha < 1$ and, for expositional ease, total innovative effort is denoted by H_{it}. The final term N_{it} represents a shock to the invention production function, which we interpret as the exogenous arrival of innovative opportunities.

Second, we assume that innovations, on average, translate into patents in a proportional manner. Thus $P_{it} = I_{it} \varepsilon_{it}$, where P_{it} is the number of patented innovations generated in a particular industry and year and ε is an independent shock determining the propensity to patent innovations. Combining this equation with eqn (9.1), we obtain:

$$P_{it} = H_{it}^{\alpha} N_{it} \varepsilon_{it}. \qquad (9.2)$$

The unobserved factor driving patenting is thus $N\varepsilon$, the product of technological opportunities and the propensity to patent.

(Hall *et al.* 1988). Furthermore, there is an institutional reason why there should not be long lags between venture capital and patenting: the ten-year lifespans of venture partnerships lead to pressure on companies to rapidly commercialize products after obtaining venture financing. Nevertheless, to explore this issue empirically, in unreported regressions we repeat the analyses in Table 9.7, including one- and two-year lagged values of the R&D and venture capital variable along with the contemporaneous variables. We find that the contemporaneous variables have the bulk of the explanatory power (and their coefficients are significantly positive), while the lagged variables have coefficients that are smaller (and insignificantly different from zero).

Third, we assume that the expected value of a new innovation for a given time period and industry is Π_{it}. We take a simple partial equilibrium approach and do not model the determinants of Π, although we have in mind that it evolves with the size of the market, as in Schmookler (1966). We assume that individual firms are small relative to the industry, and therefore take Π as given. The expected value of a new invention incorporates the fact that some, but not all, innovations will be worth patenting.

Finally, we make assumptions regarding the marginal costs of innovating that deserve discussion at greater length. In addition to the direct expenditures on R&D and venture disbursements, we assume that there are associated indirect expenses. These might include the cost of screening opportunities, recruiting managers and researchers, and undertaking the crucial regulatory approvals to sell the new product. We argue that at each point of time, there is likely to be a spectrum of projects: some will be very appropriate for a corporate research laboratory, while others will be more suited for funding by a venture capitalist in an entrepreneurial setting. Raising venture activity as a fraction of total innovative effort pushes venture capitalists into areas farther from their comparative advantage, raising their costs, while corporate researchers are able to specialize in areas they have the greatest advantage in exploiting.

More specifically, we assume that given total research effort H, and venture financing V, the venture capitalist's costs of managing the last venture-backed project is $v_{it} f_V(V_{it}/\lambda_{it}H_{it})$, while the corporation's costs of managing the last corporate-backed project is $f_R(V_{it}/\lambda_{it}H_{it})$. We assume that the venture capitalists' function fV is strictly increasing while the corporations' fR is strictly decreasing in $V/\lambda H$. The term λ_{it} governs the extent to which opportunities are conducive to venture finance. We interpret a rise in λ to mean that technological opportunities have become more radical in nature, a shift that should lower the management costs of pursuing such projects in an entrepreneurial rather than a corporate setting. The v_t term represents the venture capitalist's cost of funds, which we enter explicitly to enable us to consider the impact of the 1979 clarification of the prudent man rule (a fall in v).

From this set of assumptions, we derive several equilibrium conditions. The equilibrium level of venture capital and corporate R&D will equate the marginal cost of additional spending to the marginal benefit. Assuming that we are not at a corner solution where V or R is equal to zero,[16] the conditions are:

$$\Pi_{it}\frac{\partial I_{it}}{\partial V_{it}} = \alpha\Pi_{it}N_{it}bH_{it}^{\alpha-1} = v_t f_V\left(\frac{V_{it}}{\lambda_{it}H_{it}}\right), \tag{9.3}$$

$$\Pi_{it}\frac{\partial I_{it}}{\partial R_{it}} = \alpha\Pi_{it}N_{it}H_{it}^{\alpha-1} = f_R\left(\frac{V_{it}}{\lambda_{it}H_{it}}\right). \tag{9.4}$$

[16] An attractive feature of the model is that it can also address the empirically relevant case of $V = 0$. In that case, $\alpha\Pi_{it}N_{it}bR_{it}^{\alpha-1} \le v_t f_V(0)$, where $R_{it} = [\alpha\Pi_{it}N_{it}/f_R(0)]^{1/(1-\alpha)}$.

Through a series of mathematical manipulations,[17] we obtain the expressions

$$H_{it} = \left[\frac{\alpha \Pi_{it} N_{it}}{g_1(v_t)} \right]^{1/(1-\alpha)}, \tag{9.5}$$

$$\frac{V_{it}}{R_{it}} = \lambda_{it} \left[\frac{g_2(v_t)}{1 - b\lambda_{it}g_2(v_t)} \right], \tag{9.6}$$

where g_1 is an increasing function and g_2 a decreasing one. According to eqn (9.5), total innovative effort is decreasing in the cost of venture funds, v, but stimulated by positive shocks to either the value of inventions or the arrival of technological opportunities. Venture funding relative to corporate R&D, eqn (9.6), is increasing in the degree to which the opportunities are radical in nature, λ, and decreasing in the cost of venture funds.

A shock to λ favours venture capital relative to corporate R&D, while a jump in N not only stimulates both forms of finance but also leads to a jump in patenting conditional on the amount of innovative effort. Complicating matters, we suspect that the two shocks, λ and N, will be positively correlated. A burst of innovative opportunities will often be associated with a radical shift in the technology, a shift that small venture-financed entrepreneurs rather than large corporations will be better able to exploit. It is this potential correlation between a shock to the patent equation and a shock that favours venture finance which leads us to be sceptical of our reduced form regression results.

9.5.2. *Implications for the Estimation*

This set of equations allows us to illustrate the issues that we face in estimating the linear form of the patent production function,

$$\ln P_{it} = \alpha \ln R_{it} + \alpha b(V_{it}/R_{it}) + \ln N + \ln \varepsilon_{it}, \tag{9.7}$$

with industry dummies, year dummies, and federally funded R&D included as controls. If technological opportunities, N, are totally captured by our controls, our estimates in Tables 9.6–9.8 should be valid. Variation in Π_{it}, according to eqn (9.5), will lead to variation in H and hence R, which identifies α. Variation in the cost of funds to venture capitalists, v_t, interacted with differences across industries in λ, will cause variation in V/R which identifies b.

The more likely scenario, however, is one in which variation in technological opportunities is only partially explained by the controls. In that case, variations in H, and hence R, will be correlated with the disturbance. Similarly, variations in V/R will also be correlated with the disturbance (if λ and N are in fact correlated). Simply regressing patents on R&D and venture funding could yield biased estimates of both α and b, and will likely overstate the potency of venture capital.

---

[17] Specific steps were to (i) define $x \equiv \alpha \Pi_{it} N_{it} H_{it}^{\alpha-1}$, (ii) combine eqns (9.3) and (9.4) to get $b/v = (1/x)f_V(f_R^{-1}(x)) \equiv h(x)$, where $h(x)$ is a strictly decreasing function, (iii) solve for $x = h^{-1}(b/v) \equiv g_1(v)$, (iv) plug into eqn (9.4) to get $V/H = \lambda f_R^{-1}(g_1(v)) \equiv \lambda g_2(v)$, (v) use $x \equiv g_1(v)$ to solve for H, and (vi), recalling that $H = R + bV$, solve for V/R.

Table 9.8. *Ordinary least squares regression analysis of the linear patent production function: robustness checks*

	Using early stage financing		Using high R&D industries only	
Privately funded industrial R&D (α)	0.24	0.24	0.38	0.37
	[0.06]	[0.06]	[0.09]	[0.09]
Venture capital/privately funded R&D (αb):				
Firms receiving funding	3.74		6.98	
	[1.30]		[1.68]	
Venture disbursements		2.50		5.14
		[1.09]		[1.59]
Federally funded industrial R&D	0.02	0.01	−0.07	−0.07
	[0.01]	[0.01]	[0.04]	[0.04]
R^2	0.99	0.99	0.99	0.99
R^2 relative to dummy variable only case	0.21	0.19	0.45	0.43
Number of observations	560	560	280	280
Implied potency of venture funding (b)	15.44	10.50	18.22	13.76
	[5.35]	[4.74]	[5.95]	[5.69]

Standard errors (in brackets) are based on the Newey–West autocorrelation-consistent covariance estimator (with a maximum of three lags). In all regressions, the standard errors for the parameter b are calculated using the delta method. Year and industry dummy variables are included in each regression.

We consider two approaches to get around potential biases in our estimates of the potency of venture funding. First, we attempt to find good instruments. Our instrument for venture funding relative to corporate R&D relies on the Department of Labor's 1979 clarification of the 'prudent man' rule (discussed in Section 9.2). We argue that this clarification lowered the cost of funds to venture capitalists, much like a drop in v_t in our model. We propose an instrument based on the interaction of this 1979 change with the historical differences across industries in venture funding relative to corporate R&D.[18]

Our second approach is to use R&D to control for the unobservable term N, which is the source of our identification problems when estimating the patent production function. The basic idea is similar to Olley and Pakes (1996) and more recently Levinsohn and Petrin (1999) who use capital investment and purchased materials, respectively, to control for unobservables in a standard production function. Combining eqns (9.2) and (9.5) while noting that $R_{it} = H_{it}/(1 + bV_{it}/R_{it})$, we can solve for the patent–R&D ratio,

$$\frac{P_{it}}{R_{it}} = \left[\frac{\alpha \Pi_{it}}{g_1(v_t)} \right]^{-1} \left(1 + b \frac{V_{it}}{R_{it}} \right) \varepsilon_{it}. \tag{9.8}$$

[18] This approach also faces another challenge, which we explore in depth below. Even if our instrument for V/R is convincing, we are still faced with the endogeneity of total innovative effort. To address this issue, we consider demand-side instruments that are correlated with the value of inventions, Π_{it}, but potentially unrelated to technological opportunities.

The striking feature of eqn (9.8) is that normalizing patents by R&D eliminates technological opportunities N from the right side of the equation. We no longer identify α (which was not essential in any case), but we can now estimate the potency of venture funding b without worrying (subject to some caveats in how we treat Π) about correlation between V/R and the disturbance in the equation.

9.5.3. *Instrumental Variables Estimation*

We now turn to a more complete discussion of our instrument choice and to the results we obtain using instrumental variables techniques to estimate eqn (9.7). We start with our instrument for V/R. It is based on the Department of Labor's clarification of a rule that, prior to 1979, limited the ability of pension funds to invest in venture capital. One might initially think of capturing this shift empirically through a dummy variable taking on the value of zero through 1979 and one thereafter. The problem with this simple approach is that patenting rates across all industries may change over time for a variety of reasons, including swings in the judicial enforcement of patent-holder rights and antitrust policy. We are unlikely to be able to disentangle the shift in venture fundraising from that in the propensity to patent. As Table 9.1 makes clear, the filing of successful patent applications actually fell in the years after 1979. But this was also a period during which firms' ability to enforce intellectual property rights were under attack (Kortum and Lerner 1998).

The 1979 policy shift, however, should have had a predictably greater impact on patenting in some industries than others. Industries with a high level of venture capital prior to the policy change should have experienced a greater increase in funding, and thus a greater burst in patenting. Thus, in certain circumstances, we can use the level of venture financing prior to the shift, interacted with a dummy variable taking on the value zero through 1979 and one thereafter, as an instrumental variable.[19]

The observed relationship is likely to derive from two features of the venture industry. First, the supply of venture capitalists is quite inelastic, at least in the short run. Gompers and Lerner (1996) document that during periods with increasing inflows into venture capital, both the amount raised in the average new venture fund and the dollars managed per partner increase. They suggest that the highly specialized skills of venture capitalists can only be developed through years of experience undertaking these investments. Second, individual venture capitalists tend to specialize in particular industries. For instance, venture capitalists often have educational backgrounds that match the areas in which they invest, such as a Ph.D. in biochemistry or a master's degree in electrical engineering.

---

[19] The empirical relevance of this instrument is based on the observation that the increase in the ratio of venture capital activity to R&D following the 1979 shift was positively correlated with the level of V/R prior to the shift. A regression of y_i (the industry-specific change in the average ratio of venture capital disbursements to R&D spending between the 1985–90 period and the 1965–75 period) on x_i (the average ratio in the 1965–75 period) yields an R^2 of 0.42. The observed relationship is likely to derive from the inelastic supply of venture capitalists and the industry specialization of individual venture capitalists.

We can motivate the proposed instrument more formally by returning to the model. From eqn (9.6) we see that the impact on V_{it}/R_{it} of a change in ν_t (we argue above that ν declined dramatically in the late 1970s) is increasing in V_{it}/R_{it} itself. In particular, the derivative of V/R with respect to a change in ν in 1979 is $D_i = (-g_2'/g_2)(V_{i79}/R_{i79})(1+bV_{i79}/R_{i79})$. Historically, differences between industries in venture funding relative to R&D have been highly persistent over time. Hence the industry-specific average of V/R from 1965 through 1978, denoted A_i, should be highly correlated with D_i. To exploit this result, we propose an instrument that takes on the value of zero up through 1979 (before the effect of the policy shift is seen) but in each year after 1979, and for each industry i, takes on the value A_i.[20]

The validity of the instrument, however, requires that λ_{it} not deviate for too long from its industry-specific mean. To insure this property, we assume that $\ln(\lambda_{it})$ can be decomposed into the sum of a permanent industry component λ_i (which accounts for the persistent differences between industries in V/R) and a transitory component ω_{it}. If the transitory component is independent across time, then from 1980 it will not be correlated with A_i. Under this assumption, our instrument will not be correlated with technological opportunities, $\ln(N_{it})$, as they vary from their industry-specific means (industry and year dummies will always be included in the regressions). More generally, if ω_{it} is a moving average process of order m, then the instrument is still valid as long as it is amended by calculating A_i as the industry-specific average of V/R from 1965 only up to only m years prior to 1980. We consider this extension in two of the regressions below, for the case of $m = 5$.

As noted above, we must also contend with the endogeneity of R&D expenditures. There is no point in instrumenting for V/R while ignoring the potential correlation between R&D expenditures and the disturbance in the patent equation. The endogeneity problem, however, would be irrelevant if we already knew the value of the parameter α. Thus, before undertaking the daunting task of searching for a valid instrument for R&D, we simply fix the parameter α at some pre-assigned values and instrument for V/R.

The results are shown in Panel A of Table 9.9. Here we have instrumented for V/R in the linear specification of the patent production function, while fixing $\alpha = 0.2$ or $\alpha = 0.5$ (which straddle our estimates from Tables 9.6 and 9.7).[21] We still obtain large and statistically significant estimates of the potency of venture funding. The magnitude

---

[20] Note that our instrument for V/R is based on an average of the level of venture capital financing, A_i, over a number of years. Venture capital disbursements in each industry are 'lumpy': a single large later-round financing may account for a substantial fraction of the total financing in a given industry and year. By better capturing the mean level of financing activity in a given industry, the instrument may alleviate errors-in-variables problems, and may even lead to an increase in the coefficient on venture capital.

[21] All of the instrumental variable (IV) regressions that we report are based on the linear specification used in Tables 9.7 and 9.8. We also experimented with non-linear IV estimation based on the specification in the second and fourth regressions in Table 9.6. A feature of non-linear IV is ambiguity about what functions of the underlying instruments should be included in the instrument set. In some cases we obtained estimates of the potency of venture capital similar to the estimates reported in Table 9.9, but these estimates were not robust to dropping or adding powers of the underlying instruments. Since a comparison of Tables 9.6 and 9.7 suggests that the linear specification is more conservative in its implications about the potency of venture funding, we decided to focus on that specification.

Table 9.9. *Instrumental variable (IV) regression analysis of the linear patent production function*

	IV: 1965–78 period α = 0.20		IV: 1965–78 period α = 0.50	
Panel A: IV Regressions, constraining α				
Privately funded industrial R&D (α)	0.20	0.20	0.50	0.50
	—	—	—	—
Venture capital/privately funded R&D (α b):				
Firms receiving funding	3.06		2.51	
	[0.92]		[1.06]	
Venture disbursements		3.38		1.72
		[1.13]		[1.10]
Federally funded industrial R&D	0.01	0.01	0.02	0.02
	[0.01]	[0.01]	[0.01]	[0.01]
R^2	0.99	0.98	0.98	0.98
R^2 relative to dummy variable only case	0.19	0.14	0.07	0.07
Number of observations	560	560	560	560
Implied potency of venture funding (b)	15.28	16.89	5.02	3.45
	[4.59]	[5.63]	[2.12]	[2.21]

	IV's: 1965–78 Period and Industry GDP		IV's: 1965–75 Period and Industry GDP	
Panel B: IV Regressions, instrumenting for R&D				
Privately funded industrial R&D (α)	0.52	0.48	0.52	0.54
	[0.10]	[0.12]	[0.10]	[0.13]
Venture capital/privately funded R&D (α b):				
Firms receiving funding	2.48		2.12	
	[1.13]		[1.14]	
Venture disbursements		1.81		0.13
		[1.40]		[1.70]
Federally funded industrial R&D	0.02	0.02	0.02	0.02
	[0.01]	[0.01]	[0.01]	[0.02]
R^2	0.98	0.98	0.98	0.98
R^2 relative to dummy variable only case	0.07	0.07	0.05	−0.04
Number of observations	560	560	560	560
Implied potency of venture funding (b)	4.81	3.74	4.08	0.25
	[2.67]	[3.56]	[2.58]	[3.21]

Standard errors (in brackets) are based on the Newey–West autocorrelation-consistent covariance estimator (with a maximum of three lags). The standard errors for the parameter *b* are calculated using the delta method. Year and industry dummy variables are included in each regression.

of the estimated parameter, however, is sensitive to the assumed value of α. We find that venture capital is about fifteen times as potent as corporate R&D if $\alpha = 0.2$, but only three to five times as potent as R&D if $\alpha = 0.5$. In light of our uncertainty about the actual value of α, and given its substantial impact on the results, we attempt to instrument for R&D as well as venture capital.

The perfect instrument for R&D would be a measure of shifts in industry demand that affect the value of an invention Π_{it}, but are unrelated to technological opportunities. Since this ideal instrument is not available, we settle on an instrument that we can measure—the value of the gross industry product Y_{it}—which under certain assumptions is the same as the ideal instrument. The value of industry product is almost certainly relevant since the amount of R&D in an industry will be stimulated by an increase in the size of the market. Its validity as an instrument is less of a sure thing. In particular, the instrument will only be valid if technological opportunities (and the innovations stimulated by those opportunities) do not affect the size of the market.[22]

The regressions reported in Panel B of Table 9.9 use instruments for both venture funding relative to R&D and for R&D itself. The last two regressions in the panel also apply a modification of the instrument for V/R, as suggested above, to allow for the transitory component in entrepreneurial opportunities ω_{it} to be correlated for up to five years. Using the value of industry product as an instrument for R&D approximately doubles the estimate of α. The effect is to lower our estimates of the potency of venture funding, much like in the last two regressions in Panel A (in which α is constrained to be 0.5). The large increase in α when we instrument for R&D can be understood in two ways. One possibility is that our earlier estimates of α are biased downward (due to errors in our measure of R&D, similar to the problem discussed in footnote 20). A second possibility is that gross industry product is not a valid instrument, because it is positively correlated with technological opportunities. Since we cannot resolve these issues within the context of our IV approach, we pursue instead a very different technique for dealing with the endogeneity of venture funding.[23]

9.5.4. *Controlling for Technological Opportunities*

Our second approach for dealing with the endogeneity problem is to use R&D to control for unobserved technological opportunities. The basic idea follows from eqn (9.8): conditional on the ratio of venture capital to R&D and the expected value of an innovation, the patent–R&D ratio does not depend on technological opportunities. Taking logarithms of eqn (9.8) and linearizing around $V/R = 0$, we have,

$$\ln P_{it} - \ln R_{it} = b(V_{it}/R_{it}) - \ln \Pi_{it} + \ln \varepsilon_{it}. \tag{9.9}$$

---

[22] Such a feedback will not exist if the price elasticity of industry demand is equal to one. In this case, a fall in quality-adjusted prices associated with a process or product innovation will be just offset by the increase in demand, leaving the value of industry output unchanged.

[23] If we accept $\alpha = 0.5$, we can resolve the puzzle of the high estimates of venture-capital potency shown in Table 9.6. Redoing those non-linear regressions under the restriction that $\alpha = 0.5$ (and $\rho = 1$) yields much lower estimates of the potency of venture capital, in the range of four to five.

Table 9.10. *Ordinary least squares regression analyses of the patent–R&D ratio*

	Dependent variable			
	$\ln P_{it} - \ln R_{it}$		$\ln P_{it} - (\ln R_{it} + \ln Y_{it})$	
Venture capital/privately funded R&D (b):				
Firms receiving funding	2.39		2.96	
	[0.82]		[0.87]	
Venture disbursements		1.45		2.70
		[0.55]		[0.85]
R^2	0.97	0.97	0.97	0.97
R^2 relative to dummy variable only case	0.04	0.02	0.06	0.07
Number of observations	560	560	560	560

Standard errors (in brackets) are based on the Newey–West autocorrelation-consistent covariance estimator (with a maximum of three lags). Year and industry dummy variables are included in each regression.

(The term $\ln[g_1(v_t)/\alpha]$ is subsumed in year effects. Industry effects are also included.) One approach to estimating this equation is to subsume any variation in the expected value of inventions in the disturbance. This approach implicitly assumes, however, that shocks to venture funding relative to R&D are uncorrelated with shocks to the expected value of an invention.

Our other approach begins with Equation (9.9) but uses industry output as a proxy for the expected value of an invention, $\ln \Pi_{it} = a_0 + a_1 \ln Y_{it}$. Assuming $a_1 = 1$ (footnote 24 relaxes this assumption) we obtain the equation,

$$\ln P_{it} - (\ln R_{it} - \ln Y_{it}) = b(V_{it}/R_{it}) + \ln \varepsilon_{it}. \qquad (9.10)$$

The dependent variable can be thought of as the logarithm of the ratio of patents P to R&D intensity, R/Y. Note that our use of the value of industry output as a proxy for the expected value of an invention does not require that the value of industry output be independent of technological opportunities. Thus, we are able to avoid the most problematic assumption that was required in our instrumental variable approach.

The results from estimating eqns (9.9) and (9.10), shown in Table 9.10, are largely consistent with our findings in Tables 9.7–9.9. In all cases, venture funding is significantly more potent than corporate R&D. The estimates of b are more modest, suggesting that venture funding is between one and a half times and three times as potent as corporate R&D.[24]

---

[24] We can generalize by including $-a_1 \ln(Y_{it})$ on the right-hand side of eqn (9.9). Restricting $a_1 = 0$ we get back the specification shown in the first two columns of Table 9.10, while restricting it to be 1 yields the specification in the last two columns. If we estimate a_1 we get a value of about 0.4, while the corresponding estimate of b remains statistically significant and within the range reported in Table 9.10. We have also run regressions corresponding to the non-linear versions of eqns (9.9) and (9.10). The estimates of b are somewhat larger than those reported in Table 9.10: 3.23 [0.74], 1.86 [0.58], 4.55 [0.91], and 4.81 [0.84].

9.6. PATENTING OR INNOVATION?

While the analyses above suggest a strong relationship between venture capital and patenting on an industry level, one major concern remains. In particular, it might be thought that the relationship between venture capital disbursements and patent applications is not indicative of a relationship between venture disbursements and innovative output. It may be that the increase in patenting is a consequence of a shift in the propensity to patent innovations stimulated by the venture financing process itself. In the terms of eqn (9.7), there may be a positive correlation between the ε it and V_{it}/R_{it} terms.

Two reasons might lead venture-backed firms—or companies seeking venture financing—to patent inventions that other firms would not. First, they may fear that the venture investors will exploit their ideas. Firms seeking external financing must make extensive disclosures of their technology. While potential investors may sign non-disclosure agreements (and may be restrained by reputational concerns), there is still a real possibility that entrepreneurs' ideas will be directly or indirectly transferred to other companies. Alternatively, venture or other investors may find it difficult to discern the quality of firms' patent holdings. In order to enhance their attractiveness (and consequently increase the probability of obtaining financing or the valuation assigned in that financing), firms may apply for patents on technologies of marginal worth.

The industry-level data does not provide us much guidance here, but we can explore these possibilities by examining a broader array of behaviour by venture-backed and non-venture-backed firms. Using a sample of 530 Middlesex County firms, we examine three measures of innovative activity: Trajtenberg (1990) has demonstrated a strong relationship between the number of patent citations received and the economic importance of a patent. Using only those firms that received any patent awards prior to 1990, we compute the ratio of the number of US patent citations during the period between 1990 and June 1994 to US patents awarded between 1969 and 1989. Citations per patent provides a largely external measure of the average importance of the firms' patent awards.

The second and third measures of the intellectual property activity of firms are the frequency and extent of patent and trade secret litigation in which the firm has engaged. Models in the law-and-economics literature suggest parties are more likely to file suits and pursue these cases to trial when (i) the stakes of the dispute are high relative to the costs of the litigation, or (ii) the outcome of the case is unclear (Cooter and Rubinfeld 1989). Thus, litigation may serve as a rough proxy for economic importance, a suggestion verified empirically by Lanjouw and Schankerman (1997). We present these tabulations separately for patent and trade secret suits. These measures may provide a rough indication of the importance of both patents and trade secrets to the firm.

Table 9.11 presents univariate comparisons. There are substantial differences between the 122 venture-backed and 408 non-venture-backed firms: the venture firms are more likely to patent, have previous patents cited, and engage in frequent and protracted litigation of both patents and trade secrets. All the tests of differences in means and medians in these three categories are significant at least at the 5 per cent confidence level,

Table 9.11. *Comparisons of intellectual property activities of venture-backed and non-venture-backed firms*

	Mean		p-value, Comparison of	
	Venture-backed	Non-venture	Means	Medians
Patents, 1990 to mid-1994	12.74	2.40	0.029	0.000
Citations/patent	6.44	4.06	0.016	0.004
Intellectual property suits				
Number of suits	0.79	0.18	0.000	0.000
Number of docket filings	30.29	4.21	0.000	0.000
Patent suits only				
Number of suits	0.36	0.08	0.000	0.000
Number of docket filings	15.35	2.04	0.000	0.000
Trade secret suits only				
Number of suits	0.34	0.08	0.000	0.000
Number of docket filings	6.43	1.86	0.007	0.000

The sample consists of 530 firms based in Middlesex County, MA, of which 122 were venture-backed.

as well as when we employ regression specifications. These findings help allay fears that differences in the propensity to patent drove our findings in Sections 9.4 and 9.5. At the same time, it is important to acknowledge that while the firm-level analysis allows us to examine whether the innovative behaviour of venture-backed and non-venture firms differ on measures other than patent counts, it does not allow us to address endogeneity issues as in the industry-level analysis.

9.7. CONCLUSION

This chapter examines the impact of venture capital on technological innovation. Patenting patterns across industries over a three-decade period suggest that the effect is positive and significant. The results are robust to different measures of venture activity, sub-samples of industries, and representations of the relationship between patenting, R&D, and venture capital. Averaging across our preferred regressions, we come up with an estimate for b (the impact on patenting of a dollar of venture capital relative to a dollar of R&D) of 3.1. This estimate suggests that venture capital accounted for 8 per cent of industrial innovations in the decade ending in 1992.[25] Given the rapid increase in venture funding since 1992, and assuming that the potency of venture funding has remained constant,

---

[25] We get the estimate of $b = 3.1$ by averaging the estimates in the regressions reported in Panel B of Table 9.9, Table 9.10, and footnote 25. The ratio of venture capital disbursements to R&D (V/R) averaged over the years 1983 to 1992 is 2.9% (see Table 9.1). Our calculation of the share of innovations due to venture capital is $b(V/R)/(1 + b(V/R))$.

the results imply that by 1998 venture funding accounted for about 14 per cent of US innovative activity.[26]

In our earlier work (1998), we argued that the recent surge in patenting in the USA was most likely explained by changes in the management of innovative activities. Interpreted broadly, the growth of venture capital is one such management change. While our results help answer some questions, they pose in turn additional questions: First, what are the sources of the venture capitalists' advantage in funding innovation? Is the key source of advantage the process by which projects are chosen *ex ante*, or rather is it the monitoring and control after the investment is made?

Second, the finding of the apparently greater efficiency of venture funding in spurring innovation raises the question of why industrial R&D managers have not adopted some of the same approaches to financing innovation. Jensen (1993), for one, has argued that agency problems have hampered the effectiveness of major corporate industrial research facilities over the past several decades. What barriers have limited the diffusion of the venture capitalists' approaches?

Finally, other innovations in organizing research occurred contemporaneously. For example, central R&D facilities of large corporations have been redirected toward more applied problems (for an overview, see Rosenbloom and Spencer 1996). Is it possible to disentangle the distinct effects of the rise of venture capital from other R&D management innovations?

Appendix: Data Sources

9.A.1. *The Industry Data Set*

Patent applications. The patent data by industry are from Kortum (1992), updated using information on US patent awards by technology class in a variety of databases prepared by the USPTO. We compile from these databases the number of successful patents applied for by US inventors in each year. Because of variations in the speed with which the USPTO handles patent applications (in particular, the periodic slow-downs associated with budget crises), it is preferable to compile the number of successful applications filed each year, rather than the awards granted annually. This information is not known until all patents filed in a given year are issued. Thus, while we can be confident about essentially how many successful patent applications were filed in 1980, the number of successful applications filed in 1995 is still quite uncertain.

Concerns about data incompleteness determined the last year of the analysis. While we can project from preliminary data (e.g. the number of patent applications filed in 1992 that were awarded through 1996) how many applications filed in each year will ultimately

---

[26] Based on estimates of venture capital disbursements to all industries in 1998 (from Venture Economics) and preliminary estimates of R&D performed and funded by industry (from the NSF) we calculate that V/R increased at a 14% annual rate from 1992 to 1998. Given that V/R was 2.22% in 1992, we project that it had risen to 5.1% by 1998. Applying the same venture funding potency b of 3.1, we get the 14% number noted in the text.

be granted, we do not wish to have to make large imputations. Consequently, we only extend the analysis through 1992.

In addition to defining the time frame of the analysis, we have to consider which patents to include in the analysis. USPTO databases compile not only awards to US inventors, but also those to foreign firms and individuals seeking protection in the US market. Because we seek a proxy for the innovative output of the United States, we drop patents that were not originally filed in the USA.

As discussed in the text, the USPTO does not compile total patent applicants by industry. Even though we know the names of the applicants, many of these firms have multiple lines-of-business. Thus, we rely instead on a concordance that relates the primary classification to which the patent is assigned to the most likely industry of the inventing firm. This concordance, based on a study of Canadian patenting behaviour, employs the International Patent Classification to which the patent is assigned to determine the industry where it is likely to be used.

One challenge with both compilations of patent awards is the need to adjust the number of recent patent awards. While we exclude from the sample (as discussed above) patent applications from recent years, a few patents applied for in the early 1990s will not be awarded until the first decade of the twenty-first century. We adjust the observed counts of patent awards between 1987 and 1992 upward to reflect the number of patents that can expected to be awarded based on historical patterns. The patent data are summarized in Table 9.2.

Venture capital disbursements. The consulting firm Venture Economics compiles investments by venture capital funds (also known as disbursements). Venture capital organizations and major institutional investors provide quarterly reports to Venture Economics on their portfolio holdings, in exchange for summary data on investments and returns. These data have been collected since the formation of Venture Economics' predecessor entity, S.M. Rubel and Co., in 1961. While Venture Economics does not obtain reports on all funds, because multiple venture groups invest in a typical venture-backed firm, the database identifies at least 85 per cent of all venture capital transactions (Gompers and Lerner 1999).

We obtain Venture Economics tabulations that list total disbursements by the industry of the firm receiving the financing. The industry codes are classified according to a proprietary scheme developed by Venture Economics. We map these codes into our industry classification scheme, with the help of a concordance between the Venture Economics and the Standard Industrial Classification (SIC) codes.

One complex question is what constitutes a venture capital investment. Until the late 1970s, there were no distinct funds set up to make investments in leveraged buyout transactions. Rather, venture capital groups would invest into a wide variety of transactions: seed and early stage financings, expansion rounds of rapidly-growing entrepreneurial firms, and buyouts and other special situations (e.g. purchases of blocks of publicly traded securities). Since the 1970s, most buyout investing by private equity funds has been done through specialized funds dedicated to these transactions (e.g. Kohlberg, Kravis, and Roberts). Some venture capital funds, however, have continued to invest in buyouts (this was a particularly common phenomenon in the mid-1980s) and other special situations. Meanwhile, some groups frequently classified as buyout specialists (such as Welch, Carson, Anderson, and Stowe) also make a considerable number of venture capital investments.

We wish to focus our analysis on the relationship between innovation and investments in growing firms where the types of information problems that venture capitalists address are most critical. While many buyouts create value by eliminating inefficiencies and improving cash flows, these types of transactions are outside the focus of this chapter. The standard tabulation of venture capital investments prepared by Venture Economics includes investments by venture capital funds into both venture transactions and buyouts, as well as venture investments by groups classified as buyout funds. We undertake a special tabulation of the venture capital investments only, whether made by groups classified as venture capital or buyout funds. To insure compatibility with the other data series, we include only investments into firms based in the United States (whether the venture fund was based domestically or not). In order to test the robustness of our results, we also compile the seed and early stage investments by these funds using a similar approach. We collect both the dollar amount invested and the number of companies funded in each year. The venture capital data are summarized in Table 9.3.

R&D expenditures. We compile information on privately and federally funded R&D performed by industry from the US NSF. Both data series have been compiled since 1957 as part of the 'Survey of Research and Development in Industry', using an industry scheme based on two- and three-digit SIC codes. Occasionally, data series for smaller industries are suppressed in particular years. In these cases, it is necessary to extrapolate based on the relative level of R&D spending in previous years.[27] We slightly collapse the NSF industry scheme to insure comparability with the patent classification discussed above, for a total of twenty industries. The R&D data are summarized in Table 9.4.

Gross industry product. The Department of Commerce's Bureau of Economic Analysis has estimated gross product by industry for the two-digit SIC classes, as well as some important three-digit classes, using the current definitions of these industries. Not all three-digit SIC codes necessary for this analysis are compiled in their database. For the missing industries, we collect this information from the printed volumes of the Annual Survey of Manufacturers (ASM). While the ASM does not report gross product by industry, it does compile a related measure, value added. In each case, we examine the distribution of value added across the three-digit industry classes, and then assign the two-digit industry's gross product in a proportionate manner. Where necessary, we adjust the categories reported in these volumes to reflect today's classification structures. (For instance, prior to 1972 guided missiles were included in SIC 19, 'ordnance and accessories'. When that category was disbanded, they were moved to SIC 37, 'transportation equipment'.)

---

[27] The NSF will not report data when one or two firms account for the majority of the R&D in an industry or when firms representing more than one-half the R&D spending do not respond to the survey. Ideally, we would also have compiled expenditures by universities relevant to each industry. Associating the classes of academic research with particular industries, however, proved problematic.

9.A.2. *The Firms Data Set*

In order to assess the behaviour of firms at a more disaggregated level, we examine firms whose headquarters are in a single county, Middlesex County, Massachusetts. We include in the sample all 130 manufacturing firms based here that were publicly traded between January 1990 and June 1994, as well as a random sample of 400 such firms that were privately held. By using a sample of firms in one region, rather than a diverse array of locations, we can examine their innovative activities in more depth.[28]

Middlesex County includes much of the 'Route 128' high-tech complex, as well as concentrations of more traditional manufacturers. The first four columns of Table 9.12 contrast the mix of industrial establishments and employment in the USA and Middlesex County in 1990. The comparison indicates that the mixture of traditional industry in the county is fairly representative of the nation as a whole. Technology-intensive sectors, however, are disproportionately represented.

We include all firms in Compustat with headquarters in Middlesex County that file financial data with the US Securities and Exchange Commission for any quarter between the first quarter of 1990 and the second quarter of 1994. Following the analysis above, we confine our analysis to manufacturing firms (Standard Industrial Codes 20–39), but also include firms in SIC codes 7372 and 7373, who make packaged software and operating systems for mainframe computers.[29] We exclude shell companies that are established merely to make an acquisition and 'SWORDs,' publicly traded subsidiaries that finance R&D. After these deletions, the sample consists of 130 firms.

Publicly traded firms are likely to have different characteristics from other companies. Thus, we seek to include a representative sample of private firms as well. There is no single directory that lists all the firms in the county. Conversations with economic development officials, however, indicate that two directories taken together provide quite comprehensive coverage of manufacturing firms. George D. Hall's Directory of Massachusetts Manufacturers, which is prepared with the cooperation of the Associated Industries of Massachusetts, provides the most detailed listing of traditional manufacturers, while the Corporate Technology Directory specializes in high-tech firms. We draw 200 firms based in Middlesex County each from these directories. In both cases, the information is collected via a survey (and, in the case of Hall's, through consultation with the records of the Associated Industries of Massachusetts). All firms were required to have been in business by the end of 1989, though some exit (e.g. through bankruptcy or liquidation) during the sample period.

---

[28] In particular, we can examine not only patent filings but also intellectual property litigation. In both the federal and state court systems, intellectual property cases are often not identified as such by the courts' internal tracking systems. They are often recorded simply as 'miscellaneous tort' or 'contract' disputes, depending upon the circumstances of the case. We do not use the firms' 10-K filings with the US Securities and Exchange Commission to identify litigation for two reasons. First, we wish to include in our sample privately held firms, which need not make such filings. Second, while firms are required to report any material litigation in these filings, they are often highly selective in the suits that they actually disclose.

[29] Our rationale is that while software manufacturers are classified as service providers, their relationship with customers is more akin to that of manufacturers. The analyses below are robust to the deletion of these observations.

Table 9.12. *The distribution of firms in the analysis of venture-backed and non-venture-backed firms*

SIC Class	The USA		Middlesex County		Sample	
	Percent of establishments	Percent of employees	Percent of etablishments	Percent of employees	Percent of firms	Percent of employees
20: Food & kindred products	5.5%	8.0%	3.7%	4.3%	2.6%	8.3%
21: Tobacco products	0.0	0.2	0.0	0.0	0.0	0.0
22: Textile mill products	1.7	3.6	1.1	1.7	0.6	0.1
23: Apparel & other textiles	6.4	5.7	2.9	1.6	1.5	0.3
24: Lumber & wood products	9.3	3.9	2.2	0.7	1.3	0.1
25: Furniture & fixtures	3.2	2.8	1.7	0.5	0.8	0.0
26: Paper & allied products	1.7	3.5	1.9	3.7	0.6	0.1
27: Printing & publishing	16.8	8.6	17.7	9.4	3.2	2.8
28: Chemicals & allied products	3.3	4.8	3.8	3.3	9.1	3.2
29: Petroleum & coal products	0.6	0.6	0.5	0.1	0.2	0.0
30: Rubber & misc. plastics	4.1	4.9	3.5	3.5	2.5	0.7
31: Leather & leather products	0.5	0.7	0.4	0.1	0.2	2.7
32: Stone, clay, & glass products	4.3	2.9	2.1	1.0	0.8	0.1
33: Primary metal industries	1.8	4.0	1.0	1.4	1.3	0.5
34: Fabricated metal products	10.1	8.2	9.3	4.8	5.1	1.3
35: Industrial machinery	13.8	10.6	14.8	14.5	19.1	24.8
36: Electronic equipment	4.6	8.6	11.1	16.8	14.7	12.3
37: Transportation equipment	2.9	9.9	1.4	5.1	0.8	0.3
38: Instruments	2.7	5.3	9.7	19.4	16.4	24.9
39: Miscellaneous manufacturing	4.8	2.2	4.3	1.8	2.3	1.9
7372 & 7373: Software	1.9	0.9	7.0	6.4	17.2	15.4

We compare the number of firms and employees across manufacturing industries (two-digit Standard Industrial Code classes). We compare all firms in the USA, all those in Middlesex County, Massachusetts, and the 530 in the sample. The USA and Middlesex County figures are based on US Department of Commerce (1991). These present the number of establishments (one firm may have multiple establishments). Not all firms with fewer than twenty employees are included. The county figures are only for those employees actually working in the county. The sample columns present the number of firms, and include all employees of these firms, whether or not they work in Middlesex County.

The fifth and sixth columns of Table 9.12 compare the firms in the sample with those in the nation and county. We classify the public firms in our sample into industries using the primary SIC provided by Compustat; for the other firms, we employ the SIC code of the first-listed line-of-business in the Hall's and Corporate Technology directories. (Both directories list lines-of-business in order of importance, as reported by the firm.)[30]

We obtain a variety of information about these firms. From Compustat or the two business directories, we determine the sales and employment in 1990, as well as the year in which the firm was founded. From CRSP, we determine if and when the firm went public. We determine whether the firm was venture-backed from Venture Economics. We also use the number of patents that the firm has been awarded in the period 1969–94 (as well as citations to these awards), which we identify using Mead's LEXIS/PATENT/ALL file and the USPTO's CASSIS CD-ROM database. (We include awards to subsidiaries, R&D limited partnerships, and earlier names, which we identify through the data sources cited below.)

We finally identify all litigation involving these firms in the federal and state judicial districts that include their headquarters: the Federal District for Massachusetts and the Commonwealth of Massachusetts' Middlesex Superior Court. Both systems include every lawsuit that was open during the sample period, even if the suit was settled almost immediately after the initial complaint was filed. We identify 1144 cases that were open on 1 January 1990 or were filed between 1 January 1990 and 30 June 1994. After eliminating those cases that are very unlikely to involve intellectual property issues, we examined the remaining case files.[31] The docket records also allow us to compute the total number of docket filings by the plaintiffs, defendants, and other parties in the dispute between 1 January 1990 and 30 June 1994. (This approach to characterizing disputes was also used in the Georgetown antitrust study; see White 1988.) The records do not provide information on the extent of activity at the appellate level. Thus, they may tend to understate the magnitude of litigation in cases that are appealed.

Table 9.13 characterizes the venture-backed and non-venture-backed firms in the sample. The 122 venture-backed firms are significantly larger in sales and employment than the 408 non-venture-backed firms, and are more likely to be publicly traded. They tend to have been founded later, and (as a result) have accumulated a smaller stock of patents. The venture-backed firms are concentrated in high-tech industries. The average ratio of R&D-to-sales of all public firms that reported R&D data in 1990 with a primary assignment in Compustat to the same four-digit SIC code as

---

[30] The comparison of the sample with the federal and county data is not precise for three reasons. First, the tabulation of the sample firms shows the distribution of firms; the USA and county columns present the pattern of establishments. (Many firms will have multiple establishments.) Second, firms with less than twenty employees are only sampled in County Business Patterns, and thus are underrepresented. The two directories appear to have quite comprehensive coverage of smaller firms, who generally welcome the visibility that a listing provides. Consequently, industries with many small firms may have greater representation in the sample. Finally, the tabulation of employment in the sample firms includes employees that work in Middlesex County and elsewhere. The county tabulation presents the distribution of employees working in Middlesex County, regardless of where the parent firm has its headquarters.

[31] In addition, we could not examine nine dockets that may or may not have involved intellectual property issues. These cases had been either lost or sealed. (While most of the case files were accessible at the clerk of the court's offices at the two courthouses, we found many case files in off-site storage archives, in courthouses elsewhere in the county or state, or in the possession of judges' docket clerks.)

Table 9.13. *Characteristics of venture-backed and non-venture-backed firms*

	Mean	Median	Stan. Dev.	Minimum	Maximum
Panel A: 122 Venture-Backed firms					
Firm sales in 1990 ($ millions)	173	11	1199	0	12942
Firm employment in 1990	526	106	2103	8	20184
Year firm was founded	1977	1981	15	1880	1989
Publicly traded at end of 1989?	0.30			0	1
Patent awards, 1969–89	10	0	41	0	375
R&D/sales ratio of industry in 1990	0.11	0.10	0.08	0.00	0.38
Panel B: 408 Non-Venture-Backed Firms					
Firm sales in 1990 ($ millions)	44	2	477	0	9268
Firm employment in 1990	184	19	940	2	11768
Year firm was founded	1967	1974	25	1842	1989
Publicly traded at end of 1989?	0.11			0	1
Patent awards, 1969–89	13	0	149	0	2644
R&D/sales ratio of industry in 1990	0.06	0.04	0.06	0.00	0.38

The sample consists of 530 firms based in Middlesex County, Massachusetts. The tabulation presents the summary statistics for the 122 firms that had received venture capital financing prior to January 1990, and the 408 that did not. The 'Publicly Traded at End of 1989?' variable is a dummy that takes on the value 1.0 if the firm was publicly traded. The final item in each panel is the average ratio of R&D-to-sales of all publicly traded firms that reported R&D data in 1990 with a primary assignment in Compustat to the same four-digit SIC code as the firm.

the venture-backed firms is higher than the ratios of the companies matched to the non-venture-backed firms.

9.A.3. *Data Sources*

Patent Applications
Case-Western Reserve University, Center for Regional Economic Issues, 1997, Unpublished patent database, Cleveland.

Kortum, S. (1992), Inventions, R&D, and industry growth, Unpublished Ph.D. dissertation, Yale University.

US Patent and Trademark Office, Office of Electronic Information Products, Technology Assessment and Forecast Program, 1996, Unpublished tabulation of patenting trends in the United States, Washington, DC.

US Patent and Trademark Office, Office of Electronic Information Products, Technology Assessment and Forecast Program, 1997, All technologies report, http://www.uspto.gov/web/offices/ac/ido/oeip/taf/all_tech.pdf.

Venture Capital Disbursements
Securities Data Company, Venture Economics, Inc. (1997), Venture Intelligence Database, Boston.

R&D Expenditures
US National Science Foundation, Division of Science Resource Studies (1980), *Research and Development in Industry*—1979, US Government Printing Office, Washington, DC.

US National Science Foundation, Division of Science Resource Studies (1997), Survey of research and development in industry, http://www.nsf.gov/sbe/srs/sird/start.htm.

Gross Industry Product
Friedenberg, H.L. and Beemiller, R.M. (1997), Comprehensive revision of gross state product by industry, 1977–94, *Survey of Current Business* 77 (June), 15–41.

US Department of Commerce, Bureau of the Census, 1996 and earlier years, Annual survey of manufacturers, US Government Printing Office, Washington, DC.

US Department of Commerce, Bureau of Economic Analysis, 1997, Unpublished data file: Gross state product by industry—Original experimental estimates, 1963–1986, Washington, DC.

Yuskavage, R.E. (1996), Improved estimates of gross product by industry, 1959–94, *Survey of Current Business* 76 (August), 133–55.

Identifying Sample of Middlesex County Firms
Corporate Technology Information Services, 1994 and earlier, *Corporate Technology Directory*, Corporate Technology Information Services, Woburn, MA.

G.D. Hall Company, 1995 and earlier, George D. Hall's directory of Massachusetts manufacturers, G.D. Hall Company, Boston.

Standard and Poors' Compustat Services (1997), *Compustat Database*, New York.

Supplemental Data on Middlesex County Firms
Commerce Register, 1995 and earlier, *Massachusetts Directory of Manufacturers*, Commerce Register, Hokokus, NJ.

Dun's Marketing Services, 1995 and earlier, *Million Dollar Directory*, Dun's Marketing Services, Parsippany, NJ.

Files of the Commonwealth of Massachusetts' Middlesex Superior Court (Cambridge) and the Federal District for Massachusetts.

Gale Research, 1995 and earlier, *Ward's Business Directory of US Private and Public Companies*, Gale Research, Detroit.

Mead Data Central, LEXIS/NEXIS, Inc., 1994, PATENTS/ALL database, Dayton.

Moody's Investor Service, 1995 and earlier, *Moody's OTC Industrial Manual*, Moody's Investor Service, New York.

National Register Publishing Company, 1995 and earlier, *Directory of Leading Private Companies, Including Corporate Affiliations*, National Register Publishing Company, Wilmette, IL.

Predicasts, Inc., 1995 and earlier, *Predicasts F&S Index of Corporate Change*, Predicasts, Inc., Cleveland.

Securities Data Company, Venture Economics, Inc. (1997), *Venture Intelligence Database*, Boston.

US Department of Commerce, Bureau of the Census (1991), *Country Business Patterns, 1990*, US Government Printing Office, Washington, DC.

US Patent and Trademark Office, Office of Electronic Information Products, 1995, *Cassis Patents BIB CD-ROM Database*, Washington, DC.

References

Akerlof, G. A. (1970), 'The Market for "Lemons": Qualitative Uncertainty and the Market Mechanism', *Quarterly Journal of Economics* 84, 488–500.

Bernstein, J., and Nadiri, M. I. (1986), 'Financing and Investment in Plant and Equipment and Research and Development', in M. H. Peston and R. E. Quandt (eds.), *Prices, Competition and Equilibrium*, Oxford: Philip Allan.

Cohen, W. M. (1995), 'Empirical studies of innovative activity', in P. Stoneman (ed.), *Handbook of the Economics of Innovation and Technical Change*, Oxford: Basil Blackwell.

Cooter, R. D. and Rubinfeld, D. L. (1989), 'Analysis of legal disputes and their resolution', *Journal of Economic Literature* 27, 1067–97.

European Commission (1995), Green Paper on Innovation, Brussels: The European Union. http://europa.eu.int/en/record/green/gp9512/ind_inn.htm.

Freear, J. and Wetzel, W. E. Jr. (1990), 'Who bankrolls high-tech entrepreneurs?', *Journal of Business Venturing* 5, 77–89.

Gompers, P. A. and Lerner J. (1996), 'The use of covenants: an empirical analysis of venture partnership agreements', *Journal of Law and Economics* 39, 463–98.

—— and —— (1998), 'What drives venture capital fundraising?', Brookings Papers on Economic Activity: Microeconomics, 149–92.

—— and —— (1999), *The Venture Capital Cycle*, Cambridge MA: MIT Press.

Greenwald, B. C., Stiglitz, J. E., and Weiss, A. (1984), 'Information imperfections in the capital market and macroeconomic fluctuations', *American Economic Review Papers and Proceedings* 74, 194–99.

Griliches, Z. (1979), 'Issues in assessing the contribution of R&D to productivity growth', *Bell Journal of Economics* 10, 92–116.

—— (1986), 'Productivity, R&D, and basic research at the firm level in the 1970s', *American Economic Review* 76, 141–54.

—— (1990), 'Patent statistics as economic indicators: a survey', *Journal of Economic Literature* 28, 1661–707.

—— and Hausman, J. A. (1986), 'Errors in variables in panel data', *Journal of Econometrics* 31, 93–118.

Hall, B., Griliches, Z., and Hausman, J. A. (1988), 'Patents and R&D: is there a lag?', *International Economic Review* 27, 265–83.

Hellmann, T. and Puri, M. (1998), 'The interaction between product market and financing strategy: the role of venture capital', Mimeo, Stanford University.

Himmelberg, C. P. and Petersen, B. C. (1994), 'R&D and internal finance: a panel study of small firms in high-tech industries', *Review of Economics and Statistics* 76, 38–51.

Jensen, M. C. (1993), 'Presidential address: the modern industrial revolution, exit, and the failure of internal control systems', *Journal of Finance* 48, 831–80.

—— and Meckling, W. H. (1996), 'Theory of the firm: managerial behavior, agency costs and ownership structure', *Journal of Financial Economics* 3, 305–360.

Kortum, S. (1992), Inventions, R&D industry growth, unpublished PhD. dissertation, Yale University.

——and Lerner, J. (1998), 'Stronger protection or technological revolution: what is behind the recent surge in patenting?', *Carnegie-Rochester Conference Series on Public Policy* 48, 247–304.

——and —— (2000), 'Assessing the impact of venture capital on innovation', *RAND Journal of Economics* 31, 674–92.

——and Putnam, J. (1997), 'Assigning patents to industries: tests of the Yale technology concordance', *Economic Systems Research* 9, 161–75.

Lanjouw, J. and Schankerman, M. (1997), 'Stylized facts of patent litigation: value, scope and ownership', Working Paper no. 6297, National Bureau of Economic Research.

Levinsohn, J. and Petrin, A. (1999), 'Estimating production functions using intermediate inputs to control for unobservables', Mimeo, University of Michigan.

Myers, S. C. and Majluf, N. (1984), 'Corporate financing and investment decisions when firms have information that investors do not have', *Journal of Financial Economics* 13, 187–221.

Newey, W. and West, K. A. (1987), 'Simple, positive semi-definite, heteroskedasticity and autocorrelation consistent covariance matrix', *Econometrica* 55, 703–8.

Olley, S. and Pakes, A. (1996), 'The dynamics of productivity in the telecommunications industry', *Econometrica* 64, 1263–97.

Rosenbloom, R. S. and Spencer, W. J. (eds) (1996), *Engines of Innovation: U.S. Industrial Research at the End of an Era*, Boston: Harvard Business School Press.

Schmookler, J. (1966), *Invention and Economic Growth*, Cambridge, MA: Harvard University.

Stiglitz, J. E. and Weiss, A. (1981), 'Credit rationing in markets with incomplete information', *American Economic Review* 71, 393–409.

Trajtenberg, M. A (1990), 'Penny for your Quotes: Patent Citations and the Value of Inventions', *RAND Journal of Economics* 21, 172–87.

White, L. J. (1988), *Private Antitrust Litigation: New Evidence, New Learning*, Cambridge, MA: MIT Press.

PART III

VALUATION OF HIGH-TECH FIRMS

10

Real Options: Principles of Valuation and Strategy

HAN T. J. SMIT AND LENOS TRIGEORGIS

10.1. INTRODUCTION

This chapter provides an overview of the basic principles of quantifying the value of corporate real options and of capturing important strategic dimensions, which are at the core of strategic planning and investing under uncertainty. In the current, highly volatile, and competitive landscape, the horizon over which cash flows can be estimated confidently is shrinking, making it essential for firms to be flexible in their investment programs. The future is uncertain and the dynamic investment path unfolds as the firm's management learns, adapts, and revises investment decisions in response to unexpected market developments. An analysis of projects in a dynamic environment is often more complex than the standard Discounted Cash Flow (DCF) approaches may suggest, since they implicitly assume a static view of investment decisions and projected cash flow scenarios.[1] The real options approach is more dynamic than the traditional approaches since it is capable of incorporating not only the value of flexibility and growth opportunities but also of competitive strategies in an uncertain environment.[2]

It is well accepted by now that the value of many strategic investments does not derive so much from direct cash inflows, as it does from the options to invest in future growth. Indeed, strategic plans often encompass projects which, if measured by cash flows alone, typically appear to have a negative net present value (NPV), when in fact they may have

---

[1] The standard NPV methodology has obvious shortcomings in analysing investment opportunities whose value derives from future growth options. NPV implicitly assumes such investment decisions are a 'now or never' proposition; it does not take into account the value to 'wait and see' and alter planned investment decisions as uncertainty gets resolved over time.

[2] A number of papers have addressed the importance of managerial flexibility. Baldwin (1982) examines sequential investment strategies and interdependencies with future investment opportunities. She observes that if firms with market power wish to compensate for the loss in the value of future opportunities that result from undertaking a project now, they must require a positive premium over NPV. Myers (1987) suggests considering strategic investment opportunities as growth options, while Kester (1984) discusses qualitatively strategic and competitive aspects of growth opportunities. Dixit and Pindyck (1994), Trigeorgis (1988, 1995, 1996), Kemna (1988), Sick (1989), Smit (1996), and others discuss many corporate options and provide various expositions of the real options approach to investment.

a positive total strategic value. An early investment in research and development (R&D), for instance, may seem unattractive if its direct measurable cash flows are considered in isolation. However, the potential profits from commercialization that may result from the research (and related spin-off applications) must be properly captured by determining the value of the underlying research program. Such a strategic R&D investment should not be seen as a one-time investment at the outset; proper analysis requires explicit consideration of its follow-on commercial options (i.e. to commercialize the end product of the R&D program) and related applications. The option perspective suggests that, as information over the success of R&D is revealed, management has flexibility to proceed with, terminate, or otherwise alter its future investment plans.

The new view of investment that treats opportunities as corporate real options has enriched modern corporate resource allocation and planning. The opportunity to invest can be seen as a call option, involving the right to acquire an asset for a specified price (investment outlay) at some future time. The underlying asset may be a package consisting of the project plus the value of other embedded corporate real options (e.g. to later expand production scale, abandon the project for its salvage value, etc.). The techniques derived from option pricing can help quantify management's ability to adapt its future plans to capitalize on favourable investment opportunities or to respond to undesirable developments in a dynamic environment by cutting losses.

'Wait-and-see' flexibility is clearly important in the evaluation of many investment opportunities under uncertainty. By delaying an investment decision, new information can be revealed that might affect the desirability of the investment, while management has the option to discontinue the project if market conditions turn out to be unfavourable. From this perspective, management should wait until a project is clearly desirable, requiring a premium over the zero-NPV value, reflecting the option value of deferment. Of course, from a strategic perspective it is not always advisable to defer investment. Besides the learning advantages of postponement, waiting may involve serious disadvantages. For example, management could lose early operating cash inflows when a fixed-life project is delayed, or miss out on a competitive first-mover advantage. An earlier (or heavier) strategic investment (say, to develop a new technology) may confer upon the pioneer firm a cost or timing advantage and influence the competitor's behaviour and the resulting equilibrium in a way that strengthens the pioneer's competitive position and long-term value. In other words, early investment commitment may have strategic benefits that must be weighted against the lost flexibility value component. These benefits and the resulting implications for competitive strategy can be captured with the help of basic game theory principles in combination with option valuation.

In the organization of this chapter we find it instructive to follow a step-by-step exposition. To introduce different aspects into the analysis one at a time we start with examples of proprietary investment decisions (options) under uncertainty, and later introduce the strategic dimension of competitive reactions. Section 10.2 uses two basic numerical examples to illustrate the application of real options valuation principles to mining and to R&D programs. Section 10.3 extends the analysis using basic game theory principles to discuss other strategic and competitive aspects, especially applicable to oligopolistic, innovative (high-tech) industries like consumer electronics. Section 10.4 examines the issue of competition vs. coordination/collaboration. Section 10.5 concludes.

Table 10.1. *Quantities, prices, and operating cash inflows of a mine in various states*

Period	State (nature)	Probability q	Gold price per ounce, S	Quantity Q	Cash inflow (QS) CF (m)
0	Current		$300		
1	High	0.5	$450	4,000	$1.80
1	Low	0.5	$200	4,000	$0.80
2	High, high	0.25	$675	10,000	$6.75
2	High, low/low, high	0.5	$300	10,000	$3.00
2	Low, low	0.25	$133	10,000	$1.33

10.2. BASIC VALUATION EXAMPLES: MINING AND R&D

This section presents two prototypical applications. The first example considers the valuation of a gold mine concession, where the current project value can be estimated using a traded financial instrument (gold futures) whose probabilistic behaviour is close to that of a producing mine. The valuation of a licence to develop the mine is treated analogous to the valuation of a simple call option. In the second example, we consider whether to invest in R&D and subsequent stages of commercialization. The multi-stage R&D investment decision can be viewed as a compound option (or option on an option).

10.2.1. *Valuing a Mine Concession (Licence)*

Following Brennan and Schwartz (1985), consider a firm that must decide whether to invest in a gold mine. The decision to develop the mine is irreversible, in that after development management cannot disinvest and recover the expenditure. To keep matters simple, suppose that development and extraction can be started immediately, requiring an investment outlay, I, of $4.5 million (m). There are no variable extraction costs. The gold reserves and the production profile, Q_t, over time t, is known ahead of time: production in year 1, Q_1, is expected to be 4,000 ounces, and production in year 2, Q_2, 10,000 ounces.

Uncertainty over the value of the project is closely related to the dynamics in gold prices. Currently, gold is priced at $300 per troy ounce; next year, the price will change. For simplicity, we assume two possible end-of-period prices after one period: price increasing (with a multiplicative factor $u = 1.5$) to $S^+ = $450, or price decreasing (with a multiplicative factor $d = 0.67$) to a value of $S^- = $200. Both prices are equally likely. In the subsequent year ($t = 2$), prices may rise or decrease again, and the same multiplicative factors will apply. Table 10.1 summarizes the possible gold prices (S), extraction quantities (Q), and the resulting operating cash flows, CF $= Q \cdot S$.[3] Suppose further that the risk-free interest rate r is 4 per cent per year.

Given the value of the investment outlay, the current gold price, and the dynamics in gold prices, is this a good investment? Should management invest now, or should it wait

---

[3] Some of the numbers in Table 10.1 are rounded.

and see how gold prices will develop? For an immediate investment decision, we need to determine the opportunity cost of capital and the NPV. The required return can be estimated from a traded financial instrument (gold) whose probabilistic behaviour is close to that of the completed project. With a spot gold price of $300, the implied market-required return, k, for this risk can be derived from the expected gold prices over the next one-year period, or it can be derived from the expected gold prices over a two-year period:

$$300 = \frac{0.5 \times \$450 + 0.5 \times \$200}{1+k} = \frac{0.25 \times \$675 + 0.5 \times \$300 + 0.25 \times \$133}{(1+k)^2}. \tag{10.1}$$

The expectation of future gold prices presented above has an implied required rate of return equal to $k = 8.33$ per cent. The NPV computation below shows that the present value of the expected cash inflows equals $4.2m. The NPV of the gold mine is $4.2m − $4.5m = −$0.3m; therefore, management would not invest in such a value-destructive project.

$$\begin{aligned}\text{NPV} &= \frac{0.5 \times \$1.80m + 0.5 \times \$0.80m}{1.0833}\\ &\quad + \frac{0.25 \times \$6.75m + 0.5 \times \$3.00m + 0.25 \times 1.33m}{(1.0833)^2} - \$4.5m\\ &= \$4.2m - \$4.5m = -\$0.3m. \end{aligned} \tag{10.2}$$

Another approach to valuing the mine is to replicate the cash flows with an equivalent 'twin' security rather than estimating the twin security's required return. Consider the position of the company that owns the producing mine. The company's position is long in gold. The company could offset this position and realize the value of the field today if management could sell short gold futures that exactly match the mine's production over time. This particular project is lucrative for the corporation's shareholders if the value of the covered position exceeds the investment outlay required for the project.

Consider, for instance, the dollar revenue of the mine at $t = 2$ equal to the production times the market price over two years, $10{,}000S_2$. The company can offset the price risk of this cash flow by selling future contracts short for 10,000 ounces of gold, with a futures price $_0F_2$ and a dollar revenue $(10{,}000)_0F_2$ at $t = 2$. Since it can offset the risk of gold prices, this hedged position, $Q_2(_0F_2)$, can be seen as a certainty equivalent, CEQ_2, of the uncertain operating cash flow at $t = 2$. In eqn (10.3) the present value of the certainty-equivalent cash flows is calculated using the risk-free rate, r, as the appropriate discount-rate:

$$\text{NPV} = \frac{Q_1F_1}{1+r} + \frac{Q_2F_2}{(1+r)^2} - I. \tag{10.3}$$

What is the price of long-term contracts if they are traded in an arbitrage-free financial market? In arbitrage-free markets the expected future price, $_0F_T$, equals the current spot price of gold, S_0, plus the interest accrued until maturity T of this position, that is,

$_0F_T = (1 + r)^{T-0} S_0.$[4] Equations (10.4) and (10.5) calculate the present value of the certainty-equivalent cash flows using the theoretical futures prices, $_tF_T = (1 + r)^{T-t}S_t$, where $T - t$ is the time to maturity of the contract.

$$\text{NPV} = \frac{Q_1 S_0 (1 + r)}{1 + r} + \frac{Q_2 S_0 (1 + r)^2}{(1 + r)^2} - I, \tag{10.4}$$

$$= (Q_1 + Q_2)S_0 - I = 14{,}000 \times \$300 - \$4.5\text{m} = -\$0.3\text{m}. \tag{10.5}$$

Equation (10.5) illustrates that we can replicate the cash flows of the mine with a gold 'cash-and-carry' strategy. In other words, owning the mine is equivalent to owning a portfolio of gold. We are able to replicate the cash flows directly if we buy 14,000 ounces of gold (the total amount of the reserves) today and sell 4,000 ounces at $t = 1$ and 10,000 ounces at $t = 2$. The current market value of this strategy and the value of the mine, therefore, equals 14,000($300) = $4.2m, and the NPV of the mine equals $4.2m − $4.5m = −$0.3m.

Not surprisingly, the NPV and the certainty-equivalent valuation approaches both result in the same answer (−$0.3m). In the NPV method, the risk adjustment was carried out in the denominator through an appropriate risk-adjusted discount rate, k. In the certainty-equivalent method, the adjustment for risk is in the numerator, allowing the certainty-equivalent cash inflows to be discounted at the risk-free rate, r. Equation (10.4) reflects this relation.

As a third variation, we could also calculate an (artificial) risk-neutral probability, p, of possible gold price up (and down) movements, which would allow us to calculate the CEQ from the possible gold prices.[5] The risk-neutral probability is the one that would prevail if the underlying asset (in a risk-neutral world) were expected to earn the risk-free return ($pS^+ + (1 - p)S^- = (1 + r)S$). The risk-neutral probability, p, differs from the actual (true) probability, q. The risk-neutral probability is given by eqn (10.7) (see Trigeorgis and Mason 1987), where S^+ and S^- are the possible gold prices in the up and down states next period, and r is the risk-free interest rate.

$$S = \frac{q \times S^+ + (1 - q)S^-}{1 + k} = \frac{p \times S^+ + (1 - p)S^-}{1 + r} = \frac{CEQ}{1 + r}, \tag{10.6}$$

where

$$p \equiv \frac{(1 + r)S - S^-}{S^+ - S^-}. \tag{10.7}$$

---

[4] This assumes no convenience or dividend-like yield. Suppose that this relation does not hold and that the futures price is higher. Should this happen, a 'cash-and-carry' arbitrage opportunity is available if traders short the contract and simultaneously buy the gold. At maturity, the gold is delivered, covering the short position in the futures contract. Hence, traders are unlikely to be willing to serve this 'free lunch' for the company by selling futures.

[5] Because of the ability to replicate the mine with a specific gold position, its value is independent of investor risk attitudes and hence it is the same if investors were risk neutral.

In the computation below we apply the risk-neutral valuation of eqn (10.6) to the above mine, using the risk-neutral probability from eqn (10.7):

$$p = \frac{(1 + 0.04)300 - 200}{450 - 200} = 0.45.$$

The resulting valuation again gives the same project value of −$0.3m:

$$NPV = \frac{0.45 \times \$1.80m + (1 - 0.45) \times \$0.80m}{1.04}$$

$$+ \frac{0.45^2 \times \$6.75m + 2(0.45 \times 0.55)\$3.00m + (1 - 0.45)^2 \times \$1.33m}{1.04^2} - \$4.5m$$

$$= \$4.2m - \$4.5m = -\$0.3m.$$

So far, replication of cash flows or properly discounting them at the required return has resulted in the same answer. We next examine situations in which NPV does not give the right answer. Capital investments are not usually a 'now or never' proposition. Suppose that management can buy a one-year licence that enables it to wait for a year and see how gold prices develop before making an investment in the project. If gold prices drop and the value of the mine declines below the required investment outlay, management can allow the license to expire. Figure 10.1 illustrates how this option to defer alters the shape (distribution) of the value of the mine. At a high gold price, the value of the mine equals $6.3m (Q × S = 14,000 × $450). At that value, management would invest $4.5m and the NPV would equal $6.3m − $4.5m = $1.8m. At a low price, management would decide not to invest, as the value of the project would be only $2.8m (< $4.5m). In this case, management would allow the license to expire and the value would be truncated to zero.

The standard NPV framework, which determines the present value of the expected cash inflows and the present value of expected outlays, does not give the right answer in this case. Under uncertainty, management has the flexibility to revise the investment decision as uncertainty over the value of the project gets resolved. The future investment decision is based on future gold prices, information that is not yet known. Decision tree analysis (DTA) can in principle capture this decision flexibility that cannot be handled well by static NPV. However, to find the appropriate discount rate (cost of capital) along each branch (gold price state) is not an easy task. As in a call option, the risk of the licence changes

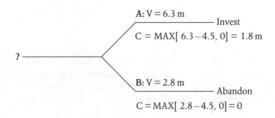

Figure 10.1. *Asymmetry in the distribution of project value due to flexibility.*

Table 10.2. *Replication of mine project value (licence) with a gold position*

	Low price ($200)	High price ($450)
7200 ounces of gold	$1.44m	$3.24m
Loan repayment (risk free)	($1.44m)	($1.44m)
Project value (licence)	0	$1.8m

each time its underlying value changes; the risk of the licence is reduced if the price of gold—and the value of the mine—increases. An option-based approach uses decision nodes (rather than passive event nodes) in modelling flexibility, with risk-neutral valuation capturing changes in risk in an appropriate manner. As with DTA, the valuation problem can be solved recursively, starting with future values and working backwards along the tree. The resulting 'certainty-equivalent' values can then be consistently discounted at the risk-free rate, r. The value of the licence in this way can be seen to equal:

$$V_0 = \frac{p \times C^+ + (1-p)C^-}{1+r} = \frac{0.45 \times \$1.8m + (1-0.45) \times 0}{1.04} = \$0.78m,$$

(10.8)

where C^+ and C^- denote the values of the option in the up $(+)$ and down $(-)$ states next period. Based on the expanded NPV criterion, the value of the licence to invest has the following components:

Expanded NPV = (static) NPV + flexibility (or option) value,

$0.78m = -\$0.3m + \$1.08m.$

The risk-neutral valuation method used above is based on an underlying ability to replicate the value of the cash flows. In this case, management can create a gold portfolio in the financial markets that replicates the future pay-off of the licence. In order to truncate the resulting pay-off, it can combine this gold portfolio with the risk-free asset. The position in gold in the replicating portfolio, N (the option delta or hedge ratio), would equal the spread in the value of the licence ($1.8m–0) divided by the spread in gold prices ($450 − $200). Table 10.2 shows that the synthetic licence consists of a position of $N = 7200$ ounces in gold and a risk-free payment of $1.44m that exactly replicates the future truncated pay-off of the mine (zero, $1.8m). If the gold price is low ($200), the value of this replicating portfolio equals 7200($200) − $1.44m = 0. If the price is high ($450), the value of the synthetic licence equals 7200($450) − $1.44m = $1.8m.

Since the licence and the replicating portfolio have the same future pay-off in each gold price state, the value of the licence today must be the current cost of constructing this replicating portfolio. Equation (10.9) estimates the value of the licence using the position in gold (7200) multiplied by the current gold price ($300) and the present value of the risk-free loan ($1.44m/1.04). This results in a $0.78m value, exactly the same as found earlier when using the risk-neutral probabilities under the risk-neutral binomial valuation method:

$$NS_0 + B = 7200 \times \$300 - \$1.38m = \$0.78m. \tag{10.9}$$

It is worth noting that in the valuation of the above gold mine we can use directly the principle of replicating future project cash flows. In R&D, however, an implementation problem with carrying out the replication argument of standard option pricing arises because a correlated financial instrument may be non-existent. Nevertheless, the methodology can still be applied for valuing the contingent claim (investment opportunity) provided there is a corresponding valuation for the underlying asset (relative valuation). In this case the issue is to determine the market value of the project to a firm if it were traded in the financial markets, which is a standard assumption in traditional capital budgeting (see Mason and Merton 1985).

10.2.2. *Valuing Research and Development*

Our second example concerns how to analyse an R&D program available to a high-tech company, and which technology strategy to pursue. As noted, R&D programs involve multiple contingent stages and thus should not be treated as isolated projects. The value of potential profits from follow-on commercial projects that may result from the research stage must be properly captured in determining the value of the underlying research program. Hence, the analysis requires explicit consideration of the project's various stages: research and product development, and future commercialization.

Figure 10.2 shows the estimated cash flows of an R&D project available to a high-technology company. Suppose the project involves a two-year upfront R&D phase,

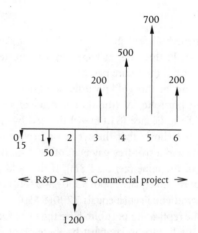

Figure 10.2. *Capital outlays (↓) and expected cash inflows (↑) for the R&D project to develop a new technology, and the potential follow-on commercial project.*

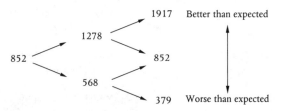

Figure 10.3. *Dynamics in the value of the commercial project (in millions).*

followed by expected cash inflows over a four-year period of commercialization. The R&D phase requires an immediate capital outlay of $15m, and an outlay of $50m as of year 1. The follow-on commercial project has expected cash inflows over the four-year period of $CF_3 = \$200m$, $CF_4 = \$500m$, $CF_5 = \$700m$, and $CF_6 = \$200m$, and requires an outlay of $I_2 = \$1,200m$ as of year 2. Even though the program appears to have a low return on investment, it may be profitable to develop the new technology to enhance the company's future market position.

What is the value of the R&D program if management were to commit to both stages immediately? Its value at the beginning of commercial phase, V_2, discounted at an opportunity cost of capital $k = 15$ per cent, is $1127m, and its NPV_2 therefore equals $1127m $-$ $1200m $=$ $-$73m. Based on the expected scenario of a static NPV analysis, the commercialization project itself does not appear to be profitable. Calculating the present value as of $t = 0$, using an opportunity cost of 15 per cent, results in a $852m value for the technology. The present value of the (certain) investment outlays for the entire program, discounted at the risk-free rate of 4 per cent, equals $1109m for the commercial stage and $63m for the R&D stage. Thus, if the firm were to commit to both stages of the program right now, the total expected net value loss would amount to $NPV = V_0 - I_0 = \$852m - (\$1109m + \$63m) = -\$320m$.

However, the firm does not have to commit to both stages immediately. Investing in R&D derives strategic value from generating the opportunity to commercialize later on, but implies no obligation to invest in the future commercial project. In other words, R&D is analogous to an option, in the sense that it creates a valuable future opportunity without committing the company to making the full investment.

Is this technology strategy worth pursuing? To answer this question, we must consider two decisions: Should the R&D be undertaken, and if so, should the technology be implemented after R&D results are known?[6] The opportunity to invest in the commercialization is like a call option with time to maturity of $t = 2$ years, and an exercise price of $1,200m. The underlying asset is the current (time zero) value of a claim on the commercial project's expected future cash inflows of $852m. Suppose that uncertainty during the R&D phase results in a yearly increase or decline with multiplicative up and down factors, $u = 1.5$ or $d = 0.67$. The dynamics in the time series of commercial project values (V) are illustrated in the event tree of Fig. 10.3.

---

[6] See Kolbe *et al.* (1991).

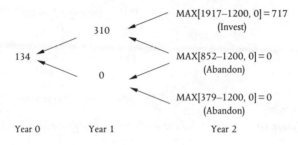

Figure 10.4. *Net value of the option to invest in the commercial project (in millions).*

As with DTA, we can value the option at the end of the tree, starting at year 2 and working backwards, using risk-neutral binomial option valuation. At the end of the R&D phase, management must decide whether to implement the technology. Consequently, the worst possible outcome for the implementation stage will be zero if the new technology is not used. Thus, at year 2, the value of the option equals the highest of: the NPV of commercialization ($V^{++} - \$1,200$m); or abandoning the technology (zero). As of year 2 this results in a net commercialization value of $717m [= 1917 − 1200] in the case events turn out better than expected, or a zero net value in the case of abandonment of the program (see the end nodes of the option valuation tree of Fig. 10.4). Under risk-neutral valuation, the current value of this claim can be determined from its expected future up and down values discounted at the risk-free interest rate ($r = 4$ per cent), with expectations taken over the risk-neutral probabilities ($p = 0.45$). Stepping back in time (to $t = 1$) results in a zero value in the low state and a $(0.45 \times \$717\text{m} + 0.55 \times 0)/1.04 = \$310\text{m}$ option value in the high state. Finally, as of year zero, the value of this growth option equals $(0.45 \times \$310\text{m} + 0.55 \times 0)/1.04 = \$134\text{m}$.

After having estimated the option of investing in commercialization, we can now consider our first question: should the R&D program be undertaken in the first place? Investment in the R&D project can be viewed as exercising a compound option. The underlying value of the R&D option is the subsequent commercialization option, which has a value of $134m. The exercise price of the R&D compound option is the present value of the R&D outlays, which equal $63m. The worst possible outcome will be zero if management decides not to develop the new technology in the first place. The value of the R&D program therefore equals MAX[0, $134m − $63m] = $71m.

Expanded NPV = −$320m + $391m = +$71m.

In this case, management is justified to invest in R&D to prove the new technology and position itself to take advantage of a future growth option, despite the negative NPV of its expected cash flows (−$320m). Management should recognize that a wider range of possible outcomes would in fact increase the option value of commercialization.

Both of the above examples were analysed assuming the project is proprietary and its value is essentially unaffected by competitive moves. The next section considers situations prevailing in oligopolistic markets where a strategic investment by a firm has a direct impact on (and/or is affected by) competitors' behaviour. An expanded or strategic analysis (often relying on game theory principles) is then called for.

10.3. STRATEGIC (EXPANDED-NPV) ANALYSIS

As noted, a strategic investment entails 'commitment value' by virtue of influencing the investment decisions of competitors (e.g. see Dixit 1980). Consider a pioneer firm that invests early and aggressively on a large scale in a new geographic market. Competitors may view this strategic investment as a threat to their future profit base in this market, and in certain states (e.g. low demand) may choose to stay out altogether or enter later at a reduced scale to avoid a market-share battle. By reducing the likelihood of competitive intrusion, the strategic project can lead to higher long-term profits for the pioneer firm.

Shared investment opportunities in oligopolistic markets are exercised with the explicit recognition that they may invite competitive reaction, which in turn can impact the value of the investment opportunity for the incumbent. Under such conditions, a strategic investment no longer represents an internal value-optimization problem under uncertainty (i.e. against nature) as in standard option models that assume an exclusive opportunity. Rather, the shared investment now involves a strategic game against both nature and competition. Such a strategic investment plan should be based on an expanded or strategic NPV criterion that incorporates not only the passive (or direct) NPV of expected cash flows from investing immediately and the flexibility value from active management (of the firm's portfolio of operating real options), but also the strategic (game-theoretic) value from competitive interactions. That is,

$$\text{Expanded (strategic) NPV} = \text{direct (passive) NPV} + \text{strategic (commitment) value}$$
$$+ \text{ flexibility value.} \qquad (10.10)$$

Table 10.3 exhibits the strategic contexts of basic game metaphors with an illustration using investment examples. In the classic 'prisoner's dilemma' context, firms have an incentive to invest immediately to avoid being pre-empted, which results in an erosion of flexibility value. The pay-off of this competitive game may be positive, but less than had they followed a coordinated wait-and-see strategy. A similar strategic context can be found in the 'grab the dollar' game, but here firms obtain a negative pay-off when they end up investing simultaneously. The 'grab the dollar' game illustrates the situation where the current market prospects are only favourable if one of the players invests but simultaneous investment results in a battle with a expected negative pay-off. Only the first player captures the dollar (e.g. patent), but when they both enter the market, they both end up losing in a battle. A dominant firm has an advantage to win this simultaneous game. The 'burning the bridges' game explains that a firm can use the threat of a battle if it has a first-mover advantage and can make the first investment commitment to capture a large portion of the market. Of course, instead of fighting for a leading position in the market, firms may sometimes find it beneficial to follow an accommodating strategy and avoid a market battle. The 'battle of the sexes' game shows that in certain cases firms have an incentive to align their strategies and cooperate.

Table 10.3. *Taxonomy of game-theory metaphors and investment applications*

Game-theory metaphor	Description (investment analogy)	Examples/applications
'Prisoners' Dilemma' (Fig. 10.5) Two people are arrested as suspects for a crime. The police puts the suspects in different cells to avoid communication. Each suspect is to be released if he testifies against the other. If neither confesses, both will get a lower punishment. The paradox is that the equilibrium outcome where both confess is worse for both prisoners, compared to the situation where neither confesses.	Innovation Race Each of two innovative firms (players) faces two possible actions: invest early or wait. Competitive pressure to be the first (e.g. to acquire a patent) induces firms to invest early; each firm has a dominant strategy to invest due to the high value of commitment, triggering a situation where both firms invest receiving their second-worst pay-off. If the two firms could coordinate their investment strategy they could share the flexibility benefits of the wait-and-see option, avoiding the inferior panic equilibrium which they rush to invest prematurely.	In high-tech industries like consumer electronics, we often see firms getting into innovation races, even forming strategic partnerships to acquire a first-mover or time-to-market advantage that erodes the value of wait-and-see flexibility from deferring investment. A noted example is the intensely competitive race in memory chip development. In February 1997 Hitachi, Mitsubishi Electric, and Texas Instruments announced they would jointly develop a one-gigabyte DRAM. NEC, which has been co-operating loosely with ATT-spin-off Lucent Technologies and Samsung, announced in June 1997 that it had developed a 4-Gb DRAM.
'Grab the Dollar' (Fig. 10.6) Each of two players has two possible actions: grab the dollar or wait. In the complete information (symmetric) version of the game, a player wins the dollar if he is the only one who grabs, but loses if both players try to grab the dollar. The pay-off of this Grab the Dollar variant is similar to the prisoner's dilemma game, but both players recognize that they have negative pay-off if they both play tough.	Innovation Race In this strategic context the market prospects are only favourable if one of the players invests, whereas simultaneous investment results in a battle with a negative expected pay-off. Either one player captures the dollar (market) or the other, but when they both enter, they both lose in the resulting battle. In many emerging, high growth industries, the possibility of each firm pursuing independent R&D activities to capture the product standard may trigger a simultaneous similar investment by competitors that results in a market battle.	Under competitive pressure to be the first (e.g. in a patent race) competitors may rush to make parallel innovation investments simultaneously, with one or both sides potentially getting hurt. For instance, Novell got hurt due to competition in networking products, Apple lost its lead as a user-friendly computer with the development of Microsoft's Windows, while in the 1980s Philips got hurt from losing the race against Matsushita over the VCR standard.

Burning the Bridge (Fig. 10.7)

Two opposing armies are asked to occupy an island between their countries, connected by bridges to both. Each army would prefer to let the island go to its opponent than fight. Army 1, who moves first, occupies the island and burns the bridge behind it (signalling its commitment to fight). Thus Army 2 has no option but let Army 1 keep the island, because it knows that Army 1 has no choice but fight back if they attack.

The paradox of commitment is winning the game by reducing your options (burning the bridge).

'Battle of the Sexes' (Fig. 10.8)

A couple must choose between going to a movie or to a play. The couple prefers going somewhere together than separately though one prefers the movie and the other the play. The couple would be better of to collaborate, sometimes going to a movie and other times to a play.

Product Standard/Preemption

Each firm (player) has two possible actions: high irreversible investment commitment or more flexible, low-effort investment. The value of early/heavy commitment is that it may set the product standard or signal to competing firms about the reduced future profitability of their options in this market. Consider a pioneer firm that makes an early, large-scale irreversible R&D investment in a new market. The firm's competitors could view this as a threat to their future profit base in the market, thus deciding to stay out or entering the market later on a reduced scale to avoid a market share battle.

Being the first in the market enables a firm to capture a larger share of the market and put followers at a strategic disadvantage. For instance, in cellular phones the early introduction of new models by a relatively small company like NOKIA preempted a significant market share (compared to larger competitors). Competitors like Philips (who formed a partnership with Lucent Technologies) could not catch up and left this market. In an extreme case, the pioneer can capture the product standard early on. For instance, Intel preempted 80 per cent of the microprocessor market with its Pentium microchip that became the product standard, forcing competitors like Digital to retreat from the market, even though Digital's Alpha chip was three or four times as powerful as the Pentium chip at a fraction of the cost.

Standardization Game

Two (alliances of) firms must choose between standard A or standard B. Everyone would be better off with one standard (avoiding a 'war of attrition'), but for one firm standard A would be the best, while for the other firm it is standard B.

In the standardization game of the high density disk, on one side was an alliance between Toshiba and Time Warner who had jointly developed a SDD; on the other side was an alliance among Philips and Sony with their MMCD. In this high-density CD battle, both sides recognized that the launch of more than one system would result in confusion and major capital waste, particularly for the losing company as well as the consumers. A standardization agreement resulted in increased productivity and expanded markets for both.

10.3.1. *Time to Launch Under Competition (Symmetric Innovation Race)*

Consider first the example of an innovation race involving a shared R&D option among two consumer electronics firms, P (Philips) and S (Sony).[7] Both firms plan to develop an interactive CD technology and expect subsequent commercialization applications. The total market value (NPV-pie) from immediate investment (whether by a single firm or shared equally among the two firms) is $400m. The additional value of the flexibility to 'wait-and-see' under demand uncertainty (had there been no competition) is $200m. This results in a total (shared) opportunity value (option pie or expanded-NPV) of $600m if the two firms could fully appropriate the flexibility value of waiting.

The 2 × 2 table in Fig. 10.5 summarizes the pay-offs (firm P, firm S) in four investment-timing scenarios: (i) when both firms invest immediately (simultaneously) they share equally the total NPV (1/2 × 400), resulting in a (200, 200) value pay-off for each firm; (ii)/(iii) when one firm (P or S) invests first while the other waits it pre-empts its competitor and captures the full NPV value (400) for itself, resulting in a pay-off of (400, 0) or (0, 400), respectively; and (iv) when both firms decide to wait they share equally the value of the investment option (1/2 × 600), resulting in a (300, 300) pay-off.

The above value–pay-off structure results in a Nash equilibrium outcome where both firms invest (200, 200). Firm P's pay-off from immediate investment (lower row) exceeds its pay-off from a wait-and-see strategy (upper row), regardless of which strategy firm S chooses (400 > 300 in left 'wait' column, 200 > 0 in right 'invest' column); that is, firm P has a dominant strategy to invest, regardless of the timing decision of its competitor. Firm S also has a dominant strategy to invest regardless of P's decision, resulting in a Nash equilibrium (*) outcome in the lower right cell, from which neither firm can improve by making a unilateral move; thus, both firms receive their second-worst pay-off of (200, 200), an example of the well-known prisoners' dilemma.[8] Obviously, here both firms

	Firm S Wait	Invest
Firm P Wait	(300, 300)	(0, 400)
Invest	(400, 0)	**(200, 200)**

Figure 10.5. *Innovation race: competitive pressure to be first induces firms to invest prematurely, even though they could both be better off waiting ('prisoners' dilemma').*

Notes: Pay-off in each cell is for (firm P, firm S). Strategies of firm P: wait (upper row) or invest (lower row). Strategies of firm S: wait (left column) or invest (right column).

[7] This prototypical example uses hypothetical numbers.

[8] In the classic prisoners' dilemma, two prisoners accused of a crime would be worse off if they both confess (200, 200) than if they do not (300, 300), but the fear of the other prisoner confessing (0, 400) puts pressure for both to do so, even though not confessing would have been preferable for both.

would be better off to collaborate or coordinate and fully appropriate the option value of waiting (300, 300).

10.3.2. *Asymmetric Innovation Race and Pre-emption*

Let us revisit the above innovation race among the two firms, P and S, but in another strategic context. If both firms invest they end up in a market share battle with a negative pay-off. Suppose now that firm P has an edge in developing the technology, although it has limited (financial or other necessary) resources at the time. Competitor S may take advantage of this resource weakness and try to win the race to market. Following Dixit and Nalebuff (1991), each firm can choose how intense an effort to make in developing this innovative technology. Less effort is consistent with a (technological) follower strategy involving lower development costs, but is more flexible (safe) in case of unfavourable developments. More effort corresponds to a (technological) leader strategy involving higher development costs that could result in earlier product launch and a first-mover cost advantage.

Figure 10.6 illustrates the pay-offs resulting if the competitors follow a (technological) leader or follower strategy (high or low R&D effort) when they are in an asymmetric power position. In this pay-off table, both sides regard a high-effort R&D battle as their worst scenario: for firm S because it is likely to loose an all-out race, and for firm P because it would incur large costs. Suppose that this situation results in a (−$100m, −$100m) pay-off.

The next-worst scenario for each competitor is to exert low effort while its competitor chooses a high-effort R&D strategy. This entails spending money with little chance of success, resulting in a pay-off of only $10m. Under firm S's technological leader strategy, it develops its interactive CD technology by exerting high effort ($200m), while firm P follows with a low-effort follower strategy. In the best scenario for firm P, both firms avoid an intense innovation race and make a low-effort investment, with firm P more likely to win due to its technological edge and lower cost (resulting in a pay-off of $200m for P, $100m for S).

Consider the equilibrium implications of an asymmetric pay-off structure as that of the 'Grab the Dollar' game in Fig. 10.6.[9] Firm P's pay-off for pursuing a low-effort R&D strategy (upper row) exceeds the pay-off of a high-effort strategy (lower row), no matter which strategy firm S chooses ($200m > $100m and $10m > −$100m). Thus, firm P has a dominant strategy to pursue low-effort R&D. Given this, firm S will pursue a high-effort R&D strategy (since $200m > $100m). The Nash equilibrium (*) outcome of this R&D rivalry game is given by the top right cell ($10, $200), where P receives its second worst pay-off. Firm P would follow a flexible, low-effort strategy, while S would follow the high-effort R&D strategy.

---

[9] This is an asymmetrical variant of the 'Grab the Dollar' game, in that both firms have a negative pay-off if they both make a high R&D effort, and there is a positive pay-off if only one of them follows a high-effort strategy. Only Firm S has a dominant position in playing this game, reflected in its higher pay-off.

Firm S

	Low	High
Low	($200m, $100m)	($10m, $200m)*
High	($100m, $10m)	(–$200m, –$100m)

(Firm P — rows)

Figure 10.6. *(Simultaneous) Innovation race with high vs. low R&D effort (asymmetric 'grab the dollar' game).*

Notes: Pay-off in each cell is for (firm P, firm S). Strategies of firm P: low-effort R&D (upper row) or high-effort R&D (lower row). Strategies of firm S: low-effort R&D (left column) or high-effort R&D (right column).

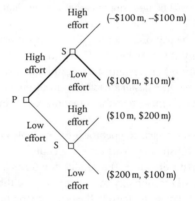

Figure 10.7. *Sequential investment game with high vs. low R&D effort ('burning the bridge').*

The following sections illustrate these ideas with a series of examples, ranging from a symmetric decision to launch an R&D project (faced by two comparable competitors), to an asymmetric game involving different degrees of R&D effort and the possibility of complete pre-emption, to a game of R&D competition versus collaboration via joint R&D ventures or strategic alliances.[10]

Consider next a similar situation (as the simultaneous innovation race of Fig. 10.6), but with the difference that firm P can make the R&D investment before firm S can decide which strategy to follow. Which R&D strategy should firm P follow? Management must now recognize that its investment decisions will directly influence competitive reaction, as illustrated in the sequential game of Fig. 10.7. The threat of a market battle could actually work in firm P's favour.

[10] See Dixit and Nalebuff (1993) for various applications of games.

If firm P pursues a flexible low-effort strategy (making a small R&D investment), firm S will respond with high effort, and firm P's pay-off will be $10m. However, if P pursues a high-effort R&D strategy, firm S can be expected to respond with low effort (since $10m > -$100m), in which case P's pay-off will be $100m. Therefore, firm P would invest heavily in R&D, signalling a credible commitment to the high-effort R&D strategy (with the competitor responding with a low-effort strategy). With such a strategic timing move, the equilibrium results in a more desirable pay-off for firm P ($100m) than that of the earlier (simultaneous) game ($10m).

This strategy represents an early exercise of a shared multi-stage R&D option and it explicitly influences both competitive behaviour and the firms' future profit base. In our strategic (expanded-NPV) framework, an immediate high-effort R&D strategy (technological leadership) has two main effects on value, with opposite sign:

(i) A standard option-value or flexibility effect. This reflects management's ability to wait to invest in the business under uncertain conditions. The large (early) investment implicit in the high-effort R&D strategy, although enhancing the value of future growth opportunities, sacrifices this flexibility value compared to a more flexible low-effort strategy.

(ii) A strategic commitment effect. A large (early) R&D investment consistent with technological leadership and a high-effort strategy can influence competitors' investment decisions and the equilibrium outcome favourably for the pioneer firm (P), giving it an asymmetric competitive edge. This must be weighted against the loss of flexibility value.

In certain cases, however, efforts to create asymmetric power positions vis-à-vis a competitor must be given up in favour of more fully appropriating the option value of a coordinated wait-and-see strategy under demand uncertainty.

10.4. COMPETITION VS. COORDINATION (STRATEGIC ALLIANCES)

In an oligopolistic industry, firms can make prior investments in R&D to increase their ability to capture the growth opportunities in the industry. This section considers the issue of whether (and when) it is optimal to compete independently or coordinate (e.g. via standardization agreements) and otherwise collaborate (e.g. via joint R&D ventures or strategic alliances) in the innovation phase, to increase the total value of growth opportunities in the industry under uncertainty. Section 10.4.1 examines the competition vs. coordination (standardization) game in the high-density disk market, while Section 10.4.2 discusses learning and across-time evolution in a given industry (consumer electronics) from a competitive mode (in VCRs) to one of strategic alliances (in the launch of the CD).

10.4.1. *Standardization in the High-Density Disk*

Consider the innovation battle for the development of the high-density disk. Initially, it might seem as if this effort would end up in a technological war. Instead, it ended up in a coordination game. On one side was an alliance between Toshiba and Time Warner, who had jointly developed a super density disk (SDD). On the other side were Philips and Sony with their multimedia compact disk (MMCD). The storage capacity of the old CD (70 mins. for a movie) had become insufficient; with new compression techniques and the use of two layers, the storage capabilities of the new-generation disk could increase ten times to 7.4 gigabytes, and even more for the Toshiba disk.[11] The new technology was expected to result in valuable growth opportunities in audio CD, CD-ROM (information storage), digital video disc (DVD), and other CD applications.

Both sides claimed victory in advance, hoping to enhance the 'commitment value' of their technology by influencing competitive behaviour. For instance, both firms made strategic moves by making advance announcements of the launch of their high-density players and disk, listing the computer producers who had chosen their systems, emphasizing the success of their R&D efforts, even providing misleading information about the capabilities of each other's systems.[12]

The game below describes the strategic context of the dilemma faced by the two parties (alliances). Each side would prefer to launch their own standard but clearly would be better off avoiding a market battle. Figure 10.8 describes the four outcomes in a 2 × 2 game. The worst pay-offs for both parties, (2, 1) and (1, 2), are for the situation in which both pursue exclusionary (adversarial) technological strategies and develop competing product standards. This would result in intense competition, but eventually uncertainty will get resolved over which one will be the winning system. The two parties would clearly be better off with a single standard to avoid a war of attrition, but each alliance would prefer their own standard to prevail. This results in pay-offs of (3, 4) or (4, 3) when both choose a standard based on SSD or on MMCD, respectively.

By recognizing the above strategic context, however, both firms will have an incentive to coordinate their product strategy to avoid a market battle. Standardization agreements

	Competition	
	Standard based on MMCD	Standard based on SDD
Standard based on MMCD	(4, 3)	(2, 1)
Philips		
Standard based on SDD	(1, 2)	(3, 4)

Figure 10.8. *The 2 × 2 competition vs. coordination game ('battle of the sexes').*

[11] Toshiba's disk, however, had the disadvantage of being double sided.

[12] For example, Toshiba announced that its competitor, Philips, would not develop a rewritable CD version. Philips called this untrue: 'Of course we are working on that. However, we have to protect the copyright first before we launch the product'. In this aggressive strategic context, the competitor's managers made threatening statements at that time, for example, 'We are in a state of war' (NRC 5-7-95).

may result in increased productivity and expanded markets for both. In the high-density CD battle, both sides recognized that the launch of more than one system would result in confusion and major capital waste, particularly for the losing company and the consumers. A 'technical working group' representing the leading firms in the computer industry investigated the competing systems and found that both the MMCD of Philips and Sony as well as the SDD of Toshiba fulfilled the requirements. The computer industry, which would benefit if the two alliances would agree on one standard, encouraged the two sides to negotiate and coordinate.[13]

10.4.2. *Learning: From Competition in VCRs to Strategic Alliances in the Launch of CDs*

In consumer electronics, firms like Philips, Sony, Matsushita, and Toshiba have a history of competing in the development of technologically innovative products, such as CD players, CDi, Walkmans, 100 Hz TVs, and the high-density disk. Innovative strategies are often accompanied by high commercial and technological risk. Such strategies may also require close contact with customers and careful monitoring of competition. It is possible that firms may compete in one product and cooperate on another. As noted, strategic alliances with some competitors that use mutual standardization agreements can help win the battle in the competition between different systems.

Consider the battle for developing a technology standard in the video recorder market. In the late seventies, the introduction of three types of video recorders resulted in intense rivalry. Philips launched the V2000 system to compete with Sony's Betamax and JVC's VHS system. Instead of following a single standard, Philips decided to make the V2000 system incompatible with VHS tapes, claiming that the advantage of reversible tapes and better slow-motion pictures was sufficient to win adequate market share. The aggressive position by these companies resulted in an intense market share battle in the video recorder market.

Figure 10.9 illustrates the market share battle between Sony, JVC, and Philips. Uncertainty concerning Philips' market share compared to the other systems is reflected by the states of nature (O). The branches in bolded type in the upper part of the tree illustrate the historic path of actions actually taken by the players involved and the resolution of uncertainty. The market for consumer video recorders increased rapidly. Sony (with its Betamax system) and JVC (with VHS) were already involved in a market share battle before Philips introduced the V2000. Philips decided not to make its system compatible with the existing VHS system, but unfortunately its claimed technical advantage was not reflected commercially in a larger market share. The existing systems had already developed a large captive market and were supported with software (movies). It should have been clear from the beginning that only one of the systems could win, and that in the end only one could

---

[13] Subsequently, the strategic moves of these firms (as reported in the press) changed from tough to accommodating. The vice-president of Philips made accommodating statements about coming to one standard. The outcome would be a new standard for the next twenty years. The expectations were that over five years 200 million pieces of CD-carrying equipment would be sold yearly. Multimedia sales would represent 10 per cent of total sales.

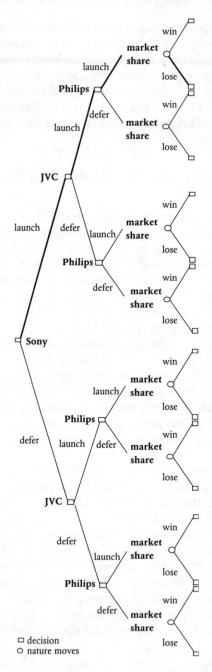

Figure 10.9. *Timing product launch with multiple competitors.*

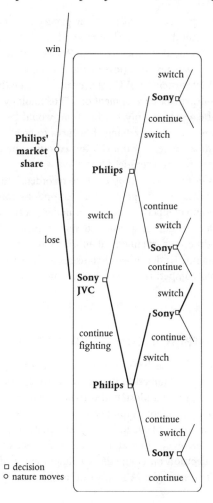

Figure 10.10. *The 'war of attrition' game.*

become the standard in the market. The other firms eventually would have to switch to this system. Hence, each player must have believed that they had at least a good chance of winning in order to be willing to participate in this battle.

The above situation could be viewed as an optimal stopping problem against competition with uncertainty over the future value of the project. In a 'war of attrition' game such as this, the winner takes all. This is more likely to occur in an industry in which economies of scale are important (see Tirole 1990: 311). Fighting is costly because it may lead to low or negative profits and R&D outlays may not be recovered. The object of the fight is to induce the rival to give up. The winning firm acquires the standard, and the losers are left wishing they had never entered the fight. Figure 10.10 illustrates the 'war of attrition' game for the video recorder market. The game ends when it becomes clear that one of the players has either quit or switched to another system. The historic path of this game is represented by the bolded-type branches. Philips suffered intense competition as unfavourable information was revealed (low market share), and in the end it switched to the VHS system. The VHS system by JVC (Matsushita) became the market standard.

By contrast, in the subsequent development of CD technology, Philips recognized that the CD player would be a success only if other firms would be willing to produce CDs and CD players. Philips and Sony exchanged licences to acquire an install-base for the CD player. The joint development of the CD turned out to be a success, resulting in a range of subsequent growth opportunities.[14]

The above examples from the launching of video recorders and the development of the CD technology clearly illustrate the potential use of options concepts and game theory principles in understanding competitive behaviour under uncertainty in such oligopolistic markets. The commitment value of a firm's strategy can be enhanced by outsmarting competition under conditions of asymmetrical information or power, as well as of technical and commercial uncertainty. Under other circumstances, however, market characteristics, demand uncertainty and competitive moves may change a firm's aggressive strategy to a collaborative one.

10.5. IMPLICATIONS AND CONCLUSIONS

This chapter has reviewed some basic valuation principles involving real options and competitive strategy analysis. Numerical examples from valuation of a licence on a mine concession and an R&D program illustrated the shortcomings of traditional NPV when management has flexibility to adapt its future contingent decisions based on the evolution of major uncertainties. In oligopolistic industries, we discussed (using basic game theory) a number of examples involving innovation races and other competitive games where the impact of a firm's decision on competitors is important in determining equilibrium outcomes and competitive strategies. A number of insights and implementation issues are summarized below.

We have shown why risk-neutral option valuation or a certainty equivalent-based approach is superior to traditional DCF or DTA, since it combines the use of decision nodes (rather than passive event nodes) to model flexibility choices while being more careful to price risk correctly in each branch (state) of the tree. In the implementation in natural resources, management can use directly the concept of replicating future cash flows. The estimated value of a producing field can be directly linked to oil futures. An insufficient set of market quotes of a correlated financial instrument (e.g. futures or forward contracts) is a general implementation problem of the option pricing methodology (and it may be non-existent in the valuation of R&D programs). However, the methodology

---

[14] A couple of decades later, it appears that the development of the CD has been a far greater success than initially expected. In 1995, total sales for the entire market using this technology came to about $50 billion. Three billion CD's and about 110 million pieces of CD-carrying equipment have been sold annually.

can still be applied provided there exists a corresponding valuation for the underlying asset.

The combined options and game theory perspective is particularly relevant for oligopolistic and innovative industries (e.g. pharmaceuticals or consumer electronics) facing high research and development costs in several phases in a technologically uncertain and competitive setting. The war of attrition in video systems, the coordination game of the CD technology, and the adversarial and accommodating strategies for the high-density disk are just a few examples of games that corporations face in real life. Firms can make prior investments in R&D to improve their competitive position and their ability to capture the growth opportunities in the industry. Patents and proprietary use of information can prevent the creation of valuable opportunities for competition. In cases of differentiated products under contrarian, quantity-type competition (e.g. in pharmaceuticals), opposition is more likely to retreat. However, it is not always wise to compete aggressively. An important aspect in corporate strategy is knowing when to coordinate strategies with competition and support rivals. When the product is homogeneous and competitive response is reciprocating, as in price competition (e.g. in the airline, the tobacco, or the food industries), adversarial strategies may result in price wars and erosion of profit margins for all sides.[15]

While adversarial strategies and a lack of coordination may result in shrinking markets, the gains from sharing information and the benefits of innovation may result in higher productivity and profits for all under certain circumstances. With an accommodating strategy, firms can work closely together (e.g. appropriating the option value of waiting more fully as well as sharing costs) and may achieve more innovation and growth. Firms often co-operate in R&D via standardization agreements, joint R&D ventures, or create other forms of strategic alliances. Philips formed several joint ventures, such as with Matsushita Electronics. A potential downside is that while these ventures may strengthen the firm's position, they may also be helping to build up new competitors.

The combined option pricing and game theory approach, when properly applied, can be a valuable tool of analysis in support of the overall corporate strategy. These quantitative tools are meant to complement the strategic thinking process and executive intuition and experience, not to replace them. Overly complicated methods are not easily adopted and face managerial resistance. Complex real-life investment problems often have to be simplified to their basic components to make the analysis more feasible. Real options valuation helps do that. To make the model easier to understand, it is more useful to use a discrete-time binomial process. Working backward in the option-game tree, decision-makers can trace the equilibrium project values and infer from the model the relative magnitude of values in the different project phases. To use the model as a practical aid to corporate planners, appropriate user-friendly software will be useful. Real options concepts and tools are being increasingly used by consulting firms and leading corporations around the world in a variety of industries. The practical use of real option analysis looks quite promising.

---

[15] As a result firms may try to differentiate their products with marketing expenses to avoid pure competition in prices.

References

Baldwin, C. (1982), 'Optimal sequential investment when capital is not readily reversible', *Journal of Finance* 37, 763–82.

Brennan, M. and Schwartz, E. (1985), 'Evaluating natural resource investments', *Journal of Business* 58, 135–57.

Dixit, A. (1980), 'The role of investment in entry deterrence', *Economic Journal* 90, 95–106.

—— and Nalebuff, B. J. (1991), *Thinking Strategically*, New York: Norton Press.

—— and Pindyck, R. (1994), *Investment Under Uncertainty*, Princeton: Princeton University Press.

Kemna, A. (1993), 'Case studies on real options', *Financial Management* 22, 259–70.

Kester, W. C. (1984), 'Today's options for tomorrow's growth', *Harvard Business Review* 62, 153–60.

Kolbe, A. L., Morris, P. A., and Teisberg E. O. (1991), 'When choosing R & D projects, go with long shots', *Research Technology Management*, 35–40.

Mason, S. and Merton, R. (1985), 'The role of contingent claims analysis in corporate finance', in E. Altman and M. Subrahmanyam (eds), *Recent Advances in Corporate Finance*, Homewood, IL: Richard D. Irwin.

Myers, S. C. (1987), 'Finance theory and financial strategy', *Midland Corporate Finance Journal* 5, 6–13.

Sick, G. (1989), 'Capital budgeting with real options', Working paper, Salomon Brothers Center, New York University.

Smit, H. T. J. (1996), 'Growth options and strategy analysis', Ph.D. Dissertation, University of Amsterdam.

Tirole, J. (1990), *The Theory of Industrial Organization*, Cambridge, MA: MIT Press.

Trigeorgis, L. (1988), 'A conceptual options framework for capital budgeting', *Advances in Futures and Options Research* 3, 145–67.

—— (1996), *Real Options: Managerial Flexibility and Strategy in Resource Allocation*, Cambridge, MA: MIT Press.

—— and Mason, S. P. (1987), 'Valuing managerial flexibility', *Midland Corporate Finance Journal* 5, 14–21.

11

The Market Valuation of Biotechnology Firms and Biotechnology R&D

JOHN R. M. HAND

11.1. INTRODUCTION

Despite its size and public importance, little academic research has sought empirically to identify or analyse the determinants of the equity market values of a growing high-tech sector of the US economy—that of biotechnology. The goal of this chapter is to take some initial steps towards obtaining that understanding by shedding light on how financial statement data in general, and R&D expenditures in particular, associate with biotech firms' equity market values, and why from an economic point of view such associations exist.

Broadly speaking, technology is the application of the scientific method and scientific knowledge to industrial or commercial objectives. Biotechnology is the application of technology, particularly genetics, to industrial or manufacturing aspects of the life sciences. Biotechnology applications include the production of drugs, synthetic hormones, and bulk foodstuffs; the bioconversion of organic waste; and the use of genetically altered bacteria.

Biotechnology falls squarely within the definition of high technology because 'high' technology distinguishes itself from 'low' technology by having three special characteristics: an intensive investment in R&D, a crucial role for knowledge capital in creating value, and high growth opportunities (Liu 2000). The largest and most important components of a biotech firm's production and investment functions are its R&D expenditures and the discoveries made by the knowledge and skill of its bioscientists and bioengineers. When successful, this knowledge produces the intellectual property and legal patents that can rapidly translate into hundreds of millions of dollars in annual sales and profits, and/or a large equity market value.

I analyse the relations between biotech firms' equity market values and the financial accounting data that are publicly available from quarterly financial statements. I do so with two goals in mind. First, a common view is that the primary drivers and indicators of

My thanks to Liz Demers, Phillip Joos, Ed Maydew, Charlie Wasley, Ross Watts, and workshop participants at the University of Rochester for valuable comments. The financial support of PriceWaterhouseCoopers and an O'Herron Scholarship is greatly appreciated.

the value created by biotechnology are 'soft' variables such as intellectual human capital, patents, strategic alliances, and joint ventures (e.g. Bratic *et al.* 2000). The validity of such a view, however, runs counter to much research in accounting that both theoretically and empirically concludes that 'hard' financial statement data should and do explain large amounts of the cross-sectional variation in firms' equity market values. As an accounting researcher, I am therefore interested in determining whether biotechnology firms are different in this regard than practically all other industries or types of firms, and if so, why.

Second, because of the size and importance of R&D to biotech firms, I am also keen to develop and test economic hypotheses about the mapping between the biotech firms' equity market values and their R&D expenditures. For reasons that I expand on later in the chapter, I hypothesize that the elasticity of biotech firms' equity market values with respect to their R&D expenditures (the 'value elasticity of R&D') will be a function of five factors: where the R&D lies in the value chain of discovery, development, and commercialization; the growth rate in R&D spending; the scale of R&D expenditures; the human capital of the firm's employees; and the maturity of the firm.

I test these hypotheses using quarterly market and financial statement data on 606 US biotech firms that were publicly traded at some time during the period 1989:q1–2000:q3. For each quarter within the sample period, I estimate a log-linear regression of the equity market value of the firm on disaggregated balance sheet, income statement, and statement of cash flows data. Disaggregating financial statement data is important for R&D-intensive companies because under US GAAP, R&D expenditures are not permitted to be capitalized and amortized into income over time, but must be immediately written off against earnings. This means that aggregate balance sheet and income statement variables such as shareholder equity and net income are biased measures of the economic position and earnings of the firm. Correlating such economically biased measures of economic position and earnings of the firm with equity market values typically results in severely misspecified regressions and counter-intuitive coefficient signs and magnitudes. These problems are mitigated if the components of shareholder equity and net income are instead used as independent variables (Zhang 2000; Hand 2001*a*).

My initial analysis therefore consists of regressing, within a contemporaneous log-linear framework, the equity values of biotech firms on their contributed capital, retained earnings, and treasury stock (three key components of shareholder equity); revenues, cost of sales, selling, general, and administrative expenses, R&D expense (four key components of net income); and dividends (from the statement of cash flows). I find that these financial statement variables together explain some 70 per cent of the variance in biotech firms' equity market values, casting doubt on the common view that the primary value drivers of biotechnology are 'soft' variables such as intellectual human capital, patents, strategic alliances, and joint ventures. Such soft variables may indeed be value-relevant—that is, incrementally informative in explaining cross-sectional variation in equity market values— but the strength of my results based on financial statement data suggests that they are unlikely to be the primary drivers of biotech firms' stock prices.

Beyond the substantial value-relevance of basic financial statement data, I further employ the log-linear regression framework to test my hypotheses concerning the determinants of the value elasticity of R&D—namely where R&D lies in the biotech value chain of discovery, development, and commercialization; the growth rate in R&D spending; the scale of R&D expenditures; the human capital of the firm's employees; and the age of the firm. I develop financial statement proxies for each of these factors and interact them with R&D expense to determine whether the factors are value-relevant. I find that the elasticity of biotech firms' equity market values with respect to R&D is significantly larger the earlier is the R&D expenditure in the value chain, and the greater is the growth rate in R&D spending. The value elasticity of R&D is also reliably decreasing in the scale of R&D expenditures, and in the maturity of the firm. However, the value elasticity of R&D appears unrelated to proxies for both the quantity and quality of employee human capital, perhaps because the quantity and quality of employee human capital is not accurately captured through financial accounting metrics.

I infer from these results that despite the typically huge uncertainty inherent in the production and investment functions of biotechnology companies, particularly with regard to R&D, investors appear to price the equity of such firms in a more sophisticated manner than would be supposed from a popular viewpoint. Investors map the components of shareholder equity and net income into equity market values for biotech firms in similar directions to non-biotech firms. Investors also seem to value the key R&D intangible in a manner that recognizes the stage that the firm's R&D is at in the value chain, the likelihood the firm will obtain property rights on its R&D, and the firm's maturity. Such sophistication would seem to bode well for the growth and accuracy of capital allocation in this growing area of high technology.

The remainder of the chapter proceeds as follows. Section 11.2 briefly explains the major attributes of biotechnology, and summarizes prior research on biotechnology firms and the stock market's valuation of R&D. Section 11.3 more fully develops the hypotheses and required proxy variables outlined above, while Section 11.4 describes the sample identification and data requirements processes, and reports descriptive statistics for the firm-quarters used in the study. Section 11.5 motivates the regression model used to test the hypotheses on the sample data, and reports the results of my empirical tests and the inferences I draw from those results. Section 11.6 concludes.

11.2. BIOTECHNOLOGY AND R&D

11.2.1. *Technology*

The American Heritage Dictionary defines technology as the application of the scientific method and scientific knowledge to industrial/commercial objectives. More loosely, technology is the set of ways that humans can reconfigure physical objects by creating new recipes for their use. Based on that definition, there is little doubt that science and technology—and the innovation they create—have in the past, and should in the future, generate new wealth. The reconfiguring of physical objects that technology makes possible boosts productivity, spawns new opportunities for profit, and ultimately drives economic growth. As Romer (1999) notes:

In 1870, average real income per person in the US was about $2,500. By 1994, average income per person had increased to about $22,500, a nine-fold increase. Everything we know about history, technology and economic theory tells us that an increase of this magnitude would not have been possible in the absence of technological change. We did not increase income per person by a factor of nine by accumulating more ox carts and water-driven mills.

Due to Romer and other 'new growth' theorists, technology is now recognized as playing a vital role in creating, sustaining, and increasing economic growth. Whereas earlier neoclassical growth theory treated scientific discovery, technology, and innovation as peripheral in economic growth, the new growth view makes them endogenous and centre-stage in importance. Assigning a primary role to scientific discovery, technology, and innovation has helped shed light on how economic growth can be sustained and even accelerated in a physical world that is characterized by diminishing returns and scarcity (Romer 1999).

11.2.2. *Biotechnology*

Broadly speaking, biotechnology is the application of technology to the life sciences. More carefully defined, biotechnology is a collection of techniques that use living cells or their processes to solve problems and to perform specific industrial or manufacturing processes. Applications include the production of drugs, synthetic hormones, and bulk foodstuffs, the bioconversion of organic waste, and the use of genetically altered bacteria.

Biotechnology per se is not new. As noted by the North Carolina Biotechnology Center (www.ncbiotech.org), since early humans began selectively breeding the best plants and animals thousands of years ago, biotech has improved people's lives. Bacteria and fungi helped make cheeses, bread, and yogurts. However, modern biotechnology was launched in 1973 and 1975 with the scientific breakthrough innovations of recombinant DNA and cell fusion, respectively.[1] Today, scientists use many biotech techniques to research new treatments for disease, create safer food products, and formulate less-damaging chemicals. Biotechnology techniques allow researchers to insert into an organism a single gene—and the desirable traits it produces—without also transferring other genes and undesirable traits. Such bioengineering is more efficient, accurate, and predictable than breeding whole organisms.

The biotech industry has emerged from its modest beginnings in the mid-1970s to be a significant force in the future of life sciences. According to the Biotechnology Industry Organization (www.bio.org), more than 250 million people worldwide have been helped by the more than 117 biotechnology drug products and vaccines approved by the US Food and Drug Administration (FDA). There are now estimated to be more than 350 biotech drug products and vaccines currently in clinical trials targeting more than 200 diseases, such as various cancers, Alzheimer's, heart disease, diabetes, multiple sclerosis, AIDS, and arthritis. Biotech is responsible for hundreds of medical diagnostic tests that keep the

---

[1] The recombination of DNA (rDNA) first occurred in 1973 when H. Boyer and S. Cohen successfully introduced genetic material from one cell into the DNA structure of another cell. In 1975, C. Milstein and G. Kohler were the first to employ cell fusion to create monoclonal antibodies. Monoclonal antibodies are highly purified proteins produced by the hybrid cell created by cell fusion. Monoclonal antibodies serve as the body's defense against disease-causing bacteria, viruses, and cancer cells (Kenney 1986; Stuart *et al.* 1999).

blood supply safe from the AIDS virus and detect other conditions early enough to be successfully treated. Consumers already enjoy biotech foods such as papaya, soybeans, and corn. Hundreds of biopesticides are being used to improve the food supply and reduce farmers' dependence on conventional chemical pesticides. Environmental biotech products make it possible to clean up hazardous waste more efficiently by harnessing pollution-eating microbes without the use of caustic chemicals. DNA fingerprinting, a biotech process, has dramatically improved criminal investigation and forensic medicine, as well as yielding significant advances in anthropology and wildlife management.

The Biotechnology Industry Organization estimates that as of December 1999 there were between 1,200 and 1,300 biotech firms in the US, of which more than a quarter were publicly held. It also estimates that the US biotech industry directly employs over 150,000 people and indirectly generated almost 300,000 other jobs via companies supplying inputs, goods, or services to the industry and biotech employees. In terms of innovative output, the total number of patents granted to US corporations, the US government, and individuals in the US has risen from 1,200 in 1985 to 5,500 in 2000 (US Patent & Trademark Office 2001). The FDA, the EPA, and the USDA regulate the biotech industry.

11.2.3. *Economic Research into Biotechnology and R&D*

11.2.3.1. *Biotechnology*
Economic (as opposed to scientific) research in the area of biotechnology has been in two main areas: intellectual human capital and strategic alliances. Research directly into valuation has been infrequent. I briefly review each area.

First, in a notable series of papers, Michael Darby and Lynne Zucker have sought to understand the business implications of the substantial intellectual human capital held by biotechnology scientists, particularly the most productive star scientists. Star scientists are scarce and immobile factors of production who are typically able to capture supranormal returns from their intellectual capital. Zucker and Darby (1996) find that where and when US star scientists were actively producing academic publications is a key determinant of where and when commercial firms began to use biotechnology. In particular, the extent of collaboration by a biotech firm's scientists with star US bioscientists is a powerful predictor of the firm's ultimate success along such dimensions as products in development, products on the market, and the number of people employed by the firm. Audretsch and Stephan (1996) find that while many university-based scientists participate in geographic networks, 70 per cent of the links between biotech companies and university-based scientists are non-local. The links between scientists and companies seem to involve many dimensions, only one of which is knowledge transfer.

Zucker and Darby (1998) also use detailed data on biotechnology in Japan to show that identifiable collaborations between particular university star scientists and biotech firms have a large positive impact on those firms' research productivity as measured by patents and products on the market. Zucker *et al.* (1998) examine the relations between the founding of US biotech firms and several factors: the intellectual capital of star scientists, the presence of great university bioscience programs, and the presence of venture capital. They find that the local number of highly productive star scientists that are actively publishing genetic sequence discoveries is the primary determinant of the timing and location of new biotech firms.

The second main area of research has sought to understand the causes and consequences of the strategic alliances among biotech firms, and between biotech firms and pharmaceutical companies. Biotech firms enter into alliances for many reasons, including accessing another firm's technology without actually purchasing the underlying assets; externally signalling an interorganizational endorsement; generating cash and revenue; and risk sharing. Lerner and Merges (1998) examine the determinants of control rights in such alliances. They argue and find evidence supportive of Aghion and Tirole's (1994) proposition that the allocation of control rights to an R&D-intensive biotech firm increases with the firm's financial resources, although the relation between control rights and the stage of the project at the time the alliance is signed is more ambiguous. Robinson and Stuart (2000) posit that the stock of prior alliances between participants in the biotech industry produces a network through which information is transmitted, and that such a network serves as a superior governance mechanism to other forms of control in inter-firm transactions. They find supportive evidence using the degree of equity participation and the amount of funding pledged in a sample of actual biotech alliance agreements.

Insofar as the valuation of biotech firms is concerned, three studies are of note. Stuart *et al.* (1999) test the hypothesis that when faced with great uncertainty about the quality of young companies, third parties rely on the prominence of the affiliates of those companies to judge the quality. They find very strong and consistent evidence that privately held biotech firms with prominent strategic alliance partners and organizational equity investors benefit from the transfer of status from those entities by going public faster and at higher valuations than do firms that lack such connections. Darby *et al.* (1999) estimate the values of star scientists and other intangibles using a technique based on option pricing, and find that such value estimates are positively correlated with biotech firms' equity market values. Finally, Joos (2002) finds that the level and rate of growth in R&D expense, R&D success, and competitive structure all help explain cross-sectional variation in market-to-book ratios for a sample of thirty-five pharmaceutical drug manufacturers that operated in the pharmaceutical preparation industry over the period 1975–98.

11.2.3.2. *R&D*

R&D has also been a strong topic of research across a wide variety of scholarly fields, including but not limited to economics, finance, and accounting. Research has focused on two major questions that are relevant to this chapter. First, how large, if any, are the future economic benefits from R&D? Over the years, many studies have documented that R&D spending increases future profitability (Grabowski and Mueller 1978; Ravenscraft and Scherer 1982; Sougiannis 1994; Nissim and Thomas 2000). Recently, Kothari *et al.* (2001) and Hand (2001*b*) have broadened the scope of this literature by investigating the riskiness and returns-to-scale of R&D. Kothari *et al.* (2001) show that R&D expenditures yield realized earnings that are more variable (i.e. benefits that are more uncertain) than do investments in PP&E, while Hand reports that expenditures on both R&D and advertising exhibit increasing profitability returns-to-scale in the sense that R&D and advertising are more profitable the larger are the magnitude of the expenditures made, particularly in the 1990s.

The second question that has been asked by scholars is how accurately the future benefits of R&D are reflected in firms' market values. The evidence suggests that although the market recognizes that R&D has future benefits (Hall 1993; Sougiannis 1994; Lev and Sougiannis 1996), it does not price R&D in a completely efficient manner (Lev and Sougiannis 1996; Chan, *et al*. 2001; Chambers *et al*. 2001).

R&D has also become a fulcrum for those who argue that the recognition and disclosure rules for intangibles under US GAAP are deficient and economically damaging. The increasing prominence of R&D, brand, and human capital intangibles in firms' business strategies in the 1990s has focused renewed attention on the inadequacies of SFAS No. 2. For example, Lev (2000, 2001) and Aboody and Lev (2001) argue that the uniform expensing of R&D and the paltry quantity and quality of R&D-related disclosure are both increasingly indefensible from an accounting standard setting point of view, and moreover create large information asymmetries that increase firms' cost of capital and provide lucrative opportunities for insiders.

11.3. HYPOTHESES

My goal in this chapter is to add to the relatively thin literature on the determinants of biotech firms' equity market values. I do so with two goals in mind. First, a common view in the business world is that the primary drivers of the value created by biotechnology activities are 'soft' factors such as the number and importance of patents; strategic alliances, partnerships, and joint ventures; the intellectual human capital of employees, particularly star scientists; and investor sentiment (e.g. Bratic *et al*. 2000). The not infrequent lack of revenues and/or positive earnings leads many to conclude that biotech valuation is far more of an art than a science.

Such a perspective implies that accounting data will be inferior to the soft variables listed above when it comes to explaining cross-sectional variation in the equity market values of biotech firms. While this implication might be true, it would run counter to a great deal of accounting research that both theoretically and empirically concludes that financial statement data per se should and do explain large amounts of the cross-sectional variation in firms' equity market values. As an accounting researcher, I am therefore interested in determining whether biotechnology firms are different in this regard than practically all other industries or types of firms, and if so, why.

Second, because of the size and importance of R&D to biotech firms, I am also keen to formulate and test economic explanations about the relations between biotech firms' R&D and their equity market values. In the subsections that follow, I present five factors that I hypothesize are determinants of the elasticity of biotech firms' equity market values with respect to their R&D expenditures (the 'value elasticity of R&D'), together with predictions as to the direction of their impact on the value elasticity of R&D. The factors I propose as determinants are based on the scientific and regulatory nature of biotechnology and prior research in several areas of economics.

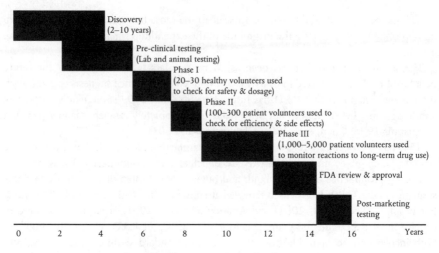

Figure 11.1. *Biotech value chain.*

Source: Ernst & Young LLP, *Biotechnology Industry Report Convergence*, 2000.

11.3.1. *Location of R&D in the Biotechnology Value Chain*

The prototypical biotechnology value chain of discovery, development, and commercial-ization is a long one, stretching as far as fifteen years from beginning work on discovery to completing the regulatory review process and post-marketing testing. The major technical steps in the biotech value chain are summarized in Fig. 11.1. They consist of discovery, pre-clinical testing, phase I–III trials, and FDA approval.

I hypothesize that the earlier R&D expenditures lie in the value chain, the greater will be the value elasticity of R&D. This is because the earlier is R&D spending in the value chain, the riskier yet larger is likely to be its ultimate pay-off. The economic value of early stage R&D is heightened beyond a simple NPV viewpoint due to the presence of real options. As shown in Fig. 11.1, discovery stage biotech R&D lies at the beginning of the chain of scientific, technical, and regulatory milestones along the way to obtaining patent protection of intellectual property. Early stage R&D therefore has more real option value than does later stage R&D because before it stretch options to accelerate vs. delay, expand vs. contract, abandon vs. continue, develop in-house vs. subcontract, and go-it-alone vs. secure a strategic alliance—many of which occur not just once along the value chain but are repeated.

I therefore predict that R&D expenditures that lie earlier (later) in the value chain will have a larger (smaller) value elasticity of R&D. Following Cumming and Macintosh (2000), who find that early-stage Canadian biotech firms spend a greater propor-tion of their expenditures on R&D than do later-stage firms, the financial statement proxy I use for location in the value chain is the ratio of quarterly R&D expense to revenues.

11.3.2. *Growth Rate of R&D Spending*

I next hypothesize that holding constant the location of R&D spending in the value chain, firms whose R&D spending is growing faster will have higher value elasticities of R&D. This is because a biotech firm seeking to discover and develop a new cure is in a race with competitors to be the first to make the discovery and secure patent protection of the successful intellectual property. I argue that it is reasonable to suppose that the faster a biotech firm is able to ramp up its spending on R&D, the higher is the probability that it will win the race and thereby secure the winner's supranormal profits. Using similar reasoning, biotech firms are also likely to spend R&D faster the larger is the anticipated size of the market for the winning intellectual property. The financial statement proxy I use for the speed with which a firm ramps up its R&D spending is the year-to-year growth rate in quarterly R&D expense.

11.3.3. *Scale of Spending on R&D*

In addition to the rate of growth in R&D spending, the scale of R&D spending may affect the value elasticity of R&D. Most research from industrial economics suggests that innovative activities such as R&D may exhibit decreasing output-denominated returns-to-scale (Scherer 1980; Acs and Audretsch 1987, 1988; Graves and Langowitz 1993). For example, Graves and Langowitz (1993) conclude that for firms in the pharmaceutical industry, increasing levels of R&D spending is positively related to the number of new chemical agreements (NCEs) produced, but at a decreasing rate. The explanation favoured by Graves and Langowitz for this result is that large R&D spending occurs in large companies, where bureaucracy, red-tape, and conservatism make it difficult for creative and inventive ideas to succeed. On the other hand, a recent large-sample study by Hand (2001*b*) finds that R&D expenditures are on average characterized by increasing profitability returns-to-scale, and that this relation has strengthened in the 1990s relative to what it was in the 1980s. Hand interprets his findings as being due to larger scale R&D expenditures leading to a disproportionately larger probability of obtaining a legal or natural monopoly on the innovation arising from the R&D. In view of the mixed results in prior research, I do not predict the sign of any economies-of-scale effects on the value elasticity of R&D. The natural financial statement proxy to use for the scale of R&D spending is the dollar amount of quarterly R&D expense.

11.3.4. *Value of Employees' Human Capital*

I also evaluate the impact that employees' knowledge and skill has on the value elasticity of R&D. The intellectual human capital of bioscientists, particularly star scientists, has been found to be an important determinant of where and when commercial firms began to use biotechnology and the ultimate success of biotech firms (Zucker and Darby 1996). Estimates of the value of star scientists are positively correlated with biotech firms' equity market values (Darby *et al.* 1999). Such results lead me to hypothesize that the value elasticity of R&D is increasing in the quantity and/or quality of employee human capital.

I measure the quantity of human capital employed by the firm using the total number of employees, and the quality of human capital by the ratio of selling, general, and administrative expenses (SGA) to the number of employees. One component of SGA is the salary cost of senior management and scientists. Although probably very noisy, I propose that the ratio of SGA to the number of employees will be proportional to the size of the average salary paid to senior management and scientists, and therefore a proxy for the quality of employee human capital.

11.3.5. *Age/Maturity of the Firm*

Finally, I examine the relation between the value elasticity of R&D and the age/maturity of the firm, but make no prediction as to the sign of the relation. Firm maturity may enhance or hinder the value elasticity of R&D. On the one hand, more mature biotech firms are less likely to attract the kinds of freewheeling star scientists who are best at discovery. Highly creative individuals may become discouraged in mature firms, and as firms mature the best researchers may be promoted to supervisory or administrative positions, leaving less capable scientists to undertake scientific discovery (Graves and Langowitz 1993). On the other hand, more mature biotech firms are likely to have greater scientific and managerial experience; more extensive networks of strategic alliances with other biotech firms as well as pharmaceutical companies and universities; more sophisticated business advisers; and less financial risk. I measure the maturity of a firm by the number of years it has been publicly traded.

11.4. FIRMS AND DATA

US biotech firms that are or were publicly traded were identified through a variety of sources that were merged to create an initial master list of potential biotech companies. The sources included both those that report information on currently traded biotech firms, and those that identify biotech firms that are no longer publicly traded, typically because of bankruptcy or acquisition.[2] The former sources included www.biospace.com, www.recap.com, Robbins-Roth (2000), the NASDAQ biotech index ($NBI), the AMEX biotech index ($BTK), and the BioSpace biotech index ($BSP). The latter sources consisted of Compustat, www.recap.com, and Robbins-Roth (2000).

The initial master list was then cross-matched with the quarterly Compustat database so as to only retain firms that were publicly traded at the end of one or more fiscal quarters beginning 1989:q1 and ending 2000:q3, and that had the minimal financial statement data needed for the study.[3] The starting date of 1989:q1 is dictated by the fact that quarterly Compustat's coverage of R&D only begins in the first quarter of 1989 (in contrast, annual Compustat reports annual R&D expense under Statement of Financial

---

[2] Clearly, restricting the sample to only biotech firms that are currently traded in public equity markets would impart potentially severe selection biases.

[3] Compustat fiscal years differ from calendar years. For example, Compustat year 1998 is defined as all fiscal year-ends that lie between 6/1/98 and 5/31/99.

Accounting Standards No. 2 starting in 1974). The ending date of 2000:q3 is the most recent quarter for which there is full data.[4] Due to the nature of the regressions I conduct in the next section of the chapter, contributed capital, retained earnings, net income, revenues, cost of sales, dividends, and the end-of-fiscal-quarter market value of common equity were required to be non-missing. Furthermore, contributed capital, revenues, cost of sales, dividends, and the end-of-fiscal-quarter market value of common equity were required to be non-negative. Finally, and importantly, since the focus of this chapter is biotech firms, large pharmaceutical (so-called 'big-pharma') firms in the master list were identified from www.phrma.org and Robbins-Roth (2000) and excluded. The final dataset consists of 606 different biotech firms with a total of 12,520 usable firm-quarter observations.

Table 11.1 lists and defines the variables used in the study by their quarterly Compustat item numbers. Income statement variables are shown in panel A, balance sheet and market-based variables in panel B, and variables from the statement of cash flows in panel C. Per these variable definitions, missing research and development expense RD was set to zero when Compustat indicated it was missing (i.e. immaterial). Since Compustat includes RD in selling, general, and administrative expenses, SGA is redefined to exclude RD when SGA is non-missing. Since cost of sales COS is defined by Compustat as total operating expenses if SGA is missing, in cases where SGA was missing COS was also set missing. This means that only a subset of firms has non-missing SGA and COS. However, the sum of COS and SGA, denoted COSGA, is readily available, being defined as COS + SGA when SGA is not missing, and max{COS − RD, 0} when SGA is missing. Core pre-tax income is defined as REV − COS − SGA − RD when SGA is not missing, and as REV − COSGA − RD when SGA is missing. All dollar amounts are restated into 2000 dollars using the CPI in December 2000.

Table 11.2 shows the numbers of biotech firms used in the study across time and SIC-defined industries. Panel A shows that the number of publicly traded US biotech firms quadrupled over the ten-year time period analysed in this study, rising steadily from 109 in 1989:q1 to 421 in 2000:q3. The number of biotech firms in any year is substantially less than the 606 firms with at least one firm-quarter observation because biotech firms are frequently bought by other firms (typically big-pharma) or they go bankrupt. According to 4-digit SIC industry classifications, panel B demonstrates that 27.1 per cent of firm-quarter observations are contributed by firms in the pharmaceutical preparations industry, 21.1 per cent are from the biological products industry, and 13.1 per cent are from *in vitro* and *in vivo* diagnostic substances. The remainder are spread out over sixty other 4-digit SIC industries, indicating that while the bulk of biotech firms are in three SIC industries, the remainder are quite spread out. In terms of exchange listing, however, diversity is less apparent: some 86.6 per cent of firm-quarters are contributed by firms that trade (or traded) on the NASDAQ.

Table 11.3 reports key economic and scientific variables for the US biotech industry as a whole, under the assumption that the biotech firms in my database comprise the entire US biotech industry. Because the last quarter for which there is complete data is 2000:q3,

---

[4] Only a subset of the sample firms have quarterly Compustat data for 2000:q4, 2001:q1, or 2000:q2. This is due to Compustat's definition of a fiscal year (in which fiscal quarters are contained).

Table 11.1. *Variable definitions per their Compustat quarterly data item numbers*

Variable	Label	Compustat quarterly data item(s)
Panel A: Income statement		
Revenue	REV	2 (net sales).
Revenue growth rate	REVGRW	REV ÷ REV lagged four quarters.
R&D expense	RD	4 (research & development expense); zero if missing. RD includes write-offs of purchased in-process R&D. Quarterly RD is only available beginning 1989:q1.
R&D growth rate	RDGRW	RD ÷ RD lagged four quarters.
SG&A expense	SGA	1 (selling, general, & administrative expense). Since Compustat includes RD in SGA, SGA is redefined to exclude RD.
Cost of sales	COS	30 (cost of sales). Since item 30 is total operating expense if SGA is missing, when SGA is missing COS is set as missing.
COS + SGA	COSGA	Set to COS + SGA when SGA is not missing. Else set to max{COS − RD, 0}.
Core (pre-tax) income	CI	REV − COS − SGA − RD.
Net income	NI	69 (net income or loss).
Panel B: Balance sheet and balance sheet-related		
PP&E	PPE	42 (net property, plant, & equipment).
Total assets	TA	44 (total assets).
Long-term debt	LTD	51 (long-term debt).
Contributed capital	CC	56 (common stock) + 57 (capital surplus).
Retained earnings	RE	58 (total common equity).
Treasury stock	TS	98 (treasury stock). Set to zero if missing.
Book equity	BVE	60 (total common equity).
Market value of equity	MVE	14 (fiscal quarter-end closing price) × 61 (common shares outstanding at fiscal quarter-end).
Number of employees	EMPL	29 (number of employees at fiscal year-end).
Panel C: Statement of cash flows		
Cash from operations	CFO	108 (net cash flow from operating activities).
Cash from investing	CFINV	111 (net cash flow from investing activities).
Cash from financing	CFFIN	113 (net cash flow from financing activities).
Dividends	DIV	89 (cash dividends). Set to zero if missing.

Table 11.2. *US biotech firms by Compustat year / quarter and SIC industry, 1989:q1–2000:q3*

Panel A: Number of biotech firms by Compustat fiscal year and quarter[a]

1989:q1	109	1992:q1	169	1995:q1	251	1998:q1	391
1989:q2	103	1992:q2	185	1995:q2	261	1998:q2	399
1989:q3	106	1992:q3	198	1995:q3	261	1998:q3	387
1989:q4	111	1992:q4	205	1995:q4	296	1998:q4	423
1990:q1	112	1993:q1	204	1996:q1	296	1999:q1	385
1990:q2	116	1993:q2	208	1996:q2	329	1999:q2	407
1990:q3	121	1993:q3	213	1996:q3	342	1999:q3	392
1990:q4	127	1993:q4	249	1996:q4	381	1999:q4	417
1991:q1	124	1994:q1	235	1997:q1	363	2000:q1	398
1991:q2	141	1994:q2	253	1997:q2	380	2000:q2	420
1991:q3	145	1994:q3	252	1997:q3	383	2000:q3	421
1991:q4	160	1994:q4	265	1997:q4	426		

Total 12,520

Panel B: 4-digit SIC composition

	4-digit SIC	SIC industry description	No. obs.	% obs.
1.	2834	Pharmaceutical preparations	3,397	27.1
2.	2836	Biological products (except diagnostic substances)	2,639	21.1
3.	2835	*In vitro* and *in vivo* diagnostic substances	1,642	13.1
4.	3841	Surgical and medical instruments and apparatus	725	5.8
5.	3845	Electromedical and electrotherapeutic apparatus	707	5.6
6.	3842	Orthopedic, prosthetic, surgical appliances and supplies	423	3.4
7.	8731	Commercial physical and biological research	396	3.2
8.	8071	Medical laboratories	291	2.3
9.	3826	Laboratory analytical instruments	279	2.2
10.	5122	Drugs, drug proprietaries, and druggists' sundries	168	1.3
11.	All others	Various ($n = 54$ four-digit SIC)	1,853	17.4
			12,520	100.0

Panel C: Exchange listing

Exchange	No. obs.	% obs.
NYSE	713	5.7
AMEX	961	7.7
NASDAQ	10,846	86.6
	12,520	100.0

[a] Sample is all biotech firms with non-missing CC, RE, NI, REV, COSGA, DIV, and MVE. All variables are defined as in Table 11.1.

Table 11.3. *Key economic and scientific innovation variables for the entire US biotech sector, 1989:q3–2000:q3*[a]

Variable	1989	1990	1991	1992	1993	1994	1995	1996	1997	1998	1999	2000
Equity market value	9,438	10,284	24,738	31,148	36,114	36,649	55,798	75,089	102,172	99,969	150,627	373,423
Total assets	5,522	6,656	9,201	14,111	14,433	16,872	19,820	27,847	33,467	41,476	49,412	75,540
Long-term debt	867	1,027	1,173	1,075	1,188	1,563	2,285	2,861	4,055	6,254	7,804	9,324
Contributed capital	4,243	5,227	8,275	14,712	16,454	19,915	22,135	30,609	35,242	41,389	50,158	69,516
Retained earnings	−940	−1,235	−2,142	−4,015	−5,687	−8,218	−9,332	−11,893	−13,813	−15,202	−19,645	−19,614
Treasury stock	42	51	41	54	60	61	89	102	142	202	509	905
R&D spending	170	215	332	519	653	799	845	1,136	1,309	1,547	1,592	2,046
Revenues	1,507	1,714	2,030	2,684	2,961	3,847	5,005	6,241	7,214	8,287	10,060	12,183
Cost of sales + SG&A	1,308	1,516	1,772	2,310	2,589	3,206	4,099	5,021	5,959	6,722	8,022	9,463
Core income	28	−17	−75	−146	−280	−158	61	83	−44	17	446	674
Net income	−86	−86	−163	−405	−423	−463	−402	−249	−475	−689	−381	−645
Dividends	8	20	96	24	20	21	27	36	40	53	48	49
Cash from operations	−255	−291	−366	−733	−1,151	−1,302	−980	−1,016	−1,234	−1,091	−1,075	298
Cash from investing	−302	−610	−1,203	−2,473	−654	−783	−1,056	−3,526	−3,190	−3,044	−3,594	−7,923
Cash from financing	490	977	2,123	3,217	1,735	1,778	2,785	5,865	4,557	3,982	3,786	15,383
No. of employees	25,270	27,838	37,227	50,474	54,431	63,679	76,977	103,737	143,661	158,268	179,417	159,671
Biotech patents[b]	1,780	1,431	1,757	2,033	2,352	2,233	2,320	3,071	4,418	6,171	6,029	5,446
Drug/vaccine approvals[c]	5	5	5	3	7	7	16	20	19	21	22	32
No. biotech firms[d]	n.a.	n.a.	n.a.	n.a.	1,231	1,272	1,311	1,308	1,287	1,274	1,311	1,273
No. publicly traded firms[e]	106	121	145	198	213	252	261	342	383	387	392	421

[a] Sample is all biotech firms with non-missing CC, RE, NI, REV, COSGA, DIV, and MVE. All variables are defined as in Table 11.1. Stock (flow) measures are as of the end of (for) the third quarter of each Compustat year. All dollar amounts are restated into 2000 dollars using the CPI in December 2000.

[b] *Source*: US Patent & Trademark Office, *Technology Profile Report*, *Patent Examining Technology Center Groups 1630–1660*, *Biotechnology*, 2000 and 2001. Number of patents refers only to those assigned to US corporations, the US government, or individuals in the US.

[c] *Source*: www.bio.org.

[d] Public and private US biotech firms. *Source*: Ernst & Young LLP, Annual Biotechnology Industry Reports, 1993–2000.

[e] US firms only. *Source*: Table 11.2.

the dollar-denominated variables shown in the upper portion of Table 11.3 are reported at or for the third quarter of each year, and are expressed in real terms using the CPI at the end of December 2000. Of the non-dollar-denominated variables, the number of employees and the number of biotech firms is as of the end of the year, while the number of US biotech patents granted and the number of drugs and vaccines approved are for the entire year.

Some striking observations emerge from Table 11.3. First, over the period 1989–2000 the market capitalization of US biotech firms rose 3,800 per cent from $9.4 billion to $373.4 billion. This was not due to simply a greater number of biotech firms being publicly traded, as the average market cap per firm rose 900 per cent from $89 million to $890 million. Second, while some of this huge increase is due to an increase in tangible assets from $5.5 billion to $75.5 billion, it seems more likely that the lion's share reflects the fruits of increased R&D spending. R&D spending rose from an annual rate of $680 million in 1999 to $8.2 billion in 2000 and under US GAAP is immediately expensed to firms' income statements rather than being capitalized as an asset and then amortized into expense over time.

The immediate expensing of the intangible R&D asset each year also explains why biotech firms' retained earnings have become more and more negative over time. Third, biotech firms have little debt, reflecting the high intrinsic risk of biotech firms as well as the reluctance of banks and other fixed-rate lending institutions to accept R&D as collateral. Fourth, while revenues have risen 700 per cent over the period 1989–2000, that has been insufficient to create positive net income for the industry in any year. Fifth, the market's strong assessment of the future cash flows expected from biotech innovations is such that biotech firms have been able consistently to tap the capital markets for financing, money they have spent not only on R&D but also on other investing activities, often the purchase of other biotech companies. Finally, the number of biotech patents granted to US corporations, the US government, and individuals in the US dwarfs the number of drug and vaccine approvals granted. This reflects not only the long lead-time between discovery and FDA approval, but also the enormous business risk of biotechnology.

An alternative perspective on the biotech industry is provided in Figs. 11.2 and 11.3. Figure 11.2 plots by year and quarter the percentage of biotech firms that were profitable according to definitions ranging from showing positive revenues to having positive net income. Although only some 90 per cent of firms at any given point in time are generating revenue, and only 30 per cent report positive core or net income, the percentages are remarkably stable over the ten-year period. The same cannot be said for most of the intensity ratios plotted in Fig. 11.3. Although the median ratio of SG&A to revenues holds very steady at just over 40 per cent, and the median market-to-book ratio rises steadily from 2.8 in 1989:q1 to 5.8 in 2000:q3, biotech firms' median level and median rate of spending on R&D, and the equity market value of their stock, rise and fall together in an almost cyclical pattern. The Pearson correlation between MVE ÷ REV and RD ÷ REV is 0.52, while that between MVE ÷ REV and the annual growth rate in R&D spending (RDGRW) is 0.32. The size of these correlations is consistent with the proposition that the cash flows expected to arise from R&D expenditures is a key driver of biotech firms' equity market values. I test this proposition more formally in the next section.

J. R. M. Hand

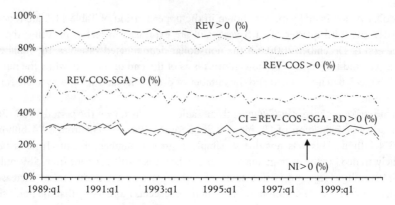

Figure 11.2. *Profitability measures for US biotech firms, 1989:q1–2000:q3.*

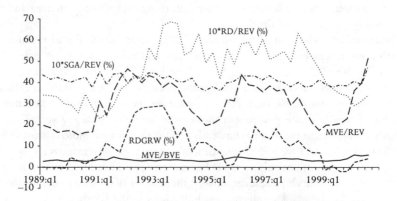

Figure 11.3. *Median intensity ratios for US biotech firms, 1989:q1–2000:q3.*

Concluding the descriptive statistics is Table 11.4. Table 11.4 reports percentiles for the data over the full period 1989:q1–2000:q3. Percentiles for general variables appear in panel A, while percentiles for various intensity measures (intensity of spending on R&D, growth rate in revenues or R&D, etc.) are in panel B. A major feature of the data in both panels is that every variable is highly right-skewed. Of firm-year observations, 89 per cent have positive revenues REV and 90 per cent spend money on R&D, but only 29 per cent report positive income NI. The median firm has been publicly traded for five years and employs ninety-five people.

The median market-to-book ratio is 3.7, likely reflecting both the biased accounting for R&D and other intangibles and an expectation on the part of the market of substantial future growth. Actual real growth rates in revenues are 15 per cent per year at the median, but 25 per cent of annual real revenue growth rates exceed 61 per cent. Biotech firms have few tangible fixed assets, with the median firm holding only 12 per cent of its total assets in PP&E. In contrast, biotech firms spend very intensively on R&D. The median

Table 11.4. *Variable percentiles for 12,520 US biotech firm-quarter observations, 1989:q1–2000:q3* [a]

Panel A: General variables [b]

Percentile	MVE	BVE	TA	LTD	REV	RD	CI	FIRM AGE	EMPL
100	$82,219	$6,130	$9,219	$1,162	$2,732	$304	$826	21	20,453
99	3,487	592	1,106	252	245	37	35	18	5,900
95	846	197	353	58	67	11	9.7	15	1,305
75	201	52	71	3.6	7.5	3.6	0.3	9	217
50	85	22	30	0.3	2.0	1.3	−1.2	5	95
25	33	8.1	13	0	0.4	0.4	−3.1	3	46
5	7.1	0.9	3.1	0	0	0	−8.6	1	14
1	2.0	−6.1	0.9	0	0	0	−17	1	6
0	0.1	−161	0.1	0	0	0	−207	0	5
% > 0	100%	97%	100%	66%	89%	90%	29%	99%	100%
No. obs.	12,520	12,519	12,519	12,366	12,520	12,520	12,520	12,520	10,804

Panel B: Intensity measures [c]

Percentile	MVE ÷BVE [d]	PPE ÷TA	COS ÷REV [e]	SGA ÷REV	RD ÷REV	REV GRW [f]	RD GRW [f]	RD ÷EMPL [g]	SGA ÷EMPL [g]
100	9,524	0.93	74	170	1,573	1,000%	1,000%	$762	$680
99	71	0.70	4.7	16	89	1,000	370	157	123
95	22	0.46	1.2	3.5	20	445	143	76	56
75	6.7	0.23	0.66	0.77	2.2	61	39	36	24
50	3.7	0.12	0.48	0.41	0.45	15	9.3	16	16
25	2.1	0.06	0.35	0.28	0.08	−12	−15	3.5	10
5	0.9	0.01	0.16	0.14	0	−70	−59	0	5.5
1	0.5	<0.01	0.04	0.04	0	−94	−86	0	3.0
0	0.1	0	0	0.01	0	−99	−99	0	0.4
% > 0	100%	99%	>99%	100%	89%	65%	60%	90%	100%
No. obs.	12,122	12,480	5,357	5,357	11,082	8,939	8,985	10,804	5,182

[a] Sample is all biotech firms with non-missing CC, RE, NI, REV, COSGA, DIV, and MVE. All variables are defined as in Table 11.1.
[b] Dollar amounts are in millions. FIRMAGE is in years. EMPL is the raw number of employees.
[c] RD ÷ EMPL and SGA ÷ EMPL are in thousands of dollars.
[d] Ratios defined using REV as the denominator are only computed when REV > 0.
[e] MVE ÷ BVE is only computed when BVE > 0.
[f] REVGRW and RDGRW are both winsorized at 1,000%.
[g] RD ÷ EMPL and SGA ÷ EMPL are in $000s per employee.

firm spends 45 per cent of its revenue on R&D, $16,000 per employee, and is growing that spending at a median real rate of 9.3 per cent per year.

11.5. EMPIRICAL TESTS

11.5.1. *Log-linear Regression Model*

The past ten years have seen a surge in the theoretical development and empirical testing of accounting-based valuation models in which equity market value is expressed as a linear function of book equity and current and/or expected future net income (Ohlson 1995; Feltham and Ohlson 1995, 1996; Barth *et al.* 1998; Dechow *et al.* 1999; Hand and Landsman 2000). Estimation of these linear models has been through OLS applied to undeflated dollar values; deflated data, where the most common deflators are the number of shares outstanding, book equity, and total assets; and in returns rather than in levels.

In this chapter I employ a different and deliberately more agnostic approach. I assume that a firm's equity market value is a Cobb–Douglas production function of its current financial statement data. Taking logs then leads to a log-linear expression for the firm's equity market value. Although log-linear models have been employed extensively in economics, particularly for valuing R&D (Hall 1993, 2000; Hall *et al.* 2001), they are rare in accounting and finance.[5]

I employ a log-linear model for two main reasons. First, in log-linear regressions the influence of anomalous or outlier observations is dramatically reduced and a greater homoscedasticity in regression residuals is achieved. These are significant concerns for biotech firms because of the high degree of skewness observed in biotech firms' equity market values, net income, book equity, etc. (Table 11.4). To finesse the reasonable concern that a minority of the data drives the magnitude and/or significance of parameter estimates, most researchers who apply OLS regression to non-logged data first identify and then winsorize or delete outliers. This potentially ad hoc process is all but unnecessary within a log-linear model because the log transformation dramatically dampens the values of previously extreme observations. My interest in this chapter is in the signs of the relations between equity market values and financial statement data, not the magnitudes of those relations. Employing an empirically robust regression method such as the log-linear specification is therefore very important. Second, recent work by Ye and Finn (2000) and Beatty *et al.* (2001) provide the beginnings of a theoretical justification for the use of log-linear valuation specifications in research that employs financial accounting data.[6]

[5] Kaplan and Ruback (1995) and Berger *et al.* (1996) are two infrequent instances of the use of log-linear models in valuation contexts in finance.

[6] Ye and Finn (2000) motivate their log-linear model of firms' equity market values, book equity, and net income by demonstrating that if the log of one plus the return on equity follows an AR(1) process, and net dividends are zero, then equity market value emerges as a multiplicative function of book equity and net income. Beatty *et al.* (2001) derive a log-linear valuation model under three structural assumptions: (1) stock valuation is first degree homogenous in underlying valuation drivers, (2) accounting constructs measure such valuation drivers with multiplicative measurement error that is conditionally lognormal, and (3) the unconditional distribution of stock values is either diffuse or lognormal.

In the somewhat agnostic approach to valuation that I have taken, the set of current financial statement data is taken to be a sufficient predictor of the present value of the expected future net cash flows accruing to the firm's common shareholders. Clearly, such a simplistic view could be made more sophisticated by including past financial statement data and/or instruments for expected future net cash flows. I limit myself to only current financial statement data for reasons of parsimony and data availability—adding past financial statement data would make the analysis quite cumbersome, and instruments for expected future net cash flows such as analyst earnings forecasts are unavailable for all but a tiny fraction of firm-years.

11.5.2. *Log-transformations of Variables*

Each variable Z in the regression is log-transformed using the following:

$$LZ = \log_e[Z + 1] \quad \text{if } Z \geq 0,$$
$$\text{but } -\log_e[-Z + 1] \quad \text{if } Z < 0 \text{ (where } Z \text{ is expressed in \$000s).} \tag{11.1}$$

This transformation is information-preserving in the sense of being monotone and one-to-one. The addition of \$1,000 to Z provides that LZ is defined when Z is zero. Equation (11.1) also ensures that negative values of core income and book equity are not discarded. Panel A of Table 11.5 reports the means and medians of the main variables used in the regressions after being log-transformed, and demonstrates that the log-transformation dramatically reduces the extreme right-skewness of the raw data found in Table 11.4.

11.5.3. *Structure of Regressions*

Table 11.6 reports the results of log-linear regressions aimed at generally determining the value-relevance of financial statement data for the equity market values of US biotech firms, and specifically testing the hypotheses outlined in Sections 11.3.1–11.3.5. The dependent variable in each regression is LMVE, the log of the firm's equity market value at the end of a given fiscal quarter.[7] Rather than pooling all available observations across firms and time, I run one regression for each of the forty-seven fiscal quarters over the period 1989:q1–2000:q3 and then base my inferences on the resulting time-series of coefficient estimates. This approach is more likely to yield unbiased inferences as to the sign and magnitude of underlying coefficients than is using pooled data, because it is highly likely that in pooled data the assumption that residuals are uncorrelated across time and across firms is severely violated. Following Fama and MacBeth (1973), I compute and report the mean coefficient estimate and a simple t-statistic on the mean.

---

[7] The end of the fiscal quarter is typically three weeks before the firm confirms its net income to the market through a quarterly earnings press release. Based on other empirical work that estimates accounting-based valuation models, the 'look-ahead' bias that this may create in the upcoming regressions should be trivial.

Table 11.5. *Means and medians of economic variables for 606 US biotech firms, 1989:q1–2000:q3*[a]

Panel A: Mean and medians of log-transformed regression variables[b]

	LMVE	LBVE	LCC	LRE	LTS	LCI	LREV	LCOS	LSGA	LRD	LDIV
Mean	11.3	9.4	10.9	−7.1	1.0	−3.2	7.0	6.9	7.7	6.5	0.3
Median	11.3	10.0	11.0	−10.1	0.0	−7.1	7.6	7.5	7.6	7.2	0.0

Panel B: Medians across sign of core income (in $ millions, unless MVE ÷ BVE)

	MVE	TA	LTD	BVE	EMPL	FAGE	DIV	CC	RE	TS	MVE÷BVE
CI < 0[c]	$79	25	0.2	18	75	5	0	64	−34	0	4.1
CI > 0[c]	105	54	1.3	34	256	7	0	42	−0.7	0	2.9
p-value[d]	<0.001	<0.001	<0.001	<0.001	<0.001	<0.001	<0.001	<0.001	<0.001	<0.001	<0.001

Panel C: Medians across sign of core income (in $ millions, unless % or ratios)

	REV	COS	SGA	RD	CI	NI	COS÷REV	SGA÷REV	RD÷REV	REV GRW	RD GRW
CI < 0	$0.9	0.5	1.3	1.7	−2.2	−2.2	0.55	0.83	1.33	8.9%	9.4%
CI > 0	12	5.5	4.1	0.5	1.7	0.8	0.45	0.31	0.05	20.6%	9.0%
p-value	<0.001	<0.001	<0.001	<0.001	<0.001	<0.001	<0.001	<0.001	<0.001	<0.001	0.54

[a] Sample is all biotech firms with non-missing CC, RE, NI, REV, COSGA, DIV, and MVE; and non-negative CC, REV, COSGA, DIV, and MVE. All variables are defined as in Table 11.1.

[b] The log transformation for variable Z is $LZ = \log_e[Z+1]$ if $Z \geq 0$ and $-\log_e[-Z+1]$ if $Z < 0$, where Z is in $000s. See Table 11.1 for definitions of data items prior to being log transformed. Number of firm-quarters where CI > 0 varies between 2,497 and 8,875 depending on the variable.

[c] Number of firm-quarters where CI < 0 varies between 2,305 and 3,645 depending on the variable.

[d] p-value on Z-statistic for Wilcoxon 2-sample rank sums testing a difference in medians (Normal approximation).

Table 11.6. *Log-linear regressions of end-of-fiscal-quarter equity market values of 606 US biotech firms on pricing variables in, or derived from, financial statements, 1989:q1–2000:q3*[a]

Independent variable[b]	Predicted sign of coefficient	Model 1	Model 2	Model 3	Model 4	Model 5	Model 6	Model 7	Model 8	Model 9
LPNIBV[c]	.(+)	0.33[d] (13.0)[e]								
LCC	(+)		0.83 (56.6)	0.6 (20.7)	0.65 (36.5)	0.54 (11.9)	0.61 (22.6)	0.56 (12.7)	0.56 (12.7)	0.64 (21.2)
LPNIRE	(+)		0.16 (19.2)	0.12 (15.6)	0.14 (15.3)	0.11 (9.0)	0.12 (14.3)	0.12 (8.7)	0.11 (8.5)	0.12 (12.9)
LTS	(−)		−0.05 (−5.9)	−0.03 (−2.7)	−0.02 (−1.5)	−0.11 (−7.7)	−0.05 (−4.4)	−0.10 (−6.9)	−0.10 (−7.1)	−0.07 (−5.3)
LCI	(+)	0.002 (0.5)								
LPOSCI	(+)		0.23 (15.8)							
LNEGCI	(−)		−0.29 (−16.3)							
LREV	(+)			0.09 (3.1)	0.02 (2.0)	0.45 (9.1)	0.24 (7.6)	0.41 (6.0)	0.41 (5.2)	0.18 (5.1)
LCOS	(−)			−0.10 (−4.8)		−0.13 (−7.1)		−0.12 (−3.8)	−0.11 (−3.8)	
LSGA	(+/−)			0.24 (9.1)		0.25 (4.1)		0.26 (4.8)	0.24 (3.1)	
LCOSGA	(+/−)				0.12 (12.9)		0.11 (9.1)			0.10 (6.6)
LRD	(+)			0.20 (11.7)	0.31 (16.3)	−0.12 (−1.4)	0.05 (1.0)	−0.17 (−1.4)	−0.16 (−1.3)	0.13 (1.6)
LDIV	(+)	0.09 (12.6)	0.16 (5.7)	0.12 (3.4)	0.13 (4.0)	0.04 (1.0)	0.08 (1.8)	0.14 (1.2)	0.16 (1.1)	0.06 (1.7)
LRD*LRDREV[f]	(+)					0.06 (6.5)	0.03 (7.1)	0.06 (4.5)	0.06 (4.3)	0.02 (4.8)

Table 11.6. *Continued*

Independent variable[b]	Predicted sign of coefficient	Model 1	Model 2	Model 3	Model 4	Model 5	Model 6	Model 7	Model 8	Model 9
LRD*LRDGRW[g]	(+)					0.03 (5.4)	0.05 (13.3)	0.03 (4.2)	0.03 (4.3)	0.04 (12.5)
LRD*LRD	(+/−)					−0.01 (−2.3)	−0.00 (−1.0)	−0.00 (−0.2)	−0.00 (−1.3)	−0.01 (−1.5)
LRD*LFIRMAGE[h]	(+/−)					−0.02 (−2.5)	0.00 (−0.2)	−0.02 (−2.3)	−0.02 (−2.2)	0.00 (0.6)
LRD*LEMPL[l]	(+)							−0.00 (−0.5)		0.01 (1.8)
LRD*LSGAEMPL[m]	(+)								0.00 (0.4)	
Number of regressions		47	47	47	47	43	43	43	43	43
Avg. adj. R^2		35%	63%	65%	65%	72%	70%	72%	72%	70%
Avg. % of fitted MVE<0[i]		0%	0%	0%	0%	0%	0%	0%	0%	0%
Avg. % RPE[j]		166%	101%	81%	90%	66%	76%	63%	63%	72%
Avg. % SRPE[k]		530%	145%	117%	129%	94%	107%	89%	89%	101%
Avg. no. observations		266	266	129	266	81	207	71	71	162

[a] Sample is all biotech firms with non-missing CC, RE, NI, REV, COSGA, DIV, and MVE; and non-negative CC, RE, NI, REV, COSGA, DIV, and MVE. All variables are defined as in Table 11.1.

[b] All variables are as per Table 11.1, with these additions: Pre-income retained earnings PNIRE = RE − NI + DIV. Pre-income book equity PNIBV = BVE − NI + DIV. LPOSCI = max{LCI, 0} and LNEGCI = min{LCI, 0}, defined only where REV > 0.

[c] The log transformation for variable Z is $LZ = \log_e[Z + 1]$ if $Z \geq 0$ and $-\log_e[-Z + 1]$ if $Z < 0$, where Z is in $000s.

[d] Mean coefficient from the quarter-by-quarter regressions.

[e] Simple Fama-MacBeth *t*-statistic (relative to a null of zero) on mean coefficient from the quarter-by-quarter regressions.

[f] $LRDREV = \log_e[1 + (100*RD/REV)]$.

[g] $LRDGRW = \log_e[RD_t/RD_{t-4}]$.

[h] $LFIRMAGE = \log_e[FIRMAGE + 1]$ where FIRMAGE is the non-negative number of years the firm has been publicly traded. Firms must have had their IPO on or after 1 January, 1980.

[i] Average percentage of fitted values of dependent variable MVE that are negative.

[j] RPE = absolute relative pricing error, defined in eqn (11.2) of Section 11.5.3.

[k] SRPE = absolute symmetrized relative pricing error, defined in eq (11.2) of Section 11.5.3.

[l] $LEMPL = \log_e[EMPL + 1]$ where LEMPL is the number of employees.

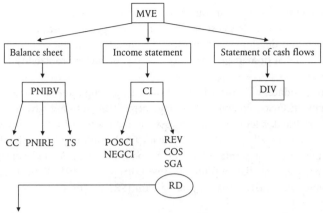

Coefficient on RD = f (RD$_t$+REV$_t$, RD$_t$+RD$_{t-4}$, RD$_t$, FIRMAGE$_t$, {#EMPL$_{t-1}$ or RD$_t$+#EMPL$_{t-1}$}).
See Table 11.1 for variable definitions.

Figure 11.4. *Structure of regressions used to test the hypotheses about the value-relevance of financial statement data, and the determinants of the value elasticity of R&D, for US biotechnology firms.*

Table 11.6 is structured as a series of different regressions that begin by using aggregate accounting data, and then move on to regressions based on decomposing the aggregate data into its major elements. A visual description of the regression structure is provided in Fig. 11.4. For example, model 1 regresses the log of biotech firms' equity market values on their book equity, core income, and dividends, while model 2 decomposes book equity into its three major components (contributed capital, retained earnings, and treasury stock) and separates positive core income from negative core income. Relative to model 2, model 3 instead disaggregates core income into revenues, cost of sales, selling, general, and administrative expenses, and R&D expense. Model 4 is similar to model 3 except that it uses the sum of cost of sales and selling, general, and administrative expenses because cost of sales and selling, general, and administrative expenses are not always separately available on quarterly Compustat. Models 1–4 therefore determine the overall relevance of financial statement data for the equity market values of US biotech firms. In contrast, models 5–9 test the hypotheses outlined in Sections 11.3.1–11.3.5 by adding to models 3 and 4 interactions between R&D and proxies for the hypothesized determinants of the value elasticity of R&D.

As noted, model 1 regresses the log of biotech firms' equity market values on their book equity, core income, and dividends. In model 1, book equity is the primary balance sheet variable, core income is the primary income statement variable, and dividends is the primary variable from the statement of cash flows. The measure of book equity I employ is denoted PNIBV, and is defined as book equity at the end of the quarter after subtracting net income earned during the quarter and adding back dividends paid out during the quarter. I use this definition of book equity instead of simply book equity at the end of the quarter because it facilitates the computation of the marginal impacts of income or the components of income on equity market value.[8] According to Table 11.1, core income is defined as revenues less cost of sales less selling, general, and administrative expenses less research and development expenses.[9] Dividends are included largely because they may act as a signal of management's expectations of future profitability or the probability of survival.

The goodness of fit of each model is assessed using three measures beyond the adjusted R^2 statistic. First, I compute the average percentage of firm-quarter observations that have negative fitted values (averaged across the time-series of quarterly regressions). All else held equal, a well-specified equity market valuation regression should ideally yield no negative fitted equity market values. Second, following Ye and Finn (2000), I compute the mean and median absolute relative pricing error (RPE) and the mean and median absolute symmetrized relative pricing error (SRPE). For a given firm, RPE and SRPE are defined by:

$$RPE_i = \left| \frac{\widehat{MVE_i} - MVE_i}{MVE_i} \right|, \quad SRPE_i = \left\{ \begin{array}{ll} \left| \widehat{MVE_i}/MVE_i - 1 \right| & \text{if } \widehat{MVE_i} \geq MVE_i, \\ \left| 1 - MVE_i/\widehat{MVE_i} \right| & \text{if } \widehat{MVE_i}, < MVE_i, \end{array} \right\}$$

(11.2)

where MVE_i is firm i's equity market value, and $\widehat{MVE_i}$ is the equity market value fitted from the regression. Both RPE and SRPE are relative measures; they are not contaminated by scaling factors associated with measurement units in the way that adjusted R^2 statistics can be (Brown *et al.* 1999). I report statistics for both RPE and SRPE because the simple relative pricing error weights overpricing more than underpricing (implying that a model that overprices stocks would appear to provide a better fit than one that underprices).[10] The symmetrized absolute relative pricing error corrects this concern in the sense that underpricing by 50 per cent yields an SRPE of the same size as overpricing by 100 per cent.

11.5.4. *Regression Results*

The regression results for model 1 indicate that book equity and dividends are strongly related to equity market values. However, core income appears entirely unrelated to equity market values! The explanation for this counterintuitive result lies in the biased nature of

[8] Clean surplus accounting under US GAAP requires that book equity at the end of the quarter includes net income. As a result, if end-of-period book equity and net income for the period are both in the regression as independent variables, then the marginal impact of net income is a function of both the coefficients on net income and book equity. Replacing book equity with pre-income book equity finesses this complexity. Note that if under clean surplus accounting, pre-income book equity is book equity at the beginning of the quarter plus new equity issued less equity repurchased less dividends declared during the quarter.

[9] I use core income instead of net income for two reasons. First, relative to net income, core income does not contain large and distortive one-time items. Second, since most biotech firms report losses, not profits, tax expense can be largely set aside.

[10] For example, suppose that $M = \$100$ and that two predicted prices $M_1 = \$150$ and $M_2 = \$50$ are being evaluated. Each predicted price deviates from the actual price by $50, and yields an RPE of 0.5. However, M_1 is overpriced by 33.3%, while M_2 is underpriced by 100%. The symmetrized RPE corrects for this. The SRPE for M_1 is 1, while the SRPE for M_2 is 0.5.

US accounting rules for intangible assets (Hand 2001*a*; Zhang 2000). Under US GAAP, virtually all expenditures on intangibles such as R&D, branding, and human capital are required to be expensed as incurred—they are not permitted to be recognized on firms' balance sheets and then amortized into expense over time as is the case with tangible fixed assets such as PP&E. The result of this is that for intangible-intensive companies such as biotech or Internet firms, reported income is highly downward-biased because a much greater expense is being recognized in income than should be the case. Indeed, Zhang (2000) argues that when spending on intangibles becomes large enough, particularly by small but fast growing companies, equity market value will become a negative, not positive, function of reported net income when net income is negative. This is exactly what Hand (2001*a*) finds to be true for Internet firms.

There are then two approaches to controlling for the distortive effects of accounting bias. The first is to allow positive and negative core income to have different coefficients (as well as different intercepts).[11] This is predicated on the assumption that firms with negative core income are much more intangible-intensive than are firms with positive core income. Evidence consistent with this assumption is shown in panels B and C of Table 11.5. For example, negative core income firm-quarter observations have a median market-to-book ratio of 4.1 as compared to 2.9 for positive firm-quarter observations (panel B). Negative core income firm-quarter observations also have a vastly greater median ratio of R&D spending to revenue—1.33 relative to 0.05 for positive core income firm-quarters.

Model 2 allows positive and negative core income to have different coefficients, at the same time as book equity is replaced by its three major components. (The two steps are done together rather than separately only for the sake of compactness, since the inferences from doing both together are the same as are found doing each separately.) Table 11.6 demonstrates that this simple control has major impacts on the results found for model 1. In model 2, the coefficient on positive (negative) core income is strongly positive (negative), supporting the accounting bias view. Also, the signs on the major components of book equity are as one would predict: those on contributed capital and retained earnings are reliably positive, while that on treasury stock (stock that has been repurchased by the company) is reliably negative. Dividends remains significant, although with a much larger standard error than in model 1, suggesting that its strong significance in model 1 may be because dividends are correlated with the specification errors created by not separating core income into positive and negative parts. Finally, the fit of model 2 is much improved over that of model 1. The adjusted R^2 of the regression increases from 35 per cent to 63 per cent; the average RPE declines from 166 per cent to 101 per cent; and the SRPE falls from 530 to 145 per cent.

---

[11] All models except model 1 also include dummy variables for those variables that can take a zero value. For example, all models except model 1 include a dummy variable set equal to one if treasury stock is zero, and zero otherwise. Dummies of this kind cover treasury stock TS, revenues REV, cost of sales COS, research and development RD, and dividends DIV. In addition, model 2 contains a dummy set equal to one if core net income CI is negative, and zero otherwise. Finally, all models except model 1 include a dummy set equal to one if retained earnings adjusted for the current quarter's net income and dividends PNIRE is negative, zero otherwise.

The second approach to controlling for the distortive effects of accounting bias is to decompose core income into its constituent parts: revenues; cost of sales; selling, general, and administrative costs; and R&D expense. This method separates out the components of core income that are much more likely not to be biased as a result of accounting rules from those that are. Falling in the unbiased category will be revenues and cost of sales; while selling, general, and administrative costs and R&D expense will be either somewhat or very biased reflections of the underlying economics. US accounting rules recognize revenue in a manner that closely reflects the underlying economics, and cost of sales is only recognized when revenues are, and also in an amount that reflects the direct cost of the sales made. This means that the value elasticity of revenues is predicted to be positive, while that of cost of sales is predicted to be negative.

In contrast, as I already argued earlier, only a small portion of R&D expense is truly an expense—that is, a benefit that is used up in the current period. Most of R&D expense is an asset—a cost with the ability or potential to provide future economic benefit to the firm. This is particularly the case for biotech firms, where the benefits from R&D are almost always obtained many years after the R&D expenditure is made. Hence the value elasticity of R&D is predicted to be positive. However, selling, general, and administrative costs are less clearly assets, because most general and administrative costs represent current period expenditures that have no future benefits (e.g. rent for an administration building). However, also included in SG&A are salaries for senior management and selling expenses. I argue that these types of costs do have future benefits, such as enhancing the likelihood that senior management will stay with the firm and creating brand intangibles, respectively. For SG&A costs, the net result of the mix of expenses and assets is unclear, leading me to make no sign prediction on the value elasticity of SG&A.

Model 3 implements this second approach to controlling for the distortive effects of accounting bias. The results shown in Table 11.6 indicate that, as predicted, the value elasticity of revenues (cost of sales) is reliably positive (negative). Also as predicted, the value elasticity of R&D is strongly positive. The value elasticity of SG&A for biotech firms is estimated to be unambiguously positive, implying that the stock market views most of SG&A as having economic benefits beyond the current quarter. Decomposing core income also improves the goodness-of-fit measures, particularly the average percentage RPE and SRPE.

Model 4 implements this same approach to controlling for accounting bias, but it does so by using the sum of cost of sales and SG&A. This is because, as noted in Table 11.1 and observed in Table 11.4, quarterly Compustat only reports SG&A for 5,357 of the 12,520 firm-quarters in my data set (the remainder of the time it is missing). It is this subset that is used in Model 3. However, quarterly Compustat always reports a cost of sales that it defines as total operating expenses if SG&A is missing. The sum of cost of sales and SG&A can therefore always be estimated by subtracting R&D expense from cost of sales if SG&A is missing. The results of estimating model 4 yield similar inferences on most coefficients to those of model 3. However, combining cost of sales and SG&A worsens the RPE and SRPE goodness-of-fit measures relative to model 3, and weakens the significance of the coefficient estimates on treasury stock and revenues.

In Sections 11.3.1–11.3.5, I hypothesized that the elasticity of equity market value with respect to R&D is a function of five factors: where the R&D lies in the biotech value chain of discovery, development, and commercialization; the growth rate in R&D spending; the scale of R&D expenditures; the human capital of the firm's employees; and the age of the firm. Models 5 and 6 test each of these predictions with the exception of that to do with the human capital of the firm's employees. That prediction I take into account and test in models 7, 8, and 9.

Using the financial statement proxies for these hypothesized factors outlined in Sections 11.3.1–11.3.5, I find as predicted that the elasticity of biotech firms' equity market values with respect to R&D is significantly larger the earlier is the R&D expenditure in the value chain, and the greater is the growth rate in R&D spending. In both model 5 and model 6, the coefficients on the proxies for the earliness of the R&D expenditure in the value chain LRD*LRDREV, and the growth rate in R&D spending LRD*LRDGRW, are strongly positive. Moreover, in model 5 the coefficients on the scale of R&D expenditures, LRD*LRD, and on the age/maturity of the firm, LRD*LFIRMAGE, are each reliably negative. While no predictions on the signs were made for the coefficients on LRD*LRD and LRD*LFIRMAGE, they indicate that empirically it appears to be the case that on average there are decreasing returns-to-scale for R&D expenditures made by biotech firms, and that the negatives of firm maturity are perceived by the stock market to outweigh the positives. I view the significance of the coefficients on LRD*LRD and LRD*LFIRMAGE in model 5 as more reliable than the insignificance of these same coefficients in model 6 because of the concerns I voiced earlier about combining cost of sales and SG&A into one variable, and the empirical fact that model 6 fits the data less well than does model 5.[12]

The final set of results augment those of models 5 and 6 by testing the hypothesis that employees' knowledge and skill have a positive impact on the value elasticity of R&D. I measure the quantity of human capital employed by the firm using the total number of employees EMPL, and the quality of human capital by the ratio of SGA to EMPL. One component of SGA is the salary cost of senior management and scientists. Although potentially quite noisy, I propose that the ratio of SGA to the number of employees will be proportional to the size of the average salary paid to senior management and scientists, and therefore a proxy for the quality of employee human capital.

These proxies are each interacted with R&D in models 7 and 8. However, both the coefficient on LRD*LEMPL and LRD*LSGAEMPL are resoundingly insignificantly different from zero, leading me to the inference that biotech firms' employees' knowledge and skill have no impact on the value elasticity of R&D. A marginally positive effect for LRD*LEMPL is found in model 9, which uses the sum of cost of sales and SG&A in place of the two separately, but as before this specification may be suspect.

---

[12] It is worth noting that in model 5, the coefficient on dividends is not reliably different from zero. This implies that its strong significance in model 1 arises only because dividends are correlated with the specification errors created by not controlling for accounting bias, and not controlling for the cross-sectional determinants of the value elasticity of R&D.

J. R. M. Hand

11.6. CONCLUSION

In this chapter I have sought to shed light on how and why the stock market values high technology by examining the pricing of 606 publicly traded biotechnology firms. Contrary to the common view that the primary value drivers of biotechnology are 'soft' variables such as intellectual human capital, patents, strategic alliances, and joint ventures, I found that simple but 'hard' balance sheet, income statement, and statement of cash flows data explain some 70 per cent of the variance in biotech firms' equity market values within a log-linear regression framework. Given the size and economic importance of R&D to biotech firms, I also analysed the mapping between the biotech firms' R&D expenditures and equity market values. I hypothesized that the elasticity of equity market value with respect to R&D is a function of five factors: where the R&D lies in the biotech value chain of discovery, development, and commercialization; the growth rate in R&D spending; the scale of R&D expenditures; the human capital of the firm's employees; and the age of the firm. Using financial statement proxies for these factors, I found that the elasticity of biotech firms' equity market values with respect to R&D is significantly larger the earlier is the R&D expenditure in the value chain, and the greater is the growth rate in R&D spending. The value elasticity of R&D is also reliably decreasing in the scale of R&D expenditures and the maturity of the firm.

In terms of future work, one logical next step would be to conduct a more sector-specific analysis of what has been done in this chapter. That is, I have assumed that it is appropriate to pool biotech firms that make pharmaceutical preparations (SIC 2834) with those that make biological products (SIC 2836) and sixty other 4-digit SICs. Such an assumption is almost certainly too restrictive, and deserving of further research.

References

Aboody, D. and Lev, B. (2001), 'The productivity of chemical research and development', Working paper, New York University.

Acs, Z. J. and Audretsch, D. B. (1987), 'Innovation, market structure, and firm size', *Review of Economics and Statistics* 69, 567–75.

—— and —— (1988), 'Innovation in large and small firms: An empirical analysis', *American Economic Review* 78, 678–90.

Aghion, P. and Tirole, J. (1994), 'The management of innovation', *Quarterly Journal of Economics* 109, 1185–209.

Audretsch, D. B. and Stephan, P. E. (1996), 'Company-scientist locational links: The case of biotechnology', *American Economic Review* 86, 641–52.

Barth, M. E., Beaver, W. H., and Landsman, W. R. (1998), 'Relative valuation roles of equity book value and net income as a function of financial health', *Journal of Accounting & Economics* 25, 1–34.

Beatty, R., Riffe, S., and Thompson, R. (2001), 'The log-linear form of stock value models based on accounting information', Working paper, Southern Methodist University.

Berger, P. G., Ofek, E., and Swary, I. (1996), 'Investor valuation of the abandonment option', *Journal of Financial Economics* 42, 257–87.

Bratic, V. W., Tilton, P., and Balakrishnan, M. (2000), 'Navigating through a biotech valuation', Working paper, PriceWaterhousecoopers LLC.

Brown, S., Lo, K., and Lys, T. (1999), 'Use of R-squared in accounting research: Measuring changes in value relevance over the last four decades', *Journal of Accounting & Economics* 28, 83–115.

Chambers, D. Jennings, R., and Thompson, R. B. (2002), 'Excess returns to R&D-intensive firms', *Review of Accounting Studies*, 7, 133–58.

Chan, L. K., Lakonishok, J., and Sougiannis, T. (2001), 'The stock market valuation of research and development expenditures', *Journal of Finance* 56, 2431–56.

Cumming, D. and Macintosh, J. G. (2000), 'The determinants of R&D expenditures: A study of the Canadian biotechnology industry', *Review of Industrial Organization* 17, 357–70.

Darby, M. R., Liu, Q., and Zucker, L. G. (1999), 'Stars and stakes: The effect of intellectual human capital on the level and variability of high-tech firms' market values', Working paper, UCLA.

Dechow, P. M., Hutton, A. P., and Sloan, R. G. (1999), 'An empirical assessment of the residual income valuation model', *Journal of Accounting & Economics* 26, 1–34.

Fama, E. and MacBeth, J. (1973), 'Risk, return, and equilibrium', *Journal of Political Economy* 81, 607–36.

—— and —— (1995), 'Valuation and clean surplus accounting for operating and financial activities', *Contemporary Accounting Research* 11, 689–732.

Feltham, G. A. and Ohlson, J. A. (1996), 'Uncertainty resolution and the theory of depreciation measurement', *Journal of Accounting Research* 34, 209–34.

Grabowski, H. G. and Mueller, D. C. (1978), 'Industrial research and development, intangible capital stocks, and firm profit rates', *Bell Journal of Economics* 9, 328–43.

Graves, S. B. and Langowitz, N. S. (1993), 'Innovative productivity and returns to scale in the pharmaceutical industry', *Strategic Management Journal* 14, 593–605.

Hall, B. H. (1993), 'The stock market's valuation of research and development investment during the 1980s', *American Economic Review* 83, 259–64.

—— (2000), 'Innovation and market value', in Barrell, R., Mason, G., and O'Mahoney M. (eds), *Productivity, Innovation and Economic Performance*, Cambridge: Cambridge University Press.

—— Jaffe, A., and Trajtenberg, M. (2001), 'Market value and patent citations: A first look', NBER Working paper No. 7741.

Hand, J. R. M. (2003a), 'Profits, losses and the non-linear pricing of Internet stocks', in Hand, J. R. M. and Lev, B. (eds), *Intangible Assets*, Oxford: Oxford University Press, 248–68.

—— (2003b), 'The increasing returns-to-scale of intangibles', in J. R. M. Hand, and B. Lev, (eds), *Intangible Assets*, Oxford: Oxford University Press, 303–31.

—— and Landsman, W. R. (2000), 'The pricing of dividends in equity valuation', Working paper, UNC Chapel Hill.

Joos, P. (2002), 'Explaining cross-sectional differences in market-to-book ratios in the pharmaceutical industry', Working paper, University of Rochester.

Kaplan, S. N. and Ruback, R. S. (1995), 'The valuation of cash flow forecasts: An empirical analysis', *Journal of Finance* 50, 1059–93.

Kenney, M. (1986), *Bio-technology: The University-industrial Complex*, New Haven: Yale University Press.

Kothari, S. P., Laguerre, T., and Leone, A. (2002), 'Capitalization versus expensing: Evidence on the uncertainty of future earnings from capital expenditures versus R&D outlays', *Review of Accounting Studies*, 7, 355–82.

Lerner, J. and Merges, R. P. (1998), 'The control of technology alliances: An empirical analysis of the biotechnology industry', *Journal of Industrial Economics* 46, 125–56.

Lev, B. (2000), 'New math for a New Economy', *Fast Company*, January–February.

—— (2001), *Intangibles: Management, Measurement, and Reporting*, Washington, DC: Brookings Institution Press.

—— and Sougiannis, T. (1996), 'The capitalization, amortization, and value-relevance of R&D', *Journal of Accounting and Economics* 21, 107–38.

Liu, Q. (2000), 'Growth opportunities, knowledge capital and leverage: Evidence from U.S. biotech firms', Working paper, University of Hong Kong.

Nissim, D. and Thomas, J. (2000), 'R&D costs and accounting profits', Working paper, Columbia University.

Ohlson, J. A. (1995), 'Earnings, equity book values, and dividends in equity valuation', *Contemporary Accounting Research* 11, 661–87.

Ravenscraft, D. and Scherer, F. M. (1982), 'The lag structure of returns to research and development', *Applied Economics* 14, 603–20.

Robbins-Roth, C. (2000), *From alchemy to IPO: The business of biotechnology*, New York: Perseus Books Group.

Robinson, D. T. and Stuart, T. (2000), 'Just how incomplete are incomplete contracts? Evidence from biotech strategic alliances', Working paper, University of Chicago.

Romer, P. (1999), 'Innovation: The new pump of growth', Blueprint: Ideas for a New Century 2 (http://www.ndol.org/blueprint).

Scherer, F. M. (1980), *Industrial Market Structure and Economic Performance*, Boston: Houghton Mifflin.

Sougiannis, T. (1994), 'The accounting based valuation of corporate R&D', *The Accounting Review* 69, 44–68.

Stuart, T. E., Hoang, H., and Hybels, R. C. (1999), 'Interorganizational endorsements and the performance of entrepreneurial ventures', *Administrative Science Quarterly* 44, 315–49.

Ye, J. and Finn, M. (2000), 'Nonlinear accounting-based equity valuation models', Working paper, Baruch College.

Zhang, X-J. (2000), 'Conservatism, growth, and the analysis of line items in earnings forecasting and equity valuation', Working paper, University of California, Berkeley.

Zucker, L. G. and Darby, M. R. (1996), 'Star scientists and institutional transformation: Patterns of invention and innovation in the formation of the biotechnology industry', *Proceedings of the National Academy of Sciences* 93, 12709–16.

—— and —— (1998), 'Capturing technological opportunity via Japan's star scientists: Evidence from Japanese firms' biotech patents and products', Working paper, UCLA.

——, ——, and Brewer, M. B. (1998), 'Intellectual human capital and the birth of U.S. biotechnology enterprises', *American Economic Review* 88, 290–306.

12

Internet Portals as Portfolios of Entry Options

ENRICO PEROTTI AND SILVIA ROSSETTO

12.1. INTRODUCTION

This chapter seeks to understand the possible foundations of the notion of platform invest-ment, a concept which has received mainstream interest in management science (for a survey see Kogut and Kulatilaka (1994)) and relate it to the strategic real option literature, a methodology to price growth opportunities. Platform investment refers to the estab-lishment of a broad logistic infrastructure which allows easier entry into related product segments and improves market responsiveness. There are well-documented examples of platform investment which have resulted in significant market advantages for the investing firms. However, to date there are hardly any theoretical treatments of the implied strategic and valuation issues. An example of a platform is a computer operating system. The explo-sion of the PC market was based on standardized software applications, which were made compatible thanks to the extreme diffusion of the DOS-Windows operating system. The company which controls the operating system is in an advantageous position to develop subsequent software applications compatible with the platform, and enjoy an immediate advantage with users.[1] Thus platform investment concerns the creation of an interme-diate infrastructure common to several types of future productive activities; this logistic

We would like to thank Frank De Jong for his comments and encouragement. We are also grateful to Jean Tirole and Bruno Biais for very helpful insights. We thank seminar participants at the Tinbergen Institute in Amsterdam, the TMR 2000 meeting in Barcelona, and the EFA00 and the AFA01 meeting. The second author acknowledges financial support from Scuola Superiore S. Anna. We retain sole responsibility for all remaining errors. Address for correspondence: Silvia Rossetto, Tinbergen Institute, Keizersgracht 482, NL-1017 EG Amsterdam, The Netherlands. e-mail: rossetto@tinbergen.nl.

[1] There are other examples of platform investment. Renowned cases are Boeing's investment in information technology and communications network processes that integrate suppliers and manufacturing plants with designers, considerably facilitating new product development. This pattern has been much adopted in the car industry: the number of their subcontractors has been significantly reduced but the productive process has become closely integrated via a common communication and productive platform. Another classic example is the information and distribution infrastructure built by Wal-Mart, targeted at rapid collection of information on customer purchases at individual shops connected with a rapid-response retail distribution system (Khanna and Tice 2000). The rapid integration in the communication and financial services industries have been predicated on the presence of strong synergies in distribution, allowing easier entry for new products.

infrastructure is not only incorporated in physical assets but also in market knowledge, customer information, and access.

Nowadays an even more central role is played by the Internet, a web of interconnected computers which allows workers to perform complex coordinated tasks and exchange information in real time. As the Internet is a global network, owners of frequently visited sites (hubs, or 'portals') enjoy a tremendous distributional capacity for information, services, and product sales. Such horizontal Internet portals, either in closed systems (such as AOL) or open access (portals such as Yahoo or general retail outlets such as Amazon) are other examples which fit the concept of platform investment.[2] These companies have gained a primary position as a focal point in a network by offering a desirable service and building a strong brand name on the Internet, while learning much about their customers' characteristics. This 'informed client database' and name recognition has created a basis for dramatic potential expansion in offering more services via the net. A portal can be seen as a hub in the network, a point of entry connected with relevant information or access to products. It lowers the cost of reaching customers and thus the cost of entry into new market segments.

This chapter builds a model of the value of the associated strategic advantages which allows us to compare the relative valuation of such 'platform stocks' versus conventional producers. In particular, the analysis allows studying the impact of demand uncertainty on strategy and valuation. Unlike the strong results of the network externalities and switching cost literature (see Klemperer (1995) for a review), in our model the innovator–early mover does not capture the market completely. The strategic implications of platform investment place our analysis in the context of the literature on strategic growth options, which examines the impact of investment to gain comparative advantages vis-à-vis competitors. The commitment of irreversible investment may confer strategic advantages as a result of lower capacity costs (Dixit 1980), operating costs (Kulatilaka and Perotti 1998a), or faster timing-to-market (Kulatilaka and Perotti 1998b). In all of these models, strategic investment increases market share and profit growth at the expense of competitors; the investing firm strengthens its post-entry position, gaining market share, and may discourage entry by competitors (Dixit 1980; Lambrecht and Perraudin 1997). In our approach we contrast platform investment to a traditional investment in productive capacity. This allows us to compare the valuation of platform firms relative to the value of established producers (old economy).[3] We therefore explicitly treat entry into a related segment, which require us to consider cross effects.

We model the advantage gained by a platform investment as a greater ease of entry (lower fixed costs) in markets for related products. The construction of a logistic platform can thus be described as the acquisition of a set of strategic entry options.[4] Another possible

[2] Vertical portals are web pages with very focused market content, such as myflowers.com. Amazon is an example of an originally vertical portal specialized in book sales which has extended itself into a broad platform (a horizontal portal), selling via the Internet all sorts of products.

[3] In related work we are studying why strategic analysis allows us to suggest that established firms may resist entry for new products because of the cross-effect with their traditional product line. This raises the issues whether Internet firms should be independent of existing brand name producers.

[4] This notion is related to the concept of a core capability or a platform investment (see Kogut and Kulatilaka 1994; Baldwin and Clark 2000).

advantage of a platform is the lower costs of access to customers, and thus a lower marginal cost. Our focus on fixed costs allows us to concentrate more on the timing of entry rather than market share. The basic model we develop is as follows. A firm considers a platform investment in a sector in which there is also a traditional incumbent. Demand is uncertain and evolves stochastically over time. Suppose that the new firm has the opportunity to make a platform investment, which allows it to produce a differentiated product and also offers the option to enter later at a reduced cost in a related market segment. The approach used here is related to the one used in Smets (1991): when market demand is low, firms prefer to wait to enter (the option of waiting to invest is more valuable than the higher profits gained), although this carries the risk of ending up being a follower. As the market expands, the attractiveness of being first increases, until a certain point when the firm decides to enter (see also Grenadier (1996) for an application to the real estate industry). Undertaking an investment under uncertainty over future demand incurs the opportunity cost of investing prior to obtaining more information (McDonald and Siegel 1986); thus the strategic value of early investment must be compared with the investment cost plus the option value of waiting (Kulatilaka and Perotti 1998*a*). However, the approach in this chapter is more complex because of the cross effects of demand due to related products. We show that depending on the degree of strategic advantage that the platform offers, the innovator decides between two different entry strategies. If the difference between the investment costs is not large, the platform firm enters just before the competitor would, inducing him to postpone its cross-entry. In this case we say that the platform firm 'owns' the option to enter as leader over a certain range of demand levels, but it is forced to exercise it before its optimal timing in order to pre-empt its competitor. If the investment cost difference is relevant, the platform firm knows that the traditional firm would not cross-enter as leader because the period of time in which it can have a leader position is not long enough to compensate for its high-investment cost. In this case the platform firm has a de facto 'monopoly' on the option to enter, in the sense that it can wait until its optimal entry timing without fearing pre-emption. Its optimal entry timing then trades off the value of the waiting-to-invest option against the higher profits from cross-entry.

In the comparative statics we focus on the effects of uncertainty (which produces the greatest difference between option- and NPV-based models of valuation). The effect of uncertainty on the strategic advantage and thus of the platform value is ambiguous, depending on which of two elements prevails: the higher the uncertainty, the higher the value to wait, but at the same time the higher the expected profits in case of immediate cross-entry. This last effect is due to two factors. First, high uncertainty increases the value of the strategic entry option more than the option value of not investing. As in Kulatilaka and Perotti (1998*a*), this is because in an oligopolistic market structure prices increase with demand; therefore, profits are endogenously convex in demand as the firm raises its margin. Because of this convexity, a mean-preserving increase in uncertainty favours investment in the strategic growth option over the waiting option.[5] Second, uncertainty increases the

---

[5] This result cannot be directly compared to the apparently contrary implications for the relative value of the waiting-to-invest option (McDonald and Siegel 1986). In the context of imperfect competition, investment has an impact on market structure and marginal profitability (Grenadier 1996; Kulatilaka and Perotti 1998), creating

time period in which the firm acts as monopolist in the entry decisions without facing any risk of entry by the competitor. Overall, the general result is unambiguous: greater uncertainty increases the strategic advantage of the platform and increases the value of the platform relative to traditional investment. Also, in absolute terms we show that the higher is uncertainty, the higher is the platform value.

Section 12.2 presents the market equilibrium under Cournot competition.[6] In Section 12.3, we describe the entry strategies of the platform firm and its competitor, and presents the main results (for the complete description, see Perotti and Rossetto (2001)). Section 12.4 describes the impact of volatility on the value of the platform. In Section 12.5 we solve the *ex ante* game finding the optimal strategy to acquire the platform. We offer at the end some concluding thoughts and ideas for further work.

12.2. THE BASIC MODEL

We consider two firms i and j competing in real time. The first is an incumbent which has invested in a traditional, specialized investment; the other one, the innovator, considers the possibility of investing in a platform infrastructure. While a platform may cover several market segments, we set this number to two for simplicity, to obtain a lower bound valuation for a platform vis-à-vis a traditional producer. More generally a platform may grant entry options into multiple market segments.

We assume that firms have complete information about the market and cost structures.[7] We also assume that there are only two differentiated products, indexed by 1 and 2. The inverse market demand functions for the two products are:

$$p_1 = \gamma - (q_{1i} + q_{1j}) - a(q_{2i} + q_{2j}), \qquad (12.1)$$

$$p_2 = \gamma - a(q_{1i} + q_{1j}) - (q_{2i} + q_{2j}). \qquad (12.2)$$

Note that the two products are partial strategic substitutes; the parameter a represents the intensity of substitution, and ranges from 0 (no substitutability) to 1 (identical products). Specialized entry into any market requires the investment of an amount I; investment in a platform costs K. In addition, a platform firm would pay I_P as the incremental investment to enter any market segment, with $I_P < I < I_P + K$. Thus there is an extra cost to build a platform, but this allows easier cross-entry thereafter.[8] Firms that compete in the same market engage in Cournot competition. When each firm produces a differentiated product, they act as monopolists in their own market, though their margins are influenced by the substitution effect between products.

---

a strong incentive for early investment, while in the traditional literature on real options the underlying market is not affected by the investment.

[6] Price competition does not result in an interesting issue since in this case neither a platform firm nor a traditional firm ever cross-enters into each other's market segment, so the platform has no value.

[7] One example of strategic entry under imperfect information is analysed in Lambrecht and Perraudin (1999).

[8] This assumption sets our analysis apart from most of the literature on strategic entry such as Smets (1991), Dixit (1980), and Huisman and Kort (1999).

The intercept of the demand function, γ, represents the size of market demand. Demand size is uncertain and evolves stochastically over time. We assume that it follows a Geometric Brownian Motion:

$$\frac{d\gamma}{\gamma} = \frac{1}{2}\left(\mu - \frac{1}{2}\sigma^2\right) dt + \frac{1}{2}\sigma \, dz. \tag{12.3}$$

In the specification, σ appears as a parameter both in the volatility and in the drift term of the demand process, in order to isolate the effect of demand uncertainty from its drift. In comparative statistic we will carry out a mean-preserving-spread analysis in the style of Rotschild and Stiglitz (1970). To this end, we define $\alpha = (2\mu - \sigma^2/2)$, so that we can rewrite the market process (12.3), as:

$$\frac{d\gamma}{\gamma} = \tfrac{1}{2}\alpha \, dt + \tfrac{1}{2}\sqrt{2(\mu - \alpha)} \, dz. \tag{12.4}$$

This formulation allows us to perform a mean preserving spread on the distribution of demand by varying its demand volatility while adjusting the drift, so that there is no change in expected demand. Oligopolistic profits under Cournot competition are convex in demand. We thus define $\gamma^2 \equiv \theta$. We can express the evolution of θ through Ito's Lemma as a Geometric Brownian motion:

$$\frac{d\theta}{\theta} = \mu \, dt + \sigma \, dz. \tag{12.5}$$

We see later that θ is linearly related to firm profits, and σ is closely related to their volatility. To ensure finite valuations, we assume that $\mu < r$, where r is the discount factor. We also assume that $\alpha < \mu(<r)$ to ensure $\sigma^2 > 0$.

We first evaluate the value of a 'platform' firm and then compare it with the value of the traditional firm.[9]

12.2.1. *Product Market Interactions*

Initially the platform firm operates in a different product segment from the competitor. This leads to a parallel differentiated monopoly. The associated profit flow is:

$$\prod_t = \frac{1}{(a+2)^2}\theta_t \equiv M\theta_t, \tag{12.6}$$

and its associated valuation of the revenues is:

$$E\left[\int_0^\infty M\theta_t e^{-rt} \, dt\right] = \frac{M}{r-\mu}\theta_t. \tag{12.7}$$

This is the discounted stream of expected profits when the underlying expected profit growth is equal to μ and there is no change in market structure.

---

[9] As the market scope is just one dimensional, the platform will cover only a line. A later version will consider a broader definition of a platform.

Both firms have the possibility to enter the competitor's market segment: for the traditional firm the cross entry will cost I, while for the platform firm the cost will be I_P (with $I_P < I$). If both firms cross-enter in each other's market (parallel duopoly), the profit flow and its expected present value are:

$$\prod_t = \frac{2}{9}\frac{1}{a+1}\theta_t \equiv D\theta_t, \tag{12.8}$$

$$E\left[\int_0^\infty D\theta_t e^{-rt}\,dt\right] = \frac{D}{r-\mu}\theta_t. \tag{12.9}$$

When a firm cross-enters as first (we term this situation an 'asymmetric duopoly'), the rival may prefer at first to wait to enter, if the waiting to invest option is more valuable than the higher profits from symmetric duopoly.[10] In this case the first firm to cross-enter enjoys higher asymmetric profits (being a monopolist in their own segment and a duopolist in the second). These extra profits are temporary: as demand increases the other firm will find it convenient to exercise the option to enter, and the market outcome will be a parallel duopoly in both products. However, the option to enter first is clearly valuable. As we will see, this is one of the advantages of building a platform.

In a asymmetric duopoly one firm operates in both segments and the other in just one. The profit flow and its expected present value for the firm present in both markets are:

$$\prod_t = \frac{1}{36}\frac{13-5a}{1+a}\theta_t \equiv L\theta_t, \tag{12.10}$$

$$E\left[\int_0^\infty L\theta_t e^{-rt}\,dt\right] = \frac{L}{r-\mu}\theta_t, \tag{12.11}$$

while the other firm earns:

$$\prod_t = \tfrac{1}{9}\theta_t \equiv F\theta_t, \tag{12.12}$$

with an expected present value of the profit of:

$$E\left[\int_0^\infty F\theta_t e^{-rt}\,dt\right] = \frac{F}{r-\mu}\theta_t. \tag{12.13}$$

Note that these profits are equal to profits under Cournot competition, as the entrant produces less in its original market for the increased cross-effect.

Because $0 < a < 1$, a firm always prefers to be in both market segments if its competitor produces just in one, while it would prefer to be a monopolist in just one market than

---

[10] In a static framework, since profits are higher under parallel monopoly ($M > D$), both firms would prefer to maintain a collusive arrangement avoiding entry under a threat of an immediate cross-entry in case the competitor enters first. However, in our dynamic framework this is not credible.

being a duopolist in both.[11] However, the option to cross-enter first grants temporarily higher returns. This can be summarized with the following relations: $F \leq D \leq M \leq L$.

Notice that since $0 < a < 1$, $L - M$ and $D - F$ are decreasing functions of a. Moreover, $L - M < D - F$: the profit increment as a result of cross-entry is never larger than the profit increment of a follower cross-entrant. Another result is that $M < L - M$: entering the second market leads to less than double monopoly profits. Finally $L - M - F < 0$: entering as leader leads to an increase in profits lower than the profits of the follower and remains in only one market.

12.3. THE DYNAMIC GAME

In this section, we study the cross-entry strategy of the platform and the traditional firm, when both firms are already operating in a different segment. Later, in Section 12.5, we go backward to analyse the acquisition strategy of the platform, and to evaluate it.

12.3.1. *The Timing of Entry*

In order to evaluate the platform firm, we first analyse the optimal entry strategies of the two firms. We can then compute the value of the platform and of the traditional firm.

For low levels of demand, there is no incentive for immediate cross entry into the other product, so both firms remain as monopolists in their own market segment (although their profits are influenced by substitution between products).

However, as demand rises, the attractiveness of entry into the second segment increases. Since the innovating firm controls a platform, it can enter the first product with a lower incremental cost than the traditional producer. Intuitively, it will have a lower threshold for entry.

Our approach to solve the game follows Smets (1991) and Grenadier (1996), in which in a symmetric duopoly a firm would enter as soon as he prefers to be a leader rather than a follower.

In such an entry game with symmetric firms, there is an ambiguity as to which firm will enter first. In our case, due to the different investment costs, the platform firm enjoys a period of monopoly on the choice to cross-enter as leader, since it knows that the traditional firm would not yet find it profitable to enter. In this period of a 'monopoly on the option to enter as leader', the innovator exercises optimally this entry option as leader by comparing the value of waiting to enter (and thus avoiding losses) to the higher profits after entry. Note the analogy in this case with the classic 'monopolistic' real option of McDonald and Siegel (1986). A difference here is that entry affects prices and market shares.

The pay-off to the platform firm of being a leader relative to being a follower, given the lower investment costs, is always higher than this pay-off for the traditional firm.

---

[11] Under some parameter values, this creates a sort of prisoner's dilemma in entry strategy. Firms would like to be able to mutually commit not to enter each other's market, but such a commitment is not credible: there is a temptation to enter.

Hence, on one side, the platform firm prefers to be a leader rather than a follower more than the traditional firm. On the other side, the traditional firm will always be a follower in the entry game. As a result, the platform firm enjoys, for a certain time interval, a monopoly on the option to enter as leader, knowing that the competitor will not move first. This is the crucial strategic entry advantage for the platform firm.

The time structure of the game is sketched in Fig. 12.1.

12.3.2. Results

We show that platform investment may lead to three different equilibria which we term: strong strategic advantage with entry, strong strategic advantage with no entry, weak strategic advantage. Weak strategic advantage obtains when the investment cost difference (i.e. the strategic advantage gained by the platform investment) is not large. The platform firm faces a cross-entry threat from the traditional firm before its optimal cross-entry timing (i.e. the entry point if it had a monopoly on the entry option). Hence, the platform firm enters just before the traditional firm would enter, but still much earlier than it would like. Before this entry point, the platform firm can still keep its option to wait because the threat of the competitor's cross-entry is not credible.

When, for the traditional firm, it becomes optimal to cross-enter, the platform firm will enter pre-emptively since it prefers to be a leader rather than a follower. Hence, when the platform firm has a weak strategic advantage, the innovator firm is forced to enter early to pre-empt its competitor.

When the investment cost difference is large enough and uncertainty is low, the equilibrium is of the form of strong strategic advantage with entry. Here the platform firm has the option to behave as a monopolist on the cross-entry option. Since the investment cost difference is large, the traditional entry firm has no incentive ever to cross-enter as leader because the platform would subsequently cross-enter so early that it is not able to recover the entry cost. Thus, the platform firm enjoys a de facto monopoly on the entry-as-leader option, and it can decide if and when to exercise it. In some case it will choose not to exercise it at all, which allows it to preclude any cross-entry and to support a parallel monopoly (strong strategic advantage without entry). The platform firm will choose to cross enter exactly when the expected profits of cross entering are higher than the wait-to-cross-enter option. When the strategic advantage is strong enough, there exists a demand threshold value such that it is optimal to exercise the option. At this point in time the profits of temporary asymmetric duopoly profits plus the subsequent parallel duopoly profits are higher than the waiting-to-cross-enter option.

When instead the investment cost difference is high (so that the platform has a strong strategic advantage), but not enough to fall into the above case, it will choose not to enter: the threshold value, such that it is optimal to exercise the option, does not exist because the waiting-to-cross-enter option is always more valuable than the expected profits from cross-entering. Hence, though the platform firm can still de facto behave as a monopolist, it never has an incentive to invest in the other market because the expected profits would be lower than in the case of parallel monopoly. The platform can here be seen as a tool

0

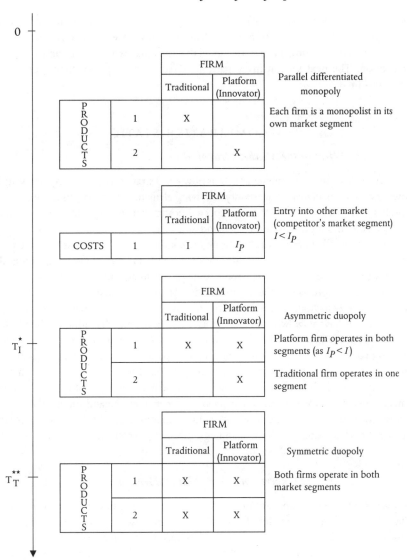

Figure 12.1. *Timing of entry.*

to avoid aggressive cross-entry, an equilibrium less desirable in some cases than parallel monopoly.

A general conclusion is that the results from the real option approach to investment do not apply trivially to circumstances of imperfect competition. When firms do not have a monopoly on the option to enter, they cannot time the entry choice of their competitors except when they have acquired their option to invest by gaining a significant entry advantage. In the next section, we study a second claim of real option literature, namely that higher uncertainty induces firms to delay new investment. Kulatilaka and Perotti (1998*a*) have already shown in a static model that the effect is ambiguous under imperfect competition. The next section investigates its effect on the optimal timing of entry in continuous time.

12.4. COMPARATIVE STATICS

12.4.1. *The Effect of the Market Growth Rate*

The interesting comparative statics concerns how entry strategy is affected by changing the growth rate and the demand uncertainty. A driving element of this analysis is the convexity of profits in demand. Because of that, expected profits increase more than proportionally to an increase in the growth rate of demand and increase with demand uncertainty. The most interesting effect of the drift term is on the conditions that distinguish between weak strategic advantage and strong strategic advantage, with and without entry. A higher drift increases the parameter space for strong strategic advantage, under which the platform firm can behave more as a de facto monopolist. At the same time, a higher drift favours less aggressive behaviour of the platform, in the sense that it increases the chance of strong strategic advantage without entry: this is due to the fact that a higher drift induces a shorter period where the platform could enjoy asymmetric profits before subsequent entry. In practice this means that in some sectors experiencing rapid expansion a platform firm would avoid cross-entry to limit direct competition. The implications of a higher drift on the critical levels for cross-entry are quite intuitive in the case of both strong and weak strategic advantage. More positive expectations for market demand induce the follower to cross-enter at lower demand levels. As a direct consequence of this, the platform firm, whether it enjoys a strong or a weak strategic advantage, enters at a lower demand level.

12.4.2. *The Effect of Uncertainty Over Market Demand*

We investigate here the impact of demand uncertainty on the timing of entry and on the value of the platform at the point of entry. Note that because of the convexity of profits in demand, expected profits increase with demand uncertainty. This higher uncertainty may encourage entry as it offers a 'more' convex pay-off from the capture of market share in the other segment, whose expected value increases with volatility. However, the value of the waiting to invest option also increases with uncertainty.[12] Uncertainty also affects the competitor entry behaviour. As we have shown, whatever the strategic advantage of the platform firm, for higher uncertainty levels the follower decides to cross-enter at higher demand values. However, because of higher volatility, this point is reached sooner and so the expected time of cross-entering of the follower is ultimately shorter (Harrison 1985).

---

[12] We do not analyse the effect of an increased risk premium as systematic risk increases, which reduces the value of entry relative to waiting to enter (Kulatilaka and Perotti 1998).

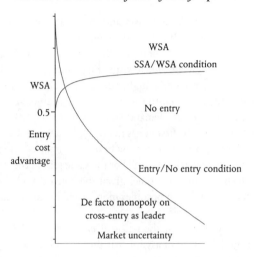

Figure 12.2. *Conditions on the type of entry.*

We analyse first the impact of uncertainty on the investment cost condition which distinguishes between strong (with and without entry) and weak strategic advantage. We next analyse its impact on the expected profits in case of strong strategic advantage with entry, with no entry, and in the case of weak strategic advantage. Later we examine the value of the platform investment and the impact of uncertainty. Figure 12.2 shows how the conditions that determine the three equilibria change with respect to uncertainty. *Ceteris paribus*, an increase in uncertainty increases the range of parameters under which the platform investment leads to strong strategic advantage. This is because the value of cross-entry as leader for the traditional firm declines, as it would enjoy a shorter period of asymmetric profits before the subsequent cross-entry by the platform firm.[13,14] Thus, in these cases, greater uncertainty enhances the strategic advantage and the value of the platform.

Under strong strategic advantage, the higher is demand uncertainty, the more the no-entry case is attractive: the gain for the platform firm to cross-enter is lower than the value of a parallel monopoly. While there is no risk that the traditional firm would enter as leader, for higher uncertainty the platform firm as follower would enter at higher demand levels. However, higher uncertainty reduces the expected time to reach the optimal demand level, thus it reduces the period in which the traditional firm would enjoy the asymmetric profits up to the point where it is no longer optimal for it to cross-enter. For the same reasoning, the period in which it could enjoy asymmetric duopoly profits is too short, and for the platform firm it is not attractive to cross-enter. Higher uncertainty induces a later

---

[13] The period of higher profits for the platform firm is longer, as its competitor has a higher entry cost.

[14] The only values of the investment ratio for which there can be a switch between strong and weak strategic advantage are between 0.44 and 0.63; for an investment cost ratio higher than 0.63 the platform firm has a weak strategic advantage; otherwise it enjoys a strong strategic advantage.

cross-entry point for both the platform firm and the traditional firm, but as uncertainty reduces the expected time to reach certain demand levels, the overall effect is such that the platform firm may now prefer no-entry parallel monopoly to direct competition.

In the case of strong strategic advantage with entry, an increase in demand uncertainty induces a platform firm to cross-enter at higher demand levels. Here the comparative static effect of greater uncertainty is similar to the case of the traditional real option theory: the higher is uncertainty, the higher the demand level at which the platform firm cross-enters. This happens for two reasons. The first one is in line with classic real option theory: higher uncertainty induces the platform firm to cross enter at higher demand levels in order to avoid the risk of losses due to weak demand. For the same reason the traditional firm waits for better demand levels. At the same time, given the convexity of the post-entry extra-profits, waiting for the platform firm becomes more attractive than immediate asymmetric profits at low market demand levels.

The value of the platform firm at the point of entry reflects the present value of the expected profits during the period of asymmetric profits plus those during the subsequent period of parallel monopoly. Both these expected profits increase with market uncertainty. Hence as higher uncertainty induces an increase of the underlying entry pay-off and an increase in option value (holding constant the pay-off), we can conclude that the platform firm value at the point of entry increases for higher uncertainty values (see Fig. 12.3). Under strong strategic advantage with no entry, the platform value is given by the present value of the profit in parallel monopoly: $M/(r - \mu)$. As an increase in uncertainty determines an increase in μ, for the mean-preserving logic we have that the higher is uncertainty, the higher is platform value.

Under weak strategic advantage, a change in uncertainty can have either a positive or negative effect on the cross-entry threshold.

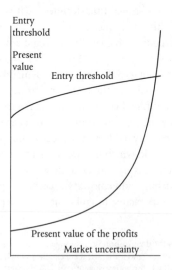

Figure 12.3. *Strong strategic advantage with entry.*

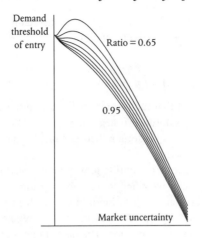

Figure 12.4. *Weak strategic advantage with entry.*

There are three elements that affect this decision. The higher the uncertainty, the higher is the option value to be a follower; at the same time, also, the pay-off to be a leader is higher (due to the endogenous convexity of the profits). The third element is the timing of the follower entry: the higher the uncertainty, the higher the entry threshold of the follower. In this case the total effect of uncertainty on the demand threshold of entry, and thus the present value of the profits of the platform firm, is not monotonic. In particular, the effect depends on the investment cost ratio, our measure of the strategic advantage gained by the platform investment. Recall that under weak strategic advantage, the timing of entry of the platform firm is exactly at the point of entry of the traditional firm as leader. When the strategic advantage is not very high, the cross-entry threshold of the traditional firm diminishes with demand uncertainty: thus, the higher the uncertainty, the earlier the platform firm is forced to enter pre-emptively. *Ceteris paribus*, because of the higher expected profit from entry (since the potential losses avoided by waiting to invest are less convex than the potential higher gains under entry), by Jensen's inequality a mean-preserving increase in uncertainty favours exercising the entry option over the waiting option.[15]

When instead the strategic advantage is higher, the total effect of uncertainty on entry behaviour is not monotonic. When uncertainty is low, as uncertainty increases the relative stability of the demand level induces the traditional firm to wait for higher demand levels. At a high-uncertainty level, the expected period of higher profits for the traditional firm increases and so it would enter at lower demand levels (see Fig. 12.4). This reasoning can also explain the non-monotonicity of the present value of the platform firm with respect to demand uncertainty: for low strategic advantage, higher uncertainty reduces firm value;

---

[15] This behaviour recalls the results in a static setting: higher profit convexity leads to a greater increase in the value of the entry option relative to the waiting to invest option (Kulatilaka and Perotti 1998).

but when the strategic advantage is high, for low uncertainty levels the present value increases, but decreases for very high uncertainty.

12.5. THE *EX ANTE* VALUE OF THE PLATFORM

Until now we have assumed that the incumbent has a traditional technology, while the platform is developed by an innovating firm at a higher cost. When would it be convenient for an innovative firm to build a platform rather than making a conventional entry? What is the *ex ante* value of a platform?

We first compute the value of the option to acquire the platform (i.e. the value of the underlying technology). Later we compute for which platform cost the innovative firm finds it optimal to buy the platform (i.e. the right to produce with the platform). Finally, we consider when it would start production in the first segment immediately, or wait for a later optimal time to start production. The demand level at which a new firm with a platform would enter the first market segment can be found following traditional real option theory, as the platform firm has the monopoly on the entry on the first market. This means computing the value of an American compound option and its exercise threshold. As the traditional firm is assumed to be the incumbent in one market segment, the platform firm will find it optimal to avoid direct competition and enter initially in the other market segment.[16] Going backwards in the game it is then possible to calculate the demand threshold to acquire a platform. For this we rule out the possibility that the traditional incumbent firm is capable of building the platform, and we assume that a platform can be built only by one firm.[17] If there are many firms with the opportunity to invest in the unique technology to build the platform, the option to acquire the platform will be exercised as soon as the expected profits rise above the investment cost.[18] At the point when the firm invests in the platform, it will not be necessary to choose to enter a market segment. When the costs to build a platform are low, the firm will tend to buy the platform early and wait for a higher demand level to enter the market segment. In particular, depending on the parameters, for example low drift, low uncertainty, high discount rate, low product differentiation, a new firm will invest in the platform and in the first product simultaneously; alternatively, the new firm will invest in the platform but not invest immediately in the first product, waiting instead for better market conditions.

In a highly volatile market, expected margins are high; the firm then prefers to guarantee for itself a strategic advantage by acquiring the platform. At the same time as it waits longer (i.e. for a better level of market demand) to become active in the market. The impact of

[16] Either in strong or weak strategic advantage the platform firm would never choose to enter first the same market segment as the incumbent. Subsequent cross-entry would be more attractive as the profit jump would be higher; however, this does not compensate for the lower profit flow during the first part of the game when the two firms compete in the same market.

[17] An additional argument is that an incumbent firm would not build a platform just to enter the second market, as traditional entry would be cheaper. In contrast, a new firm can use the platform to enter both segments, so it finds it convenient to acquire it for lower demand values than the incumbent firm.

[18] This is the perfect competition case, again different from the classical real option investment environment where the firm holds a monopoly on the investment opportunity.

uncertainty on the platform value is unambiguously positive. Qualitatively these results are the same either in strong and weak strategic advantage. Quantitatively in weak strategic advantage, the demand threshold is higher both to enter the first market segment and to buy the platform. More importantly, the condition on the investment costs of the platform that distinguishes between buying and entering in the same instant, or in two different moments, is more stringent under weak strategic advantage than under strong strategic advantage: the firm will tend to buy the platform and enter simultaneously more under a weak strategic advantage.

For the comparative statics, it can be shown that the higher is the uncertainty, the higher is the value of the platform. The demand is more volatile, the more it becomes attractive to secure control of the platform even without the immediate profits of the first product. At the same time, the platform acquisition will occur earlier.

12.6. CONCLUSION

We have considered a strategic logistic investment under dynamic uncertainty on future consumer demand. An innovative firm acquires a productive and distributive platform to gain entry advantages. We study the subsequent entry decision in specific products and compute the value of the option to wait to invest against the (temporarily) higher profits of immediate entry. We can rationalize a much greater value for platform firms relative to traditional producers, especially over market size.

Investing in a platform means acquiring a 'strategic cross-entry option', a concept related to the 'strategic growth option' (Kulatilaka and Perotti 1998a). On the other hand, platform investment involves absorbing significant demand uncertainty. Therefore, the value of not committing funds to platform investment increases with demand uncertainty. The most striking result we obtain is that in general, in a regime of higher volatility of demand, platform strategic advantage increases. In fact the platform firm may end up 'controlling' the entry options, and behaving more as a de facto monopolist. In our context, greater uncertainty means greater risk but also greater opportunities thanks to the early (cross-)entry advantage gained by acquiring the platform. Platform investment turns out to have several strategic effects. It may grant a competitive advantage to enter earlier into competitors' market segments; but it also eliminates the possibility of simultaneous entry and may help avoiding undesirable 'excessive' competition equilibria.

Our surprising results concerning the positive effect of uncertainty on the value of investment are driven by the oligopolistic market structure. Firms with market power respond to higher demand by increasing both output and prices; therefore, profits are endogenously convex in demand. High volatility gives more weight to potential high profits than to the possibility of suffering losses due to low demand. Since the potential losses avoided by waiting to invest are less convex than the potential gains from entry, more uncertainty (in the sense of a mean-preserving spread in demand) reduces the threshold of expected future demand at which the firm finds it attractive to enter, and increases the value of the entry option relative to the waiting to invest option. A current drawback is the very simplified notion of the platform we have adopted. In future research we wish to model both a multidimensional platform as well as the initial decision on the platform size.

296 *E. Perotti and S. Rossetto*

Moreover, a broader platform may allow entrance in unrelated market segments without cross-effects. In the case of Internet web sites, the analysis of a horizontal portal implies a greater dimensionality of the set of strategic entry options and thus a correspondingly higher value for a platform firm relative to a traditional producer. We plan to develop a more specific interpretation for Internet portals in future work.

Intuitively, the optimal platform size (which is related to the potential range of differentiated products) depends on the fact that the greater is the initial differentiation, the weaker are the cross-price effects. The firm in charge of the platform may become dominant in some products as later innovators face either higher entry costs or a time disadvantage relative to the platform-owner, and may choose therefore a more limited range of entry among products. The outcome of this decision is not trivial, as it depends on product features and expected market demand evolution.

References

Baldwin, C. Y. and Clark, K. B. (2000), *Design Rules: The Power of Modularity*, Cambridge, MA: MIT Press.

Dixit, A. (1980), 'The role of investment in entry deterrence', *Economic Journal* 90, 95–106.

Grenadier, S. R. (1996), 'The strategic exercise of options: development cascades and overbuilding in real estate markets', *Journal of Finance* 51, 1653–79.

Harrison, J. M. (1985), *Brownian Motion and Stochastic Flow Systems*, New York: John Wiley and Sons.

Huisman, K. J. and Kort, P. M. (1999), 'Effects of strategic interactions on the option value of waiting', Discussion Paper, Center Tilburg University.

Khanna, N. and Tice, S. (2000), 'Strategic response of incumbents to new entry: the effect of ownership structure, capital structure, and focus', *Review of Financial Studies* 13, 749–79.

Klemperer, P. (1995), 'Competition when consumers have switching costs: an overview with applications to industrial organization, macroeconomics, and international trade', *Review of Economic Studies* 62, 515–39.

Kogut, B. and Kulatilaka, N. (1994), 'Options thinking and platform investment: investing in opportunity', *California Management Review* 36, 52–71.

Kulatilaka, N. and Perotti, E. (1998a), 'Strategic Growth Options', *Management Science* 44, 1021–31.

—— and —— (1998b), 'Time-to-market capability as Stackelberg growth option', in *Innovation and Strategy: New Developments and Applications in Real Options*, Oxford: Oxford University Press.

Lambrecht, B. M. and Perraudin, W. (1997), 'Real option and preemption', Working paper, Judge Institute, Cambridge University.

—— and —— (1999), 'Real options and pre-emption under incomplete information', Working paper, Judge Institute, Cambridge University.

McDonald, R. and Siegel, D. (1986), 'The value of waiting to invest', *Quarterly Journal of Economics* 101, 707–28.

Perotti, E. and Rossetto, S. (2001), 'Strategic advantage and the optimal exercise of entry options', Discussion Paper 3061, CEPR, London.

Rotschild, M. and Stiglitz, J. (1970), 'Increasing risk I: A definition', *Journal of Economic Theory* 2, 225–43.

Smets, F. (1991), 'Exporting versus FDI: the effect of uncertainty, irreversibilities and strategic interactions', Discussion paper, Yale University.

13

The Dotcom Premium: Rational Valuation or Irrational Exuberance?

MICHAEL COOPER AND P. RAGHAVENDRA RAU

13.1. INTRODUCTION

How do you value a high-tech firm? This question is important, given the extreme run-up in prices for high-tech firms in the latter half of the previous decade, in particular for Internet firms. In the first quarter of 2000, Internet firms alone formed over 5 per cent of the market capitalization of all US public companies. Was this an irrational bubble or due to rational expectations of extremely high future growth rates for high-tech and Internet companies? This has been a matter of some controversy in the academic literature.

Several studies (Demers and Lev 2001; Hand 2003, 2001; Core *et al.* 2003) have focused on whether investors were using rational valuation models to value Internet firms. These authors regress Internet-specific variables (usually related to web traffic) on a market value measure, after controlling for economic fundamental variables. They find that web traffic measures have additional explanatory power beyond traditional measures of firm growth. Specifically, web stickiness and the number of unique visitors both play important roles. However, typical fundamentals are also important in valuing these firms and moreover, the relationship does not disappear after the Internet crash in March 2000. Schwartz and Moon (2000) argue, in addition, that high-tech and Internet firms should not be valued using standard valuation models since these models neglect the strategic/real options available to these firms.

In contrast, there is an increasing body of literature documenting investor irrationality at both the firm and industry level. Rashes (2001) examines the co-movement of MCI and MCIC, stocks with similar ticker symbols. He finds a significant correlation between returns, volume, and volatility at short frequencies. Arbitrageurs appear to be limited in their ability to eliminate these deviations from fundamentals. Huberman and Regev (2001) document that a *New York Times* article on the development of new cancer-curing drugs by EntreMed caused EntreMed's stock price to quadruple over one day. The potential breakthrough in cancer research already had been reported, however, in the journal *Nature*, and in various popular newspapers several months earlier. Enthusiastic public attention seemed to induce a permanent rise in share prices, even though no genuinely new information had been presented.

Was the rise in prices in high-tech and especially Internet firms an example of such investor irrationality? There are many famous examples of what we now believe to have been manias, or speculative bubbles in asset prices. For example, Mackay (1841) documents bubbles across time and in different markets, ranging from the Dutch tulip bulb craze in the 1630s to the South Sea Bubble in the 1710s. More recently, Sobel (1965) reports similar manias in the USA in the 1850s with railroad and mining stocks and in the 1960s with science and technology stocks. The common feature in all these manias appears to be that the industries are new 'glamour' industries with both an enormous growth potential and uncertainty. Consequently, investors appear to be extremely anxious to buy shares of any firms that are involved in these industries. Investors may even be frantic to buy shares in firms that are at best only loosely, if at all, connected to the current glamour industry.

One way to distinguish between the rational valuation explanation and the irrational exuberance explanation is to examine firms that investors perceive as new firms in the glamour industry, though there is no accompanying change in cash flows. One such set of firms are firms that announce cosmetic name changes without any change in their underlying cash flows.

This kind of name change behaviour appears to be relatively common in 'glamour' industries. For example, there was an incredible growth in stock prices for firms in the railroad and mining industries in the 1850s; the automobile industry in the 1910s; airplane firms in the late 1920s; the high-tech industry in the 1960s; bio-genetic firms in the 1980s; and in more recent times, the dotcom firms of the late 1990s. In all of these growth periods, investors appeared extremely interested in 'getting a piece of the action', often times at the expense of due diligence. For instance, during the airplane 'craze', investors rushed to purchase shares of Seaboard Airlines, which turned out to be a renamed railroad stock (Gordon 2001).

Previous papers on the effect of name changes (Bosch and Hirschey 1989; Karpoff and Rankine 1994) have concluded that there is little effect from unconditional corporate name changes on firm value, an unsurprising result given that the underlying cash flows to the firms have not changed.

In this chapter, we report the effects on individual firm stock prices of one special type of name change—that of companies that change their name to a dotcom name during the Internet boom period of 1998 and 1999. This research, originally appearing in Cooper *et al.* (2001), documents that Internet firms which simply add a '.com' to their names earned significant abnormal returns on the order of 53 per cent for the five days around the announcement date. Cooper *et al.* argue that their results are driven by a degree of investor mania—investors were eager to be associated with the Internet at all costs during the 1998 and 1999 run-up. They find that the announcement period returns are similar across all firms, regardless of the firms' true level of involvement with the Internet. Thus, Cooper *et al.* provide strong evidence that conditional name changes have a profound effect on firm value, lending support to the irrational exuberance explanation of the Internet bubble.

The remaining sections of this chapter are organized as follows. In Section 13.2, we provide some background on the initial study of Cooper *et al.* (2001). In Section 13.3, we discuss the unique data used in the study. In Section 13.4, we discuss their event study to examine the effects on shareholder wealth to firms that add a dotcom to their name. We also analyse a number of determinants of the abnormal returns, including a firm's level of involvement with the Internet, the impact on shareholder wealth of major versus minor name changes, and the role of volume in increasing returns after the name change. Finally, in Section 13.5, we conclude.

13.2. WARNING SIGNS OF A BUBBLE ABOUT TO BURST: SOME ANECDOTAL EVIDENCE

During the month of November 1999, we wrote the following in Cooper *et al.* (2001) concerning our finding of large increases in stock prices following firms adding a dotcom to their names:

At this point in time, we cannot know with any degree of certainty if the increase in firm value for the dotcom firms is rational, perhaps due to investor expectations of large future payoffs to such firms, or if it is simply a speculative bubble that may deflate in the future. However, the fact that we see firms, which derive apparently little or none of their revenue from the Internet experiencing large dotcom effects, suggests some degree of investor irrationality.

Speculative bubbles are, of course, only known to be speculative based on *ex post* knowledge, but this real-time quote certainly illustrates a predilection towards forecasting a future crash of Internet stocks. Were we in an Internet bubble at the time? Perhaps one of the clearest signs of the obsessive focus of investors on Internet firms was the rabid degree of media attention our paper was subject to following the publication in the *New York Times* of an article reporting the results of Cooper *et al*. On 15 August 1999, an approximately half-page article summarizing our research was published in Marc Hulbert's regular *Sunday NY Times* business-section column. On the following Monday morning, we were inundated with inquires from the press. The intensity and number of inquiries was absolutely overwhelming. We received hundreds of phone calls and e-mails (this despite the fact that an incorrect web address was published for us in the *NY Times* article). By Monday night we had already been interviewed by countless sources, and crews were flying in to our location to film TV interviews on Tuesday. By the end of the week, the results of our study had appeared in hundreds of newspaper articles, and we had TV interviews on CNBC and NBC, radio interviews on NPR, and many other sources. Though this certainly was not the first time that an academic paper has received popular press interest, what struck us as obsessive was the intensity of the interest; there were even reports of an Oregon town that legally changed its name from Halfway to Half.com town (Kane 2000). We had inquiries from at least one company that added a dotcom to its name as a direct result of our research.

13.3. DATA AND METHODOLOGY

Our sample consists of all publicly traded companies on the NYSE, Amex, Nasdaq, and the OTC Bulletin Board (OTCBB) that changed their names between June 1, 1998 and

Table 13.1. *Sample description*

Initial number of firms in sample	147
Deleted due to mergers and acquisitions	37
Deleted due to new stock issuance, uncertain event date, spin-offs, going private before name change	15
Total number of remaining firms	95

	First of either effective or announcement dates
Total remaining firms after deletions	95
Category 1: Pure Internet Companies	29
Category 2: Companies which have some prior involvement in the Internet and change their names to 'better' reflect this involvement	31
Category 3: Companies which change their focus completely from non-Internet to Internet	25
Category 4: Companies whose core business is not Internet-related	10

This table describes the sample of companies that changed their name to dotcom names between June 1998 and July 1999. Firms are divided into subcategories based on their level of involvement with the Internet. The categories are Category 1: Pure Internet companies; Category 2: Companies which have some prior involvement in the Internet and change their name to 'better' reflect this involvement; Category 3: Companies which change their focus completely from non-Internet to Internet; Category 4: Companies whose core business is not Internet-related. Because of the difficulty in obtaining exact announcement dates, the announcement day (day zero) is defined as the first available information on the name change, whether from an announcement or effective trading day.

July 31, 1999.[1] The new name has to be either a dotcom name (e.g. Wareforce.com), a dotnet name (e.g. Docplus.net Corporation), or has to include the word Internet in it (e.g. Internet Solutions for Business Inc.) As reported in Table 13.1, this results in an initial sample of 147 firms, only one of which, Speedus.com Inc, is listed on NASDAQ. The remaining firms are listed on the NASDAQ OTC Bulletin Board. We exclude stocks that experience a contaminating news event such as a merger, issuance of stock, earning announcement, etc. during the event window period.

Since these are mostly extremely small capitalization companies, it is difficult to obtain current stock price information and company profiles from traditional academic sources such as CRSP, Compustat, etc. Most of our sources of information on these companies are from the Internet. The appendix reports the data sources utilized in our study.

We use published company profiles, SEC filings, and contemporaneous news releases, as well as the company homepages, to classify the firms in our sample into four major

---

[1] We search for name changes in websites such as http://www.otcbb.com/dynamic/; http://www.nasdaq.com/; or http://www.nyse.com/. See the Appendix for a complete listing of data sources.

categories. We use these categories to determine what types of firms are most affected by name changes and why. These categories are:

1. Pure Internet companies, which do all their business on the Internet;
2. Companies that have some prior involvement with the Internet and change their names to better reflect this involvement;
3. Companies that change their focus from non-Internet related businesses to Internet-related; and
4. Companies whose core business is not Internet-related.

The number of firms under each category is listed in Table 13.1.

In many cases, we do not have information on the actual announcement date, or the earliest announcement we find coincides with the effective date[2] (the date when the firm actually started trading on the exchange under a different name).[3] In these cases, we also examine SEC records for name change filings. The SEC requires firms to file a form 8K when a company changes its name. However, the SEC does not currently punish firms that do not file. In fact, when we examined 8K forms, we could only find three firms in our sample that had filed with the SEC.[4] Because of this difficulty in obtaining exact announcement dates for many of the firms in our sample, we define the announcement day (day zero) as the first available information on the name change, whether from an announcement or effective trading day.[5] To the extent that the actual announcement day is before the date we use as our event date in our sample, our tests are biased towards accepting the null hypothesis of no abnormal returns in the event windows.

Stock price data for individual firms are collected from three independent sources: Financialweb.com, Bloomberg, and Dow Jones Interactive. Stock prices and volumes are adjusted for stock splits. Interestingly, one of our three data sources, Financialweb.com, belongs to our sample. We collect price and volume data for the 151-day period from $t = -30$ to $t = +120$ for the sample of 95 firms.

We then compute abnormal returns in two ways. First, we compute abnormal returns relative to a price-matched control group of firms selected from all OTCBB Internet firms that did not change their name between June 1998 and August 1999. Specifically, we identify, using the OTCBB website, Bloomberg company profiles, and firm names and

---

[2] The OTCBB requires that firms should provide notification of a name change in a letter sent prior to the effective date (there is no rule on the minimum amount of time prior to the effective date). It then includes all known name changes in the daily list at least one trading day before the effective change date specified in the letter. If a firm has already changed its name effectively, they include the new name of that firm as soon as possible. These daily lists are distributed to market makers before the effective dates so that they can adjust their records. The effective name change is usually the next trading day. Thus, there are 2–5 days between the time the letter with all pertinent information is received and the effective date, which is published on the OTCBB website.

[3] The announcement dates were taken from the earliest newswire information releases regarding these changes. The sources of these releases are listed in the Appendix.

[4] The OTCBB introduced a new rule in January 1999, which states that companies that are delinquent in filing appropriate documents with the SEC will be de-listed. However, there appears to be a transition period until this rule comes into force and, thus, most of our sample has not complied with filing the 8K forms.

[5] We also analyse the sample of firms for which we are able to identify announcement dates. In addition, we analyse firms for which day zero is defined as the effective date and firms for which day zero is defined as the effective date for firms with announcement dates. The results are qualitatively similar.

Table 13.2. *Name changes to dotcom firm*

Old name	Old ticker	New name	New ticker	Date of change	Minor ticker/ name change
AFFILIATED ADJUSTERS INC	AFAJ	DOT COM ENTERTAINMENT GROUP INC	DCEG	8-Feb-99	
ALL AMERICAN CONSULTANT AIRCRAFT INC	AACA	MARKETCENTRAL.NET CORP	MKTS	3-Mar-99	
ALLIANCE TECHNOLOGIES INC	ALTL	STEREOSCAPE.COM INC	SSCP	11-Feb-99	
ALTERNATIVE ENTERTAINMENT INC	BOYS	BOYSTOYS.COM INC	GRLZ	4-Jan-99	
AMERICAN ALLIANCE CORP	AMRE	WHATSONLINE.COM	WHAT	20-May-99	
AMERICAN INDUSTRIAL MINERALS GP	AIMG	NETWORTHUSA.COM	EBUX	6-Apr-99	
AMERICAN REALTY MGMT SVCS CORP	AMRO	BIB.NET CORP	BIBN	15-Jun-99	
APC TELECOMMUNICATIONS	APCI	INNOFONE.COM	INNF	25-Mar-99	
ASIA MEDIA COMMUNICATIONS	ASMC	MYWEB.COM	MYWB	28-Apr-99	
ATLANTA TECHNOLOGY GROUP INC	ATYG	DOCPLUS.NET CORPORATION	ATYG	21-Jan-99	•/
AUCTION TELEVISION NETWORK INC	ATVW	BIDNOW.COM INC	BIDN	3-Feb-99	
AUSTIN UNDERGROUND INC	AUUG	SALEOUTLET.COM	SLET	5-Mar-99	
AUTO NETWORK GP	ANWK	AUTO TRADECENTER.COM	AUTC	7-May-99	
AXXESS INC	AXXS	FINANCIALWEB.COM INC	FWEB	6-Jan-99	
BORAXX TECHNOLOGIES	BRXX	QUAD X SPORTS.COM	QXXX	13-Mar-99	
BRIDGEPORT COMMUNICATIONS	BPOT	WEALTHHOUND.COM	WLTH	22-Jul-99	
BUFFALO CAPITAL VI	BUFJ	ISOLVER.COM	ISLV	7-Jun-99	
BUFFALO CAPITAL VII	BUFK	WORKFIRE.COM	WKFR	11-Jun-99	
CARV INDUSTRIES INC	CARV	CARV.COM INC	CARVD	14-Dec-98	•/•
CELLULAR VISION	CVUS	SPEEDUS.COM INC	SPDE	5-Jan-99	
CENTAUR TECHNOLOGIES	CJAZ	TRADERALERT.COM	TTOP	20-May-99	
CHOPP COMPUTER CORPORATION	CHPP	ANTS SOFTWARE.COM	ANTS	18-Feb-99	
COMGEN CORPORATION	CGEE	PLANET 411.COM CORPORATION	PFOO	16-Feb-99	
COURTLEIGH CAPITAL INC	CTLH	STOCKUP.COM INC	SKUP	22-Feb-99	
DATA GROWTH INC	TFGI	PHOTOLOFT.COM GROUP INC	LOFT	26-Feb-99	
EDUVERSE ACCELERATED LEARNING SYSTEMS	EDUV	EDUVERSE.COM	EDUV	11-Jun-99	•/•
EJH ENTERTAINMENT	TIXXD	FINDEX.COM	FIND	7-May-99	
EQUITY GROWTH SYSTEMS	ETSY	AMERINET GROUP.COM	ABUY	21-Jul-99	
FIELDCREST CORPORATION	FLCR	SOFTLOCK.COM INC	SLCK	10-Aug-98	
FINELINE PRPTS	FNLN	FINELINE PROPERTIES.COM	FNLND	7-May-99	•/•

Table 13.2. *Continued*

Old name	Old ticker	New name	New ticker	Date of change	Minor ticker/ name change
FLORIDA DIET SERVICES	FLDT	WWW.EBIZNET.COM INC	BIZN	8-Dec-98	
FLORIDA VENTURE FUND INC	FLVN	INFORMATION HIGHWAY.COM INC	IHWY	24-Feb-99	
FOODQUEST INTERNATIONAL CORPORATION	FDQI	DEALCHECK.COM INC	DEAL	21-Jan-99	
FRONTIER FINANCIAL HOLDINGS	FDIR	EVISION USA.COM	EVIS	29-Apr-99	
GCST CORP	GCCT	RBID.COM	RBID	15-Apr-99	
GOLDEN PHARMACEUTICALS	GPHI	DOCSALES.COM	DOCP	12-Jul-99	
GOLF BALL WORLD	GBLL	QORUS.COM	QRUS	17-May-99	
HALO HOLDINGS OF NEVADA	HALO	A1 INTERNET.COM	AWON	21-May-99	
HEALTHY CHOICE	HYCH	IMAGIN.NET INC	ITOY	13-Nov-98	
HENLEY GP	HNLY	CIS.COM	CISI	27-May-99	
HHHP INC	HHHP	W COLLECT COM INC	WCLT	16-Feb-99	
HOME CARE AMERICA	HCAI	BIZROCKET.COM	BIZR	7-Jun-99	
HONOR ONE CORPORATION	HNRO	ALPHA TRADE.COM	EBNK	8-Jan-99	
IMN FINL CORP	IMNF	APPONLINE.COM	APLY	14-May-99	
INFO CENTER INTERNATIONAL INC	IFCR	BUDGETHOTELS.COM INC	BUDH	12-Mar-99	
INTERACTIVE PROCESSING INC	IAPI	WORLDTRADESHOW.COM	WTSW	16-Mar-99	
INTERNATIONAL BARTER CORP	IBCX	UBARTER.COM	UBCN	27-Apr-99	
INTERNATIONAL FOOD & BEVERAGE INC	IFDB	INTERNET BUSINESSES INTERNATIONAL INC	IBUI	2-Mar-99	
I-TECH HLDNGS GP	IHGP	STOCKGROUP.COM HLDNGS	SWEB	11-May-99	
JRL RESOURCES CORPORATION	JRLR	FIRST ECOM.COM INC	FECC	5-Mar-99	
LAL VENTURES CORP	LALV	CYBEROAD.COM CORP	FUNN	10-May-99	
LOTUS ENTERPRISES	LUTS	CLUBCHARLIE.COM	CLUC	21-May-99	
MAGIG LANTERN GP	MGIL	CASINOBUILDERS.COM	CSNO	20-May-99	
MDM VASCULAR SYSTEM INC	YBET	CASINOLIVE.COM CORPORATION	YBETD	17-Feb-99	
MICROCAP FINANCIAL SERVICES	MFSI	GLOBALNET FINANCIAL.COM	GLBN	14-Apr-99	
NDS SOFTWARE INC	NDSS	HOMESEEKERS.COM INC	HMSK	10-Jul-98	
NEROX ENERGY	NROXD	E*TWOMEDIA.COM	ETMD	18-Dec-98	
NEW GENERATION FOODS	NGNF	CREDITRISK MONITOR.COM	CRMZ	11-May-99	
NORTH AMERICAN NATURAL	NANR	PINKMONKEY.COM INC	PMKY	25-Jun-98	
NU MED SURGICAL	NMDS	NUTRICEUTICALS.COM CORPORATION	JCOM	12-Mar-99	
OKANE INTL ENTERPRISES	OKNI	SUPERWARE.COM	SUPW	30-Apr-99	
PALMER MEDICAL INC	PLMI	EDATENOW.COM INC	EDNC	8-Feb-99	
PANTHEON TECHNOLOGIES	PTTK	CANCEROPTION.COM	CAOP	10-May-99	

Table 13.2. *Continued*

Old name	Old ticker	New name	New ticker	Date of change	Minor ticker/ name change
PANTHER RESOURCES	PTHR	PHANTOMFILM.COM	PHLM	22-Jun-99	
PRIMESOURCE COMMUNICATIONS HLDNGS	PSCM	PRIMEHOLDINGS.COM	PRIM	28-Jul-99	
PROGRESSIVE GENERAL	PSUG	CRYS*TEL TELECOMMU-NICATIONS.COM	CYSS	21-Dec-98	
PUB SINGIN' INC	PBSG	FREEREALTIME.COM	FRTI	11-Sep-98	
QCS CORP	QCSC	SOURCINGLINK.NET	SNET	20-Jul-99	
RLD ENTERPRISES INC	RLDS	GO-RACHELS.COM CORPORATION	RACH	28-Jan-99	
RLN REALTY ASSOCIATES INC	MAAX	NETMAXIMIZER.COM	MAAX	5-Mar-99	•/
SBB INC	SBBI	USA TALKS.COM INC	USAT	7-Aug-98	
SCORE MEDICAL CORPORATION	SCRE	IMATTERS.COM	IWEB	17-Mar-99	
SECURITIES RESOLUTION ADVISORS INC	PAID	SALES ONLINE DIRECT INC	PAID	23-Mar-99	•/
SUNCOM TELECOMMUNICATIONS	SNLMF	VIRTUALSELLERS.COM	VDOTF	1-Jun-99	
SUNRISE EXPRESS INC	SUEX	WORLD COMMERCE ONLINE	WCOL	5-Oct-98	
SYCO COMICS & DISTRIBUTION INC	SYCD	SYCONET.COM INC	SYCD	3-Feb-99	•/•
SYSTEMS COMMUNICATIONS INC NEW	SCMID	HITSGALORE.COM INC	HITS	24-Mar-99	
TAO PARTNERS	TAOL	INETVISIONZ.COM	INVZ	6-May-99	
TECHNOLOGY HORIZONS	THCX	CDKNET.COM INC	CDKX	18-Dec-98	
THE NEW YORK BAGEL EXCHANGE INC	EBOT	WEBBOAT.COM, IN	EBOT	1-Feb-99	•/
TOUCH-IT INC NEW	TOCHD	GLOBAL CYBER	GCSC	15-Mar-99	
TRANSCO RESEARCH CORP	TRSD	GEOTELE.COM	GEOL	28-May-99	
UNIVERSAL REDUCTION MELTING TECHNOLOGIES	ISFB	INTERNET SOLUTIONS FOR BUSINESS INC	ISFB	19-Mar-99	•/
US AMATEUR SPORTS INC	USSP	ECOM ECOM.COM	USSP	5-Jan-99	•/•
US-WORLD LINK	USWL	US-WORLDLINK.COM	USWL	4-Aug-99	•/•
VENTECH INTL CORP	VTEC	VDO.COM	VDOO	16-Jun-99	
WAREFORCE ONE INC	WFRC	WAREFORCE.COM INC	WFRC	12-Jan-99	•/•
WATT COMM INTL	WATC	VIVA GAMING & RESORTS.COM	VIGA	14-May-99	
WESTERGAARD ONLINE SYSTEMS INC	WSYS	WESTERGAARD.COM INC	WSYS	3-Mar-99	/•
YOU BET INTERNATIONAL INC	UBET	YOUBET.COM INC	UBET	20-Jan-99	•/•

This table reports the old name and ticker, the new name and ticker, and the event date for firms that change their names to dotcom names. The last column marks firms that have undergone minor name changes or minor ticker changes.

websites, 207 Internet firms that did not change their names over this period. For each of the 95 firms in our dotcom sample, we then match the closest firm in the Internet non-name change sample on price over a two-week window around the event date for the dotcom sample firm. We refer to this control group as the 'Internet control group'. The abnormal return for each firm in our dotcom sample is then calculated as the difference between the returns it earns and the returns earned by its price-matched control firm.

We also compute market-adjusted abnormal returns relative to the Amex Inter@ctive Week Internet index. The Amex Inter@ctive Week Internet index (also known as the @Net Index) is a value-weighted index, created in August 1995, as a free service by the magazine Inter@ctive Week as a benchmark measure of the performance of Internet-related companies. The index, which originally comprised thirty-seven companies in 1995, represents a broad range of companies involved in providing Internet infrastructure and access, developing and marketing Internet content and software tools, and conducting business over the Internet. Among the better known of the fifty-one current Index components are Cisco Systems (CSCO), America Online (AOL), Yahoo! (YHOO), Amazon.com (AMZN), and eBay (EBAY). Note that all figures quoted in the text reflect the first type of adjustment. Whenever we use the Amex Index, we mention this explicitly.

13.4. RESULTS

13.4.1. *Descriptive Statistics*

Table 13.2 provides a list of the firms in our sample. We could not find any name changes to dotcom names before June 1998. After this, approximately seven firms per month changed to dotcom names on average, with a clear increase in name changes in 1999. Most of our announcements cluster in the first five months of 1999, with over 70 per cent of the firms in our sample announcing name changes during this period. The majority of dotcom name change firms are firms that have some Internet-related business already and are changing their names to better reflect this focus (category 2), followed closely by category 1 firms, pure Internet companies. As examples of a name change, consider Alternative Entertainment Inc and Courtleigh Capital Inc, respectively. Alternative Entertainment Inc changed its name to Boystoys.com on January 4, 1999 and its ticker from BOYS to GRLZ. Similarly, on 22 February 1999, Courtleigh changed its name to the optimistic 'Stockup.com' and changed its ticker symbol from CTLH to SKUP.

We sort our data into four quartiles based on the −30 day price and volume, respectively, to examine the evolution of price and volume for the high and low price and volume companies, respectively. Both the price per share and the average daily trading volume increase dramatically from before to after the name change, especially for the firms in the lowest price and volume quartiles. The average price per share for all firms 15 days before the announcement of the name change is $2.79, increasing to $4.20 on day +15. The average volume of shares traded for all firms is 58,943 on day −15, rising to 70,971 shares on day +15.

Most of these price increases come from our lowest price and volume firms. The average firm in the highest-price quartile (based on day −30 prices) increases in price from

$6.79 to $7.32 over the -15 to $+15$ day window, an increase of 7.8 per cent. In contrast, the average firm in the lowest-price quartile increases its share price from $0.41 to $1.11 over the same period, an increase of 170 per cent. The average firm in the next-highest price quartile increases its share price from $1.76 to $3.19, an increase of 81 per cent. Similarly, when we sort our firms into quartiles based on day -30 volume, firms in the highest volume quartile increase their share price from $4.24 to $5.20, an increase of 23 per cent. Firms in the two lowest-volume quartiles increase their average share price from $3.44 to $4.59 (quartile 2) and $1.70 to $3.25 (quartile 1), increases of 33 per cent and 91 per cent, respectively. Much of the increase in share price for the lowest volume quartile comes in the period immediately around the announcement date. Over the -2 to $+2$ day period; for example, firms in this quartile increase in price from $2.47 to $4.77, an average increase of 93 per cent.

13.4.2. *Do firms that change their names to dotcom names earn abnormal returns?*

Table 13.3 reports cumulative abnormal returns (CARs) relative to the price-matched Internet-control-group sample (panel A) and to the AMEX Inter@ctive Week Internet index (panel B) for various event windows for all firms and for the four firm categories. Each cell reports the average CAR across firms for the respective event windows and the associated t-statistics.[6] The CARs are also graphed in Fig. 13.1.

---

[6] The abnormal returns, using the Amex Inter@ctive Index, earned by each firm are computed as

$$AR_{it} = R_{it} - R_{mt}, \quad t = -30, \ldots, +30,$$

where R_{it} is the return for firm i for day t and R_{mt} is the index return for that day. We then compute the CAR for various event windows. For example, the event window from $t = -15$ to $t = -2$ is

$$CAR = \sum_{t=-15}^{-2} \sum_{i=1}^{N} \frac{AR_{it}}{N},$$

where N is the number of firms. This method implicitly assumes that the portfolio of stocks is rebalanced every period to give equal weighting in each security. The corresponding t-statistics that measure whether the CAR is significantly different from zero over the $t = l$ to $t = k$ window are calculated using the dependence adjustment method as described by Brown and Warner (1985) with a holdout period $t = -30$ to $t = -16$:

$$t = \sum_{t=l}^{k} AR_t / \sqrt{\sigma_{\text{holdout}}^2 \times M},$$

where $\sigma_{\text{holdout}}^2$ is the variance of the abnormal return computed over the holdout period and M is the number of days from $t = l$ to k. Abnormal returns and t-statistics for the Internet-control-group adjustment are computed similarly, except that AR_t is calculated on the aggregate level:

$$AR_t = \frac{\sum_{i=1}^{N} R_{it} - \sum_{j=1}^{N} R_{jt}}{N},$$

where R_{it} and R_{jt} are the return on the dotcom firm i and its corresponding matched firm j from the Internet control sample for day t, and N is the number of firms.

Table 13.3. *Cumulative abnormal returns subsequent to name changes*

	Event period						
	1	**2**	**3**	**4**	**5**	**6**	**7**
	−15 to −2	0 to 1	−2 to +2	+2 to +15	+1 to +30	+1 to +60	+1 to +120
Panel A: CARs adjusted by Internet control group							
All	31	18	53	20	11	23	28
(N = 95)	(4.53)	(7.31)	(13.13)	(3.30)	(1.10)	(1.66)	(1.40)
Cat. # 1	23	27	36	30	46	59	44
(N = 29)	(3.42)	(10.51)	(8.88)	(4.95)	(4.62)	(4.23)	(2.2)
Cat. # 2	32	14	105	21	−7	−31	−74
(N = 31)	(4.81)	(5.72)	(25.78)	(3.55)	(−0.76)	(−2.19)	(−3.7)
Cat. # 3	21	9	14	7	−18	−2	40
(N = 25)	(3.11)	(3.85)	(3.47)	(1.09)	(−1.88)	(−0.18)	(2.03)
Cat. # 4	76	30	23	18	38	140	243
(N = 10)	(11.11)	(11.83)	(5.77)	(2.92)	(3.87)	(9.94)	(12.15)
F-test:	0.226	0.874	0.484	0.732	0.209	0.005	0.000
χ^2-Test:	0.719	0.882	0.007	0.568	0.410	0.004	0.000
Panel B: CARs adjusted by Amex Inter@ctive Internet Index							
All	42	25	63	12	10	30	42
(N = 95)	(5.40)	(8.55)	(13.8)	(1.59)	(0.89)	(1.90)	(1.86)
Cat. # 1	27	31	44	20	26	37	35
(N = 29)	(3.46)	(10.8)	(9.54)	(2.59)	(2.33)	(2.31)	(1.54)
Cat. # 2	44	19	115	13	−9	−7	−18
(N = 31)	(5.78)	(6.67)	(25.1)	(1.65)	(−0.82)	(−0.43)	(−0.79)
Cat. # 3	31	18	22	−2	−5	13	44
(N = 25)	(4.03)	(6.36)	(4.70)	(−1.3)	(−0.46)	(0.79)	(1.98)
Cat. # 4	101	38	42	22	53	153	214
(N = 10)	(13.09)	(13.15)	(9.19)	(2.90)	(4.75)	(9.60)	(9.52)
F-test:	0.286	0.848	0.493	0.641	0.297	0.002	0.001
χ^2-Test:	0.461	0.614	0.001	0.383	0.102	0.001	0.006

This table reports market adjusted cumulative abnormal returns, expressed in per cent, relative to a price-matched control sample consisting of OTCBB Internet firms and to the AMEX Inter@ctive Week Internet index, respectively. The CARs are calculated for various event windows for companies that changed their name to dotcom names, between June 1998 and July 1999. Each cell reports the average CAR across all firms for the respective event windows. T-statistics are reported in parentheses. T-statistics significant at the 5% level are bolded. The categories are Category 1: Pure Internet Companies; Category 2: Companies which have some prior involvement in the Internet and change their name to 'better' reflect this involvement; Category 3: Companies which change their focus completely from non-Internet to Internet; Category 4: Companies whose core business is not Internet-related. We report p-values for tests of the null hypothesis of equality of means across firm categories and equality of medians across firm categories using an F-test and Kruskal and Wallis χ^2-test, respectively.

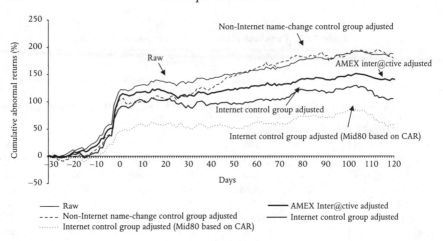

Figure 13.1. *Cumulative abnormal returns earned around the announcement date by firms changing their names to dotcom names.*

The dotcom effect is remarkably strong across all firms. The CARs are positive and significant across all event windows surrounding the announcement date, for firms announcing name changes between June 1998 and July 1999. For example, in panel A of Table 13.3, over the 5-day period from day -2 to day $+2$, all firms earn a strongly statistically significant abnormal return of 53 per cent. Over the entire 61-day period from day -30 to day $+30$, all firms earn a significant 89 per cent, with a t-statistic of 6.2 (not reported in the table). We observe similar striking abnormal returns in all periods surrounding the announcement day.

Is the dotcom effect a candidate for a profitable trading strategy? To the extent that an investor can identify in real time the announcements and/or effective dates from the websites in the Appendix, then the returns from the first few days after day zero suggest that the answer is yes. For example, on day $+1$, the firms earn an average excess return of 9 per cent, and on day $+2$, the firms earn 4.51 per cent. Thus, over the $+1$ to $+2$ period, a trader would have earned almost 14 per cent (t-statistic $= 5.30$). Since we do not have intra-day data, we cannot know the effects of the bid–ask spreads on our return calculations. Obviously, a judicious use of limit orders would be warranted in attempting to implement such a trading strategy.

Figure 13.1 and columns 5–7 of Table 13.3 show that when firms change their name to a dotcom name, the increase in firm value is permanent within the event window. For example, we do not see a significant reduction in CARs from day $+1$ to day $+120$, suggesting that the firms do indeed experience a permanent value increase. There is no post-announcement negative drift, implying that the increase in value due to the name change is permanent. This is in contrast to Karpoff and Rankine (1994) who find that a small initial positive stock price reaction to name changes is reversed within a few trading days after the announcement date. It is also in contrast to Bosch and Hirschey (1989) who find a negative post-announcement drift.

13.4.3. *Robustness Checks*

We also calculate the abnormal returns and t-statistics for samples that exclude the outliers, on the basis of the abnormal returns earned, and on the basis of the price and the volume of shares traded. To exclude outliers on the basis of the abnormal returns earned, we compute the overall CAR for each firm from the -30 to the $+120$ period and exclude all firms above the 90th percentile and below the 10th percentile. Similarly, to exclude outliers on price or volume, we exclude all firms above the 90th percentile and below the 10th percentile. Our results are robust to this trimming methodology. The greatest decrease in performance is seen when we exclude firms on the basis of the abnormal returns they earned over the entire -30 to $+120$ day period. Figure 13.1 shows that excluding the firms earning the highest and the lowest 10 per cent of abnormal returns ('Internet control group adjusted Mid80 based on CAR'), still earns the remaining firms an statistically significant average of 25 per cent and 42 per cent over the 5- and 11-day period, respectively, surrounding the announcement date. Excluding the firms with the lowest and highest -30 day price earns the remaining firms statistically significant abnormal returns of 60 per cent and 71 per cent over the 5- and 11-day periods, respectively. Excluding the firms with the lowest and highest -30 day volume earns the remaining firms statistically significant abnormal returns of 70 per cent and 95 per cent over these two periods, respectively.

Since most of our firms trade on the OTCBB, it is a fair assumption that these are very small firms. It may be possible that the existence of news, any news, for these tiny companies might have a positive effect on the stock prices of these companies if there was little trading or investor interest in them before the news of the name change.[7] To address this concern, we examine a similar group of non-Internet related companies that change their names/ticker symbols and check the price effects of these changes. We use these firms to create a control group, which we will refer to as the 'non-Internet name-change' control group.[8]

This control group earns an insignificant abnormal return of 2 per cent over the -30 to $+30$ event window. In Fig. 13.1 we report the difference between the Amex Inter@ctive Week Internet index-adjusted abnormal returns earned by the dotcom name change sample and the OTCBB index-adjusted abnormal returns earned by our non-Internet name change

---

[7] The *Wall Street Journal* (Buckman 1999) reports, for example, that NEI WebWorld Inc., a Dallas printing company in bankruptcy proceedings and whose stock was involved in an alleged Internet stock scam, soared nearly 1,170 per cent on December 16, a day after news of the alleged scheme broke. According to the *WSJ*, the reason for the surge was that the stock's name was in the news—even though the news was not positive. Apparently, the mere mention of NEI's name in the media seemed to prompt web 'momentum' investors to jump in, generating enough trading in the stock to propel its price through the roof.

[8] The name change control group is constructed by identifying all OTCBB firms over the May 1998 to August 1999 period that experience non-Internet related name changes. After eliminating firms with confounding events, our sample consists of 249 firms. For each of the 95 firms in our dotcom sample, we then match with the closest firm in the non-Internet name change sample on price over a two-week window around the event date for the dotcom sample firm. This results in a 95 firm control group. The CARs for this control group are calculated using an OTCBB constructed index. To construct the index, we eliminate all OTCBB firms that are either in the dotcom sample or in the control sample. This results in approximately 6,000 remaining firms. We then draw a random sample of 400 firms (sampling without replacement). Of the 400 firms, we delete those that have more than 50 per cent missing return data over the sample period, giving us a final sample of 274 firms. Our OTCBB index is constructed by equally weighting all available daily returns for these 274 stocks.

control group. This difference is plotted in Fig. 13.1 as the 'non-Internet name-change control group adjusted' CAR. Over the 5- and 11-day period surrounding the announcement date, the dotcom firms earn significant excess returns of 64 and 72 per cent, respectively, relative to the excess returns of the non-Internet name change sample; 120 days after the name change, the difference between the two samples is a statistically significant 180 per cent. Thus, these results suggest that the dotcom name change effect is not simply attributable to the the arrival of any news for small firms, but rather an Internet-related dotcom effect.

From Table 13.3, in the pre-event period of day −15 to day −2, firms exhibit a pre-event run up in returns, earning a statistically significant CAR of 31 per cent. This has several implications for our interpretation of the results. One explanation is that there may be some information leakage before the actual name change. Another explanation is that the actual announcement date is before the event date we identify for the firm. Both these explanations bias us towards accepting the null hypothesis that the sample firms do not earn excess returns in the event windows. A third explanation is that these companies may have high betas. Using the market model instead of the control group adjustment or a simple market adjustment to compute abnormal returns might be a better adjustment for risk in this case; perhaps this would have a negative impact on both the average excess returns and the statistical significance of the results.

Using the AMEX Inter@ctive Week Internet index, we first compute the betas for the 95 firm sample from days −90 to −31. Using the pre-event period to estimate betas, and applying a requirement that each firm have no more than 25 per cent missing returns, we are able to compute betas for 19 of the 95 firms.[9] For these 19 firms, the average (median) beta is 0.74 (0.85), and the Amex Inter@ctive market-model adjusted CAR for the −2 to +2 window is 35 per cent (t-statistic = 5.48) and 62 per cent (t-statistic = 6.42) for the −5 to +5 window. We also estimate market model abnormal returns using three other Internet indexes: the Dow Jones (DJ) Internet Commerce Index, the DJ Composite Index, and the DJ Internet Services Index. The results with these indexes are qualitatively similar to the Amex Inter@ctive index adjustments. Hence our results are robust to various market model risk adjustments.

Alternatively, the high-abnormal returns earned by the name change firms may be driven by an upward bias in calculated CARs. This bias may be attributable to two sources: one, a failure to adjust for transaction costs emanating from the bid–ask spread, and two, a bid–ask bounce effect (Conrad and Kaul 1993). To address these two issues, we follow two approaches.

First, we collect, when available, event date, day −30, and day +30 closing bid–ask spread data from Bloomberg for our full sample of 95 firms. We then estimate

---

[9] The market model results, using pre-event betas, are robust to variations on the non-missing return screens ranging from requiring 50 to 75 per cent non-missing observations. We also estimate betas and the parameters of the market model using post event data (days +31 to +180) for a subsample of 52 firms announcing their name change before 1 April 1999, a procedure that increases the number of firms for which we can calculate betas. For the 50 firms remaining, the average (median) beta is 0.20 (0.13), and the Amex Inter@ctive market-model adjusted CAR for the −2 to +2 window is 192 per cent (t-statistic = 14.14) and 202 per cent (t-statistic = 10.05) for the −5 to +5 window.

AMEX Inter@ctive Week adjusted CARs by inversely weighting each firm by its relative event day bid–ask spread (where the relative spread is calculated as $(ask_t - bid_t)/((ask_t + bid_t)/2))$. Second, we estimate an average excess holding period return (HPR) by calculating each firm's HPR, subtracting the HPR of the Inter@ctive Week index, and then averaging across firms. To calculate each firm's HPR, we use the conservative assumption of 'buying' at the day 30 ask price and 'selling' at the day +30 bid price.

For the event date, day −30, and day +30, Bloomberg has bid–ask data for 90, 91, and 92 firms in our sample, respectively. The event-day average (median) relative bid–ask spread is a fairly large 24 per cent (10.8 per cent). However, the inversely weighted bid–ask spread CARs are still quite large, at 158 per cent (*t*-statistic = 5.73) for the day −30 to +30 window. The 158 per cent is larger than the non-spread-Amex Inter@ctive-adjusted CARs of 109 per cent, suggesting that firms with smaller relative bid–ask spreads experience a greater dotcom effect. Our results with HPR are similar. The 60-day window average HPAR is 104 per cent (*t*-statistic = 1.63). These results suggest that the dotcom effect is robust to a microstructure-induced upward bias in returns.

13.4.4. *The Dotcom Effect: Is it a Rational Response or Evidence of an Irrational Bubble?*

Is the dotcom effect a rational response from investors? It may certainly be the case that the majority of firms in our sample are small firms, neglected for the most part by analysts, and for which the vast majority of investors are unaware of the firm's involvement with the Internet. The switching of the firm name to a dotcom name may serve as a swift, inexpensive method for a firm to signal its involvement with the Internet. Then, once investors realise that the firm is an Internet firm, they apply a 'premium' to the company's stock. Of course, this implies that markets are not semi-strong efficient.

The question we wish to answer is this: is the premium economically sensible? Are the dotcom premiums akin to a speculative bubble (Shiller 1984; Summers 1986; Gilles and LeRoy 1997) or is it rational to the extent that investors are simply impounding expectations of large future pay-offs to Internet firms' stock prices? Most of the papers that attempt to examine if the time variation in expected returns is rational or the result of speculative bubbles study the relation between long horizon returns and dividend and earning yields (Fama and French 1988; Campbell and Shiller 1988). In this study, since we do not have long horizon returns nor do the vast majority of our firms pay dividends or even have positive earnings, these types of tests are not applicable.

Instead, to ascertain the extent to which the dotcom effect is at least consistent with a very loose definition of rationality, we adopt some simple and admittedly ad hoc tests. First, we examine the relation between abnormal returns and the extent to which the firm is indeed an Internet firm and how much of the firm's business is derived from the Internet. Second, we examine if the abnormal returns vary across the degree of name and ticker change. Third, we examine whether firms earn higher returns in up markets or in periods when they cluster in announcing name changes, as opposed to down markets or in periods when they do not cluster.

Table 13.4. *Abnormal returns and major versus minor name changes*

	−15 to −2	0 to 1	−2 to 2	2 to 15	−30 to 30
Panel A: Firms with major and minor name changes					
CAR of major (N = 87)	40	25	59	13	92
CAR of minor (N = 8)	43	−1	11	12	34
P-value	(0.86)	(0.064)	(0.059)	(0.94)	(0.20)
Panel B: Firms with major and minor ticker changes					
CAR of major (N = 81)	39	25	61	12	95
CAR of minor (N = 14)	43	7	16	11	30
P-value	(0.82)	(0.13)	(0.090)	(0.89)	(0.038)

This table reports comparisons of AMEX Inter@ctive Week Internet index-adjusted abnormal returns, expressed in per cent, for firms that undergo major or minor name and/or ticker changes. Each cell reports the average cumulative abnormal return for major changes, minor changes, and the *p*-value for the null hypothesis that the abnormal returns are the same across major and minor changes.

In the first test, concerning a firm's level of business operations on the Internet, we might expect that firms whose core business is not Internet related (Category 4) should exhibit much lower returns than other firms, that firms for which the name change should be less of a surprise (Category 1, pure Internet companies) should also have lower returns than other firms, and that firms for which the change to a dotcom name signals their switch to a larger emphasis on the Internet (Categories 2 and 3) should have larger returns. The results in Table 13.3 are not consistent with these conjectures. The bottom row of Table 13.3 provides parametric *F*-statistics and non-parametric Kruskal–Wallis test-statistics to test this hypothesis. Across the event windows, we reject the null for the *F*-test twice and reject the null three times for the medians test. Thus, there is no consistent pattern across different firm categories for different event windows.

When we examine longer horizon returns in Table 13.4, a clearer pattern emerges. We find that in two of the event windows, days +1 to +60 and days +1 to +120, we are able to reject the null that all categories of firms have the same excess returns. However, the returns across categories appear to run opposite to our hypothesis. In the +1 to +60 and +1 to +120 windows, Category 4 firms, which we expected to have lower returns, have much higher returns. Category 2 and 3 firms, which we expected to have higher returns, have the lowest returns. Overall, the results across different firm categories suggest that at shorter horizons, market participants appear to apply a similar positive price premium across all companies changing their names to dotcom names, regardless of a company's level of involvement with the Internet. In the longer horizon, firms that have less involvement with the Internet have the greatest returns following a dotcom name change. The small size of the sample prevents us from drawing any robust conclusions but a mere association with the Internet seems enough to provide a firm with a large and permanent value increase.

For the second test, we examine the differences in abnormal returns across firms with major or minor name and/or ticker changes. One possible hypothesis concerning the relation between abnormal returns and the degree of a name change is that we might expect that if investors were more rational, the abnormal returns earned by the firm would be higher if the name change and/or ticker change was major. This is because a major name change may be a way of signalling a focus on the Internet and, therefore, indicating that the company should be 'rationally' priced as such (assuming Internet stock return premiums are rational). Another possible hypothesis, related to investors being less rational, is the idea that firms with major name changes represent new firms to Internet 'crazed' day traders and, as such, these day traders pounce on the 'new' dotcom firms, dramatically increasing the trading volume and consequently bidding up the price. We use the data in Table 13.2 to perform the classifications. We classify 8 firms as not having major name changes and 14 firms as not having major ticker changes. Indeed, it seems the majority of our sample firms take on new names and ticker symbols when they switch to dotcom names. In Table 13.4, we report the results of major and minor name and ticker change comparisons. The abnormal returns show a pattern of increased returns for the major name and ticker change firms, although the significance levels for tests comparing the differences vary across different event windows. For example, in the five days surrounding the name change, firms with major name changes experience Amex Inter@ctive Week Internet index-adjusted returns of 59 per cent compared to just 11 per cent for the 8 firms with minor name changes, a difference significant at the 6 per cent level. Overall, when we examine the average excess returns in Table 13.4, across panels A and B, the major name and ticker change firms have higher excess returns in eight out of the ten event windows. However, the higher excess returns are significantly different at the 10 per cent level in only 4 out of the 10 windows.

One way to distinguish between the two name change hypotheses (rational versus irrational) is to examine what proportion of the minor name or ticker change companies are companies that derive very little of their business from the Internet (Category 4 firms). We might expect to see that if investors are rationally pricing Internet firms based on their degree of involvement with the Internet, then Category 4 firms should represent a large number of the firms with low returns (i.e. minor name and ticker changes). However, we find the opposite: none of these minor name or ticker change companies are companies in Category 4—companies that have nothing to do the Internet. This supports the Internet day trader hypothesis.

Third, we examine whether firms earn greater abnormal returns in up-markets or in periods when firms cluster their name change announcements. If investors are reacting rationally, there should be no difference in the excess returns earned by the firms in these periods to returns earned in down markets or in non-clustering periods.

We compare the size of the effect in 'up' and 'down' markets by calculating the monthly index return for the Amex Inter@ctive Week Internet index for each of the 15 months from June 1998 to July 1999. We then rank the months according to the average return on the index. Unfortunately, there isn't really a pronounced down period for the Amex Internet index during the period covered by this chapter. We compute CARs for all firms with announcement dates in the top eight months (where the index earned returns ranging from 6.6 to 34.6 per cent). We repeated this procedure for those firms with announcement dates in the bottom seven months (where the index return ranged from −11 to 5.1 per cent). 45 firms announced name changes in 'up' markets, while 50 firms announced name changes in 'down' months. Over an 11-day window surrounding the name change, the firms earn 81 per cent in the up months and 42 per cent in the down months. However, the difference, while large in magnitude, is not significant, with a p-value of 0.34.

We also check to see if firms are attempting to take advantage of perceived 'hot' market periods, akin to the hot issue market phenomenon in IPOs (Ritter 1984), by clustering their name changes in periods where investor passion for Internet stocks appears to be greatest. We compute the average abnormal returns earned by the firms in the months for which the greater number of name changes occurred (January–March 1999 and May 1999) and compare these to the returns earned by the firms in the non-clustering months. In the months with less name change activity, the average day −30 to +30 excess return is 31 per cent. In the months with greater numbers of name changes, the firms earn average excess returns of 118 per cent. The difference between the returns in high name change months vs. low name change months is significant (t-statistic = 2.47, p-value = 0.016).

13.4.5. *Determinants of the Cross-section of Abnormal Returns*

In this section, we examine the determinants of the cross-section of daily abnormal returns to see if the cross-sectional dispersion is related to the level of trading activity and price per share. Large positive differences in the relation between volume and abnormal returns from before to after the dotcom name change announcement may indicate an increased awareness by traders that the stock is now an Internet company. The name change may bring the firm to the attention of individual day traders and on-line traders discussing and trading stocks on Internet stock-chat rooms. Because of the relatively small capitalization of these firms, we may see a price pressure effect after the announcement date that is manifested as a positive and significant relation between shares traded and abnormal returns. Thus, we estimate the following pooled regression model using OLS:

$$AR_{it} = \alpha + \beta_1 D_{pre} \Delta \text{Volume}_{it} + \beta_2 D_{post} \Delta \text{Volume}_{it} + \beta_3 D_{pre} \text{Price}_{it} + \beta_4 D_{post} \text{Price}_{it} + \varepsilon_{it},$$

where AR_{it} is the Amex Inter@active Week Internet index adjusted abnormal return for firm i on day t for $t = -15$ to $+15$, D_{pre} is a dummy variable equal to 1 (0) if the abnormal return is from day −15 to day −1 (day 0 to day +15), D_{post} is a dummy variable equal to 1 (0) if the abnormal return is from day 0 to 15 (day −15 to −1), $\Delta \text{Volume}_{it}$ is the growth rate in volume[10] for firm i, defined as day t volume minus the average volume for days $t − 16$ to $t − 30$, all divided by the average volume for days $t − 16$ to $t − 30$, and Price$_{it}$ is the price of firm i on day t. To control for heteroscedasticity in the variances of the model's errors, we use the White (1980) method to calculate a consistent covariance matrix.

---

[10] This volume measure is similar to measures used in Conrad *et al.* (1994). We also estimate the abnormal return regression using individual firm raw daily volume and find similar results.

Table 13.5. *Pooled regression model of relation between trading volume and abnormal returns*

RHS Variables	Beta (p-value)
$B_1 D_{pre} \Delta Volume_{it}$	0.208 (0.074)
$B_2 D_{post} \Delta Volume_{it}$	0.643 (0.0002)
$B_3 D_{pre} Price_{it}$	0.465 (0.008)
$B_4 D_{post} Price_{it}$	−0.005 (0.982)
Test of equality of pre- and post-volume and price betas	p-value
Volume $H_0 : B_1 = B_2$	0.037
Price $H_1 : B_3 = B_4$	0.094

This table presents the results of a pooled regression model to determine the effects of contemporaneous volume and price per share on daily abnormal returns in the pre- and post-announcement periods. The model is:

$$AR_{it} = \alpha + \beta_1 D_{pre} \Delta Volume_{it} + \beta_2 D_{post} \Delta Volume_{it} + \beta_3 D_{pre} Price_{it} + \beta_4 D_{post} Price_{it} + \varepsilon_{it},$$

where AR_{it} is the Amex Inter@active Week Internet adjusted abnormal return for firm i on day t, with $t = -15$ to $+15$, D_{pre} is a dummy variable equal to 1 (0) if the abnormal return is from day -15 to day -1 (day 0 to day $+15$), D_{post} is a dummy variable equal to 1 (0) if the abnormal return is from day 0 to $+15$ (day -15 to -1), $\Delta Volume_{it}$ is the growth rate in volume for firm i, defined as day t volume minus the average volume for days -16 to -30, all divided by the average volume for days -16 to -30, and $Price_{it}$ is the price of firm i on day t. p-values of T-statistics, adjusted for heteroscedasticity, are in parentheses. Point estimates are multiplied by 100.

The results are presented in Table 13.5. The pre-announcement period growth-rate-in-volume beta is relatively small, at 0.208, and marginally significant, while the post-beta is much larger, at 0.643, and significant (p-value $= 0.0002$). Thus, the growth rate in volume in the post announcement period has a positive correlation with the daily abnormal returns, suggesting a price-pressure effect. The pre- and post-betas on growth in volume are statistically different (p-value $= 0.037$), suggesting a difference in the importance of a price pressure effect in the pre- and post-announcement period. To examine price pressure effects across firm categories, we estimate a separate regression (not reported in the tables) in which we interact the firm category with post announcement volume. We find a much larger post-announcement period volume beta for Category 4 firms (beta $= 2.74$) relative to the other categories. Thus, while we cannot know for sure who to attribute the increases in trading volume to, our evidence is consistent with the popular press notion of an Internet day trader price pressure effect. This effect is strong across all firms, but especially strong for the firms whose dotcom name change announcements (Category 4) are likely to have been more of a surprise. Finally, the level of abnormal returns in the pre-announcement period is linked to the price of the firm. Larger priced firms have greater abnormal returns prior to the name change. In contrast, the post name change price beta is insignificant. Thus, both the pre- and post-price betas suggest that it is not likely that the dotcom effect is related to microstructure problems associated with smaller priced stocks.

13.5. CONCLUSION

We find that companies that change their name to a dotcom name earn significant abnormal returns on the order of 53 per cent for the five days around the announcement date. The effect is not transitory; there is no post-event negative drift. These results contrast with evidence in previous literature on corporate name changes, such as Bosch and Hirschey (1989) or Karpoff and Rankine (1994) who find an insignificant excess return around the announcement date, with a positive pre-announcement drift followed by a negative post-announcement drift.

We argue that our results are driven by a degree of investor mania—investors seem to be eager to be associated with the Internet at all costs. This is supported by the fact that our announcement returns are similar across all firms, regardless of the company's actual involvement with the Internet. Evidence of investor mania seems especially true when we consider the finding that firms with little or no sales generated from the Internet, experience the greatest long-horizon returns. The returns to firms announcing dotcom name changes are much greater during the months in which more name changes occur, suggesting some degree of a 'hot' name change period effect. A mere association with the Internet seems enough to provide a firm with a large and permanent value increase.

Our evidence in this chapter lends more support to the investor mania hypothesis than to the rational pricing hypothesis. In this sense, this chapter adds to a growing body of evidence documenting irrational investor behaviour, both at the aggregate and at the individual level. When valuing high-tech firms in general, therefore, it may be necessary to consider both irrational investor sentiment as well as the underlying fundamentals of the firm.

Appendix: Data Sources

Nasdaq OTC board:	http://www.otcbb.com/dynamic/
Nasdaq listings:	http://www.nasdaq.com/
Company profiles	http://www.hoovers.com/
	http://www.siliconinvestor.com/
	Bloomberg
	Company web pages
Company news	http://www.siliconinvestor.com/
	Dow Jones Publications Library
	http://www1.newsalert.com/
Stock splits	http://investor.cnet.com/
	Bloomberg
SEC filings	http://freeedgar.com/
	http://www.sec.gov/edgarhp.htm
Historical prices	http://www.financialweb.com/
	Bloomberg
	Dow Jones Interactive
Market capitalization	Bloomberg
	Datastream
Bid–ask spreads	Bloomberg

References

Bosch, J. and Hirschey, M. (1989), 'The valuation effects of corporate name changes', *Financial Management* 18, 64–73.

Brown, S. J. and Warner, J. B. (1985), 'Using daily stock returns: The case of event studies', *Journal of Financial Economics* 14, 3–31.

Buckman, R. (1999), 'In the wild world of internet postings, sometimes bad news is good news', *Wall Street Journal*, December 17, C18.

Campbell, J. Y. and Shiller, R. S. (1988), 'The dividend-price ratio and expectations of future dividends and discount factors', *Review of Financial Studies* 1, 195–227.

Conrad, J., Hameed, A., and Niden, C. (1994), 'Volume and autocovariances in short-horizon individual security returns', *Journal of Finance* 49, 1305–29.

—— and Kaul, G. (1993), 'Long-term market overreaction or biases in computed returns?', *Journal of Finance* 48, 39–63.

Cooper, M. J., Dimitrov, O., and Rau, P. R. (2003), 'A rose.com by any other name', *Journal of Finance* 56, 2371–88.

Core, J. E., Guay, W. R., and van Buskirk, A. (2001), 'Market valuations in the new economy: An investigation of what had changed', *Journal of Accounting and Economics*, 34, 43–67.

Demers, E. and Lev, B. (2001), 'A rude awakening: Internet shakeout in 2000', *Review of Accounting Studies*, 20, 331–59.

Fama, E. F. and French, K. R. (1988), 'Dividend yields and expected stock returns', *Journal of Financial Economics* 22, 3–25.

Gilles, C. and LeRoy, S. (1996), 'Bubbles as Payoffs at Infinity', Board of Governors of the Federal Reserve System, Finance and Economics Discussion Series.

Gordon, J. S. (2001), *The Business of America*, New York: Walker & Co. Inc.

Hand, J. R. M. (2003), 'Profits, losses and the non-linear pricing of internet stocks', Working paper, in J. Hand, Intangible Assets: values, incomes and risk, Oxford: Oxford University Press.

—— (2001*b*), 'The role of economic fundamentals, web traffic and supply and demand in the pricing of U.S. internet stocks', Working paper, *European Finance Review*, 5, 295–317.

Huberman, G. and Regev, T. (2001), 'Contagious speculation and a cure for cancer: A non-event that made stock prices soar', *Journal of Finance* 56, 387–96.

Kane, M. (2000), 'Oregon town changes name to dotcom', *ZDNET News fron ZDWire*, January 20.

Karpoff, J. M. and Rankine, G. (1994), 'In search of a signaling effect: The wealth effects of corporate name changes', *Journal of Banking and Finance* 18, 1027–45.

Mackay, C. (1841), *Extraordinary popular delusions and the madness of crowds*, New York: Barnes & Noble Books.

Rashes, M. S. (2001), 'Massively confused investors making conspicuously ignorant choices (MCI-MCIC)', *Journal of Finance* 56, 1911–27.

Ritter, J. R. (1984), 'The "hot issue" market of 1980', *Journal of Business* 57, 215–40.

Schwartz, E. and Moon, M. (2000), 'Rational pricing of Internet companies', *Financial Analysts Journal* 56, 62–75.

Shiller, R. (1984), 'Stock Prices and Social Dynamics', Brookings Papers on Economic Activity 2, 457–510.

Sobel, R. (1965), *The Big Board: A History of the New York Stock Market*, New York: Free Press.

Summers, L. H. (1986), 'Does the stock market rationally reflect fundamental values?', *Journal of Finance*, 41, 591–601.

White, H. (1980), 'A heteroskedasticity-consistent covariance matrix estimator and a direct test for heteroskedasticity', *Econometrica*, 48, 817–38.

14

The Liquidation Preference in Venture Capital Investment Contracts: A Real Option Approach

DIDIER COSSIN, BENOÎT LELEUX, AND ENTELA SALIASI

14.1. INTRODUCTION

Valuing early stage high-tech growth-oriented companies is a challenge to current valuation methodologies. This inability to come up with robust point estimates of value could potentially lead to a breakdown of market liquidity. This is not what is witnessed: indeed, billions of dollars of early stage venture capital has been poured into promising start-ups in Europe and the USA over the last couple of years. So, how do venture capitalists cope with the valuation uncertainties? The pioneering work of Sahlman (1990) pointed the way to the solution, or at least the 'coping' mechanism used: instead of expending useless amounts of time and effort coming up with a better estimate of an inherently uncertain future, efforts are redirected towards (1) the design of investment contracts which materially skew the distribution of pay-offs in favour of the venture investors, and (2) an active involvement in the development process of the invested company. In effect, limitations in valuation abilities are addressed by designing the investment contracts as baskets of real options instead of linear pay-off functions and by directly intervening in the underlying processes. The key items outlined by Sahlman (1990) in the relationship between venture capitalists and entrepreneurial ventures include (1) the staging of the commitment of capital; (2) the use of convertible securities instead of straight equity investments; and (3) anti-dilution provisions to secure the investor's equity position in the company. The work of Cossin *et al.* (2003) details how to value the different dimensions of these contracts using a real-options technique. In this chapter, we pay closer attention to the liquidation preference that underlies most of the actual convertible securities design.

Liquidation preferences appear in venture contracts in different formats. Most often, it is constructed as a participating feature in the convertible preferred securities design used to finance a majority of the venture investments, whereby the first tranche of capital obtained in an exit is entirely committed to the investor group and any residual is then distributed pro rata to the actual equity ownership. The participating feature usually disappears once the exit valuations are sufficiently high to guarantee the outside investors a solid return on their initial investments. Two examples are presented below from actual venture capital term sheets that closed in 2001.

Preference: In case of merger, reorganization, or transfer of control of e-docs, first pay cost of preferred stock. Participating goes away on valuation that corresponds to $50 million. Thereafter preferred and common share on as-converted basis [a series A first round funding of $4 million at a pre-money valuation of $6 million].

Liquidation preference: Upon the occurrence of a liquidation event, the series A preferred stock investors shall be entitled to receive in preference to the existing preferred stock investors and the common stock investors an amount equal to the initial purchase price per share of series A preferred stock plus all accrued but unpaid dividends. Thereafter, and after payment of the purchase price in respect of the other series of preferred stock, any remaining proceeds shall be allocated pro rata among the holders of the common stock and the series A preferred stock, treating the investors in the series A preferred stock on an as-converted basis, until the series A preferred stock holders shall receive an aggregate on their initial investment of 150 per cent. A merger, consolidation, dissolution, winding up, change of control, or sale of the assets shall be deemed to be a liquidation event ('liquidation event') [a series A first round funding of $6.5 million at a pre-money valuation of $3 million].

The participating preferred debentures or preferred stock investment format provides the venture capitalist with preferences in liquidation, a feature reinforced by the accruing dividends, as shown in the second example above. The accruing dividends are not meant to be paid unless the exit mechanism is not rich enough to provide adequate returns to the investors. In such circumstances, for example, liquidation, accruing dividends (often 10–20 per cent per annum) guarantee a disproportionate share of the assets to the venture capital investors. Very high, out of the money liquidation preference features have been known to be implemented in order to skew values even more towards the venture capitalist (or a specific member of a syndicate). The net effect of the preferred equity format with accruing dividend is to skew the pay-off distribution in case of liquidation.

This chapter investigates this common feature of venture capital investment contracts from an option pricing perspective. First of all, analogies are drawn to standard real option models. Second, these models are described in detail and mathematically developed to provide closed-form pricing solutions if possible. Third, numerical methods with common venture capital parameters are used to 'calibrate' the formulae and obtain a more intuitive estimate of the value of each feature of the contracts. Finally, inferences are drawn from the previous sections for future contract design by valuing the above covenant altogether.

The chapter is organized as follows. Section 14.1 introduces the VC contract and the important contractual feature of the liquidation preference. Section 14.2 discusses three crucial assumptions for the ongoing model such as the discount rate for non-priced project risk, firm value as the underlying diffusion process, and most importantly the VC ownership stake. Section 14.3 focuses on the liquidation preference as a package of liquidation right and automatic conversion. It is important to note that the analytical and numerical solutions do take account of the complete interdependence of the liquidation right and conversion optionality, defining the conversion option's strike price equal to the initial investment price (conversion price) plus the liquidation right. Moreover this section looks at the importance of automatic conversion versus liquidation right and the conditions driving their relative importance, as well as provides a sensitivity analysis of liquidation preference to firm's characteristics. The liquidation preference sets up the framework for the VC exit pay-off and the conditions (event) under which it is exercised. Of course, further features of VC contracts should be included for an overall design and the reader is referred to the background work of Cossin *et al.* (2003). A further specification allows us to account for more flexibility in the assumptions made and most importantly it includes a much richer pay-off structure and early exit in a discrete time framework. The last section concludes.

14.1.1. *General Notation*

I_{t_i}	Investment cost per stage
ρ	Discount rate per stage
r	Risk-free interest rate
α	Drift of the firm value process per stage adjusted for VC non-financial contribution
V_t	Value of the project
x_{t_i}	VC ownership stake in each stage
$\varphi(V_t)$	VC contract value at the beginning of each stage
$\delta = \rho - \alpha$	VC capital cost

14.2. GENERAL FRAMEWORK

Option pricing is a powerful tool in approaching the pricing of venture backed projects such as R&D or IT projects where future returns are highly uncertain. The technique used here investigates the liquidation preference feature of classical VC contracts. The mathematical model involves only one state variables, the project value. Empirical results (Gompers 1995) and research studies (Berk *et al.* 1998) have shown that the systematic risk as well as the volatility levels are highest early in the life of a project and decrease as the project approaches completion. As per Myers and Howe (1997), cited in Berk *et al.* (1998), the cost of capital should decrease through the life of the project, due to the higher 'leverage' of the project early in its life. In order to study the impact of these factors in the contracting value process, we consider stepwise parameters such as volatility, drift rates, and VC value added. The VC value added is a crucial component in valuing the venture project contract, since it captures the VC dual role in financing the project as well as offering his/her non-financial contribution. The existence of the VC value added leads to major implications, which make the private equity investment different from an outside equity financing. As in the case of an option on a dividend paying stock, the VC (equivalent to the option holder) faces the early exercise problem. The VC deals with this issue by staging the required investment amount in discrete time. Furthermore, staging in itself incorporates two options: the option to drop the project if the performance is not good, as well as the option to continue investing if the expected future value of the project exceeds its cost. The second implication concerns the capital or opportunity cost of the VC contribution to active monitoring of the project, which should be rewarded by some higher ownership stake in the final venture project's pay-offs. While the staging so important in VC investments will necessarily impact valuations, we abstract from it here (but provide solutions linking staging and liquidation preference in our background paper previously quoted).

We achieve closed-form solutions under the growing perpetuity and other additional rigid assumptions like no firm value restructuring for additional cash inflow (jumps in case of new investments). Furthermore, although the VC value added is beneficial for the firm value, that is, it increases the probability of success of the venture project, it is costly for the VC. This will lead VCs to a premature exit from the venture backed project, if no additional reward (in terms of a higher ownership stake) is accounted for. Exogenously preset project and stage duration enable us to release the perpetuity assumption as well as to allow for firm value restructuring and to define the VC ownership stake dependent on his capital cost. At the end of each predefined stage, the VC revises his investment policy maximizing his pay-off given the future uncertainty concerning the project. Although we approach in our discussions the issue of staging and its interaction with the liquidation preference, this chapter focuses more on the liquidation preference. The reader interested in the staging issue in more detail than treated here is referred to Cossin *et al.* (2003).

14.2.1. *Discount Rate*

Salhman (1990) mentions that

in theory, the required rate of return on an entrepreneurial investment reflects the risk-free interest rate in the economy, the systematic risk of the particular asset and the market risk premium, the liquidity of the asset, and compensation for the value added by the supplier of capital. This last adjustment is required to compensate the VC for monitoring and playing an active role in management. In practice, the use of high-discount rates reflects the well-known bias in financial projections made by entrepreneurs. Because few firms ever do so well as their founders believe they will, projections can be lowered or a higher interest rate can be used ....

Hence there exists a $\delta = \rho - \alpha > 0$. The role of the VC value added (his supportive non-financial contribution) affects the probability of success. The drift of the venture project α is defined as the sum of a drift of a similar project plus the VC value added given its involvement in the project. The larger the VC contribution, the higher the project's drift. The interpretation δ is similar to the dividend yield for an financial option holder. The holder (VC) incurs the cost of its value added, unless he converts his preferred holdings in common stocks.

A crucial but realistic assumption concerns the stochastic changes in the project value which cannot be 'spanned' or replicated from the existing assets in the economy. First, the underlying state variable in this model is a non-traded asset. The contingent claim approach is based on the assumption of no arbitrage argument. Hubalek and Schachermayer (1999) conclude that any number in $(0, \infty)$ is a possible price for a derivative (option in our case) written in a surrogate asset (a closely related but not identical to the underlying asset), without violating the non-arbitrage arguments. The message of their theorem is that: whenever one applies the non-arbitrage argument methodology to real options whose underlying asset is not a traded asset one must be very aware that preferences, subjective probabilities, come into play. Therefore the riskless portfolio cannot be constructed making use of the discount rate per stage, ρ, which account for the decisionmaker's subjective valuation of risk.[1] Furthermore, the risk free rate cannot cover the VC's cost in providing the value added. Consequently, in order for us to use the contingent claim approach (but not in a risk-neutral environment), we make use of the dynamic programming argument as per Dixit and Pindyck. The VC contract value fluctuations are captured through the stochastic evolution of the project value, which is the underlying state variable of the model.

14.2.2. *Firm Value as the Diffusion Process*

The main characteristic of this type of investment is that the project value is not concerned with the discounted value of future cash flows, but with the future investment opportunities that this project provides. Hence the project value follows a stochastic process in itself.

Let V_t denote to the firm value at date t. The dynamics for V_t under the objective probability measure follows the diffusion process defined as

$$dV_t = \begin{cases} V_t(\rho - \delta)\,dt + V_t\sigma\,dW_t & \text{if } t \neq t_i, \\ I_{t_i} & \text{if } t = t_i, \end{cases} \tag{14.1}$$

where $(\rho - \delta)$ is the drift parameter, $V_t^2\sigma^2 > 0$ is the instantaneous variance, and $dW_t \sim N(0, dt)$ is a classical increment for a Wiener process, under the objective probability measure.

14.2.3. *VC Ownership Stake*

As mentioned in the very first sections, the VC plays a dual role in the venture project. First s/he contributes in financing the project and secondly s/he brings value added in terms of a non-financial contribution which positively affects the probability of success. Nonetheless these actions are costly for the VC, consequently s/he is entitled to an additional reward. The role of the VC value added and its capital cost is evident in the presence of the discounted future projections under the objective probability measure:

$$\tilde{E}_t\left[e^{-\rho(T-t)}\left(V_t\exp^{\left(\alpha - \frac{\sigma^2}{2}\right)(T-t)+\sigma(W_T-W_t)}\right)\right] = V_t e^{-\delta(T-t)}. \tag{14.2}$$

Following Sahlman (1990), at the beginning of each stage i the VC calculates the owner-ship stake of the firm value that s/he is entitled to, given his financial and non-financial

---

[1] Dixit and Pyndick (1996: 121).

contribution. At $t = t_1$, the ownership stake x_{t_1} is given by[2]

$$x_{t_1} = \frac{I_{t_1}}{V_{t_1}^+ e^{-\delta(T-t_1)}},$$ (14.3)

for $V_{t_1}^+ = V_{t_1}^- + I_{t_1}$, for $V_{t_1}^-$ ($V_{t_1}^+$) denoting firm value before (after) investment takes place. The firm value at time $t = t_1$ is increased by the amount of cash inflow at I_{t_1}. Therefore the higher ownership stake $\left(I_{t_1}/V_{t_1}^+ e^{-\delta(T-t_1)}\right) > \left(I_{t_1}/V_{t_1}^+\right)$ rewards the VC for his capital cost, $\delta > 0$.

At the contractual time t_1, the VC expects the firm value driven by the drift rate α and discounted by ρ. Assuming that I_{t_2} is committed at time $t = t_1$, by the time that investment takes place $t = t_2$, it will be $I_{t_2} * e^{rt_1}$. Moreover since $I_{t_2} * e^{r(t_2-t_1)}$ it will be part of the firm value at t_2 it will be discounted by the VC cost $e^{-\delta(T-t_2)}$ that he will incur in the following stage. The ownership stake x_{t_2} is given by[3]

$$x_{t_2} = \frac{I_{t_2} * e^{r(t_2-t_1)}}{V_{t_2}^+ * e^{-\delta(T-t_2)}},$$ (14.4)

for $V_{t_2}^+ = V_{t_1}^+ e^{\alpha(t_2-t_1)} + I_{t_2} * e^{r(t_2-t_1)}$. Hence the VC ownership stake x_{t_2} is determined from the growth on the firm value during $(t_2 - t_1)$ and the level of capital cost that the VC will incur during the second period. Therefore the VC ownership stake is an endogenously defined variable:

$$x_{t_i} = x(\delta, \rho, t, I_{t_i}, V_t).$$ (14.5)

At the exit date, the VC ownership stake is a linear combination of each individual stake:

$$x_{tot} = x_{t_1} + x_{t_2}.$$ (14.6)

The marginal reward for the VC's non-financial contribution for each stage is as follows:

$$\Delta x_{t_1} = \frac{I_{t_1}}{V_{t_1}^+} (e^{\delta(T-t_1)} - 1)$$ (14.7)

---

[2] The expected firm value at time of investment t_1 is given by the following expression

$$E_{t_1}\left[e^{-\rho(T-t_1)} \left((V_{t_1} + I_{t_1}) \exp^{\left(\alpha - \frac{\sigma^2}{2}\right)(T-t_1)+\sigma(W_T-W_{t_1})} \right) \right] = V_{t_1}^+ e^{-\delta(T-t_1)}.$$

[3] The expected firm value at time of investment t_2 is given by the following expression

$$E_{t_2}\left[e^{-\rho(T-t_2)} \left(V_{t_1}^+ e^{\alpha(t_2-t_1)} + I_{t_2} * e^{r(t_2-t_1)} \right) \exp^{\left(\alpha - \frac{\sigma^2}{2}\right)(T-t_2)+\sigma(W_T-W_{t_2})} \right]$$

$$= V_{t_2}^+ e^{-\delta(T-t_2)}.$$

and

$$\Delta x_{t_2} = \frac{I_{t_2} * e^{r(t_2-t_1)}}{V_{t_2}^+}(*e^{\delta(T-t_2)} - 1). \tag{14.8}$$

The VC holds the option to convert his securities (convertible preferred debentures or convertible preferred stocks) into common shares if the upside potential gain by converting is larger than the loss in value of giving up the liquidation right. For a conversion ratio equal to one, the amount that the VC has to pay is equivalent to the initial investment I_{t_1} (assuming an at-the-money liquidation preference). In a two stage environment, reaching the next stage means deciding whether to further invest and be entitled to the accumulated ownership stake x_{tot}, or convert at a x_{t_1} stake exercising the liquidation preference (liquidation right + automatic conversion). S/he will continue investing in the project only if the expected discounted pay-off from this strategy brings higher value than exercising the liquidation preference at that moment.

Proposition 14.1. *The effects on the VC ownership stake level of the changes in different parameters are as follows:*

$$\frac{\partial x}{\partial \delta} > 0 \quad \text{and} \quad \frac{\partial^2 x}{\partial \delta^2} > 0, \tag{14.9}$$

implying that the VC ownership stake is a convex increasing function of the capital cost. The importance of the investment timing is captured from the first and the second derivative of the VC stake with respect to the investment time, while having a fixed final exit date T.

$$\frac{\partial x}{\partial t_i} < 0 \quad \text{and} \quad \frac{\partial^2 x}{\partial t_i^2} > 0 \tag{14.10}$$

The later the VC decides to invest, the lower will be his stake. In other words the VC ownership stake is a decreasing convex function of the investment time. Given

$$\frac{\partial x}{\partial I_{t_i}} > 0 \quad \text{and} \quad \frac{\partial^2 x}{\partial I_{t_i}^2} < 0, \tag{14.11}$$

the VC ownership stake increases at a decreasing rate for increasing investment levels. Lastly

$$\frac{\partial x}{\partial V_t} < 0 \quad \text{and} \quad \frac{\partial^2 x}{\partial V_t^2} > 0 \tag{14.12}$$

says that the VC claim on project value is lower if the project value at that moment is higher.

14.3. LIQUIDATION PREFERENCE

The venture capitalist seeks convertible preferred stocks or convertible debentures over common stocks. The convertible holder is senior in liquidation rights to common stock holders. In a liquidation situation, the venture capitalist has the right to put the stock or debenture to the company for a certain predefined price and get cash in return, or ask for redemption of the holdings in very specific situations, like merger, trade sale, public offering, purchase price, etc. We consider two main aspects of a liquidation preference:

1. Liquidations—including an acquisition or merger—entitle the VC to share the upside potential of the project or to receive up to his original investment amount. To put in other words, the VC requires the maximum value left up to its original investment (and any unpaid dividend) if any, or he may choose to convert into common shares and redraw its holdings before a merger or reorganization liquidation happens.
2. In the case of a public offering (IPO) the VC is required to convert (automatic conversion) into common stocks and leave the company according to the contractual provisions.

From the VC prospects, s/he would like to maximize the value of his/her holdings in case the project is successful or recoup the maximum possible value in case of project liquidation. Usually the liquidation right entitles the VC to collect its original investment I, if there is enough money in the company, or the remaining value V_t after the creditors and before all the other shareholders' claims, whereas the automatic conversion is part of the upside potential from conversion in case of good performance $\max(xV_T - I, 0)$. It is important to note at this point that although liquidation preference may look like a package of the upside potential from conversion and liquidation right, it is less valuable than the linear sum of the option components given that the VC has to give up the liquidation right $\min(V_T, I)$ to buy the automatic conversion option. Note that x can be either the absolute upside sharing of the VC (in the case of convertible debentures) or the relative gain in upside sharing by going from convertible preferred to common stock. In the extreme case where $x = 0$, the VC will convert only when forced (e.g. by the arrival of an IPO). This is an issue that is covered in more detail in Cossin *et al.* (2003). We treat here a stylized case that corresponds more exactly to the situation of convertible debenture (a form of financing that is widely used in VC contracts, notably in Europe).

The VC payoff at time T is given as:

$$\varphi(V_T) = \max(xV_T - I, \min(V_T, I)). \tag{14.13}$$

Figure 14.1 shows that the VC will convert his holdings only if the upside potential from converting is high enough to pay for the loss of the downside protection linked to the liquidation right. This expression can be simplified to:

$$\varphi(V_T) = \max(xV_T - I - \min(V_T, I), 0) + \min(V_T, I), \tag{14.14}$$

$$\varphi(V_T) = \max(xV_T - I + \max(-V_T, -I), 0) + \min(V_T, I), \tag{14.15}$$

$$\varphi(V_T) = \max(\max(xV_T - I - V_T, xV_T - I - I), 0) + \min(V_T, I), \tag{14.16}$$

$$\varphi(V_T) = V_T + \max(xV_T - I - V_T, xV_T - 2I) - \max(V_T - I, 0). \tag{14.17}$$

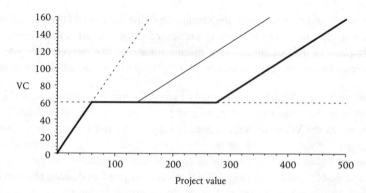

Figure 14.1. *VC pay-off value. The bold solid line stands for the VC pay-off value,*
$\max(xV_T - I, \min(V_T, I))$, *for any realization of project value V_T. The thin solid line on the right is the*
upside potential coming from the conversion optionality $\max(xV_T - I, 0)$. Note the parameters are:
$\delta = 0.05, \alpha = 0.35, \sigma = 0.6, r = 0.04, V_0 = 100, I = 60, T = 3\,yr$. *These parameters lead to a*
critical value of $V_T^* = 275.2$, where $V_T^* = \frac{2I}{x}$ and $x = 43.6\%$.

Proposition 14.2. *The VC final pay-off at $t = T$ can be written as:*

$$\varphi(V_T) = \begin{cases} V_T + (xV_T - I - V_T)^+ - (V_T - I)^+ \\ \\ V_T + (xV_T - 2I)^+ - (V_T - I)^+ \end{cases} \begin{cases} V_T & \text{if } V_T \le I, \\ V_T - (V_T - I)^+ & \text{if } I < V_T \le 2I, \\ & \text{if } V_T > 2I. \end{cases}$$

Proof. For any $V_T \le I$

$$V_T + (xV_T - I - V_T)^+ - (V_T - I)^+ = V_T \qquad (14.18)$$

equivalent to

$$(xV_T - I - V_T)^+ = 0. \qquad (14.19)$$

The only possibility for which $(xV_T - I - V_T)^+ > 0$ would imply an $x > 2$, which is in contradiction to the requirement that the VC cannot ask more than the project value as a whole, hence $x \in [0, 1]$. Consequently $(xV_T - I - V_T)^+ = 0$. Moreover for $V_T \le I$ one has $(V_T - I)^+ = 0$. The VC pay-off is then given by

$$\varphi(V_T) = V_T - 0 + 0 = V_T. \qquad (14.20)$$

For $I < V_T \le 2I, (xV_T - I - V_T)^+ = 0$ given that the only possibility to have $(xV_T - I - V_T)^+ > 0$ is for $x > \frac{3}{2}$, which once again is in contradiction to the VC ownership stake satisfying the requirement $x \in [0, 1]$. The VC pay-off for this case is as follows

$$\varphi(V_T) = V_T + (xV_T - I - V_T)^+ - (V_T - I)^+ = V_T - (V_T - I)^+. \qquad (14.21)$$

$\square$

14.3.1. *Infinite Horizon Case/Endogenous Threshold Exit Level*

Pushing the analysis further, one can solve for the VC pay-off process in an infinite horizon case. Closed-form solutions are available. The timing of the investment becomes then endogenous to the model, and is determined by a smooth pasting condition. The optimal stopping time τ_i is then given by

$$\tau = \{\inf t \geq 0 \mid V_t \geq V^*\}. \tag{14.22}$$

The pricing process uses the dynamic programming argument. The idea is to start from the end of the project life and fold recursively to the present. In a perpetual framework it reduces to the finding of the optimal thresholds V^* to exit. Once the boundary conditions are known, we work backwards toward the initial contracting time, $t = 0$.

The VC contract whose terminal pay-off is a piecewise linear function of the terminal price of the underlying asset is similar to a package option—that is, a combination of standard options and underlying asset. For $t = \tau$

$$\varphi_1(V_\tau) = (xV_\tau - 2I)^+ \tag{14.23}$$

and

$$\varphi_2(V_\tau) = (V_\tau - I)^+ \tag{14.24}$$

the VC pay-off is defined as:

$$\varphi(V_\tau) = V_\tau - \varphi_1(V_\tau) - \varphi_2(V_\tau). \tag{14.25}$$

Proposition 14.3. *In an infinite horizon case, the VC contractual pay-off at $t \in [0, \tau]$, given the liquidation right and automatic conversion value, is as follows:*

$$\varphi(V_t) = \begin{cases} V_t & \text{if } V_t \leq I, \\ V_t - \dfrac{I}{u-1}\left(\dfrac{V_t}{V_A^*}\right)^u & \text{if } I < V_t \leq 2I, \\ V_t - \dfrac{I}{u-1}\left(\dfrac{V_t}{V_A^*}\right)^u + \dfrac{2I}{u-1}\left(\dfrac{V_t}{V_B^*}\right)^u & \text{if } V_t > 2I, \end{cases} \tag{14.26}$$

for option components $\varphi_i(V_t)$ equal to

$$\varphi_1(V_t) = \frac{2I}{u-1}\left(\frac{V_t}{V_B^*}\right)^u, \tag{14.27}$$

$$\varphi_2(V_t) = \frac{I}{u-1}\left(\frac{V_t}{V_A^*}\right)^u, \tag{14.28}$$

V_A^* *would be the threshold below which VC is entitled only to the liquidation right and has zero (if $V_A^* \leq 2I$) or very low (if $V_A^* > 2I$) upside potential from conversion:*

$$V_A^* = \left(\frac{u}{u-1}\right)I,$$

V_B^* represents the upper optimal threshold level to exit the project:

$$V_B^* = \left(\frac{u}{u-1}\right)\frac{2I}{x}. \tag{14.29}$$

This is equivalent to saying that for any $V_t \geq V_A^*$ the liquidation right $\varphi_2(V_t) = I$. For any $V_A^* < V_t < V_B^*$ the VC pay-off includes a positive value due to conversion possibilities. Lastly for $V_t \geq V_B^*$ the final pay-off at the exit is given by

$$\varphi(V_\tau) = I + (xV_\tau - 2I) = (xV_\tau - I). \tag{14.30}$$

Proof. Define the upside potential to convert the holdings in common stocks and downside protection to exercise the liquidation right as follows:

$$\varphi_1(V_\tau) = (xV_\tau - 2I)^+,$$
$$\varphi_2(V_\tau) = (V_\tau - I)^+.$$

Hence the partial differential equation for each of the options are:

$$\tfrac{1}{2}\sigma^2 V_t^2 \varphi_{ivv}(V_t) + (\rho - \delta)V_t\varphi_{iv}(V_t) - \rho\varphi_i(V_t) = 0. \tag{14.31}$$

Identify the general solution as $\varphi_1(V_t) = BV_t^u$ and $\varphi_2(V_t) = AV_t^u$. It is important to note that $u > 1$. The polynomial root u is computed as:

$$u = \frac{-\left((\rho - \delta) - \frac{\sigma^2}{2}\right) + \sqrt{\left((\rho - \delta) - \frac{\sigma^2}{2}\right)^2 + 2\sigma^2\rho}}{\sigma^2}. \tag{14.32}$$

The boundary conditions of value matching (vm) and smooth pasting (sp) for the upside potential are as follows:

$$AV_\tau^u = V_\tau - I \qquad \text{vm,}$$
$$BV_\tau^u = xV_\tau - 2I \qquad \text{vm,}$$
$$AV_\tau^{u-1}u = 1 \qquad \text{sp,}$$
$$BV_\tau^{u-1}u = x \qquad \text{sp.}$$

These four equations determine the four unknowns, critical values of the project that trigger liquidation :

$$A = \frac{1}{u}V_A^{*1-u},$$
$$B = \frac{x}{u}V_B^{*1-u},$$
$$V_A^* = \left(\frac{u}{u-1}\right)I,$$
$$V_B^* = \left(\frac{u}{u-1}\right)\frac{2I}{x}.$$

For $V_t < V_A^*$ the VC pay-off is determined from the liquidation right, for $V_A^* \leq V_t < V_B^*$ is as if the VC would hold a riskless bond plus the option to convert for high firm value, whereas for $V_t \geq V_B^*$, the VC converts its holdings and exits the venture project. $\square$

The pricing is carried out under two crucial implicit assumptions:

1. The VC optimizes his/her position, by choosing the upper threshold level such as to maximize its pay-off at the exit of the venture, once the project value is known. In other words the VC has all the bargaining power in deciding when and how to end the venture project. In reality, exit options in a venture project may be limited. The board of directors is the only entity to have the power to initiate exit. The VC will be entitled to a certain degree of control right over exit only towards the end of the venture project's life. Kaplan and Stromberg (2003) provide empirical evidence of this phenomenon. Thus the actual design followed here applies better to VC dominated firms.

2. When the VC provides some value added in terms of reducing the level of asymmetric information, co-managing the project, etc., s/he is at the same time occurring some additional cost apart from investing in the project. Consequently s/he is induced to have an early exit from the venture. Obviously the VC would like to minimize this cost, by equalizing it to zero and by providing no value added. The reality shows that the VC does have a dual role and we do have to account for that.

Although the assumptions under which the VC pay-off value is derived are rigid, it provides some useful insights into understanding the value of this very important contractual feature.

Figure 14.2 considers a large versus a small stakeholder. The larger the ownership stake of the VC in the project, the larger is its pay-off at the exit. The liquidation preference

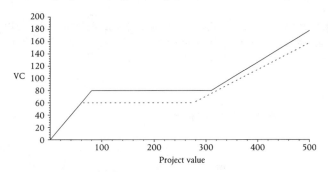

Figure 14.2. *VC ownership stake and project value. Large (solid line) versus small (dashed line) VC ownership stake. Small stakeholder case: VC invests 60 unit in a 100 unit worth company, hence is entitled to $x_1 = 43.6\%$ stake. Large stakeholder case: VC invests 80 unit equivalent to a $x_2 = 51.6\%$ stake. In order to convert, the VC requires the project value to be high enough to compensate for his liquidation right and the conversion price. The larger the ownership stake, the higher the required firm value, given the more valuable liquidation right. Note that the parameters are: $\delta = 0.05, \alpha = 0.35, \sigma = 0.6, r = 0.04, I(x_1) = 60, I(x_2) = 80, T = 3yr, V_0 = 100$. These parameters lead to the respective cirtical values:*
$$V_{2,T}^* = 310.1 > V_{1,T}^* = 275.2.$$

entitles the VC to a large pay-off if the venture project performs well, reducing the downside losses if the project performs poorly. It is important to note that in both VC contracts, the pay-off for the liquidation right is similar. Nonetheless the pay-offs are quite different for the upside part. The more the VC invests, the larger its stake on the company, the more he can gain if the project is successful. The required exit (critical) firm value is positively related to the investment level.

Figure 14.3 is a simple realization of the VC contract value at any time t, for different firm values. The VC holds a convertible security which allows him a share of the upside potential (=automatic conversion) as well as to the liquidation right. Whereas for low performance his contract value is equal or almost equal to the firm value, the gap in between is large in case of a good performance. One may think of it as a reward (punishment) for the entrepreneur if the project is successful (a failure).

Figure 14.4 represents the VC contract value as the sum of the liquidation right $\min(V_t, I)$, plus the opportunity to convert $(xV_t - 2I)^+$. The VC pay-off at the exit

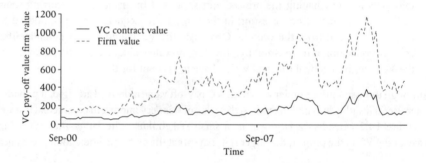

Figure 14.3. *VC contract value and firm value. VC pay-off versus firm value. Note that the parameters used are as follows:* $\alpha = 0.35, \delta = 0.05, \sigma = 0.6, V_0 = 100, V_0^+ = 160.$

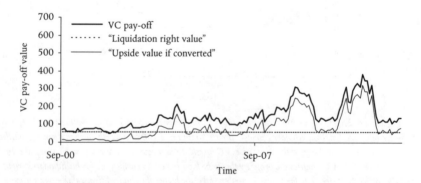

Figure 14.4. *VC pay-off value, liquidation value, and conversion value. The VC contract value is the sum of the liquidation right,* $\min(V_t, I)$*, plus the opportunity to convert,* $\max(xV_t - 2I, 0)$*. Note that the parameters are:* $\alpha = 0.35, \delta = 0.05, \sigma = 0.6, V_0 = 100, V_0^+ = 160.$

is equal to the firm value or initial investment in case of poor performance, or to the converted value for good performance.

Moreover the figures shed light on the relative importance of each component (automatic conversion and liquidation right) of the liquidation preference for different project performance levels.

14.3.2. *Liquidation in Finite Horizon Case*

In order to derive the closed form solution equation (14.26), we attributed no role to the entrepreneur in deciding the conditions under which the VC may liquidate his/her position. Furthermore we assumed that the VC non-financial contribution in the project had no impact on the VC ownership stake. This section releases these rigid restrictions in the model by assuming: First, an exogenously predefined project life as well as the duration of each stage. To put it differently, the VC is allowed to exit only at some preset discrete event, which may correspond to the end of each financing stage. Second, the model accounts for an additional reward for the VC capital cost.

As already mentioned the liquidation pay-off has two main components, the upside potential coming from the conversion possibility and the liquidation right, $\min(V_t, I_{t_1})$. The upside potential is implied by the automatic conversion. The VC would convert his holdings into common stock against a cost equal to the initial investment amount, only if the conversion value covers the investment cost. The way to proceed is to use dynamic programming and to work recursively. This model considers an up front financing. At $t = 0$, the VC meets the entrepreneur and both enter into a contractual agreement which will last up to time $T = 3$ years, the VC exit point. If the project has been successful until the end of the contractual period the VC exercises his liquidation preference at $t = T$. The VC pay-off value, in case of an acquisition or merger exit event, is defined as

$$\varphi(V_T, T) = \max(x_{t_1} V_T - I_{t_1}, \min(V_T, I_{t_1})). \tag{14.33}$$

In case an IPO (assumed to have no lock up period) takes place at date T, then the VC pay-off at the exit is as follows:

$$\varphi(V_T, T) = \max(x_{t_1} V_T - I_{t_1}, 0). \tag{14.34}$$

So far we focus on the possibility of an exit defined as in eqn (14.33), given that it also includes the possibility of an IPO without any lock up period.

Date	0		T	
* sign the contract		* VC payout (1)		
* VC disburse I_{t_1}	$max(x_{t_1} V_T - I_{t_1}, \min(I_{t_1}, V_T))$		caption [E]	
		or		
		* VC payout (2)		
		$max(x_{t_1} V_T - I_{t_1}, 0)$		

Figure 14.5. *Timing of events.*

14.3.2.1. *Pricing in Finite Differences*

The idea of pricing the liquidation right in a finite horizon case is to replace the partial derivative occurring in the partial differential equation by finite-difference approximations. It is already known by now that the VC pay-off function $\varphi(V_t, I, t, \rho, \sigma)$ of the derivative satisfies the following PDE:

$$\frac{\partial \varphi}{\partial t} + (\rho - \delta)V_t \frac{\partial \varphi}{\partial V} + \frac{1}{2}\sigma^2 V_t^2 \frac{\partial^2 \varphi}{\partial V^2} - \rho\varphi = 0. \tag{14.35}$$

Define:

$$X_t = \ln V_t, \tag{14.36}$$

then X_t satisfies the PDE:

$$\frac{\partial \varphi}{\partial t} + \left(\rho - \delta - \frac{1}{2}\sigma^2\right)\frac{\partial \varphi}{\partial X} + \frac{1}{2}\sigma^2 \frac{\partial^2 \varphi}{\partial X^2} - \rho\varphi = 0. \tag{14.37}$$

For (i,j), indicating time steps and space steps respectively, the discretization of this PDE gives:

$$0 = \frac{\varphi_{i+1,j} - \varphi_{i,j}}{\Delta t} + \left(\rho - \delta - \frac{1}{2}\sigma^2\right)\frac{\varphi_{i+1,j+1} - \varphi_{i,j-1}}{2\Delta X}$$
$$+ \frac{1}{2}\sigma^2 \frac{\varphi_{i+1,j+1} - 2\varphi_{i+1,j} + \varphi_{i+1,j-1}}{\Delta X^2} - \rho\varphi_{i,j}. \tag{14.38}$$

Equivalently:

$$\varphi_{i,j} = \frac{p_u\varphi_{i+1,j+1} + p_m\varphi_{i+1,j} + p_d\varphi_{i+1,j-1}}{1 + \rho\Delta t} \tag{14.39}$$

with

$$p_u = \frac{\Delta t}{2}\left(\frac{\sigma^2}{\Delta X^2} + \frac{\rho - \delta - \frac{1}{2}\sigma^2}{\Delta X}\right),$$

$$p_d = \frac{\Delta t}{2}\left(\frac{\sigma^2}{\Delta X^2} - \frac{\rho - \delta - \frac{1}{2}\sigma^2}{\Delta X}\right),$$

$$p_m = 1 - p_u - p_d.$$

That is, by discretization of the PDE we get a trinomial tree with up, middle, and down probabilities specified by p_u, p_m, and p_d, respectively. The number of asset steps is implicitly determined by the time steps and the boundary conditions:

$$M = \frac{\ln V_{\max} - \ln V_{\min}}{\Delta x}. \tag{14.40}$$

Hence time and asset steps depend on each other. Such specification is necessary to have convergence and stability of the explicit finite difference pricing method $\Delta x = \sqrt{\Delta t}$, where $\Delta t = \frac{T}{W}$, W is the number of time steps exogenously defined. Working in a grid means imposing additional conditions. We choose the set of Neumann boundary conditions such as:

$$\varphi(i, M * \Delta x) = \varphi(i, M * \Delta x) + (V(M * \Delta x) - V(M * \Delta x - 1)),$$

$$\varphi(i, 0) = \varphi(i, 0 + 1).$$

At maturity the VC pay-off is given by eqn (14.33):

$$\varphi(W * \Delta t, j) = \max(x_{t_1} * \exp^{X_{W*\Delta t}} - I_{t_1}, \min(\exp^{X_{W*\Delta t}}, I_{t_1})). \tag{14.41}$$

Moreover, some additional refinements (restructuring) are needed on the firm value process V_t once the VC disburses I_{t_1} at date zero.

14.3.2.2. *Numerical Results*
Table 14.1 studies the importance of each component of liquidation preference. The liquidation preference is a package of liquidation rights plus the automatic conversion. The value of the automatic conversion is lower than the value of the upside potential, since it incorporates the liquidation right in the strike price. The results of Table 14.1 are compatible with Proposition 14.1. Table 14.1 indicates that the VC expected contract value at the end of the venture is very sensitive to the financing level. The more the VC disburses in the project, the larger is the ownership stake in a successful project. The amount invested is positively related to the VC ownership stake and to the after money project value (higher cash inflow). Furthermore the liquidation right limits the VC downside losses in case of poor performance, in other words limits the risk of incurring large losses. The initial project value plays an ambiguous role: first it reduces the VC ownership stake, since his/her financing amount is relatively less important for a higher firm value, and secondly it implies larger expected firm value at time T. Whereas the first plays a negative role on the VC ownership stake x_{t_1} the second one has a positive impact on project value V_T. Any increase in uncertainty implies higher values as the project value increases and there is negligible impact on the downside part. The marginal increase in the upside more than compensates for the drop in liquidation rights which serves as a cushion for any potential losses. A higher project drift α means higher future firm value, hence both components of the liquidation preference will experience an increase in their respective values. The more the VC is involved in terms of non-financial contribution, the higher will be his/her stake on the end pay-off due to a higher capital cost. Lastly, the timing of the exit T ($1 \to 3$ years) determines not only the value of the liquidation preference but also its decomposition in terms of the importance of upside value ($36.057 \to 171.471$) vs liquidation right ($59.687 \to 58.66$). Obviously the longer the project life, the higher the probability that the project value will hit the upper threshold which makes possible the convertibility feature. Furthermore the liquidation right becomes less important as the expected project duration increases.

Table 14.1. *VC contract value*

Parameters		VC stake x_{t_1}	VC Contr. Value[1]	Liquidation Right[2]	Automatic Convers.[3]	Upside Potential[4]
I_{t_1}	40	0.332	141.661	39.572	102,09	126.241
	60	0.436	193.926	58.66	135,27	171.472
	80	0.516	245.83	77.387	168,44	216.703
V_0	80	0.497	190.987	58.363	132,62	168.895
	100	0.436	193.926	58.66	135,27	171.472
	120	0.387	193.318	58.906	134.41	170.583
σ	0.4	0.436	159.885	59.95	99,94	147.205
	0.6	0.436	193.926	58.66	135,27	171.472
	0.8	0.436	225.709	56.083	169,63	198.157
α	0.2	0.436	120.295	56.954	63.34	89.592
	0.35	0.436	193.926	58.66	135,27	171.472
	0.4	0.436	229.312	59.017	170.30	209.694
δ	0	0.375	175.409	58.66	116,75	149.579
	0.05	0.436	193.926	58.66	135,27	171.472
	0.1	0.506	216.609	58.66	157,95	197.332
T	1	0.394	71.976	59.687	12.29	36.057
	3	0.436	193.926	58.66	135,27	171.472
	4	0.458	312.237	58.568	253,67	293.307

1. $\varphi(V_T, T) = \max(x_{t_1} V_T - I_{t_1}, \min(V_T, I_{t_1}))$
2. $\varphi_2(V_T, T) = \min(V_T, I_{t_1})$
3. $\varphi_1(V_T, T) = \max(x_{t_1} V_T - 2I_{t_1}, 0)$
4. $\max(x_{t_1} V_T - I_{t_1}, 0)$

The table shows how the VC contract value (estimated at time zero) reacts to changes in parameters. Note the drift rate, the VC additional cost, and the volatility are respectively 0.35, 0.05, and 0.6. The risk free rate is 0.04, the initial firm value 100 units, and an initial investment of 60 units. The time horizon is three years. In bold is the base case.

14.4. CONCLUSION

Venture capitalist play a complex and multi-faceted role in the financing of new ventures. Particularly critical and unique is their direct hands-on interventions, which can significantly affect the value of their ownership stakes above and beyond their financial contributions. This ability to intervene directly (through board seats and other direct interaction with the venture management) on the underlying value process is a defining characteristic of the venture capital world not captured in models of 'arm's length' external equity investments. Any omission of these non-financial contributions (e.g. by failing to recognize additional rewards) would lead to early exercise of the exit option. We integrate this feature into our model and analyse the value of the liquidation preference based on a simple real options model. The liquidation preference clause limits the downside risk of the venture capitalist while leaving the upside potential unadulterated. The liquidation preference is thus a package of conversion optionality and liquidation right. Exercising the automatic conversion implies giving up the liquidation preference. Hence the automatic conversion constitutes only a fraction of the upside potential, given the higher conversion strike price. The relative importance of these features is a function of firm characteristics and project duration, as classically expected in a real options framework.

We obtain values in closed form for the perpetual case and analyse non perpetual situations using numerical analysis (finite differences). We thus provide the tools to understand better this important venture capital contract feature. Ultimately, while this was not the direct goal of this chapter, solutions of the style we suggest could lead to optimization programmes and better overall contract design (as the feature described here is currently not well analysed from an economic point of view). Nonetheless, in order to fully understand the impact of this classical contractual feature, the other option-like covenants of VC contracts should be analysed as well and the interaction between the different dimensions (staging, antidilution, and liquidation preference, notably) be fully understood. As outlined by Kaplan and Stromberg (2003), venture capital contracts are best seen as flexible contractual mechanisms for the contingent reallocation of control, ownership, and cash flow rights. But for this complex package of real options to attain its goal of optimally balancing incentives, risk protections, and the sharing of the upside potential, we need to be able to look at the basket of options as a basket, not a collection of individually priced options. A first attempt at this can be found in our background work (Cossin *et al.* 2003), but this is just a first glimpse at the complex universe of venture capital investment contracts. The contribution from the real options approach should not be underestimated though, and it holds the promise of significant advances in the understanding of the true value added of contractual features which have often been part of 'boilerplate' contracts for decades, with little understanding of their effect on the investors' wealth or behaviour.

References

Berk, J. B., Green, R.C., and Naik, V. (1998), 'Valuation and return dynamics of new ventures', NBER Working Paper 6745.

Cossin, D., Leleux, B., and Saliasi, E. (2003), 'Understanding the economic value of legal covenants in investment contracts: A real-options approach to venture equity contracts', Working Paper, University of Lausanne.

Dixit, A. K. and Pindyck, R. S. (1996), *Investment under Uncertainty*, Princeton: Princeton University Press.

Gompers, P. (1995), 'Optimal investment, monitoring, and the staging of venture capital', *Journal of Finance* 50, 1461–89.

Hubalek, F. and Schachermayer, W. (1999), 'The limitations of no-arbitrage arguments for real options', Working Paper, Vienna University of Economics and Business Administration.

Kaplan, S. and Strömberg, P. (2000), 'Financial contracting theory meets the real world: An empirical analysis of venture capital contracts', *Review of Economic Studies*, 70, 251–83.

Myers, S. C. and Howe, C. D. (1997), 'A life cycle model of pharmaceutical R& D', Technical Report, Program on the Pharmaceutical Industry, Massachusetts Institute of Technology.

Sahlman, W. A. (1990), 'The structure and governance of venture capital organizations', *Journal of Financial Economics* 27, 473–521.

PART IV

VENTURE CAPITAL EXITS AND IPOS

15

The Extent of Venture Capital Exits: Evidence from Canada and the USA

DOUGLAS J. CUMMING AND JEFFREY G. MACINTOSH

15.1. INTRODUCTION

Venture capitalists are a highly specialized group of investors with expertise in the financing of small- and medium-sized enterprises. Both because of a lack of positive cash flow, and because the agency costs associated with entrepreneurial finance are pronounced, high-growth (and usually technology-based) firms rarely have access to bank borrowing, particularly in the early stages. Because of their specialized skill set, venture capitalists are uniquely positioned to resolve informational asymmetries, police moral hazard problems, and offer value-added services such as finding suitable legal, accounting, marketing, investment banking, and other services, identifying strategic partners, hiring managers, participating in strategic decisions, and providing technical and operating advice (Sahlman 1988, 1990; MacIntosh 1994; Amit *et al.* 1997, 1990, 1993; Gompers and Lerner 1999*a*).

Much research has focused on the role of venture capital financial contracts in mitigating agency costs and informational asymmetries between venture capitalists and entrepreneurial firms (e.g. Admati and Pfleiderer 1994; Lerner 1994; Gompers 1995, 1998; Cornelli and Yosha 1997; Gompers and Lerner 1999*a*; Kaplan and Strömberg 2000). However, there is a comparative dearth of research examining issues associated with venture capital exits. Black and Gilson (1998) and Jeng and Wells (2000) have documented the importance of the relation between venture capital finance and stock markets. Related research has analysed the relationship between venture capital finance and initial public offerings (e.g. Barry *et al.* 1990; Megginson and Weiss 1991; Zingales 1995; Lin and Smith 1997; Black and

We owe special thanks to Stefanie Franzke, Aditya Kaul, Paul Halpern, Gary Lazarus, Ted Liu, Mary Macdonald, Frank Mathewson, Vikas Mehrotra, Corrine Sellars, Kashi Nath Tiwari, and Ralph A. Winter for helpful comments and discussions. We are also grateful for comments from seminar participants at the University of Alberta Institute for Financial Research Workshop (October 1999), the ABN AMRO International Conference on Initial Public Offerings, Amsterdam (July 2000), the Canadian Law and Economics Association Annual Conference, Toronto (September 2000), the Eastern Finance Association, Charleston (April 2001), the University of Western Ontario, ASAC (May 2001), the Multinational Finance Society, Lake Garda (June 2001), the University of Frankfurt Center for Financial Studies (CFS) (July 2001), the University of Hamburg Institute for Law and Economics Workshop (July 2001) and the Australian Banking and Finance Conference (December 2002). Related work appears in Cumming and MacIntosh (2003), 'A cross-country comparison of full and partial venture capital exits', *Journal of Banking and Finance*, 27, 511–48.

Gilson 1998; Gompers and Lerner 1999*a*, *b*; Petty *et al.* 1999; Cumming and MacIntosh 2003*a*). In earlier work, we examine the complete range of exit vehicles, including acquisition exits, secondary sales, buybacks, and write-offs (Cumming and MacIntosh 2003*a*).

This chapter seeks to extend our earlier work by examining the question of why venture capitalists sometimes make a full exit (i.e. sell all of their holdings in the investee firm) and sometimes make a partial exit (i.e. sell some but not all of their holdings, as discussed further below). In our earlier work, we suggest that the choice of exit vehicle is heavily influenced by the ability of potential new owners to resolve information asymmetries both in valuing the firm and in monitoring management after the VC effects an exit, in addition to their ability to resolve owner–manager agency conflicts post-exit. The central organizing theme of this chapter is similar; we suggest that a VC will choose to make a partial exit where information asymmetry between firm insiders and outsiders (i.e. potential buyers) is high, in order to signal the quality of the investment to potential buyers. We also suggest that, in some circumstances, a VC will choose to effect a partial exit in order to bring on board a new active investor with specialized skills that existing investors do not possess.

We test our theories concerning the importance of the degree of information asymmetry and the probability of a partial exit by looking at a number of variables that we posit are associated with the extent of information asymmetry between firm insiders and outsiders. These include the type of exit, whether the firm is in a high-tech industry, the stage at which the initial investment was made, the duration of the investment, the availability of capital to venture capitalists, and the firm's growth rate.

In the spirit of Black and Gilson (1998) and Jeng and Wells (2000), one of our primary interests is in the international comparison of the relationship between private and public equity markets. We find significant differences in exit behaviour between Canada and the USA. These differences are likely attributable to a combination of market and regulatory factors that differ between the two countries.

This chapter is organized as follows. Section 15.2 recaps the types of exits used by venture capitalists. Section 15.3 distinguishes between full and partial exits in each exit context. Section 15.4 develops a theory of partial exits. Section 15.5 documents institutional and legal differences between Canada and the United States that may affect the choice of exit strategy. The data are discussed in Section 15.6, and the empirical evidence is presented in Section 15.7. Conclusions follow in Section 15.8.

15.2. TYPES OF EXIT VEHICLES EMPLOYED BY VENTURE CAPITALISTS

In general, VCs will exit their investments by one of the following five methods. In an initial public offering (IPO) the firm sells shares to members of the public for the first time. The VC will typically retain its shares at the date of the public offering, selling shares into the market in the months or years following the IPO. Alternatively, following the IPO the VC may dispose of its investment by making a dividend of investee firm shares to the fund's owners. Despite the fact that the VC will not usually sell more than a small fraction of its shares at the time of the IPO (if any at all), exits effected by sales subsequent to the IPO are (following common usage) classified as IPO exits.

The VC may also sell the entire firm to a third party, which we refer to below as an acquisition exit. Typically, the buyer is a strategic acquirer—a larger entity in the same or similar business to the acquired firm that wishes to meld the firm's product or technology with its own (either vertically or horizontally). Strategic acquisitions often involve the merger of two corporations with some prior contractual relationship, such as in the supply of inputs or the licensing of a particular technology (MacIntosh 1994).

This form of exit may be effected in a number of different ways. For example, the transaction may be structured as a sale of all the shares in return for cash, shares of the acquirer, or other assets. Alternatively, the transaction may be structured as a sale of the firm's assets or as a merger between the investee firm and purchasing firm (or a subsidiary thereof).

In an exit effected by way of secondary sale, the VC will sell its shares to a third party—typically a strategic acquirer, and in some cases another VC. A secondary sale differs from an acquisition exit in that only the shares of the VC are sold to the third party; the entrepreneur and other investors will retain their investments. Where the purchaser is a strategic acquirer, it will often be seeking a window on the firm's technology, with a view to possibly effecting a complete acquisition of the firm sometime in the future.

In a buyback exit, the VC will sell its shares to the entrepreneur and/or the company.

A write-off typically involves the failure of the entrepreneurial firm. The VC may continue to hold shares in a non-viable or barely profitable enterprise in the case of a write-down, as discussed below.

15.3. FULL AND PARTIAL VENTURE CAPITAL EXITS

An exit may be full or partial. In the case of IPOs, the VC will rarely sell its holdings at the date of the IPO, for reasons explored further below. By convention (and in accord with how industry data is collected by the Canadian Venture Capital Association and Venture Economics in the USA; see Section 15.6), a full exit is defined as one in which the VC fully disposes of its holdings within one year of the date of the IPO. A partial exit involves a sale of at least some of the VC's holdings within one year of the IPO, with retention of some of its holdings beyond the one-year period. A full acquisition exit involves the sale of the entire firm for cash; in a partial acquisition exit, the venture capitalist receives (often illiquid) shares in the acquirer firm instead of cash. In the case of a secondary sale or a buyback exit (in which the entrepreneur buys out the venture capitalist), a partial exit entails a sale of only part of the venture capitalist's holdings. A partial write-off involves a write down of the investment.

In a write-off exit, the VC makes a decision to spend no further time or effort bringing the investment to fruition, and essentially walks away from it. Indeed, many write-offs involve the bankruptcy and consequent disappearance of the firm. Given that a partial exit is one in respect of which the VC disposes of some of its holdings, a partial write-off appears to be a contradiction in terms. Nonetheless, the Canadian Venture Capital Association and Venture Economics defines a partial write-off as a situation in which the VC takes a write-down of the investment on its books. When this occurs, it is virtually certain that the investment is a 'living dead' investment—that is, one involving a viable but marginally profitable enterprise which lacks sufficient upside potential for the VC to continue to devote time and attention to it. While distinguishing between full write-offs and partial write-offs thus provides useful information, partial write-offs are somewhat distinct from partial exits in the case of IPOs, secondary sales, and buybacks. We thus consider the sample with and without write-offs in our empirical analysis.

The case of partial acquisition exits is also unique. An acquisition exit is, definitionally, an event in which the entire firm is sold, typically to a strategic acquirer that intends to merge the target firm into its own operations. Such sales frequently involve the payment of cash consideration to the outgoing shareholders of the purchased firm. Thus, on its face, it seems impossible to imagine that an acquisition could be a partial acquisition. Nonetheless, in certain situations, the acquisition exit may resemble a partial exit. At a broad level of generality, there are four types of acquisition exits: (a) acquisitions by public companies with deep public markets; (b) acquisitions by public companies that are thinly traded; (c) acquisitions by private companies; (d) acquisitions by the investee firm of another firm.

In any of these cases, the consideration received by the VC for selling its shares may be (and often is) shares. In the first case, shares received by the VC are tantamount to cash, since the shares may freely be sold into the public market. Such exits are thus properly classified as full exits. In the second case, the shares can also be converted into cash by a sale into the public market. However, depending on the degree of illiquidity of the acquirer's stock, the VC may be able to convert to cash only over a lengthy period of time, or perhaps (if the market is very illiquid) not at all. Thus, the VC remains invested in the combined operations of its original investee firm and those of the acquirer. This type of transaction resembles a partial exit in that the VC's ability to influence and control the operations of the investee firm are reduced commensurately with the VC's reduction in equity ownership (although not linearly[1]). It also resembles a partial exit in that, following the transaction, the VC retains an indirect interest in the investee firm's assets that is less substantial than the direct interest it formerly held.

In the third case, shares of a private company are necessarily very illiquid. In addition to the absence of a ready market in which to sell the shares, private companies typically have constitutional or contractual restrictions on the ability of any shareholder to resell its shares (such as requirements for board and/or shareholder approval of a share transfer). This type of exit again resembles a partial exit. In the fourth case, the investee firm acquires, and subsequently merges with, another firm. If the acquired firm is small relative to the acquiring firm, then there is no exit at all. If the acquired firm is large compared to the acquirer (as is typically the case in a transaction structured as a reverse takeover[2]) then

---

[1] Key control thresholds in equity ownership are 33.34% (conferring the ability to block a two-thirds resolution), 50.1% (conferring *de jure* control), and 66.67% (conferring the power to pass supermajority resolutions, but this threshold is subject to jurisdictional variation, and variation arising from supermajority requirements in the corporation's constitution). Also, the VC may no longer possess a seat or seats on the board, and may also sacrifice previously held rights arising from shareholder agreements.

[2] A reverse takeover is one in which shareholders of the nominal target corporation are paid in shares in the acquirer corporation. Following the takeover, the two corporations are merged, with shareholders of each

the transaction is either a full or partial exit, depending on the liquidity of the shares received as consideration for the transaction.

While our data sample indicates those situations in which share consideration is received, it does not indicate the identity or nature of the purchaser, nor whether that purchaser is a public or a private company. Thus, we are unable to make the fine distinctions between different types of acquisition exits that we would have preferred to make. As a saw-off, we have classified all acquisition exits in which share consideration is received as 'partial acquisitions', which assumes that there is at least some degree of share illiquidity in the average acquisition exit.

Once again, we have empirically tested the data both with and without partial acquisition exits. As detailed below, this makes little difference to our results. In addition, we empirically investigate the relationship between the receipt of a share consideration and a number of other variables.

In addition, in the empirical analysis in Section 15.7, we first regress the dependent variable (extent of exits) on (*inter alia*) all of the exit types in our sample, except acquisitions. Acquisitions are excluded given (as explained above) that a partial acquisition exit is somewhat different in type than other forms of partial exit. Second, we segregate each type of exit, and regress the extent of exit on various other factors that we hypothesize to affect the extent of exit. This allows us to check for the possibility that partial and full exits have somewhat unique meanings across different types of exit, and also provides a check on the robustness of our other empirical results.

15.4. A THEORY OF PARTIAL EXITS

In previous work (Cumming and MacIntosh 2003*a*), we provide a more general theory of venture capital exits. This is briefly summarized as follows. VC investors are active, value-added investors. They bring not merely capital to the table, but knowledge, skill, and a network of legal, accounting, investment banking, marketing, and other contacts that are useful to a fledgling enterprise. We hypothesize that a VC will exit from an investment when the projected marginal value added as a result of the VC's efforts, at any given measurement interval, is less than the projected marginal cost of these efforts. By 'effort' we mean all of those things that VCs can do to add value to an enterprise. By 'cost' we mean all the direct and overhead costs associated with creating value, the costs of monitoring and periodically re-evaluating the investment, as well as the opportunity cost associated with alternative deployments of capital. By 'projected' we mean to suggest that the VC will take into account not merely present cost and effort, but a summation of all future costs and efforts. By 'measurement interval', we mean those points in time (whether quarterly, yearly, or otherwise) at which the VC formally or informally reassesses its continued commitment to an investment. Below, we refer to the projected costs of maintaining the investment as the 'maintenance costs'.

corporation receiving shares in the merged entity. The end result is that the shareholders of the former target will hold the majority of shares in the merged entity, giving them control.

In general, we predict that this exit condition will tend to be satisfied, and the VC will effect an exit, when its skill set is exhausted, when the maintenance costs of the investment increase unexpectedly, or when the VC's potential value added diminishes sharply (owing, for example, to an internal event such as a failure of the firm's technology, or to an external event like a competitor's invention of a superior product). This will be subject to considerations relating to the VC's opportunity cost of investment, however. We hypothesize that the VC will exit its investment even when the potential value added exceeds the investment's maintenance cost, if the VC can sell the investment to a party with a greater ability to add value (such as a strategic acquirer). Regardless of ability to add value, there may also be windows of opportunity for the VC to sell into the public market when valuations for technology firms are particularly high.

When would we expect to observe partial exits? Initially, a partial exit appears to be an odd phenomenon. A partial exit, involving the disposition of some, but not all, of the VC's investment, will lower the VC's potential upside profit commensurately with the lessening of the VC's equity stake. It will also dilute the VC's ability to exercise powers of control over the enterprise—powers that can be useful in bringing discipline to management and maximizing the value of the investment. It will not, however, substantially decrease the VC's maintenance costs. Such costs are relatively fixed; that is, the cost of maintaining an investment, per dollar of investment, increases less than proportionately with the size of the investment. In short, as the size of the VC's investment decreases, it sacrifices economies of scale in investing. We thus expect that partial exits will be made only in a small number of special situations, which we summarize here and elaborate below. As will be seen in most of these situations, the purpose of the partial exit is to mitigate information asymmetries arising between the VC as seller and the outside buyer(s).

15.4.1. *Partial Exit as a Signal of Quality*

There is abundant evidence in the finance literature that partial ownership retention is a signal of quality (e.g. Leland and Pyle 1977; Lin and Smith 1997; Gompers and Lerner 1999*a*). Partial retention is a credible signal of quality because it is less expensive for the VC to maintain an ownership interest in a high-quality firm than in a low-quality firm. We thus hypothesize that a VC may choose a partial exit in preference to a full exit in order to signal the quality of the firm and sell shares at a value closer to the firm's true worth. Clearly, the value of the signal will vary with the degree of information asymmetry between (selling) insiders and (purchasing) outsiders. Below, we formulate hypotheses about the degree to which information asymmetry will vary with the investee firm's book and market values, stage of development, and degree of asset intangibility. We also generate hypotheses concerning the degree of information asymmetry and whether the investment is staged or syndicated, the duration of the VC's investment, and the different types of exit vehicles used.

15.4.1.1. *Signalling and Increases in Capital Available to the Venture Capital Industry*
When the pool of capital available to the VC industry expands, this will create opportunities for VC managers to expand the pool of capital under administration, increasing VC returns.

In the short run, however, this will stretch managerial resources, resulting in redeployment of managers from some old investments to new investments. We hypothesize that this will result in a shorter duration of investment than would otherwise have been the case for those investments exited, increasing the value of a partial exit as a signal of quality.

15.4.1.2. *Bringing on Board a New Active Investor with Specialized Skills*

We hypothesize that, in connection with investments that are of less than 'home run' quality, a VC may wish to bring in another active investor to facilitate monitoring and strategic decisionmaking. This will involve a sale of part of the VC's shares to the new investor, and hence a partial exit. In this situation, a partial exit may also be used to signal quality to the incoming strategic acquirer or other purchaser.

15.4.1.3. *Signalling and Grandstanding*

Grandstanding is a phenomenon that likely enhances the likelihood of a partial exit. Gompers (1996) finds that younger VC firms will prematurely exit portfolio investments in order to build a track record that will facilitate further fundraising efforts. We suggest that the theory of grandstanding can be used to explain not merely why we observe some exits when we do, but also the manner in which they are exited (i.e. by a partial, rather than a full, exit).

Grandstanding necessarily involves exit of some investments at an earlier stage than would otherwise be the case. *Ceteris paribus*, an exit taken early in the life of the investee firm will be associated with heightened information asymmetry, since the prospects of younger firms are generally less predictable than those of older, more established firms which have already proved their product and/or established the quality of management. Thus, when we observe grandstanding, we are also likely to observe a heightened probability of a partial exit.

There may be another way in which grandstanding may lead to a heightened probability of a partial exit. The best of all worlds for a young VC firm would be to be able to retain all promising investments while simultaneously establishing a track record. However, establishing a track record necessarily requires that at least some investments be exited. It may be that instead of exiting promising investments fully, the VC will believe that it can simultaneously establish a track record and retain a part interest in promising investments. On this view, partial exit is a compromise between establishing a track record sufficient for the purposes of future capital raising efforts, and remaining involved in those investments that still have significant upside potential.

15.4.2. *Type of Exit Vehicle*

Different exit vehicles are associated with different degrees of information asymmetry between insiders and outsiders. We expect to see partial exits used more frequently in connection with exit vehicles for which the new owners face large hurdles in resolving informational asymmetry. In this subsection, we summarize our previous research on the extent of information asymmetry associated with different forms of exit (Cumming and MacIntosh 2003a).

15.4.2.1. *Initial Public Offerings*

Initial public offerings (IPOs) involve the sale of shares of a company to public investors, typically (but not always) accompanied by a listing on a stock exchange. We hypothesize that this form of exit will be accompanied by the greatest information asymmetry between the firm and its new owners. This is partly a product of the relatively unsophisticated nature of public buyers. While all but the smallest IPOs are sold mainly to institutional investors, institutional money managers will not possess the same degree of expertise in any particular technology as strategic acquirers, which are typically the purchasers in both acquisition exits and secondary sales. Nor will they be as knowledgeable as the entrepreneur herself, in the case of a buyback. Thus, public buyers will be the least sophisticated purchasers.

Public buyers will also suffer from free-rider problems. The incentive of each is to rely on other buyers to set an accurate IPO price. It is well known that this free-rider problem carries over into post-IPO monitoring of the firm's activities. By contrast, exits via acquisitions, secondary sales, and buybacks all result in considerable concentration in post-exit shareholdings.

These problems will be all the more acute with respect to technology issues, in which information asymmetry between insiders and outsiders is high, and for which the skill and knowledge deficit is most pronounced. About three-quarters of all VC investments are made in technology investments (Macdonald and Associates, Venture Economics, Gompers and Lerner 1999*a*).

The skill and knowledge deficit and the free-rider problem will be abridged by the investment bankers (and other professionals associated with the offering, such as lawyers and accountants) who will use their knowledge and expertise to price IPOs, and hence to protect public investors. The very fact that an investment banker is willing to bring an issue to market is a signal of the issue's quality; indeed, the more reputable the investment banker, the more potent the signal of quality (Megginson and Weiss 1991). Investment bankers, however, like institutional money managers, tend to be generalists,[3] who will in turn rely heavily on their technology analysts in determining whether to underwrite a particular offering. Despite their specialized skills, however, these analysts are unlikely to be able to replicate the knowledge and experience of a strategic acquirer, or the firm's insiders. Thus, even the presence of expert market intermediaries will leave more information asymmetry in the case of IPOs than with respect to acquisition exits, secondary sales, and buybacks. Because a partial exit mitigates information asymmetry, we hypothesize that partial exits will be used more often in association with IPOs than with other forms of exit in the tests using the full sample of all exits in the empirics (see Table 15.4 in Section 15.7).

In the empirics we also consider the subsample of IPO exits separately (see Table 15.5 (Panel A) in Section 15.7), and consider factors that affect the extent of IPO exits. These factors are discussed further in Sections 15.4.3–15.4.8.

---

[3] This is more frequently the case in Canada than in the USA. Almost all underwriters in Canada are generalists. Even Yorkton Securities, the investment banker with perhaps the best claim to be a technology boutique, still does approximately 30% of its business in traditional industries. Moreover, it does not specialize in any one segment of the technology market. By contrast, in the USA, boutique underwriters more frequently concentrate on technology offerings, or even on particular types of technology offerings.

15.4.2.2. *Acquisition Exits*

As noted earlier, an acquisition exit involves the sale of the entire firm to a third party, typically a strategic acquirer. We classify any acquisition exit where share consideration is paid to the VC as a partial exit. Given it is somewhat unique, in the empirical analysis (Section 15.7) of the extent of exit for all exits together (Table 15.4), we therefore suppress the acquisition exits variable to avoid problems of collinearity across different exit types.

We perform tests in Section 15.7 on the sub-sample of acquisition exits to determine when share as opposed to cash consideration is likely to be paid (see Table 15.5 (Panel B)). Because of collinearity problems, we were able to run regressions on the set of acquisition exits in our sample only with a limited number of variables, namely technology versus non-technology investments, market/book ratio, investment duration, and a variable for market conditions (discussed further in Section 15.4.8). We hypothesize that we will observe more partial exits (i.e. those in which share cash consideration is received) with technology investments. Technology investments are riskier than non-technology investments, and therefore more difficult to value. This creates a valuation risk that will be borne by those who continue to hold shares in the investee firm, whether directly or indirectly (i.e. through share ownership of the purchaser). Giving share consideration is a way of splitting this risk between purchaser and seller. This in turn avoids at least two moral hazard problems. First, the vendor will be tempted to misrepresent the value of the firm to the acquirer. Remaining indirectly invested in the investee firm through holding the acquirer's shares attenuates this risk. Second, the seller(s) possess skills and knowledge that has continuing value to the purchasers. Remaining invested provides an incentive to communicate this information and, more generally, to continue to work as far as possible to make the investee firm work.

In addition, technology firms dominate our sample. Most acquirers of technology firms will also be technology firms, and such firms are notoriously strapped for cash. This also makes the use of share consideration preferable to cash consideration.

We also hypothesize that a high market/book ratio is consistent with a fast growth firm, and such firms are more likely to be characterized by uncertainty as to future earnings and profitability than firms with slow but steady growth. We thus hypothesize that high market/book ratios will be associated with more partial exits, to signal quality.

Finally, longer duration of investment will tend to be associated with a more mature firm with less information asymmetry, and a lower degree of valuation risk. We thus hypothesize that the longer the duration, the less frequently we will observe partial exits.

15.4.2.3. *Secondary Sales*

Instead of selling the entire firm, the VC may sell all or part of its investment to another venture capitalist or a strategic acquirer in a secondary sale. As we have suggested elsewhere, a secondary sale is likely to be an inferior form of exit to an acquisition exit (Cumming and MacIntosh 2003a). Generally speaking, a strategic acquirer will prefer to purchase 100 per cent of the firm, since then it has much greater freedom to use the firm's assets and technology unhindered by legal obligations to other owners. While this will not always be the case (the acquirer may desire nothing more than gaining a window on the firm's technology), we believe that it will be the case more often than not.

Moreover, because in a secondary sale the buyer will purchase less than 100 per cent of the firm, the incentive and ability to monitor the managers post-exit will be less than in connection with a strategic acquisition (lowering the value of the purchase to the acquirer). In addition, a bilateral agency problem arises between two previously unrelated owners of the firm—the entrepreneur and the new owner. There is no guarantee that this relationship will work well.

A secondary sale will also typically involve sale of the VC's shares but not the entrepreneur's. This may be indicative of a breakdown in the relationship between the entrepreneur and VC (i.e. the parties are not 'working on the same team') (MacIntosh 1997). This is frequently associated with a lack of clear direction and purpose—and hence an investment that is floundering.

In some (relatively infrequent) cases, secondary sales will be made to other VCs. This will probably occur most often when a venture capital fund nears the end of its lifecycle (typically ten years) and investments must be liquidated in an orderly fashion. This is clearly a scenario that the VC would prefer to avoid, since a forced sale may be a fire sale. Nonetheless, there may be firms that, as the end of the fund's existence approaches, are ready neither for an IPO nor a strategic sale. In this situation, a secondary sale may be the best that can be achieved.

We nonetheless hypothesize that a partial secondary sale may be value enhancing. A partial secondary sale to a strategic acquirer or other VC is similar to a syndication of the investment, given that it will bring on board an additional skilled monitor. A VC may be willing to entertain a partial secondary sale when it would not be willing to entertain any other form of exit, where the investee firm has a promising future, but where the skill set of management and of the current team of active investors is inadequate to develop fully the firm's potential.

While our data sample does not disclose the identity of the purchasers in secondary sales, anecdotal evidence suggests that purchasers in secondary sales are usually strategic purchasers—in many cases with a view to making a future acquisition if the technology proves successful. In such cases, the buyer will be a skilled monitor. If we can assume that maintenance costs are spread equally among all active investors (and that free-rider problems do not corrupt this equal allocation of monitoring responsibility), then the maintenance costs of each active investor will be proportionately reduced by the partial sale of the VC's shares and the arrival of the new active investor. Thus, while a secondary sale will necessarily reduce the seller's upside, it may also reduce the seller's maintenance cost by a commensurate amount. Even if it does not, the new active investor may sufficiently enhance the upside to justify the VC's sale of part of its shares.

We nevertheless suggest that this type of value-enhancing secondary sale will tend to be confined to investments without significant home-run potential. If the VC views the investee firm as a suitable candidate for an IPO, it is unlikely that it will accede to a secondary sale of part its interest. Such a sale will reduce the upside potential commensurate with the proportion of shares sold. Since IPOs typically yield the greatest return on investment, this reduction in upside will likely dominate any advantages secured from obtaining a new active monitor.

Another way of putting this is that the act of bringing a new specialized monitor on board suggests that the VC is not entirely confident about the firm's future under current stewardship, and/or the potential of its technology—and hence its ability to take the firm to an IPO. Very likely, the strategic acquirer will harbour thoughts of ultimately purchasing the entire firm, should its product prove successful. Thus, any further attempts to take the firm public are likely to lead to material conflicts between the firm's investors, diverting management's focus and damaging the business.

In summary, we suggest that a partial secondary sale is a superior form of exit vehicle to a full secondary sale. We have argued that full secondary sales will tend to occur in situations where the investment is floundering. By contrast, the investment is likely to be relatively healthy in situations in which we observe a partial secondary sale, although probably not of home-run potential.

We also considered that partial secondary sales may be effected in situations of high information asymmetry, in order to induce the strategic acquirer to purchase. This explanation for partial secondary exits does not suggest that partial exits will be of higher quality than full secondary exits. However, we note that strategic acquirers are likely to be able to resolve information asymmetries quite effectively on their own, mitigating the efficacy of a partial VC exit to signal quality. Thus, we suggest that partial secondary sales will more often be designed to bring on board a new specialized monitor than to overcome information asymmetries.

For the reasons expressed above, we hypothesize that a secondary sale is more likely to be effected as a partial than as a full exit. This hypothesis is tested in our full sample estimates (see Table 15.4 in Section 15.7.1).

In the empirical analysis in Section 15.7, we also consider the subsample of secondary sale exits to consider the factors that affect the extent of exit for secondary sale exits alone (see Table 15.5 (Panel C) in Section 15.7.1). The factors that affect the extent of exit for the sub-sample are discussed in Sections 15.4.3–15.4.8.

15.4.2.4. *Buybacks*

In a buyback exit, share ownership is concentrated in the hands of the entrepreneur. In other associated work (Cumming and MacIntosh 2003*a*), we hypothesize that buybacks are an inferior form of exit reserved for cases in which the investment is a 'living dead' or 'lifestyle' company that satisfies the entrepreneur's desire for profit but has virtually no home-run potential. Because informational asymmetry is eliminated (by definition), the need for a partial exit is mitigated. Although buybacks do not suffer from problems of informational asymmetry, they put a large strain on the firm's and/or entrepreneur's cash resources, and thus almost by definition will not involve companies with high valuations.

In such cases, the VC will have a clear preference for a full exit. However, consistent with the theory that these are living dead investments and the firm is only modestly successful and possessing only limited ability to generate cash flow, the entrepreneur (with or without external borrowing) may not have the resources to effect a full buyout.

For this reason, our null hypothesis is that buybacks will be associated with an elevated probability of a partial exit. This hypothesis is tested in the full sample estimates (see Table 15.4 in Section 15.7.1).

In the empirical analysis in Section 15.7, we also segregate the sub-sample of buy-back exits to determine the factors that affect the extent of buybacks separately (see Table 15.5 (Panel D) in Section 15.7.2). These factors are discussed further below in Sections 15.4.3–15.4.8.

15.4.2.5. *Write-offs*
An investment will be fully written off when the VC determines that there is little or no prospect of ever recovering its initial investment. A 'partial write-off', in our data set, is a write-down on the books of the company. In this situation, the VC recognizes that the investment still has value, but lacks the significant upside potential that motivates venture capital investing. When a write-down occurs, the VC will likely spend very little or no further effort in bringing the investment to fruition. In the parlance of the VC, it is a 'living dead' or 'walking wounded' investment. As partial write-offs signal the VC has poor quality firms remaining in their portfolio, we hypothesize that write-offs will more often be full write-offs. This hypothesis is tested in the full sample estimates (see Table 15.4 in Section 15.7.1).

A partial write-off is somewhat unique in that it entails nothing more than a write down of the book value of the investment. In the empirical analysis in Section 15.7 we therefore also segregate the sample of write-offs to consider separately the factors that lead VCs to write down an investment rather than completely writing it off (see Section 15.7.2). Unfortunately, because of collinearity problems, we were unable to regress the extent of write-off against any variables save duration and market conditions (see Section 15.4.8), and thus report only our hypothesis in relation to those variables (Table 15.5 (Panel E)). We hypothesize that the longer the investment duration, the less likely an investment will be written-off, as opposed to being written-down. This is because an investment of longer duration has survived more periodic profitability evaluations than an investment of shorter duration. Periodic re-evaluations act as a screen to cull the least desirable investments from the VC's portfolio. The worst investments are likely to be culled in one of these periodic re-evaluations, while investments of at least living dead quality (i.e. those that are written down rather than written off) will survive but ultimately be written-down.

15.4.2.6. *The Direction of Causality in the Relationship between Exit Vehicle and Extent of Exit*
Above, we assumed that the choice of exit vehicle affects the extent of exit. However, it may also be the case the extent of exit affects the choice of exit vehicle. This potential for endogeneity is considered in the empirical analysis (and see also Cumming and MacIntosh 2001*b*, 2003*a*).

15.4.3. *Development Stage and the Benefits of a Partial Exit*

Information asymmetry between firm insiders and outsiders varies substantially with the stage of the firm's development at the time when the investment is made (e.g. Gompers and

Lerner 1999*a*). However, it is the degree of information asymmetry at the time of exit that will be a factor in determining whether to make a full or partial exit. It may be, however, that there is some correlation between the stage at which the investment is made and the degree of information asymmetry at the time of exit. When investments are made at an early stage (particularly at the seed or start-up stages, and perhaps the expansion stage; for definitions of the stages of development, see, for example, MacDonald 1992; Venture Economics 1993–1996; or MacIntosh 1994), informational asymmetries are high. Further, the rate at which informational asymmetry is resolved will be high in the first few years following the investment. For later stage investments (buyout, turnaround), however, the information asymmetry will be comparatively low—and the rate at which informational asymmetry is resolved will also be low. Thus, for any duration of investment, early stage investments will be characterized by a higher degree of unresolved informational asymmetry than later stage investments. This puts a premium on partial exits as a signal of quality.

Put somewhat differently, there is good evidence that VC involvement in an investee firm is a signal of the investment's quality (Sahlman 1990; Megginson and Weiss 1991; Gompers and Lerner 1999*a*). However, we hypothesize that VC involvement in early stage investments sends a more ambiguous signal regarding quality than VC involvement in later stage investments. When a VC makes an initial investment, the VC will use a filter to separate those investments that are worthy of investing in from those that are not. This may be called the 'threshold criterion for investment' (TCI); only those firms that meet the TCI will receive funding. Once the investment is made, it will periodically be re-evaluated to determine if the investment will be continued (i.e. not exited). We call the continuance criterion the 'threshold criterion for continuance' (TCC). We hypothesize that the TCC at any given stage in the firm's existence will be lower than the TCI. This is plausible because once the investment has been made, the VC's managers will acquire expertise with respect to the investee firm that is necessarily to some degree firm-specific—such as gaining familiarity with the quality of management, the firm's technology, etc. By themselves, the sunk costs associated with acquiring this firm-specific knowledge are economically irrelevant and will not figure in any decision to continue or exit. Nonetheless, these early investments in the acquisition of firm-specific information create knowledge assets that will lower the continued cost of monitoring the firm and maintaining the investment. Thus, the TCC will be less than the TCI, and a VC's decision to continue an investment will be a less potent certification of quality, at any given stage, than a decision to embark upon a fresh investment. This enhances the need to signal quality via a partial exit. Our null hypothesis is thus that the earlier the stage at which the investment is made, the more likely it is that a partial exit will be used, although we do not regard this as a strong hypothesis.

15.4.4. *Venture Capital Investment*

VC involvement with an investee firm is a signal of quality to outside investors. There is also evidence that this signal is more potent the longer the duration of the investment. Megginson and Weiss (1991), for example, show that short-term IPO underpricing is less pronounced when VC investment duration is longer. We thus hypothesize that the lengthier the duration of investment, the less will be the need to signal quality to outsiders via a partial exit. In short, we expect to observe a positive relationship between duration and the extent of exit.

15.4.5. *Increases in Available Capital and the Benefits of a Partial Exit*

In other work, we hypothesize (and present evidence showing) that increases in the total amount of capital available in the venture capital industry lowers the average duration of venture capital investments (Cumming and MacIntosh 2001*b*). Because venture capital investors are value-added investors, the expertise of VC managers lies at the very heart of venture capital investing (Sahlman 1990; Gompers and Lerner 1999*a*). However, managerial expertise necessarily takes time to develop, and this means that in the short run the supply of skilled venture capital managers is restricted. Since VCs are commonly compensated by the receipt of some percentage (usually 20 per cent; see Sahlman 1990) of the increase in the value of assets under management, there is a strong incentive to expand the pool of capital, even if this entails a premature exit from previous investments (Gompers 1996). Thus, when the pool of available capital expands, VCs have an incentive to redeploy managers from old to new investments.

We hypothesize that increases in available capital will increase the proportion of partial exits. Anything that results in unanticipated divestment will shorten the average duration of VC investments; that is, some proportion of the VC's portfolio will be exited at an earlier stage than would otherwise have been the case.[4] Firms at an earlier stage in their development will be characterized by heightened information asymmetry. Thus, the proportion of firms in which a partial exit will serve as a valuable signal of quality will increase. We therefore hypothesize that expansion in the pool of available capital will result in an increase in the proportion of exits taken as partial exits.

15.4.6. *Firm Growth Rate and the Benefits of a Partial Exit*

For each investment in our sample, we have the investment or 'book' value, and the exit or 'market' value. We can thus compute the ratio of market to book value. A high market to book value has an ambiguous effect on the extent of exit. Investments with a high market to book value are likely to be the highest quality investments in the VC's investment portfolio. If so, such investments will be characterized by relatively little informational asymmetry, mitigating the need for a partial exit to signal quality. On the other hand, investments with a high market to book value are likely to be high-growth firms, and high-growth firms are typically characterized by a great deal of uncertainty as to future value, leading one to believe that they will possess a high degree of information asymmetry, and that a partial exit will be useful in mitigating this asymmetry. We hypothesize that the second effect will be the stronger, and thus our null hypothesis is that firms with a high market to book ratio will be more likely to be partially than fully exited.

---

[4] The empirical results in Section 15.7 are not materially affected by the inclusion of both the variables for investment duration and capital available for investment.

Since the very basis for effecting a partial exit, however, is to achieve a higher exit value, there is the potential for endogeneity with this variable. In the empirical analysis, we thus test for endogeneity.[5]

15.4.7. *Technology v. Non-technology Investee Firms*

Over the period of time covered by our sample, approximately 70 per cent of all venture capital investments were made in technology companies (i.e. those developing innovative technologies) and 30 per cent in traditional sectors (see, for example, Canadian Venture Capital Association, 1992–1995; Venture Economics, 1992–1995). Compared to traditional industrial sectors, technology companies are characterized by greater asset intangibility, and heightened informational asymmetry and agency costs (Hart and Moore 1994; Helwege and Liang 1994; Noe and Rebello 1996; Gompers and Lerner 1999a). Thus, we hypothesize that a greater proportion of partial exits will be observed for technology-based firms.

15.4.8. *Other Possible Reasons for Partial Exit*

In the survey data (described in Section 15.6), we are able to partition the data into exits that were pre-planned from the date of investment, and exits that were inspired by unsolicited offers, market conditions, or 'other reasons'. Due to problems of collinearity, these variables are not included in the full sample estimates (see Table 15.4 in Section 15.7.1). Nevertheless, where possible, we include some of these variables in the econometric models using the data for the separate sub-samples in Table 15.5 (see Section 15.7.2).

15.5. LEGAL AND INSTITUTIONAL DIFFERENCES ACROSS CANADA AND THE USA

Previous research has documented regulatory differences across Canada and the USA, and stressed the impact of such differences on small and medium sized enterprises (MacIntosh 1994; see also Gillen 1992 and Halpern 1997; on Canadian regulation, see Levin 1995; and Gompers and Lerner 1999a, on US regulation). This subsection only briefly highlights some of the more important differences–securities regulation and government sponsorship of venture capital[6]—as they pertain to full versus partial exit strategies without going

---

[5] In the empirical analysis quality is proxied by the value the VC receives for the investment (market value divided by book value). There is potential for endogeneity with this variable if a partial exit leads to a different full exit value (tests for endogeneity in the empirical analysis in Section 15.7 suggested that this was insignificant). Generally, however, causation is expected to run from quality to the extent of exit, as quality is associated with lower informational asymmetry, which in turn diminishes the need for a partial exit strategy. Further, note that in partial exits for IPOs, secondary sales, and buybacks, the data only indicate the proceeds received from the shares sold; thus, the proceeds will be lower than that for the sale of the whole company. This will bias the results in favour of finding an association between low proceeds and partial exits. We have therefore adjusted the market values upward by the typical fraction received in the case of partial exits for IPOs, secondary sales, and buybacks in the empirical analysis in Section 15.7. See also note 12, *infra*.

[6] VCs will pay capital gains tax regardless of the exit vehicle selected (MacIntosh 1994). Nevertheless, there may be tax incentives for partial exits if VCs want to defer tax until their next taxation year (Levin 1995). Such a

into an in-depth analysis of regulatory differences across the two countries discussed in other sources (e.g. MacIntosh 1994). Market liquidity is addressed in Section 15.5.1. Section 15.5.2 assesses the effect of escrow requirements and hold periods. Underwriter specialization is considered in Section 15.5.3. Canadian tax assistance for Labour Sponsored Venture Capital Funds is analysed in Section 15.5.4. The predicted impact of these factors for the Canadian and US empirical evidence (see Sections 15.6 and 15.7 below) is assessed.

15.5.1. *Market Liquidity*

It is well known that investors value liquidity (i.e. immediacy, or the benefit of selling quickly at or close to the last quoted price), and that the prospect of buying into an illiquid market raises a firm's cost of capital. We also posit that the greater the degree of information asymmetry at the time of a primary market sale, the greater will be the prospective cost of illiquidity to investors. Greater information asymmetry will broaden the prospective distribution of investment returns, as well as second, third, and higher order confidence intervals associated with return assessments. This will lead investors to put a higher premium on a nimble exit from the investment on the arrival of new, unfavourable information.

We further posit that the greater the degree of illiquidity in a firm's secondary market trading, the more valuable will be partial exit. This is because, in signalling the firm's quality, a partial exit reduces the investor's prospective assessment of the breadth of the distribution of returns.

There is reason to believe that Canadian markets for smaller firms are less liquid than their American counterparts (MacIntosh 1994). Regulatory constraints are more binding in Canada, leaving small firms with fewer trading options than in the USA. There are also fewer traders in the smaller Canadian market, leading to a lower probability of finding a counterparty with which to trade. Further, there is at least anecdotal evidence that Canadian dealers provide small firms with less vigorous secondary market support (such as actively maintaining a market in the firm's securities). On this footing, we thus hypothesize that partial exits will have greater value in the Canadian market than in the US market.

15.5.2. *Escrow Requirements and Hold Periods*

Of particular importance to IPO exits are regulatory escrow requirements and hold periods. Escrow requirements are designed to ensure that managers and key investors remain involved in an enterprise for some period of time after the firm goes public. In Canada, escrow rules of both the securities regulators and the stock exchanges typically require

---

strategy, however, would mitigate the venture capitalist's certification effect of a partial exit. Mixing of taxation factors and certification strategies send mixed signals to all new owners regarding the rationales underlying the partial exit. It is more likely that the VCs will delay the entire exit until the next taxation year, rather than pursue a partial exit strategy, if there is an underlying taxation motive so that the benefits of signalling through partial exits are not mitigated.

that venture capitalists escrow some or all of their holdings (i.e. deposit them in holding accounts controlled by a third party) for a period following an IPO. This period may be as long as four or five years (but is typically one or two years). By contrast, in the USA, escrow requirements are typically negotiated between the underwriter and the VC, with the most usual escrow period being six months.

Securities regulators also impose hold periods on any investor purchasing securities in an exempt market transaction prior to the date of the firm's IPO. Such requirements are designed to prevent a 'back-door distribution', in which exempt investors (i.e. those who may purchase without the issuer having to put together a prospectus) purchase securities for the purpose of funnelling them to non-exempt investors. Like escrow requirements, hold period requirements vary between Canada and the USA. In Canada, hold periods range from six to eighteen months, and will typically be twelve or eighteen months for post-IPO shares[7] (MacIntosh 1994). Importantly, the hold periods start to run from the date of the IPO, rather than the date of the initial purchase. In the USA, hold periods in our data period (1992–95) would typically have been two years.[8] However, these are measured from the date of the initial purchase, so that for the majority of VC investors the hold periods will already have expired prior to the date of the public offering.

Canadian hold period restrictions on venture capital sales may sometimes be circumvented (Gillen 1992; MacIntosh 1994). For example, Ontario securities law allows the firm to start the hold period tolling by filing a prospectus outside of the context of an IPO and while the firm is still private (Gillen 1992, c.8; OSA s.53(2)). A reverse takeover bid may also be used to take a company public and circumvent resale restrictions (MacIntosh 1994: 111). Further, the VC may sell after the IPO by taking advantage of exemptions from the resale restrictions (e.g. one 'control person', which will generally include a VC, may sell to any other control person; see Gillen 1992: ch. 7; and MacIntosh 1994: ch. 5, for additional discussion). Nonetheless, these are relatively rare events, and it remains true that it is generally more difficult for Canadian venture capitalists to fully dispose of their investments following IPOs due to escrow and hold period requirements (MacIntosh 1994).

These differences in escrow and hold period requirements will clearly impact our results in respect of IPOs; because of these requirements, we expect more partial exits in connection with IPOs in Canada than in the USA. Obviously, these regulatory requirements also cloud the interpretation of our empirical results in respect of Canadian IPOs; an abundance of partial exits can be attributed to regulatory requirements, and not the desire to signal the worth of the investment.

---

[7] Securities regulation in Canada varies by province. Hence, hold periods may vary. The absence of a uniform approach has proved to be 'cumbersome and confusing for issuers and their investors' (Tucker 1999). The Canadian securities administrators have recently adopted a more uniform approach across jurisdictions; however, for the most part, securities held by professional venture capital fund managers will be treated no better under the new regime than the old one, despite repeated submissions by the Canadian Venture Capital Association.

[8] SEC Rules 144 and 145. In April 1997, these hold-period requirements were lowered to one year after the purchase of restricted stock, with some restrictions between the first and second years; see SEC 17 CFR Part 230 [Release No. 33-7390; File No. S7-17-95].

With respect to the US results, we encounter a different problem. Recall that in our data, a full exit is one in which all shares are sold within a year of the IPO. If VCs often exit after the expiry of their negotiated escrow periods, then we will record their exits as full exits, even where they have held the securities for some months after the IPO. Thus, we will have under-reporting of partial exits. Our data thus biases our empirical tests against finding that an IPO exit increases the chances of a partial exit.

15.5.3. *Underwriter Specialization*

With few or no exceptions, Canadian underwriters are generalists rather than specialists. By contrast, in the USA, many small firm underwriters specialize in technology offerings, or even in particular types of technology offerings (MacIntosh 1994; Cumming and MacIntosh 2003*a*). Generalist underwriters are less able to credibly certify the quality of initial public offerings. Since underwriter certification and VC certification (via a partial exit) are likely to be substitutes, we expect to observe more partial IPO exits in Canada than in the USA.

15.5.4. *Canadian Tax Assistance for Labour Sponsored Venture Capital Funds*

Our US data derives from private venture capital firms funded mostly by pension funds and wealthy individuals. The Canadian data, by contrast, is from a mix of both private and Labour Sponsored Venture Capital Corporations (LSVCCs). LSVCCs are created pursuant to relevant legislation in eight of the Canadian provinces. An LSVCC must have a labour union as sponsor, and the union will nominally control the fund's board of directors. However, the union will invariably contract out the management function and play a nominal role on the board of directors. For all intents and purposes, the union collects a fee from the managers of the fund for agreeing to rent its name to the fund. Such funds are capitalized exclusively by the contributions of individuals (often consisting of tax-sheltered retirement accounts), and such contributions have largely been induced by generous tax credits given to investors by both the federal and provincial governments (Vaillancourt 1997). Typically, LSVCCs cannot invest in firms with more than 50 per cent of assets or wages paid outside the sponsoring province. LSVCCs are created with the dual mandate of maximizing profits and creating employment growth, although most funds have publicly stated that they will be run solely in the interest of profit maximization (MacIntosh 1994).

LSVCCs have enjoyed tremendous growth since their introduction in the 1980s. Between 25 per cent and 50 per cent of the new capital flowing into the industry was raised by LSVCCs in each of the years covered by our exit data (1992–95; see the Canadian Venture Capital Association's annual reports). LSVCCs pay a penalty (20 per cent of contributions[9]) if they do not invest contributed funds in an entrepreneurial firm within a certain amount of time (from one to three years, depending on the jurisdiction).

---

[9] Additional penalties may be imposed, including revocation of the LSVCC fund's registration.

We expect these differences between US funds and Canadian LSVCC funds (which constitute an unknown proportion of our sample) to lead to differences in exit behaviour. Perhaps the most worrying difference is that many of the LSVCCs are recent in origin (most having been formed in the first half of the 1990s). This, coupled with the rapid expansion of the pool of venture capital in Canada, almost certainly means that LSVCC managers are less skilled on average than their US counterparts participating in our survey. Indeed, some LSVCC funds have hired graduates directly from MBA programs to work as venture capital managers. The relative absence of skill of these new managers will be at its greatest in relation to exits. Most venture capital investments take a period of years to bring to fruition, and many of these new managers will have had little experience with exits.

In our view, this lack of experience is likely to create an abundance of noise in our Canadian data. Lack of skill will likely lead to a certain amount of randomization in exit behaviour, a randomization that will not be present with more experienced US managers. This in turn is likely to make it more difficult to find statistically significant results in the Canadian data.

Abstracting away from the randomization element, the probability that Canadian managers are younger and less skilled depreciates the degree of certification that derives from VC involvement with a given investment. This enhances the utility of a partial exit as an alternative means of certifying quality.

However, as noted, there are legislated requirements that LSVCC funds turn investors' contributions into portfolio investments within limited periods of time. This abridges the time during which due diligence may be undertaken, leading to a preference for more mature (and less risky) later stage investments. Such investments are characterized by less information asymmetry, lowering the utility of a partial exit.

The LSVCC preference for later stage investments is exacerbated because over our test period (1992–95; see Section 15.6), investors were free to withdraw their funds within five years (increased in 1997 to 8 years) from the date of the investment. This contrasts with US funds, in which investors have a ten-year lock-in, and the fund is (subject to extensions with the approval of investors) wound up at the end of this period. The somewhat shorter horizon confronting LSVCCs may enhance the preference for later stage investments, which can be exited sooner and, at any time, turned into cash more readily than early stage investments. There are three complicating factors, however. Although during our test period, the LSVCC funds faced possible withdrawals by investors after five years, this does not mean that all investors would withdraw simultaneously. First, not all investor contributions are made at the same time. Second, not all investors will withdraw after the end of the five year lock-in, although one might predict that many will, because what attracted most investors to LSVCCs is not investment potential so much as the extraordinarily generous tax credits. If that is the case, once the tax benefits have been secured, it is likely that many investors in LSVCCs will withdraw their funds. Third, LSVCCs are perpetual, like commercial corporations. They do not terminate after ten years, as most US funds do. If the LSVCC does not think that it will face significant redemptions after the end of its investors' lock-ins, it might well favour early stage investments that take longer to bring to fruition.

There is evidence to support the view that LSVCCs have in fact favoured later stage investments (Macdonald 1992). This factor alone suggests less of a need for partial exits to signal quality, since later stage investments will be more mature firms with established track records, reducing information asymmetry.

We indicated earlier that VCs will sometimes exit an investment at an inopportune time simply because the end of the fund's life is approaching. Since LSVCCs are perpetual, the only constraint that would produce a similar result is if the fund suffered from large and unpredicted redemptions (which it might do at any time, if its profitability is poor; Berkowitz and Kotowitz 1993). During the test period (1992–95; see Section 15.6), most investors were still under lock-ins, and we thus do not expect to see forced redemptions for LSVCC funds in this period.

15.5.5. *Summary*

Reduced market liquidity in Canada should lead to a greater number of partial exits to signal quality. A lesser degree of underwriter specialization should also lead to greater use of partial exits, as should the relative inexperience of Canadian venture capital managers. One mitigating factor is the later stage of investments taken on by LSVCC managers. Nonetheless, overall, we expect a greater use of partial exits in Canada to signal the quality of VC investments. Enhanced escrow and hold period requirements will also result in more partial IPO exits in Canada; not to signal quality, but merely to comply with regulatory requirements.

The data used to test these propositions and the comparative effects of regulation in the two countries are described in Section 15.6. Empirical evidence follows in Section 15.7.

15.6. DATA

Survey data over the 1992–95 period from 112 venture capital exits in the US and 134 venture capital exits in Canada are used to test the hypotheses developed herein. The IPO exits data are publicly available. With respect to acquisitions, secondary sales, buybacks, and write-offs, private data were collected through the facilities of Venture Economics in United States, and the Canadian Venture Capital Association (CVCA) in Canada. Participation by surveyed venture capitalists was completely voluntary.[10]

The confidentiality of the data imposes some limitations on our empirical tests. For example, although we know that an IPO exit was partial or full, we do not know the exact date of the sales of securities that led to the partial or full exit. The data nevertheless provide a first look at full and partial exits across all exit vehicles, and at the factors that affect the extent of exit for the complete class of VC exits.

---

[10] Factors that may induce self-selection reporting bias of private data (acquisitions, secondary sales, buybacks, and write-offs) across Canada and the USA are likely to be the same in the two countries; therefore self-selection bias, if it exists, should not affect the comparative cross-country results. The Canadian Venture Capital Association (1993–1996) reports the total dollar values of the exits in Canada for each exit vehicle; Venture Economics (1993–1996) only reports the total dollar values of IPO and acquisition exits. Additional industry data (such as the extent of each exit) is not available in the Venture Economics (1993–1996) and Canadian Venture Capital Association (1993–1996) annual reports; nevertheless, the available industry data do not suggest significant discrepancies between the Canadian and US samples and industry data. See also notes 12 and 13, *infra*.

Table 15.1 summarizes the US data by the choice of exit vehicle. The US sample comprises approximately 10 per cent of the US exits in the Venture Economics database over this period (see Venture Economics, 1993–1996, and notes 11 and 13).[11] Eighty-seven of the 112 US exits were full exits. Partial exits are observed across all the exit types, although (as indicated above) a partial exit in the case of an acquisition or a write-off has a different meaning than in other exit contexts. Full exits in the USA were most common among write-offs, and least common among buybacks. Twenty-seven per cent of the US IPOs are partial exits.[12] Table 15.2 summarizes the Canadian data, which comprise 32 per cent of the exits in the CVCA database over the 1992–95 period (see Canadian Venture Capital Association, 1993–1996, and note 11). Buybacks are more frequent in Canada than in the USA. In contrast to the US data, full exits are also relatively more common for buybacks in Canada (perhaps because Canadian VC investments are, on average, smaller than their US counterparts, suggesting smaller investee firms and greater ease with which the entrepreneur can buy out the VC). The data on the average investment values, exit values, gross and real returns, variation in real returns, duration, and whether the firm was in a high-technology industry are also summarized in Tables 15.1 and 15.2. Section 15.7 relates this and other firm-specific data summarized in Table 15.3 to the extent of exits in Canada and the USA.

15.7. EMPIRICAL EVIDENCE

As discussed in Section 15.4.2, partial exits may be considered for all exits taken together, or for the sub-samples of each exit vehicle separately. In Table 15.4 we present the econometric regressions for all exits taken together.[13] In Table 15.5, we present the results for the sub-samples of IPOs, acquisitions, secondary sales, buybacks, and write-offs, respectively. In all cases, the binary left-hand side variable, the extent of exit, was recorded as follows: full exits received the value '1', and partial exits were noted with a '0'. Thus, significant positive coefficients indicate a greater likelihood of a full exit, while significant

---

[11] While the total number of secondary sale, buyback, write-off, and other exits are unknown in the USA, we base our estimate on the total number of IPO and acquisition transactions reported by Venture Economics over the test period. 'Other' exits comprise a mixed exit strategy (e.g. part buyback and part secondary sale). The exact details of the few other exits in Canada and the USA are unknown; dummies for 'other' exits are not included in the empirical analysis. The market values for partial exits have been adjusted to reflect the full market values, assuming an average 68.9% distribution of shares for partial exits (see also notes 6 and 13). The empirical results in Section 15.7 are robust to a wide variety of adjustments to the full market values for partial exits.

[12] The statistics may suggest a bias towards self-reporting of full exits, however, there is similar evidence. Gompers and Lerner's (1999a: Table 13.1) US sample of IPOs (1978–93) indicates that the median percentage of VC holdings distributed was 100% in the first distribution, and the first VC distribution occurred within a median of 0.9 years from the time of the IPO. For all IPO distributions, VCs distributed a median of 68.9% of their holdings within a median time of 1.02 years.

[13] We suppress a dummy variable for the 'other' exits (see note 11) to avoid perfect collinearity problems. But the inclusion of all five other exit vehicles still generates collinearity problems in estimation, given the fact that there are only a couple of 'other' exits, and even fewer 'other' partial exits. Because acquisition exits are somewhat unique (see Section 15.4.2.2), we also suppress the acquisition exits dummy variable to avoid problems of collinearity across variables for different exit types. We nevertheless assess the factors that affect the extent of acquisition exits in Table 15.5b in Section 15.7.2. Moreover, for the full sample combining US and Canadian data, note that a dummy variable equal to 1 for Canada (not reported) was insignificant in all the regressions, and did not materially affect the other coefficients. There were insignificant degrees of freedom for interaction dummies.

Table 15.1. *US venture capital exits data summarized by exit vehicle* [a]

Exit vehicle	Number of portfolio companies	Average duration (years)	Technology industry		Extent of exit		Full sample including partial exits					Sample excluding partial exits				
			No	Yes	Partial	Full	Average investment [b]	Average exit value [b]	Average gross real return (%)	Average annual real return (%)	Variance in real return (%)	Average investment [b]	Average exit value [b]	Average gross real return (%)	Average annual real return (%)	Variance in real return (%)
IPO	30	4.7000	12	18	8	22	2,035,036	12,565,880	464.6397	54.9152	51.1517	2,052,934	13,058,260	506.1595	44.4932	14.9276
Acquisition	30	5.1667	9	21	6	24	1,720,349	3,859,077	143.0386	57.8286	754.7467	1,640,617	3,017,889	119.8723	67.2604	943.0674
Secondary sale	9	6.3333	2	7	3	6	519,931	1,005,871	54.8768	-7.5650	6.6850	428,671	242,123	-42.3940	-9.7570	4.3797
Buyback	6	4.0000	5	1	5	1	784,397	2,687,449	145.0423	24.7910	3.2665	2,634,352	10,265,360	289.6732	40.4996	0.0000
Write-off	33	4.3636	15	18	2	31	1,984,068	92,500	-97.8450	-90.0070	4.8772	2,032,191	98,468	-97.7050	-89.3620	5.1315
Other	4	2.7500	2	2	1	3	1,112,445	1,539,990	35.2761	34.0191	83.9444	1,355,079	1,712,773	-8.1910	-9.8670	10.3594
Total	112	4.7500	45	67	25	87	1,714,030	4,706,597	147.3815	5.6146	256.6047	1,568,089	3,796,201	109.9431	-2.5835	304.8443

[a] *Source*: Venture Economics.
[b] Real US Dollars (base year = 1990). CPI data source: International Financial Statistics, Label 11/64; available at www.chass.utoronto.ca.
Partial exit market values are adjusted to reflect full values. Real returns are calculated assuming investment at the beginning of the year, and exit at the end of the year, reflecting the lowest possible estimate.

Table 15.2. *Canadian venture capital exits data summarized by exit vehicle*[a]

Exit method	Number of portfolio companies	Average duration (years)	Technology industry		Extent of exit		Full sample including partial exits					Sample excluding partial exits				
			No	Yes	Partial	Full	Average investment[b]	Average exit value[b]	Average gross real return (%)	Average annual real return (%)	Variance in real return (%)	Average investment[b]	Average exit value[b]	Average gross real return (%)	Average annual real return (%)	Variance in real return (%)
IPO	36	5.8611	3	33	20	16	1,464,087	5,170,185	1385.8530	27.8282	9.8247	1,520,666	3,536,233	187.5823	21.5102	8.6706
Acquisition	16	6.9375	9	7	1	15	1,945,386	3,271,514	84.5848	13.3089	2.9498	1,998,818	3,353,662	85.0041	13.7993	3.1193
Secondary sale	12	3.0833	0	12	5	7	402,144	968,181	165.6950	54.8972	90.2764	304,109	581,065	157.8125	18.0877	8.0910
Buyback	41	6.3415	30	11	7	34	668,245	808,686	66.9712	3.8207	1.5041	729,096	879,255	41.7198	2.5680	1.5212
Write-off	27	4.0741	18	9	1	26	332,038	3,821	−97.1010	−92.0440	4.3792	338,780	3,968	−96.9890	−91.7380	4.5280
Other	2	6.0000	2	0	1	1	2,412,731	3,687,627	60.1537	9.5346	0.1692	2,766,431	3,492,890	42.1686	12.4435	0.0000
Total	134	5.5299	62	72	35	99	969,012	2,169,579	399.0807	−3.2530	33.8738	937,431	1,459,018	43.6362	−16.2390	24.9186

[a] *Source*: Canadian Venture Capital Association.

[b] Real Canadian Dollars (base year = 1990) converted to US Dollars. CPI data source: CANSIM, Label P700000; available at www.chass.utoronto.ca. Foreign exchange rates from CANSIM, label B3400. Values expressed in US dollars for comparative purposes only. Returns were computed in Canadian dollars and do not reflect exchange rate changes. Partial exit market values are adjusted to reflect full values. Real returns are calculated assuming investment at the beginning of the year, and exit at the end of the year, reflecting the lowest possible estimate.

Table 15.3. *Relations across investment variables and the extent of venture capital exit* [a]

	Investee Firm Characteristics							Investment characteristics		Reason for Exit			
	Seed	Start-up	Early stage	Expansion	Buyout	Turnaround or SP [b]	Technology	Avg. Duration	Avg. Market/Book	Market Conditions	Unsolicited Offer	Pre-planned	Other
USA													
Full Exits	20	18	23	22	1	3	51	4.6552	2.2637	33	9	21	23
Partial Exits	7	2	2	12	1	1	16	5.0800	3.2050	5	1	13	6
Canada													
Full Exits	4	34	7	48	2	4	47	5.1818	1.4364	18	26	21	34
Partial Exits	2	9	8	13	1	2	26	6.5143	15.0448	15	3	14	3

[a] See Tables 15.1 and 15.2 for relations across choice of exit vehicle and extent of exit.
[b] SP stands for secondary purchases. There were no secondary purchases in the Canadian data. There were no turnaround investments in the US data.

Table 15.4. *Logit estimates of the extent of exits in Canada and the USA*

	USA			Canada			Full sample estimates		
	Coefficient	t-statistic	p-value[a]	Coefficient	t-statistic	p-value[a]	Coefficient	t-statistic	p-value[a]
Constant	2.5415	1.7109	0.0871	2.3416	1.5120	0.1305	1.7849	2.0421	0.0411
IPO	−0.5653	−0.8049	0.4209	−2.2167	−2.2954	0.0217	−1.1766	−2.4555	0.0141
Secondary sale	−0.0745	−0.0767	0.9389	−2.5584	−2.1063	0.0352	−1.0788	−1.7274	0.0841
Buyback	−3.2569	−2.4566	0.0140	−0.4808	−0.5334	0.5938	−0.8364	−1.5009	0.1334
Write-off	1.5403	1.6986	0.0894	0.5694	0.4243	0.6714	1.1194	1.5491	0.1214
Technology	−1.4559	−2.1294	0.0332	0.3345	0.4744	0.6352	−0.6341	−1.5760	0.1150
Duration	−0.0542	−0.4343	0.6641	−0.0973	−1.2427	0.2140	−0.0851	−1.6360	0.1018
Market/book	0.0514	0.7094	0.4781	−0.1694	−1.7701	0.0767	−0.0283	−0.5932	0.5530
Seed	0.5762	0.4564	0.6481	1.4040	0.8697	0.3844	0.9533	1.1733	0.2407
Start-up	1.7609	1.2686	0.2046	0.3771	0.3286	0.7425	1.4116	1.8354	0.0664
Early stage	2.1683	1.5422	0.1230	−0.5629	−0.4531	0.6505	1.0899	1.3588	0.1742
Expansion	0.1150	0.0941	0.9250	0.4802	0.4262	0.6700	0.7645	1.0686	0.2852
Fundraising	−0.0003	−1.2266	0.2200	0.0003	0.3842	0.7008	−0.0001	−0.9457	0.3443

[a] Two-sided test.

negative coefficients indicate a greater likelihood of a partial exit.[14] Akaike and Shwartz information criteria were used to infer the appropriateness of the included right-hand side variables in each of the regressions. We present only the logit estimates; probit regressions (*inter alia*) did not materially affect the results. In Section 15.7.1 we discuss the full sample estimates. The results for each exit separately are considered in Section 15.7.2.

15.7.1. *Full Sample Estimates*

The US logit estimates (Table 15.4) suggest that partial exits are neither more nor less likely for IPOs, although they have the expected negative sign. As noted earlier, this may be a product of our definition of partial exit, which records as a full exit any exit in which all the VC's shares are sold within a year of the IPO. It is likely that many VC's sell their shares after the expiry of the six-month escrow period.

By contrast, the Canadian data as well as the full sample estimates indicate (at the 5 per cent level of significance) that IPO exits tend to be partial exits. Unfortunately, as we indicated earlier, this may reflect the more onerous escrow and hold periods in Canada, and cannot uniquely be attributed to a desire to signal the quality of the investee firm.

In respect of secondary sales, we hypothesized that partial secondary sales are more likely to be an efficient form of exit than full secondary sales. We thus expect a negative coefficient. While we find a negative coefficient in the US data, it is not statistically significant. However, the Canadian coefficient has the expected sign and is significant at

[14] Durbin–Wu–Hausman tests (see Davidson and MacKinnon 1993: 235–42) were used to test for the effect of possible endogeneity with some of the explanatory variables. Instruments used included the geographic location (US states and Canadian provinces) of the investee firms. There was no significant evidence of endogeneity.

Table 15.5. *Logit estimates for Canada and the USA*

	USA			Canada			Full sample estimates		
	Coefficient	t-statistic	p-value[a]	Coefficient	t-statistic	p-value[a]	Coefficient	t-statistic	p-value[a]
Panel A: Logit estimates of the extent of venture capital IPO exits in Canada and the USA									
Constant	−1.7464	−0.6011	0.5478	3.8845	1.4746	0.1403	−0.9414	−0.6502	0.5155
Technology	−1.3741	−0.7716	0.4404	−1.0835	−0.6401	0.5221	−0.2668	−0.3236	0.7463
Duration	0.0232	0.1079	0.9141	0.0507	0.2950	0.7680	−0.0646	−0.6511	0.5150
Market/book	0.1686	1.1524	0.2492	−0.5356	−2.3978	0.0165	−0.0269	−0.4409	0.6593
Seed	−1.0031	−0.6911	0.4895	8.4458	1.8914	0.0586	0.2351	0.2283	0.8194
Start-up	0.9551	0.5821	0.5605	0.1227	0.1052	0.9162	0.7264	0.9571	0.3385
Early stage	2.8746	1.4570	0.1451	−1.9273	−1.4485	0.1475	0.2104	0.2799	0.7795
Fundraising	0.00002	0.0255	0.9796	−0.0003	−0.1914	0.8482	0.0004	1.4318	0.1522
Market conditions	4.3553	1.9961	0.0459	−1.3877	−0.8020	0.4225	1.1070	1.0651	0.2868
Pre-planned exit	1.9696	1.2263	0.2201	−0.6243	−0.3426	0.7319	1.1470	1.2025	0.2292
Panel B: Logit estimates of the likelihood of cash consideration in venture capital acquisition exits in Canada and the USA									
Constant	16.3158	2.0161	0.0438	3.9083	1.3993	0.1617	3.9789	2.9397	0.0033
Technology	−5.7817	−1.7299	0.0836	N/A[b]	N/A[b]	N/A[b]	−0.4488	−0.4577	0.6471
Duration	−1.7639	−1.9076	0.0564	−0.1461	−0.6908	0.4897	−0.2197	−1.6636	0.0962
Market/book	−0.6524	−1.8228	0.0683	−0.0783	−0.1057	0.9158	−0.2134	−1.5004	0.1335
Market conditions	−1.8654	−0.9307	0.3520	N/A[b]	N/A[b]	N/A[b]	−1.1553	−1.0449	0.2961
Panel C: Logit estimates of the extent of venture capital secondary sale exits in Canada and the USA									
Constant	8.7239	0.8487	0.3960	−0.2319	−0.2139	0.8306	3.4863	1.4486	0.1474
Duration	0.1528	0.4005	0.6888	0.5147	1.0835	0.2786	0.2716	0.9795	0.3273
Market/book	−4.5011	−0.7136	0.4755	−0.1801	−0.6207	0.5348	−0.4544	−1.7349	0.0828
Fundraising	−0.0014	−0.8524	0.3940	N/A[b]	N/A[b]	N/A[b]	−0.0010	−1.2967	0.1947
Market conditions	−3.2965	−0.6533	0.5136	N/A[b]	N/A[b]	N/A[b]	−1.7177	−1.0815	0.2795
Panel D: Logit estimates of the extent of venture capital buyback exits in Canada and the USA									
Constant	−4.1615	−0.8387	0.4017	3.3246	1.8021	0.0715	4.9667	2.9692	0.0030
Technology	N/A[b]	N/A[b]	N/A[b]	−0.4461	−0.4109	0.6812	−0.0239	−0.0241	0.9808
Duration	−1.0598	−0.4219	0.6731	−0.2537	−1.9289	0.0537	−0.2151	−1.8143	0.0696
Market/book	1.7273	0.5900	0.5552	−0.0703	−0.3117	0.7552	−0.0309	−0.1558	0.8762
Fundraising	N/A[b]	N/A[b]	N/A[b]	0.0017	1.2522	0.2105	−0.0014	−2.1257	0.0335
Pre-planned	N/A[b]	N/A[b]	N/A[b]	−2.3292	−1.4464	0.1481	−1.9042	−1.3994	0.1617
Unsolicited offer	N/A[b]	N/A[b]	N/A[b]	−1.0873	−0.7297	0.4656	−0.4738	−0.3403	0.7336
Panel E: Logit estimates of the likelihood of venture capital write-offs v. write-downs in Canada and the USA									
Constant	3.7177	2.0021	0.0453	5.9173	2.1892	0.0286	4.5620	3.3746	0.0007
Duration	−0.2676	−0.7603	0.4471	−0.5285	−1.5436	0.1227	−0.4225	−1.7465	0.0807
Market conditions	0.1290	0.0875	0.9303	N/A[b]	N/A[b]	N/A[b]	0.5814	0.4075	0.6836

[a] Two-sided test.
[b] Not Applicable. Variable excluded to avoid collinearity problems. Similarly, variables not shown were excluded to avoid collinearity problems.

the 5 per cent level. The full sample also has the expected sign and is significant at the 10 per cent level.

That the Canadian data showed significance, while the US data did not, is consistent with the view that Canadian VCs have a lower average skill level. Lower skill levels make it more likely that a Canadian VC will make a partial secondary sale in order to effect a mini-syndication, bringing on board a new specialized monitor, whether it be another VC or a strategic acquirer. It is also consistent with other factors noted in Section 15.5 that make a partial exit a more potent signal of quality in the Canadian context.

With respect to buybacks, we noted earlier that information asymmetries are minimal or non-existent, leaving little role for a partial exit as a signalling device. We also noted, however, that buyback exits are likely to be made in the case of living dead investments. The buyback may thus overstretch the resources of the entrepreneur and/or investee firm (including the capacity to borrow), leading to a heightened probability that a partial exit will be made. In Table 15.4, all three data samples indicate a negatively signed coefficient, in accord with this hypothesis. However, only the US sample estimates are statistically significant (two-sided p-value equal to 0.0140). This may be the product of the relative size of US and Canadian investments; Tables 15.1 and 15.2 show that the average VC investment in the US is nearly twice as large as the average VC investment in Canada. A buyback effected in the USA will thus put more strain on the entrepreneur's resources, leading to a greater likelihood of a partial exit.

We also note that buybacks are used with much greater frequency in Canada than in the USA (i.e. 41 vs. 6 buyback exits in samples of relatively equal size; see Tables 15.1 and 15.2). This is consistent with the hypothesis that Canadian VCs possess, on average, a lower degree of skill than their US counterparts, and consequently breed a higher proportion of living dead investments (although there are somewhat fewer write-offs in Canada than in the USA).

The US data suggest that write-offs are more likely to occur than write-downs. While this result is not confirmed in the Canadian data or the total sample, the small number of write-downs yields a low degree of statistical power.

In the US data, the logit estimates indicate (with a p-value of 0.0332) that technology firms are more likely to be partially exited, as predicted. The Canadian data, however, is not supportive.[15] This is puzzling, since we had predicted that a partial exit would have greater value in the Canadian context.

In respect of investment duration, we hypothesized that the longer the duration of the investment, the less the degree of information asymmetry between insiders and outsiders, and the lesser the need for a partial exit. Thus, we expected a positive coefficient on duration. However, we encounter negative coefficients in all three data samples. The negative coefficient is on the borderline of statistical significance at the 10 per cent level. It may be that as duration increases beyond a certain value, a negative signal of quality is sent to the market. This would be the case, for example, if potential buyers take the view that overholding of investments results from an inability to exit profitability, because of low quality. The lack of a monotonic relationship would work against a finding of statistical significance.

Similarly, the data do not confirm our weak hypothesis of a relationship between the stage at which the initial investment was made and the extent of exit. Only one coefficient

---

[15] The particular type of technology industry did not affect the results.

achieved statistical significance (at the 10 per cent level of significance) and it was wrongly signed.

We had predicted that the greater the availability of capital for investment, the greater the likelihood that some investments will be prematurely liquidated, enhancing the value of a partial exit as a signal of quality. We find no support for this hypothesis.

We also hypothesized that the higher the market/book ratio, the higher the firm's growth rate, and the greater the uncertainty about future profitability. We thus expected a partial exit to be a useful signal of quality (i.e. we expected a negative coefficient). While the Canadian data was supportive at the 10 per cent level, neither the US data nor the full sample were supportive.[16] This result, however, is consistent with our hypothesis that a partial exit has more signalling value in the Canadian context.

15.7.2. Sub-sample Estimates with each Exit Vehicle Segregated

As discussed above, some right-hand side variables were necessarily excluded in the estimates using the smaller sub-samples of the different exit types separately in order to avoid estimation problems arising from perfect collinearity. We are nevertheless able to include some of the variables associated with the reasons for exit in the survey data (see Sections 15.4.8 and Section 15.6) that were excluded in the full sample estimates to avoid collinearity problems.

Table 15.5 (Panel A) considers the extent of exit for the sub-sample of IPOs. The US evidence indicates that market conditions are the only significant determinant of the extent of IPO exits. Consistent with related research, an exit based on market conditions was more likely to be a full exit.[17] The Canadian evidence, by contrast, indicates that full IPO exits are more common among seed investments. This is not in accord with our weak hypothesis respecting the stage of development and the extent of exit (Section 15.4.3).

In Canada, there are also few variables that achieve statistical significance. However, the greater the market/book ratio, the greater the likelihood of a partial exit, consistent with our hypothesis.[18] This evidence is consistent with a partial exit having a greater value in the Canadian context.

Table 15.5 (Panel B) provides the logit estimates for the separate sample of acquisition exits in Canada and the USA. Some of the included variables for Table 15.4 were necessarily excluded in Table 15.5 (Panel B) to avoid perfect collinearity problems, and in the end we were able to regress the extent of exit only on the variables technology, market/book ratio, investment duration, and the real interest rate. We were also able to include a dummy variable for survey respondents indicating when an exit was prompted by market conditions, but this variable is insignificant. Earlier, we hypothesized that we would observe more partial exits in connection with technology firms, high market/book firms, and investments of lesser duration. In the US sample, we find evidence that technology investments and higher market/book investments are indeed associated with a greater

---

[16] The particular type of technology industry did not affect the results.

[17] Gompers and Lerner (1999a) consider the extent of IPO exits in much more detail.

[18] DWH tests did not indicate endogeneity problems; see note 14, supra.

likelihood of a partial exit. However, contrary to expectation, we find that a partial exit is more likely the longer the investment duration. As indicated above, this may suggest that the relationship between the extent of exit and duration is more complicated than we have hypothesized.

Despite the US results, none of the independent variables were significant in the Canadian data in Table 15.4. This is consistent with the view that Canadian and US acquisition markets are far from fully integrated.

We also considered the sub-sample of secondary sale exits alone in Table 15.5 (Panel C), where we were able to regress the extent of exit on the duration, market/book, fundraising, and market conditions variables. While the results are generally insignificant, in the combined sample partial secondary sales were more likely the greater the market/book ratio, as expected (see Sections 15.4.2.3 and 15.4.6).

In respect of US buybacks (Table 15.5 (Panel D)), none of the variables achieved statistical significance. In the Canadian sub-sample and the combined sample, the results suggest that the longer the duration of investment, the greater the likelihood of a partial buyback, contrary to expectation. This may be further evidence that as duration increases beyond a certain threshold, potential buyers assume that the investment is of relatively low quality, enhancing the need for a partial exit to signal quality.

We also predicted that the greater the amount of venture capital fundraising, the greater the likelihood that some investments will be prematurely liquidated, and the greater the need for a partial exit to signal quality. The results for the combined sample (but not for either sub-sample) support this hypothesis at the 5 per cent level of significance.

Table 15.5 (Panel E) segregates the write-off data for regression purposes. Unfortunately, all of the right-hand side variables except investment duration and market conditions had to be suppressed to avoid problems of colinearity. The combined Canada and US data indicate at the 10 per cent level of significance that the longer the investment duration, the more likely the investment will be written down than written off. This is consistent with the intuition that investments that are held for a long time lie somewhere in the upper range of the living dead; that is, with sufficient promise to maintain the VC's interest, but insufficient results to secure a favourable exit.

15.8. CONCLUSION

In this chapter, we theorized that the extent of exit (partial or full) could be predicted by the degree of information asymmetry between firm insiders and outsiders (i.e. potential buyers). This theory led us to hypothesize certain relationships between the extent of exit and the type of exit, including whether the firm is in a high-tech industry, the stage at which the initial investment was made, the duration of the investment, the availability of capital to venture capitalists, and the firm's growth rate. Overall, we find evidence in support of some, but not all of our hypothesized relationships. In particular, we find support in the Canadian data for the hypothesis that secondary sales and a high market/book ratio are predictors of a partial exit. We find support in the US data for the hypothesis that buybacks, technology investments, and expansion of the pool of capital available for investment are predictors of partial exits. Curiously, however, in no case do we find support for our hypothesized relationships in both Canada and the USA. We believe that some of these differences are explicable. For example, that a buyback is more likely to result in a partial exit in the USA and not in Canada is consistent with the higher average investment made by US venture capitalists in their investee firms, which diminishes the entrepreneur's ability to use her own resources to buy out the VC.

Similarly, that IPOs tend to be associated with partial exits in Canada but not the USA may be a product in part of our definition of what constitutes a partial exit in the IPO context. While (following convention) we defined a partial exit as one in which the VC sells only part of its holdings within a year of the IPO, anecdotal evidence suggests that many US VCs will hold their investments for the contractual escrow period, typically six months, after which they will sell the balance of their holdings. From an economic point of view, this ought to be regarded as a partial rather than a full exit. It may also be that Canada's more demanding regulatory environment is partly responsible for the difference in US and Canadian results. The more onerous hold and escrow periods in Canada require the VC to stay invested for a longer period of time.

Other differences in our empirical results between the two countries are less easily explained. We posited a number of factors (such as a less efficient capital market, lower average VC skill, and a variety of institutional factors) that would lead us to believe that a partial exit would have more value in Canada than in the USA. Our result in relation to the significance of the market/book ratio is in keeping with this hypothesis, as is the result pertaining to secondary sales. However, the insignificance of the technology variable in Canada (and significance in the USA) is contrary to this intuition; if a partial exit has a greater value in Canada, we should have observed the reverse result. Thus, our theoretical predictions about differences between the two countries are only partly supported by the data. It may be that the Canadian results are contaminated by noise resulting from the lower average skill level of Canadian VCs, given that lower skill will tend to introduce some randomness into exit decisions.

That there are demonstrable differences in the results between Canada and the USA is in itself significant, as it suggests that even if our theory is incomplete, exit behaviour in the two countries does indeed differ in light of different institutional, regulatory, and market contexts.

References

Admati, A. R. and Pfleiderer, P. (1994), 'Robust financial contracting and the role of venture capitalists', *Journal of Finance* 49, 371–402.
Amit, A. R., Brander, J., and Zott, C. (1997), 'Venture capital financing of entrepreneurship in Canada', in P. Halpern, (ed.), *Financing Innovative Enterprise in Canada*, Calgary: University of Calgary Press, 237–77.
——, Glosten, L., and Muller, E. (1990), 'Entrepreneurial ability, venture investments, and risk sharing', *Management Science* 36, 1232–45.
——, ——, and —— (1993), 'Challenges to theory development in entrepreneurial research', *Journal of Management Studies* 30, 815–34.

Barry, C. B., Muscarella, C. J., Peavy, J. W. III, and Vetsuypens, M. R. (1990), 'The role of venture capital firms in the creation of public companies: evidence from the going public process', *Journal of Financial Economics* 27, 447–71.

Berkowitz, M. K. and Kotowitz, Y. (1993), 'Incentives and efficiency in the market for management services: a study of Canadian mutual funds', *Canadian Journal of Economics* 26, 850–66.

Black, B. S. and Gilson, R. J. (1998), 'Venture capital and the structure of capital markets: banks versus stock markets', *Journal of Financial Economics* 47, 243–77.

Canadian Venture Capital Association (1993–1996), *Venture Capital in Canada: Annual Statistical Review and Directory*, Toronto: Canadian Venture Capital Association.

Cornelli, F. and Yosha, O. (1997), 'Stage financing and the role of convertible debt', London Business School Working Paper No. 253–1997.

Cumming, D. J. and MacIntosh, J. G. (2003*a*), 'Venture capital exits in Canada and the United States', *University of Toronto Law Journal* 53, 101–200.

—— and —— (2001*b*), 'Venture capital investment duration in Canada and the United States', *Journal of Multinational Financial Management* 11(4–5), 445–63.

Davidson, R. and MacKinnon, J. G. (1993), *Estimation and Inference in Econometrics*, New York: Oxford University Press.

Gillen, M. R. (1992), *Securities Regulation in Canada*, Scarborough, Ontario: Carswell.

Gompers, P. A. (1995), 'Optimal investment, monitoring, and the staging of venture capital', *Journal of Finance* 50, 1461–89.

—— (1996), 'Grandstanding in the venture capital industry', *Journal of Financial Economics* 42, 133–56.

—— (1998), 'Ownership and control in entrepreneurial firms: an examination of convertible securities in venture capital investments', Mimeo, Harvard University.

—— and Lerner, J. (1999*a*), *The Venture Capital Cycle*, Cambridge, MA: MIT Press.

—— and —— (1999*b*), 'Conflict of interest in the issuance of public securities: evidence from venture capital', *Journal of Law and Economics* 42, 1–28.

Hart, O. and Moore, J. (1994), 'A theory of debt based on the alienability of human capital', *Quarterly Journal of Economics* 109, 841–79.

Halpern, P. (1997), *Financing Growth in Canada*, Calgary: University of Calgary Press.

Helwege, J. and Liang, N. (1994), 'Is there a pecking order? Evidence from a panel of IPO firms', Finance and Economic Discussion Series 94-22, Board of Governors, Federal Reserve System.

Jeng, L. A. and Wells, P. C. (2000), 'The determinants of venture capital fundraising: evidence across countries', *Journal of Corporate Finance* 6, 241–89.

Kaplan, S. N. and Strömberg, P. (2000), 'Financial contracting theory meets the real world: an empirical analysis of venture capital contracts', Working Paper, University of Chicago.

Leland, H. and Pyle, D. (1977), 'Informational asymmetries, financial structure and financial intermediation', *Journal of Finance* 32, 371–87.

Lerner, J. (1994), 'The syndication of venture capital investments', *Financial Management* 23, 16–27.

Levin, J. S. (1995), *Structuring Venture Capital, Private Equity, and Entrepreneurial Transactions*, Boston: Little, Brown.

Lin, T. H. and Smith, R. L. (1997), 'Insider reputation and selling decisions: the unwinding of venture capital investments during equity IPOs', *Journal of Corporate Finance* 4, 241–63.

MacDonald, M. (1992), *Venture Capital in Canada: A Guide and Sources*, Toronto: Canadian Venture Capital Association.

MacIntosh, J. G. (1994), 'Legal and institutional barriers to financing innovative enterprise in Canada', Monograph prepared for the Government and Competitiveness Project, Discussion paper 94-10, School of Policy Studies, Queen's University.

—— (1997), 'Venture capital exits in Canada and the United States', in P. J. Halpern (ed.), *Financing Growth in Canada*, Calgary: University of Calgary Press, 279–356.

Megginson, W. and Weiss, K. (1991), 'Venture capitalist certification in initial public offerings', *Journal of Finance* 46, 879–903.

Noe, T. H. and Rebello, M. J. (1996), 'Asymmetric information, managerial opportunism, financing and payout policies', *Journal of Finance* 51, 637–60.

Petty, J. W., Martin, J. D., and Kensinger, J. W. (1999), *Harvesting Investments in Private Companies*, Morristown, NJ: Financial Services Research Foundation, Inc.

Sahlman, W. A. (1988), 'Aspects of financial contracting in venture capital', *Journal of Applied Corporate Finance* 1, 23–36.

—— (1990), 'The structure and governance of venture capital organizations', *Journal of Financial Economics* 27, 473–521.

Tucker, D. (1999), *Proposed National Escrow Regime Enterprise*, Toronto: Canadian Venture Capital Association, 2–3.

Vaillancourt, F. (1997), 'Labour-sponsored venture capital funds in Canada: institutional aspects, tax expenditures and employment creation', in P. Halpern (ed.), *Financing Growth in Canada*, Calgary: University of Calgary Press, 571–92.

Venture Economics Investor Services (1993–1996), *Venture Economics Annual Review*, Toronto: Securities Data Co.

Zingales, L. (1995), 'Insider ownership and the decision to go public', *Review of Economic Studies* 62, 425–48.

16

Greenhorns, Yankees, and Cosmopolitans: Venture Capital, IPOs, Foreign Firms, and US Markets

EDWARD B. ROCK

16.1. INTRODUCTION

What is the connection between a venture capital industry, a well-developed stock market, and a nation's securities regulation and corporate law? Bernie Black and Ron Gilson, in a comparative look at the USA, Germany, and Japan, observe that the USA has both an active venture capital industry and a well-developed stock market, while Germany and Japan have neither.[1] This, they suggest, is far from accidental. Rather, they argue, 'venture capital can flourish especially—and perhaps only—if the venture capitalist can exit from a successful portfolio company through an initial public offering (IPO), which requires an active stock market'.

Israel provides an important and revealing case study for this theory, because Israel has an extremely active venture capital industry but a relatively undeveloped local stock market, at least for IPOs. Over the last decades, two exit options for Israeli venture capital have developed: IPOs on the NASDAQ and acquisition by foreign firms. In this chapter, I use the Israeli experience to gain insight into the connection between national venture capital and national stock markets in a globalizing economy.

The ability of Israeli companies to go public on the NASDAQ is a striking and important phenomenon that has important implications in a number of areas. First, as mentioned, it casts light on the issue flagged by Black and Gilson, namely the link between venture capital and domestic capital markets. Second, it provides insight into the structure of global capital markets and, in particular, the relatively small magnitude of cross-border transaction costs. The Israeli case demonstrates that those costs are not so high that firms cannot tap foreign capital markets routinely, and even change their 'citizenship', without changing

Thanks to Rann Marom, Mark Lesnick, Estee Solomon Gray, and participants in the June 2000 conference organized by the Cegla Institute. This chapter first appeared in Theoretical Inquires in Law (2001). The data in this article are current as of June 2000, with aggregate figures for 1999.

[1] See Black and Gilson (1998).

their operations. Third, it demonstrates the inevitability of interjurisdictional choice for corporate charters at the start-up margin.

Finally, a striking conclusion of this case study is that Israeli firms can and do 'pass' as US firms. If Israeli firms can do so, so can German and Japanese firms, once they learn how.

16.2. BLACK AND GILSON: THE LINK BETWEEN VENTURE CAPITAL AND IPOs

Black and Gilson argue that venture capital requires an exit and, in particular, requires exit in the form of an IPO. Venture capitalists provide both early stage financing and a host of non-financial services, including management advice, reputational capital, networking, and cross-fertilization. In addition, they provide a bridge between the firm and both product and capital markets, playing a central role in positioning the company, determining how to present the company to the product markets and financial markets, and determining the optimal timing of a public offering or sale. Capital and non-capital contributions are linked. The capital contribution makes the other services provided to the portfolio company more credible (i.e. the venture capitalists or VCs put their money where their mouths are). The capital contribution also provides the power within the firm that forces the entrepreneurs largely to accept the VC's advice.

But the VC's non-capital inputs have special value to early-stage companies and depend importantly on the VC's ability to exit. As Black and Gilson explain, as the portfolio company's management gains its own experience, proves its skill, and establishes its own reputation, the relative value of the venture capital provider's management experience, monitoring, and service as a reputational intermediary declines. Thus, by the time the portfolio company succeeds, the venture capital provider's non-financial contributions can be more profitably invested in a new round of early stage companies.[2]

Exit is also important to the investors in the VC fund. It provides: an objective benchmark against which to measure the VC's performance; an objective benchmark to measure the performance of a VC investment in comparison to other investments; and the ability to reallocate funds from less successful to more successful VCs.

But why is the IPO a particularly valuable means of exit (aside from the availability of sometimes facially implausible valuations)? After all, even in the absence of a market for IPOs, VCs could exit by selling the firm to a larger company. Why is it important for there to be two, rather than one, exit routes? Black and Gilson's answer is that the IPO uniquely permits the VCs to exit while leaving the entrepreneurs in control. This option, they argue, is necessary for the negotiation of an incentive-compatible implicit contract at the time of the original venture capital investment. They argue further that this implicit contract provides the entrepreneur with incentives not easily duplicated if sale of the portfolio company is the only exit option.

This provides a neat explanation for the importance of IPOs to venture capital contracting, but how does it relate to Germany and Japan? An interesting feature of the Black and

---

[2] See Black and Gilson (1998: 255) (footnote omitted).

Gilson analysis is its generality: nothing rests on the exit option being located in the same country as either the venture capitalist or the portfolio firm. In what sense are Germany and Japan consistent with this analysis? What is the link between a national venture capital industry and a national capital market? This chapter uses the Israeli experience to explore this question.

16.3. ISRAELI VENTURE CAPITAL: A THUMBNAIL SKETCH

16.3.1. *Funding*

Israeli venture capital went from negligible to significant during the 1990s. In 1991, there was one venture capital operation, the $29 million Athena Venture Partners Fund.[3] By the middle of the decade, two things had become clear: first, that Israeli hi-tech firms could go public on the NASDAQ; second, that foreign firms would acquire Israeli firms at impressively high prices.

This led to an acceleration of venture capital investing. According to a recent Dun & Bradstreet report, the assets of Israeli venture capital funds were $2.6 billion at the end of 1998 and had increased by 53 per cent to $4 billion by the end of 1999.[4] The leader in the survey was Star Ventures Capital Management, with capital of $590 million, followed by Evergreen Canada Israel Investments ($370 million), Jerusalem Venture Partners ($260 million), and Tamir Fishman ($255 million).

Most of the venture capital money is foreign, with much of that apparently coming from the USA. For example, Giza Venture Capital lists, as investors, 'GE Equity, a wholly owned subsidiary of GE Capital, Deutsche Bank Alex Brown, NIB Capital, Bessemer Trust, the Dow Employees' Pension Fund, and Credit Suisse First Boston Asset Management'.[5] The significant Canadian presence largely reflects the Bronfman family's long-standing interest (and investments) in Israel. Funds also include European, Asian, and Israeli capital.

The increase in venture funds raised has been followed by an increase in funds invested. In 1997, $429 million was invested. In 1998, $667 million. In 1999, $1.01 billion was invested in Israeli start-ups.[6] In 2000, $3.2 billion was invested.[7]

These numbers, while large in absolute terms, need to be placed in perspective. For example, the $1.01 billion invested in 1999 can be compared to 1999 venture capital investments in the USA by region. According to PWC, in 1999, the amounts invested are shown in Table 16.1.

In US terms, then, Israel would be considered a significant region, but not a leading one: somewhat larger than Philadelphia; significantly smaller than New York; and, like everywhere, dwarfed by Silicon Valley.

---

[3] Birth of a VC Nation, Red Herring, at http://www.redherring.com/mag/issue31s/birth.html.
[4] See Gerstenfeld (2000: 21).   [5] Giza Venture Capital, Fund Investors, at www.gizavc.com.
[6] Kesselman and Kesselman, PriceWaterhouseCoopers Money Tree Survey for Q4, 1999 (2000).
[7] Kesselman and Kesselman, Price WaterhouseCoopers Money Tree Survey for Q4, 2000 (2001). I have not updated the comparative figures in Table 16.1 to include 2000 because it was an unsettled year for venture capital investing and, moreover, an unsettled year for Israel. While it is true that the amounts invested in Israel in 2000 were larger than in 1999, the same is true about venture investments everywhere.

Table 16.1. *1999 venture capital investments*

Region	Investments ($ in millions)
Silicon Valley	13,430.8
New England	4,139
NY Metro	2,523.1
Southeast	2,461.6
LA/Orange County	2,356.8
DC/Metroplex	1,662.1
Midwest	1,552.3
Northwest	1,528.8
Texas	1,519.6
Colorado	1,305.8
Israel	1,001
San Diego	952.3
Philadelphia Metro	704.0
North Central	607.1
South West	359.5
Upstate NY	201.6
South Central	134.9
Sacramento/N Cal	133.5

16.3.2. *A Very Short and Incomplete History*

Arguably, Israeli hi-tech and venture capital grew out of a common US root. On one account, Israeli venture capital, at least in the technology sector, can be traced to the early investments by Discount Investments, the investment arm of Israel's Discount Bank. Beginning in the early 1960s, under the leadership of Dan Tulkowsky, Discount Investments began to invest in start-ups. Around the same time, Uzia Galil founded Elron Electronics Industries, which managed to attract early investments from Discount Investments and the Rockefeller Brothers Fund. Subsequently, Tulkowsky and Galil jointly co-founded Elscint, a medical imaging manufacturer, which produced an early CAT scan.[8] In the early 1970s, while searching for additional capital for Elscint, Tulkowsky met Fred Adler, a New York-based VC who was among the founders of the modern VC industry. Adler acquired 5 per cent of Elsinct.[9]

Flash forward a few years to 1980. Aryeh Finegold, an Israeli who had worked for Intel, founded Daisy Systems, a computer-assisted engineering firm and a very early Israeli Silicon Valley start-up. Finegold found his way to Adler, who provided early venture capital, recruited additional investors, and became Chairman of the Board.[10]

---

[8] See Briggs (1983: 134).   [9] *Id.*
[10] Thomas P. Murphy, Flowers from the Desert, Forbes, 31 Jan. 1983, at 104.

After Daisy's early success, and subsequent failure, Finegold returned to Israel, where he founded Mercury Interactive, a company that will be discussed in more detail below. Meanwhile, in 1981, Dan Tulkowsky's son Gideon, a Wharton MBA, went to work for Adler & Company in New York. Dan and Gideon Tulkowsky, along with Galil and Adler, subsequently co-founded Athena Venture Partners, the first Israeli venture capital fund. Athena provided seed capital for a variety of firms, including Finegold's Mercury Interactive and Gilat Satellite Networks Ltd. In 1990, Gideon Tulkowsky, while continuing to manage Athena's investments, also founded Veritas. Athena was wound up in 1997.

True to its American roots and investors, Israeli venture capital functions according to the familiar American pattern. Deals are structured according to the same templates, often using the same or closely related documents, in English, prepared by lawyers who have practised in the USA. Indeed, the fundamental legal documents originate with Adler's lawyers in New York, modified to take into account local peculiarities.

Hand in hand with the venture capitalists have come the other essential intermediaries. Many of the prominent hi-tech investment bankers have Israeli operations, including Hambrecht & Quist, Robertson Stephens, Lehman Brothers, and Goldman Sachs. Likewise, major US law and accounting firms have opened branches in Israel or affiliated with Israeli firms.

16.3.3. *Exit Options: IPOs and Acquisitions*

As Gilson and Black emphasize, exit options are critical to the venture capital process. The two principal exit options for Israeli start-ups, like other start-ups, are IPOs on the NASDAQ or acquisition by another firm.

Israeli companies, aided by VCs and investment bankers, have been strikingly successful in going public on the NASDAQ. According to NASDAQ,

Nasdaq® lists 96 Israeli companies—more companies than from any other country outside of North America—and the dollar value of equity trading in Israeli stocks will be approximately $44 billion in 1999. NASDAQ Israeli stocks are up 59.7 per cent in 1999 through November 19. In 1999, 10 Israeli companies have raised more than $1 billion on NASDAQ. Since 1995, 88 per cent of all equity capital raised in the US by Israeli companies has been on NASDAQ. The most recent Nasdaq listing from Israel was Partner Communications (October 27, 1999), which raised $525 million and listed with a market cap of $2.5 billion.[11]

Also impressive have been the prices that foreign firms have been willing to pay to acquire Israeli start-ups. The most recent and most impressive acquisition is Lucent Technologies' agreement to acquire Chromatis Networks, a two-year-old Israeli-based optical networking firm, for nearly $5 billion in stock.[12] But this is the latest in a series of increasingly rich transactions, as Table 16.2 indicates, which is recently published in Ha'aretz.[13]

---

[11] NASDAQ, *Israeli Prime Minister Barak Opens The Nasdaq Stock Market*, http://www.nasdaq.com/reference/sn_barak_112299.stm.

[12] *Lucent to Buy Chromatis, an Optical Networks Concern*, N.Y. Times, 1 June 2000, at C4. Lucent's stock has since declined in value significantly.

[13] *Ha'aretz*, 2 June 2000, at 6 (North American weekly edition).

Table 16.2. *Recent foreign acquisitions*

Israeli company	Acquiring company	Price (in $million) (at time deal announced)	Date
Chromatis	Lucent	4,645	5/00
DSPC	Intel	1,600	10/99
New Dimension	BMC	675	2/99
Tridium	VerticalNet	500	3/00
Mirabilis	AOL	407	6/98
Memco Software	Platinum Technology	400	3/99
Bioscience	Johnson & Johnson	400	9/97
Libit	Texas Instruments	365	6/99

In a country the size of Israel, such high-price and high-profile acquisitions have an electrifying impact. AOL's 1998 acquisition of Mirabilis (inventor of the popular chat program ICQ) for $287 million in cash, with the possibility of an additional $120 million, generated wide coverage, in part because of its 1990s Cinderella character.[14] In classic fashion, the firm was founded by three scruffy post-army twenty-somethings, two of whom had dropped out of high school. After only a couple of years, they were suddenly worth $60 million each. In addition to these high-profile acquisitions, there have been numerous smaller deals that are routinely reported in the financial pages of the leading papers.

16.4. THE LINK BETWEEN VENTURE CAPITAL AND CAPITAL MARKETS

Over the last decade, then, the classic path has been paved from Israeli start-up to exit (either through IPO or acquisition), all without the Tel Aviv Stock Exchange (TASE) playing an important role.[15] One might conclude from this that when firms are valuable to participants in US capital markets, intermediaries will emerge to make the connections. The key players, as in the USA, are the VCs and the investment bankers. In the space of ten years, the critical venture capital infrastructure has been put into place and has almost entirely bypassed the local stock exchange. The Israeli experience thus provides at least a prima facie counter-example to any claim that a country's venture capital industry depends on a country likewise having an IPO market of its own.

Such a conclusion would not be too surprising, especially with regard to technology companies. With customers in the USA and Europe and relevant technologies that know no language, it matters little where the research and development operations or corporate headquarters are located. For such companies, there is little reason to think that the

---

[14] Saul Hansell, America Online to Buy Internet Chat Service for $287 Million, N.Y. Times, 9 June 1998, at D3.   [15] For some of the reasons lying behind the TASE's unimportant role, see Licht (2001).

relationship between a country's venture capital industry and its domestic IPO market will be determinative.

The Israeli experience is consistent with this conclusion and calls into question any strong claim of a link between venture capital and a domestic IPO market. But a closer look at the Israeli examples suggests that reality is interestingly more complex. On closer examination, such a link may be closer than might appear at first glance.

So far, I, like others, have blithely talked about the ability of Israeli technology start-ups to raise capital on US markets. But what does it mean to be an 'Israeli' technology company, as opposed to a California technology company? There are two ways to make a match between an Israeli entrepreneur and a US investor. One is to pave the way for US investors to invest in Israeli companies. The other is to pave the way for Israeli companies to become, or to pretend to be, US companies. It is to the interplay between these two dimensions that I now turn.

It is worth flagging a closely related phenomenon that is just beyond the scope of this chapter. There is a group of Israeli-born, Hebrew-speaking entrepreneurs in Silicon Valley who form a loosely knit network. This group has started companies that can also be characterized as 'Israeli' companies. As we will see, some Silicon Valley Israeli entrepreneurs have chosen to return to live in Israel where they have started some very successful companies, which have subsequently gone public on the NASDAQ. As one would expect, there is substantial overlap between the overseas and domestic Israeli networks, with a variety of bridging organizations such as the California Israel Chamber of Commerce. One finds much the same phenomenon among Indian-born entrepreneurs. The interaction between overseas and domestic ethnic entrepreneurial networks is an important topic in its own right that casts additional light on the mechanisms and patterns of cross-border financing transactions.

16.4.1. *Who are Those Guys?*

The aggregate figures on Israeli success in using the NASDAQ, as impressive as they may be, must be placed in context. First, how significant is the phenomenon? Second, what do we know about the companies?

Of the nearly 100 companies identified by NASDAQ as 'Israeli NASDAQ companies', only ten have a market capitalization in excess of $1 billion, another eight have market capitalizations between $500 million and $1 billion, with an additional thirty-three with market capitalization between $100 million and $500 million. If we take $1 billion in market capitalization as the lower bound of publicly traded companies with a significant profile,[16] then the group looks like what is shown in Table 16.3. The next band of companies is shown in Table 16.4.

---

[16] A market capitalization of $1 billion is a reasonable lower bound for publicly-traded companies with a significant profile, especially given the valuations of technology companies. It is the generally accepted lower bound for 'mid cap' companies. Moreover, as of June 2000, NASDAQ had 659 companies with market caps in excess of $1 billion. NASDAQ, Market Statistics—Growth of $1 Billion + Companies, http://www.nasdaq.com/about/ms_groofb.stm.

Table 16.3. *Israeli NASDAQ companies with market capitalization > $1 billion (25 May 2000)*

Company	Market cap. (15/5/00; in $million)	Incorporation and headquarters	Business	Number of analysts	IPO
AudioCodes Ltd. (AUDC)	1,239	Inc.: Israel HQ: Yehud, Israel	Packet voice networking	5	1999
Check Point Software Technologies (CHKP)	11,382	Inc: Israel HQ: Ramat GanH	Software security	17	1996
Comverse (CMVT)	10,654	Inc.: NY HQ: NY & Ramat GanH.	Voice mail	17	1986
ECI Telecom (ECIL)	2,419	Inc.: Israel HQ: Petach Tikva	Telecom	10	1983
Electronics for Imaging (EFII)	2,482	Inc.: Delaware HQ: Foster City, CA	Printing	7	1992
Gilat Satellite Networks (GILTF)	1,470	Inc.: Israel HQ: Petach Tikva	Satellite communications	12	1993
Mercury Interactive (MERQ)	4,578	Inc.: Delaware HQ: Sunnyvale, CA	Software testing	15	1993
Orbotech (ORBK)	1,472	Inc.: Israel HQ: Nes Ziona	Circuit boards	5	1984
Partner Communications (PTNR)	1,205	Inc.: Israel HQ: Rosh Ha'ayin	Mobile telecom	3	1999
Teva (TEVA)	5,690	Inc.: Israel HQ: Petaeh Tikva	Pharmaceuticals	11	1982
Amdocs (NYSE: DOX)[fn17]	14,680	Inc.: Guernsey HQ: Chesterfield, MO	Telecom customer care and billing	10	1999

Table 16.4. *Israeli NASDAQ companies with market capitalization $500 million to $1 billion*

Company	Market Cap. (25 May 2000; $million)
BackWeb Technologies (BWEB)	515
DSP Group (DSPG)	731
Elron Electronic Industries (ELRNF)	613
M-Systems Flash Disk Pioneers (FLSH)	533
Galileo Technology (GALT)	560
Israel Land Development Company (ILDCY)	749
NICE-Systems Inc. (NICE)	687
Zoran Corp (ZRAN)	505

16.4.2. *Who Owns Those Guys?*

Who are the shareholders of these firms? In order to understand the process by which Israeli firms go public on the NASDAQ, it is important to figure out who the target audiences are.

Who are the shareholders of these companies? As it happens, one can develop a pretty good sense from piecing together various items of publicly available information. While these figures are approximate and always changing, especially in the newly public firms, they do give a ballpark estimate. In Table 16.5, I provide the distribution of shares between insiders, who I define to include directors and officers as a group (which will include, for example, venture capitalists with a director on the board) and outside institutional shareholders. At least so far as the publicly-available information suggests, all of the outside institutional investors are US firms.

16.4.3. How do They Market Themselves?

The above shareholding profile has a striking implication. Without exception, the audience is a relatively small group of US institutional investors. In most of the cases, the top ten outside shareholders account for almost all of the shares and almost all are US institutional investors. For these companies, 'going public on the NASDAQ' is equivalent to convincing this small group of investors to buy shares.

The exceptions are interesting. Partner Communications is, in essence, a partly owned subsidiary of Hutchison Whampoa of Hong Kong. ECI Telecom is controlled by two Israeli conglomerates. Amdocs has a close relationship with Southwestern Bell.[17]

Disclosure documents and websites are both means by which companies present themselves to the US investing community. One can thus learn a lot about how companies see themselves and how they market themselves by looking at what they tell the US investing public as they try to raise funds, comply with US disclosure requirements, or market their products. The 'Israeli' companies on the NASDAQ can be classified into three groups: the 'greenhorns', the 'yankees', and the would-be 'cosmopolitans'. As we will see, companies have an enormous amount of flexibility in how they present themselves, while complying with disclosure requirements.

16.4.3.1. The Greenhorns
Among the most 'Israeli' of the Israeli companies are Teva Pharmaceuticals and ECI Telecom. In their public profile, these companies present themselves as Israeli companies who compete vigorously in international markets.

16.4.3.1.1. Teva Pharmaceuticals. Teva Pharmaceuticals is, arguably, the best known and most successful of the traditional Israeli companies that have tapped foreign capital markets. It is the largest pharmaceuticals company in Israel and markets a range of pharmaceuticals around the world, with a particular focus on generics. It recently acquired US generic maker Copley Pharmaceuticals and the Canadian generic drug-maker Novopharm. Its sales over the last twelve months were approximately $1.3 billion, with earnings of approximately $127 million. Its stock has traded between $22.68 per share and $52.12 per share over the last year and is currently trading at around $47 per share,

---

[17] Amdocs, a NYSE company, is included because it manifests many of the same characteristics as the Israeli NASDAQ companies.

Table 16.5. *Israeli > $1 billion market cap.: incorporation and ownership profile*

Company	Incorporation	Principal shareholders
AudioCodes	Israel	Insiders: N.A. Institutions: 68% Top 10 : 45 %
Amdocs	Guernsey	Insiders: 65% [Including Southwestern Bell (SBC): 21%, Welsh, Carson (NYC): 20%] Top 10 outside institutions: 24% (Float: 35%)
Check Point	Israel	Insiders: 30% Institutions: 70% Top 10: 32%
Comverse	NY	Insiders: 4% Institutions: 86% Top 10: 45% Record holders: 2,103 Beneficial holders (approx): 30,000
ECI Telecom	Israel	Insiders: 0.6% Israeli institutions: 46.7% Foreign Institutions: 46% Top 10 Foreign Investors: 24%
Electronics for Imaging	Delaware	Insiders: 2.7% Institutions: N.A. Top 10: 64% Record holders: 348
Gilat Satellite Networks	Israel	Insiders: 5.78% Institutions: 89% Top 10: 43%
Mercury Interactive	Delaware	Insiders: 7% Institutions: N.A. Top 10: 32% Record holders: 30,600
Orbotech	Israel	Insiders: N.A. Institutions: N.A. Top 10: 64%
Partner Communications	Israel	Insiders: 72% Institutions: 17% Top 10: 13%
Teva	Israel	Insiders: 13.5% Institutions: 70% Top 10: 30%

which yields a market capitalization of approximately $5.7 billion. Teva is incorporated in Israel, and its ADRs have traded on the NASDAQ since 1982. As such, it need only file an annual Form 20-F and need not file quarterly 10-Q forms or annual proxy statements.

As one reads through Teva's 20-F, its Israeli connection is prominent. Starting with its incorporation in Israel and principal executive offices in Petach Tikva, one turns to the description of the business. The 20-F describes Teva as follows:

Teva Pharmaceutical Industries Ltd. is a fully integrated pharmaceutical company producing drugs in all major therapeutic categories, with a leading position in the US generics market. As the largest pharmaceutical company in Israel, Teva has successfully utilized its integrated production and research capabilities to establish a worldwide pharmaceutical business focusing on the growing demand for generic drugs and opportunities for proprietary branded products for specific niche therapeutic categories. Through its wholly-owned subsidiary, Teva Pharmaceuticals USA, Inc., Teva is among the leading generic drug companies in the United States.[18]

The description goes on to state, in the fourth paragraph, that:

Teva's operations are conducted directly and through subsidiaries in Israel, Europe, the United States and several other countries. Teva was incorporated in Israel on February 13, 1944 and is the successor to a number of Israeli corporations, the oldest of which was established in 1901. Teva's executive offices are located at 5 Basel Street, P.O. Box 3190, Petach Tikva 49131 Israel, telephone number 972-3-9267267, telefax number 972-3-9234050.[19]

When the 20-F describes Teva USA, the wholly owned US subsidiary, it emphasizes the connections with the Israeli parent company:

Teva USA manufactures products in a variety of dosage forms, including tablets, capsules, ointments, creams and liquids. In 1998, Teva USA sold 24 products in 45 dosage forms which were produced by Teva in Israel and accounted for 38% of the total sales of Teva USA. Through the coordinated efforts of research and development staff in Israel and the United States, Teva is constantly expanding the range of generic products sold by Teva USA. As of June 15, 1999, the Company had pending before the FDA applications for approval of 23 generic products (including 7 applications filed by Biovail Corporation International) and had under development approximately 50 products. The Company's product development strategy emphasizes introducing its generic products upon the patent expiration date of the equivalent brand name pharmaceutical. The Company believes that a broad line of products will continue to be of strategic significance as the generic industry continues to grow and as it experiences the effects of consolidation among buying groups, including managed care providers, large pharmacy chains and wholesaling organizations. During 1998, Teva and Teva USA received FDA approvals to manufacture and market 9 additional generic drugs, although some are tentative approvals subject to future patent expirations.[20]

---

[18] Teva, Form 20-F for the fiscal year ended 31 Dec., 1998, Item 1, available at SEC Edgar database [hereinafter Teva 1998 Form 20-F].   [19] *Id.*   [20] *Id.*

The Israeli character of Teva is likewise apparent in the lengthy description of applicable Israeli regulation, the description of the complicated tax structure applicable to the company in Israel, and the description of the complicated taxation of Israeli and non-Israeli shareholders. Likewise, there is a lengthy discussion of Israeli inflation and its effects on the company. The Israeli character of the firm is further emphasized in the description of the management of the company. It starts with the board itself, which has twenty-five members, all but two of whom are clearly Israelis. The two exceptions are William Fletcher and Harold Snyder, respectively President and Senior Vice-President of Teva Pharmaceuticals USA, Inc., the wholly owned US subsidiary.

In the description of the directors, all of the classic prestigious identifying affiliations are highlighted: degrees from Hebrew University, Tel Aviv University, or the Technion; and high military rank and position.[21] The disclosed relations among the directors and managers reflect the rather incestuous relationships that characterize a small economy like Israel:

(1) Ruth Cheshin and Eli Hurvitz are sister and brother in-law; (2) Dan Mirkin's wife and Yaacov Y. Salomon are first cousins of Eli Hurvitz's wife and Ruth Cheshin; (3) Eli Hurvitz and Chaim Hurvitz are father and son; (4) Israel Levin and Prof. Meir Heth are first cousins; (5) Haim Bental is Amir Elstein's uncle; (6) Harold Snyder and Beryl Snyder are father and daughter.[22]

Teva's website is to like effect. In the section 'about us', the geographic scope of Teva's operations is represented by a map in which Israel is dead centre. Similarly, the rest of the web page continues in the 'national champion' style, manifesting great pride in the corporation's Israeli-ness. All of Teva's press releases bear either a Jerusalem or Petach Tikva dateline. The standard, boilerplate description of the company contained in the press releases likewise features Teva's connection to Israel. Finally, the telephone and fax numbers given in the 'contact us' section are Israeli numbers.

All in all, the Teva Form 20-F and website paint a consistent picture of an Israeli company whose shares are traded on the NASDAQ. This is reflected in the analysts' views of Teva. MSN's Money Central describes Teva as 'Israel's top drug firm'.[23] Multex's Stock Snapshot characterizes Teva as 'the largest producer of branded as well as generic human pharmaceuticals in Israel'.[24]

Interestingly, however, other, less-emphasized portions of the 20-F suggest that the centre of gravity of the company is not so clear. In the description of Teva's production, we find out that it has production facilities in Israel, the Netherlands, the USA, and Italy. We subsequently discover that of its 6,000 employees, 2,500 are based in Israel, while 1,250 in the USA, 630 in Holland, 290 in the UK, and 950 in Hungary.

---

[21] Thus, for example, one learns that Meir Amit is 'the former Head of the Israeli Mossad, President of Koor Industries Ltd., Minister of Communications and a Major General (res.)'. Teva 1998 Form 20-F, *supra* note 18, Item 10. One possible explanation for the size and the politically well-connected character of the Teva board is that pharmaceuticals in Israel are subject to price regulation. *Id.*   [22] *Id.*

[23] Moneycentral.msn.com/invest/research/profile.asp?symbol=teva.

[24] Multex.com, Inc., Stock Snapshot, Teva Pharmaceuticals, Inc. (20 May 2000), available at www.multex.com.

Sales paint a similarly ambiguous picture: 'Consolidated sales in 1998 amounted to $1,115.9m, practically unchanged from 1997. Sales outside Israel amounted to $862.5m in 1998 and constituted 77 per cent of total sales, as compared to 75 per cent of total sales in 1997. Sales outside Israel increased by 4 per cent, while sales in Israel declined by 11 per cent'. By geographic area, Israel represents 23 per cent of total sales, North America 46 per cent, and Europe 26 per cent.

16.4.3.1.2. *ECI Telcom.* ECI Telecom presents itself similarly. ECI Telecom Ltd. 'designs, develops, manufactures, markets and supports end-to-end digital telecommunications solutions for today's new services and converging networks. The Company's products create bandwidth, maximize revenues for network operators, expand capacity, improve performance and enable new revenue-producing services'.[25] Incorporated in Israel, ECI Telecom is controlled by the Clal and Koor industrial groups, trades on the Nasdaq, and has a market cap of approximately $2.5 billion.

As one reads through its Form 20-F, one is again struck primarily by its foreignness: par value in New Israeli Shekels; Israeli government subsidies for research and complicated royalties resulting from that support; extensive description of the implications of Israeli employment law; discussion of 'conditions in Israel' and the effect of reserve service obligations on employees; lengthy descriptions of complicated shareholder agreements; withholding tax on payment of dividends unless a tax treaty is in effect; a largely Israeli board of directors.[26]

ECI's website, by contrast, is far more cosmopolitan.[27] There are far fewer references to Israel than in Teva's website. Almost all of the website focuses on business matters (products, customers, offices, etc.). That said, there are still significant references: the dateline of the press releases is Petach Tikva; the investor relations contact is an Israeli telephone number; general contract addresses include both a US address and an address in Israel.

This is similarly reflected in the analyst reports. Merrill Lynch classifies ECI Telecom as 'Israel: Telecom Equipment—Wireline'.[28]

16.4.3.2. *The Yankees*
Other Israeli firms look, sound, and feel like US companies. Indeed, these firms arguably are US companies. They include two of the largest and most successful Israeli companies: Comverse and Mercury Interactive. Comverse and Mercury Interactive are both incorporated in the US and thus file the same SEC disclosure documents as any other US firm.

16.4.3.2.1. *Mercury Interactive* Mercury Interactive is a 'leading provider of integrated performance management solutions that enable businesses to test and monitor their Internet

---

[25] ECI Telecom, Ltd., 1998 Form 20-F, available in the S.E.C. Edgar database.   [26] *Id.*
[27] www.ecitele.com.
[28] Tal Liani, Comment, ECI Telecommunications, Merrill Lynch (28 Jan. 2000) (on file with the author).

applications'.[29] It went public in 1993 on the NASDAQ national market and currently has a market capitalization of approximately $4.5 billion. In the last twelve months, it has traded at between $14.688 and $134.5 per share, with recent prices at around $85 per share.

Mercury's SEC disclosure documents give little hint that it has more than a casual relationship with Israel. It is incorporated in Delaware, its principal executive offices are in Sunnyvale, California, and, so far as the SEC is concerned, it is as American as Coca Cola. If one examines Mercury's Form 10-K for the fiscal year ending 31 December 1999, one discovers, on page six, that Mercury's primary research and development facility is located near Tel Aviv. Interestingly, this is presented as an advantage, not as a risk factor:

Performing research and development in Israel offers a number of strategic advantages. Our Israeli engineers typically hold advanced degrees in computer-related disciplines. Operation in Israel has allowed us to enjoy tax incentives and research subsidies from the government of Israel. Geographic proximity to Europe, a strategic market for Mercury, offers another key advantage.[30]

It turns out that the research and development group consisted of 226 employees. When one puts this together with the description of personnel,[31] one discovers that, at that time, there were a total of 857 employees, of which 362 were based in the Americas. Israel is next mentioned on page fourteen, in connection with funding of research and development. We learn that Mercury received $1.6 million of research grants in 1998 from the Israeli Office of the Chief Scientist, but received no grants in 1999.

The description of the executive officers is likewise silent on an Israeli connection. Although Amnon Landan, the President, CEO, and Chairman of the Board, is Israeli, there is no mention of that fact in the 10-K. Similarly, Moshe Egert's Israeli origins are not mentioned.

Turning to Mercury's proxy statement, one finds that its five directors are: Aryeh Fine-gold, Igal Kohavi, Amnon Landan, Yair Shamir, and Giora Yaron. While the five's Israeli roots are not hidden, they are conspicuously not emphasized, especially in comparison to a company like Teva. Aryeh Finegold, one of the founding members of the Israeli Silicon Valley mafia, is described as:

A founder of the Company, has served as Chairman of the Board of Directors since the Company's incorporation in July 1989, served as Chief Executive Officer from July 1989 until January 1997 and served as President from July 1989 until October 1995. Previously, Mr. Finegold was President, Chief Executive Officer and Chairman of the Board of Directors of Ready Systems, Inc. He also co-founded Daisy Systems, Inc., serving as its President and Chief Executive Officer. Previously, Mr. Finegold was a product line architect in the microprocessor division at Intel Corporation.[32]

Daisy Systems was an early Israeli Silicon Valley start-up, which pioneered computer-assisted design. The descriptions of the other members of the Board likewise bristle with indications that the directors are insiders in Israeli business, especially hi-tech. According

---

[29] Mercury Interactive Corp., Form 10-K, at Item 1 (22 Mar. 2000), available at SEC Edgar database.
[30] Id. at 6.   [31] Id. at 9.
[32] Mercury, Proxy Statement, 26 May 1999, at 2, available at SEC Edgar database.

to the proxy statement, Kohavi has served as Chairman of the DSP Group (David Gilo's Silicon Valley-based operation) and Chairman of Polaris, an Israeli-based venture capital fund. Yair Shamir is a former CEO of Elite, the Israeli food products company, an identity that provides a slightly discordant link to the old economy but that reflects the extent to which, in Israel, 'old economy' firms have engaged in venture capital investments.

While to the insider, the Israeli connections are obvious, more interesting is what is not mentioned. There is no mention of military rank or undergraduate degrees. There is no mention of where the directors live. There is no mention of where the board meetings are held.

Mercury Interactive's website carries forward this same strategy.[33] On the homepage, there is no mention of Israel at all. Likewise, the 'Company' page is entirely silent. All press releases carry the Sunnyvale, California dateline. The only contact addresses or numbers are in the USA.

As judged by analysts' reactions, Mercury has been spectacularly successful in its efforts to 'pass' as a normal, Silicon Valley technology company. In the Merrill Lynch analyst updates, Mercury is categorized as 'United States: Server & Enterprise Software'.[34] In the Multex Stock Snapshot, Israel is not mentioned even once.[35] Mercury is identified as a US corporation, with headquarters in Sunnyvale. Similarly, in the Multex ACE consensus estimate (a summary of analyst recommendations), there is again no mention at all of Mercury's Israeli connection.[36] Mercury is a Yankee company and, to the analysts, every bit as American as the Silicon Valley firms founded by expatriate Israelis. Indeed, in 1999, Mercury appeared as number 36 on Fortune Magazine's list of 'America's Fastest Growing Companies'.[37]

But now compare Mercury and Teva. In operational terms, they are equally Israeli or equally non-Israeli. Simple calculations based on the annual reports indicate that at Mercury, 220 of 857 employees are based in Israel. Meanwhile, at Teva, 2,500 of 6,000 employees are based in Israel. At both companies, the vast majority of the sales are made in the US and Europe. At both companies, the directors are Israelis who, I believe, live in Israel. Finally, my guess is that all the board meetings for both firms are held in Israel.

16.4.3.2.2. Comverse. Comverse is even more successful at passing as a US corporation than Mercury. It is a New York corporation with its corporate headquarters in Woodbury, NY. The annual meeting is held in New York. Its principal shareholders are large US institutions: FMR, Putnam, and AIM. Although Comverse has significant operations in Israel, they are presented in a 'by the way' style. The impression conveyed is of a US company that has operations in Israel, not the other way around. As such, it is not so very

---

[33] www-heva.mercuryinteractive.com.

[34] See, for example, Christopher Shilades and Peter Goldmacher, Comment, Mercury Interactive Corp, Merrill Lynch (1 Mar. 2000) (on file with the author).

[35] Multex.com, Inc., Mercury Interactive Corp., Stock Snapshot (20 May 2000) (on file with the author).

[36] Multex.com, Inc., ACE Consensus Estimates, Mercury Interactive Corp. (20 May 2000) (on file with the author).

[37] Cora Daniels *et al.*, Fortune's One-Hundred Fastest Growing Companies, Fortune, 6 Sept. 1999, at 90.

different from how, say, Intel is presented in its 10-K. Intel has a large fabrication plant in Israel and is thus subject to some level of locational risk.

Kobi Alexander, Chairman of Comverse, is quoted as explaining that 'Comverse is not an Israeli company; it is an international company with a strong presence in Israel'.[38] In the same context, he pointed to its Woodbury, NY headquarters and its recent inclusion in the Standard & Poor's 500. But, according to the *New York Times*, he quickly added that, '[T]he heart and soul of the company is in Israel—including the vital research and development division'.[39]

Like Mercury, Comverse's website is consistent with this strategy.[40] Throughout, there is no mention of Israel; press releases carry the Woodbury, NY dateline; and all contact numbers are to the Woodbury, NY headquarters site.

Like Mercury, Comverse is not perceived by the analyst community as an Israeli corporation at all. For example, in a five-page analyst report on the company by US Bankcorp Piper Jaffray, in which the analyst reiterates a strong buy recommendation, there is not one mention of Israel.[41] Comverse's international success in marketing its products is trumpeted, including new contracts with the largest mobile operator in China, where Comverse has been operating since 1993; a new contract with the British digital phone operator, One 2 One; and a new contract with Telecom Italia Mobile. Finally, in the report's 'Company Description', Comverse is described as follows:

Incorporated in October 1984, Comverse designs and manufactures communication systems and software for multimedia communications and information processing applications. Comverse has three product lines: (1) enhanced services platforms for service providers, (2) digital monitoring systems for intelligence agencies, and (3) call recording systems and related technologies for call centres. The Company has more than 330 customers across wireline/wireless service providers worldwide.[42]

16.4.3.3. *The Cosmopolitans?*
To what extent must firms choose to be either Israeli or American? Can firms present themselves as 'global' or Israeli cosmopolitan? Two very successful firms have tried to forge such an identity: Check Point and Amdocs.

16.4.3.3.1. *Check Point.* Check Point Software Technologies provides Internet network security products. It is incorporated in Israel. Its ordinary shares have traded on the NASDAQ national market since March 1996, in the range of $11.50 per share to $237.00 per share. In June 1999, it traded at around $230 per share, which gave it a market capitalization of around $17 billion.

Gil Shwed, one of the founders of Check Point, is an advocate of maintaining Israeli incorporation. 'That is who we are', he is quoted as saying in a *New York Times* article, 'We are a global company that operates from both Israel and the United States, and the fact that

[38] William A. Orme, The New Israel: Land of Milk and Money, N.Y. Times, 16 Apr. 2000, at C1.
[39] *Id.*   [40] www.comverse.com.
[41] Edward R. Jackson, Equity Research Notes: Comverse Technology, US Bancorp Piper Jaffray, 1 June 2000 (on file with the author).   [42] *Id.*

we are Israelis is a fact'.[43] Shwed suggest that rather than Israeli companies incorporating in the US, 'a better model would be Nokia of Finland or Ericsson of Sweden—global companies competing successfully from small countries'.[44]

How does Check Point project this image? Like the Mercury board, the Check Point board is small and technology-oriented. Three co-founders of the company serve on the Board. In addition to the three insiders, there are two VCs and a European technology guru. The financial statements, audited by an Ernst & Young affiliate, are prepared in accordance with US GAAP.

Leaving aside the board size and membership, Check Point's Form 20-F actually looks a lot like Teva's. As with Teva, there is lengthy discussion of Israeli tax law and of the tax consequences under US tax law of investing in shares of an Israeli firm, discussions that are almost entirely absent from the Comverse and Mercury disclosure documents. Similarly, there are discussion of Israeli corporate law and its effects on the possibility of a takeover.[45]

Check Point's website almost completely ignores its Israeli connections.[46] All press releases carry the dateline of the Redwood City, California headquarters. In the boilerplate description of the company that appears in press releases, there is no mention of Israel. Contact numbers are the California office.

How do analysts view Check Point? Like Mercury and Comverse, Check Point is largely treated as a 'regular' company. When one looks at the analyst reports, one finds either that no mention is made of the firm being Israeli or cursory reference (e.g. 'Israel-based Check Point' (Morgan Stanley Dean Witter)).[47]

16.4.3.3.2. *Amdocs* Amdocs introduces itself as follows:

We are a holding company incorporated under the laws of the Island of Guernsey. Our global business, conducted through subsidiaries, is to provide information system solutions to major tele-communications companies in Europe, North America and the rest of the world. Our ordinary shares are publicly traded on the New York Stock Exchange under the symbol 'DOX'. In the USA, our main sales and development centre is located in St. Louis, Missouri. The executive offices of our principal subsidiary in the USA are located at 1390 Timberlake Manor Parkway, Chesterfield, Missouri 63017, and the telephone number at that location is (314) 212-8328.[48]

---

[43] Orme (2000).   [44] *Id.*

[45] Check Point Software Technologies Inc., Form 20-F for the fiscal year ended 31 Dec 1999, available at SEC Edgar database.   [46] www.checkpoint.com.

[47] Gilat Satellite Networks, also incorporated in Israel, has used another method to convey its 'American' face: its 1998 annual report uses a baseball theme throughout! In a cautionary lesson on the difficulty of passing as American, the cover of the annual report depicts a pitcher shown from behind holding a ball, with the caption 'A Whole New Ballgame'. Upon seeing this cover, my colleague Michael Wachter commented that the pitcher seemed to be 'hiding the ball' and getting ready to throw the investors a curve ball. 'Who would invest in such a company?' he wanted to know.

[48] Amdocs, Form 20-F for the fiscal year ended 31 Dec 1999, Item 1, available at SEC Edgar database.

There is no mention of Israel at all in the 'GENERAL' section, and almost none in the 'OVERVIEW' section of the 20-F. It mentions, for example, in passing that 'we have global recruitment capabilities and have development centres in Israel, the USA, Cyprus and Ireland'.[49]

It is only when one reaches the description of the employees that one discovers that:

As of September 30, 1999, we employed on a fulltime basis approximately 4,400 software and information technology specialists, engaged in research, development, maintenance and support activities, and approximately 600 managers and administrative professionals. We employ over 3,000 software and information technology specialists in Israel, with the remaining located in North America, Europe and the Asia–Pacific region. We often maintain teams of employees at a customer's premises to work on specific projects.[50]

16.5. IMPLICATIONS

16.5.1. *What is the Question?*

I opened this chapter with the question of the relationship between a country's venture capital industry and its IPO market and, in particular, the case of Israel. In this initial presentation of the question, I took as unproblematic that one could talk of Israeli venture capital, Israeli companies, and the Israeli IPO market.

But two out of the three assumptions are, it turns out, problematic. As described above, it is not clear that it is correct to speak blithely either about an 'Israeli' venture capital industry or 'Israeli' companies. As I described in more detail above, the Israeli 'venture capital' industry, while arguably centred in Tel Aviv, does not stop sharply at Israel's borders. Much of the capital fuelling it and much of the expertise flow easily across the friendly border between Israel and the USA.

Even more striking and intriguing is the description of firms as 'Israeli' firms. The Israeli experience suggests that at a fundamental level, companies can choose their nationality and how to present themselves to the world. Whether the centre of gravity is in Israel or the USA, a company categorized as an 'Israeli' company can present itself as a US company (Mercury, Comverse), an Israeli company (Teva, ECI Telecom), or possibly a 'global' company (Amdocs, Check Point). Likewise, of course, Intel has operations all over the world, including a large facility in Israel, yet chooses to present itself as a US company.

Finally, the relevant investor community, at least at the early stages, is small and overwhelmingly American. For all of the major, new Israeli players, outside shareholding is very concentrated, and concentrated in the hands of a relatively small group of US institutional investors. Put differently, if a firm convinces this group that it has a good company, it does not seem to matter much what kind of accent it has.

---

[49] Amdocs, Form 20-F for the fiscal year ended 31 Dec 1999, Items 5, 9.   [50] *Id.* Item 12.

16.5.2. *Legal Restrictions on Self-definition?*

Can it really be this easy? Do 'Israeli' hi-tech firms really have the ability to choose to be American? Are there any appreciable legal barriers to self-definition when firms have significant operations in Israel, the USA, and Europe?

The answer seems to be that it really is. When firms have their operations spread over several jurisdictions, it means that whatever a jurisdiction's view of chartering freedom, this important subset of companies can choose to incorporate in any of their centres of activity (at least). From the US side, there is no difficulty, because of the internal affairs doctrine. But even from the Israeli side, which requires that firms with their centre of gravity in Israel be treated as Israeli corporations for both corporate governance and tax purposes, there is also no real impediment. Teva and Mercury have more or less the same percentage of their employees in Israel. For any of these firms, success will inevitably result in substantial operations in both the US and Europe. Even under Israeli law, one can structure the firm to allow for foreign incorporation. Under US securities law, the disclosure requirements depend on jurisdiction of incorporation. Foreign issuers can issue shares in the USA so long as they comply with SEC disclosure obligations.[51] The SEC considers all foreign companies that have securities listed on a US exchange (including American Depositary Receipts (ADRs)) or have made a public offering of securities under the 1933 Act as having voluntarily entered the US market.[52] If a private foreign issuer[53] registers securities under the 1933 Act, then, as with domestic issuers, it becomes subject to the 1934 Act's periodic disclosure obligations by virtue of section 15(d).[54] For issuers that are already publicly traded, entry into the US disclosure regime can be accomplished through a number of channels. First, listing securities or ADRs[55] on a national exchange is deemed by the SEC to constitute a voluntary entry into the USA and results in the registration requirement and accompanying disclosure obligations.[56] Teva, for example,

---

[51] The prohibition in section 5 of the 1933 Act on the offer or sale of unregistered securities applies equally to foreign issuers. Section 6 likewise anticipates the registration of securities of foreign issuers. Neither section 3 nor section 4 provides any categorical exemption for the sale of foreign issues. Securities Act of 1933, Sections 3–6, 15 USC. Section 77a, 77c–f (1994).

[52] Securities Act Release No. 33-6360, 1981, SEC Lexis 278 (20 Nov. 1981).

[53] Rule 405 of the 1933 Securities Act, 17 C.F.R. Section 230.405 (2000), defines 'foreign private issuer' to include all foreign issuers, except foreign governments, and excludes issuers when: more than 50 per cent of the shares are held directly or indirectly by residents of the US; and either the majority of the executive officers or directors are US citizens or residents or more than 50 per cent of the assets are located in the US or the business is principally administered in the USA. Rule 3b-4 of the 1934 Securities Exchange Act, 17 C.F.R. Section 240.3b-4 (2000), has a parallel definition.   [54] 15 USC. Section 780(d) (2000).

[55] American Depositary Receipts 'are negotiable certificates issued by a US bank or trust company . . . [which] represent an ownership interest in a foreign private issuer's securities deposited, usually outside the United States, with a financial institution as depositary' (Saunders 1993: 48). See also Moxley (1962: 22–23). The principal advantages of investing in a foreign issue through an ADR rather than directly are that the depositary 'facilitates (i) the payment of dividends to security holders, (ii) the transfer of ownership of deposited securities and (iii) communications between the foreign private issuer and security holders' (Saunders 1993: 52 n.12). In addition, ADRs avoid foreign inheritance taxes and probate in foreign courts. Loss and Seligman (1990).

[56] Securities Act Release No. 33-6360, *supra* note 52; NASD Manual (CCH) 1803, at 1564 (1991); Foreign Securities, Securities Act Release No. 6433, [1982 Transfer Binder] Fed. Sec. L. Rep. (CCH) ¶ 83,272 (28 Oct 1982). See Foreign Securities, Securities Act Release No. 6493, [1983–1984 Transfer Binder] Fed. Sec. L. Rep. (CCH) ¶ 83,435 (6 Oct. 1983).

lists ADRs on the NASDAQ. Second, an issuer may voluntarily register in order to be able to trade on the NASDAQ. Indeed, listing a security, including an ADR, on NASDAQ will necessarily trigger the registration obligation.[57]

But foreign private issuers do not have to meet the full disclosure obligations that a US firm must. The principal differences are that foreign private issuers need only file annual reports (on Form 20-F).[58] In addition, Form 6-K requires that foreign private issuers furnish information that the issuer either is required to make public in its domicile or has filed with a foreign stock exchange and that the exchange has made public or information that it has distributed to its security holders.[59] One important substantive difference relates to accounting principles: foreign issuers need not comply with US GAAP or Regulation S-X if the financial statements are presented in accordance with the generally accepted accounting principles of the foreign issuer's domicile and a reconciliation of the differences in measurement items is provided.[60] A second difference is the reporting of compensation to and transactions with directors and officers, where the issuer need only disclose aggregate compensation to the management group and the interest of management in certain transactions 'to the extent that the registrant discloses to its shareholders or otherwise makes public the information specified in this Item'.[61]

For Israeli firms, the effect of these differences is that rather than having to file quarterly 10-Q s, Annual Reports (Form 10-K), and annual Proxy Statements (Schedule 14A), they need only file the annual Form 20-F. Because the Form 20-F need only be filed within six months of the close of the fiscal year,[62] an investor may find him or herself in May 2000 relying on the 20-F for the fiscal year ending 31 December 1998. This, for example, is the case with Check Point. By contrast, for domestic issuers, the annual Form 10-K must be filed within ninety days of the end of the fiscal year covered; the quarterly Form 10-Q must be filed within forty-five days of the close of the quarter; and the annual Proxy Statement when delivered to shareholders. Thus, for the Israeli firms we have been discussing, one can get much less information from the normal databases. The greater flexibility in accounting standards makes no difference: from their inception, all these firms prepare their financial reports in compliance with US GAAP.

Under US securities law, then, the disclosure burdens on a firm are less if the firm defines itself as an Israeli firm rather than a US firm. Likewise, for the investor community, one gets substantially less information about an Israeli firm than a US firm.

This has two implications. First, it means that a partial version of the portable reciprocity proposals put forward by Choi and Guzman[63] and Roberta Romano[64] are, in fact, already part of US securities law. Foreign firms interested in raising money in US capital markets have a (small) menu of options from which to choose, namely two: foreign versus domestic incorporation.

[57] Rule 12g3-2(d), Securities Exchange Act of 1934, 17 C.F.R. Section 240.12g3-2(d) (2000).
[58] See Securities Exchange Act of 1934 Form 20-F, General Instructions, 17 C.F.R. Section 249.220f (2001) [hereinafter Form 20-F]; see also Securities Exchange Act of 1934 Form 6-K, 17 C.F.R. Section 249.306 [hereinafter Form 6-K].   [59] Form 6-K, General Instructions.
[60] Form 20-F.   [61] *Id.* Items 11, 13.   [62] *Id.* General Instructions A(b).
[63] See Choi and Guzman (1998).   [64] See Romano (1998).

Because of these differences, the scope of the foreign private issuer exclusion becomes significant. The 1934 Exchange Act Rule 3b-4(c) defines a 'foreign private issuer' to be:

any foreign issuer other than a foreign government except an issuer meeting the following conditions: (1) More than 50 per cent of the issuer's outstanding voting securities are directly or indirectly held of record by residents of the United States; and (2) Any of the following: (i) The majority of the executive officers or directors are United States citizens or residents; (ii) More than 50 per cent of the assets of the issuer are located in the United States; or (iii) The business of the issuer is administered principally in the United States.[65]

On this definition, Mercury and Comverse clearly do not qualify as they are incorporated in the USA. But what about Check Point, which, like other Israeli companies that go public on NASDAQ, has greater than 50 per cent of its shares held by US residents? Item (ii) is a hard sort of provision to apply to a new economy company like Check Point. Where is its intellectual property located? None of its other assets amount to much of anything.

The remaining items can be manipulated. So long as Check Point keeps these requirements in mind and continues to be run by Israelis who are both citizens and residents of Israel, with corporate headquarters in Israel, then it will qualify as a 'foreign private issuer'. As such, it will be able to choose between complying with 20-F as a foreign private issuer or reconfiguring itself to fall outside of Rule 3b-4 and thus subjecting itself to the full disclosure requirements that fall on US firms. The SEC, in Rule 3b-4, is concerned with companies that are run in the USA that pretend to be foreign, not companies that are run abroad that pretend to be American.

Overall, then, the foreign private issuer definition provides a limited natural experiment on issuer choice. Israeli firms (and other foreigners, of course) can choose between 20-F and full-scale reporting. Casual empiricism suggests that both kinds find American investors and, moreover, that there is little if any evidence that the US investors particularly care. Although there are differences in the information available, I find no evidence that any of the analysts are concerned about the difference. If, in fact, investors do care about the level of disclosure above some threshold—which, I think, really is what is at stake in the issuer choice/portable reciprocity discussion, despite the amusing references to Panamanian or Russian disclosure standards—then one should be able to find some evidence here. It is also possible that investors should care but do not.

16.5.3. *Potential Factors Driving the Choice*

Given this freedom, how does a firm choose its identity? What drives that decision? Anecdotal evidence from Israel suggests that taxes figure prominently:

'Most start-ups that consult with a lawyer or accountant these days are immediately warned against setting up headquarters in Israel and are told to look for offices in America instead', says Yigal Ehrlich, president of IVA [Israel Venture Association]. In his view, the main incentive for moving abroad is the more comfortable tax environment.[66]

---

[65] 17 C.F.R. Section 240.3b-4(c) (2001).
[66] Judy Maltz, Go West, Young Techies, Jerusalem Rep., 13 Mar. 2000, at 41. See also Orme, *supra* note 38 ('Almost all venture capitalists—Israeli and foreign alike—are requiring new companies to establish

For example, the Israeli tax on a founder's capital gains is 50 per cent, while the maximum rate in the USA is 28 per cent. It is unclear, however, whether incorporating outside of Israel is sufficient to take advantage of this lower rate or whether the firm must also be run abroad. Lucent's recent $4.8 billion stock acquisition of Chromatis, a US-incorporated Israeli start-up, provides a high-profile test case that raises a host of important issues.

But even leaving aside tax considerations, we have seen that for companies like Mercury and Comverse, incorporation in the USA is clearly part of a larger investor relations and product market strategy. These sophisticated hi-tech entrepreneurs seem to have realised that they can use their freedom of choice to adopt an identity that will be familiar to the target investors and customers, without limiting themselves significantly.

An additional consequence of the choice is felt at the level of corporate governance. Incorporating in Delaware or New York provides firms with greater flexibility than under Israeli corporate law.

In addition, product markets seem to play a significant role, at least in some untried sectors. For nearly all of the successful Israeli NASDAQ firms, the USA is their most important or one of their most important product markets. As the jurisprudence of 'gun jumping' under the Securities Act suggests, there is a very fine line between marketing products and marketing securities, and one can assist the other.[67]

To put the point somewhat differently, consider QXL, a company advised by Jerusalem Global Partners, a Jerusalem-based investment banking and venture capital firm. QXL is a European version of eBay. Much of its venture capital was provided by Jerusalem Global. When QXL went public, it went public on the London AIM rather than the Nasdaq. Why? Apparently because European investors had heard of it and were therefore a target audience.

16.5.4. *Why isn't Everyone American?*

Leaving aside product market considerations, are there reasons not to follow the Mercury or Comverse approach? Is the Check Point decision anything more than idiosyncratic?[68] Here, the answers may depend on company-specific factors. Mercury Interactive provides software-testing software. Comverse provides voice mail and customer service software. By contrast, Check Point is a provider of Internet security products. Does it benefit from an Israeli accent and link (if only in the biographies of the founders) with the Israeli military?

In a gushing *New York Times* article, much is made of this connection, in particular as a source of cutting-edge technology.[69] 'Their success at finding civilian applications for military hardware and software is hailed as a ploughshares paradigm for this military-obsessed nation, which is just beginning to anticipate the possibility of a different and

their headquarters in the United States, as a prelude to a NASDAQ offering or a takeover by an American multinational.')

[67] See Securities Act Release No. 5180, 36 Fed. Reg. 16,506 (16 Aug. 1971).

[68] One person told me that Check Point had little early venture funding. By the time it was funded, it had already started operations as an Israeli corporation; to change at that point would have triggered significant tax liabilities.   [69] See Orme (2000).

peaceful future'.[70] The article then quotes analysts as saying that the military origins may better protect Israeli companies from a high-tech market implosion.

Check Point, however, does not make much of its Israeli connection. There is little on its website that ties it to Israel. None of the product descriptions seem to do so. In the 'Corporate Information & News' area, there is likewise little, although if one digs deeply enough bits and pieces come out, but only grudgingly. For example, the corporate profile identifies Redwood City as the US headquarters and Ramat Gan as the 'worldwide headquarters', without making clear which is the head headquarters or that Check Point is an Israeli corporation.

16.5.5. *Entrepreneurs and Investors*

Let me close with a speculation. What is the difference for an Israeli entrepreneur between incorporating in Israel versus the USA? Between living in Silicon Valley and Israel? The fact that the TASE does not serve as an important IPO venue for these entrepreneurs is utterly irrelevant. When the customers are mainly in the USA, the alternative to living in the USA is spending a lot of time on airplanes. But that does not seem to be the whole story.

So what is going on? The bottom line is that investors, especially investors in the 'new economy', seem to be willing to invest with entrepreneurs who 'get it' and not with those who do not. What is meant by 'getting it'? A variety of things, but one of them is that the entrepreneur understands how the game is played: the value that a venture capitalist brings to the table, both in terms of developing a company and in selling the company to the wider investor community in an IPO; the value of alliances with other companies and how to build these alliances through advisory boards, joint ventures, common VCs, etc.; the value of employees who have connections with other key players; and a dozen other things that seasoned entrepreneurs in Silicon Valley understand but which ex-Israeli air force pilots may not believe.

The pressure of venture capitalists on entrepreneurs to try to 'pass' as American, to relocate to the USA and to incorporate in the USA, is all a shorthand way of capturing—and teaching—the set of understandings that are taken for granted by the repeat players. While one can find examples of firms that succeed without playing the game and of firms that play the game but fail, my guess is that the reason that Israeli entrepreneurs are told to incorporate in Delaware and to be as 'American' as possible is that it is part and parcel of getting into the right mindset, social set, business set, and investor set. The decisions to incorporate in the USA, to set up a corporate headquarters in the Valley, or to seek investments from prominent Silicon Valley VCs are important both for what they contribute and for how they teach the entrepreneurs what it takes to succeed. As such, they signal to investors that this is a company that understands what it takes to succeed today.

[70] *Id.*

When one compares Mercury and Teva's disclosure documents, one comes away with the overwhelming impression that the key differences are not state of incorporation at all but, rather, mindset. Mercury is very much 'new economy'. It understands what the new economy is about; it understands what investors are looking for and what the markets care about. The structure and descriptions of the boards of directors of the two companies could not be more different. Teva's gigantic board filled with pillars of the Israeli military and industrial establishment contrasts strikingly with Mercury's small, technologically oriented board. The descriptions of directors maps this: in reading about Teva's board, we learn who was a former head of the Mossad; in reading about the Mercury board, we learn who was involved in successful start-ups and who understands the new technologies.

To call that mindset 'American' is obviously a distortion: it is probably far more common among Israeli entrepreneurs than among Louisiana entrepreneurs. But, that said, for better or for worse, the 'new economy' is, at heart, an American phenomenon. The success of Israeli companies compared to German or Japanese companies may be, at least in part, a reflection of the 'Americanization' of Israeli society.

From this perspective, the real question is not how it is that Israeli companies manage to raise capital on the NASDAQ. The real question is 'What about the Germans? The Japanese?' In a world of global product markets and global capital markets, in which we know from the Israeli experience that transaction costs of cross-border capital flows are not prohibitively high, how come we do not see an equal number of German and Japanese technology companies going public on NASDAQ?

Here, the role of an IPO market may re-enter as a mechanism for educating entrepreneurs. The Israeli case study shows that these critical pedagogic and certification functions can be served by another country's capital market. But a national IPO market is another way to provide these functions and may be more accessible for entrepreneurs, say in Germany and Japan, who may not watch as much American television as Israelis, who may not study in the USA as often, and thus who may not be as quick to pick up the American way of doing things. For those entrepreneurs, it may take the development of a domestic IPO market to teach these lessons. More likely, however, they will learn from NASDAQ too, with the return of more and more US-educated MBAs who seek their fortunes in developing German or Japanese companies for eventual IPOs on the NASDAQ. Just as Goldman Sachs follows the money to Israel, it follows it to Frankfurt and Tokyo. Indeed, this may already be happening.

References

Amdocs, Form 20-F for the fiscal year ended 31 Dec. 1999, Item 1, available at SEC Edgar database.
Black, B. S. and Gilson, R. J. (1998), 'Venture capital and the structure of capital markets: banks versus stock markets', *Journal of Financial Economics* 47, 243–77.
Briggs, J. A. (2000), 'We need entrepreneurs, not military heroes', *Forbes,* 7 Nov. 2000, at 134.
Check Point Software Technologies Inc. (1999), Form 20-F for the fiscal year ended 31 Dec. 1999, available at SEC Edgar database.

Choi, S. J. and Guzman, A. T. (1998), 'Portable reciprocity: rethinking the international reach of securities regulation', *Southern California Law Review* 71, 903–51.

Cora D. *et al.* (1999), 'Fortune's one-hundred fastest growing companies', *Fortune,* 6 Sept. 99.

ECI Telecom Ltd. (1998), Form 20-F, available in the S.E.C. Edgar database.

Gerstenfeld, D. (2000), 'D & B: Local VC Funds Managed $4b', *Jerusalem Post,* 22 March, 12.

Giza Venture Capital, Fund Investors, www.gizavc.com.

Ha'aretz, 2 June 2000, at 6 (North American weekly edition).

Hansell, E. (1998), 'America online to buy Internet chat service for $287 million', *NewYork Times,* 9 June, D3.

Jackson, E. R. (2000), 'Equity research notes: comverse technology', US Bancorp Piper Jaffray (1 June).

Kesselman and Kesselman (2000), PriceWaterhouseCoopers Money Tree Survey for Q4, 1999.

Liani, T. (2000), 'Comment, ECI Telecommunications', Merrill Lynch (28 January).

Licht, A. (2001), 'David's dilemma: a case study of securities regulation in a small open market', *Theoretical Inquiries in Law* 2, 673–709.

Loss, L. and Seligman, J. (1990), *Securities Regulation,* Boston: Little, Brown & Co., 3rd edition.

Maltz, J. (2000), 'Go west, young techies', *Jerusalem Rep.,* 13 March, 41.

Mercury Interactive Corp., Form 10-K, at Item 1 (22 Mar. 2000), available at SEC Edgar database.

Mercury, Proxy Statement, 26 May 1999, at 2, available at SEC Edgar database.

Moneycentral.msn.com/invest/research/profile.asp?symbol=teva.

Moxley, R. C. (1962), 'The ADR: an instrument of international finance and a tool of arbitrage', *Villanova Law Review* 8, 22.

Multex.com Inc., ACE Consensus Estimates, Mercury Interactive Corp. (20 May) (on file with the author).

Multex.com Inc. (2000), 'Mercury Interactive Corp., Stock Snapshot' (20 May).

Multex.com Inc. (2000), 'Stock Snapshot, Teva Pharmaceuticals, Inc.' (May 20), available at www.multex.com.

Murphy, T. P. (1983), 'Flowers from the desert', *Forbes,* 31 Jan., 104.

NASDAQ (1999), 'Israeli Prime Minister Barak Opens The Nasdaq Stock Market', http://www.nasdaq.com/reference/sn_barak_112299.stm.

New York Times (2000), 'Lucent to Buy Chromatis, an Optical Networks Concern', 1 June, C4.

Orme, W. A. (2000), 'The new Israel: land of milk and money', *New York Times,* 16 April, C1.

Red Herring, (1991), 'Birth of a VC Nation', Red Herring, available at http://www.redherring.com/mag/issue31s/birth.html.

Romano, R. (1998), 'Empowering investors: a market approach to securities regulation', *Yale Law Journal* 107, 2359–430.

Saunders, M.A. (1993), 'American depositary receipts: an introduction to U.S. capital markets for foreign companies', *Fordham International Law Journal* 17, 48–62.

Shilades, C. and Goldmacher, P. (2000), 'Comment, Mercury Interactive Corporation', Merrill Lynch (1 Mar. 2000).

Teva (1998), Form 20-F for the fiscal year ended 31 Dec. 1998, available at SEC Edgar database.

17

Lock-in Agreements in Venture Capital-backed UK IPOs

SUSANNE ESPENLAUB, MARC GOERGEN, ARIF KHURSHED,
AND LUC RENNEBOOG

17.1. INTRODUCTION

It is widely believed that one of the reasons for the impressive success of the American new economy is the availability of venture capital (VC) providing ample funds for innovative firms. There is a growing body of literature on the impact of VC involvement on various aspects of the process and performance of initial public offerings (IPOs) such as the survivor profile, initial and long-term returns, and the operating performance of issuing firms (Megginson and Weiss 1991; Jain and Kini 1995, 1999, 2000; Brav and Gompers 1997*a*, *b*). Recently, some researchers (Bradley *et al.* 2000; Field and Hanka 2001) have focused on yet another aspect of VC involvement in the IPO process, that is, their involvement with so-called lock-in (or in the USA, lock-up) agreements contained in IPO prospectuses. These studies have so far exclusively focused on the US capital market. This chapter extends the analysis into lock-in agreements of British VC-backed IPO companies.

A lock-in agreement is a formal contract between the original shareholders of the issuing firm and the underwriter (called sponsor in the UK), whereby the original shareholders undertake not to sell their shares for a given period of time after the listing. The first day on which these shareholders can sell their shares is called the lock-in expiry day.

With the exception of the study by Espenlaub *et al.* (2001), there has been no work on lock-in agreements in the UK. Yet the UK is of particular interest given the different institutional and legal framework. In addition, UK lock-in agreements are much more diverse than the US ones. For instance, while lock-in periods are virtually standardized at 180 days in US IPOs (Bradley *et al.* 2000; Field and Hanka 2001) there is much greater diversity in the UK.

This chapter looks at the impact of VC presence on the characteristics of the lock-in contract and also on the abnormal returns realized around the expiry of directors' lock-in agreements using a sample of 186 UK IPOs issued during 1992–98. The lock-in agreements may help to reduce agency problems and information asymmetry that arise in IPOs. With insiders such as management and other major shareholders being restricted from selling their holdings, lock-in agreements ensure that these insiders maintain a significant interest in the firm after the IPO. This helps to align the interests of the old and new shareholders. In addition, the presence of VCs may act as a substitute for or alternatively as a complement to the lock-in agreements imposed on these insiders. We also examine the share-price performance of IPOs with and without VC backing around the time of the expiry of the lock-in agreements, and find significant differences between the two sub-samples.

The rest of the chapter is organized as follows. In Section 17.2 we review the literature on lock-in agreements. Section 17.3 presents examples of the lock-in agreements contained in the prospectuses of VC-backed UK IPOs and gives an overview of the regulations in the UK relating to lock-in agreements. In Section 17.4, we describe the data and the sample used in the large-scale studies reported in Section 17.5, which gives detailed descriptive statistics describing the manifold types of lock-in agreements observed in the UK, and Section 17.6, which reports the results of an event-study examining the abnormal returns of IPOs with and without VC backing around the expiry of directors' lock-in agreements. Finally, Section 17.7 presents a summary of four case studies of UK IPOs: two with VC backing, one issued by a firm in an industry classified as high tech, and two firms without VC backing, again one in the high-tech sector. Section 17.8 concludes the chapter.

17.2. LITERATURE SURVEY

The venture capital industry is crucial in the creation of new firms. VCs not only provide the necessary capital but their presence also signals quality as they are usually heavily involved with decisionmaking and monitoring the firm (e.g. Barry 1994; Jain and Kini 2000). Barry *et al.* (1990) examine IPOs of VC-backed companies in the USA between 1978 and 1987 and find that VCs perform intensive monitoring. They also report that, consistent with this monitoring role, VCs hold substantial shareholdings, and in many cases retain their investments well beyond the IPO contrary to the commonly held view of IPOs being an exit route. They also find that VCs often serve on the boards of the firms they invest in, typically holding two board seats or one third of the total. Megginson and Weiss (1991) focus on the 'certification hypothesis' formally developed by Booth and Smith (1986) and the role of VCs in 'certifying' the value of issuing firms and the quality of company information reported at the IPO. They find evidence to support their hypothesis that VC backing may reduce the asymmetry of information between the issuing firm and investors and hence lower the costs of going public. In this context, VCs play a similar part as underwriters and auditors, in that, as repeat players in the IPO market, they may be able to commit themselves credibly to the accuracy and completeness of disclosed information as false certification would lead to the loss of valuable reputation. In addition, the services of VC certification are costly to the issuing firm in terms of the very high returns VCs generally expect on their investments and the stringent conditions they impose on portfolio companies, such as the right of the VC to replace the entrepreneur as a manager under certain conditions. The cost, stringency, and limited availability of VC backing may act as a screening device as only high-quality firms that expect to gain most from VC involvement seek investment by VCs.

Jain and Kini (2000) argue that the presence of VCs influences the managers' decisions on strategic resource allocation and report evidence that VC backing increases the post-IPO survival time of firms.

Recent studies have examined the lock-in agreements entered into by the existing shareholders of IPO companies. One aspect of interest is the length of the lock-in periods agreed upon by directors and VCs. Obviously, the longer the lock-in period the longer everyone has to wait to sell their holdings. The length of the lock-in is especially important to venture capitalists who frequently seek to use the IPO as an exit route (e.g. Jain and Kini 2000; Khurshed 2000). Brav and Gompers (2000) argue that since adverse-selection problems are less severe in firms with VC backing, the length of the lock-ins for these firms should be smaller. They find empirical evidence to support this conjecture. For a sample of US IPOs issued during 1988–96, they find that the average lock-in period of VC backed firms is 191 days as compared to 264 days for firms without VC backing. Surprisingly, they also find that the percentage of shares locked in is higher for VC backed firms than for other firms. Similarly, Brau *et al.* (2001) and Bradley *et al.* (2000) find that on average the length of the lock-in period is shorter for VC-backed firms than for non-VC backed firms.

Finally, a growing body of literature focuses on the stock-returns performance of IPO firms at the time of the lock-in expiry reporting evidence of abnormal returns around the expiry date. Brav and Gompers (2000) examine a sample of US IPOs and find a statistically significant average abnormal return of −0.59 per cent and a significant average buy-and-hold return of −1.35 per cent on the lock-in expiry date. A cross-sectional study reveals that VC-backed firms suffer a price decline that is almost five times higher than that suffered by other firms (−2.55 and −0.57 per cent, respectively). This is a surprising result, and the authors argue that it may be due to the downward pressure on stock prices of large-scale selling by VCs seeking to exit the company at the time of lock-in expiry. Field and Hanka (2001) find similar results, which show that at the time of lock-in expiry the stock price drops on average by −2.9 per cent for the VC-backed firms as compared to −0.9 per cent for firms without VC backing. Bradley *et al.* (2000) also find that the decline in stock prices of VC-backed IPOs at lock-in expiry is much more substantial than for other IPOs. They conduct an in-depth cross-sectional study of VC-backed and other firms, controlling for differences in underwriter reputation, and find that VC-backed firms have consistently lower stock returns than other firms around lock-in expiry.

17.3. LOCK-IN AGREEMENTS IN THE UK

When a company offers shares in an IPO, insiders frequently agree to abstain from selling shares for a specified period of time after the IPO date, commonly referred to as the lock-in period. The lock-in agreement is negotiated between the sponsor(s) of the issue and the issuing firm. Lock-in agreements in the UK are typically phrased as follows:

The directors/selling shareholders have undertaken not to dispose of any ordinary shares without the prior consent of the underwriters at any time prior to the date of publication of the company's financial results for a specified financial year, except in limited specific circumstances.

In the USA, there is a trend towards a standardized lock-in period of 180 days. Brau *et al.* (2001) show that 69 per cent of IPOs in 1998 chose lock-in periods of exactly 180 days compared to only 20 per cent in 1988. Field and Hanka (2001) also find that lock-in periods were standardized at about 180 days during the 1990s.

By contrast, there is wide variation in lock-in agreements in the UK, not only with respect to the length of the lock-in period but also with respect to the other characteristics of the agreement. To appreciate the complexity of lock-in agreements in the UK, consider the following lock-in agreements of two randomly chosen UK companies with venture-capital backing. One is a high-tech research company, Vision Group, set up in 1990 by a university scientist to develop and commercialize highly integrated camera chip technology and floated in 1995. The other is a carpet-retailing company, Carpetright, launched in 1988 by MFI and an entrepreneur (Sir Philip Harris) with long experience in running a similar business and floated in June 1993. In Carpetright, the involvement of venture-capital backers came about when the company raised capital for expansion from NatWest Ventures and Phildrew Ventures in 1989 and 1990. In the case of Vision, no details are given in the prospectus of the origin of the involvement of the venture-capital backer. The lock-in agreements in the prospectus of Vision Group are as follows:

In terms of Letters of Undertaking dated 8th, 27th, and 28th March, 3rd and 4th April 1995 respectively granted by each of Mr. A. Macpherson, the University Court of the University of Edinburgh, Q.F. Realisations Limited, Mr. D. Renshaw and Donnelly (the 'Locked-in Shareholders'), the Locked-in Shareholders have agreed not to dispose of in aggregate 15,386,072 Ordinary shares until after the publication of the Company's accounts for the financial period ending 31st July 1996. In terms of the Placing Agreement, the Directors have agreed not to dispose of any Ordinary shares during the above period. The restrictions contained in the letters of undertaking and the Placing Agreement do not apply in certain cases being, inter alia, (i) transfers which Sharps have approved in writing and (ii) transfers in connection with certain offers for the whole or any part of the issued share capital of the Company.[1]

While the lock-in agreements for Vision are contained in the placing agreement at the back of the prospectus in Part 4 entitled 'Additional Information', the prospectus of Carpetright gives the lock-in agreements in an unusually prominent position, in the first part of the document together with the Details of the Flotation (p. 24). The underwriting agreement is dated 8 June 1993, and the lock-in agreements are worded as follows:

Each of the Directors has undertaken not to sell further shares until the publication of Carpetright's preliminary results for the year ending 30 April 1994, other than with the consent of County NatWest. Sir Philip Harris and Harris Ventures Limited have undertaken that they will not, together, other than with the consent of County NatWest, sell more than two and a half per cent of the ordinary

---

[1] A. Macpherson, and D. Renshaw are shareholders, but are not directors, (Renshaw is predicted to own 5% of the post-IPO equity, while Macpherson is not listed as a substantial shareholder holding 3 per cent or more). Q.F. Realisations Ltd: the venture-capital backer, part of the Quantum Fund. Donnelly Corporation, a US vehicle components manufacturer, became a minority shareholder in Vision's trading subsidiary, VVL, providing the company with increased funds for investment in vision applications. VVL and Donnelly also entered into an agreement to develop automotive vision products. Sharps: Albert E. Sharp, the sponsor, underwriter and stockbroker to the issue.

share capital of the Company in the first year following this period or more than five per cent of the ordinary share capital in total in the two years following this period.[2]

In many lock-in agreements, as in the examples above, there are separate lock-in agreements for different groups of initial shareholders. Directors are typically more likely to agree to lock-in periods than other shareholders, including institutional backers such as venture capitalists (see also Tables 17.5 and 17.6).

Lock-in contracts not only differ in length but also in the way they specify the expiry date of the lock-in agreements. They are either expressed in terms of a specific future calendar date, a certain period after flotation, or relative to the occurrence of other announcements or events in the company's financial year (e.g. the publication of the (preliminary) results or the annual-report release date). In the latter case, the precise timing of the lock-in expiry is to some extent under the control of the company's management.

Agreements may also involve a combination of company-event specific ('relative') dates and calendar dates or periods, as in the case of the agreement entered into by the chairman-cum-CEO of Carpetright, Sir Philip Harris. This particular agreement extends the initial lock-in period of the directors, defined as the period until the publication of the preliminary results for the current financial year, by a further one to two calendar years. Agreements may also provide for a gradual release of the retained equity from the lock-in provision by granting the disposal of parts, but not all, of the retained share stakes after one or several initial periods. An example is again the agreement by Harris, which limits his share sales to 2.5 per cent and 5 per cent of the company's shares in the first and second calendar year, respectively, after the expiry of the first lock-in period.

Contrary to the US where there are no rules about lock-in periods (Ofek and Richardson 2000), in the UK there are rules applying to certain types of companies seeking a listing on the London Stock Exchange (LSE). Companies that are or have been subject to compulsory lock-in periods are of three types: mineral companies, scientific research based companies, and innovative high growth companies. Until January 2000, both mineral companies and scientific research based companies, which did not satisfy the minimum age requirement of three years, were subject to compulsory lock-in periods.

Chapters 19 and 20 of the Listing Rules deal exclusively with mineral companies and scientific research based companies, respectively. Since January 2000, mineral companies that do not satisfy the minimum age of three years have had to make a prominent statement in their prospectus whether lock-in agreements exist for the directors and substantial shareholders. In the case where there is no lock-in agreement for one or more directors or substantial shareholders, the prospectus must clearly specify the absence of such a contract and state the reasons for its absence. Before January 2000, the directors as well as other senior employees of mineral companies, which did not satisfy the minimum age

---

[2] Sir Philip Harris (later Lord Harris) launched Carpetright together with the MFI Furniture Group in 1988. After two years as non-executive chairman, Harris took over as chairman and CEO of Carpetright in 1990. Carpetright was founded after the takeover in 1988 of the former Harris family business, Harris Queensway Plc. Harris took over as chairman and CEO of Harris Queensway in 1964 and expanded the company internally and by acquisition from three shops in 1957 to ninety-three when it was floated in 1978. When Harris Queensway was taken over in 1988, Harris sold his entire stake. The company failed in 1990. Harris Ventures Ltd: a company controlled by a trust of which Sir Philip Harris is a beneficiary.

requirement, were obliged either not to sell shares in the IPO or not to sell shares for a period of two years commencing on the first trading day. Major shareholders[3] were not allowed to sell shares in the IPO, or alternatively were not allowed to sell during the period of six months beginning on the first trading day or the period until the publication of the semi-annual results, whichever was longer. In addition, they could not dispose of more than 40 per cent of their holdings during the two years following the first trading day. All shareholders other than directors or major shareholders were not permitted to sell more than 20 per cent of the securities for which the application for listing had been made.

In January 2000, a new chapter—Chapter 25—was added to the Listing Rules. Chapter 25 relates to so called innovative high growth companies. Although these companies are not required to have any lock-in contracts, they have to publish a statement in their prospectus if they have a trading record of less than three years. The statement must contain the details of existing agreements or, if no agreements exist, the statement must specify the reasons for their absence.

Table 17.1 contains a summary of the rules about lock-in agreements.

17.4. DATA AND LARGE-SCALE SAMPLE

The sample used for the large-scale study into UK lock-in agreements consists of 188 IPOs issued by UK-incorporated companies on the LSE during January 1992 to December 1998. IPOs by financial and investment companies were excluded. IPOs were classified as VC backed if they were included in the list of IPOs backed by members of the British Venture Capital Association (BVCA). Sample companies are defined as high tech if they are included in the so-called techMARK segment of the LSE.[4] The sample was selected by initially selecting all companies on techMARK that conducted a new issue during 1992–98, excluding new issues other than IPOs (such as rights issues, introductions, and transfers from the lower tier, the Unlisted Securities Market, to the upper tier, the Official List). However, this sample would have been biased towards IPOs that survived at least until the opening of techMARK in 1999. Moreover, inclusion into techMARK is not automatic and companies are required to apply for admittance. As a result, the high-tech sample was extended to include any companies that went public during 1992–98 and at the time of the IPO satisfied the techMARK criteria (see footnote 4), but have since been de-listed or have not joined techMARK for other reasons.

---

[3] A major shareholder is a person who holds at least 10 per cent of the class of securities that will be listed on the LSE or is a person who has the right to appoint one of the directors of the firm.

[4] TechMARK is a market within the official market of the LSE. It went live on 4 November 1999 with over 190 UK and international companies from a wide range of FTSE industrial sectors, whose success depends on technological innovation. The market is open to innovative technology companies with a primary or dual primary listing in London, irrespective of their size, industry, or location. The purpose of techMARK is to create a new way for growing technology companies to access capital to finance expansion.

Table 17.1. *Lock-in agreements imposed by the LSE on certain types of firms with a trading record of less than three years for the period of 1993–99*

Type of company	Type of shareholder		
	A. Directors, senior employees, and their associates	B. Shareholders holding more than 10%	C. Other shareholders
Mineral company	Either: no shares to be sold in the IPO	Either: no shares to be sold in the IPO	Sales must not exceed 20% of the total number of shares
	Or: no shares to be sold during the two years after the first day of trading	Or: no shares to be sold during the six months after the first day of trading or the publication of the first semi-annual or annual results. Not more than 40% of their stake within two years of first day of trading	
Scientific research based company	*idem*	*idem*	*idem*

The non-high-tech sample was selected by choosing companies randomly from the KPMG New Issue Statistics, excluding financial and investment companies and companies on techMARK. Eliminating issues for which prospectuses are not available from Companies House leaves 105 IPOs issued by companies not classified as high-tech.

Two high-tech companies were excluded from the analysis because we were unable to identify whether they had VC backing or not, resulting in a final sample of 81 high-tech and 105 other companies (not classified as high-tech).

Data on the lock-in agreements were extracted from the IPO prospectuses, and data on the daily returns of the IPOs and the market index (the FT All Share Index) were obtained from Datastream.

17.5. DESCRIPTIVE STATISTICS ON LOCK-IN AGREEMENTS

Panel A of Table 17.2 provides information about the frequency of ownership by directors and other shareholders as well as information about the frequency of lock-in agreements for these two types of shareholders. The table shows that in virtually all firms directors own substantial equity stakes. This is the case across all the samples. Also, most firms (92 per cent) have lock-in agreements applying to their directors. There are slight

Table 17.2. *Ownership and lock-in agreements for directors and other shareholders*

Firms …	81 high-tech firms		105 other firms		Total for 186 firms
	48 VC-backed firms	33 non-VC backed firms	55 VC-backed firms	50 non-VC backed firms	
Panel A: Frequency of ownership and lock-in agreements					
Without ownership by the directors	0	1	0	1	2
With ownership by the directors	48	32	55	49	184
Thereof with locked-in directors' shares	45	29	53	43	170
Without other shareholders	2	10	0	3	15
With other shareholders	46	23	55	47	171
Thereof with locked-in other shareholders	31	19	32	27	109

Panel B: Z-test for the equality between the proportion of firms with locked-in directors/other shareholders for the VC-backed firms and the proportion for the non-VC backed firms

	High-tech sample	Low-tech sample
Directors	0.537	1.480
Other shareholders	−1.525	0.083

Panel C: Z-test for the equality between the proportion of firms with locked-in directors/other shareholders for the high-tech firms and the proportion for the low-tech firms

	VC-backed sample	Non-VC backed sample
Directors	−0.615	0.398
Other shareholders	0.962	2.397**

Figures shown in Panel A are the number of firms satisfying a certain criterion. The tests in Panels B and C are based on the assumption of a binomial distribution.
**Statistically significantly different from zero at the 5% level.

differences across the samples in the proportions of firms with locked-in directors. Among VC backed firms, 94 per cent of high-tech firms and 96 per cent of other firms lock in directors. These proportions are somewhat lower for firms not backed by VCs: 91 per cent for high-tech firms and 88 per cent for other firms. While these differences may be economically significant at least in the case of firms not in the high-tech sector, Panel B of Table 17.2 shows that these differences are not statistically significant.

Panel A of Table 17.2 also reports the ownership and frequency of lock-in agreements for other shareholders, that is, non-managerial shareholders. Only 15 out of 186 firms do not have non-managerial shareholders. Across all the samples, the majority of firms (64 per cent) have lock-in agreements applying to their other shareholders. This indicates that it is much more common for directors than for other shareholders to agree to lock-in periods. Comparing high-tech to other firms, we observe that other shareholders are more likely to be subject to lock-ins in high-tech firms than in other firms.

In the case of firms without VC backing, the proportion of firms that lock in other (non-managerial) shareholders is significantly higher among high-tech than among other firms, with the difference being statistically different from zero at the 5 per cent level. In firms with VC backing, the difference between the proportion of locked in other shareholders in high-tech and other firms is not significant. This indicates that venture capitalists are relatively less likely to face lock-in agreements than other non-managerial shareholders. This could be due to two separate factors. First, some venture capitalists escape such agreements because of their affiliation to the sponsor/underwriter. The potential conflicts of interest arising in the case of IPOs sponsored and underwritten by financial firms affiliated with a VC backer of the issuing company are examined in Gompers and Lerner (1997b) for the US, Hamao et al. (2000) for Japan, and Espenlaub et al. (1999) for the UK. In the case of Carpetright examined in Section 17.7, there is such an affiliation between a VC backer and the IPO sponsor, and the affiliated VC backer indeed manages to avoid being locked in. Second, venture capitalists are repeat investors in private firms, most of which will eventually go public, and venture capitalists have a valuable reputation at stake if they act against the interests of the new shareholders acquiring shares in the IPO. Investors may not buy shares in IPOs backed by venture capitalists who were previously involved with issues that reduced the wealth of new shareholders. As a result, such reputational considerations may limit the conflicts of interest between VC backers and IPO investors, reducing the need to lock in venture capitalists.

Table 17.3 records the average proportions of shares locked-in by the directors and other shareholders. In general, the percentage of locked-in shares in firms without VC backing is higher than in firms with VC financing. However, this may be due to the fact that the figures in Table 17.3 are calculated as the ratio of the number of locked-in shares over the total number of shares outstanding immediately after the IPO. Therefore, the figures may not reflect the lower level of ownership dispersion in firms without VC backing. For the high-tech firms, there is indeed a statistically significant difference in the percentage of equity sold in the IPO between VC-backed firms and firms without VC backing. On average, the former sell 39 per cent of their equity in the initial offering whereas the latter sell only 31 per cent.

In Table 17.4, the locked-in shares are reported as a proportion of the shares owned by each type of shareholder. For example, for the directors the percentage is the proportion of shares locked in by the directors out of the total number of shares owned by the directors immediately after the IPO. Table 17.4 shows that there is no longer a difference between high-tech firms with and without VC backing in terms of the proportion of directors' shares that are locked in. However, there is now a significantly higher proportion of locked-in directors' shares in VC-backed firms as compared to firms without VC backing in the sample of firms not classified as high tech. This suggests that there is no evidence that venture-capital backing of IPOs acts as a substitute for lock-in agreements. To the contrary,

Table 17.3. *Shares locked in by the directors and by other shareholders as a proportion of shares outstanding*

Average proportion	81 high-tech firms		105 low-tech firms		
	48 VC-backed firms	33 non-VC backed firms	55 VC-backed firms	50 non-VC backed firms[1]	Average for the 186 firms
Panel A: Average proportion of shares locked-in					
Shares locked in by the directors	16%	35%	22%	28%	24%
Shares locked in by the other shareholders	23%	21%	17%	20%	20%

Panel B: t-statistics for differences in means between VC-backed and non-VC backed firms

	High-tech firms	Low-tech firms
Shares locked in by the directors	−3.680***	−1.359
Shares locked in by the other shareholders	0.365	−0.710

Panel C: t-statistics for differences in means between high-tech firms and low-tech firms

	VC-backed firms	Non-VC backed firms
Shares locked in by the directors	−2.015**	1.222
Shares locked in by the other shareholders	1.112	0.151

Proportions are calculated as a percentage of the total number of shares outstanding immediately after the IPO.
[1] For one non-high tech/non-VC firm (Cox Insurance Holdings) we are unsure about the percentages locked in by directors and other shareholders, as the prospectus only specifies the total amount of shares locked in.
*** and ** stand for statistical significance at the 1% and 5%, respectively.

there is some evidence (for firms not operating in high-tech industries) that venture-capital backing of the IPO results in a higher proportion of locked-in directors' shares. There may be two reasons for this. First, the underwriter of a VC-backed IPO may expect heavy sales by the VC in the period after the IPO and decide to lock in the directors' shares in order to limit the downward pressure of the VC's disposals on stock prices. Second, if VCs do not sell out completely in the IPO, as reported by Barry *et al.* (1990), they may seek to align the directors' interests with their own by locking the directors in.

Table 17.5 contains statistics about the frequency of the different types of lock-in agreements for the directors. Some firms may have more than one agreement. As mentioned

Table 17.4. *Shares locked in by the directors and shares locked in by other shareholders as a proportion of their ownership*

Average proportion	81 high-tech firms		105 low-tech firms		Average for the 186 firms
	48 VC-backed firms	33 non-VC backed firms	55 VC-backed firms	50 non-VC backed firms[1]	
Panel A: Average proportion of shares locked-in					
Shares locked in by the directors	79%	84%	96%	85%	90%
Shares locked in by the other shareholders	51%	69%	46%	40%	55%

Panel B: t-statistics for differences in means between VC-backed and non-VC backed firms

	High-tech firms	Low-tech firms
Shares locked in by the directors	−0.609	−1.932***
Shares locked in by the other shareholders	−1.572	0.548

Panel C: t-statistics for differences in means between high-tech firms and low-tech firms

	VC-backed firms	Non-VC backed firms
Shares locked in by the directors	−2.773*	−0.101
Shares locked in by the other shareholders	0.500	2.402**

Proportions are calculated as a percentage of the total number of shares owned by the category of shareholders.
[1] For one non-high tech/non-VC firm (Cox Insurance Holdings) we are unsure about the percentages locked in by directors and other shareholders, as the prospectus only specifies the total amount of shares locked in.
***, **, * stand for statistical significance at the 1%, 5%, and 10% level, respectively.

above, lock-in agreements may contain either an absolute date, that is, a precise date such as 1 March 2001, or a relative date, such as the date of publication of the annual results. There are three broad categories of lock-in agreements: simple agreements, that is, agreements which specify a single date (Panel A of Table 17.5); staggered agreements which, in addition to a first lock-in period, specify one or more additional periods during which only a given percentage of the shares can be sold or during which sales can only happen with the consent of the sponsor (Panel B); and agreements which specify a combination of an absolute date and a relative date and expire on the later of these two dates, for example, 'until 30 April 2000 or the publication of the interim results, whichever is later' (Panel C).

Table 17.5 shows that the distribution of the agreements of the three types is approximately the same across the samples. However, about a third of agreements in the high-tech firms—with and without VC-financing—do not allow the directors to sell before the expiry of an absolute date, whereas for the low-tech firms a third of the agreements specify

Table 17.5. *Types of lock-in agreements for directors of all the firms*

Type of lock-in agreement	81 high-tech firms		105 other firms	
	48 VC-backed firms	33 non-VC backed firms	55 VC-backed firms	50 non-VC backed firms
Panel A: Simple lock-in agreements				
Publication of half yearly results	9.3%	2.8%	3.6%	6.1%
Publication of preliminary results	9.3%	5.6%	16.4%	10.2%
Publication of annual results	11.1%	16.7%	27.3%	30.6%
One month after publication of preliminary results	0.0%	2.8%	0.0%	0.0%
One month after publication of annual results	7.4%	5.6%	0%	0.0%
Absolute date	31.5%	33.3%	12.7%	22.4%
Until an absolute date, the publication of the half yearly results, or the publication of the annual results, whichever is longer	0.0%	0.0%	0.0%	0.0%
Total	68.6%	66.8%	60.0%	69.3%
Panel B: Staggered lock-in agreements (in addition to a first lock-in period during which sales are prohibited, these agreements include one additional period during which only a given percentage of the shares can be sold or during which sales can only happen with the consent of the sponsor)				
Publication of half yearly results	0%	2.8%	1.8%	2.0%
Publication of preliminary results	11.1%	0.0%	9.1%	4.1%
Publication of annual results	3.7%	5.6%	7.3%	4.1%
One month after publication of preliminary results	0.0%	0.0%	0.0%	0.0%
One month after publication of annual results	0.0%	5.6%	0.0%	0.0%
Absolute date	1.9%	2.8%	5.5%	4.1%
Total	16.7%	16.8%	23.7%	14.3%
Panel C: Combination of one absolute date and one relative date (e.g. 'until 30 January 1994 or the publication of the preliminary results, whichever is later')				
Publication of interim/half yearly results	0%	2.8%	1.8%	0.0%
Publication of preliminary results	1.9%	2.8%	0.0%	0.0%
Publication of annual results	0.0%	0.0%	5.5%	0.0%
One month after publication of preliminary results	0.0%	0.0%	0.0%	0.0%
One month after publication of annual results	0.0%	0.0%	0.0%	0.0%
Total	1.9%	5.6%	7.3%	0.0%
Panel D: Other types				
No lock-in	5.6%	8.3%	3.6%	6.1%
Not clear	1.9%	0.0%	0.0%	2.0%
Other	5.6%	2.8%	5.5%	8.2%
Total	13.1%	11.1%	9.1%	16.3%
Total number of agreements	54	36	55	49

This table shows the types of lock-in agreements. As one firm can have more than one type of lock-in agreement and as others may have no ownership by directors, the number of agreements may differ from the number of firms. In some firms some directors are subject to lock-in agreements, whereas other directors are not bound by such an agreement. All percentages are expressed as percentages of the total number of contracts.

the relative date of the publication of the annual results (Panel A). To some extent, this result may appear counter-intuitive as one would expect that, given the higher uncertainty about future profits, the directors of high-tech firms should be locked in until a date relative to the publication of new financial information about the company. Conversely, one could argue that absolute expiry dates are binding and legally enforceable whereas relative dates allow the directors to have a certain discretion to fix the actual date. For example, if the lock-in expires on the day of the publication of the company accounts, the directors have considerable discretion over the precise timing of the expiry date. In fact, the actual expiry may occur at any time during a period of several months. Hence, if the intention is to make sure that the directors hold shares in the company until a certain date, lock-in agreements with a relative expiry date should be avoided, as this type of agreement provides too much leeway to the directors.

Table 17.6 is similar to Table 17.5, but focuses on the agreements entered into by other (non-managerial) shareholders. Likewise, there is a higher incidence of simple agreements specifying an absolute date in the high-tech firms than in the low-tech firms (Panel A). The main difference between VC-backed firms and non-VC backed firms in each industry group seems to be the higher incidence of agreements that expire on the date of the publication of the annual results in firms without VC-financing.

17.6. DURATION OF LOCK-IN PERIODS AND EXPIRY-DATE EVENT STUDY

We examine the stock performance of venture-backed and other IPOs around the dates when the directors' lock-in agreements expired using an event study. The sample consists of the stocks with absolute expiry dates for lock-ins (i.e. the expiry date defined in terms of calendar dates or periods). The study analyses the informational content of the expiry of directors' lock-ins and the effect of VC backing on this informational content. This study focuses on directors' expiry dates for two reasons. First, directors are the second most important shareholder type in quoted UK firms after institutional investors. Although the latter are more important in terms of the accumulated shareholdings, they do not necessarily exercise their voting rights. Hence, in the average UK firm, it is the directors who control the firm and the main agency problem tends to be the potential expropriation of (minority) shareholders by the management of the firm (Goergen and Renneboog 2001*a*, *b*; Franks *et al.* 2001). Second, especially in younger firms, directors and founders may also assume an important leadership role (Morck *et al.* 1988). Therefore, directors are more informed than other shareholders, and there tends to be a greater informational asymmetry between directors and outside shareholders than between other existing shareholders and new shareholders.

Hence, if the abnormal returns at lock-in expiry are at least partly due to information asymmetries between insiders (directors) and outsiders, the expiry of directors' lock-ins is likely to have a greater impact on share prices than the expiry of the lock-ins of other shareholders, including venture capitalists. Further, if VC backing of the IPO company reduces these information asymmetries, then *ceteris paribus* the stock returns of VC-backed IPOs should show less adverse performance around the expiry of directors' lock-ins than those of IPOs without VC backing.

Table 17.6. *Types of lock-in agreements for other shareholders for all the firms*

Type of lock-in agreement	81 high-tech firms		105 other firms	
	48 VC-backed firms	33 non-VC backed firms	55 VC-backed firms	50 non-VC backed firms
Panel A: Simple lock-in agreements				
Publication of half yearly results	7.3%	3.6%	14.3%	3.1%
Publication of preliminary results	5.5%	0.0%	9.5%	6.3%
Publication of annual results	3.6%	14.3%	19.0%	28.1%
One month after publication of preliminary results	0.0%	0.0%	0.0%	0.0%
One month after publication of annual results	0.0%	0.0%	0.0%	0.0%
Absolute date	25.5%	28.6%	16.7%	28.1%
Until an absolute date, the publication of the half yearly results, or the publication of the annual results, whichever is longer	9.1%	7.1%	0.0%	0.0%
Total	51.0%	53.6%	59.5%	65.6%
Panel B: Staggered lock-in agreements (in addition to a first lock-in period during which sales are prohibited, these agreements include one additional period during which only a given percentage of the shares can be sold or during which sales can only happen with the consent of the sponsor)				
Publication of half yearly results	0.0%	0.0%	4.8%	3.1%
Publication of preliminary results	0.0%	0.0%	21.4%	0.0%
Publication of annual results	0.0%	0.0%	0.0%	6.3%
One month after publication of preliminary results	0.0%	0.0%	0.0%	0.0%
One month after publication of annual results	0.0%	7.1%	0.0%	0.0%
Absolute date	5.5%	3.6%	2.4%	3.1%
Total	5.5%	10.7%	28.6%	12.5%
Panel C: Combination of one absolute date and one relative date (e.g. 'until 30 January 1994 or the publication of the preliminary results, whichever is later')				
Publication of interim/half yearly results	9.1%	0.0%	2.4%	3.1%
Publication of preliminary results	3.6%	0.0%	0.0%	0.0%
Publication of annual results	1.8%	0.0%	2.4%	0.0%
One month after publication of preliminary results	0.0%	0.0%	0.0%	0.0%
One month after publication of annual results	0.0%	0.0%	0.0%	0.0%
Total	14.5%	0.0%	4.8%	3.1%
Panel D: Other types				
No lock-in	27.3%	28.6%	4.8%	9.4%
Not clear	1.8%	0.0%	0.0%	3.1%
Other	0.0%	7.1%	2.4%	6.3%
Total	29.1%	35.7%	7.2%	18.8%
Total number of agreements	55	28	42	32

This table shows the types of lock-in agreements. As one firm can have more than one type of lock-in agreement and as others may have no ownership by other shareholders, the number of agreements may differ from the number of firms. In some firms some shareholders are subject to lock-in agreements whereas other shareholders are not bound by such an agreement. All percentages are expressed as percentages of the total number of contracts.

IPOs with expiry dates specified relative to other company announcements or events are excluded as it is difficult to disentangle the effects on stock returns of the lock-in expiry from the effects of the simultaneous company announcements or events relative to which the lock-in expiry is defined. In addition, for a significant proportion of those companies it is impossible to identify *ex post* (i.e. after the expiry date) the precise dates of the expiry announcement or the related company announcements or events using the available UK data sources (such as Sequencer and the *Financial Times*). The total sample comprises 54 companies with clear-cut expiry dates (specified in terms of simple or staggered lock-in agreements, or both).[5] In the case of staggered agreements, and consequently multiple lock-in expiry dates, the earliest expiry date was selected for the analysis. Two IPOs were excluded from the analysis due to a lack of share-price data; neither was venture-capital backed and both were issued by firms not classified as high-tech. Of the remaining 52 companies used in the event study, 28 had venture-capital backing before flotation. Of these 28 companies, 19 are classified high-tech, and of the 24 firms without VC backing, 13 are high-tech (see Table 17.7).

17.6.1. *Descriptive Statistics of Event-study Sample and Length of Lock-in Periods*

Brav and Gompers (2000) argue that since adverse-selection problems are less severe in firms with VC backing, the lock-in periods for these firms should be shorter. Their empirical results support this. For a sample of US IPOs during 1988–96, the average length of the lock-in period for VC-backed firms is 191 days compared to 264 days for firms without VC backing. Other US studies report similar results (Bradley *et al.* 2000; Brau *et al.* 2001).

We examine the length of the lock-in periods for the sample of 52 companies with absolute expiry dates. The results are presented in Table 17.7. For the 52 companies as a whole, the average lock-in period is 561 days, and the median lock-in period is 730 days. The shortest lock-in period is 158 days, but only four companies in the sample chose lock-in periods of 180 days or less (the fifth shortest period was 345 days). Thus, it appears that the directors of UK companies (or more specifically, those directors who select absolute lock-in expiry dates) typically agree to substantially longer lock-in periods than their US counterparts irrespective of the presence or absence of VC backing. Moreover, contrary to the findings of US studies, we find no evidence that the differences in lock-in periods between UK firms with and without venture-capital backing are statistically significant. In fact, the average lock-in period is exactly the same (561 days) for firms with and without VC backing. Looking at the sub-samples of high-tech companies and other companies separately, the mean lock-in periods do differ between

---

[5] The discrepancies between the number of firms with absolute expiry dates (54) and the number of agreements by the directors of those firms specifying absolute expiry dates (56) underlying the figures in Table 17.5 is due to the fact that the directors of two firms entered into two separate agreements both specifying absolute expiry dates, one in terms of a simple lock-in agreement and one staggered.

Table 17.7. *Descriptive statistics of event-study sub-sample*

Lock-in periods (duration in calendar days)			
Industrial Sector	**Firms without VC backing**	**VC-backed firms**	**All firms**
High-tech firms			
Obs.	13	19	32
Mean	594	613**	605
Standard Error	76	43	40
Median	730	730	730
Min/Max	180/1095	158/731	158/1095
Other firms (not high-tech)			
Obs.	11	9	20
Mean	522	449**	489
Standard Error	63	57	43
Median	481	365	366
Min/Max	169/730	350/767	169/767
All Firms			
Obs.	24	28	52
Mean	561	561	561
Standard Error	50	37	30
Median	730	727	730
Min/Max	169/1095	158/767	158/1095

The sub-sample comprises the 52 companies with absolute expiry dates used in the event study. Two IPOs were dropped from the sub-sample of 54 due to lack of share-price data; both are 'other firms' issued in 1992 and 1993, respectively, with directors' lock-in expiry dates in 1995.
** Difference in means between VC-backed high-tech and VC-backed other firms is statistically different from zero at the 5% level.

firms with and without VC backing. However, these differences are not statistically significant.[6]

While it appears not to matter whether a firm has VC backing or not, there is however a difference in lock-in periods between high-tech and other firms. Specifically, there is evidence that, among UK companies with venture-capital backing, the directors of high-tech firms choose longer lock-in periods than those of other firms. A one-tailed t-test confirms that the average lock-in period of VC-backed high-tech firms is statistically significantly longer than that of other VC-backed firms at the 5 per cent level. It could be argued that high-tech companies are more prone to information asymmetries between company insiders and outsiders than other firms. Therefore, this result suggests that the insiders of firms with greater information asymmetries choose longer lock-in periods either to credibly signal favourable private information about the company to uninformed

[6] The smallest p-value for the t-test of the differences in means between the sub-samples with and without VC backing is 0.4; this occurs for the sub-sample of firms not classified as high-tech.

outsiders (Courteau 1995; Brau *et al.* 2000) or as a 'commitment device' (Brav and Gompers 2000) to assure uninformed IPO investors that they will refrain from expropriating these investors' interests. It is interesting to note that a significant difference in lock-in periods between high-tech and other firms only arises in the VC backed sub-sample. This suggests that for UK companies VC backing at best serves to reduce minor informational problems as may be found among firms not classified as high tech. By contrast, for firms facing substantial information asymmetries (such as those in the high-tech sector), VC backing does not serve to reduce information asymmetries, at least not by itself. Instead, it needs to be complemented by other mechanisms, such as locking in directors for longer periods.

17.6.2. *Event-study Methodology*

The abnormal returns surrounding the lock-in expiry are estimated according to the standard event-study methodology (e.g. Brown and Warner 1980, 1985).[7] The returns measure used is daily discrete total returns (in percentages), including dividend payments, based on daily returns indices (data type RI)[8] from Datastream:

$$R_t = \frac{RI_t - RI_{t-1}}{RI_{t-1}} * 100.$$

The abnormal return (AR) is the market-adjusted return:

$$AR_{it} = R_{it} - R_{mt},$$

where R_{mt} is the daily discrete total return on the market portfolio proxied by the FTSE All Share Index, and R_{it} is the discrete total return on the stock of firm i on day t. The average abnormal return (AAR) is calculated as:

$$AAR_t = \frac{1}{n_t} \sum_{i=1}^{n_t} AR_{it},$$

where n_t represents the number of stocks or firms in the sample on day t.

The lock-in expiry day is Day 0, and average abnormal returns are cumulated over several periods: first, for the period from forty trading days before to forty trading days after Day 0, and second, for periods immediately around Day 0. The cumulative abnormal return (CAAR) from start day t_s to the end day t_e is calculated as:

$$CAAR_{(t_e \cdot t_s)} = \sum_{t=t_s}^{t_e} AAR_t.$$

---

[7] For many helpful comments and suggestions on event-study methodology, we are grateful to Norman Strong.

[8] RI_t is defined as

$$RI_t = RI_{t-1} * \left(\frac{P_t + D_t}{P_{t-1}} \right) \tag{17.1}$$

where P_t and P_{t-1} are the share prices on day t and $t-1$, and D_t is the dividend payment associated with ex-date t

To determine the statistical significance of the CAARs over the 81-day window around the lock-in expiry, we use both cross-sectional t-statistics with standard errors calculated from cross-sectional data of the sample firms' CAAR, and Brown and Warner's (1980) Crude Dependence Adjustment Test:

$$\frac{\text{CAAR}_{(t_e \cdot t_s)}}{se(\text{AAR}_t)\sqrt{t_e - t_s + 1}},$$

where the standard errors are calculated from time-series data:

$$se(\text{AAR}) = \sqrt{\frac{\sum_{t=-40}^{+40}(\text{AAR}_t - \overline{\overline{A}})^2}{80}} \quad \text{and} \quad \overline{\overline{A}} = \frac{1}{81}\sum_{t=-40}^{+40}\text{AAR}_t.$$

In Tables 17.9 and 17.10, the start day t_s is Day -40 and the end day t_e ranges from -40 to $+40$.

17.6.3. *Results on Lock-in Expiry Abnormal Returns*

The findings of the event study are reported in Tables 17.8–17.10 and illustrated in Figures 17.1 and 17.2. Table 17.8 reports the market-adjusted (cumulative) abnormal returns for alternative, relatively narrow test windows of one, two, three, and eleven days immediately around the expiry of the directors' lock-in agreements. The statistical significance of the (cumulative) abnormal returns is assessed using cross-sectional t-statistics (not reported).

Tables 17.9 and 17.10 show the returns performance over a wider 81-day window around the expiry date (Day 0). Table 17.9 reports the daily AARs, median abnormal returns, and CAARs for the entire event-study sample of fifty-two stocks over the

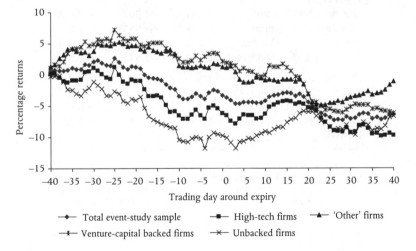

Figure 17.1. *Cumulative abnormal returns around lock-in expiry date (Day 0).*

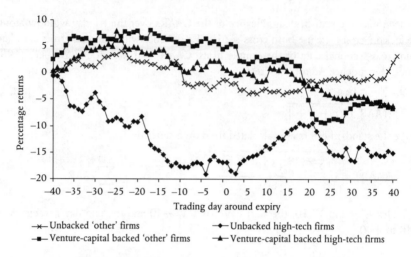

Figure 17.2. *Cumulative abnormal returns around lock-in expiry date (Day 0).*

Table 17.8. *Performance immediately around lock-in expiry date (Day 0)*

Pre-IPO backing Industrial Sector	Firms without VC backing	VC-backed firms	All firms
Other firms (not high-tech)			
One-day (Day 0) return	−0.028	−0.967	−0.451
Two-day (0, +1) return	−0.677	−0.571	−0.630
Three-day (−1, +1) return	−0.273	−1.122	−0.655
Eleven-day (−5, +5) return	−1.945	−3.017	−2.427
High-tech firms			
One-day (Day 0) return	−0.251	−1.307	−0.878
Two-day (0, +1) return	−0.314	−1.753	−1.168
Three-day (−1, +1) return	−1.232	−1.773	−1.553
Eleven-day (−5, +5) return	0.322	−1.532	−0.779
All Firms			
One-day (Day 0) return	−0.149	−1.198***	−0.714
Two-day (0, +1) return	−0.481	−1.373***	−0.961*
Three-day (−1, +1) return	−0.792	−1.564***	−1.207
Eleven-day (−5, +5) return	−0.717	−2.010	−1.413

The table shows the abnormal returns on IPOs with and without venture-capital backing of either industry sector (high-tech and other firms) immediately around the lock-in expiry date for three narrow windows (day zero only, days −1 to 0, days −1 to +1) and one wider window (days −5 to +5). The calculations of the AAR and CAAR and the cross-sectional *t*-statistics shown in this table are explained in Section 17.6.2 on research design.
* Statistically significantly different from zero at the 10% level (two-tailed *t*-test).
*** Statistically significantly different from zero at the 1% level (two-tailed *t*-test).

Table 17.9. *Performance around lock-in expiry date*

Day relative to lock-in expiry	AAR (percentage)	Median abnormal return in (percentage)	CAAR (%)	Cross-sectional t-statistic for CAAR	Crude-dependence adjusted t-statistic for CAAR
−40	0.543	−0.043	0.543	1.418	1.190
−39	0.268	0.262	0.811	1.568	1.257
−38	−0.089	0.022	0.722	1.101	0.914
−37	−0.088	−0.013	0.633	0.624	0.694
−36	0.166	−0.126	0.799	0.555	0.783
−35	0.275	−0.100	1.074	0.678	0.961
−34	−0.186	−0.128	0.888	0.570	0.736
−33	−0.022	−0.375	0.866	0.529	0.671
−32	0.814	0.155	1.680	0.923	1.228
−31	−0.175	−0.217	1.505	0.816	1.043
−30	0.610	0.014	2.115	1.055	1.398
−29	0.200	0.025	2.314	1.042	1.465
−28	−0.417	−0.079	1.897	0.822	1.154
−27	−0.359	0.177	1.538	0.581	0.901
−26	−0.138	−0.001	1.400	0.530	0.792
−25	1.270	−0.142	2.669	0.896	1.463
−24	−0.629	−0.204	2.040	0.723	1.085
−23	−0.826	−0.517	1.214	0.435	0.627
−22	−0.366	−0.373	0.848	0.305	0.427
−21	0.434	0.231	1.282	0.454	0.629
−20	−0.101	−0.037	1.182	0.422	0.565
−19	−0.212	−0.335	0.969	0.376	0.453
−18	−0.956	−0.617	0.013	0.005	0.006
−17	−0.411	−0.115	−0.398	−0.133	−0.178
−16	−0.202	−0.211	−0.600	−0.198	−0.263
−15	−0.087	−0.104	−0.687	−0.222	−0.296
−14	−0.242	−0.300	−0.929	−0.294	−0.392
−13	−0.579	−0.345	−1.508	−0.467	−0.625
−12	−0.632	−0.140	−2.141	−0.641	−0.872
−11	−0.223	−0.133	−2.364	−0.729	−0.946
−10	−1.102	−0.302	−3.466	−1.009	−1.365
−9	−0.394	−0.176	−3.860	−1.125	−1.496
−8	−0.044	0.074	−3.904	−1.139	−1.490
−7	0.401	0.019	−3.503	−1.033	−1.317
−6	0.501	−0.050	−3.001	−0.907	−1.112
−5	−0.460	−0.244	−3.462	−1.053	−1.265
−4	−0.426	−0.078	−3.888	−1.150	−1.401
−3	1.043	0.013	−2.846	−0.866	−1.012
−2	0.429	0.271	−2.417	−0.732	−0.849

Table 17.9. *Continued*

Day relative to lock-in expiry	AAR (percentage)	Median abnormal return in (percentage)	CAAR (%)	Cross-sectional t-statistic for CAAR	Crude-dependence adjusted t-statistic for CAAR
−1	−0.246	−0.289	−2.664	−0.780	−0.923
0	−0.714	−0.086	−3.377	−0.961	−1.156
1	−0.248	−0.219	−3.625	−1.015	−1.226
2	−0.446	−0.161	−4.070	−1.150	−1.361
3	−0.600	−0.002	−4.670	−1.290	−1.543
4	0.025	−0.121	−4.645	−1.230	−1.518
5	0.231	−0.059	−4.414	−1.161	−1.427
6	−0.045	−0.041	−4.459	−1.165	−1.426
7	−0.028	−0.045	−4.488	−1.158	−1.420
8	−0.072	0.034	−4.560	−1.156	−1.428
9	0.058	−0.082	−4.502	−1.149	−1.396
10	0.277	−0.090	−4.226	−1.086	−1.297
11	0.708	0.179	−3.517	−0.900	−1.069
12	0.138	0.004	−3.379	−0.852	−1.018
13	0.114	0.018	−3.265	−0.829	−0.974
14	0.291	0.047	−2.974	−0.755	−0.879
15	0.044	−0.117	−2.930	−0.747	−0.858
16	−0.091	−0.101	−3.020	−0.759	−0.877
17	−0.372	0.078	−3.393	−0.833	−0.977
18	0.281	−0.312	−3.111	−0.745	−0.888
19	−0.474	−0.296	−3.585	−0.855	−1.015
20	−0.896	−0.325	−4.481	−1.046	−1.258
21	−0.618	−0.245	−5.100	−1.192	−1.420
22	−0.351	−0.296	−5.451	−1.257	−1.505
23	−0.725	−0.336	−6.175	−1.370	−1.692
24	−0.403	−0.253	−6.579	−1.462	−1.789
25	−0.317	−0.207	−6.896	−1.481	−1.861
26	−0.408	−0.271	−7.304	−1.547	−1.956
27	0.059	0.111	−7.245	−1.515	−1.926
28	−0.117	−0.132	−7.362	−1.501	−1.943
29	0.579	−0.053	−6.783	−1.381	−1.777
30	−0.362	−0.240	−7.145	−1.436	−1.859
31	0.118	−0.133	−7.027	−1.397	−1.816
32	0.634	−0.043	−6.393	−1.338	−1.640
33	0.218	−0.031	−6.175	−1.271	−1.574
34	−0.193	0.161	−6.368	−1.280	−1.612
35	−0.795	−0.368	−7.163	−1.411	−1.801
36	0.221	0.076	−6.942	−1.385	−1.734
37	−0.243	−0.310	−7.185	−1.414	−1.783

Table 17.9. *Continued*

Day relative to lock-in expiry	AAR (percentage)	Median abnormal return in (percentage)	CAAR (%)	Cross-sectional t-statistic for CAAR	Crude-dependence adjusted t-statistic for CAAR
38	0.205	0.014	−6.979	−1.347	−1.721
39	0.533	−0.027	−6.446	−1.274	−1.580
40	0.011	−0.032	−6.436	−1.263	−1.568

This table gives the results of an event study using all sample IPOs with clear-cut, absolute expiry dates, excluding two stocks with missing data. The final event-study sample comprises fifty-two stocks. Returns data are available for all these firms for the entire 81-day period around the expiry of the directors' lock-in agreement. AAR and CAAR and t-statistics are calculated as detailed in Section 17.6.2 on research design.

period from Day −40 to Day +40 around the expiry day, Day 0. The statistical significance of the cumulative average abnormal returns is assessed using both standard cross-sectional t-statistics and Brown and Warner's (1980) Crude-Dependence Adjustment Test. Table 17.10 reports CAARs separately for IPOs with and without venture-capital backing and by industry sector (high-tech and other firms). The results reported in Tables 17.9 and 17.10 are also shown in Figures 17.1 and 17.2. In addition to the CAARs for the entire event-study sample, Figure 17.1 also illustrates separately the CAARs for stocks with and without venture-capital involvement and for high-tech and other firms.

As shown in Table 17.8, there is some evidence of negative abnormal stock-returns in the days around the expiry day, in the sense that almost all the returns measured are negative. However, most of these abnormal returns are statistically not significantly different from zero. While the magnitudes of the CAARs for the event-study sample as a whole range from −0.7 to −1.4 per cent depending on the specific test window, only one of these returns, the two-day return for Days 0–1, turns out to be statistically different from zero (and only at the 10 per cent level).

It appears, however, that there is a significant difference between IPOs with and without venture-capital backing, pooling the two industrial categories, high tech and other firms. Specifically, the CAARs for the VC-backed stocks are lower for all windows for the entire sample and separately for each industry sector (except for the two-day return); and for the sample of twenty-eight VC-backed stocks, the CAARs are statistically significantly less than zero at the 1 per cent level for the narrow one-to three-day windows around the expiry date. For the VC-backed stocks, the CAARs range from −1.2 to −1.6 per cent (and even to −2 per cent for the 11-day window, but this result is not statistically significant), while the corresponding CAARs for the stocks without VC backing range only from −0.2 per cent to −0.8 per cent. An examination of the median CAARs (not reported) shows similar results: the medians of stocks with VC backing are always lower than those of stocks without VC backing, but the magnitudes of the median returns and

Table 17.10. *Cumulative AAR (in percentage) around lock-in expiry date: firms with(out) venture-capital backing by industrial sector*

Day relative to lock-in expiry	Firms without venture-capital backing		Venture-capital backed firms	
	High-tech firms	Other firms	High-tech firms	Other firms
−40	−0.567	0.282	0.486	2.584
−39	−0.683	0.389	0.922	3.250
−38	−1.720	1.723	0.404	3.698
−37	−3.477	1.638	0.746	5.105
−36	−6.264	2.327	2.146	6.290
−35	−6.450	2.220	2.851	6.790
−34	−6.882	1.529	3.123	6.609
−33	−7.251	1.253	3.631	6.283
−32	−5.956	1.392	4.818	6.440
−31	−4.822	1.047	4.176	5.565
−30	−3.747	1.949	4.372	6.019
−29	−5.479	2.860	4.842	7.569
−28	−6.744	3.110	4.750	6.876
−27	−9.157	3.434	5.477	6.353
−26	−9.051	3.427	5.062	6.284
−25	−8.425	4.106	7.844	6.014
−24	−8.881	3.927	6.159	6.814
−23	−10.077	2.800	4.931	7.739
−22	−10.235	2.221	4.538	7.389
−21	−9.089	2.195	4.840	7.637
−20	−9.331	1.982	4.756	7.841
−19	−8.285	2.082	3.980	6.621
−18	−11.117	1.608	3.664	6.433
−17	−13.581	1.553	3.529	7.969
−16	−14.209	0.950	4.006	7.438
−15	−14.622	0.912	4.299	6.959
−14	−15.434	0.962	4.365	6.534
−13	−16.568	1.769	3.179	6.343
−12	−17.584	2.245	1.904	6.266
−11	−16.944	1.304	1.609	5.827
−10	−17.675	−1.908	1.115	5.482
−9	−17.805	−2.220	0.292	5.516
−8	−17.805	−2.578	0.176	5.941
−7	−17.197	−2.011	0.982	4.986
−6	−16.810	−1.948	1.980	5.140
−5	−17.087	−2.173	0.651	5.960
−4	−19.126	−3.059	1.170	6.430

Table 17.10. *Continued*

Day relative to lock-in expiry	Firms without venture-capital backing		Venture-capital backed firms	
	High-tech firms	Other firms	High-tech firms	Other firms
−3	−16.417	−2.533	2.220	5.680
−2	−15.668	−1.743	2.291	5.960
−1	−16.586	−1.339	2.271	5.410
0	−16.836	−1.367	0.964	4.443
1	−16.900	−2.016	0.518	4.839
2	−18.509	−1.904	0.081	5.375
3	−18.958	−3.263	−0.315	5.056
4	−17.160	−3.148	−0.209	2.235
5	−16.488	−3.894	0.448	2.123
6	−15.891	−3.609	−0.079	1.768
7	−15.750	−3.847	−0.299	2.154
8	−15.366	−3.249	−1.505	2.998
9	−14.942	−2.917	−1.477	2.253
10	−13.778	−3.502	−1.254	2.415
11	−14.213	−3.513	0.955	2.485
12	−13.314	−3.425	0.827	2.148
13	−12.201	−4.049	0.613	2.414
14	−12.532	−3.599	1.244	2.691
15	−11.180	−3.500	0.447	2.556
16	−10.576	−3.306	−0.154	2.192
17	−10.236	−3.206	−1.089	1.402
18	−9.378	−2.427	−1.311	1.304
19	−9.769	−1.359	−1.456	−1.868
20	−9.898	−1.432	−2.265	−5.064
21	−9.425	−1.885	−2.795	−7.647
22	−10.938	−1.553	−2.364	−8.804
23	−12.582	−1.291	−3.168	−9.240
24	−13.186	−1.120	−3.890	−9.382
25	−14.835	−0.965	−3.983	−8.826
26	−15.473	−1.280	−4.580	−8.616
27	−15.492	−0.582	−4.726	−8.794
28	−15.655	−0.704	−4.754	−9.027
29	−14.123	−0.944	−4.819	−7.463
30	−16.306	−1.119	−4.580	−6.695
31	−16.666	−1.473	−4.206	−5.849
32	−13.993	−1.286	−4.360	−5.949
33	−13.351	−1.048	−4.463	−5.691
34	−14.494	−0.455	−4.743	−5.290
35	−15.505	−1.293	−5.560	−5.674

Table 17.10. *Continued*

Day relative to lock-in expiry	Firms without venture-capital backing		Venture-capital backed firms	
	High-tech firms	Other firms	High-tech firms	Other firms
36	−15.132	−0.980	−5.481	−5.485
37	−15.543	−0.830	−5.990	−5.401
38	−15.557	0.466	−5.889	−5.990
39	−14.646	2.193	−5.852	−6.417
40	−15.065	3.290	−6.116	−6.535

The table breaks down the results of the event study using all sample IPOs with clear-cut, absolute expiry dates for firms with and without IPO venture-capital backing by industrial sector. Excluding two stocks with missing data leaves a final event-study sample comprising fifty-two stocks: twenty-eight IPOs with and twenty-four without venture-capital backing. Of the venture-capital backed IPOs, nineteen were issued by high-tech firms, and of the IPOs without venture-capital backing, thirteen were issued by high-tech firms. Returns data are available for all these firms for the entire 81-day period around the expiry of the directors' lock-in agreement. AAR, CAARs and *t*-statistics are calculated as detailed in the Section 17.6.2 on research design.

of the differences between the two sub-samples are smaller than the (differences in the) average returns. The lack of statistical significance of the CAARs of VC-backed stocks for the two industry sectors (high-tech and other firms) separately may be due to the small size of the sub-samples.

The findings of significantly lower abnormal returns for VC-backed IPOs compared to others is consistent with the results reported by US studies. As outlined in the literature review above, Brav and Gompers (2000) report that the price decline around the lock-in expiry of VC-backed firms is almost five times higher than that of firms without VC backing (−2.55 and −0.57 per cent, respectively). Field and Hanka (2001) find similar results and report an average return of −2.9 per cent at the lock-in expiry for VC-backed firms as compared to only −0.9 per cent for non-VC backed firms. Bradley *et al.* (2000) also find that, controlling for differences in underwriter reputation, VC-backed firms show consistently worse stock returns around the lock-in expiry than firms without VC backing.

Brav and Gompers suggest that this may be due to downward pressure on the share price as a result of large share disposals by venture capitalists exiting the company after the expiry of their lock-ins. However, this argument does not (fully) explain our findings. As shown in Tables 17.2–17.6, in the UK, the lock-in agreements of directors and other shareholders, such as VCs, differ considerably both in frequency and in the details of the agreement. This event study focuses on the expiry of directors' lock-in agreements, and the expiry dates for directors is very likely to differ from that of VCs (if in fact they agree to lock-ins). As a result, the difference in the abnormal returns around the lock-in expiry date between stocks with and without VC backing is unlikely to be due to price pressure from VC selling. Instead they may be indicative of differences in the informational contents of the expiry of directors' lock-ins and also of other announcements or events occurring at that time, such as announcements of share trading by directors and others.

Examining the wider 81-day window around lock-in expiry (forty days on either side of Day 0) in Table 17.10 indicates that it is high-tech firms without VC backing that underperform in the run-up to the expiry date from Day -40 to -4. The performance of both other stocks without VC backing and of venture-capital backed stocks in either industry sector are substantially better prior to the expiry date. However, while for high-tech firms without VC backing there is no further deterioration in the CAARs after the expiry date, the CAARs of the other three sub-samples in Table 17.10 and Fig. 17.2 all decline after Day 0. The most striking deterioration in CAARs in the period after expiry occurs for venture-capital backed firms not classified as high-tech. This is also the sub-sample with the worst performance in the window from Day -5 to Day $+5$ (see also Table 17.8).

The reasons for these differences in pre-expiry CAARs are not clear. One possible explanation for the differential pre-expiry performance high-tech firms with no VC backing is that these firms have a relatively lower credibility with investors due to high information asymmetries and the absence of VC certification. Hence, they may choose to disclose information about prospective post-expiry directors' sales at an earlier stage, that is, before the expiry, to spread the adverse impact on stock prices over a longer period. This issue will require further investigation.

17.7. CASE STUDIES

This section details lock-in agreements of four companies that conducted IPOs on the London Stock Exchange during 1992–95. By focusing on a small number of companies we intend to shed further light on the structure and rationale underlying the lock-in agreements. The sample comprises one company of each type; that is, it comprises two firms with and two firms without venture-capital backing, and in each category there is one company classified as high-tech (see the section on sample selection) and one 'other' firm (not classified as high-tech).

Cases 1 and 2 refer to companies without venture-capital backing; Case 1 is a non-high-tech company whereas Case 2 a high-tech company. The lock-in agreements of the venture-capital backed IPOs: Cases 3 (not high-tech) and 4 (high-tech) were also cited above in the section on lock-in agreements in the UK. The performance of the return indices of the case-study IPO stocks are shown in Fig. 17.3. Further background details of the case studies and the full wording of the lock-in agreements are given in the Appendix.

17.7.1. *Case 1: Ryland*

The business was founded in 1951 by the Whale family, and it remained family owned until its flotation in 1994. It is a distributor of motor vehicles (i.e. not high-tech) based in

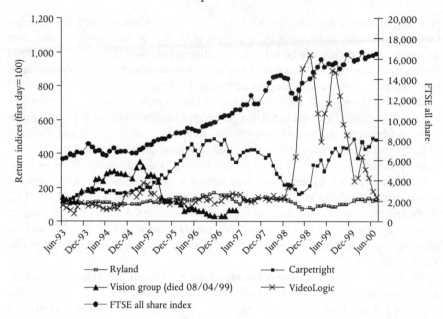

Figure 17.3. *Performance of the return indices of the case-study IPO stocks and of the FT all share index (June 1993–2001).*

the English Midlands. The company had no venture-capital backing, and sought a flotation to reduce its gearing and obtain access to external equity capital to increase its range of franchises. Following the IPO in 1994, the family stake was reduced from 65 to 39 per cent.

The first part of the lock-in agreement (which is part of the placing agreement on the penultimate page of the prospectus under Additional Information) states that:

Each of the Vendors, other than MPE, has undertaken not to dispose of any further Ordinary shares (without the prior written consent of Sharps), until publication of the Company's audited accounts for the year ending 30 April 1995 and until publication of the Company's audited accounts for the year ending 30 April 1996 to dispose of shares through Sharps.[9]

This part of the lock-in agreement refers to the vendors. The prospectus states that 'certain existing shareholders' will sell shares in the IPO. The disposals amount to a trifling 0.1 per cent of the enlarged share capital, raising £0.75m for the vendors. However, from the prospectus it is impossible to determine exactly who the 'vendor shareholders' are, and specifically whether the directors are among them. In fact, the prospectus predicts the numbers of ordinary shares owned by the three share-owning directors (including the two Whales) to increase after flotation. Part of this increase may be due to a reorganization of

[9] MPE: an institutional investor. Sharps: Albert E. Sharp, the sponsor and underwriter to the issue.

the company's share capital just before the IPO (and conditional on admission to the stock market). Besides the interest of MPE, an institutional investor owned by HSBC predicted to hold 11 per cent of the enlarged equity share capital after flotation (plus a number of deferred shares), there are no other substantial shareholdings of 3 per cent or more either before or immediately after the IPO.

MPE entered into a separate lock-in agreement:

MPE has undertaken not to dispose of any further Ordinary shares (without the prior written consent of Sharps) during the period of six months from Admission and for a period of 12 months from Admission to dispose of Ordinary shares only through Sharps (other than in certain specified circumstances).

If one concludes that the lock-in agreements actually apply to the directors and the founding family, one could argue that these agreements are motivated by a concern over the large retained stakes of the founding family (who retain 39 per cent of the equity after the IPO) and the institutional investor MPE (11 per cent). These share retentions may be interpreted by the market as a favourable signal of insiders' information about the value of the firm (Leland and Pyle 1977). The lock-in agreements render the signal credible by making it costly to imitate for lower-quality types (see e.g. Courteau 1995). The lock-in agreements may also be intended to allay fears in the market of pressures on the company's stock price resulting from large share disposals by existing shareholders after the IPO.

However, the interesting feature in this case is that the lock-in agreements and the further details given in the prospectus are so opaque as to make it impossible to conclude whether the directors and the founding family are in fact locked in or not.

17.7.2. *Case 2: VideoLogic*

VideoLogic was founded in 1985 by Anthony (Tony) Maclaren as a division of Teletape Video Limited. VideoLogic's main business is the development of multimedia technology for PCs. Avesco Plc (according to its website, a provider of specialist services to the corporate, presentation, entertainment, and broadcast markets) acquired VideoLogic in 1989. Derek Maclaren, the father of Tony Maclaren, joined VideoLogic in 1986 and at the time of the flotation in July 1994 was the chairman. The two Maclarens were re-appointed as directors in March 1994. VideoLogic had no venture-capital or other institutional backers apart from Avesco at the time of flotation.

VideoLogic was floated on the Official List of the LSE on 6 July 1994 as a result of a demerger from Avesco. The IPO consisted of a placing of shares and a priority subscription offer to Avesco shareholders.

Part 10 of the prospectus, entitled 'Additional Information', gives the lock-in agreements as part of the offer and underwriting agreement (p. 75):

The Underwriting Agreement also contains restrictions on sales by any of D.A.E. Maclaren, A.E. Maclaren or Mr. Murray of any of their shares in the Company in the 12 month period following the date of Admission (or, in the case of D.A.E. Maclaren, until the date of cessation of his employment by the Group if earlier) and on A.E. Maclaren in respect of half of his shares in the Company in the 12 months thereafter.

Mr. Murray is the chairman of Avesco, but does not sit on the board of VideoLogic, and he, along with 'certain other directors and employees of Avesco', sold shares in VideoLogic through the IPO. The prospectus states that Derek and Tony Maclaren have declared that they would subscribe to shares in VideoLogic and immediately after flotation are predicted to hold 0.6 and 1.18 per cent, respectively, of the share capital. Derek Maclaren states his intention to retire as a director (see p. 23 of the prospectus) as soon as a successor is found, but agrees to act as chairman until at least 31 March 1995 (the end of the next financial year).

It is not clear why the lock-in agreement attaches so much importance to the holdings of the Maclarens, given their small size. Tony Maclaren is subject to a longer, staggered lock-in agreement given his key role as chief executive (and founder). A possible reason for the lock-in agreement is the pre-IPO performance of the company: the prospectus reports that during the three financial years before the IPO, VideoLogic made operating losses. The lock-ins may have been intended as signals of favourable inside information. However, the company continued to make a loss in 1995.

17.7.3. *Case 3: Carpetright*

Carpetright was launched in 1988 by MFI, a UK chain of furniture stores, and an entrepreneur (Philip Harris) with long experience in running a similar business. The company was floated in June 1993. In Carpetright, the involvement of venture-capital backers came about when the company raised capital for expansion from NatWest Ventures and Phildrew Ventures in 1989 and 1990. The IPO was a placing and offer for sale sponsored and fully underwritten by County NatWest. The reasons for flotation given in the prospectus (p. 24) were to allow some existing shareholders (specifically MFI, which sold its entire interest in the flotation) to realize their investment, to enable wider employee share ownership, and to redeem existing preference shares.

The lock-in agreements (which are given on p. 24 of the prospectus along with the reasons for the flotation) affect only the directors of the company:

Each of the Directors has undertaken not to sell further shares until the publication of Carpetright's preliminary results for the year ending 30 April 1994, other than with the consent of County NatWest. Sir Philip Harris and Harris Ventures Limited have undertaken that they will not, together, other than with the consent of County NatWest, sell more than two and a half per cent of the ordinary share capital of the Company in the first year following this period or more than five per cent of the ordinary share capital in total in the two years following this period.

Notably, the venture backers' holdings were not locked in, and based on the first annual report published after the IPO (in June 1994), it appears that both venture capitalists liquidated their holdings during the first year of trading. An interesting feature arises from the association between one of the venture capitalists, NatWest Ventures, and the sponsor/underwriter, which may have resulted in conflicts of interest (as argued in Section 17.3).

Philip Harris is clearly the crucial shareholder in Carpetright, which is reflected in the lock-in agreements. The experience with his previous business, Harris Queensway Plc, may explain both the extensive lock-in of his shareholding and the prominent position of the lock-in agreement. Harris sold his entire holding in Harris Queensway in a takeover, and other shareholders of Harris Queensway who did likewise benefited from the acquisition. By contrast, those shareholders who held on to their stakes lost their money when the company failed in 1990. As a result, it may have seemed necessary to Carpetright and its advisers to draw investors' attention to Harris's share stake and lock-in agreement. His retention of a substantial stake together with his lengthy lock-in must have been intended and understood by the market as a positive signal.

17.7.4. *Case 4: Vision Group*

The company was set up in 1990 by a university scientist to develop and commercialize highly integrated camera chip technology. It went public on 12 April 1995 via a placing, raising about £5 million. None of the existing shareholders, including the venture-capital backer, Q.F. Realisations, sold any of their shares in the IPO. The proceeds from the placing were intended to reduce the level of debt and to buy out a royalty agreement with the University of Edinburgh. VVL, the trading subsidiary of Vision Group[10], was set up at the beginning of 1990 by Professor Peter Denyer, the managing director, and Roy Warrender, the commercial director, with institutional support to develop and commercialize specialist electronic cameras ('highly integrated camera chip technology'). The technology used by VVL was developed by Peter Denyer during the 1980s, and in 1992 Denyer's research team from the University of Edinburgh joined VVL.

According to the prospectus the largest shareholder immediately after flotation was Donnelly Corporation, a US vehicle components manufacturer, who became a minority shareholder of VVL in 1993, providing the company with increased funds for investment in vision applications. Two out of the three non-executive directors were directors of Donnelly Corporation. The second largest shareholder was Q.F. Realisations Limited, part of the Quantum Fund, a venture capital firm. Peter Denyer's held the largest directors' share stake (6.76 per cent). Other directors' shareholdings were Roy Warrender's (5.08 per cent) and the non-executive chairman's (James Millar; 0.05 per cent). Two further individuals are given as substantial shareholders: David Renshaw (5.10 per cent) and Michael Underwood (3.55 per cent). A. Macpherson, who is listed in a lock-in agreement, is not given either as a director or a substantial shareholder.

The lock-in agreements are found in the section on 'placing arrangements' in Part IV (Additional Information), Section 17.10(b) (p. 50) of the IPO prospectus (there is also a brief mention in the 'placing' section of Part I of the prospectus):

In terms of Letters of Undertaking dated 8th, 27th and 28th March, 3rd and 4th April 1995 respectively granted by each of Mr. A. Macpherson, the University Court of the University of Edinburgh, Q.F. Realisations Limited, Mr. D. Renshaw and Donnelly ('the 'Locked-in Shareholders'), the Locked-in Shareholders have agreed not to dispose of in aggregate 15,386,072 Ordinary shares

---

[10] Vision Group itself has never traded, but it holds all of VVL and the firm holding the Employees Trust.

until after the publication of the Company's accounts for the financial period ending 31st July 1996. In terms of the Placing Agreement, the Directors have agreed not to dispose of any Ordinary shares during the above period. The restrictions contained in the letters of undertaking and the Placing Agreement do not apply in certain cases being, inter alia (i) transfers which Sharps have approved in writing and (ii) transfers in connection with certain offers for the whole or any part of the issued share capital of the Company.

All the shares of directors are locked in, as well as almost all the shares held by other pre-IPO shareholders with stakes in excess of 5 per cent, and the lock-in period is the same for the directors and the other shareholders. The total number of locked-in shares represents about 62 per cent of the equity outstanding immediately after the IPO.

Given that the lock-in expiry date is defined relative to a company event, the publication of the company report for the year ending on 31 July 1996, this raises the question as to how accurately outsiders can predict this date. There is no information as to the precise date in the IPO prospectus. However, the expiry period will obviously exceed a calendar year. One reason why the lock-in agreement is specified relative to the publication of the 1996 company accounts may be similar as in the case of VideoLogic: in each of the previous three years before the IPO the company had made losses. However, Professor Denyer stated (*Financial Times*, 13 March 1995, p. 20) that he expected the firm to break even by the end of the 1996 financial year.[11]

The annual report for 1995 reveals that the stakes of some of the other shareholders (Q.F. Realisations and the University of Edinburgh) that were locked in had decreased. All other stakes, including the ones of the directors, were unchanged. The directors' holdings also remained unchanged over the following year. On 19 November 1996, along with a profit announcement, the company also announced a rights issue to raise expansion finance. Most of the new shares were taken up by institutional investors. Interestingly, none of the locked-in shareholders took up their rights. As a result, institutional ownership increased by more than 10 per cent to more than 50 per cent in total, while directors' holdings decreased.

17.8. CONCLUSION

This chapter has examined the impact of venture-capital backing of UK companies issuing shares at flotation on the characteristics of the lock-in agreements entered into by the existing shareholders, and on the abnormal returns realized around the expiry of the directors' lock-in agreements. The study examines the lock-in agreements of a sample of 186 UK IPOs issued during 1992–98. 103 of these companies had venture-capital backing at the IPO. The sample is also broken down into firms classified by industrial sector: of 103, VC backed companies, 48 are high-tech, and among the 83 firms without VC backing, 33 are high-tech.

We find that lock-in agreements in the UK show much more variety in terms of the contractual detail than US agreements. For instance, unlike in the USA, where lock-in

---

[11] However, the IPO prospectus only mentions under 'Current trading and prospects' that '[...] revenues from the Group's standard products continue to grow [...]'

periods are usually defined in terms of 'absolute' calendar dates or periods (following admission or a calendar date), UK agreements more commonly define expiry relative to another company announcement or event. The lock-in periods agreed upon by the directors of IPO companies are also on average substantially longer in the UK than in the USA, where lock-in periods have become standardized at around 180 days. By contrast, the average period in the UK is 561 days (for the sub-sample of directors' agreements that define the lock-in expiry in terms of an 'absolute' calendar date). Lock-in periods are particularly long for venture-backed high-tech companies. By contrast, for firms not in the high-tech sector, venture-capital backing appears to reduce the directors' lock-in periods. This suggests that for UK IPOs venture-capital backing does not serve as a substitute for lock-in agreements.

Examining the proportion of locked-in directors' shares, we find it to be significantly higher in VC-backed firms as compared to firms without VC backing in the sample of firms not classified as high tech. Again, this suggests that for firms likely to face only moderate information asymmetries (i.e. those not in high-tech industries), venture-capital backing of the IPO is not used as a substitute for, but rather as a complement to, lock-in agreements. The higher proportion of locked-in directors' shares among VC-backed companies (not in the high-tech sector) may be because the underwriters of VC-backed IPOs expect heavy sales by the VCs in the period after the IPO and decide to lock in the directors' shares and in order to limit the downward pressure of the VC's disposals on stock prices. Alternatively, if VCs do not sell out completely in the IPO, as reported by Barry *et al.* (1990), they may seek to align the directors' interests with their own by locking the directors in.

We also examine the share-price performance of IPOs with and without VC backing around the time of the expiry of the lock-in agreements, and find significant differences between the two sub-samples. The CAARs for the VC-backed stocks are lower for most of the short windows around the expiry date we examine, both for the sample as a whole and separately for each industry sector. For the sample of twenty-eight VC-backed stocks, the CAARs are statistically significantly less than zero at the 1 per cent level for the narrow one- to three-day windows around the expiry date. For the VC-backed stocks, the CAARs range from −1.2 to −1.6 per cent (and even to −2 per cent for the eleven-day window, but this result is not statistically significant), while the corresponding CAARs for the stocks without VC backing range only from −0.2 to −0.8 per cent. The findings of significantly lower abnormal returns for VC-backed IPOs compared to others is consistent with the results reported by US studies (Bradley *et al.* 2000; Brav and Gompers 2000; Field and Hanka 2001). However, while Brav and Gompers suggest that this may be due to downward pressure on the share price as a result of large share disposals by venture capitalists exiting the company after the expiry of their lock-ins, this argument cannot (fully) explain our findings because our event-study focuses on the expiry of directors' lock-in agreements, as opposed to those of VCs. Our analysis shows that the lock-in agreements of directors and other shareholders, such as VCs, differ considerably both in frequency and in the details of the agreement. Hence, the expiry date for directors is very likely to differ from that of VCs (if in fact they agree to lock-ins). As a result, the difference in the abnormal returns around the lock-in expiry date between stocks with and without VC backing is unlikely to be due to price pressure from VC selling. Instead they may be indicative of differences in the informational contents of the expiry of directors' lock-ins and also of other announcements or events occurring at that time, such as announcements of share trading by directors and others.

Finally, we examine four UK companies in detail: two with VC backing (one issued by a firm in an industry classified as high tech), and two firms without VC backing (again one in the high-tech sector). A number of interesting aspects of the lock-in agreements are observed and interpreted. In one case, the agreements are phrased so opaquely as to make it impossible to determine exactly who is locked in. In another case, the lock-in agreement may have been used to show the founder's commitment not to exit the company as he did in an earlier venture which subsequently failed. Finally, poor pre-IPO earnings performance may motivate companies, particularly growth companies in the high-tech sector, to lock-in existing shareholders in order to signal favourable inside information.

Appendix A: Case Studies

17.A.1. *Carpetright*

17.A.1.1. *Sub-sample: Not high-tech, with VC Backing*

The company published its annual report for the fifty-two weeks up to 1 May 1993 around 24 May 1993 (date of Chairman's Statement) and a pathfinder prospectus on 25 May 1993. The IPO was a placing and offer for sale sponsored and fully underwritten by County NatWest (SG Warburg acted as the stockbroker). Shares were offered at a price of 148p per ordinary share. The IPO consisted of a placing of over 39m ordinary shares of which 13.7m were offered to the public. Up to 1.37m (10 per cent of post-IPO shares) were reserved to meet applications by directors and company employees. Of the 39.2m shares marketed, 32.4m were sold on behalf of existing shareholders and 6.8m to raise funds for the firm.

Although the offer price, had been set at the top end of expectations, the flotation was predicted to go well (*FT*, 9 June 1993). The offer closed on 16 June 1993, and share dealing commenced on the Official List on 23 June 1993 (as predicted in the prospectus) with the share price closing at 165.5p. Turnover on that day was noted to be heavy at 22.7m (*FT*, 24 June 1993). The reason given for this in the *FT* (17 and 24 June 1993) was that some institutions may have been buying in the aftermarket because the share allocation (detailed in an article in the *FT* on 23 June 1993) had favoured smaller investors, and the placing of shares with institutions had left some institutional investors with fewer shares than they had wanted, so that there were some large institutional applications in the public offer.

The reasons for flotation given in the prospectus (p. 24) were 'to allow the Vendors to realize part of their investment and wider participation by Carpetright's employees in the future ownership of the Company', and the net proceeds of the issue of approx. £8.9m were also to be used to redeem the existing redeemable preference shares.

There were comments on the fact that investors in an earlier business floated by the Carpetright Chairman-cum-CEO had lost money. This was the Harris family business,

Harris Queensway, which was taken over in 1988 (when Harris sold out after a failed MBO) and eventually failed in 1990.

Soon after the takeover of Harris Queensway, Harris went on to launch Carpetright together with MFI in 1988. Harris promised that unlike with his previous venture Harris Queensway, which expanded rapidly through acquisitions and outside carpet retailing, Carpetright would not attempt to diversify outside the carpet business (*FT*, 24 April 1993).

The prospectus gives a detailed list of the numbers of shares being sold by each vendor (p. 61). MFI, which together with P. Harris launched the company in 1988, is predicted to sell its entire interest in the flotation.

Following completion of the IPO, the prospectus predicts that the Chairman-cum-CEO, Sir Philip Harris, will control 20.8 per cent of the enlarged share capital (directly and through Harris Ventures Ltd), and the venture capital backers, NatWest Ventures and Phildrew Ventures, who contributed expansion capital in 1989 and 1990, will retain holdings of 5.0 and 4.4 per cent. The prospectus notes that Phildrew Ventures' remaining holding is non-beneficial and re-registered in the names of the underlying investors.

The lock-in agreements (p. 24) affect only the directors of the company:

Each of the Directors has undertaken not to sell further shares until the publication of Carpetright's preliminary results for the year ending 30 April 1994, other than with the consent of County NatWest. Sir Philip Harris and Harris Ventures Limited have undertaken that they will not, together, other than with the consent of County NatWest, sell more than two and a half per cent. of the ordinary share capital of the Company in the first year following this period or more than five per cent. of the ordinary share capital in total in the two years following this period.

Sir (later Lord) Philip Harris is clearly the crucial shareholder in Carpetright, which is reflected in the lock-in agreements. He has continued to hold a substantial share stake until the present day (2003). Investors in the IPO and thereafter may have been particularly nervous about large share sales by Harris given the experience with his previous business, Harris Queensway, where investors who sold shares during the takeover as Harris did, made money, but those who held on to their stakes lost out when the company failed in 1990.

Notably, the venture backers' holdings were not locked in, and based on the first annual report published after the IPO (in June 1994), it appears that both venture capitalists liquidated their holdings during the first year of trading (the only substantial shareholdings besides directors' are Provident Mutual Life Assurance Association with 4.04 per cent and Laurentian Financial Group Plc with 3.37 per cent). In the case of Phildrew Ventures, it is possible that the underlying investors had retained their holdings but were not substantial shareholders. The fact that one of the venture capitalists, NatWest Ventures, is an associate of the sponsor/underwriter creates the potential for conflicts of interest.

To examine the incidence of directors' trading in the stocks of the companies they run, both before and after the expiry of the directors' lock-in agreements, we used a database called Directus. Our version of the database covers all share dealings from the early 1990s to the end of 1998. The database collects data based on the notifications by directors of their share dealings to the LSE.

If a director sells shares before the expiry of the lock-in agreement, this can mean either that the agreement was lifted with the agreement of the sponsor/underwriter, or that the director broke the agreement.

In the case of Carpetright, the first share transaction by a director recorded on Directus took place on 11 July 1994, which is clearly after the publication of the preliminary results for the year ending 30 April 1994 (the annual report was signed on 21 June 1994), and hence after the expiry of the directors' lock-in agreement. The first transaction by P. Harris was a purchase in January 1995, and his first share sale occurred at the end of March April 1995 consisting of 8,000 shares (0.01 per cent of the issued shares at flotation). The next two transactions by Harris are recorded in 1996: one is the exercise of executive options and this is followed by the sale of same number of shares (that is, reducing Harris's shareholding to the pre-exercise level). The first major share disposal by Harris (of 4m shares) occurs in January 1997, approximately six months after the expiry of his lock-in. In conclusion, all the lock-in agreements were adhered to.

17.A.2. *Ryland Group Plc*

17.A.2.1. *Sub-sample: not high-tech, no VC Backing*
Ryland Group Plc was floated on the LSE via a placing on 22 September 1994. At the time of listing, the Ryland Group was one of the four largest privately owned groups of companies in the UK motor distribution industry, by turnover. At the time of the listing, the reason given for placing was to reduce the company's gearing, to make further investment and to consider acquisition opportunities as they arise, to increase the company profile, and to encourage employee share ownership.

The business was founded over fifty years earlier by the grandfather (the late H. W. Whale in Birmingham) of the chairman at the time of flotation (Peter Whale). In 1966 the founder's son, W. J. Whale, took over and commenced expansion of the Group's activities, converting the business into a broadly based motor group. In May 1990, following the death of W. J. Whale, his eldest son Peter Whale became Chairman and Chief Executive.

Immediately following the placing, Peter Whale and Nick Whale (P. Whale's younger brother) owned 39 per cent of the outstanding shares in the company. The third executive director, K. Hampson, owned only 0.5 per cent of the outstanding shares. There was one other investor; MPE (an institutional investor owned by HSBC), holding 11 per cent of the issued equity share capital after flotation.

The lock-in agreements state:

Each of the Vendors, other than MPE, has undertaken not to dispose of any further Ordinary shares (without the prior written consent of Sharps), until publication of the Company's audited accounts for the year ending 30 April 1995 and until publication of the Company's audited accounts for the year ending 30 April 1996 to dispose of shares through Sharps. MPE has undertaken not to dispose of any further Ordinary shares (without the prior written consent of Sharps) during the period of six months from Admission and for a period of 12 months from Admission to dispose of Ordinary shares only through Sharps (other than in certain specified circumstances).

The prospectus reports that during the last three financial years of 1992, 1993, and 1994, the company made profits of £0.27m, £0.77m, and £2.04m, respectively. These results were impressive despite the length and breadth of the UK economic recession at that period of time. The firm continued to perform well until 1999, when it made a profit of £12.6m. In 2000 it had been experiencing problems with losses of £5.9m in 2000. The finance director, Keith Hampson, put this down to the confusion created by the Competition Commission's inquiry into new car pricing. 'The general public want and deserve price cuts. They weren't forthcoming and so people stayed away' (*The Times*, 5 October 2000, p. 67). He added that the September fuel crisis had an impact on both sales and the service and parts business. The interim figures of 2000 showed a modest profit of £1.12m.

The audited accounts for the year ending 30 April 1995 were published shortly after 24 July 1995 (the date of signing of chairman's report). The directors' interests from the annual report of 1995 show that none of the directors had sold any shares during the vendors' lock-in period. The institutional investor MPE also held on to its shares beyond the lock-in expiry date. The annual report further tells that there were no changes in the director's interests between 30 April 1995 and 21 July 1995.

The first transaction recorded on Directus is a share sale by P. Whale at the end of July 1995, which is after expiry of the vendors' lock-in (i.e. the publication of the accounts for the year ending 30 April 1995; the report was signed on 24 July 1995).

17.A.3. *VideoLogic Group Plc*

17.A.3.1. *Sub-sample: High-tech, no VC Backing*

VideoLogic was floated on the Official List of the LSE on 6 July 1994 as a result of a demerger from Avesco. VideoLogic's main business is the development of multimedia technology for PCs. The official reason for the demerger was that it was felt that Video-Logic's activities were very different from the ones of the other divisions of Avesco and that therefore a demerger would make sense. The real reason seems to have been that Avesco was making huge losses before the demerger and that they hoped reduce these losses by selling off VideoLogic. However, Avesco's losses after the demerger were even more substantial (see *Financial Times*, 30 November 1994, p. 50).

VideoLogic's origins go back to 1985, when Tony Maclaren started the business as a division of Teletape Video Limited. Avesco acquired VideoLogic in 1989. Derek Maclaren, the father of Tony Maclaren, joined VideoLogic in 1986. At the time of the demerger, Derek Maclaren was the chairman and Tony Maclaren the chief executive of VideolLogic.

Derek and Tony Maclaren were expected to subscribe to the offer, and immediately after the demerger they were predicted to hold 0.6 and 1.18 per cent, respectively, of VideoLogic's ordinary shares. The offer agreement specifies the following:

The Underwriting Agreement also contains restrictions on sales by any of D.A.E. Maclaren, A.E. Maclaren or Mr Murray of any of their shares in the Company in the 12 month period following the date of Admission (or, in the case of D.A.E. Maclaren, until the date of cessation of his employment by the Group if earlier) and on A.E. Maclaren in respect of half of his shares in the Company in the 12 months thereafter.

At the time of the demerger, Mr. Murray was the chairman of Avesco, but he had no seat on the board of VideoLogic. Along with certain other directors and employees of Avesco, he was expected to sell shares pursuant to the IPO.

Derek Maclaren stated his intention to retire as a director (see p. 23 of the prospectus) as soon as a successor could be found. He agreed to act as chairman until at least 31 March 1995 (the end of the subsequent financial year). Although the Maclarens' share stakes after flotation were small, the lock-in agreement attached a lot of importance to them. Tony Maclaren is subject to a longer, staggered lock-in agreement given his key role as chief executive (and founder). The lock-in agreement specified an absolute expiry date (6 July 1995), although Derek Maclaren had the opportunity to sell as early as 31 March 1995 if he retired.

The prospectus reports that during the last three financial years of 1992, 1993, and 1994, VideoLogic made operating losses of £1.0 m, £0.6 m, and £5.3 m, respectively. In the *Financial Times* of 15 December 1994 (p. 29), Derek Maclaren was quoted as saying that 'the company had considered whether to go for short-term profits or to continue investing in the research needed for the multimedia breakthrough'. Mr. Maclaren said that the latter was the right option as otherwise the company would jeopardize a deal with NEC.

The two Maclarens had been re-appointed as directors in March 1994. The company continued to make a loss even in the financial year after the IPO (1995). Derek Maclaren finally resigned on 27 March 1996, and Geoff Shingles was appointed as the new chairman.

The database of directors' dealings, Directus, does not record any transactions for the directors from flotation until the summer of 1998, that is, around two years after the expiry of the longest lock-in period.

17.A.4. *Vision Group Plc*

17.A.4.1. *Sub-sample: High-tech with VC Backing*
Vision Group went public on 12 April 1995 via a placing raising about £5m. None of the existing shareholders sold any of their shares in the IPO. The proceeds from the placing were intended to reduce the level of debt and to buy out a royalty agreement with the University of Edinburgh. VVL, the trading subsidiary of the Vision Group,[12] was set up at the beginning of 1990 by Professor Peter Denyer, the managing director, and Roy Warrender, the commercial director, with institutional support to develop and commercialize specialist electronic cameras ('highly integrated camera chip technology'). Applications include among others video conferencing, toys, machine vision, and surveillance. The technology used by VVL was developed by Peter Denyer during the 1980s. In 1992, Peter Denyer's research team from the University of Edinburgh joined VVL.

In terms of directors' share stakes post-IPO, Peter Denyer held the largest stake with 6.76 per cent. The other directors' shareholdings were by Roy Warrender (5.08 per cent)

---

[12] Vision Group itself has never traded, but it holds all of VVL and the firm holding the Employees Trust.

Table 17.11. *Ownership structure and lock-in agreements of Vision Group Plc*

Shareholder	% of shares immediately after the IPO	Lock-in agreement
Donnelly Corporation	31.95	Yes
Q.F. Realisations Limited	8.12	Yes
The University Court of the University of Edinburgh	6.01	Yes
David Renshaw	5.10	Yes
The Equitable Life Assurance Society	4.05	No
Michael Underwood	3.55	No

and James Millar (0.05 per cent), the non-executive chairman. The holdings of the other shareholders are reported in Table 17.11.

The second largest shareholder in the firm is Q.F. Realisations Limited, part of the Quantum Fund, a venture capital firm. The Vision Group Employees Trust holds about 2 per cent of the shares after the placing. The trustees are the non-executive chairman and the three non-executive directors.

Two out of the three non-executive directors were directors of the largest shareholder, that is, Donnelly Corporation, a US vehicle components manufacturer. Donnelly became a minority shareholder of VVL in 1993. Donnelly's main interest is in the development of a camera that would replace or supplement the rear view mirrors in cars. With respect to the representation of Donnelly on the board of directors, there is a material contract that requires:

[...] R.D. Warrender and P.B. Denyer to support the continuing representation of Donnelly on the Board such that, while Donnelly continues to hold more than 25 per cent of the issued Ordinary shares they will vote for the re-election of two directors nominated by Donnelly and while Donnelly continues to hold more than 15 per cent of the issued Ordinary shares they will vote for the re-election of one director nominated by Donnelly.

Although Donnelly is the controlling shareholder, the relationship between the firm and Donnelly is at arm's length.

The lock-in agreement can be found in section b of the 'placing arrangements' section of the IPO prospectus (there is also a brief mention in the 'placing' section of Part 1 of the prospectus):

In terms of Letters of Undertaking dated 8th, 27th, and 28th March, 3rd and 4th April 1995 respectively granted by each of Mr. A. Macpherson, the University Court of the University of Edinburgh, Q.F. Realisations Limited, Mr. D. Renshaw and Donnelly ('the 'Locked-in Shareholders'), the Locked-in Shareholders have agreed not to dispose of in aggregate 15,386,072 Ordinary shares until after the publication of the Company's accounts for the financial period ending 31st July 1996.

In terms of the Placing Agreement, the Directors have agreed not to dispose of any Ordinary shares during the above period. The restrictions contained in the letters of undertaking and the Placing Agreement do not apply in certain cases being, inter alia (i) transfers which Sharps have approved in writing and (ii) transfers in connection with certain offers for the whole or any part of the issued share capital of the Company.

The total number of shares owned by the directors is therefore locked in, as well as almost all the shares held by other pre-IPO shareholders with stakes in excess of 5 per cent. In the case of Vision Group, the lock-in period is the same for the directors and the other shareholders. The total number of locked-in shares represents about 62 per cent of the equity outstanding immediately after the IPO.

Given that the lock-in expiry date is relative to a company event, i.e. the publication of the company report for the year ending on 31 July 1996, this raises the question as to how accurately outsiders can predict this date. As the company went public more than three months before its financial year end (the prospectus contains accounting information up to 31 January 1995), it is difficult to have a clear idea of the expiry date after studying the IPO prospectus. However, the expiry period will obviously exceed a calendar year. The reason why the lock-in agreement is relative to the publication of the 1996 company accounts is probably that in each of the previous years (1993, 1994, and until 31 January 1995) Vision had made losses on ordinary activities. In this line of thought, Professor Denyer stated (*Financial Times*, 13 March 1995, p. 20) that he expected the firm to break even by the end of the 1996 financial year.[13]

Surprisingly, the annual report for 1995 reveals that the stakes of some of the other shareholders that were locked in had decreased: on 15 September 1995 Q.F. Realisations holds 7.31 per cent (8.12 per cent) and the University of Edinburgh held 5.41 per cent (6.01 per cent). All other stakes, including the ones of the directors, were unchanged. The 1995 accounts were signed by the Company Secretary and the auditors on 27 September 1995. There was a profit announcement by Peter Denyer a day later, which was published in the *Financial Times* on 29 September. Interim figures for 1996 were announced on 19 April. There was also an article in the *Sunday Times* of 17 November 1996 (p. 7), which reports that an analyst had stated that the balance sheet was 'cash positive'.

The 1996 company report was approved by the auditors on 19 November 1996. This time it took much longer from the end of the financial year to the publication of the report than in the previous year. The reason may be that in the previous year the IPO prospectus already contained the audited accounts up to 31 January 1995. The directors' holdings remained unchanged. On 31 October 1996, the holdings of the other locked-in shareholders were slightly lower with 30.43 per cent for Donnelly, 6.50 per cent for Q.F. Realisations, 5.15 per cent for the University of Edinburgh, and 4.86 per cent for David Renshaw. The *Independent* (p. 26) and *Financial Times* (p. 24) of 20 November 1996 mentioned the profit announcement for the year 1996. On 19 November 1996, along with the profit announcement the company also announced a 3-for-19 rights issue to raise £11.5m to expand its production facilities in response to the high demand for

[13] However, the IPO prospectus only mentions under 'Current trading and prospects' that '[...] revenues from the Group's standard products continue to grow [...]'

its electronic camera. Most of the new shares were taken up by institutional investors. As a result, institutional ownership increased by more than 10 per cent to more than 50 per cent in total.

In terms of directors' trading, there were no sell transactions before or at the expiry of the lock-in period.[14] The only transactions recorded by Directus for Vision Group from floatation until the end of 1998 were buy transactions.

As none of the locked-in shareholders took up their rights, their percentage stakes decreased as a result of the rights issue. The *Financial Times* mentions that after the rights issue Donnelly's stake was 25.6 per cent. In the *Sunday Times* of 24 November 1996, Peter Denyer is quoted as saying that:

Strategically, we have reached a watershed. At the time of our flotation in April 1995, we forecast that we would be hitting breakeven on a monthly basis for the first time by our year-end this July. In fact, we came very close to that and have gone modestly into the black in the first quarter of the current year to end October.

References

Barry, C. B., Muscarella, C. J., Peavey, J. W., and Vetsuypens, M. R. (1990), 'The role of venture capital in the creation of public companies: evidence from the going-public process', *Journal of Financial Economics* 27, 447–71.

Barry, C. B. (1994), 'New directions in research on venture capital finance', *Financial Management* 23, 3–15.

Booth, J. and Smith, R. (1986), 'Capital raising, underwriting and the certification hypothesis', *Journal of Financial Economics* 15, 261–81.

Bradley, D. J., Jordan, B. D., Roten, I. C., and Yi, H. C. (2000), 'Venture capital and IPO lock-up expiration: an empirical analysis', *Journal of Financial Research*, 24, 465–93.

Brau, J. C., Carter, D. A., Christopher, S. E., and Key, K. G. (2000), 'Market reaction to the expiration of IPO lock-in provisions', Working paper, George Mason University.

Brau, J. C., Lambson, V. E., and McQueen, G. (2001), 'Why lockups?', Working paper, Brigham Young University.

Brav, A. and Gompers, P. A. (1997*a*), 'The long-run underperformance of initial public offerings: evidence from venture and non-venture capital backed companies', *Journal of Finance* 52, 1791–821.

————(1997*b*), 'Myth of reality? Long-run underperformance of initial public offerings: Evidence from venture capital and nonventure capital-backed IPOs', *Journal of Finance* 52, 1791–812.

————(2000), 'Insider trading subsequent to initial public offerings: Evidence from expirations of lock-in provisions', Working paper, Duke University.

Brown, S. J. and Warner, J. B. (1980), 'Measuring security price performance', *Journal of Financial Economics* 8, 205–58.

————(1985), 'Using daily stock returns: The case of event studies', *Journal of Financial Economics* 14, 3–32.

---

[14] All of the directors were still in their posts around the lock-in expiry.

Courteau, L. (1995), 'Under-diversification and retention commitments in IPOs', *Journal of Financial and Quantitative Analysis* 30, 487–517.

Espenlaub, S., Goergen, M., and Khurshed, A. (2001), 'IPO lock-in agreements in the UK', *Journal of Business Finance and Accounting* 28, 1235–78.

Espenlaub, S., Garrett, I., and Mun, W. P. (1999), 'Conflicts of interest and the performance of venture-capital-backed IPOs: a preliminary look at the UK', *Venture Capital—International Journal of Entrepreneurial Finance* 1, 325–49.

Field, L. C. and Hanka, G. (2001), 'The expiration of IPO share lockups', *Journal of Finance* 56, 471–500.

Franks, J., Mayer, C., and Renneboog, L. (2001), 'Who disciplines management in poorly performing companies?', *Journal of Financial Intermediation* 10, 209–48.

Goergen, M. and Renneboog, L. (2001a), 'Strong managers and passive institutional investors in the UK', in F. Barca and M. Becht (eds), *The Control of Corporate Europe*, Oxford: Oxford University Press.

——— (2001b), 'United Kingdom', in K. Gugler (ed.), *Corporate Governance and Economic Performance*, Oxford: Oxford University Press, 184–200.

Gompers, P. A. and Lerner, J. (1997a), 'Venture capital and the creation of public companies: do venture capitalists really bring more than money?', *Journal of Private Equity* 1, 15–30.

——— (1997b), 'Conflict of interest and reputation in the issuance of public securities: evidence from venture capital', Working Paper, Harvard University.

Hamao, Y., Packer, F., and Ritter, J. (2000), 'Institutional affiliation and the role of venture capital: evidence from initial public offerings in Japan', *Pacific-Basin Finance Journal*, 8, 529–58.

Jain, B. A. and Kini, O. (1995), 'Venture capitalist participation and the post-issue operating performance of IPO firms', *Managerial and Decision Economics* 16, 593–606.

——— (1999), 'The life cycle of IPO firms', *Journal of Business Finance and Accounting* 26, 1281–307.

——— (2000), 'Does the presence of venture capitalists improve the survival profile of IPO firms?', *Journal of Business Finance and Accounting* 27, 1139–76.

Khurshed, A. (2000), 'Discussion of the survival profile of IPO firms', *Journal of Business Finance and Accounting* 27, 1177–83.

Leland, H. and Pyle, D. (1977), 'Informational asymmetries, financial structure and financial intermediation', *Journal of Finance* 32, 371–87.

Megginson, W. L. and Weiss, K. A. (1991), 'Venture capitalist certification in Initial Public Offerings', *Journal of Finance* 46, 879–903.

Morck, R., Shleifer, A., and Vishny, R. (1988), 'Management ownership and market valuation. An empirical analysis', *Journal of Financial Economics* 20, 293–315.

Ofek, E. and Richardson, M. (2000), 'The IPO lock-in period: implications for market efficiency and downward sloping demand curves', Working paper, New York University.

18

The Effect of Market Conditions on Initial Public Offerings

RAGHURAM RAJAN AND HENRI SERVAES

18.1. INTRODUCTION

Why are initial public offerings (IPOs) underpriced (Ibbotson 1975), and why does the average underpricing vary over time? Why do IPOs come to market in clusters creating the appearance that firms are taking advantage of windows of opportunity (Ibbotson and Jaffe 1975)? Why do IPOs perform poorly in the long run (Ritter 1991)? There are many models with rational agents which explain why underpricing occurs.[1] Most of these, however, are based on idiosyncratic factors specific to a firm—for example, the information asymmetry between issuer and potential investors. Consequently, they do not explain why there are market-wide cycles in underpricing.[2] Some economists have offered explanations for the long term underperformance of IPOs and fluctuations in the number of IPOs coming to market. Seyhun (1992) concludes from the trading patterns of insiders in IPOs that *ex post* bad luck cannot explain the poor long run performance of IPOs, because insiders seem to be able to identify the issues that will fare badly. He argues that poor long run performance is due to the fact that offerings are bought at too high a price.[3]

We thank Jay Ritter and Mike Vetsuypens, and I.B.E.S. for allowing us to use their database. Comments by Tim Loughran, Mitchell Petersen, Jay Ritter, René Stulz, Robert Vishny, and Marc Zenner on a previous draft were very helpful as were comments of participants in seminars at the University of North Carolina at Chapel Hill, INSEAD, the NBER Spring 1993 Corporate Finance meeting, and VPI. We thank Andrew Curtis for helpful research assistance.

[1] Allen and Faulhauber (1989), Baron and Holmstrom (1980), Benveniste and Spindt (1989), Beatty and Ritter (1986), Carter and Manaster (1990), Grinblatt and Hwang (1989), Rock (1986), and Welch (1989, 1992) offer explanations based on asymmetric information between one class of participants in the IPO process and another. Tinic (1988) argues that underpricing is a response to legal penalties, and Hughes and Thakor (1992) develop models where the threat of litigation could lead to underpricing under certain circumstances. Brennan and Franks (1997), Habib and Ljunqvist (2001), Aggarwal *et al.* (2002), and Loughran and Ritter (2002, 2003) focus on agency-based explanations. Ritter (2001) and Ritter and Welch (2002) review the theories.

[2] But see Nanda (1990), who argues that cyclical conditions in the real economy result in cyclical investment opportunities and consequently market-wide cyclicality in information asymmetries. Whether the magnitude of the cyclical fluctuations in information asymmetries can explain the fluctuations in volume and underperformance is an open question.

[3] Schultz and Zaman (2001), on the other hand, find no evidence of insider selling in Internet-related IPOs.

Loughran and Ritter (1995) show that the volume of IPOs is highest near market peaks and that there is greater underperformance following high volume. In other words, firms take advantage of a time-varying propensity of investors to overpay. The recent boom and bust of the IPO market, which was mainly driven by Internet and high-tech companies, is a good example of this propensity (Ritter and Welch 2002).

This chapter starts with the hypothesis that all three phenomena—cycles in underpricing, long-run underperformance, and fluctuations in IPO volume—are related to common factors. This link, between underpricing and the latter two phenomena, has received relatively little attention.[4] The reason may lie in the fact that while there are plausible explanations of underpricing based on the behaviour of rational agents (though these may not explain the cycles), explanations of fluctuations in IPO volume and long-run underperformance hint at some form of irrational behaviour by investors. Since the irrational behaviour is not specifically modelled, the links between the phenomena are hard to see. Therefore, we begin by writing down a simple model where some investors are irrational (or quasi-rational) in specific ways, and we establish how the three phenomena are related to the common irrationalities.

A potential criticism of explicit models relying on irrational behaviour is that a specific form of irrationality can be set up to explain every phenomenon, and consequently these models explain nothing. This is not to say that irrational or quasi-rational explanations of what are anomalies in the traditional economist's rational model should not be given a fair trial. What is important, however, is that with a limited number of degrees of freedom the 'irrational' economist should derive a number of testable implications that exceed the degrees of freedom. This makes the models of irrationality falsifiable, and perhaps more acceptable. Clearly, there are fewer restrictions on the kind of behaviour the 'irrational' economist can assume (though the variety of agency costs assumed in the corporate finance literature or the utility functions assumed in the equity premium literature suggest that this is not a monopoly of the 'irrational' economist). But here it is imperative that the 'irrational' economist provide additional direct evidence that the suggested behaviour is plausible.

In our model two specific forms of irrationality are time-varying; we assume that the fraction of investors who chase trends (also called positive feedback traders) varies over time, and that investors have a propensity to overpay for the stocks of certain industries at times (we term this 'investor sentiment'). A model with such 'irrational' behaviour could also be thought of as a reduced form of a model with rational investors, but with imperfections like short investor horizons, agency costs, or incomplete contracts. For instance, Scharfstein and Stein (1990), Bikchandani et al. (1992), and Welch (1992) show that investors may rationally ignore their own information and follow the decisions of other investors. This could explain trend-chasing and fads for certain industries.[5] Institutional managers may have an incentive to 'window-dress' their year-end portfolios so as to preserve their jobs. This could lead to excessive prices being paid for 'glamour' stocks.[6]

[4] See, however, Ljunqvist et al. (2001).

[5] Grinblatt et al. (1995) provide evidence of trend chasing (also termed 'momentum' investing) among institutional investors.

[6] We do not claim, however, that all such behaviour is necessarily rational. Investors may irrationally extrapolate past growth into the future (see Sirri and Tufano 1998; Lakonishok et al. 1994), or they may sell certain investments because the nominal yield is too low.

To restrict our degrees of freedom we adapt a well known theoretical model proposed by De Long, Shleifer, Summers, and Waldmann (DSSW) (1990) in a different context. Furthermore, because the number of correlations predicted are greater than the number of irrationalities assumed, the model is falsifiable. We then test the empirical predictions using data on firm-commitment initial public offerings between 1975 and 1987.

The empirical results indicate that common factors appear to partially explain all three phenomena. While some of the correlations we find are not particularly surprising in light of the previous research, the existence of common factors explaining both underpricing and long run underperformance or IPO volume is, to the best of our knowledge, new. While we can only guess as to why the market conditions we postulate vary over time, we believe that a contribution of this chapter is to suggest a disciplined way of investigating potential irrationalities in the IPO market.

The remainder of the chapter is organized as follows. In Section 18.2, we adapt De Long *et al.* (1990) to model the underwriter's pricing decision. We test the empirical implications in Section 18.3. Section 18.4 discusses the results and evidence from research on analyst forecasts that supports our analysis. Section 18.5 concludes.

18.2. THEORY

18.2.1. *The Model*

We consider a world with four dates: 0, 1, 2, and 3. At date 0, an investment bank wants to sell one completely divisible share of stock in a firm which is going public. The investment bank is assumed to act entirely in the interests of the firm, so we assume away any agency costs between the two. The stock pays a risky liquidating dividend of $\omega + \epsilon$ at date 3. The long-term shock to dividends, ϵ, is realized at date 3, and is distributed normally with mean 0 and variance σ_ϵ^2. ω is a measure of the firm's short-term prospects, and is distributed uniformly $U[-W, W]$. The sequence of events on the other dates is discussed shortly.

18.2.1.1. *Investors*

We assume there are three types of investor: First, there are rational speculators who set their demand for the share so as to maximize date 3 wealth. These investors maximize a mean-variance utility function with unit coefficient of risk aversion. Second, there are passive investors whose demand depends on the difference between the price and their expectation of the intrinsic value of the shares, v, so that at each date t, demand is given by $\gamma + \alpha/2(v - p_t)$ where $\alpha = 1/\sigma_\epsilon^2$. We term the price insensitive portion of their demand, γ, investor sentiment. Finally, trend chasers have demand proportional to past price movements, with factor of proportionality θ, which we term feedback risk. At date t, their demand is given by $\theta(p_{t-1} - p_{t-2})$.[7]

---

[7] We do not take a stand on who these investors are. A possible interpretation is that passive investors are institutions like mutual funds and pension funds, rational speculators are hedge funds, and trend chasers are small investors.

18.2.1.2. Information and Sequence of Events

Not all investors are in the market at all times. At date 0, the investment bank sets a price of p_0 at which it will offer the share to passive investors who have expressed their intent to purchase. At date 1, the issue opens on the market and the entire supply of 1 share hits the market. At this date, rational speculators trade with passive investors and the investment bank in determining the market price. We also assume that rational speculators know the realization ω at this date.[8] Clearly, the equilibrium market price, p_1, when the issue opens may be different from the offer price. At date 2, all investors (including the feedback traders) participate in the market. ω is publicly revealed and price p_2 obtains. Finally, ϵ is revealed at date 3.

18.2.1.3. Investor Demand

At date 2, rational speculators face uncertainty about ϵ. Their demand for the stock is given by

$$D_2^r = \frac{(\omega - p_2)}{2\sigma_\epsilon^2} = \frac{\alpha}{2}(\omega - p_2), \tag{18.1}$$

where $\alpha = 1/\sigma_\epsilon^2$. Passive investors demand $\gamma + \alpha/2(\omega - p_2)$. Trend chasers will demand $\theta(p_1 - p_0)$. As in DSSW, we impose a stability restriction that

$$\alpha > \theta. \tag{18.2}$$

At date 1, positive feedback traders have not had the opportunity to see price movements and do not trade (in other words, they trade only after the open).[9] The only demand is from speculators and passive investors. Finally, at date 0, passive investors demand $D_0^P = \gamma - \alpha/2p_0$.

18.2.1.4. The Investment Bank's Objective

The investment bank wants to maximize the proceeds it gets from selling the share. For simplicity, we assume that the underwriter sells the share at the minimum of the offer price p_0 and the market price p_1.[10] The expected proceeds are:

$$\begin{aligned} p_0 \quad &\text{if } p_1 \geq p_0, \\ p_1 \quad &\text{if } p_1 < p_0. \end{aligned} \tag{18.3}$$

---

[8] This does not necessarily imply that rational speculators have superior information about the firm. Instead of being a component of the final dividend, ω could be information about date 2 market conditions.

[9] Thus positive feedback investors see the underpricing/overpricing of the stock and then formulate their demand. The sequence of events is similar to Welch's theory of cascades, where initial purchases by some investors draw in many others.

[10] Nothing depends on this assumption, though it simplifies the algebra. In practice, the price p_0 is the maximum price that the bank is legally allowed to sell shares at. If all the shares are not sold at date 0, then the investment bank sells the remaining shares at time 1, at the minimum of p_0 and the time 1 price, p_1. One way of thinking about our assumption is that the underwriter has to stabilize the issue at the offer price (see Hanley et al. 1993). It thus buys back stock it has pre-sold to investors at the offer price even though the market price may be lower. However, it does not buy back stock which investors have bought from other investors in the market.

This is tantamount to the investment bank having sold a call option on the shares. But, interestingly, it controls the price movement of the underlying asset when it sets the exercise price p_0. The object of the exercise that follows is to determine the price p_0 the investment bank sets so as to maximize expected proceeds.

18.2.2. *Equilibrium*

Equating supply and demand at date 2,

$$1 = \gamma + \alpha/2(\omega - p_2) + \alpha/2(\omega - p_2) + \theta(p_1 - p_0). \tag{18.4}$$

Also, because rational speculators face no residual uncertainty between dates 1 and 2, they must drive the prices at both dates to equal each other. Setting $p_1 = p_2$ in (18.4), we get

$$p_1 = -\frac{(1-\gamma)}{\alpha - \theta} - \frac{\theta}{\alpha - \theta} p_0 + \frac{\alpha}{\alpha - \theta} \omega. \tag{18.5}$$

Note that the lower the price p_0, the higher is the price p_1. This is because rational speculators rationally anticipate the date 2 demand of trend-chasers and bid up the date 1 price if the offer price is low. Now it is easy to derive the expected proceeds at date 0:

$$p_1 \geq p_0 \quad \text{if } \omega \geq p_0 + \frac{1-\gamma}{\alpha} = \bar{w}. \tag{18.6}$$

Thus the expected proceeds are

$$\frac{1}{2W} \int_{-W}^{\bar{W}} p_1 \, dw + \frac{1}{2W} \int_{\bar{W}}^{W} p_0 \, dw. \tag{18.7}$$

On expanding and substituting from (18.6) and (18.5), this works out to

$$p_0^2 \frac{-\alpha}{4W(\alpha - \theta)} + p_0 \left(\frac{1}{2} - \frac{2(1-\gamma)\alpha - 2\theta W\alpha}{4W\alpha(\alpha - \theta)} \right) - \frac{(1-\gamma)^2}{4W\alpha(\alpha - \theta)}$$
$$- \frac{2(1-\gamma) + \alpha W}{4(\alpha - \theta)}. \tag{18.8}$$

The offer price p_0 that maximizes expected proceeds is then

$$p_0^* = W - 2\frac{\theta W}{\alpha} - \frac{(1-\gamma)}{\alpha}. \tag{18.9}$$

Therefore, on average there is an observed run up in the price at the open if

$$E_0(p_1) - p_0^* = \left(\frac{\theta}{\alpha - \theta} - 1 \right) W > 0. \tag{18.10}$$

That is, if

$$\theta > \alpha/2, \tag{18.11}$$

what is usually reported in empirical studies is the underpricing which is the run up in price normalized by the offer price. The expected underpricing is

$$\frac{(2\theta - \alpha)W}{(\alpha - \theta)\left(W - \frac{2\theta W}{\alpha} - \frac{1-\gamma}{\alpha}\right)}. \tag{18.12}$$

The following is immediate:

Result 18.1. Underpricing is observed, on average, if $\theta > \alpha/2$. The expected underpricing increases in the feedback risk θ and decreases in the investor sentiment γ.

The intuition is simple. If the offer price is high relative to the intrinsic value, passive investors are not likely to demand much. In anticipation of selling by trend-chasers, rational speculators will sell at date 1 unless their private information, ω, is particularly good. The underwriter will then have to offer the share at a much lower price. As the underwriter is limited on the upside by the offer price, but has to bear all the cost of a fall in price, it buys insurance against feedback risk, θ, by underpricing. Clearly, the need to buy this insurance decreases if investor sentiment will keep the price high anyway, so underpricing decreases in γ.

Expanding (18.7) and substituting from (18.5), we obtain the expected revenue in terms of the offer price p_0^*. Then using the envelope theorem,

$$\mathrm{dRevenue}(p_0^*, \theta, \gamma)/d\theta = \delta\mathrm{Revenue}(p_0^*, \theta, \gamma)/\delta\theta$$

$$= \frac{\bar{W} + W}{(\alpha - \theta)^2}\left(-\frac{(1-\gamma)}{2} - \frac{\alpha p_0^*}{2} - \frac{W\alpha}{2}\right) < 0. \tag{18.13}$$

Similarly, it can be shown that $\mathrm{dRevenue}(p_0^*, \theta, \gamma)/d\gamma > 0$.

Result 18.2. The expected proceeds from the initial public offering decrease in feedback risk and increase in the extent of investor sentiment.

Our model also throws light on the relation between long-term performance, market sentiment, and feedback risk. From simple algebra we get the difference between the realized value at date 1, ω, and the price p_1 is

$$\frac{(1-\gamma)}{\alpha} + \frac{\theta}{(\alpha - \theta)}\left(W - \frac{2\theta W}{\alpha}\right) - \frac{\theta}{\alpha - \theta}\omega. \tag{18.14}$$

The expected long-term return to a particular stock (as measured from the opening market price) consists of three terms. The first term arises from investor sentiment which imparts an optimistic bias to the offer price and a negative bias to long-term returns. The second term stems from the effect of deliberate underpricing on feedback trading. If issues, in general, are underpriced ($\theta > \alpha/2$), this term contributes negatively to long-term returns. Finally, the third term represents the destabilizing effect of speculators who anticipate overreaction by feedback traders. Taking expectations over ω, and differentiating we see that:

Result 18.3. The expected long run return increases in feedback risk if $\theta < k$ and decreases in feedback risk if $\theta > k$, where $\alpha(\sqrt{2} - 1)/\sqrt{2} = 0.29\alpha$. Expected long run returns decrease in investor sentiment γ.

While the effect of sentiment on long-run returns is clear, the effect of feedback risk is a little more subtle. When feedback risk is low, the optimally set offer price tends to be higher than intrinsic worth. Because there are few feedback traders who will sell short, the opening price is not much different from the offer price, and long-run performance is poor as the price declines to the intrinsic worth. But as feedback risk increases, long-term returns improve at first. This is because even though the offer price continues to be set higher than intrinsic worth, the opening price is lower (than when feedback risk is smaller) because speculators dump stock in anticipation of later feedback selling. Thus long-run returns improve. Eventually, of course, feedback risk increases to the point where the offer price is quite low relative to intrinsic worth. Now feedback traders are expected to go long in the stock, so that feedback risk pushes the average opening price above the intrinsic worth of the stock. Thus expected long-run returns start falling with feedback risk. Note finally that if underpricing is observed on average so that $\theta > \alpha/2$, long-run returns should always decrease with θ.

Finally, we can make some predictions about the volume of trading at date 2. Note first that passive investors will not trade at date 2 because they get no new information nor does the price change. All trading at date 2 is between the speculators and the feedback traders who enter the market. Therefore, the expected volume of trading is exactly equal to the expected absolute value of feedback trader demand which is

$$\theta E[\text{abs}(p_1 - p_0)] = \theta E \left[\text{abs} \left(\frac{-\alpha W}{\alpha - \theta} + \frac{2\theta W}{\alpha - \theta} + \frac{\alpha\omega}{\alpha - \theta} \right) \right]$$

$$= \left(\frac{-\alpha W}{\alpha - \theta} + \frac{2\theta W}{\alpha\theta} \right) \quad \text{if} \quad \theta > \alpha/2.$$

Therefore, if underpricing is observed on average so that $\theta > \alpha/2$, then:

Result 18.4. The expected trading volume at date 2 increases with feedback risk θ.

18.3. DATA AND EMPIRICAL TESTS

The sample consists of all firm commitment[11] initial public offerings between 1975 and the second quarter of 1987 in the databases compiled by Ritter (1984, 1991), Loughran and Ritter (1995), and Barry *et al.* (1991).[12] In addition, we obtain accounting data from Compustat and stock prices and trading volume from CRSP.

---

[11] In a firm commitment offering, the investment bank purchases the entire issue from the firm. In a best efforts contract, the investment bank makes its best effort to sell the issue but has no obligation to do so.

[12] A number of criteria were used to exclude IPOs in these samples: combination offerings in which a 'unit' composed of both shares and warrants were offered, closed end mutual funds, real estate investment trusts

Table 18.1. *Average underpricing and standard deviation of underpricing by year of going public*

Year	Average underpricing	Cross-sectional standard deviation of underpricing	N
75	−0.0088	0.0432	11
76	0.0030	0.0846	28
77	0.0660	0.1543	20
78	0.1413	0.1890	24
79	0.1351	0.4070	49
80	0.2899	0.5555	125
81	0.1186	0.3439	320
82	0.1032	0.1867	107
83	0.1100	0.2575	651
84	0.0662	0.2015	336
85	0.0877	0.1466	276
86	0.0785	0.1719	551
87 (six months)	0.0677	0.1326	227
	Average = 0.1003	Average = 0.2557	Total = 2725

Underpricing is computed as: (first aftermarket price—offer price)/offer price. Only firm commitment offers are included in the sample.

Table 18.1 clearly demonstrates two well-known 'anomalies' associated with initial public offerings: first, issues are underpriced on average—the price at the close of the first trading day exceeds the offer price by 10.03 per cent. The underpricing (computed by subtracting the offer price from the first closing price and dividing by the offer price) varies over time, with an average of 29 per cent in 1980 and −1 per cent in 1975. The second 'anomaly' is that the number of issues coming to market varies considerably, with large numbers in 1981, 1983, and 1986. Table 18.2 demonstrates a third 'anomaly': initial public offerings underperform a number of plausible benchmarks. For instance, while the average return (exclusive of the first-day return) over a three year holding period for the IPOs in our sample is 22.7 per cent, they underperform the smallest NYSE/AMEX size decile portfolio by 10.4 per cent.[13] We also matched each IPO with a seasoned NYSE, AMEX, or NASDAQ firm in the same industry (defined at the two-digit S.I.C. level) with the closest possible size.[14] Again the IPOs underperform, on average by 20.3 per cent.

(excluded only by Ritter), and conversions of mutuals to stock (Barry *et al.* 1993). Ritter collected his sample based on announcements in *Going Public: The IPO Reporter*, whereas Barry *et al.* collected their sample based on public announcements in the *Wall Street Journal* and the Dow Jones News Wire. Loughran and Ritter (1995) purchased listings of IPOs from IDD Information Services and Securities Data Company for the 1985–90 period.

[13] Returns of firms that are de-listed within three years of their IPO are counted until de-listing.

[14] Each year we rank all stocks belonging to a two-digit S.I.C. industry that have been listed on the CRSP NYSE/AMEX/NASDAQ database for at least three years by their market value of equity. For each IPO that takes place during the following year, we find the seasoned firm in the same industry with the closest market

Table 18.2. *Average three-year performance according to several benchmarks, by year of going public*

Year	Raw return	NYSE/Amex adjusted return	NYSE/Amex smallest decile adjusted return	Matched firm adjusted return
75	0.5822	0.2913	−0.5193	−0.1041
76	0.9004	0.6871	0.0267	0.0478
77	1.9805	1.6065	0.9913	0.6026
78	1.2302	0.7628	0.5198	0.0025
79	0.4789	0.1236	−0.1608	−0.2467
80	0.4357	0.0122	−0.8022	−0.6156
81	0.1062	−0.2373	−0.8428	−0.7446
82	0.3194	−0.3552	−0.6741	−0.5624
83	0.1912	−0.3088	−0.0127	−0.1779
84	0.6237	−0.1483	0.2630	0.0724
85	0.1323	−0.3852	−0.0870	−0.1170
86	0.0862	−0.2858	0.0461	−0.0365
87 (six months)	−0.0336	−0.3660	0.0742	−0.1498
	0.2274	−0.2243	−0.1036	−0.2033

Returns are computed for 756 trading days starting from the second trading day. The adjusted returns are computed by subtracting the three-year return on NYSE/Amex (value weighted), the smallest decile of NYSE/Amex, and a matched firm from the three-year raw return. The firm closest in size (traded on NYSE, Amex, or Nasdaq) to the IPO firm from the same two-digit SIC industry is used as a matching firm if it has been listed for at least three years. If firms are de-listed, returns are only computed until the de-listing.

Finally, it should be noted that the underperformance is largely concentrated in the latter years of the sample, especially in the 1980s.

18.3.1. *Empirical Predictions*

Given the simplicity of the model, we can only have confidence about the predictions of the signs of correlations rather than the magnitude of any effects (though we can check if the effect is economically important). We know from Table 18.1 that stocks have been underpriced on average in every year after 1975. This suggests that $\theta > \alpha/2$. The empirical predictions that follow from this are:

1. The extent to which a stock is underpriced is positively related to feedback risk θ and negatively related to the investor sentiment γ.
2. The long-term excess returns measured from the open should be negatively related to θ and to γ.

value of equity at the end of the previous year. If the matching firm is de-listed when the IPO firm is still trading, we substitute another matching firm, chosen according to the same procedure, on the day after de-listing of the original matching firm. This is similar to the procedure followed by Ritter (1991).

3. The volume of trading on the second day after the issue should be positively related to the amount of feedback risk θ.[15]

4. Because firms would want to tap markets so as to maximize expected proceeds, the number of firms coming to market should vary positively with factors enhancing the expected revenue. So the number of firms coming to market in a certain period should be negatively related to θ and positively related to γ.

18.3.2. *Proxies for Market Conditions*

Because there is little previous work on this subject, the proxies that we use for investor sentiment and feedback risk are bound to be subjective. However, we will attempt to convince the reader that our proxies are reasonable.

We have interpreted sentiment as the price-inelastic portion of demand for specific securities. More specifically, investors may be over-optimistic about particular industries— oil and gas companies in the early 1980s, computer and biotechnology companies in the late 1980s, casino stocks in the early 1990s, and technology and Internet stocks in the late 1990s and early 2000. If so, the willingness to pay historically high prices (relative to book value or earnings) for seasoned firms in that industry may proxy for sentiment for an IPO in that industry. We therefore calculate two measures of sentiment.

Our first measure is the relative market to book for the industry at the time of the IPO. This is calculated as follows: we compute an equally weighted cross-sectional average of the market to book value of equity in the quarter before the IPO for all Compustat firms which have been in existence for at least three years, and are in the same two-digit S.I.C. industry as the IPO.[16] We then divide this number by the market to book ratio averaged for all seasoned firms on Compustat to obtain RELMBK. We thus obtain a measure of whether the market is willing to pay high multiples for firms in that industry, relative to all firms in the market. Unlike Loughran and Ritter (1995) or Lakonishok *et al.* (1994), we do not use the market to book for the specific firm being brought to market, because that is endogenous in our model.[17]

As our second measure, we compute HISTMBK, which is a measure of whether the industry is trading at historically high multiples. This is calculated as follows: we compute

---

[15] Clearly, there is no reason why the dates in the model have to correspond to actual trading dates. An example of what we have in mind is that feedback traders are individual investors who read about the price run up in the newspapers the day after the issue opens and place their orders subsequently. The turnover on the first day is contaminated by speculative traders taking positions and passive investors 'flipping' their stock. However, the third day could also do. Eventually, all the feedback traders will have traded so that trading volume will reach its long run equilibrium and there will be no feedback component. This is why we think that turnover on the second day corresponds best with turnover on date 2 of the model.

[16] We use S.I.C. codes provided by Compustat. A potential problem here is that Compustat determines the most likely S.I.C. based on the firm's business in the most recent year of existence. However, there is no reason to believe that this would systematically bias our results.

[17] Clearly, investors may be faddish about other aspects of an IPO than the industry the firm belongs to. For instance, interest in small firms (as well as expectations of their growth) may increase, leading investors to pay higher prices for small firm earnings relative to the price they are willing to pay for large firm earnings. If investors are increasingly attracted by the small size of the IPOs, then our equally weighted industry measure will partially reflect this increase.

an equally weighted cross-sectional average of the market to book value of equity in the quarter before the IPO for all Compustat firms which have been in existence for at least three years, and are in the same two-digit S.I.C. industry as the IPO. We divide this by the same measure averaged over all quarters in the five years surrounding the IPO. HISTMBK will be highest when the industry is trading at high prices relative to its normal levels. In a sense, RELMBK captures the cross-sectional aspects of sentiment while HISTMBK captures the time series aspects.[18]

A direct proxy for feedback risk is the turnover (the volume of trading divided by the number of shares issued) on the second day.[19] Clearly, the turnover may be affected by a number of factors other than feedback risk. For example, it is possible that trading volume is associated with the price change on the first day of trading. Thus, an appropriate measure of feedback risk is the residual from a regression of turnover on these factors.

We compute our measure of feedback risk THETA as follows. We regress the second day turnover on a measure of size—the log of the dollar volume of the offering (measured at the offer)—a measure of risk—the standard deviation of the stock's returns computed over the 100 day window starting the day after the IPO—measures of price volatility—the absolute price movement from the offer to the open (normalized by the offer) and its square—the measures of sentiment RELMBK and HISTMBK defined above, and indicator variables for the industry the firm is in. There is no reason to expect the coefficient estimates to be stable so we compute different estimates for three different time periods: 1975–79, 1980–84, 1985–87.[20] We define the feedback risk THETA for an IPO coming to market in January 1978 as follows. We estimate the model

$$\text{Second Day Turnover} = \alpha + \beta[\text{Explanatory Variables}] + \epsilon$$

using all IPOs between 1975 and 1979 (except for those in the month of January 1978). We find the median prediction error using the estimated model for all IPOs coming to market in January 1978. This is our measure of feedback risk θ for all firms coming to market in January 1978.

18.3.3. *The Effect of Market Conditions on Underpricing*

According to our theory, underpricing should be positively correlated with feedback risk and negatively correlated with investor sentiment. Also, past work (see Ritter 1984) has shown that the degree of underpricing is related to the size of the firm going public. We proxy for size with the log of the dollar value of equity outstanding. In addition, Ritter identifies a number of variables that proxy for risk including the aftermarket standard

---

[18] Lowry (2002) employs the discount on closed-end funds as a measure of investor sentiment.

[19] In an earlier version of this chapter, we used the cross-sectional variance of underpricing to proxy for feedback risk. The problem with that measure is that it cannot be computed for periods with very few IPOs and it may reflect the variety of firms coming to market rather than market conditions.

[20] We also computed feedback risk as the median prediction errors for IPOs coming to market in that month where the estimation was performed over the five years prior to the IPO. The results are qualitatively similar. We also reduced the window of estimation to three years and obtained similar results.

Table 18.3. *Summary statistics*

Variable	N	Mean	Standard deviation	Min	Max
Underpricing	2725	0.1003	0.2557	−0.625	4.0000
LT rets NYSE/AMEX adj.	2505	−0.2243	1.5031	−2.14	36.55
LT rets small firm adj.	2505	−0.1036	1.5309	−3.23	37.07
LT rets match. firm adj.	2239	−0.2033	1.9139	−23.63	23.59
Feedback risk	2749	−0.064	0.0112	−0.0479	0.0721
RELMBK	2521	1.1802	0.3565	0.394	2.937
HISTMBK	2520	1.0747	0.1368	0.686	1.576
LSIZEEQ	2478	10.32	1.1385	4.723	14.899
STD	2487	0.0295	0.0131	0.0024	0.1240
USES	1385	6.812	7.1770	0	30
RISKS	786	44.29	29.60	0	98
UNCER	640	42.69	41.65	0	910

Computation end definition of variables:

Underpricing: (first aftermarket price−offer price)/offer price.

LT rets NYSE/AMEX adj.: Three year returns of the IPO firm (excluding the first day return) minus the value weighted NYSE/Amex returns.

LT rets small firm adj.: Three year returns of the IPO firm (excluding the first day return) minus the returns of the smallest decile of stocks on the NYSE and Amex.

LT rets match. firm adj.: Three year returns of the IPO firm (excluding the first day return) adjusted for the performance of a matching firm in the same industry (two-digit SIC) and closest in size.

Feedback risk: Median abnormal turnover on the second trading day for all firms going public in the same month as the IPO firm.

RELMBK: Average equity market to book ratio for seasoned firms in the industry (listed at least three years) at the end of the month prior to the IPO, divided by the equity market to book ratio for all seasoned firms in the market at the end of that month.

HISTMBK: Average market to book ratio for seasoned firms in the industry (listed at least three years) at the end of the month prior to the IPO, divided by the same measure averaged over all months in the five years surrounding the IPO.

Lsizeeq: Logarithm of the market value of the equity based on the offer price.

Std: Standard deviation of stock returns computed over the 100-day window starting on the second day of trading.

Uses: Number of uses of proceeds listed in the prospectus (only available for IPOs in Ritter's 1975–1984 database).

Risks: Number of risk factors listed in prospectus (only available for IPOs in Ritter's 1975–84 database).

UNCER: Aftermarket return standard deviation for the first twenty trading days, as a percentage (only available for IPOs in Ritter's 1975–1984 database).

deviation of the stock's returns, the number of uses listed in the prospectus, and the number of risk factors listed in the prospectus.[21]

Table 18.3 reports summary statistics for the above variables and Table 18.4 reports correlations for some of these variables. In Table 18.5 column (i), the dependent variable is the realized underpricing while the explanatory variables are feedback risk, the measures of

---

[21] We compute the standard deviation of stock returns over the 100-day window starting the day after the IPO. The other variables are only available for the firms included in Ritter's original database.

Table 18.4. *Correlation matrix for selected variables*

	Underpr.	Feedback risk	RELMBK	HISTMBK	LSIZEEQ	Std	Uses	Risks
Feedback risk	0.1589							
RELMBK	0.0570	0.0385						
HISTMBK	0.0429	0.0001	0.3547					
LISIZEEQ	−0.0743	−0.0174	0.0075	0.0752				
STD	0.1592	−0.0022	0.1464	0.0523	−0.0679			
USES	0.2796	−0.0223	0.1490	0.1237	−0.5679	0.5647		
RISKS	0.0207	0.0233	−0.0286	−0.0138	−0.1036	0.0751	0.0026	
UNCER	0.1550	0.0453	0.0504	−0.0002	−0.1684	0.3162	0.2554	−0.0314

All variables have been defined in Table 18.3.

sentiment, and the aftermarket standard deviation of the stock's return. We exclude penny stocks from this analysis because they are associated with extreme levels of underpricing. Underpricing is positively related to feedback risk ($\beta = 2.62$, t-statistic $= 7.78$). The economic magnitude of this relationship is also significant. A one standard deviation increase in feedback risk increases underpricing by 15.7 per cent of its standard deviation. Consistent with previous research, we also find a positive relation between underpricing and the aftermarket standard deviation of stock returns.

The results on sentiment are not consistent with our predictions. Our model predicts a negative coefficient for both the time series component, HISTMBK, and the cross-sectional component, RELMBK, but both coefficients are not significantly different from zero.

In Table 18.4 column (ii) we add the log of firm equity size to the model as an additional explanatory variable. Firm size also proxies information asymmetry and risk. As the extent of underpricing increases in the amount of information asymmetry and risk, we should find underpricing negatively related to size. This is indeed the case. In column (iii), we also include Ritter's measures of risk: USES, RISKS, and UNCER (though we drop STD which is similar to UNCER). We lose a lot of our observations (we have these measures only for Ritter's dataset) so these results must be interpreted with caution. There is a small decline in the coefficient on the feedback proxy, but it remains highly significant. The coefficient on RELMBK now becomes negative, as predicted by the model, but it is not significant at traditional levels. Contrary to our predictions, however, the coefficient on HISTMBK is now positive and significant. Nevertheless, the economic effect of sentiment on underpricing is small. A one standard deviation increase in both sentiment measures increases underpricing by less than 4 per cent of its standard deviation.[22,23]

---

[22] The small effect of sentiment on underpricing relative to the effect of feedback risk may not be entirely unexpected from the theory. Unlike feedback risk, sentiment does not affect the price movement at the open but does affect the offer price. Because we define underpricing as the price movement at the open normalized by the much larger offer price, we would expect factors affecting the numerator to have larger effect than factors affecting the denominator.

[23] Adding penny stocks to the regression has no qualitative effect on the coefficients for sentiment and feedback risk.

Table 18.5. *Cross-sectional regression of underpricing on measures of feedback trading*

	(i)	(ii)	(ii)
INTERCEPT	−0.0205	0.0800*	−0.1335
	(0.032)	(0.047)	(0.121)
FEEDBACK RISK	2.6203***	2.6016***	2.1511***
	(0.337)	(0.340)	(0.797)
RELMBK	0.0087	0.0096	−0.0302
	(0.012)	(0.013)	(0.022)
HISTMBK	0.0371	0.0455	0.1448**
	(0.030)	(0.030)	(0.064)
STD	2.3716***	2.2644***	
	(0.317)	(0.320)	
LOG EQUITY		−0.0103***	0.0110
		(0.003)	(0.010)
USES			0.0031*
			(0.002)
RISKS			0.0001
			(0.0003)
UNCER			0.0001
			(0.0002)
Adj. R^2	0.0529	0.0552	0.0279
N	2158	2134	459

*** Significant at the 1% level.
** Significant at the 5% level.
* Significant at 10% level.
The dependent variable, underpricing, is computed as: (first aftermarket price—Offer price)/Offer price).
FEEDBACK RISK is measured as median abnormal turnover on the second trading day for all firms going
public in the same month as the IPO firm. RELMBK is the average equity market to book ratio for seasoned
firms in the industry (listed at least three years) at the end of the month prior to the IPO, divided by the market
to book ratio for all seasoned firms in the market at the end of that month. HISTMBK is the average market
to book ratio for seasoned firms in the industry (listed at least three years) at the end of the month prior to the
IPO, divided by the same measure averaged over all months in the five years surrounding the IPO. Industry
is defined at the two-digit SIC code level. STD is the standard deviation of stock returns computed over the
100-day window starting the second trading day. LOG EQUITY is the logarithm of the market value of the
equity based on the offer price. USES is the number of uses of the proceeds listed in the prospectus. RISKS
is the number of risk factors listed in the prospectus. UNCER is the aftermarket return standard deviation for
the first twenty trading days, expressed as a percentage. Penny stocks (offer price < \$1) are excluded from the
analysis. Standard errors are in parentheses.

Regression model: UNDERPRICING $= a + b_1$ FEEDBACK RISK $+ b_2$ RELMBK

$+ b_3$ HISTMBK $+ b_4$ STD

$+ b_5$ LOG EQUITY $+ b_6$ USES $+ b_7$ RISKS $+ b_8$ UNCER

18.3.4. *The Effect of Market Conditions on Long-term Performance*

The model predicts that the excess long-term return on an IPO, as measured from the opening price p_1, should be negatively related to sentiment. Sentiment or over-optimism drives price above fundamentals. When prices revert to fundamentals in the long run, returns are more negative for issues that came to market during periods when sentiment was high. Our model also predicts that if feedback risk is high enough so that issues are underpriced, long-term excess returns should decrease in feedback risk.

To test these predictions, we first determine the three-year returns for each IPO net of a benchmark. We use the three different benchmarks discussed earlier: the returns on the NYSE/AMEX value weighted index, the returns on the NYSE/AMEX smallest decile, and the returns of a seasoned firm from the same industry as the IPO and with the closest market capitalization to it. We then regress these excess returns on our measures of feedback risk and sentiment. Note that it is hardly surprising that the time series measure of sentiment which includes the future realized market to book for the industry will be negatively correlated with long-run returns. Therefore, we do not include this measure as an explanatory variable in the regression. The estimates are reported in Table 18.6.

Because long-term excess returns are notoriously volatile, it is not surprising that the explanatory power of these regressions is small. The sign of the sentiment and feedback

Table 18.6. *Cross-sectional regression of long-term returns on measures of feedback trading and investor sentiment*

	NYSE/Amex adjusted	NYSE/Amex smallest decile adjusted	Matching firm adjusted
INTERCEPT	0.2571**	0.6800***	0.2016
	(0.1164)	(0.117)	(0.145)
FEEDBACK RISK	−7.026**	−9.9240***	−4.8821
	(2.877)	(2.905)	(3.611)
RELMBK	−0.4365***	−0.7246***	−0.3639***
	(0.094)	(0.095)	(0.117)
Adjusted R^2	0.0116	0.0302	0.0045
N	2275	2275	2199

*** Significant at the 1% level.
** Significant at the 5% level.
NYSE/Amex adjusted returns are computed as: Raw 756 trading day return for IPO firm – return on CRSP value weighted NYSE/Amex index over the same period. NYSE/Amex smallest decile adjusted returns are computed as: Raw 756 trading day return for the IPO firm – return on smallest decile of NYSE/Amex firms over the same period. Matching firm adjusted returns are computed as: Raw 756 trading day return for the IPO firm – return on the seasoned firm (listed at least three years) in the industry which is closest in size. Industry is defined at the two digit SIC code level. FEEDBACK RISK is measured as median abnormal turnover on the second trading day for all firms going public in the same month as the IPO firm. RELMBK is the average market to book ratio for seasoned firms in the industry (listed at least three years) at the end of the quarter prior to the IPO, divided by the market to book ratio for all seasoned firms in the market at the end of that quarter.

Regression model: LONG TERM RETURNS $= a + b_1$ FEEDBACK RISK $+ b_2$ RELMBK coefficients are the expected ones for all three benchmarks and five out of six are significant at least at the 5 per cent level. We also include the following measures of business conditions (see Fama and French 1989; Choe *et al.* 1993): the dividend yield at the time of issue, the default spread (the difference between yields on Baa bonds and Aaa bonds) at the time of issue, and the term spread (the difference between yields on ten-year Treasury bonds and Treasury bills) at the time of issue. We do this to check if general business conditions drive the poor IPO excess returns. While the explanatory power of the regressions goes up moderately (R^2 of 0.015 when the dependent variable is NYSE/AMEX adjusted returns, 0.057 for smallest decile adjusted returns, 0.011 for matched firm adjusted returns), the coefficients on sentiment and feedback risk continue to be highly significant in five out of six cases (regressions are not reported). They always have the expected sign. A similar result obtains when the market to book ratio for the market at the time of the issue is included in the regression models.

The noise in returns can be reduced by forming portfolios. We group the IPOs into sixty-four portfolios on the basis of the sentiment (RELMBK), feedback risk, and the size quartile the IPO falls in. We include size because size is a predictor of realized returns. We then regress the median return on each portfolio on the median sentiment, feedback risk, and size measure for the IPOs in that portfolio. These regressions are reported in Table 18.7. As expected, the explanatory power of these portfolio regressions is much higher than the regression on individual IPOs. The long-term excess returns decrease with sentiment (at the 1 per cent level and independent of the benchmark), decrease with feedback risk (but statistically significant only in the regression explaining NYSE/AMEX smallest decile adjusted returns), and increase with the size of the firm. Note that the size of these coefficients does not change much, even after we form portfolios and include our measure of size. The economic importance of these effects can be gauged from the following numbers. Despite the fact that feedback risk is not always significant in the portfolio regressions, it is economically important. In Table 18.7, a one standard deviation increase in feedback risk for a portfolio reduces its NYSE/AMEX adjusted long-run returns by 14 per cent of its standard deviation. The corresponding numbers for NYSE/AMEX smallest decile-adjusted returns is 20 per cent, and for matched firm adjusted returns it is 15 per cent. The effect of sentiment is even larger. A one standard deviation increase in RELMBK reduces NYSE/AMEX adjusted long run returns by 40 per cent, NYSE/AMEX smallest decile adjusted returns by 42 per cent, and matched firm adjusted returns by 33 per cent of their corresponding standard deviations. It is also useful to compare these effects to the effect that size has. A one standard deviation increase in feedback risk has about 40 per cent of the effect that a standard deviation increase in log size has, while sentiment has about the same effect as size, on long-run returns.

Note that sentiment is important even when returns are adjusted by returns on matched firms within the same industry. This suggests that sentiment for an industry may have a special influence on the price of IPOs, over and above its influence on the price of seasoned firms. Finally, the coefficient on size may simply reflect the poor performance of small firms over the 1980s.

It is interesting to compare these findings with previous work. Seyhun (1992) performs a time-series analysis, regressing the (monthly) average long-run excess returns

Table 18.7. *Cross-sectional regression of long-term returns on measures of investor sentiment and feedback trading for sixty-four portfolios*

	NYSE/Amex adjusted	NYSE/Amex smallest decile adjusted	Matching firm adjusted
INTERCEPT	−1.4130***	−1.5503***	−0.9788**
	(0.342)	(0.384)	(0.387)
FEEDBACK RISK	−4.2758	−7.341**	−4.6561
	(3.121)	(3.507)	(3.534)
RELMBK	−0.5634***	−0.6455***	−0.4019***
	(0.125)	(0.141)	(0.142)
LOG SIZE EQUITY	0.1456***	0.1830***	0.1220***
	(0.0302)	(0.034)	(0.0342)
R^2	0.4065	0.4545	0.2400
N	64	64	64

*** Significant at the 1% level.
** Significant at the 5% level.
NYSE/Amex adjusted returns are computed as: Raw 756 trading day return for IPO firm − return on CRSP NYSE/Amex index over the same period. NYSE/Amex smallest decile adjusted returns are computed as: Raw 756 trading day return for the IPO firm − return on smallest decile of NYSE/Amex firms over the same period. Matching firm adjusted returns are computed as: Raw 756 trading day return for the IPO firm − return on the seasoned firm (listed at least three years) in the industry which is closest in size. Industry is defined at the two digit SIC code level. FEEDBACK RISK is measured as median abnormal turnover on the second trading day for all firms going public in the same month as the IPO firm. RELMBK is the average market to book ratio for seasoned firms in the industry (listed at least three years) at the end of the quarter prior to the IPO, divided by the market to book ratio for all seasoned firms in the market at the end of that quarter. Firms are divided into sixty-four portfolio according to quartiles of FEEDBACK RISK, RELMBK, and LOG SIZE EQUITY. These regressions use the portfolio medians of these three variables as explanatory variables. Standard errors are in parentheses.

Regression model: LONG TERM PORTFOLIO RETURNS

$$= a + b_1 \text{ FEEDBACK RISK } + b_2 \text{ RELMBK } + b_3 \text{ LOG SIZE EQUITY}$$

against average initial returns, the standard deviation of initial returns, the dollar volume of the issue, and the number of initial offerings in the month. He concludes, from evidence on inside trades around the IPO, that long-term underperformance stems from investors paying too high a price at the offer. Also, he finds a weak positive relationship between long-term excess returns and underpricing, whence he argues that long-term underperformance is not due to overreaction by investors after the opening.

While our finding that sentiment can explain a large portion of the long-term underperformance is consistent with his findings that investors overpay, the importance of feedback risk in our results suggests overreaction. (Note that by omitting the first day returns from our measure of long-run underperformance, we do not introduce a mechanical relationship between underpricing and long-run underperformance.) One reason why our results may differ from Seyhun's is that he treats underpricing as a primitive while it is endogenous in our model. For instance, underpricing in the model is negatively correlated with sentiment which in turn is negatively correlated with long-run excess returns. So the positive correlation between underpricing and long-run returns that Seyhun finds may simply be because underpricing is proxying for an omitted variable.

Loughran and Ritter (1995) argue that low long run returns may be explained by two factors: (i) IPOs come to market near market peaks; and (ii) IPO firms have high market to book ratios, which are associated with lower returns. Clearly, (i) can only explain the low raw returns, not the low excess or matched returns. As for (ii), we show in the next section that IPOs have high market to book ratios because they come to market when their industries have high market to book ratios. But as the matched firm excess returns show, IPOs still underperform relative to seasoned firms in the same industry (also see the evidence from analyst forecasts discussed in Section 18.4). Our analysis confirms the fact that relative market to book ratios can partly explain long-term underperformance, although we measure market to book ratios at the industry level, not the firm level. This enables us to abstract from potentially priced risk factors such as financial distress, which may explain low market to book ratios at the individual firm level. In addition, we show that there is another factor—feedback trader risk—which is an important determinant of long term returns.

18.3.5. *Market Conditions and Windows of Opportunity*

Our model suggests that if their intent is to maximize proceeds from the issue, firm managers and investment bankers will bring IPOs to market when sentiment is high, and when feedback risk is small. Over 40 per cent of our sample comes from initial public offerings in five high-tech or sunrise industries, namely computer software, electrical and electronics devices, computer hardware, electronic measurement and testing equipment, and pharmaceuticals, chemicals, and biotechnology. An additional 3 per cent comes from the oil and natural gas industry. Table 18.8 shows the annual number of firms coming to market in the thirteen industries with more than fifty IPOs in our sample. In the computer software industry there is a clustering of IPOs in 1983–84 and another in 1986. In oil and natural gas there is a clustering of issues in 1980–81. Such strong industry patterns in the IPOs coming to market suggest the 'opening of a window of opportunity'. We examine below if our measures of sentiment and feedback risk can partially explain these windows.

The dependent variable in the regressions in Table 18.11 is the number of IPOs coming to market in a quarter in a two-digit S.I.C. industry. We have observations for fifty quarters (from the first quarter of 1975 to the second quarter of 1987), and we restrict ourselves to industries which have, on average, at least one IPO per quarter. This leaves us with thirteen two-digit S.I.C. industries. We pool the observations and, because the dependent variable is censored at zero, we use a one sided censored tobit model to estimate the coefficients. The explanatory variables in the regression are our measures of sentiment and feedback risk. The estimates are reported in Column 1 of Table 18.11, with summary statistics and correlations in Tables 18.9 and 18.10.

Table 18.8. *Number of IPOs by year for industries with at least fifty IPOs in the sample*

							SIC						
	13	28	35	36	38	48	50	58	60	61	67	73	80
1975	0	2	2	0	0	0	0	0	0	0	0	1	0
1976	1	0	9	3	1	0	0	1	0	0	1	3	0
1977	1	1	3	2	3	0	0	0	0	0	0	1	1
1978	0	1	4	5	2	0	0	0	0	0	0	3	0
1979	9	2	8	7	8	1	0	1	1	0	1	4	2
1980	24	5	15	19	10	3	4	1	0	1	5	2	1
1981	49	14	32	45	35	5	9	10	0	0	2	38	7
1982	1	3	16	14	12	5	1	9	0	1	2	23	3
1983	1	37	69	65	62	13	24	29	18	50	16	102	34
1984	0	14	34	40	17	11	10	11	22	14	24	51	22
1985	2	8	17	17	14	8	8	7	22	13	24	22	11
1986	0	25	24	23	19	16	12	8	6	10	21	43	11
1987	0	9	14	10	14	3	7	5	1	2	5	16	5
Total	88	121	247	250	197	65	75	82	70	91	101	309	97

Industry definitions

SIC 13 = oil and gas extraction
SIC 28 = chemicals and allied products
SIC 35 = computer hardware and industrial machinery
SIC 36 = electronics and electrical equipment
SIC 38 = instruments and related products
SIC 48 = communications
SIC 50 = durable goods—wholesale

SIC 58 = eating and drinking places
SIC 60 = depository institutions
SIC 61 = nondepository credit institutions
SIC 67 = holding and other investment offices
SIC 73 = software and business services
SIC 80 = health services

The effect of an increase in sentiment is to increase significantly the number of initial public offerings coming to market. Keeping in mind that this is a censored regression and the marginal effects reported are for the latent variable rather than the actual dependent variable, a one standard deviation increase in sentiment (RELMBK) for an industry increases the number of IPOs from that industry in the quarter by 1.37, which is 31 per cent of the standard deviation of the dependent variable. A one standard deviation increase in HISTMBK increases the number of IPOs from that industry in the quarter by 1.8, which is 41 per cent of the standard deviation of the dependent variable. This is consistent with the predictions of the model.[24]

As predicted, the coefficient on feedback risk is negative but it is not significant at conventional levels. This relationship does not, however, appear to be spurious. When we estimate the coefficients on an industry by industry basis, ten of the thirteen coefficients are negative. It is possible, though, that the relationship is non-linear. When we include the square of feedback risk in the regression, the explanatory power of the model increases

[24] Other recent papers on the relationship between industry market-to-book ratios and IPO activity are Pagano *et al.* (1998) and Lowry (2002).

Table 18.9. *Summary statistics and correlation coefficients for variables used in the 'hot issue' tests*

Variable	Mean	Standard deviation	Minimum	Maximum
NUMQ	2.758	4.406	0	35
FEEDBACK RISK	−0.0053	0.011	−0.032	0.025
RELMBK	1.134	0.343	0.51	2.898
HISTMBK	1.002	0.134	0.637	1.480
MARKETMBK	1.004	0.988	0.767	1.198
INVGTH	3.799	0.593	2.47	6.038
INVGTH$_{-3}$	3.821	0.583	2.495	5.608

NUMQ is the number of IPOs coming to market in a quarter in a (two digit) industry. FEEDBACK RISK is measured as median abnormal turnover on the second trading day for all firms going public in the same quarter as the IPO firm. RELMBK is the average equity market to book ratio for seasoned firms in the industry (listed at least three years) at the end of the previous quarter, divided by the market to book ratio for all seasoned firms in the market at the end of that quarter. HISTMBK is the average market to book ratio for all seasoned firms in the industry (listed at least three years) at the end of the quarter prior to the IPO, divided by the same measure averaged over all quarters in the five years surrounding that quarter. MARKETMBK is the equally weighted equity market to book ratio for all seasoned firms in the market in the previous quarter, divided by the same measure averaged over all quarters in the five years surrounding that quarter. INVGTH is the average over all seasoned firms in the industry of the three-year sum of annual investment to sales ratios (i.e. the current year and the next two years) divided by the investment to sales ratio in the previous year. INVGTH$_{-3}$ is INVGTH lagged three years. Only observations for the thirteen industries with an average of at least one IPO per quarter (i.e. at least fifty IPOs) are included. The investor sentiment and feedback trader measures are re-computed on a quarterly basis for this analysis.

and the coefficients for feedback risk and squared feedback risk are significantly negative at the 1 per cent level. A one standard deviation increase in feedback risk from zero reduces the number of firms coming to market in a quarter in that industry by 45 per cent of its standard deviation.[25]

The effect of sentiment on issues coming to market, together with the results on long-run underperformance of IPOs from the previous section, suggests that IPOs come to market when their industry is 'overvalued' relative to the rest of the market. Does this effect persist even when we correct for Ritter and Loughran's finding that IPOs come to market when the overall market peaks? To check this possibility, we include the equally weighted average of the market-to-book equity ratio for all seasoned firms in the market in the quarter before the IPO, divided by the same measure averaged over all quarters in the surrounding five years. The estimates are reported in column (iii) of Table 18.11. The coefficients on the sentiment variables remain highly significant, suggesting that they have

[25] We also included two-digit industry dummies in our regression models, without affecting the qualitative nature of our results.

Table 18.10. *Correlation coefficients for variables used in the 'hot issue' tests*

	NUMQ	FEEDBACK RISK	RELMBK	HISTMBK	MARKETMBK	INVGTH
FEEDBACK RISK	−0.0016					
RELMBK	0.2265	0.0146				
HISTMBK	0.3303	0.0198	0.2546			
MARKETMBK	0.2873	0.0105	0.0009	0.7669		
INVGTH	0.0598	0.0826	0.1951	0.1933	0.1046	
INVGTH_−3	0.1405	−0.1044	0.2775	−0.0768	−0.0900	−0.0429

NUMQ is the number of IPOs coming to market in a quarter in a (two-digit) industry. FEEDBACK RISK is measured as median abnormal turnover on the second trading day for all firms going public in the same quarter as the IPO firm. RELMBK is the average equity market to book ratio for seasoned firms in the industry (listed at least three years) at the end of the previous quarter, divided by the market to book ratio for all seasoned firms in the market at the end of that quarter. HISTMBK is the average market to book ratio for all seasoned firms in the industry (listed at least three years) at the end of the quarter prior to the IPO, divided by the same measure averaged over all quarters in the five years surrounding that quarter. MARKETMBK is the equally weighted equity market to book ratio for all seasoned firms in the market in the previous quarter, divided by the same measure averaged over all quarters in the five years surrounding that quarter. INVGTH is the average over all seasoned firms in the industry of the three-year sum of annual investment to sales ratios (i.e. the current year and the next two years) divided by the investment to sales ratio in the previous year. INVGTH_−3 is INVGTH lagged three years. Only observations for the thirteen industries with an average of at least one IPO per quarter (i.e. at least fifty IPOs) are included. The investor sentiment and feedback trader measures are re-computed on a quarterly basis for this analysis.

an independent influence on the number of IPOs coming to market, even after correcting for the level of the market. However, the economic magnitude of the market to book ratio for the market is larger than the effect of the sentiment variables. A one standard deviation change in the market's market to book increases the number of firms coming to market by 154 per cent of its standard deviation. A one standard deviation change in both sentiment variables increases the number of firms coming to market by 55 per cent of its standard deviation. Note, however, that the inclusion of the average market to book for the market raises the explanatory power of the regression, a finding consistent with Loughran and Ritter (1995).

Is RELMBK a proxy for the investment opportunities in the industry? To check this possibility, we include a measure of the growth in investments that take place in the industry in the year of the IPO and the two years following it.[26] For industry i in year t, we compute INVGROWTH as follows, where the summation is over all seasoned firms j in that industry:

$$\frac{1}{n_i} \sum_{\text{firms } j\in i} \frac{\frac{\text{investment}_{j,t}}{\text{sales}_{j,t}} + \frac{\text{investment}_{j,t+1}}{\text{sales}_{j,t+1}} + \frac{\text{investment}_{j,t+2}}{\text{sales}_{j,t+2}}}{\frac{\text{investment}_{j,t1}}{\text{sales}_{j,t1}}}.$$

[26] The quarterly Compustat data on investments is very sparse, so we are forced to use annual data.

Table 18.11. *Tobit regression of number of IPOs coming to market during a quarter*

Variable	(i)	(ii)	(iii)	(iv)	(v)
INTERCEPT	−17.08***	−14.74***	−18.83***	−23.47***	−28.58***
	(2.042)	(2.024)	(2.835)	(3.644)	(4.920)
FEEDBACK RISK	−15.14	−77.97***	−75.94***	−66.96***	−65.65**
	(24.12)	(27.96)	(27.83)	(10.49)	(28.42)
FEEDBACK RISK SQUARED		−9439***	−9252***	−8360***	−8075***
		(1754)	(1751)	(1751)	(1800)
RELMBK	4.002***	3.948***	4.503***	3.281***	4.857***
	(0.786)	(0.772)	(0.815)	(0.867)	(0.808)
HISTMBK	13.325***	12.095***	6.659**	8.335**	5.934*
	(2.000)	(1.967)	(3.256)	(3.294)	(3.175)
MARKETMBK			8.864**	7.763*	14.624***
			(4.259)	(4.242)	(4.632)
INVGTH				−0.0277	
				(0.456)	
INVGTH$_{-3}$				1.4547***	
				(0.484)	
DIVYLD					0.1091
					(0.413)
TERMSPR					0.8005***
					(0.193)
DEFSPR					1.5522***
					(0.552)
Pseudo R^2	0.0319	0.0433	0.0449	0.0460	0.0563
N	624	624	624	612	624

***Significant at the 1% level.
**Significant at the 5% level.
*Significant at the 10% level.
The dependent variable is the number of IPOs coming to market in a quarter in a (two-digit) industry. FEEDBACK RISK is measured as median abnormal turnover on the second trading day for all firms going public in the same quarter as the IPO firm. RELMBK is the average equity market to book ratio for seasoned firms in the industry (listed at least three years) at the end of the previous quarter, divided by the market to book ratio for all seasoned firms in the market at the end of that quarter. HISTMBK is the average market to book ratio for seasoned firms in the industry (listed at least three years) at the end of the previous quarter, divided by the same measure averaged over all quarters in the five surrounding years. MARKETMBK is the equally weighted equity market to book ratio for all seasoned firms in the market in the previous quarter, divided by the same measure averaged over all quarters in the five years surrounding that quarter. INVGTH is the average over all seasoned firms in the industry of the three-year sum of annual investment to sales ratios (i.e. the current year and the next two years) divided by the investment to sales ratio in the previous year. INVGTH$_{-3}$ is INVGTH lagged three years. DIVYLD is the S&P 500 dividend yield. TERMSPR is the difference between the yield on ten-year treasury bonds and treasury bills. DEFSPR is the difference between the yield on Baa and Aaa bonds. DIVYLD, TERMSPR, and DEFSPR are obtained from Citibase. Only observations for the thirteen industries with an average of at least one IPO per quarter (i.e. at least fifty IPOs) are included. The investor sentiment and feedback trader measures are re-computed on a quarterly basis for this analysis. Only the estimates from a pooled Tobit estimation are reported. The coefficient on the constant and industry dummies are not reported. Standard errors are in parentheses.

Regression model: NUMBER OF IPOs IN QUARTER q in INDUSTRY i

$$= a + b_1 \text{ FEEDBACK RISK} + b_2 \text{ FEEDBACK RISK SQUARED} + b_3 \text{ RELMBK}_{i,q}$$

$$+ b_4 \text{ HISTMBK}_{i,q} + b_5 \text{ MARKETMBK}_q + b_6 \text{ INVGTH}_{i,q} + b_7 \text{ INVGTH}_{i,q-3}$$

$$+ b_8 \text{ DIVYLD} + b_9 \text{ TERMSPR} + b_{10} \text{ DEFSPR}$$

INVGROWTH and RELMBK are significantly positively correlated ($\rho = 0.20$, $T = 5.8$). But the raw correlation between INVGROWTH and the number of IPOs coming to market is an insignificant 0.06. Furthermore, the coefficient estimate for INVGROWTH (Table 18.11, column (iv)) is negative and does not reduce the coefficient for the sentiment variables—which suggests they are not measuring the same thing. We also compute INVGROWTH lagged three periods, which is a proxy for the past growth in the industry. The raw correlation between INVGROWTH$_{-3}$ and the number of IPOs coming to market is 0.14 which is significant at the 1 per cent level. INVGROWTH$_{-3}$ is also more strongly correlated with RELMBK ($\rho = 0.27$). When we include INVGROWTH$_{-3}$ in the regression, the coefficient is significant and positive (Table 18.11, column (iv)). Therefore, the number of IPOs coming to market is significantly related to past investment growth in that industry, but not to future investment growth.

Finally, we include the dividend yield, the term spread, and the default spread, which are measures of general business conditions proposed by Fama and French (1989) and Choe *et al.* (1993). We included these variables with a dual purpose. First, if they proxy for time varying risk premiums, as suggested in Fama and French, we will be able to establish the importance of our proxies after correcting for the nominal level of the stock market. Second, these variables may also proxy for the general level of investment opportunities that Choe *et al.* find to be important. As shown in column (v) of Table 18.11, the term spread and the default spread are significantly correlated with the number of firms coming to market. Interestingly, the coefficients of feedback risk and feedback risk squared remain negative and significant and the coefficients on our measures of investor sentiment remain positive and significant.

18.4. DISCUSSION

We know that returns are negatively correlated with a firm's market to book ratio (see Fama and French (1992) for references). Our measures of sentiment are based on the market to book ratio, but attempt to correct for the level of the market (in the cross-sectional measure) and for the historical level of the industry (in the time-series measure). While some readers may not find it surprising that these adjusted measures are still negatively correlated with long-run returns, the evidence that these measures are correlated with the volume of IPOs coming to the market is perhaps more novel. The finding that these measures are important even after we add the level of the market adds to the evidence in Loughran and Ritter (1995).

It is also well known that trading volume is correlated with price volatility (see Lo and Wang (2000) for references). In deriving our measure for feedback risk, we attempt to correct for price volatility and other relevant factors (see Section 18.2). Furthermore, our measure is market-wide rather than firm-specific. Still some readers may not find it surprising that our proxy labelled 'feedback risk' is positively correlated with firm specific initial price movements. Perhaps more interesting is that it also has some explanatory power for long-run returns and the volume of IPOs coming to market. These correlations suggest that the phenomena may be related, which is something the previous literature has not focused on. We believe that more convincing tests of the phenomena we seek to understand can only come from more direct data. The most direct evidence of investors' behaviour would be from an analysis of who trades around IPOs and what their expectations are.

An alternative source of data, though still one step removed from actual investors, is analyst forecasts. Rajan and Servaes (1997) provide detailed evidence on the frequency and accuracy of analysts forecasts for IPOs. They find that analyst following increases with underpricing, after controlling for firm size.[27] These analysts then make over-optimistic earnings forecasts for the two fiscal years after the IPO. Forecasts errors average 2.4 per cent of the stock price before making industry adjustments, and 1.8 per cent of the stock price after making industry adjustments, where only seasoned firms (more than three years since their IPO) are used to construct the industry sample. This indicates that there is an IPO over-optimism effect and that this effect persists even after adjusting for industry over-optimism.

Rajan and Servaes (1997) also find that this over-optimism on the part of analysts is reflected in the behaviour of the firm's stock price, which supports the notion that investors rely on analyst forecasts in making their decisions. The stocks with the worst aftermarket performance are those where analysts were most over-optimistic and *vice versa*.[28]

Related evidence is also presented by Teoh *et al.* (1998) who find that the long-run underperformance of IPOs is related to earnings management by these companies. The companies with the most extensive use of discretionary accruals have the worst post-issue performance. If analysts do not fully incorporate the implications of these accrual policies into their earnings predictions, this could lead to the results described above.

Overall, these results on analyst following, together with our findings, support the notion that there is systematic over-optimism in the IPO market, which contributes to the anomalies we are addressing.

18.5. CONCLUSION

Much of what we have done is exploratory. There clearly is enormous scope for improvement—in examining the robustness of the kinds of proxies used, in refining the institutional details of the model, in providing more detailed evidence (and perhaps more rational explanations) of this kind of irrational behaviour, and in explaining why this behaviour varies with time.

---

[27] Of course, this result suggests that there may be benefits to underpricing instead of simply costs. The promoter may find it advantageous to create a large initial price run-up in the stock, not simply to attract feedback traders but also to attract attention. Underpricing need not only signal quality (Allen and Faulhaber 1989; Welch 1989; Jegadeesh *et al.* 1993) so as to ease future equity issuances, but may make the issue a 'story stock' which could cause information producers like the media and analysts to examine the firm more closely, attracting clients to the firm and prestige to the owner (see Demers and Lewellen 2003). In turn, this will boost the price of the promoter's remaining stock. This raises the possibility that the objective function we have specified for the promoter (the investment bank/firm) may be incorrect. Perhaps promoters care as much about the short-term aftermarket price of the issue as they care about the proceeds raised through the offering. Such a change to the objective function will weaken the negative relationship between the numbers coming to market and feedback risk.

[28] See also Michaely and Womack (1999) for an analysis of analyst recommendations in IPOs.

An important criticism of models of (seemingly) irrational behaviour is that while they explain any-and everything *ex post*, they do not help predict behaviour. Clearly, if we are allowed one irrationality per phenomenon, we can explain anything. In this chapter we restrict our degrees of freedom, first, by adapting a well-known theoretical model developed in a different context, and second, by deriving over-identifying restrictions from the model. It appears that our proxies for feedback risk and investor sentiment have some power in explaining well-known anomalies associated with initial public offerings.

At the very minimum, a contribution of this chapter is to call attention to the possibility that common factors explain both underpricing and long-run underperformance/IPO volume. Some may choose to call our proxies for feedback and sentiment 'risks'. However, risk based explanations cannot, thus far, account for the relationships between the phenomena that we document. For instance, why should initial underpricing or IPO volume be influenced by systematic risks? But we also recognize important shortcomings of this chapter; we cannot precisely identify why the market conditions we postulate vary over time, and we assume without any basis that the conditions are independent. Elucidation of these matters requires a much better understanding of the micro-foundations of investor behaviour, and much better data on how the population of investors varies over time. In a sense, we have only pushed the puzzles associated with IPOs one step further. But our chapter provides a systematic basis for thinking about IPO anomalies, and adds to the evidence (see Loughran and Ritter (1995), for example) that they do not necessarily have different explanations from other anomalies in the stock market.[29] There is obviously scope for further research.

References

Aggarwal, R., Krigman, L., and Womack, K. (2002), 'Strategic IPO underpricing, information momentum, and lockup expiration selling', *Journal of Financial Economics*, 66, 105–37.

Allen, F. and Faulhaber, G. (1989), 'Signalling by underpricing in the IPO market', *Journal of Financial Economics* 23, 303–23.

Baron, D. and Holmstrom, B. (1980), 'The investment banking contract for new issues under asymmetric information: Delegation and incentive problem', *Journal of Finance* 35, 1115–38.

Barry, C., Muscarella, C., and Vetsuypens, M. (1991), 'Underwriter warrants, underwriter compensation and the costs of going public', *Journal of Financial Economics* 29, 113–35.

Beatty, R. and Ritter, J. (1986), 'Investment banking, reputation, and the underpricing of initial public offerings', *Journal of Financial Economics* 15, 213–32.

Benveniste, L. and Spindt, P. (1989), 'How investment bankers determine the offer price and the allocation of new issues', *Journal of Financial Economics* 24, 343–61.

Bikchandani, S., Hirshleifer, D., and Welch, I. (1992), 'A theory of fads, fashion, custom, and cultural change as informational cascades', *Journal of Political Economy* 100, 992–1026.

[29] For instance, the importance of the market to book factor (Fama and French 1992), alternatively termed the underperformance of 'glamour' stocks (Lakonishok *et al.* 1993), and the underperformance of seasoned equity issues (Loughran and Ritter 1995).

Brennan, M. and Franks, J. (1997), 'Underpricing, ownership, and control in initial public offerings of equity securities in the U.K.', *Journal of Financial Economics* 45, 391–413.

Carter, R. and Manaster, S. (1990), 'Initial public offerings and underwriter reputation', *Journal of Finance* 45, 1045–67.

Choe, H., Masulis R., and Nanda, V. (1993), 'Common stock offerings across the business cycle: Theory and evidence', *Journal of Empirical Finance* 1, 3–31.

De Long, B., Shleifer, A., Summers, L., and Waldmann, R. (1990), 'Positive feedback investment strategies and destabilizing rational speculation', *Journal of Finance* 45, 379–95.

Demers E. and Lewellen, K. (2003), 'The marketing role of IPOs: Evidence from internet stocks', *Journal of Financial Economics*, 68, 413–37.

Fama, E. and French, K. (1989), 'Business conditions and expected returns on stocks and bonds', *Journal of Financial Economics* 25, 23–49.

———— (1992), 'The cross-section of expected returns', *Journal of Finance* 46, 427–66.

Grinblatt, R. and Hwang, C. (1989), 'Signalling and the pricing of new issues', *Journal of Finance* 45, 393–420.

Grinblatt, M., Titman, S., and Wermers, R. (1995), 'Momentum investment strategies, portfolio performance, and herding: a study of mutual fund behavior', *American Economic Review* 85, 1088–105.

Habib, M. and Ljunqvist, A. (2001), 'Underpricing and entrepreneurial wealth losses in IPOs: theory and evidence', *Review of Financial Studies* 14, 433–58.

Hanley, K., Kumar, A., and Seguin, P. (1993), 'Price stabilization in the market for new issues', *Journal of Financial Economics* 34, 177–97.

Hughes, P. and Thakor, A. (1992), 'Litigation risk, intermediation, and the underpricing of initial public offerings', *Review of Financial Studies* 5, 709–42.

Ibbotson, R. (1975), 'Price performance of common stock issues', *Journal of Financial Economics* 2, 235–72.

—— and Jaffe, J. (1975), 'Hot issue markets', *Journal of Finance* 30, 1027–42.

Jegadeesh, N., Weinstein, M., and Welch, I. (1993), 'An empirical investigation of IPO returns and subsequent equity offerings', *Journal of Financial Economics* 34, 153–75.

Lakonishok, J., Shleifer, A., and Vishny, R. (1994), 'Contrarian investment, extrapolation and risk', *Journal of Finance* 49, 1541–78.

Lo, A. and Wang, J. (2000), 'Trading volume: Definitions, data analysis, and implications of portfolio theory', *Review of Financial Studies* 13, 257–300.

Loughran, T. and Ritter, J. (1995), 'The new issues puzzle', *Journal of Finance* 50, 23–51.

———— (2003), 'Why has IPO underpricing increased over time?', Mimeo, University of Florida.

———— (2002), 'Why don't issuers get upset about leaving money on the table in IPOs?', *Review of Financial Studies*, 15, 413–43.

Lowry, M. (2002), 'Why does IPO volume fluctuate so much?', *Journal of Financial Economics*, 67, 3–40.

Ljunqvist, A, Nanda V., and Singh, R. (2001), 'Hot markets, investor sentiment, and IPO pricing', Mimeo, New York University.

Michaely, R. and Womack, K. (1999), 'Conflict of interest and the credibility of underwriter analyst recommendations', *Review of Financial Studies* 12, 653–86.

Nanda, V. (1990), 'IPO underpricing and the business climate', Mimeo, University of Chicago.

Pagano, M., Panetta, F., and Zingales, L. (1998), 'Why do companies go public? An empirical analysis', *Journal of Finance* 53, 27–64.

Rajan, R. and Servaes, H. (1997), 'Analyst following of initial public offerings', *Journal of Finance* 52, 507–29.

Ritter, J. (1984), 'The "hot issue" market of 1980', *Journal of Business* 32, 215–40.

—— (1991), 'The long-run performance of initial public offerings', *Journal of Finance* 46, 3–27.

—— (2001), 'Investment banking and securities issuance', in G. Constantinides, M. Harris, and R. Stulz (eds), *Handbook of the Economics of Finance*, Amsterdam: North-Holland.

—— and Welch, I. (2002), A review of IPO activity, pricing, and allocations, *Journal of Finance*, 57, 1795–1828.

Rock, K. (1986), 'Why new issues are underpriced', *Journal of Financial Economics* 15, 187–212.

Scharfstein, D. and Stein, J. (1990), 'Herd behavior and investment', *American Economic Review* 80, 465–79.

Schultz, P. and Zaman, M. (2001), 'Do the individuals closest to internet firms believe they are overvalued?', *Journal of Financial Economics* 59, 347–81.

Seyhun, N. (1992), 'Information asymmetry and price performance of initial public offerings', Mimeo, University of Michigan.

Sirri, E. and Tufano, P. (1998), 'Costly search and mutual fund flows', *Journal of Finance* 53, 1589–622.

Teoh, S., Welch, I., and Wong, T. (1998), 'Earnings management and the long-run market performance of initial public offerings', *Journal of Finance* 53, 1935–74.

Tinic, S. (1988), 'Anatomy of initial public offerings of common stock', *Journal of Finance* 43, 789–822.

Welch, I. (1989), 'Seasoned offerings, imitation costs, and the underpricing of initial public offerings', *Journal of Finance* 44, 421–49.

—— (1992), 'Sequential sales, learning, and cascades', *Journal of Finance* 47, 695–732.

The Rise and Fall of the European New Markets: On the Short- and Long-run Performance of High-tech Initial Public Offerings

MARC GOERGEN, ARIF KHURSHED, JOSEPH A. MCCAHERY,
AND LUC RENNEBOOG

19.1. INTRODUCTION

As recently as a decade ago, primary equity markets in continental Europe provided investors with low levels of transparency and corporate governance standards (La Porta *et al.* 1997). This contrasts sharply with common law jurisdictions, where investors have long enjoyed significantly higher levels of investor protection. Certainly, continental European countries have law regimes that differ from Anglo American jurisdictions, particularly in terms of disclosure. New comparative research on securities markets has shown that some legal systems give investors more protection against fraud and expropriation than others and has suggested that the control of information asymmetry is an essential precondition for the establishment of a strong capital market. As a minimum, increasing the level and scope of disclosure is likely to be significant. Higher quality disclosure, which gives the investors a higher level of protection, increases the accuracy of asset pricing, which is likely to have an impact on investor confidence (Fox 2000).

The corporate governance regimes of most continental European countries place emphasis on rules and regulations protecting stakeholders, such as creditors and employees, in sharp contrast with the common law countries' reliance on judicially enforced legal rules to protect investors. At a first glance, the weakness of the rules protecting minority investors from asymmetric information and opportunism makes it harder for capital markets in continental Europe to raise the external funds to support a higher rate of initial public offerings (IPOs) for high-growth, start-up businesses. Given the limits on the ability

The authors wish to thank the Euro.NMs for providing information and in some cases data for this study. We would especially like to thank Massimo Grosso from Nuovo Mercato for his kind help. We are also grateful to Marie Thérèse Camilleri Gilson for research assistance. All remaining errors are those of Arif Khurshed. Part of this research was funded by a Social Science Small Grant (SGS/00624/G) from the Nuffield Foundation and by the Netherlands Organization for Scientific Research and by the European Commission (Project no. HPSE–CT–2002–00146).

of firms to raise funds, reform-minded policymakers possess a number of alternatives that can generate rapid changes tailored to meet the regulatory needs of issuers and investors.

Previous research has shown that one way to increase investor protection in continental Europe would be for individual country regulators to generate a range of investor protections within the context of a mandatory disclosure regime and supply a more effective set of enforcement mechanisms (Bratton and McCahery 2001). Even though it would be important to improve the disclosure requirements in company law and provide more effective enforcement mechanisms to protect investors and creditors at the national level, it is quite obvious that such a distinctive shift in the legal system is a lengthy process. Despite the efficiency benefits that greater investor protection would bring to equity markets, regulators will not, because they lack sufficient incentives, commit themselves to revise regulations that could lead to a distinctive shift in the legal system (Coffee 2001). Further, even if EU regulators have the incentives and resources to devise harmonized legal protections that benefit investors, the revisions will not necessarily make expropriation more difficult (Bebchuk and Roe 1999; Hopt 2002).

Harmonization of corporate law in the EU, of course, is not the only way that investor protection can be improved. Given the practical difficulties of enhancing transparency and disclosure practices, corporate governance deficiencies may be addressed alternatively by establishing *ex ante* stock markets that guarantee better levels of shareholder protection and high levels of disclosure (Pagano 1998). Indeed, this is precisely the route taken by Europe's 'new stock markets', that is, the *Nieuwe Markt* (NMAX) in Amsterdam, Euro.NM Brussels, the *Neuer Markt* in Frankfurt, the *Nuovo Mercato* in Milan, and the *Nouveau Marché* in Paris, the latter being the first of the European New Markets (Euro.NMs). Although this is not a solution for the official markets, which are obliged to comply with the mandatory terms of the EU issuer disclosure regime (Moloney 2002), the Euro.NMs alliance imposed additional restrictive disclosure measures on new issuers in order to promote investor protection and investor confidence.

Triggered to a large extent by the impressive emergence of high-tech businesses in the USA, the Euro.NMs sought to emulate the NASDAQ, a highly liquid exchange that has high disclosure and transparency standards (Röell 1998). Thus, as with the NASDAQ, the combination of stricter disclosure rules and less stringent entry requirements (regarding age, size, and minimum profitability requirements) than companies face on first-tier markets led to the development of a very active IPO market in Europe. In Germany, for example, the *Neuer Markt*, which created the most stringent disclosure regime, accounted for the largest share of capital raised in IPOs compared to Europe's other new markets (Bottazzi and Da Rin 2002). It is noteworthy, however, that not all new market segments have pursued a high-disclosure listings strategy (Jenkinson and Ljungqvist 2001). An alternative, embraced by the UK, is to eliminate exchange-based listings rules and transfer authority to the stock exchange regulator, which establishes the minimum rules governing admissions (Macey and O'Hara 2002). For example, this regulatory arrangement gives the London Stock Exchange some discretion over which applicants, subject to their satisfying the minimum requirements, are admitted to trade on the Alternative Investment

Market (AIM). As can be seen in Table 19.2, the AIM imposes less stringent disclosure requirements on the issuer.

In general, despite the higher transaction costs generated by the higher disclosure and reporting requirements of the new markets, there is ample evidence that issuing firms benefit from higher disclosure standards in the form of lower costs of capital (Romano 2001). Moreover, the evidence suggests that some firms floating on the Euro.NMs in the late 1990s were able to diversify their shareholdings rapidly after setting up their company (Jenkinson and Ljungqvist 2001). Diversification is particularly important since the models developed by Kahn and Winton (1996) and Bolton and von Thadden (1998) predict that firms with high growth rates and volatile cash flows will go public early in their lifecycle and thus allow the founders to diversify their investments.

This chapter focuses on the initial offerings in the Euro.NMs which are largely under-researched markets. We study the short- and long-run performance of Euro.NM IPOs. *Ex ante* it is difficult to formulate a hypothesis about whether or not initial under-pricing in the Euro.NMs is higher or lower than underpricing in the regular markets. On the one hand, stronger disclosure requirements on the Euro.NMs reduce the degree of asymmetric information between insider and outsider shareholders such that credible offer prices are more likely to be set and underpricing tends to be lower than on the regular markets. On the other hand, the entry requirements are less stringent for the Euro.NMs than for the regular markets, where some of the smaller firms and those with short trading histories would not be admitted. This implies that more uncertainty about the correct offer price (maybe resulting in more severe underpricing) is to be expected for the Euro.NMs. Which of the two effects applies is an empirical matter which we investigate in this chapter. We document that the average underpricing measured on the first day ranges from as low as 4 per cent in France to a staggering 86 per cent in the Netherlands. We argue that the large differences in underpricing across the Euro.NMs can be explained in terms of differences in industry distributions. Our results confirm the findings that sectors with a high degree of information asymmetry will be significantly underpriced (Ljungqvist *et al.* 2001). We also examine the long-run performance of IPOs on the Euro.NMs over the period 1996–2000. Whether or not the long-term price correction for the Euro.NMs is stronger or weaker than that for the regular markets may depend on the degree of initial price reaction (underpricing). We also investigate the effect of the bursting of the 'Internet bubble' in 2000. Although, there are numerous studies on the long-run performance of IPOs on Europe's main equity markets, this is the first study that explores the long-run performance of the Euro.NM IPOs.

This chapter is organized as follows. Section 19.2 outlines the history and performance of the Euro.NMs. Section 19.3 analyses the listing and disclosure standards of these markets. In our discussion, we emphasize that the few discernable differences between the set of listing and disclosure requirements among the new markets are unlikely to serve as the basis for an institutional explanation for the higher underpricing during the bull market of 1996–2000. In Section 19.4, we provide data on the short-run underpricing and consider alternative theories for the high short-run underpricing on the Euro.NMs. We also document the long-run underperformance of the Euro.NM IPOs and discuss a number of explanations for this phenomenon. Section 19.5 concludes.

19.2. RISE AND FALL OF THE EUROPEAN
NEW MARKETS

Section 19.2.1 focuses on the competition between stock exchanges that has led to the increasing irrelevance of national boundaries. Increased competition has led to the creation of new market segments which have new listing and disclosure rules that facilitate the capital raising process for high-growth, start-up companies. In Section 19.2.2, we describe the creation of the Euro.NMs in Belgium, France, Germany, Italy, and the Netherlands. We discuss the common regulatory features of the alliance of Euro.NMs, showing that the adoption of lower entry requirements and more stringent disclosure rules played an important step in the development of these exchanges. We argue that there are a number of reasons why the listing and disclosure rules played little or no role for the high underpricing of IPOs on the Euro.NMs.

19.2.1. *Competition between Exchanges*

In the past, exchanges were natural monopolies and there was little competition for listings (Mahoney 1997). Within this framework, the relationship between stock exchanges and firms applying for a listing was viewed as giving rise to a long-term contract in which stock exchanges supplied liquidity, corporate governance rules, clearing and monitoring services, and a signalling function to investors in exchange for listing fees (Macey and O'Hara 1999). However, the globalization of securities markets has recently led to a growing number of companies seeking to raise capital across borders and financial markets becoming more integrated. At the most general level, the forces shaping the competition between exchanges are a direct result of technological innovation, elimination of cross-border capital controls, and the introduction of new trading systems. An immediate consequence of the changes that have taken place is the diminished role of exchanges as the dominant supplier of high-quality corporate governance rules and monitoring, signalling, and clearance services. It is important to underline the obvious fact that because there are alternatives to products and services supplied by exchanges, it is reasonable to assume that exchanges will face increasing competition from automated trading systems, where it is possible to trade securities generally listed on exchanges (Steil 1996; DiNoia 1998).

While in the USA there has been strong competition between equity markets for a long time, competition among exchanges in much of continental Europe goes back to the mid-to-late 1980s only (Macey 2001). Some have noted that the competition between European exchanges has led to significant reductions in trading fees—which have benefited investors—and a proliferation of trading mechanisms which increase market liquidity (Pagano 1998). In the context of competitive capital markets, exchanges present issuers with a choice of listing requirements, trading systems, and trading and listing fees (Santos and Scheinkman 2000). These are offered by profit-maximizing exchanges in order to maintain their competitive advantage (Biais and Faugeron-Crouzet 2002; Foucault and Parlour 1999).

Unfortunately, there are significant differences in the level and quality of competition between the main and secondary markets in Europe. For the most part, the effective absence of competition within countries between first- and second-tier exchanges was a primary cause (along with inadequate investor demand) of the undercapitalized state of European small- and medium-sized enterprises (SMEs) (Röell 1998). Moreover, it should be pointed out that the focus of Europe's first-tier exchanges on large, blue-chip firms reduced the attractiveness of the second-tier exchanges, which made it difficult for these exchanges to attract listings from firms that would be eligible to list on a first-tier exchange. Naturally, the most obvious way for the second-tier markets to compete with the rival first-tier exchanges was to become an independent exchange, like NASDAQ, which could provide a home for high-tech firms in Europe that would normally apply for a US listing. To a large extent, the emergence of the Euro.NMs, along with NASDAQ Europe (Easdaq) and AIM, is best seen as an attempt to pursue such a strategy.

19.2.2. *Euro.NMs*

In 1996/97, the Euro.NMs were launched in order to facilitate the financing of innovative companies with a high-growth potential, which were the type of companies that continental European listing rules would have excluded earlier. The Euro.NMs were developed to provide European equity issuers with an alternative to the—at the time—shining example of NASDAQ. Consequently, the Euro.NMs established admissions, listings, and disclosure regulation, trading procedures, and operational standards as a means to achieve an efficient decentralized market which reduced the barriers to flotation for SMEs and provided start-up ventures with the best possible access to risk capital (Avgerinos 2000). The Euro.NMs also adopted a dual trading system consisting of a mix of a quote-driven and order-driven system, to ensure adequate market liquidity. By creating greater liquidity for the shares of SMEs and setting high listing and disclosure standards, the New Markets also aimed at attracting institutional investors.

The French New Market (*Nouveau Marché*) was the first to be created and commenced operating on 14 February 1996 as an alternative, independent investment market governed by its own organizational and operating rules while trading and clearing is done by SBF-Paris (*Société des Bourses Françaises*). At the end of 2001, the total market capitalization of the 164 companies listed on the *Nouveau Marché* was €15 billion. Only 7 per cent of these firms came from foreign jurisdictions. Table 19.1 shows the growth in IPO activity on the Euro.NMs from the start until 2000. The table reports only true IPOs and hence excludes (i) transfers from the OTC, (ii) firms already listed on Easdaq, (iii) introductions (admissions to the listing without any sale of shares), (iv) rights issues, and (v) firms with missing share prices. However, the table includes foreign listings[1] and dual listings with NASDAQ and other non-European markets. In its first two years of trading, the *Nouveau Marché* attracted fourteen and seventeen IPOs, respectively. IPO activity picked up in 1998 when thirty-nine firms applied for a listing and the trend continued until 2000 when fifty firms were granted a listing. Venture capital activity, moreover, increased during the 1990s as a result of the opening of the *Nouveau Marché*.

---

[1] A foreign listing is, for example, an Israeli firm, not listed in Israel, going public on the *Neuer Markt*.

Table 19.1. *Number of IPOs on the Euro.NMs*

Year	Euro.NM Brussels	*Nouveau Marché*	*Neuer Markt*	*Nuovo Mercato*	NMAX (Amsterdam)
1996	—	14	—	—	—
1997	1	17	11	—	3
1998	6	39	41	—	8
1999	6	30	130	6	1
2000	3	50	143	21	2
Total	16	150	325	27	14

This table includes the number of recently introduced IPOs on the Euro.NMs. The numbers exclude (i) transfers from the OTC, (ii) firms already listed on Easdaq, (iii) introductions, (iv) rights issues, and (v) firms with missing share prices.

Source: List adapted from the data provided by the Euro.NMs as well as *Hoppenstedt* and *Deutsche Bank AG* for Germany.

As a consequence of the increasing demand for equity investment in Germany, the *Deutsche Börse* established the *Neuer Markt* on 10 March 1997 to meet the financing needs of young companies which were not catered for by the existing markets, that is, the Official Market (*Amtlicher Markt*) and the Regulated Market (*Geregelter Markt*). The *Neuer Markt* is legally part of the Regulated Market, which was created in 1986. However, technically, the *Neuer Markt* is not a market organized by public authorities, but is privately organized and benefits therefore from a greater flexibility in terms of tailoring its regulation to improve investor protection. This approach yielded positive results as the *Neuer Markt* soon proved successful in attracting new issues (Jenkinson and Ljungqvist 2001). The number of firms seeking a *Neuer Markt* listing took off with eleven flotations and rose spectacularly to 143 in 2000. By the end of 2000 (see Table 19.1), 325 companies were listed and the market capitalization was in excess of €50 billion. Becker and Hellmann (2000) have documented how the *Neuer Markt* undoubtedly contributed to the deepening of the venture capital market, which has matured in recent years.

On 25 March 1997, the Amsterdam Exchanges created a new market segment (the New Market of Amsterdam Exchanges (NMAX)), which developed its own rules for listing eligibility. This initiative was soon followed by the Brussels Exchange, which created Euro.NM Brussels on 11 April 1997. In comparison to their French and German counterparts, the Euro.NMs of Amsterdam and Brussels have only achieved modest success. The total number of IPOs on the Dutch and Belgium markets was sixteen and fourteen, respectively. Also, by contrast with the *Nouveau Marché* and *Neuer Markt*, the firms listed on the Dutch and Belgian new markets had little if any venture capital support. Bottazzi and Da Rin (2002) suggest that the absence of venture capital-supported IPOs in the Dutch market is explained by the long recognized tradition of Dutch firms listing on the NASDAQ.

The youngest Euro.NM is the Milanese *Nuovo Mercato* that was created by Opengate SpA, an Italian IT services group on 17 June 1999, and is operated by *Borsa Italiana*. Whilst the *Nuovo Mercato* has only twenty-seven listed companies, it included Tiscali, one of Europe's largest Internet service providers in 2000.

It is worth pointing out that Easdaq, which was established in June 1996 to provide a market for a broad range of high-tech growth companies, was unable to compete successfully in terms of size, liquidity, and performance against the Euro.NMs and was taken over by NASDAQ in 2001. Moreover, the two high-growth markets in the UK (the AIM created in June 1995, and the Techmark[2] started in November 1999) have been unable to match the performance of the Euro.NMs.

Indeed, the early success of the Euro.NMs has been remarkable: at the end of May 2000, 438 companies from thirteen countries were listed across all the Euro.NMs, the total amount of new capital raised exceeded €23.5 billion, and the total market capitalization was around €234 billion. Of the 438 firms, twenty-seven were dually listed on NASDAQ and on seven other markets. The market performance has also been very impressive with the official Euro.NM All-share Index rising by 561 per cent since the start of 1998 until March 2000 (Grant Thornton 2002), just prior to the market crash.

At the end of March 2000, the Belgian, Dutch, and French Euro.NMs announced that they were merging to form EuroNext. The inability to harmonize five sets of listing rules, the involvement of five different national regulators, and inefficient cross-border trading led to the breakup of the Euro.NMs in December 2000. Consequently, the five Euro.NMs were reduced to three: the German *Neuer Markt*, the Italian *Nuovo Mercato*, and EuroNext.[3]

Since the dissolution of the Euro.NMs, the new markets have suffered particularly badly from the decline in technology stocks with losses on some markets exceeding 80 per cent. In 2001, there were virtually no new issues with fewer than twenty IPOs down from more than 200 in 2000. In 2001, the Nuovo Mercato had a liquidity of 11 per cent (measured by turnover of shares as a percentage of total market capitalization), *Neuer Markt* 6 per cent, the *Nouveau Marché* 4 per cent, AIM 3 per cent, and NASDAQ Europe 1 per cent (Grant Thornton 2002). Clearly the growth rate of the New Markets has slowed down. Unsurprisingly, *Deutsche Börse AG* announced on 27 September 2002 that the *Neuer Markt*, which has seen its market capitalization decline by more than 95 per cent of its value in the last two and a half years and has suffered from a series of insider trading and manipulation scandals,[4] would be closed for trading in 2003. The *Independent* newspaper quoted on 27 September 2002 Alastair Duffy (Aegon Asset Management) saying that 'high-growth companies that needed a lot of finance would look for a listing on *Neuer Markt*—it was a high-profile index. But companies listed on it have had issues with fraud, directors being jailed, and some of the business models have been very suspect. It became the last place you would want to list a business because of the negative associations'. One of the problems of the *Neuer Markt* was that the regulator could not force shareholders to comply with the mandatory lock-in period. Still, lock-in periods were considered as important

---

[2] TechMark is not an independent exchange but is a segment of the Official List of the London Stock Exchange.

[3] At the beginning of 2002, the Borsa de Valores de Lisboa e Porto merged with EuroNext. Furthermore, the Bourse de Luxembourg has an agreement about cross-membership and cross-access with EuroNext.

[4] For example, the top executives of EM.TV & Merchandising face trial on charges that they manipulated the share price (*New York Times*, 27/9/2002). The boss of Comroad, Bodo Schnable, was also charged with share manipulation as almost all the sales reported in the firm's 2001 annual report were fictitious (*Financial Times*, 27/9/2002).

mechanisms to reduce asymmetric information between old and new shareholders: forcing the incumbents to keep their holdings over a certain time after the IPO makes it more likely that any private information becomes public (Espenlaub *et al.* 2001; Brav and Gompers 2000). The need for compulsory lock-ins is particularly important for firms subject to higher asymmetric information such as the young and high-tech firms of the Euro.NMs.

The decision to discontinue the *Neuer Markt* is part of a wider shake-up of the way German companies are listed. Companies will have to comply with a set of rigorous reporting standards. Technology stocks will be brought to the main exchange, where companies will be listed on different segments according to their size. A segment for small- to mid-cap companies will sit underneath the blue chip constituents of the DAX.

Probably, further consolidation is inevitable given the failure of the New Markets to attract foreign companies.[5] There can be little doubt that consolidation will most likely be a natural consequence of the introduction of the European Commission's new disclosure regime, which is designed to transform the Listing Particulars Directive and Public Offers Directive. The new regime is based on the introduction of enhanced, uniform disclosure standards for public offers of securities, the introduction of a shelf-registration document, and the adoption of a multilateral admissions system. Ultimately, even though the new proposed disclosure regime is designed to benefit companies that raise capital on Europe's national exchanges, the evidence suggests that the proposed removal of the distinction between the official and second-tier markets and the requirement for the approval of prospectuses will have a costly impact on SMEs and the performance of the new markets (Moloney 2002).

19.3. LISTING AND DISCLOSURE REQUIREMENTS

In this section, we briefly discuss the economics of listing rules and then describe the main features of the listing and disclosure requirements for the Euro.NMs. As noted earlier, one of the main reasons for the success of the Euro.NMs in developing a more active IPO market is the enhanced listing and disclosure requirements imposed on issuer firms (see Table 19.2). Although in this section we find some differences in regulation between the markets, we argue that these differences are minor and cannot be the main reason for the substantial differences in the short- and long-run performance of IPOs.

From the outset, it is important to note that exchanges provide an important service consisting of a screening of the information provided by the firm applying for a listing. The quality of this information is important, as analysts and investors will use it to evaluate the performance and prospects of the firm. In establishing listing requirements, stock exchanges aim to safeguard the interests of investors by requiring the disclosure of sufficient information about the applicant for a listing. Typically, exchanges will establish minimum

---

[5] NASDAQ Europe suffers even more from low liquidity. Innogenetics (listed on NASDAQ Europe) claimed that its share price suffered from the low liquidity of NASDAQ Europe and applied for a listing on EuroNext Brussels. The announcement of the listing triggered a positive announcement reaction of 19.2% which can be attributed to the higher liquidity provided by that market. An earlier transfer (for liquidity reasons) by Melexis from NASDAQ Europe to EuroNext had a similar price reaction.

quantitative standards—minimum number of shares outstanding, average trading volume, market value of outstanding shares, and public shares outstanding—financial criteria, and disclosure requirements. It is generally acknowledged, however, that stock exchanges do not, for many reasons, provide a financial assessment of the filings of the applicant firms. Even though stock exchanges will only evaluate applicant firms on a going concern basis, the issuer's choice of exchange, nevertheless, will signal important information to investors about the firm. In this analysis, it is assumed that the branding of listing rules will have a direct effect on the level of competition between exchanges for listings (Macey and O'Hara 2002). The proliferation of exchanges will offer firms applying for a listing a greater variety of choice of listing rules (Santos and Scheinkman 2000; Foucault and Parlour 2001). The most direct effect of the competition of exchanges in the design of listing rules is that high-disclosure exchanges will attract more firms than low-disclosure exchanges (Huddart *et al.* 1999). This argument rests on the assumption that liquidity traders will choose to trade in firms listed on high-disclosure exchanges. In turn, corporate insiders, who control the listing decision, will follow the flow of liquidity to the exchanges where the trading costs are lowest. In a closely related paper, Boot and Thakor (2001) show that, since high-quality firms will benefit from a better disclosure of certain types of information, exchanges will have to revise their disclosure regimes upwards, to be able to attract sufficient numbers of high-quality listing firms. There is another argument in favour of improved disclosure standards: the benefit of higher standards for issuing firms is that the listing reduces the firms' cost of capital (Fox 2001).

Despite the ongoing competition between the Euro.NMs and the other second-tier exchanges (e.g. NASDAQ Europe, AIM, and the TechMark), there has recently been substantial convergence in terms of new listing regulations. The rules, among other things, require the filing of quarterly reports, the provision of continually updated information, and the submission of financial statements that must be reported in US GAAP, IAS, or a national version of GAAP. Detailed economic research of firms listed on the *Neuer Markt* has revealed that the differences in the bid–ask spread and share turnover across IAS and US GAAP are statistically insignificant (Leuz 2002). The implication is that US GAAP and IAS are equivalent in terms of quality. Interestingly, nearly every new market in Europe allows listed firms to adopt either IAS or GAAP. From the perspective of an issuer, the Euro.NMs' admission and listing obligations are rigorous and quite extensive. For example, the rules are also reasonably stringent with respect to lock-in periods, the issuing prospectus, and disclosure of transactions by managers. Yet, in other respects, the admissions rules are not very stringent: the issuer size requirements, minimum proceeds, and trading history rule allow young, small firms (like, e.g., innovative high-growth companies) to seek a listing.

In the remainder of this section, we focus on the listing and disclosure criteria for the two largest exchanges in the Euro.NMs alliance: the *Neuer Markt* and *Nouveau Marché*. We noted earlier that the Euro.NMs have substantially converged in terms of their disclosure and transparency requirements and operational standards so as to make their markets attractive to investors. In particular, the enhanced level of transparency that the *Neuer Markt* and *Nouveau Marché* demand of issuing firms can be seen as an advantage, particularly if listing firms expect to attract the support of institutional investors.

Table 19.2. *Listing and disclosure requirements and regulation on the Euro.NMs, NASDAQ Europe, AIM, and TechMark*

	Neuer Markt	Nouveau Marché	NMAX (Amsterdam)	Euro.NM Brussels	Nuovo Mercato	Nasdaq Europe (formerly Easdaq)	AIM	TechMark
Accounting standards	US GAAP or IAS	French GAAP and IAS (regarding consolidation rules); US GAAP conversion permitted	US GAAP or IAS	US GAAP or IAS	Italian GAAP or IAS	US GAAP or IAS	UK GAAP, US GAAP, or IAS	UK GAAP, US GAAP, or IAS
Interim reporting requirements	Quarterly	Turnover quarterly and accounts bi-annually	Quarterly	Quarterly	Quarterly	Quarterly	Bi-annually	Quarterly
Lock-in period	6 months	80% of shares for 12 months or 100% for 6 months	80% of shares for 12 months	80% of shares for 12 months or 100% for 6 months	80% of shares for period of 12 months	80% of shares for 12 months or 100% for 6 months	12 months	No mandatory lock-in period
Market capitalization	€5 m minimum	€5 m minimum	No minimum requirement	€15 m minimum	No minimum requirement	€0.50 m depending on route to admission	No minimum requirement	€775,000 minimum
Initial equity required	€1.5 m minimum	€1.5 m minimum	€5 m minimum	€5 m minimum	€5 m minimum	Minimum of €20m depending on route to admission	No minimum requirement	No minimum requirement
Previous trading history	Minimum of 3 years financial statements, some exceptions allowed	No minimum but 3 years of financial statements preferred	Minimum of 3 years of financial statements	Minimum of 3 years of financial statements	Minimum 1 year trading, some exceptions allowed	0–2 years depending on route to admission	No minimum requirement	Minimum of 3 years financial statements
Past profitability	No minimum requirement	No minimum requirement	No minimum requirement	No minimum requirement	No minimum requirement	€0–1m depending on route to admission	No minimum requirement	No minimum requirement
Foreign company rules	Articles of association must conform to rules of issuer's home jurisdiction	No change	No change	No change	Admission dependent on positive ruling from *Borsa*; audited financial statements must be submitted for equivalence declaration	No change	No change	Listed rules are modified
Reporting language	German and English	French	Dutch and English	French and Dutch or English	Italian	English	English	English
Interview with exchange	No	No	No	No	Yes	Only in listing appeal	No	Yes

Table 19.2 states the criteria that issuers must satisfy in order to list on the *Neuer Markt* and *Nouveau Marché*. In terms of prerequisites for admission, the rules on the two markets are very similar. First, the issuer must have at least €1.5m of equity capital. Second, the minimum number of shares issued must be at least 100,000 and the minimum market capitalization must be at least €5m. Third, there must be a minimum free float of 20 per cent. Firms are required to have a market maker to provide liquidity support. Fourth, at least half of the shares offered in the IPO must be primary shares, that is, shares that increase the firm's equity. In contrast to the *Neuer Markt*, which has a six-month lock-in period for all shares, the *Nouveau Marché* subjects insiders to a lock-in of 80 per cent of their shares for a period of twelve months or 100 per cent of their shares for six months. The listing prospectus of firms applying to either market has to contain information about: (1) the issuer, its share capital, and business; (2) the assets, financial position, and profit and loss statements; (3) associated companies and affiliates of the issuer; (4) board(s) of directors; and (5) recent developments, business prospects, and risk factors. In terms of continuing obligations for issuers, both markets have established strict disclosure regimes.[6]

The early success of the *Neuer Markt* and *Nouveau Marché* depended on several factors. One of the most important factors is the stringent disclosure regime aimed at protecting minority investors. The listing rules for both exchanges are more extensive than those applicable to listed securities on the Official Exchanges. There is evidence that having a good reputation for high corporate governance and minority shareholder protection correlates with increased size, performance, and liquidity of a securities market. In turn, the state of the market, its size, and liquidity also contribute to the expansion of the market for IPOs.

19.4. PRICING ANOMALIES OF EURO.NMs' IPOs

This section starts with a general description of the characteristics of IPOs (Section 19.4.1) listed on the Euro.NMs. It then investigates the traditional pricing anomalies: short-run underpricing (Section 19.4.2) and long-run underperformance (Section 19.4.3) of the companies floated on the Euro.NMs. We explore the various theoretical explanations for short-run underpricing and long-run underperformance which rely upon issue method and the institutional environment. Still, our analysis shows that none of these analyses provide a sufficient explanation. We argue that determinants such as industry characteristics, age and size of the firm, and behavioural accounts serves to predict both initial and long-run underpricing of IPOs on the Euro.NMs.

---

[6] *Neuer Markt* firms must issue a quarterly report within two months after each quarter, and disclose annual financial statements within three months after the end of the business year according to IAS or US GAAP. Issuers listed on the *Nouveau Marché* are required to publish quarterly reports (and semi-annual accounts) and an audited annual financial statement, according to IAS or US GAAP, where a reconciliation table is provided. Both markets also require that firms provide investors with information about share transactions by managers, the company, and the directors. Issuers are also asked to disclose management reports, summons for annual general meetings, the announcement of distributions, and payment of dividends and the issuing of new shares, as well as the exercise of conversion, subscription, and rights. Finally, issuing companies must also honour the Takeover Code.

19.4.1. *Sample Description, Data Source, and Euro.NM IPO Characteristics*

In this chapter, we include the whole population of the IPOs from all five Euro.NMs starting from the first date of trading until the end of 2000. Firm-specific information, such as the firms' names, the date of the initial trading, the offer price, and other listing particulars, were obtained directly from the Euro.NMs' exchanges. For the German market we completed the data using the annual volumes of the *Hoppenstedt Aktienführer* and data from *Deutsche Bank AG*. The first-day share prices, weekly share prices, as well as information on industrial sectors, were obtained from Datastream. Information on the age of the firms was collected from the IPO prospectuses and *Hoppenstedt* for Germany.

Table 19.3 reveals that the IPOs on the Euro.NMs are significantly younger than IPOs on the first- and second-tier markets. For example, the average IPO on the *Neuer Markt* is less than eight years old whereas the average age of German IPOs on the Official and Regulated Markets amounts to more than forty-nine years (Goergen and Renneboog 2003). Those floated on the Brussels market are the oldest with an average age of thirteen years. The average size varies substantially across markets: the market capitalization of the average (median) French firm is 4.6 (2.5) times smaller than the average (median) German IPO.

Table 19.3. *Characteristics of Euro.NMs' IPOs*

	Belgium	France	Germany	Italy	The Netherlands	All the Euro.NMs
Age (in years)	12.6	8.9	7.7	NA	9.9	8.0
	(5)	(54)	(287)		(11)	(357)
Average market capitalization on first trading day (in million €)	9.2	84.6	388.1	656.4	NA	306.7
	(13)	(144)	(280)	(27)		(464)
Median market capitalization on first trading day (in million €)	6.9	43.9	124.6	230	NA	102.7
	(13)	(144)	(280)	(27)		(464)
IPOs with book building	NA	94.3%	100.0%	96.3%	22.2%	96.8%
		(140)	(321)	(27)	(9)	(497)
Book-building ratio	NA	0.7	0.8	0.5	1.0	0.7
		(130)	(318)	(25)	(2)	(475)

This table shows some characteristics of companies listed on the Euro.NMs. Age is calculated as the number of full years between the year of foundation and the year of the flotation. The book-building ratio is calculated as the ratio of the difference between the offer price and the book-building low to the difference between the book-building high and the book-building low. Market capitalization is the market capitalization of the firm at the end of the first day of trading. For Germany, data were not available for most of the foreign firms listed on the *Neuer Markt*. The number of firms for which information of a characteristic is available is given in parentheses.

Book-building was used as the pricing method for all the IPOs, except for about 78 per cent of the Dutch IPOs which used the fixed price method. The book-building ratio in Table 19.3 is calculated as the ratio of the difference between the offer price and the book-building low to the difference between the book-building high and the book-building low. The book-building ratio ranges from 0 to 1 if the price was set within the book-building range. A ratio of 0 means that the offer price was set to the lower bound of the book-building range and a ratio of 1 means that it was set equal to the upper bound. In a few cases, the initial book-building range was different from the final book-building range, and as a result the offer price was outside the initial range. For these cases, the ratio will either be negative (if the final range was lower) or higher than 1 (if the final range was higher).[7] The median ratio for each market was exactly 1, except for the Italian market which had a median ratio equal to its mean of 0.5. The fact that for most IPOs the offer price was set at the top end of the book-building range may reflect the overoptimism of investors in the new economy IPOs. Aussenegg *et al.* (2002) analyse IPOs on the NASDAQ and the *Neuer Markt*. They find that contrary to underwriters on the NASDAQ, underwriters on the *Neuer Markt* do not set the offer price above the price range and do not therefore use the information collected during the book-building process.[8]

The industry distribution of the Euro.NMs IPOs is reported in Table 19.4. Except for the small Brussels market, most of the IPOs are in the new economy sectors of telecommunications, Internet, and software, and other high-tech sectors such as electronic equipment or pharmaceutical and medical appliances. In the French and German markets, more than 90 per cent of the listed firms can be classified as high-tech and almost a third of the IPOs are software firms. In contrast, the majority of German IPOs on the Main and Regulated Markets during the 1980s came from relatively mature industries such as electricals, mechanical engineering, packaging and paper, and motor components (Goergen 1998).

19.4.2. *Short-run Underpricing of Euro.NMs' IPOs*

One of the most widely documented pricing anomalies is short-run IPO underpricing, that is, the phenomenon that the price at the end of the first trading day is substantially above the offer price. This observation, namely that firms fail to capture a substantial amount of external funds by setting too low an offer price, has been made in almost all markets worldwide for the 1970s and 1980s (for an international overview, see Loughran *et al.* 1994). This phenomenon continued through the 1990s with Rajan and Servaes (1997), amongst others, providing evidence that average initial returns of up to 16 per cent were a regular feature of the US new issue market. One of the main reasons why the average degree of underpricing varies across countries is the existence of different pricing methods. For French firms that went public in 1992–98, underpricing averaged

[7] We found the following negative (higher than one) book-building ratios: 2 (3) IPOs on the *Nouveau Marché*, 1 (11) IPOs on the *Neuer Markt*, 0 (2) IPOs on the *Nuovo Mercato*, and 0 (0) IPOs on the Amsterdam market. Information on the book building arrangements was not available for the Brussels market.

[8] In contrast, we find about eleven cases where the offer price is outside the initial price range. This difference in results may be due to the fact that Aussenegg *et al.* (2002) base themselves on the final book-building range, whereas we consider the initial range.

Table 19.4. *Industries with the highest frequency of Euro.NM IPOs—the top-10 rankings*

Belgium		France		Germany		Italy		The Netherlands	
Banks	19% (3)	Software	29% (43)	Software	29% (90)	Other business	26% (7)	Software	29% (4)
Electrical equipment	13% (2)	Computer services	12% (17)	Internet	12% (36)	Internet	19% (5)	Computer services	29% (4)
Steel	13% (2)	Telecom fixed line	9% (13)	Electronic equipment	11% (33)	Computer services	11% (3)	Business support	14% (2)
Broadcasting	13% (2)	Electronic equipment	8% (12)	Business support	7% (21)	Software	7% (2)	Electrical equipment	7% (1)
Retailers e-commerce	13% (2)	Media agencies	3% (5)	Computer services	6% (20)	Broadcasting	7% (2)	Household appliances + housewares	7% (1)
Eng. contractors	6% (1)	Pharmaceuticals	3% (4)	Broadcasting	5% (17)	Telecom fixed line	7% (2)	Household products	7% (1)
Household products	6% (1)	Computer hardware	2% (3)	Media agencies	4% (13)	Chemicals, speciality	4% (1)	Medical equipment + supplies	7% (1)
Clothing + footwear	6% (1)	Other distributors	2% (3)	Other health care	3% (9)	Distrib. ind. comps.	4% (1)		
Textiles + leather goods	6% (1)	Retail, hardlines	2% (3)	Telecom fixed line	3% (9)	Electronic equipment	4% (1)		
Other financial	6% (1)	Other financial	2% (3)	Auto parts	2% (5)	Publishing + printing	4% (1)		
				Chemicals, speciality	2% (5)	Business support	4% (1)		
				Pharmaceuticals	2% (5)	Banks	4% (1)		

This table shows the percentage of Euro.NMs' firms of our sample by industry. Number of firms is shown between brackets.

Source: Datastream.

13 per cent (Derrien and Womack 1999) whereas for German IPOs introduced over the period of 1970–93 this number amounted to 9 per cent (Ljungqvist 1994). Dutch IPOs floated in 1985–98 were underpriced by 17 per cent (Van Frederikslust and Van der Geest 2001), whereas Rogiers *et al.* (1993) reported underpricing by about 10 per cent for a sample of twenty-eight IPOs on the Brussels stock exchange. Cherubini and Ratti (1992) reported that the seventy-five Italian IPOs introduced over the period 1985–91 were underpriced by a formidable 27 per cent.

A small number of mostly unpublished papers have looked at the short-run performance of IPOs on the Euro.NMs. Manigart and De Maeseneire (2000) analysed all the IPOs floated on Euro.NMs and Easdaq (now NASDAQ Europe) prior to the end of 1999 and found that the average initial underpricing was 36 per cent. Another study limited to Internet IPOs on the Euro.NMs found that the underpricing was about 70–85 per cent for German and French IPOs (Arosio *et al.* 2000). The *Nuovo Mercato* IPOs were underpriced by about 24 per cent on their first day of trading (Arosio *et al.* 2001). Aussenegg *et al.* (2002) tested the informational role of book-building as advanced by the model by Benveniste and Spindt (1989) on a sample of Internet, software, and computer IPOs floated between January 1999 and December 2000 on NASDAQ and the *Neuer Markt*. They found evidence of rents being earned by those investors providing information during the book-building process on NASDAQ, whereas no such rents were earned on the *Neuer Markt*.

Table 19.5 reports the degree of underpricing for the five markets. Underpricing is calculated as the difference between the share price at the end of the first day (first week) of trading and the offer price divided by the offer price. At first sight, the numbers in Panel A seem puzzling, as average underpricing measured on the first day ranges from a low 4 per cent in France to a staggering 86 per cent in the Netherlands. The range narrows down to between 5 and 65 per cent, if one measures underpricing at the end of the first week of listing. When IPOs on the Brussels market, which has attracted older firms and firms from more mature industries, are excluded, first-week underpricing is within the range

Table 19.5. *Initial returns of firms floated on the Euro.NMs (1996–2000)*

	Belgium	France	Germany	Italy	The Netherlands	All Euro.NMs
Panel A: Average first-day returns						
First-day return (%)	10.36	4.19	43.32	18.84	86.07	31.17
First-week return (%)	5.38	25.10	54.27	36.88	64.47	44.18
Sample size	13	144	319	26	11	513
Panel B: Median first-day returns						
First-day return (%)	2.18	0.00	8.00	0.00	90.07	0.19
First-week return (%)	0.00	8.38	30.95	1.25	38.38	18.04

This table presents the average and median first-day and first-week returns of firms floated on the Euro.NMs. The first-day return is calculated as the ratio of the trading price at the end of the first day of trading (or the first trading price available) over the offer price minus 100%. First-week underpricing is calculated as the ratio of the trading price at the end of the first week of trading (or the closest day to this) over the offer price minus 100%.

of 25–65 per cent. This suggests that a higher degree of underpricing (in comparison to the main markets) is typical for high-tech firms for which value uncertainty and asymmetric information between management and external investors are high.

The higher first-day (first-week) average underpricing of 31.2 per cent (44.2 per cent) as compared to the first-tier continental European markets is entirely due to the *Neuer Markt* and NMAX, as levels of underpricing on the *Nouveau Marché* and the Italian and Belgian Euro.NMs are similar to those reported for the main markets. Panel B of Table 19.5 reports that, from the perspective of the median firm, there is hardly any first-day underpricing in Belgium, France, and Italy, with modest underpricing for the *Neuer Markt*. However, median first-week underpricing is significant apart for Belgium and Italy.

The distributions of first-day and first-week initial returns of the (high-tech) Euro.NMs firms (see the histograms for the French and German markets in Figs 19.1–19.4) differ substantially from those of the main markets and differ across the Euro.NM exchanges. The distribution for the *Nouveau Marché* shows that a large proportion of IPOs, namely about 60 per cent, are over- rather than underpriced. The proportion of IPOs with negative initial returns is about 40 and 60 per cent at the end of the first day for the *Neuer Markt* and the *Nouveau Marché*, respectively, and about 25 and 35 per cent at the end of the first week. This is very different from what studies on the main markets have found. For example, Ritter (1997) reports that for the US only one out of eleven IPOs had negative first-day initial returns.

Why is underpricing of German and Dutch Euro.NM high-tech firms four- to five-times larger than that of firms on their main markets, and why are there large differences across the Euro.NMs? We need to ask whether differences in listing and disclosure rules

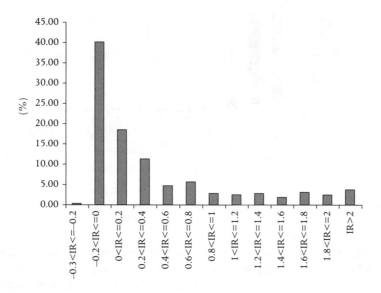

Figure 19.1. *Histogram of first-day initial market-adjusted returns for the German Neuer Markt.*

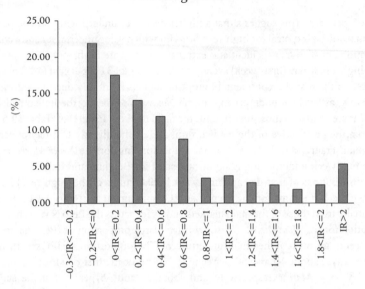

Figure 19.2. *Histogram of first-week initial market-adjusted returns for the German* Neuer Markt.

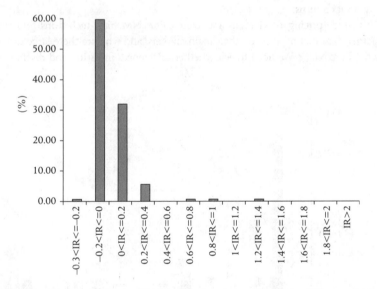

Figure 19.3. *Histogram of first-day initial market-adjusted returns for the French* Nouveau Marché.

between the main markets and among the Euro.NMs can account for the differences in the initial performance. As hypothesized in Section 19.1, stronger disclosure rules on the Euro.NMs than on the main markets and the resulting reduction in asymmetric information are expected to lead to less underpricing on the Euro.NMs. We have documented that

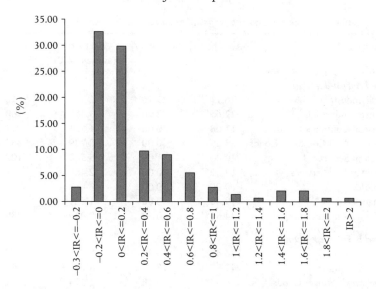

Figure 19.4. *Histogram of first-week initial market-adjusted returns for the French* Nouveau Marché.

this is not the case. Thus it seems that the listing requirements, which are more lenient for the new markets than for the main markets, can be responsible for a more cautious setting of the offer price resulting in higher underpricing on the Euro.NMs. Still, listing rules cannot explain the differences in short-run underpricing across the Euro.NMs. First, since the listing rules for both markets are virtually identical, they cannot account, to any significant extent, for the wide divergence in performance between the Euro.NMs. Second, we are sceptical that other legal/institutional explanations, such as differences in rules concerning litigation risk and the probability of litigation in the countries concerned, shed light on the pattern of underpricing on the *Nouveau Marché* or *Neuer Markt*. Unlike the USA, the legal liability of underwriters is not economically significant in continental Europe (Jenkinson and Ljungqvist 2001).

Apart from listing rules—largely equivalent to IPO characteristics like age, size, trading and profit history—differences in industry distribution also explain differences in initial underpricing between Euro.NMs and the main markets, on the one hand, and between the Euro.NMs, on the other. Table 19.6 documents that the degree of underpricing varies substantially across industries. For example, information technology and cyclical services were significantly underpriced by 34.5 and 40.5 per cent, respectively, whereas underpricing in the non-cyclical services industry and cyclical consumer goods were only 14.22 and 11.7 per cent (not significantly different from zero). Underpricing is exceptionally high for the Dutch new market (NMAX) compared to the other Euro.NMs (Table 19.5). This difference can be partially explained by the different flotation method. Whereas all the other Euro.NMs use the book-building method, the Dutch uses mainly the fixed-price method. As the fixed-price method does not allow the firm (and its underwriter) to

Table 19.6. *Initial returns of firms floated on the Euro.NMs by industry (1996–2000)*

Industry	Average (%)	Median (%)	t-statistic (average ≠ 0)	Sample size
Panel A: First-day returns				
Basic Industries	26.11***	25.76	2.563	10
General Industrials	27.65***	2.96	3.350	60
Cyclical Consumer Goods	11.68	0.00	1.521	11
Non-Cyclical Consumer Goods	23.29***	0.00	2.729	33
Cyclical Services	40.46***	1.09	5.500	102
Non-Cyclical Services	14.22***	0.00	2.469	29
Utilities	0.00	0.00	—	2
Financials	19.40*	0.00	1.821	14
Information Technology	34.50***	0.13	7.939	239
Panel B: First-week returns				
Basic Industries	36.45***	39.38	5.215	10
General Industrials	42.27***	18.29	4.739	60
Cyclical Consumer Goods	56.92**	3.18	1.974	11
Non-Cyclical Consumer Goods	40.28***	14.77	3.471	33
Cyclical Services	52.30***	12.97	5.519	102
Non-Cyclical Services	35.61***	17.46	4.135	29
Utilities	15.70***	15.70	10.547	2
Financials	23.65*	5.38	1.652	14
Information Technology	45.28***	23.91	9.394	239

This table presents the average and median first-day and first-week returns of firms floated on the Euro.NMs, by industry. The first-day return is calculated as the ratio of the trading price at the end of the first day of trading (or the first trading price available) over the offer price minus 1. First-week underpricing is calculated as the ratio of the trading price at the end of the first week of trading (or the closest day to this) over the offer price minus 1. ***,**,* stand for statistical significance at the 1, 5, and 10% level.

collect more information about how potential investors value its shares, more substantial underpricing can be expected in the Dutch new market.

19.4.3. *Long-run Performance of Euro.NMs' IPOs*

To date there is no study investigating the long-run performance of IPOs on the Euro.NMs. The many papers investigating long-run returns for the main markets in Europe report usually significantly negative market-adjusted returns (for a review see Jenkinson and Ljungqvist 2001). Van de Hoeijen and Van der Sar (1999) find that IPOs on the Amsterdam Exchanges underperform the market benchmark over the five years after their listing by 17.9 per cent. For Germany, Ljungqvist (1997) reports that over the three years after their listing IPOs underperform the market by about 12 per cent. A sample of IPOs introduced on the French market during 1996–98 generates three-year returns of 10 per cent below the market (Chahine 2001). For the USA, the picture is similar: Ritter (1991), Rajan and Servaes (1997), Carter *et al.* (1998), among others, have all shown that US IPOs underperform the market benchmarks by between 17 and 49 per cent in the long run.

We calculate long-run returns for periods of between one and five years using data from Datastream. To avoid the impact of the initial underpricing and that of price support by the underwriter, the first four weeks of trading were excluded. We opted for weekly returns rather than the traditionally used monthly returns as some of the Euro.NM IPOs have less than three years of share prices. We use two different methodologies and two different benchmarks as a robustness check on our results. First, we use the market-adjusted cumulative abnormal returns (CARs), which are defined as follows for the case of the three-year period:

$$\text{CAR} = \sum_{t=5}^{t=156} \frac{1}{N} \sum_{i}^{N} AR_{i,t},$$

where $AR_{i,t} = R_{i,t} - R_{m,t}$ is the abnormal return for firm i in month t and N is the number of firms in the sample. $R_{i,t}$ stands for the actual return of firm i and $R_{m,t}$ is the market return. To assess the statistical significance of the CARs, we use t-statistics based on Brown and Warner's (1980) Crude Dependence Adjustment Test in order to correct for cross-sectional dependence:

$$t - stat = \frac{\text{CAR}_t}{\sqrt{t \cdot \left(\sum_{5}^{156} \left(\overline{AR}_t - \text{CAR}_{152}/152 \right)^2 \right)/151}},$$

where CAR_t is the cumulative abnormal return until month t, CAR_{152} is the cumulative abnormal return for the 152 weeks after the IPO, and $\overline{AR}_t$ is the average abnormal return in month t.

Second, we use Buy-and-Hold returns (BHRs) as in Ritter (1991). For the case of the three-year period (152 weeks), holding returns are computed as:

$$\text{BHR}_i = \prod_{t=5}^{t=156} \left(1 + R_{i,t} \right) - 1,$$

where $R_{i,t}$ is the raw return on firm i over the event week t. This measures the total return from a buy-and-hold strategy where the IPO is purchased four weeks after the listing and is held until the earlier of either its third-year listing anniversary or its date of de-listing. We also adjust the BHR for market movements. For both the CARs and BHRs, we face the problem of the choice of an appropriate market benchmark for the Euro.NM firms. We opt for the FTSE Eurotop 300 and FTSE Euromid indices. According to FTSE, the Eurotop 300 is a widely accepted European benchmark, which measures the performance of Europe's largest 300 companies in terms of market capitalization. The Euromid represents the medium-capitalization companies across Europe and consists of all the companies in the FTSE World Europe index minus the FTSE Eurotop 300 companies.

For each of the firms introduced on the Euro.NMs from the first year of the exchange until 2000, we calculate market-adjusted returns as well as BHRs, measured over the period starting one month after the IPO and covering periods of one to five years (if applicable). Panel A of Table 19.7 shows the performance of firms listed on the *Nouveau Marché*: there is statistically significant underperformance by more than 20 per cent in the first two years. Although longer-term returns are also negative, they are not statistically significant from zero. The BHRs are substantially negative and even reach −50 per cent over a five-year period. It should be noted that these results include the effect of the bursting high-tech and dotcom bubble of March 2000. On the right-hand side of panel A, we largely exclude the consequences of the bursting of the dotcom bubble by investigating the performance over one year and two years for the IPOs introduced during the period 1996–99. As a result, entirely different results are obtained: in the first year, the market-adjusted returns are between 18 and 31 per cent, depending on the benchmark. Over the first two years after the IPO, the results are significantly positive or insignificantly different from zero, depending on the market benchmark.[9]

A similar picture can be sketched for the *Neuer Markt* where underperformance after the IPO is even worse: the share prices of firms introduced during 1997–2000 experienced market-adjusted price decreases of between 40 per cent (BHRs) and 60 per cent (CARs) over a two-year period (Panel B of Table 19.7). For a smaller sub-sample for which we can calculate returns over three and four years, we find that the negative price correction amounts to around 64 per cent (BHRs) and 173 per cent (CARs). Excluding the market crash from the year 2000 (right-hand side of Panel B), we find strongly positive one-year returns, which substantially decline over a two-year period when the effect of the bursting dotcom bubble becomes apparent for part of the sample (the IPOs introduced in 1999). The situation on the Brussels, Amsterdam, and Milan Euro.NMs (Panels C–E) is similar.[10]

Table 19.8 in the Appendix shows long-run underpricing by industry: the negative price correction in years three to five is larger in those industries characterized by high initial underpricing.

The evidence presented in Section 19.4.1 (that IPO volume and initial returns are highly correlated (as in Lowry and Schwert 2002)), and in this section (that a severely negative performance correction takes place three to five years subsequent to the IPO) is consistent with the existence of a speculative bubble.

[9]   The data presented in Panel A exclude ten outliers with returns of over 200% (excluding initial underpricing): Soitec, A Novo, Valtec, Egide, Wavecom, FI System, IT Link, Kalisto, Coheris, Metrologic. The inclusion of these firms gives a significantly positive return of 33% for year one and 51% for the three-year period. For Panel B, we excluded the following outlier firms which had abnormal returns of more than 200%: EMTV & M NMBL, Mobilcom, Morphosys, Dlogistics, Advanced Optics Network, MWG-Biotech, Parsytec, Teleplan, and CE Consumer Electronics.

[10]   For each of the Amsterdam, Brussels, and Milan markets, one outlier firm was removed. Prolion (NMAX) gave a return of around 800 per cent in its first year of trading (603 per cent in the first two years and 545 per cent in the first three years of listing). The impact of one firm was such that without removing it from the sample the first year-average returns were 33.53 per cent, but its removal brought the returns down to −29.33 per cent (significant). International Brachytherapy (Brussels Euro.NM) had a return of 461 per cent in its first year. Open Gate (*Nuovo Mercato*) achieved a return of 173 per cent in the first year of listing.

Table 19.7. *Long-run returns for Euro.NMs' IPOs (1996–2000)*

	IPOs introduced during 1996–2000 No. of years after the IPO					IPOs introduced during 1996–99 No. of years after the IPO	
	1 year	2 years	3 years	4 years	5 years	1 year	2 years
Panel A: Nouveau Marché							
CAR (FTEU 300)	−21.43***	−25.66***	−27.77	−23.61	−31.63	8.15	11.60
adjusted)	(−2.43)	(−2.32)	(−1.61)	(−1.06)	(−1.11)	(0.80)	(0.02)
CAR (FTE MIDI)	−19.00***	−21.45*	−27.68	−26.67	−43.21	17.51*	23.92*
adjusted)	(−2.20)	(−1.93)	(−1.60)	(−1.20)	(−1.51)	(1.77)	(1.76)
BHR (FTEU 300)	−1.80	−16.58	−39.86***	−47.79***	−52.88***	20.59*	4.33
adjusted)	(−0.09)	(−1.57)	(−3.22)	(−4.52)	(−5.91)	(1.72)	(0.29)
BHR (FTE MIDI)	1.81	−9.89	−34.68***	−42.25***	−50.35***	31.17***	19.61
adjusted)	(0.20)	(−0.93)	(−2.79)	(−3.99)	(−5.91)	(2.58)	(1.36)

	IPOs introduced during 1997–2000 No. of years after the IPO					IPOs introduced during 1997–99 No. of years after the IPO	
	1 year	2 years	3 years	4 years	5 years	1 year	2 years
Panel B: Neuer Markt							
CAR (FTEU 300)	−13.09	−59.97***	−76.66***	−152.92***		28.67***	−29.98*
adjusted)	(−1.52)	(−4.99)	(−5.794)	(−4.95)		(2.32)	(−1.65)
CAR (FTE MIDI)	−13.75	−65.94***	−83.78***	−172.62***		36.39***	−32.97*
adjusted)	(−1.54)	(−5.29)	(−6.12)	(−5.58)		(2.80)	(−1.70)
BHR (FTEU 300)	−7.44	−36.23***	−53.81***	−57.33***		21.89***	−16.06
adjusted)	(−1.36)	(−5.18)	(−11.33)	(−18.07)		(2.72)	(−1.37)
BHR (FTE MIDI)	−7.57	−40.47***	−59.38***	−64.13***		29.91***	−15.67
adjusted)	(−1.34)	(−5.65)	(−12.27)	(−19.24)		(3.71)	(−1.32)
Panel C: NMAX (Euro.NM Amsterdam)							
CAR (FTEU 300)	−38.71***	−68.37***	−65.17	−81.22***		−12.10	−46.18*
adjusted)	(−2.26)	(−2.37)	(−1.09)	(−2.51)		(−0.71)	(−1.85)
CAR (FTE MIDI)	−39.89***	−62.76***	−65.95	−83.86		−11.55	−37.83
adjusted)	(−2.26)	(−2.14)	(−1.11)	(−1.41)		(−0.65)	(−1.48)
BHR (FTEU 300)	−29.33***	−52.38	−37.24*	−56.43***		−20.07*	−47.78***
adjusted)	(−2.58)	(−2.59)	(−1.65)	(−5.37)		(−1.79)	(−2.37)
BHR (FTE MIDI)	−31.08***	−46.92***	−35.84	−57.48***		−20.22*	−39.55*
adjusted)	(−2.54)	(−2.30)	(−1.34)	(−3.95)		(−1.78)	(−1.77)
Panel D: Euro.NM Brussels							
CAR (FTEU 300)	5.57	−33.2	−95.57*			12.22	30.09
adjusted)	(0.26)	(−1.02)	(−1.76)			(0.56)	(0.41)
CAR (FTE MIDI)	3.16	−34.93	−107.08*			14.44	31.59
adjusted)	(0.17)	(−1.07)	(−1.94)			(0.66)	(0.43)
BHR (FTEU 300)	−14.59	−50.75***	−69.95***			−6.92	−40.91*
adjusted)	(−0.90)	(−2.75)	(−9.07)			(−0.35)	(−1.79)
BHR (FTE MIDI)	−15.98	−52.09	−77.81***			−5.54	−39.58*
adjusted)	(−0.97)	(−2.80)***	(−7.85)			(−0.28)	(−1.78)

	IPOs introduced during 1999–2000 No. of years after the IPO					IPOs introduced during 1999 No. of years after the IPO	
	1 year	2 years	3 years	4 years	5 years	1 year	2 years
Panel E: Nuovo Mercato							
CAR (FTEU 300)	−34.56**	−22.77				52.82	38.26
adjusted)	(−2.12)	(−0.71)				(0.74)	(0.44)

Table 19.7. *Continued*

	IPOs introduced during 1997–2000 No. of years after the IPO					IPOs introduced during 1997–99 No. of years after the IPO	
	1 year	2 years	3 years	4 years	5 years	1 year	2 years
CAR (FTE MIDI	−43.85***	−33.19				55.66	30.82
adjusted)	(−2.58)	(−1.01)				(0.77)	(0.35)
BHR (FTEU 300	−26.51***	−32.39***				27.79	−18.05
adjusted)	(−3.07)	(−5.08)				(1.03)	(−0.99)
BHR (FTE MIDI	−34.93***	−41.87***				30.32	−24.95
adjusted)	(−3.53)	(−6.31)				(1.10)	(−1.34)

This table presents the long-term performance of firms floated on the Euro.NM for one to five years after the flotation on each of the five Euro.NM markets. CAR stands for cumulative abnormal return adjusted for one of two indices: the FTSE Eurotop 300 or the FTSE Euromid indices. The Eurotop 300 is a widely accepted European benchmark, which measures the performance of Europe's largest 300 companies in terms of market capitalization. The Euromid represents the medium capitalization companies across Europe and consists of all the companies in FTSE World Europe index minus the FTSE Eurotop 300 companies. BHR stands for buy and hold returns. Both the CAR and BHR are calculated for several years starting one month subsequent to the flotation. In parentheses, Brown and Warner *t*-statistics are given for the cumulative abnormal returns and the skewness-adjusted *t*-statistics are given for the BHR. ***,**,* stand for statistical significance at the 1, 5, and 10% level.

19.5. CONCLUSION

In 1996/97, the European New Markets were launched in order to facilitate the financing of innovative companies with high-growth potential. These were the type of companies that continental European listing rules would have excluded previously. Consequently, the Euro.NMs established admissions, listings, and disclosure regulation, trading procedures, and operational standards as a means to achieve an efficient decentralized market which reduced the barriers to flotation for SMEs and provided start-up ventures with the best possible access to risk capital. We find that Euro.NM IPOs are substantially younger than IPOs on the main markets. Except for the Belgian market, Euro.NM IPOs also come from different industries, mainly high-tech industries.

The initial returns we documented in this chapter are remarkable in four ways. First, underpricing is on average two- to three-times higher than that on the main markets. It should be noted that the Euro.NMs were created during a surging IPO-wave and about two years before the bursting of the dotcom bubble. Second, the distribution of the initial returns is very different from that of IPOs on the established markets. In particular the proportion of IPOs with negative initial returns is much higher. Third, in the period starting one month after the IPO and ending three to five years after the flotation, the BHRs and the cumulative abnormal returns of firms introduced on the European New Markets are strongly negative and even substantially more negative than long-term returns on the main markets. Fourth, even across Euro.NMs, we find large differences in short- and long-run performance. Underpricing ranges from only 4 per cent on the *Nouveau Marché* to 86 per cent in the Netherlands. The differences in underpricing also induce differences in the long-term price corrections.

It is puzzling that underpricing and long-term performance between the Euro.NMs are so different. What we can largely rule out are differences in regulation: those differences are only minor and cannot account for the major discrepancies in performance across markets. Furthermore, the flotation method cannot explain differences either as most firms introduced on the Euro.NMs (with exception of NMAX) used the book-building method. We have shown that the performance discrepancies can largely be explained by differences in firm and industry characteristics. Small deviations in industry distribution (especially in terms of the weight of Internet and telecoms firms) can already account for significant performance differences between the Euro.NMs. Ljungqvist and Wilhelm (2002) show for a sample of US IPOs that more fragmented ownership, lower pre-IPO insider ownership stakes, lower equity stakes held by venture capitalists and investment banks, and directed share programmes can already explain some changes in performance across time. Furthermore, the agency conflicts between issuers and investment banks may also account for the differences in IPO performance over time and across markets. Loughran and Ritter (2001) and Biais *et al.* (2002) offer the conjecture that issuers grew complacent as valuations spiralled.

Finally, the larger underpricing and stronger market correction in the Euro.NMs compared to the main markets suggests that a higher degree of uncertainty (resulting from more lenient listing rules in the Euro.NMs) and investor irrationality were present in the New Markets.

Appendix

Table 19.8. *Industrial analysis of long-run performance of Euro.NMs' IPOs (1996–2000)*

	No. of years after the IPO				
	1 year	2 years	3 years	4 years	5 years
Panel A: Basic Industries (code 10)					
CAR (FTEU 300 adj.)	−28.51 (−1.00)	−51.76 (−1.40)	−53.75 (−1.03)	−48.49 (−0.49)	16.19 (0.14)
CAR (FTE MIDI adj.)	−28.02 (−1.02)	−23.21 (−0.58)	−21.23 (−0.37)	−15.74 (−0.16)	41.52 (0.34)
BHR (FTEU 300 adj.)	−11.56 (−0.44)	−36.25*** (−2.34)	−51.30*** (−4.40)	−63.40*** (−4.07)	−60.42*** (−4.34)
BHR (FTE MIDI adj.)	−8.75 (−0.28)	−30.05* (−1.74)	−46.37*** (−473)	−56.20*** (−4.82)	−57.46*** (−6.65)
Panel B: General Industries (code 20)					
CAR (FTEU 300 adj.)	3.68 (0.31)	−15.35 (−0.89)	−51.21*** (−2.41)	−76.05*** (−2.45)	−169.44*** (−2.76)
CAR (FTE MIDI adj.)	6.36 (0.52)	−14.40 (−0.82)	−55.72*** (−2.56)	−84.98*** (−2.67)	−184.84*** (−2.96)
BHR (FTEU 300 adj.)	16.16 (1.09)	−12.53 (−0.88)	−38.46*** (−3.11)	−40.00*** (−3.66)	−44.99*** (−2.51)
BHR (FTE MIDI adj.)	19.49 (1.24)	−10.60 (−0.68)	−38.33*** (−3.06)	−40.99*** (−3.28)	−47.21*** (−4.70)
Panel C: Cyclical Consumer Goods (code 30)					
CAR (FTEU 300 adj.)	−57.94*** (−2.63)	−39.83 (−1.06)	−47.50 (−1.13)	−65.69 (−1.23)	−68.97 (−0.80)
CAR (FTE MIDI adj.)	−56.92*** (−2.62)	−32.55 (−0.87)	−47.43 (−1.14)	−66.47 (−1.28)	−83.08 (−0.99)
BHR (FTEU 300 adj.)	−40.92*** (−3.01)	−59.08*** (−10.79)	−64.97*** (−8.02)	−65.42*** (−5.04)	−64.14*** (−5.81)
BHR (FTE MIDI adj.)	−38.56*** (−2.68)	−50.74*** (−5.60)	−60.93*** (−9.92)	−59.82*** (−9.04)	−62.09*** (−8.39)
Panel D: Non-cyclical Consumer Goods (code 40)					
CAR (FTEU 300 adj.)	4.83 (0.30)	4.47 (0.19)	−2.59 (−0.08)	42.20 (0.85)	14.89 (0.21)
CAR (FTE MIDI adj.)	6.13 (0.39)	4.07 (0.18)	−10.03 (−0.31)	34.55 (0.69)	−2.51 (−0.04)
BHR (FTEU 300 adj.)	24.98 (1.16)	−10.31 (−0.67)	−28.26*** (−2.10)	−26.69*** (−2.07)	−27.69*** (−2.07)
BHR (FTE MIDI adj.)	27.08 (1.19)	−8.68 (−0.46)	−29.32*** (−2.25)	−26.94*** (−2.09)	−29.89*** (−2.28)
Panel E: Cyclical Services (code 50)					
CAR (FTEU 300 adj.)	−0.99 (−0.10)	−50.70*** (−3.22)	−63.94*** (−2.46)	−60.56* (−1.85)	−63.03 (−1.48)
CAR (FTE MIDI adj.)	−1.05 (−0.10)	−52.45*** (−3.25)	−70.51*** (−2.68)	−70.85*** (−2.13)	−83.31** (−1.96)
BHR (FTEU 300 adj.)	−4.71 (−0.49)	−28.75*** (−2.44)	−50.94*** (−5.65)	−54.34*** (−6.35)	−54.00*** (−6.31)
BHR (FTE MIDI adj.)	−1.96 (−0.20)	−28.96*** (−2.47)	−52.84*** (−6.07)	−56.30*** (−6.80)	−56.62*** (−6.86)
Panel F: Non-cyclical Services (code 60)					
CAR (FTEU 300 adj.)	−17.46 (−1.16)	−22.28 (−0.67)	−102.71* (−1.81)	−59.46 (−0.55)	

	1 year	2 years	3 years	4 years	5 years
CAR (FTE MIDI adj.)	−22.62 (−1.46)	−28.91 (−0.86)	−119.19*** (−2.09)	−78.78 (−0.72)	
BHR (FTEU 300 adj.)	32.43 (0.96)	−20.49 (−1.07)	−51.04*** (−5.27)	−52.84*** (−5.61)	
BHR (FTE MIDI adj.)	27.54 (0.79)	−25.35 (−1.27)	−59.78*** (−6.07)	−61.12*** (−6.50)	
Panel G: Utilities (code 70)					
CAR (FTE 300 adj.)	27.06	35.76			
CAR (FTE MIDI adj.)	17.22	23.29			
BHR (FTE 300 adj.)	5.27	0.23			
BHR (FTE MIDI adj.)	−3.85	−9.54			
Panel H: Financials (code 80)					
CAR (FTE 300 adj.)	−20.67 (−0.85)	−30.17 (−0.76)	−120.23* (−1.65)	−177.20** (−2.07)	
CAR (FTE MIDI adj.)	−22.57 (−0.91)	−35.13 (−0.89)	−133.73* (−1.83)	−195.96*** (−2.27)	
BHR (FTE 300 adj.)	−10.60 (−0.43)	−46.21*** (−5.19)	−55.55*** (−8.16)	−56.93*** (−8.01)	
BHR (FTE MIDI adj.)	−12.25 (−0.46)	−51.17*** (−4.82)	−62.61*** (−9.31)	−64.89*** (−8.98)	
Panel I: Information Technology (code 90)					
CAR (FTE 300 adj.)	−27.29*** (−3.21)	−64.51*** (−5.01)	−100.07*** (−4.80)	−153.23*** (−5.14)	−155.28*** (−3.19)
CAR (FTE MIDI adj.)	−30.21*** (−3.58)	−70.84*** (−5.49)	−111.91*** (−5.35)	−172.48*** (−5.73)	−181.05*** (−3.73)
BHR (FTE 300 adj.)	−18.53*** (−3.35)	−38.72*** (−4.65)	−55.64*** (−10.38)	−62.13*** (−18.26)	−61.78*** (−18.44)
BHR (FTE MIDI adj.)	−20.48*** (−3.50)	−42.92*** (−9.87)	−61.62*** (−11.19)	−68.81*** (−20.71)	−68.79*** (−20.71)
Panel J: Other industries					
CAR (FTE 300 adj.)	−0.17 (0.00)	−46.38 (−1.18)	−47.03 (−0.67)	−10.91 (−0.12)	25.88 (0.22)
CAR (FTE MIDI adj.)	12.99 (0.48)	−30.39 (−0.77)	−31.74 (−0.45)	2.04 (0.02)	30.90 (0.25)
BHR (FTE 300 adj.)	4.63 (0.14)	−50.74 (−1.05)	−52.05 (−0.67)	−42.55*** (−0.47)	−103.43*** (−4.94)
BHR (FTE MIDI adj.)	19.97 (0.52)	−29.41 (−0.58)	−27.96 (−0.33)	−18.27 (−0.18)	−8.24*** (−3.92)

This table shows the long-run performance over one to five years for all companies floated on the EuroNMs by industry. CAR stands for cumulative abnormal return adjusted for one of two indices: the FTSE Eurotop 300 or the FTSE Euromid indices. The Eurotop 300 is a widely accepted European benchmark, which measures the performance of Europe's largest 300 companies in terms of market capitalization. The Euromid represents the medium capitalization companies across Europe and consists of all the companies in FTSE World Europe index minus the FTSE Eurotop 300 companies. BHR stands for buy and hold returns. Both the CAR and BHR are calculated for several years starting one month subsequent to the flotation. In parentheses, Brown and Warner *t*-statistics are given for the cumulative abnormal returns and the skewness-adjusted *t*-statistics are given for the BHR. ***, **, * stand for statistical significance at the 1, 5, and 10% level.

References

Arosio, R., Bertoni, F., and Giudici, G. (2001), 'The good, the bad and the ugly…everyone wants to join the Nuovo Mercato', Working paper, Politecnico di Milano and University of Bergamo.

——, Giudici, G., and Paleari, S. (2000), 'Why do (or did?) internet-stock IPOs leave so much money on the table?', Working paper, Politecnico di Milano.

Aussenegg, W., Pichler, P., and Stomper, A. (2002), 'Sticky prices: IPO pricing on NASDAQ and the *Neuer Markt*', Working paper, Boston College.

Avgerinos, Y. (2000), 'Towards a pan-European securities market for SMEs: The Easdaq and Euro.NM models', *European Business Law Review* 11, 8–26.

Bebchuk, L. and Roe, M. (1999), 'A theory of path dependence in corporate ownership and governance', *Stanford Law Review* 52, 127–52.

Becker, R. and Hellmann, T. (2001), 'The genesis of venture capital—lessons from the German experience', Working paper, Stanford University Graduate School of Business.

Benveniste, L. and Spindt, P. (1989), 'How investment bankers determine the offer and price allocation of new issues', *Journal of Financial Economics* 24, 343–61.

Biais, B., Bossaerts, P., and Rochet, J.-C. (2002), 'An optimal IPO mechanism', *Review of Economic Studies* 69, 117–46.

—— and Faugeron-Crouzet, A.-M. (2002), 'IPO auctions: English, Dutch, French, and internet', *Journal of Financial Intermediation* 11, 9–36.

Bolton, P. and von Thadden, E.-L. (1998), 'Blocks, liquidity and corporate control', *Journal of Finance* 53, 1–25.

Boot, A. W. and Thakor, A. V. (2001), 'The many faces of information disclosure', *Review of Financial Studies* 14, 1021–57.

Bottazzi, L. and Da Rin, M. (2002), 'Venture capital in Europe and the financing of innovative companies', *Economic Policy*, 34, 231–269.

Bratton, W. and McCahery, J. (2001), 'Incomplete contracts theories of the firm and comparative corporate governance', *Theoretical Inquiries in Law* 2, 745–82.

Brav, A. and Gompers, P. (2000), 'Insider Trading Subsequent to Initial Public Offerings: Evidence from Expirations of Lock-Up Provisions', Working paper, Duke University and Harvard University.

Brown, S. and Warner, J. (1980), 'Measuring security price performance', *Journal of Financial Economics* 8, 205–58.

Carter, R., Frederick, H., and Singh, A. (1998), 'Underwriter reputation, initial returns, and the long-run performance of IPO stocks', *Journal of Finance* 53, 285–311.

Chahine, S. (2001), 'Long run underperformance after IPOs and optimistic analysts forecasts', Working paper, Nantes Atlantique.

Cherubini, U. and Ratti, M. (1992), 'Underpricing of Initial Public Offerings in the Milan Stock Exchange', Mimeo, Banca Commerciale Italiana.

Coffee, J. (2001), 'The coming competition among securities markets: which strategies will dominate', Working paper, Columbia University Law School.

Derrien, F. and Womack, K. L. (1999), 'Auctions vs. book building and the control of underpricing in hot IPO markets', Working paper, Dartmouth College.

DiNoia, C. (1998), 'Competition and integration among stock exchanges in Europe: network effects, implicit mergers and remote access', Working Paper, Wharton School of Business.

Espenlaub, S, Goergen, M., and Khurshed, A. (2001), 'IPO Lock-in Agreements in the UK', *Journal of Business Finance and Accounting* 28, 1235–78.

Foucault, T. and Parlour, C. (1999), 'Competition for listings', CEPR Discussion Paper No. 2222.

Fox, M. (2000), 'The securities globalization disclosure debate', *Washington University Law Quarterly* 78, 567–96.

—— (2001), 'The issuer choice debate', *Theoretical Inquiries in Law* 2, 563–612.

Goergen, M. (1998), *Corporate Governance and Financial Performance—A Study of German and UK Initial Public Offerings*, London: Edward Elgar.

—— and Renneboog, L. (2003), 'Why are the levels of control (so) different in German and UK companies? Evidence from initial public offerings', *Journal of Law, Economics, and Organization* 19, 141–75.

Grant Thornton (2002), 'European new markets guide 2002', Grant Thornton working paper series, London.

Hopt, K. (2002), 'Common principles of corporate governance in Europe', in J. A. McCahery, P. Moerland, T. Raaijmakers, and L. Renneboog (eds), *Corporate Governance Regimes: Convergence and Diversity*, Oxford: Oxford University Press.

Huddart, S., Hughes, J., and Brunnermeier, M. (1999), 'Disclosure requirements and stock exchange listing choice', *Journal of Accounting and Economics* 26, 237–69.

Jenkinson, T. and Ljungqvist, A. (2001), *Going Public: The Theory and Evidence on How Companies Raise Equity Finance*', Oxford: Oxford University Press.

Kahn, C. and Winton, A. (1996), 'Ownership structure, speculation and shareholder intervention', *Journal of Finance* 53, 99–129.

La Porta, R., Lopez-de-Silanes, F., Shleifer, A., and Vishny, R. (1997), 'Legal determinants of external finance', *Journal of Finance* 52, 1131–50.

Leuz, C. (2002), 'Information-asymmetry based evidence from Germany's new market', Working paper, Wharton School, University of Pennsylvania.

Ljungqvist, A. (1997), 'Pricing initial public offerings: Further evidence from Germany', *European Economic Review* 7, 1309–20.

—— (1994), 'Under-pricing and long-term performance of German initial public offerings 1970–1993', Working paper, Nuffield College, Oxford.

—— Jenkinson, T., and Wilhelm, W. (2001), 'Global integration in primary equity markets: the role of US banks and US investors', Working paper, New York University Stern School of Business.

—— and Wilhelm, W. (2001), 'IPO pricing in the dot-com bubble', Working paper, New York University Stern School of Business.

Loughran, T. and Ritter J. (2001), 'Why has IPO underpricing increased over time?', Working paper, University of Florida.

——, ——, and Rydqvist, K. (1994), 'Initial public offerings: international insights', *Pacific-Basin Finance Journal* 2, 165–99.

Lowry, M. and Schwert, G. W. (2002), 'IPO market cycles: bubbles or sequential learning', *Journal of Finance* 57, 1171–200.

Macey, J. (2001), 'Regulatory competition in the US federal system: banking and financial services', in D. Esty and D. Geradin (eds), *Regulatory Competition and Economic Integration: Comparative Perspectives*, Oxford: Oxford University Press.

—— and O'Hara, M. (1999), 'Regulating exchanges and alternative trading systems', *Journal of Legal Studies* 28, 17–54.

—— and —— (2002), 'The economics of stock exchange listing fees and listing requirements', *Journal of Financial Intermediation* 11, 297–319.

Mahoney, P. (1997), 'The exchange as regulatory', *Virginia Law Review* 83, 1453–500.

Moloney, N. (2002), *EC Securities Regulation*, Oxford: Oxford University Press.

Manigart, S. and De Maeseneire, W. (2000), 'A first evaluation of Easdaq and Euro.NM and their initial returns', Working paper, University of Ghent.

Pagano, M. (1998), 'Changing microstructure of European equity markets', in G. Ferrarini (ed.), *European securities markets: the investment services directive and beyond*, The Hague: Kluwer Law International.

Rajan, R. and Servaes, H. (1997), 'Analyst following of initial public offerings', *Journal of Finance* 52, 507–29.

Ritter, J. R. (1991), 'The long-run performance of initial public offerings', *Journal of Finance* 46, 3–27.

—— (1997), 'Initial public offerings', in D. Logue and J. Seward (eds), *Handbook of Modern Finance*, New York: Research Institute of America.

Röell, A. (1998), 'Competition among European exchanges: recent developments', in G. Ferrarini (ed.), *European Securities Markets: The Investment Services Directive and Beyond*, The Hague: Kluwer Law International.

Rogiers, B., Manigart S., and Ooghe, H. (1993), 'An empirical examination of the underpricing of initial public offerings on the Brussels stock exchange', Working paper, Vlerick School of Management, University of Ghent.

Romano, R. (2001), 'The need for competition in international securities regulation', *Theoretical Inquiries in Law* 2, 387–562.

Santos, T. and Scheinkman, J. (2000), 'Competition among exchanges', Working paper, University of Chicago.

Steil, B. (1996), '*The European Equity Markets*', London: Royal Institute for International Affairs and European Capital Markets Institute.

Van de Hoeijen, H. and Van der Sar, N. (1999), 'De performance van aandelenintroducties op de Amsterdamse effectenbeurs', *Maanblad voor Accountancy and Bedrijfseconomie* 73, 120–32.

Van Frederikslust, R. and Van der Geest, G. (2001), 'Initial returns and long-run performance of private equity-backed initial public offerings on the Amsterdam stock exchange', Working paper, Rotterdam School of Management, Erasmus University.

Author Index

Subject Index

Brussels 465, 469, 475, 476, 484
buybacks 14, 341, 346, 349–50, 358, 359, 365
  partial 367
buy-ins 49
buyouts 3, 142, 216, 349
  leveraged 37, 49
BVCA (British Venture Capital Association) 401

CAARs (cumulative average abnormal returns)
  412–20, 427
California 79
  Redwood City 387, 393
  Sunnyvale 384, 385
  see also Silicon Valley
California Israel Chamber of Commerce 377
call options 45, 232–3, 235, 441
Canada 13, 53, 111 n., 137, 138, 151
  biotech firms 258
  extent of exits 340–70
  patents 193 n., 215
  see also LSVCCs
capital increases available 344–5, 352
capital gains tax 138, 143, 145, 150, 392
capital markets 29–53, 390
  bank-centred 41, 42, 51, 54–5
  link between VC and 372, 373, 376–88
  vibrant and liquid 171
Carpetright 399, 400, 404, 424–5, 428–30
CARs (cumulative abnormal returns) 306–11, 483,
  484
  see also CAARs
cash 83, 95, 100
  build-up of reserves 96
  firms notoriously strapped for 347
  strain on entrepreneur's resources 349
'cash-and-carry' strategy 231
cash flows 16, 18, 76, 96, 227–8, 261, 273
  certainty-equivalent 231
  cosmetic name changes and 298
  expected 236, 269
  free 124
  future 265, 269, 322
  IPOs and 70–1
  limited ability to generate 349
  negative 135
  positive, lack of 339
  replication of 230, 232, 234
  uncertain 230
  volatile 466
casino stocks 446
causality problem 203–11
causation 51, 53
CCIP (Paris Chamber of Commerce and Industry)
  165
CDs (compact disks) 240, 241, 243, 245–8
  see also MMCDs
Centros case (1999) 165, 181

CEOs (chief executive officers) 11, 79, 122, 123,
  124, 126, 128, 385
  right to remove 43
certainty-equivalent method 231, 233
certification 357, 420
'certification hypothesis' 397
Channel Islands 164
  see also Guernsey; Jersey
charter amendments 112
Check Point Software Technologies 386–7, 388,
  389, 391, 392–3
China 386
choice 96, 117, 122, 134, 173
  entry 289
  interjurisdictional 372
  optimal 65, 66, 68, 120, 124
  suboptimal 118, 119, 120
Chromatis Networks 375, 392
clawback provision 7
Coasian bargaining 118–20, 126, 128
Cobb-Douglas production function 200, 268
collinearity problems 347, 350, 353, 366, 367
commercialization 228, 229, 235, 236, 240, 253,
  258, 277, 399
  future 234
common stock 74, 123–4, 321, 324, 325, 328
company law 151, 164, 167
  EC directives on 168
comparative advantage 18, 46, 204
compensation 4, 7, 62, 65, 76, 79, 90, 117, 173
  aggregate, disclosure of 390
  contingent 98, 172
  implicit 94
  incentive 114
  optimal 16
  postponing 96
  shares 138
competition 19, 29, 179, 237, 247
  coordination and 243–8
  Cournot 284, 286
  direct 290, 292
  exchanges 467–8, 472
  foreign 3
  imperfect 289, 290
  intense 248
  monitoring of 245
  R&D 242
  regulatory 157–8, 178–82
  time to launch under 240–1
Competition Commission 431
competitive advantage 228, 467
competitive disadvantage 15
competitiveness 37
Compustat 218, 219, 260–1, 273, 276, 300, 443,
  446, 447